REVOLUTIONARY MOVEMENTS IN WORLD HISTORY

FROM 1750 TO THE PRESENT

REVOLUTIONARY MOVEMENTS IN WORLD HISTORY

FROM 1750 TO THE PRESENT

VOLUME 1: A–G

JAMES V. DEFRONZO
EDITOR

A B C • C L I O

Santa Barbara, California • Denver, Colorado • Oxford, United Kingdom

Library of Congress Cataloging-in-Publication Data
Revolutionary movements in world history : from 1750 to present / James V. DeFronzo, editor.
     p.   cm.
   Includes bibliographical references and index.
     ISBN 1-85109-793-7 (alk. paper) — ISBN 1-85109-798-8 (ebook)   1. History, Modern.
2. Revolutions.   I. DeFronzo, James.

D295.R49 2006
303.6'4—dc22

                                                                   2006009532

10   09   08   07   06   05 / 10   9   8   7   6   5   4   3   2   1

Media Editor: Ellen Rasmussen
Media Resources Manager: Caroline Price
Production Editor: Vicki Moran
Editorial Assistant: Alisha Martinez
Production Manager: Don Schmidt
Manufacturing Coordinator: George Smyser

This book is also available on the World Wide Web as an ebook.
Visit abc-clio.com for details.

ABC-CLIO, Inc.
130 Cremona Drive, P.O. Box 1911
Santa Barbara, California 93116–1911

This book is printed on acid-free paper ∞.
Manufactured in the United States of America

Contents

Entries

VOLUME 3: R–Z

Maps

Contributors

Advisor
Cyrus Ernesto Zirakzadeh
University of Connecticut
Storrs, CT

Contributors
Howard Adelman
Griffith University
Brisbane, Queensland
Australia

David E. Adleman
University of Idaho
Moscow, ID

Ali Abdullatif Ahmida
University of New England
Biddeford, ME

Ayad Al-Qazzaz
California State University
Sacramento, CA

Craig Baxter
Juniata College
Huntingdon, PA

Marc Becker
Truman State University
Kirksville, MO

Angie Beeman
University of Connecticut
Storrs, CT

Leigh Binford
Benemérita Universidad
    Autónoma de Puebla
Puebla
Mexico

P. Richard Bohr
College of Saint Benedict and Saint
    John's University
St. Joseph, MN

Hamit Bozarslan
Ecole des Hautes Etudes en
    Sciences Sociales
Paris
France

Roger Brown
Saitama University
Saitama City, Saitama Prefecture
Japan

Malcolm Byrne
National Security Archive
Washington, DC

Henry F. Carey
Georgia State University
Atlanta, GA

Clayborne Carson
Stanford University
Stanford, CA

Francesco Cavatorta
Dublin City University
Dublin
Ireland

David Chandler
Monash University
Melbourne
Australia

James G. Chastain
Ohio University
Athens, OH

Albert K. Cohen
University of Connecticut
Storrs, CT

James DeFronzo
University of Connecticut
Storrs, CT

Judith Ewell
College of William and Mary
Williamsburg, VA

John Foran
University of California, Santa
    Barbara
Santa Barbara, CA

Will Fowler
University of St. Andrews
St. Andrews
United Kingdom

Andrew S. Fullerton
University of Connecticut
Storrs, CT

Venelin I. Ganev
Miami University of Ohio
Oxford, OH

John D. Garrigus
University of Texas at Arlington
Arlington, TX

Gordon Gauchat
University of Connecticut
Storrs, CT

Paul A. Gilje
University of Oklahoma
Norman, OK

Jungyun Gill
University of Connecticut
Storrs, CT

Roger S. Gocking
Mercy College
Dobbs Ferry, NY

Anthony Gorman
University of London
London
United Kingdom

Alexander Groth
University of California, Davis
Davis, CA

Josef Gugler
University of Connecticut
Storrs, CT

Geoffrey C. Gunn
Nagasaki University
Nagasaki
Japan

Ahmed H. Ibrahim
Missouri State University
Springfield, MO

George Joffe
Cambridge University
Cambridge
United Kingdom

Sanjay Joshi
Northern Arizona University
Flagstaff, AZ

Colin H. Kahl
University of Minnesota
Minneapolis, MN

Stathis N. Kalyvas
Yale University
New Haven, CT

Eran Kaplan
University of Cincinnati
Cincinnati, OH

Mark N. Katz
George Mason University
Fairfax, VA

Damien Kingsbury
Deakin University
Geelong
Australia

Mikolaj Stanislaw Kunicki
Institute for Human Sciences
Vienna
Austria

George Lawson
University of London
London
United Kingdom

J. J. Lee
New York University
New York, NY

Namhee Lee
University of California, Los
    Angeles
Los Angeles, CA

Deanna Lee Levanti
Braintree, MA

Anatol Lieven
New America Foundation
Washington, DC

Richard A. Lobban, Jr.
Rhode Island College
Providence, RI

Jean-Michel Mabeko-Tali
Howard University
Washington, DC

Theresa M. Mackey
Virginia Community College
Annandale, VA

James I. Matray
California State University, Chico
Chico, CA

Brian C. Melton
Liberty University
Lynchburg, VA

Valentine M. Moghadam
UNESCO
Paris
France

Evan Braden Montgomery
University of Virginia
Charlottesville, VA

Michael Mulcahy
University of Connecticut
Stamford, CT

Carlo Nasi
Universidad de los Andes
Bogota
Colombia

Malyn Newitt
King's College London
London
United Kingdom

Michael R. Nusbaumer
Indiana University-Purdue
    University at Fort Wayne
Fort Wayne, IN

Borden Painter
Trinity College
Hartford, CT

Stacie Pettyjohn
University of Virginia
Charlottesville, VA

Roger Price
University of Wales
Aberystwyth
Wales

Jennie Purnell
Boston College
Chestnut Hill, MA

Nathan Gilbert Quimpo
University of Amsterdam
Amsterdam
Netherlands

Kumar Ramakrishna
Nanyang Technological University
Singapore

Mike Rapport
University of Stirling
Stirling
Scotland

James F. Rinehart
Troy University
Troy, AL

Paul A. Rodell
Georgia Southern University
Statesboro, GA

Donald Rothchild
University of California, Davis
Davis, CA

Steven C. Rubert
Oregon State University
Corvallis, OR

Peter Rutland
Wesleyan University
Middletown, CT

L. Sabaratnam
Davidson College
Davidson, NC

Roland Sarti
University of Massachusetts
Amherst, MA

Paul Khalil Saucier
Northeastern University
Boston, MA

Eric Selbin
Southwestern University
Georgetown, TX

Deric M. Shannon
University of Connecticut
Storrs, CT

Julie Shayne
Emory University
Atlanta, GA

Priscilla M. Shilaro
West Virginia University
Morgantown, WV

James Sidbury
University of Texas at Austin
Austin, TX

Paul E. Sigmund
Princeton University
Princeton, NJ

Richard Stahler-Sholk
Eastern Michigan University
Ypsilanti, MI

Lynn Stephen
University of Oregon
Eugene, OR

Jill Stephenson
University of Edinburgh
Edinburgh
Scotland

Stephen M. Streeter
McMaster University
Hamilton, Ontario
Canada

Martin Stuart-Fox
The University of Queensland
Brisbane
Australia

Gebru Tareke
Hobart and William Smith
   Colleges
Geneva, NY

Arlene B. Tickner
Universidad de los Andes and
   Universidad Nacional
Bogotá
Colombia

Thomas Turner
Formerly of the National
   University of Rwanda
Dubuque, IA

Frédéric Volpi
University of St. Andrews
St. Andrews
Scotland

Veljko Vujačić
Oberlin College
Oberlin, OH

Samuel Watson
United States Military Academy
West Point, NY

Kathleen Weekley
University of Wollongong
Wollongong
Australia

Timothy P. Wickham-Crowley
Georgetown University
Washington, DC

Teresa Wright
California State University, Long
     Beach
Long Beach, CA

Cyrus Ernesto Zirakzadeh
University of Connecticut
Storrs, CT

Preface

Revolutionary movements, conflicts, successful revolutions, the transformations they attempt to bring about, and the support or opposition they provoke are all fascinating topics for a wide range of academic fields, including anthropology, economics, history, political science, psychology, and sociology, as well as for people in general. My interest in revolutions stems from several experiences including the U.S. Civil Rights movements and the conflict over U.S. involvement in Vietnam. As undergraduates, Roger Gocking, author of the entry on the Ghana's Independence Revolution, and I founded the Youth Interracial Council at Fairfield University whose participants from several colleges, such as Manhattanville College, and highschools, such as Convent of the Sacred Heart in Noroton, CT, helped run community centers and tutoring programs, discussion panels, and fund raising musical performances in Connecticut and New York. Some of us also participated in in the university's Upward Bound Program for local highschool students (I taught an English grammar and literature course). Roger and I, along with approximately fifty other students, organized what was apparently the first anti-Vietnam War demonstration at the university and participated in the great 1967 New York City anti-war demonstration led by the Reverend Martin Luther King Junior. When we graduated, my younger brother Donald, later mayor of New Britain, CT, and currently state senator and sponsor in 2005 of the state's first public campaign financing election law, carried on in the Youth Interracial Council. Work in the Youth Interracial Council resulted in the award of the university's Saint Ignatius Loyal Medal. Roger headed to Stanford University and eventually became a college professor and expert on West African history. I enrolled at Indiana University. For three years I taught as a lecturer in Sociology at Indiana University's branch campus in Fort Wayne (Indiana University-Purdue University at Fort Wayne), participating in local social movement activity and writing for the city's activist newspaper, the *Fort Wayne Free Press*. As a graduate student at Indiana University, a course on social conflict by Professor Austin T. Turk provided an opportunity for me to write a very long paper on revolution, guerilla warfare, and related topics, which was later published in a book, *Focus on Sociology* (Dubuque, IA: Kendall/Hunt), edited by professors Arnold O. Olson and Sushil K. Usman. Research for this paper and a short volunteer course on revolution which I taught one semester at IU in Fort Wayne, and later study, including work for the political crime section of my criminology course, resulted in the creation of the other large course, which with criminology, I taught every semester at the University of Connecticut for more than twenty years, Revolutionary Social Movements Around the World. This led to my writing a textbook for the course and similar courses, Revolutions and Revolutionary Movements (1991, 1996, 2007 forthcoming, Boulder CO: Westview). Most likely this book led to Mr. Simon Mason of ABC-CLIO asking me to prepare a proposal and to serve as general editor for this project, *Revolutionary Movemens in World History: From 1750 to the Present*. After more than a year of discussing the project with Simon and developing the proposal, the project began at the beginning of 2004. I have been tremendously impressed at the depth of knowledge of our contributors and working on this project was always extremely interesting and educative.

STRUCTURE OF THE ENCYCLOPEDIA

The encyclopedia includes two major types of entries, which appear in alphabetical order: revolution entries and theme or concept entries. The revolution entries—on revolutions and social movements—range in length from about 4,000 to 15,000 words and are divided into six main sections: Chronology; Background; Context and Process of Revolution; Impacts; People and Organizations; and References and

Further Readings. The theme or concept entries deal with topics related to revolution, such as colonialism and neo-colonialism, human rights and revolution, ideology and propaganda,, student movements and revolutions, war and revolution, women and revolution, terrorism, and theories of revolution. These entries generally range in length from about 3,000 to 4,500 words. Two longer theme entries deal respectively with documentaries on revolutions and revolution as the subjects of feature films.

ACKNOWLEDGMENTS

Above all, I am extremely grateful to our authors for the exceptional quality of the entries they wrote.

But many people in addition to the authors contributed directly or indirectly to the production of this encyclopedia. At ABC-CLIO I would particularly like to thank Simon Mason who invited me to develop the proposal for this project and who contributed valuable guidance, information, suggestions, and ideas for the project. Simon's colleagues at ABC-CLIO who also played important roles include, in alphabetical order, Ron Boehm, Valerie Boyajian, Craig Hunt, Alex Mikaberidze, Vicki Moran, Ellen Rasmussen, Wendy Roseth, Vicky Speck, Art Stickney, and Peter Westwick. Others at ABC-CLIO also contributed significantly and deserve appreciation. I would particularly like to thank Wendy, who was my direct contact and project editor for much of time.

Professor Cyrus E. Zirakzadeh of the University of Connecticut's Political Science Department, author of the entry on "The Spanish Revolution and Counter-Revolution," served as my advisor for this project and provided very important guidance and suggestions.

Jack Goldstone of George Mason University, who had edited the earlier *Encyclopedia of Political Revolutions* (Congressional Quarterly) and published a number of important works on revolution, and with whom I worked as an academic consultant on a documentary series on revolutions, provided valuable advice and suggestions from his own experience as an editor. Both Jack and Douglas Goldenberg-Hart of Congressional Quarterly also consented to allow several authors who had written for the earlier encyclopedia to write entries for this project.

My friend and former teaching assistant Jungyun Gill, author of the entry on "Student and Youth Movements, Activism and Revolution," provided valuable assistance, including important insights on Korean history and society, which helped me in the editing of the Korea entries. There are many UCONN students and faculty members to whom I would like to express thanks, in part for encouraging the creation of my revolutions' course, such as then Sociology Department Head Mark Abrahamson, and my book on revolutions that preceded this encyclopedia. In particular, my good friend Professor Al Cohen, the brilliant and well-known criminologist and author of the entry on "Terrorism" for this encyclopedia, provided much encouragement and many useful suggestions in the course of many conversations.

Many family members and other friends also provided important encouragement and assistance. I particularly would like to thank my brother and sister-in-law, Don and Diane DeFronzo, and their children, David and Karen, and my sister, Margaret Pastore, her friend David Timm, and her son, Michael. Thanks also to my parents, Armand and Mary Pavano DeFronzo, my uncle and aunt, Francis and Lenneye DiFronzo, my uncle and aunt, Alexander and Angie Pavano DiFronzo, my aunt Doris Pavano Pitts, and my cousin, Connie Manafort, and all my other cousins for their encouragement. Deanna Levanti (Americorps and graduate of UMASS), who researched and wrote the valuable entry on "Documentaries and Revolution," which lists hundreds of documentaries and the sources from which these may be obtained, provided much encouragement, as did her mother and stepfather, Sue and Tom Ryan, her brothers, Mathew and Evan, and her father, Charles Levanti.

Others who provided important encouragement were my wonderful and long-time friends Professor Jane Prochow, Massey University, New Zealand; and John McVarish of Hull, Massachusetts. John's daughter, Heather, was, to the best of my knowledge, first college student (James Madison University) to read one of the entries for the encyclopedia, the entry on the Iranian Revolution, which was used as a model for all revolution entries. Heather's reaction to it was very positive, enthusiastic, and encouraging. Professor Lance Hannon of Occidental College and Villanova University, another good friend, former teaching assistant, and coauthor on other projects, also provided valuable encouragement as well as suggestions for authors.

I would also like to thank my good friend, Professor Roger Gocking, Mercy College, author, as noted earlier, of the entry on "Ghana's Independence Revolution," for his valuable encouragement and assistance. Other good friends provided encouragement for this project. Thanks to Wendy Kimsey, my former teaching assistant, and her husband, David Fowler, their daughters, Zoe and Hannah, and Steve Merlino, also my former teaching assistant, and his wife, Kathy Mangiafico. Thanks also to Professor Walter Ellis and his wife Becky Ellis of Hillsboro College, Ted Rhodes and Joni Pascal and their children, Jesse and Rachel, and Sue Cook Ringle and Ken Ringle and their sons Dylan and Carter, and John Pearlman, and George Relue, a great friend and the cofounder, along with Ted Rhodes, and editor of the *Fort Wayne Free Press*.

I would also like to express gratitude to Professor William Doyle of the University of Bristol, Professor Josef Gugler of the University of Connecticut, author of the entry on "The Cinema of Revolution," Professor George Lawson of the London School of Economics, author of the entries on "Reform, Rebellion, Civil War, Coup D'état, and Revolution" and "Trends in Revolution," and Professor Roland Sarti of the University of Massachusetts, author of the entry on the "Italian Risorgimento," for their valuable suggestions of several authors.

Introduction

A *social movement* is a collective effort by a relatively large number of people to bring about, resist, or reverse social change. A *revolutionary movement* is a type of social movement whose leaders advocate structural change, the replacement of one or more major social institutions, such as a society's political system or its economic system. Social movements with goals not including structural change are generally called *reform movements* rather than revolutionary movements. *Revolution* is the term for a revolutionary movement that succeeds and accomplishes structural change.

Students of revolution disagree on whether other characteristics should be included in the definition. Some insist that a true revolution must involve participation by the large mass of a society's population. Others assert that only structural change brought about by violence qualifies as revolution. Still others argue that although violence is not a necessary element, only social transformations through illegal means should be labeled revolutions.

The editor of this encyclopedia does not agree with narrowing the conception of revolution by including any of these restrictions. The preference here is for a definition of revolutionary movement based solely on advocacy of institutional change and for revolution as the achievement of institutional change.

The revolutions and revolutionary movements covered in this project include many that were characterized by large-scale popular participation, illegal rebellion against existing governments, and violence, such as the Russian Revolution of 1917 and the Chinese and Vietnamese revolutions, and others that lacked one or more of these aspects. The political revolutions in Eastern Europe in 1989 and later in the Soviet Union, for example, were largely non-violent. And democratic elections brought leftist coalitions, supported in part by movements advocating structural economic change to power legally in Spain in 1936 and Chile in 1970. The resulting governments were crushed by right-wing counter-revo-

lutions spearheaded by the military and permitted or even aided by foreign powers. Efforts of people to structurally change their societies through legal democratic means merit the term *revolutionary*. In fact, it could be argued that the reason for the historic link between past revolutions and violence was precisely that democratic means to accomplish institutional change did not exist in many societies until recently.

WHAT MAKES REVOLUTION POSSIBLE?

Historically revolutionary movements were likely to occur and succeed when five factors were present simultaneously. One key element was the development of a high level of discontent with the existing political or economic systems among a large sector of a society's population. This popular or mass discontent has typically been the result of one of three processes: (1) A decline in living standards due to rapid population growth, economic problems or policies, war, or other factors; (2) a change in the moral acceptability of existing living standards in that people come to believe that their lives could and should be better (such a change in viewpoint can result from messages communicated by recognized moral authorities, such as religious leaders, or contact with people from other societies); (3) a period of general improvement in living standards followed by a significant decline (the period of improvement raises people's expectations for future improvements, which are frustrated by the later deterioration of economic conditions).

In order for the discontent to lead to a revolutionary movement, people must come to believe that their troubles are due not only to the current government leaders, but also to one or more of their society's social institutions. Directing blame in this way is often the result of the efforts of leaders of revolutionary movements and the ideologies they put forth. In the past, revolutionary leadership has often developed from a division within the so-called elite sector of a society. Elites are people with culturally defined characteristics qualifying them for leadership positions in society in general. In many societies these include at minimum high levels of intelligence, education, and talent. Elite members of society can become alienated from existing institutions for a number of reasons. Occasionally young people with elite traits become morally outraged at aspects of the social system or repressive government policies. Others may turn against the pre-revolutionary regime because they feel themselves to be the targets of discrimination or barred from opportunities due to the nature of the political, social, or economic systems.

Whatever the reason, the existence of a division within the elite sector, the second factor in successful revolutionary movements, simultaneous with mass discontent creates the possibility that dissident elite persons may provide leadership and organization for the members of the discontented mass of the population, along with an ideology to motivate, mobilize, and guide them. Such an ideology typically includes a systematic criticism of the existing regime and its policies, an explanation of the need for the revolutionary movement, a plan for overthrowing the governing group, and proposals for revolutionary changes to society. In order for a revolution to succeed, the revolutionary ideology should be characterized by a concept that provides a basis for unifying different groups and social classes in a revolutionary alliance to oust the existing regime.

The unifying motive constitutes a third important factor in successful revolutionary movements. A unifying theme may be hatred for a particular ruler, but nationalism in some form has usually served most effectively as a motive unifying different population groups against either colonial regimes or indigenous rulers or governments perceived as serving foreign interests.

A fourth essential element for the success of a revolutionary movement is the deterioration of the legitimacy and coercive capacity of the state. This may be due to devastating defeat in war blamed on the existing government, as was the case in the Russian Revolution of 1917, a state financial crisis such as that which contributed to the occurrence of the French Revolution in 1789, or loss of faith in a personalized dictatorship such as characterized the Cuban Revolution against the Batista regime in the 1950s. In such situations the pre-revolutionary government lacks the capacity to suppress revolutionary movements.

The fifth crucial factor is whether or not other nations intervene to help suppress a revolutionary movement. If the world is permissive toward a revolutionary movement in a particular society, in that other nations are unwilling or unable to assist an existing government in the repression of rev-olutionaries, then the revolutionary movement has a chance of success.

Some students of revolution have stressed the importance of one of these factors, for example the breakdown of state authority, over the others. The orientation here is that a successful revolution almost always has involved the simultaneous presence of all five factors: mass discontent; a division among elites with some becoming revolutionary leaders; the development, propagation, and widespread acceptance of an ideology that in the process of defining the problems of the old regime and calling for its overthrow is able to unify different social groups and classes in support of the revolutionary effort; the deterioration of the coercive capacity of the state; and a world context at least temporarily permissive towards the revolutionary movement.

TRENDS IN REVOLUTION

Social conflict over political systems may be as old as civilization. The ancient Greeks experienced forms of democracy, oligarchy, and dictatorship. The Romans at one time abolished monarchy to create a republic. Senators opposed to the establishment of a dictatorship under Caesar killed him and lost a civil war and their own lives in an attempt to preserve the republic. At some point conflict among social elites for control of government came to resemble little more than a circulation of leadership personnel, and Europeans began referring to the revolving of competing elites in and out of control of government as "revolution." But gradually, with the coming of the philosophical concepts of the Enlightenment and the growing belief in the ability of humanity to control nature and alter society, revolution came to mean changing the system of government or other institutions, including the form of a society's economic system.

The American Revolution shifted the type of government in the former colonies from monarchy to republic and attempted to guarantee a wide range of freedoms and rights to citizens, although limited initially to white males. The French Revolution not only changed the form of government, at least temporarily, and abolished privileges of certain groups, such as the aristocracy and the clergy, it also involved proponents of sweeping economic transformations whose aspirations were largely frustrated, although their ideas and efforts inspired later generations of revolutionaries. The French Revolution's "rights of man and the citizen" concepts constituted a type of transnational revolutionary ideology threatening monarchal regimes throughout Europe. The monarchies reacted by forming a grand international counter-revolutionary military coalition to defeat Napoleon and crush the French Revolution. This international anti-revolutionary alliance functioned to some degree in the 1820s, 1830s, and

1840s to repress new multinational revolutionary efforts motivated both by ideals of the French Revolution and aspirations for national liberation.

Marx's historical materialist concept of socialism appealed to a wide range of intellectuals attracted by an ideology that not only supported the creation of what appeared to be a morally superior form of society, but also offered an apparently scientific analysis which seemed to demonstrate that socialism, and eventually communist utopia, were not only achievable but inevitable. The success of the Marxist Russian revolutionaries in seemingly bringing about the first social revolution in which workers and peasants actually seized state power and control of the economy, and destroyed the old ruling class, inspired revolutionaries in many other countries. But the Communists' establishment of one party rule sowed the seeds of Stalin's brutal dictatorship and, ultimately, contributed to discrediting their revolutionary model.

Lenin's theories of revolution and imperialism long held wide appeal for revolutionaries in many developing countries seeking to free themselves from colonial rule. Communist movements in China and Vietnam effectively became the vehicles of their people's national liberation, greatly contributing to their staying power long after the fall of Communist governments in Eastern Europe and the U.S.S.R. Although Marxism-Leninism became a major transnational revolutionary ideology for decades after the Russian Revolution, it eventually lost ground to non-Marxist nationalism, revolutionary democratic ideologies, and Islamic fundamentalism, especially after the 1991 disintegration of the Soviet Union.

FUTURE REVOLUTIONS?

Will the future be characterized by the number of revolutions that occurred in the past? Students of revolution disagree. Goodwin (2001, 273), refers to the period of 1945–1991 as an "age of revolutions" and offers arguments regarding why revolutions should become less frequent. He notes that some claim that growth in the power of multinational corporations and financial institutions has reduced the relative power of the state in many countries, making control of the state less valuable to potential revolutionaries seeking to bring about change. He also discusses what he considered the more plausible explanation, that without the example of the U.S.S.R. as a powerful industrialized alternative to a capitalist system, the attractiveness and feasibility of revolution decrease. However, Goodwin (273) believes that the spread of democracy, in part the result of certain revolutions of the Cold War period that "helped destroy European colonialism, toppled some of the century's most ruthless dictators and humbled the superpowers," is most responsible for the decline of revolution. He argues that democracies offer the opportunity for voters to punish offensive government officials and to "win concessions from economic and political elites," thus reducing motives for revolution (277). But he qualifies his argument in a telling way by saying that the movements and revolutions least likely to occur are those that "would seriously challenge the capitalist world-system" (274). This assessment clearly points to an external element affecting the frequency of revolutions, not the internal attribute of whether a society's government is democratic or non-democratic.

Many of the "new" democracies of the recent wave of democratization from the late 1980s on, including Chile and Guatemala, had been democracies in the past, but military revolts overthrew the earlier democratic systems, often with great violence and loss of life. Those who had friends or family members killed, imprisoned or abused, or who were themselves the victims of torture, rape, or other mistreatment by members of the armed forces or police (who were virtually never punished) were profoundly affected. Victims of these types of crimes in any society generally avoid engaging in behaviors that they perceive will put them at risk of further victimization. Such is also the case for people who have survived such crimes and suffered repression and the loss of democracy because they favored a particular economic or political policy. If they know that the perpetrators of the crimes against them were not punished—and that these people or others like them are free to commit the same crimes again—they are not likely to even consider repeating the political choices that led to their plight. So in some cases, lack of visible revolutionary aspirations may not have been due to the new democracies, but rather to the lingering fear of state terrorism among their citizens.

Selbin (2001, 290) refers to the wave of democratization of the late twentieth century as "wider," but not necessarily "deeper." Focusing mainly on Latin America, he suggested that poverty and inequality have been increasing and so the motivation for revolutionary change should also be increasing. Selbin (286) stated that neo-liberal economic "globalization…appears strikingly similar to what was once called 'imperialism.'" He also noted (285–286) that "democratic institutions and free markets are not, in any broad historical perspective, natural allies" and as "neo-liberalism fails to deliver on its promise, revolution will become more likely."

In assessing the possible relationship between democracy and revolution, a question that must be asked is whether any revolutionary movement would seek to overthrow a genuinely democratic system, that is, one in which the military is committed to a democratic constitution and obedient to the elected government. If revolutionaries could win popular support, they would most likely not attempt to overthrow the democratic system, but rather use democracy and elections to take power and to carry out their plans for social change without resorting to the dangerous and costly option of violence.

Whether more revolutions will occur in the future cannot be forecast with certainty. The pace of the occurrence of revolutions may have at least temporarily slowed, perhaps not so much due to the wave of democratization as to the maintenance of a generally non-permissive international stance towards revolutionary economic change, particularly on the part of a number of U.S. administrations. The orientation of the United States towards implementing true democracy in other nations and respecting the electoral will of the people in those democracies is essentially the key to determining whether the pace of revolutionary change will accelerate or decline. A major implication is that elections in the United States may determine how permissive or non-permissive the world environment is towards revolutionary change. As has been widely noted, it was no accident that both the Iranian and Nicaraguan revolutions occurred during the human rights–focused U.S. administration of Jimmy Carter. After the reduction of what appeared to be previous near unconditional U.S. support for the pre-revolutionary right-wing regimes in both countries, opponents of these governments were apparently encouraged to mount or escalate major revolutionary efforts.

Real democracy is inherently revolutionary in societies where the majority of the population is impoverished and perceive themselves to be the victims of economic exploitation and/or imperialism. Non-permissive world contexts in the form of the actions of nations opposing radical change have blocked revolutionary movements on numerous occasions. In the twenty-first century, the answer to the question regarding whether revolutionary movements and change re-emerge as a prominent features of world history may be found within the world's wealthiest and most powerful nation.

See Also American Revolution; Chilean Socialist Revolution, Counter-Revolution, and the Restoration of Democracy; Chinese Revolution; Democracy, Dictatorship and Fascism; East European Revolutions of 1989; Elites, intellectuals and Revolutionary Leadership; French Revolution; Iranian Revolution; Nicaraguan Revolution; Reform, Rebellion, Civil War, Coup D'état and Revolution; Russian Revolution of 1917; Russian Revolution of 1991 and the Dissolution of the U.S.S.R.; Spanish Revolution and Counter-Revolution; Student and Youth Movements, Activism and Revolution; Theories of Revolution; Transnational Revolutionary Movements; Trends in Revolution; Vietnamese Revolution

References and Further Readings

Brinton, Crane. 1965. *The Anatomy of Revolution.* New York: Vintage.

DeFronzo, James. 1996. (3rd edition forthcoming in 2007) *Revolutions and Revolutionary Movements.* Boulder, CO: Westview Press.

Foran, John. 2005. *Taking Power: On the Origins of Third World Revolutions.* Cambridge, UK: Cambridge University Press.

———. "Theories of Revolution." Pp. 868–872 in *Revolutionary Movements in World History: From 1750 to the Present* edited by James DeFronzo. Santa Barbara, CA: ABC-CLIO.

Goldfrank, Walter L. 1986. "The Mexican Revolution." Pp. 104–117 in *Revolutions: Theoretical, Comparative, and Historical Studies,* edited by Jack A. Goldstone. San Diego, CA: Harcourt Brace Jovanovich.

Goldstone, Jack A., ed. 1986, 1994. *Revolutions: Theoretical, Comparative, and Historical Studies.* Fort Worth, TX: Harcourt Brace College Publishers.

———. 1998. *The Encyclopedia of Political Revolutions.* Washington DC: Congressional Quarterly.

———. 2001. "An Analytical Framework." Pp. 9-29 in *Revolution: International Dimensions,* edited by Mark N. Katz. Washington DC: Congressional Quarterly Press.

———, Ted Robert Gurr, and Farrokh Moshiri, eds. 1991. *Revolutions of the Late Twentieth Century.* Boulder CO: Westview Press.

Goodwin, Jeff. 2001. "Is the Age of Revolution Over?" Pp. 272—283 in *Revolution: International Dimensions,* edited by Mark N. Katz. Washington DC: Congressional Quarterly Press.

Gurr, Ted Robert. 1970. *Why Men Rebel.* Princeton NJ: Princeton University Press.

Katz, Mark N. 1999. *Revolutions and Revolutionary Waves.* New York: Saint Martin's Press.

———, ed. 2001. *Revolution: International Dimensions.* Washington DC: Congressional Quarterly Press.

———. 2006. "Transnational Revolutionary Movements." Pp. 872–876 in *Revolutionary Movements in World History: From 1750 to the Present* edited by James DeFronzo.

McAdam, Doug, Sidney Tarrow and Charles Tilly. 2001 *Dynamics of Contention.* Cambridge, UK: Cambridge University Press.

Selbin, Eric. 2001. "Same as It Ever Was: The Future of Revolution at the End of the Century." Pp. 284-297 in *Revolution: International Dimensions,* edited by Mark N. Katz. Washington, DC: Congressional Quarterly Press.

Skocpol, Theda. 1979. *States and Revolutions.* Cambridge: Cambridge University Press.

REVOLUTIONARY MOVEMENTS IN WORLD HISTORY

FROM 1750 TO THE PRESENT

Afghanistan: Conflict and Civil War

CHRONOLOGY

Early modern era

1866–1935 Mahmud Tarzi. Key figure among the modernizing intelligentsia that emerges after the ruthless rule of King Abdur Rahman (1880–1901). Advocates social reforms, expansion of education, and improvements in the status of women in the Afghanistan of classic patriarchy.

1872–1919 Habibullah Khan. Ruler who attempts social reforms, including an upper limit on marriage expenditures. This measure is designed to end practices that often led to indebtedness of households.

1892–1960 King Amanullah Khan. In 1921–1922, he institutes a progressive family law and schooling for girls; abolishes slavery. Queen Soraya appears in public unveiled. His reform program meets armed resistance, and he is overthrown in a rebellion in 1928.

Continued attempted reforms

1940s, 1950s Two girls' high schools and Malalai College established.

New restrictions on *walwar* (bride-price or *mahr*).

1964 Constitution under Zahir Shah and Prime Minister Daoud gives women equality and right to vote.

Formation of People's Democratic Party of Afghanistan (PDPA) and Democratic Organization of Afghan Women (DOAW).

1970s Four women from DOAW elected to parliament, including Anahita Ratebzad and Massouma Esmati Wardak.

1971 A new marriage law proclaimed but not enforced.

1973 Daoud overthrows Zahir Shah and establishes a republic.

1977 New constitution establishes equality and sets minimum age of marriage: sixteen for girls and eighteen for boys.

Saur (April) Revolution and the new reform program

1978   PDPA comes to power in April, with Noor Mohammad Taraki as the first president and Hafizullah Amin as vice president of the Democratic Republic of Afghanistan.

DRA announces a reform program; the most controversial elements are decrees number six (to end mortgages and indebtedness), seven (to end "buying and selling of girls," early marriage, and levirate), and eight (redistribution of land).

1978–1979   Tribal-Islamic rebellion emerges; *Mujahidin* (fighters of holy war) groups are organized to combat the leftist government in Kabul.

1979   In July, at the urging of advisor Zbigniew Brzezinski, U.S. president Jimmy Carter approves CIA plan to arm tribal-Islamic opposition. Armed rebellion grows.

In September, President Taraki is killed on orders of Hafizullah Amin.

Internationalized civil conflict

In December, Soviet army intervenes on side of Kabul government.

1980–1985   Babrak Karmal is DRA president. Reagan administration pours billions of dollars into military support for the "freedom fighters"; support for Mujahidin also comes from Pakistan, Iran, Saudi Arabia, and "*jihadis*" from Algeria, Egypt, etc.

1986   DOAW becomes All-Afghan Women's Council; Dr. Najibullah becomes president.

1987   New constitution accepted in November reiterates equality of women and men. Social organizations expand, as do women's roles. Literacy and education expand for females. Women in Kabul are unveiled.

Peshawar, Pakistan, is site of refugee camps, Mujahidin exile headquarters. Schooling is discouraged for girls above age ten. Separate widows' camp. All women are veiled.

1988–1990   The last Soviet troops leave Afghanistan under orders of Gorbachev. Dr. Najibullah changes name of PDPA to National Homeland Front (*Hizb-e Vatan*) and DRA to Republic of Afghanistan. Seeks national reconciliation. United States, Pakistan, and Iran continue to support Mujahidin.

Islamists take control

1992   In April, Mujahidin take control of Kabul; new regulations for women.

1996   In September, Taliban hang Dr. Najibullah, institute new gender regime. United States initially finds "nothing objectionable" in Taliban; interest by the Clinton administration in UNOCAL oil pipeline deal.

1997   International condemnation of Taliban, feminist action by RAWA, WAPHA, Feminist Majority, European feminists, and parliamentarians.

2000–2001   Sanctions against Taliban for harboring Osama bin Laden; widespread poverty, malnutrition, drought in Afghanistan; a new wave of refugees; destruction of the mountain Buddhas.

United States supports "Northern Alliance" of ex-Mujahidin fighting the Taliban.

On September 9, 2001, Ahmad Shah Massoud, former Mujahidin commander and leader of the United Front opposition to Taliban rule in Afghanistan, is assassinated.

Terrorist attacks in October–November. Northern Alliance gains ground. Bonn Agreement concluded. Post-Taliban interim government under Hamid Karzai includes two women, Sima Samar and Soheila Siddiqi.

The Karzai era

2002   Quest for bin Laden continues. ISAF concentrates on Kabul's security; Northern Alliance warlords control the rest of Afghanistan. Loya Jirga (traditional assembly) convenes to create a new constitution.

2003   Loya Jirga and constitutional assembly continue their work. American occupation continues.

2004   In January–September, new constitution formally adopted. Upsurge of violence in run-up to elections.

               In October, elections are held and Karzai is elected president amid charges of irregularities.

2005   In September, first legislative elections since 1969 are held in Afghanistan.

INTRODUCTION

Afghanistan's attempted revolution was launched by a coup in April 1978, when a military unit sympathetic to the beleaguered People's Democratic Party of Afghanistan (PDPA), whose officials had been imprisoned and faced execution, seized control of the presidential palace. Power was quickly turned over to the civilian government of Noor Mohammad Taraki, who represented the radical Khalgh faction of the PDPA. An audacious reform program with socialist overtones was announced but was soon met by tribal and Islamist resistance. The internationalization of the ensuing conflict and civil war, followed by the installation of two Islamist regimes, dashed the revolutionaries' plans for social progress and foreclosed the opportunity for modernization and development in Afghanistan. It also triggered the proliferation of weapons, drugs, and Islamist fighters in the region and beyond.

Afghanistan was the last proxy battle of the Cold War. It altered the face of East-West relations, encouraged the Islamic resurgence, and undermined prospects for modernization. The failure of the revolution prevented the advancement of women, who remain economically dependent on the men in their families and locked into a kin-based patrilineal family structure.

BACKGROUND: CULTURE AND HISTORY

Afghanistan is a predominantly rural country with a traditional social structure of tribes and ethnolinguistic groups. Of these, Pashtuns are the largest, at 44 percent of the population; the Tajiks comprise 25 percent, Hazaras 10 percent, Uzbeks 8 percent, and other minorities 13 percent. Major languages spoken are Pashtu and Dari (the Afghan dialect of Farsi, Persian). The vast majority of the population is Muslim: 84 percent are Sunni and 15 percent are Shias, with only 1 percent listed as "other" (www.afghansite.com). Most adhere to the Sunni Hanafi school of Islamic jurisprudence. Kin-based extended families are patrilocal and patrilineal, characterized by male domination within the family (classic patriarchy) and gender relations remain patriarchal. The main systems of production are nomadic pastoralism, herding and farming, settled agriculture, and small industry, with very limited urbanization. Difficulties with modernization include weak state capacity, center-periphery tensions, and limited legal reform and infrastructural development. In the nineteenth century the tribes united to resist British attempts at colonization, and they united again in the late twentieth century against a pro-Soviet left-wing government. Nevertheless, Afghanistan is still socially and politically fragmented.

Historically, the population of Afghanistan has been fragmented into myriad ethnic, linguistic, religious, kin-based, and regional groupings. The bases of the social structure are the *qawm* (communal group) and the *qabila* (tribe). These microlevel social and political affiliations based on primordial ties have been structural impediments to nation building and economic development. In this social structure—which may be termed *tribal feudalism*—ethnic, religious, and tribal divisions have impeded class formation, maintained provincial patterns of local independence and hostility toward the central government, and perpetuated the use of violence in place of political negotiations. Afghanistan's rugged physical environment also served to isolate communities and create microenvironments. Members of the same ethnic group and tribe who resided in different locations had to adapt to separate microenvironments, which could lead different kin-based groups within the same tribe and ethnic group to use different modes of production. For example, the Durrani Pushtuns that anthropolgist Nancy Tapper studied in the 1970s were primarily agriculturalists, while the Sheikhanzai Durrani Pushtuns, the subject of another anthropologist Tavakolian's research, were primarily pastoralists (Nyrop and Seekins 1986, 105).

The fragmentation and stagnation of the Afghan economy originated during the periodic Turkish invasions of the medieval era, which wreaked havoc on town and country alike. Later, when the country became involved in early international trade, it participated not as a producer of commodities but as a facilitator of transit trade. The early trade routes between China, Central Asia, the Arab states, and Turkey, as well as those between Europe, Russia, and India, cut across Afghan territory, giving rise to what are today the major Afghan cities—Kabul, Herat, Kandahar, and Mazar-e Sharif—and to the emergence of an urban commercial sector geared to servicing caravans and organizing transportation of goods. In Afghanistan, economic links between the towns

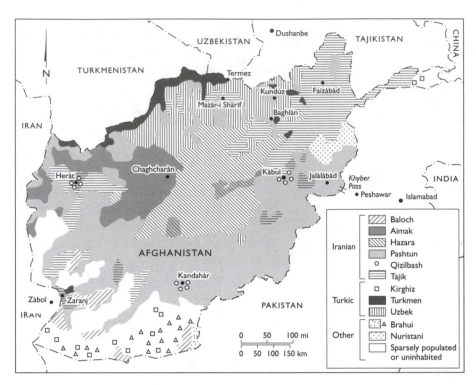

Afghanistan, showing the areas where major ethnolinguistic groups are located.

were initially as undeveloped as their links with the surrounding rural areas. Competition from the Russians and the British in the nineteenth century inhibited further development. The reorientation of trade toward export production (of agricultural raw materials and carpets) at the end of the nineteenth century reinforced the stagnation of the national industrial sector. Other important factors in Afghanistan's economic and social underdevelopment are its rugged terrain, making transportation hazardous and costly, the absence of central authority and a taxation system, and the persistence of tribalism and pastoral nomadism (Nyrop and Seekins 1986, 140–185; Gibbs 1986, 36–95; Gregorian 1969, 19–24; Gangovsky 1985, 182–184).

The development planning that began in the 1950s did not reduce the by-then deeply entrenched dichotomies between rural and urban areas and between foreign trade and domestic production. This was mainly because Afghanistan remained a prototypical weak state, inasmuch as the central authorities were not able to realize their goals or to regulate social relations and use resources in determined ways (Urban 1988).

Afghanistan's experience with modernization and social reforms has been a tortuous one. Since the mid nineteenth century, various governments and rulers have tried to develop the infrastructure and extend schooling, end usurious forms of lending, and discourage excessive expenditure on bride-price and marriage celebrations as a way of preventing rural indebtedness. Mohammad Hashim Kamali (1985)

writes that combating pernicious custom in the area of matrimonial law constituted a major preoccupation of the statutory legislation that Afghanistan has experienced in this field ever since at least the 1920s.

The reformer Mahmud Tarzi (1866–1935), royal adviser and editor of *Siraj al-Akhbar Afghaniyah,* a biweekly paper and forum for the "Young Afghans," appealed for compulsory education, including that of girls. He devoted a series of articles to famous women in history that discussed the many abilities of women. Since in his view the health, welfare, and education of Afghan families were essential to Afghan progress, he also attacked the extravagant expenditures incurred in connection with multiple marriages, which often financially ruined families due to interest rates as high as 75 percent on the loans that they took out (Gregorian 1969, 172).

Reform initiatives in government authority either resulted in tribal rebellion or could not be implemented outside the confines of Kabul's elite social groups. Government attempts to improve and standardize educational curriculum were not successful. The *mullahs,* especially those outside Kabul, opposed the government's control of education, the teacher-training center, and the teaching of English and of modern subjects in general (Gregorian 1969, 198). Habibullah's son, King Amanullah, introduced an audacious reform program, but it was defeated. The king was forced to abdicate in 1928 by a tribal rebellion opposed to schooling for girls, restrictions on polygyny, and prohibition of the brideprice (Nawid 1999).

Social reforms were not attempted again until the 1950s. During the long reign of Zahir Shah (1933–1973), very little modernization, social change, or meaningful legal reform took place, in contrast to developments in neighboring Iran. The 1964 constitution guaranteed education and political rights for women and men alike, but these were enjoyed by only the small urban elite, mainly in Kabul. The Civil Code 1977 (*Qanun-e Madani*), which was introduced as a decree law under President Daoud, enacted statutory marriageable ages for boys and girls, thereby indirectly outlawing child marriage. Some restrictions were also imposed on polygamy and divorce (Kamali 1985, 86–87).

Afghan nationalism has been incipient at best, as the concepts of nation-state and national identity are absent from much of the population, though nationalism has been promoted by modernizing elites since the nineteenth century (Gregorian 1969; Canfield 1989; Hyman 2002). During most of the country's modern history, the fragmented groupings waged war on each other. Battles were fought principally over land and water, sometimes over women and honor, usually over sheer power. Interethnic hostility among Afghans has been widely discussed in the literature. Anthropolgist Nancy Tapper describes ethnic identity in terms of claims of religiously privileged descent and superiority to all other ethnic groups. Durrani women, for example, were absolutely prohibited from marrying men of a "lower" ethnic status (Tapper 1984, 304).

One of the few commonalities in this diverse country is Islam. Yet Afghan Islam is a unique combination of practices and precepts from the Sharia and tribal customs, particularly Pakhtunwali, the tribal code of the Pashtuns. Anthropological studies in the 1970s found that the absence of inheritance rights for women—which is contrary to Islamic law—was integral to the complex web of the tribal exchange system. The practice of usury, banned under Islamic law, was widespread, keeping rural households in almost perpetual indebtedness. Exorbitant expenditure in marriages was another source of the rural household's debt accumulation. The Islamic dower or *mahr* (*walwar* in Pushtu) was abused in the Afghan tribal-patriarchal context. The *mahr,* a payment due from groom to bride, is an essential part of the Islamic marriage contract. In the Quran the *mahr* is a nominal fee. In many Muslim countries its purpose is to provide a kind of insurance for the wife in the event of divorce or widowhood. But in tribal Afghanistan, *walwar* was understood to be compensation to the bride's father for the loss of his daughter's labor in the household and was part of the groom's ownership claim over his wife. It was essentially the price for a girl. The heaviest expenses any household had to bear were concerned with marriage. The choice of bride, the agreed bride-price, and the usurious rates of moneylenders could plunge a household into debt and poverty (Tapper 1984; Kamali 1985).

In the 1970s, Afghanistan's central social unit was the extended family, in which the senior man had authority over everyone else, including younger men, and an age-based hierarchy existed among the women. These extended families were characterized by restrictive codes of behavior, sex-segregation, and the association of female virtue with family honor. Women's mobility was extremely circumscribed, since they were confined largely to the household; if they appeared in public it was in a tent-like covering with a net over the eyes, called the *burqa* or *chadori.* Among the Pashtuns in particular, women and children were considered property belonging to a male (Tapper 1984). A strict sexual division of labor assigned to women the role of producer of carpets and reproducer of children. Due to higher-than-normal rates of mortality among women and girl-children, at the end of the 1970s the population of Afghanistan was 48.6 percent female and 51.4 percent male (Centlivres-Demont 1994, 335).

In a patriarchal context, marriage and bride-price are transactions between households, an integral part of property relations and the exchange system. In Afghanistan, marriage, forced or voluntary, was a way of ending feuds, cementing a political alliance between families, increasing a family's prestige, or accumulating wealth. In such a social structure, the rights of individuals were moot—and those of women and young girls virtually nonexistent.

CONTEXT AND PROCESS OF REVOLUTION

On the eve of the 1978 revolution, the Afghan government relied heavily on foreign aid—as much as 80 percent for its development expenditure (Griffiths 1981, 136). Arable land was in short supply and patterns of ownership highly inequitable, with a few families (including families of some of the men who would become Mujahidin leaders) owning vast acreage on which peasants sharecropped. Agricultural productivity was low, and the system of food distribution inefficient; thus food shortages were common. Between 94 and 98 percent of women were illiterate, and Afghanistan lagged considerably behind its neighbors Pakistan and Iran, not to mention the republics of the Soviet Union, on almost every social indicator. Thus the men and women of the pro-Soviet People's Democratic Party of Afghanistan (PDPA), which had been formed in 1965, were eager for more profound and rapid change (Moghadam 2003).

In the 1970s, Kabul was a hotbed of radical politics. Nationalists, Communists, monarchists, Islamists, and ethnic-based groupings sought to recruit new members, vied for influence, competed with each other, and sometimes fought each other. Schools and universities were sites of ideological battles, recruitment drives, and ethnic rivalries. The Left was far from united. Maoists, Trotskyists, and pro-Soviet Communists were bitter rivals. The PDPA had split into two factions: the more radical and Pashtun-dominant Khalgh group, and the Parcham group, dominated by Persian speakers who advocated gradualism (Halliday 1978). A Maoist schoolteacher named Meena formed the Revolutionary Association of Women of Afghanistan (RAWA) in 1977.

Between the 1950s and 1970s, Afghanistan received little attention in Washington, but increasing Soviet influence and the growth in popularity of the PDPA began to alarm Cold Warriors. After overthrowing his cousin and patron, Zahir Shah, in 1973, Prime Minister Daoud sought more Soviet assistance for development purposes. At the same time, he was hostile to the PDPA. Following a trip to Iran, then ruled by the anti-Communist Shah Mohammad Reza Pahlavi, Daoud clamped down on the PDPA, imprisoning most of its leadership. This action precipitated a takeover of the state apparatus by a military unit sympathetic to the PDPA.

The uprising came as a surprise to many PDPA members, who felt that the party was not prepared to assume political power. Given the circumstances, however, they prepared a program of political, economic, and social reform (personal communication from Jamila Palwasha, Utrecht, Holland, October 17, 2004). At the helm were President Noor Mohammad Taraki and his deputy Hafizullah Amin, both from the Khalgh faction. An eight-point reform program, the "Saur [April] Revolution," was launched, and the Democratic Republic of Afghanistan (DRA) came into being.

Three decrees—Numbers 6, 7, and 8—were the main planks of the program of social and economic reform. Decree Number 6 was intended to put an end to land mortgage and indebtedness; Number 7 was designed to stop the payment of bride-price and give women more freedom of choice in marriage (it specifically forbade forced engagements or marriages, requiring instead the full consent of the parties involved, and it banned giving a girl in engagement or marriage in exchange for cash or for commodities [Beattie 1984, 186]); Number 8 consisted of rules and regulations for the confiscation and redistribution of land.

The PDPA government also embarked upon an aggressive literacy campaign led by the DOAW, whose function was to educate women, bring them out of seclusion, and initiate social programs. PDPA activists organized literacy classes in the villages for men, women, and children, and by August 1979 the government had established 600 new schools (Katsikas 1982, 231).

The audacious program of revolutionary change, state-building, and women's rights aimed at the rapid transformation of a patriarchal society and a power structure based on tribal and landlord authority. This led one commentator to write: "The novel character of the new regime [in Afghanistan] soon became apparent. It committed itself to land reform, to equality of the nationalities, to emancipating women, to a solution of the nomadic question. So it was that at a time and in a place suspected by few, and in a country renowned only for colonial war and narcotic plenitude, a revolutionary process of some description had begun" (Halliday 1978, 3).

The emphasis on women's rights on the part of the PDPA reflected (a) their socialist/Marxist ideology, (b) their modernizing and egalitarian outlook, (c) their social base and origins—urban middle-class professionals educated in the U.S., U.S.S.R., India, and Western and Eastern Europe, and (d) the influence of women members of the PDPA, such as Anahita Ratebzad (see below). But land reform, cancellation of peasants' debts, and marriage reform threatened vested rural interests and patriarchal structures that benefited the large landowners, the religious establishment, and money lenders. In the summer of 1978, Afghans began to pour into Pakistan, citing the forcible schooling of their daughters as the reason. An Islamist opposition began organizing and conducted several armed actions against the government in the spring of 1979.

The year of the Afghan revolution was also the year of massive anti-Shah street demonstrations in Iran and military intrigues in Pakistan. In Iran, the anti-Shah movement turned into an Islamic revolution, while in Pakistan, a military coup overthrew the secular government of Zulfiqar Ali Bhutto and installed the Islamist General Zia-ul-Haq. Afghanistan was now surrounded by Islamist states hostile to Communism, and they began to encourage resistance to the progressive reform program of the Kabul government.

At the same time, the United States became alarmed by Soviet influence in Afghanistan. The Carter administration authorized CIA funding of the rebellion in July 1979, six months before the Soviet intervention. As Zbigniew Brzezinski, President Carter's national security adviser, stated in a January 1998 interview with the French magazine *Nouvelle Observateur*: "According to the official view of history, CIA aid to the mujahidin began during 1980, that is, after the Soviet army invaded Afghanistan. But the reality, secretly guarded until now, is completely otherwise." The goal was to lure Moscow, then deeply troubled by the spread of Islamic fundamentalism in the Soviet central Asian republics, into the "trap" of Afghanistan (Brzezinski 1998; Cordovez and Harrison 1995, 103; Gibbs 2000, 241–242; Coll 2004).

Internal battles within the PDPA and hostility between its two wings, Parcham and Khalgh, contributed to the government's difficulties. In September 1979, President Taraki was killed on the orders of his deputy, Hafizullah Amin, a ruthless and ambitious man who imprisoned and executed hundreds of his own comrades and further alienated the population. Leaders in the U.S.S.R. became alarmed that Amin's actions were provoking a wider Islamist rebellion that po-

Rebel soldiers known as Mujahidin (fighters of holy war) rest high in the mountains in the Kunar province of Afghanistan in May 1980. Though the soldiers were comprised of warring, noncohesive factions, the Soviet invasion of Afghanistan was finally repelled in 1989, 10 years after the conflict began. (AP/Wide World Photos)

tentially could spread to Islamic areas in the Soviet Union. In December 1979, following months of requests for assistance from Kabul, the Soviet army intervened. Amin was killed and succeeded by Babrak Karmal, who initiated what is called "the second phase" (*marhale-ye dovvom*), predicated upon a more gradualist approach to change. Even so, the Mujahidin continued their attacks, encouraged by Pakistan, the United States, Saudi Arabia, and China. U.S. officials rebuffed U.N. efforts to bring about a negotiated settlement and developed a covert military aid program for the Mujahidin. In turn, Soviet aircraft carried out bombing raids on rebel sites that resulted in considerable destruction as well as further migration. The refugee population, concentrated in Peshawar, eventually ballooned to about 2 million Afghans. Refugees also went to the Islamic Republic of Iran, which encouraged the rebellion.

The 1980s saw efforts by the Reagan administration to maintain a favorable image for the rebels in the news media;

Soviet leader Mikhail Gorbachev's attempts to extricate the Red Army from Afghanistan; the impact of the war on Pakistan, including an explosion in unrestrained arms and drug trafficking; U.S. contact with and manipulation of Islam and tribal politics; the genesis and results of USAID's (U.S. Agency for International Development) unorthodox Cross-Border Humanitarian Assistance Program designed to aid citizens and rebels inside "liberated" areas of Afghanistan; massive amounts of money and guns for the *jihad;* and the impact on Afghanistan, its infrastructure and its people, of a war which took over 1 million lives and uprooted nearly half the country's population. The CIA, the KGB, Pakistan's ISI (Inter-Services Intelligence), and Saudi Arabia's General Intelligence Department all operated in Afghanistan. They primed Afghan factions with cash and weapons, secretly trained guerrilla forces, funded propaganda, and manipulated politics. In the midst of the struggles, bin Laden conceived and built his transnational network (Coll 2004). U.S. military aid to the "resistance" began under the Carter administration and increased substantially under President Reagan, with Saudi Arabia matching U.S. aid. Barnet Rubin estimates "approximately $5 billion in weapons sent to the mujahidin during 1986–1990". (Rubin 1995, 179–180) Military aid had the overall aim of exhausting and ultimately destroying the Soviet Union (Pilger 2003, 47).

At the same time, CIA director William Casey gave his backing to a plan put forward by Pakistan's intelligence agency to recruit people from around the world to join the Afghan *jihad*. More than 100,000 Islamic militants were trained in Pakistan between 1986 and 1992, in camps overseen by the CIA and MI6 (British intelligence), with the SAS (British Special Air Service) training future al-Qaeda and Taliban fighters in bomb-making and other violent techniques (Pilger 2003, 47). Their leaders were trained at a CIA camp in Virginia in what was called Operation Cyclone, which continued even after the Soviets had withdrawn in 1989 (Pilger 2003, 47).

The last of the Soviet troops left Afghanistan in early February 1989, and the Kabul government and its military managed to withstand the U.S./Pakistan/Saudi-funded Mujahidin and their Arab allies until 1992. The government of Dr. Najibullah, previously a functionary in the Khad, or political police, who succeeded Babrak Karmal as head of the PDPA and president of Afghanistan in 1986, sought international support for a peace settlement, but very little was forthcoming in the face of U.S. opposition. In June 1990 the PDPA held a party congress and voted to change its name to Hezb-e Vatan (Homeland Party) to emphasize nationalism and reconciliation. But this and similar measures proved futile. The defection of a general led to the weakening of the military, and Kabul succumbed in late April 1992. The Saur Revolution was over.

IMPACTS

The impacts of the Afghan revolution were both positive and negative domestically and largely negative internationally. The positive domestic impacts included the growth of social organizations and opportunities for women (Moghadam 1994; 2003). Thus a number of women who became prominent in the post-Taliban era were products of the educational and employment opportunities of the DRA. Literacy and education expanded, too. For example, just before the Saur Revolution, according to official sources, 98 percent of women and 95 percent of men were illiterate. In 1985–1986, however, efforts at literacy produced some 118,000 newly literate persons (Rahimi 1991, 38).

The negative internal impact was the emergence of an armed counter-revolution, which led to Soviet intervention and massive movements of refugee populations to Iran and Pakistan, from which the Taliban emerged. The impact of the conflict included rural and infrastructural damage; the prolif-

eration of weapons and narcotics under the control first of the Mujahidin, then the Taliban, and later the Northern Alliance warlords; a huge growth in the population of widows (the notorious adverse sex ratio of the past was reversed, in favor of women); and the eventual substitution of American occupation for Soviet occupation. Internationally, the negative impacts of the counter-revolution included the proliferation of armed Islamist fighters in Central Asia, the Middle East, and southeast Asia. Islamist groups began to fill the void created by the collapse of the Soviet Union and the ideology of Communism, and the defeat of the Soviet Union in Afghanistan encouraged them to wage battles in Algeria and elsewhere.

The December 1979 Soviet intervention in Afghanistan became a seminal event in the history of the Cold War. It represented the largest Soviet military operation since World War II. The invasion was also decisively important for the United States. It was during the Afghan crisis that President Jimmy Carter shifted U.S. policy from detente to Cold War confrontation. In addition to the hostage crisis in Iran, the Afghan situation may have contributed to Carter's defeat in the 1980 election and the implementation of a much more aggressive foreign policy under Ronald Reagan, whose principal objective was the collapse of the Soviet Union. The nine-year-long military engagement became traumatic for the Soviet Union and may have contributed to Gorbachev's "new thinking": glasnost and perestroika internally, a new foreign policy externally. And of course the conflict was especially important for the people of Afghanistan, who experienced an internationalized war and enormous suffering. For Afghans, devastation and suffering continued after the withdrawal of Soviet troops in early 1989 and the downfall of the left-wing government in late April 1992 during the years of internecine warfare and lawlessness under the Mujahidin (1992–1996), during the repressive years of the Taliban (1996–2001), and during the American bombing campaigns to drive out the Taliban and capture Osama bin Laden and al-Qaeda members responsible for the September 11, 2001, tragedies in the United States.

Following the U.S. invasion, representatives of Afghan political factions (excluding Communists) met in Bonn, Germany, in December 2001. The Bonn Agreement established the basic framework of a new government for Afghanistan and provided for "the establishment of a broad-based, gender-sensitive, multiethnic and fully representative government . . . with due regard to the ethnic, geographic and religious composition of Afghanistan and to the importance of participation of women" (www.afghangovernment.com/AfghanAgreementBonn.htm).

The Islamic Transitional State of Afghanistan, whose leadership included warlords and tribal leaders and a nominal interim president, Hamid Karzai, launched a constitution-making exercise in accordance with the principles of the Bonn

UN Afghanistan envoy Lakhdar Brahimi signs a UN-brokered Afghanistan deal under the eyes of Afghanistan leaders in Koenigswinter near Bonn December 5, 2001. In rear row are (right to left) German Foreign Minister Joschka Fischer, German Chancellor Gerhard Schroeder and UN deputy Afghanistan envoy Francesc Vendrell. Afghan rivals struck a landmark accord to set aside two decades of war and form a post-Taliban government led by Pashtun chief Hamid Karzai to steer their shattered nation toward democracy. (Reuters/Corbis)

Agreement, such as "the right of the people of Afghanistan to freely determine their own political future in accordance with the principles of Islam, democracy, pluralism and social justice" (www.afghangovernment.com/AfghanAgreementBonn.htm). The Bonn Agreement stipulated that "free and fair elections" to choose a "fully representative government" would be held no later than two years from the date of the convening of the constitution creating Loya Jirga (a traditional assembly which convened in June 2002). Islamist elements, however, remained strong, and Hamid Karzai conceded to their insistence that his outspoken minister of women's affairs, Sima Samar, considered to have made "blasphemous" utterances while abroad, be removed from her post. She was replaced by Habiba Sorabi. The two other women in government were Dr. Suhaila Siddiq, the minister of public health, and Prof. Mahbuba Huquqmal, the minister of state for women's issues.

During the Loya Jirga, in December 2003, a female delegate from the western province of Farah, where women face some of the worst abuses, was temporarily thrown out when she complained that the same warlords from the old days were in charge in the "new" Afghanistan. Malalai Joya dared to speak out about "the treatment of women in her country and of the creeping dominance of drug-dealing tribal warlords over the assembly and the country itself. They were the ones who destroyed our country. They should be tried in international and national courts. If our poor people forgive these criminals, history will never forgive them, their criminal activities have all been recorded in history" (UNIFEM 2003, 14–16). Joya's microphone was cut off as dozens of male delegates rushed toward constitutional assembly chair Sighbatullah Mojadeddi's platform, some shouting "Death to Communism!" and "Kick the Communists out of the tent!" Mojadeddi had Joya removed.

Adopted in January 2004, the new constitution grants equal rights to women, even promising two parliament seats in each province to women. It mandates a directly elected president and a two-chamber national assembly. (The first presidential elections were held in October 2004, and parliamentary and local elections were scheduled for 2005.) But Mojadeddi, the constitutional assembly chairman, insisted on including references to Islamic law. Thus the country is now the "Islamic Republic of Afghanistan." There is to be a system of civil law, but no law will be contrary to the beliefs and provisions of Islam, a provision that many believe opens the door to the introduction of Sharia law, which, in its strict interpretations, penalizes various forms of "immorality" and punishes crimes with executions and amputations.

During 2004, heavy fighting between rival militias raged on in the north of Afghanistan. In the south, civilian deaths caused by U.S. assaults against presumed al-Qaeda sites caused resentful locals to turn against Karzai's government. The government of Hamid Karzai remained dependant on the U.S. for its security and financial viability.

In 2004, Afghanistan remained a poor, pastoral country. Conflicts have rendered the country bereft of economic, social, and political resources and awash in narcotics. President Karzai ran a shell of a government with Mujahidin warlords in the cabinet of ministers. The position of women in Afghanistan continued to be abysmal. They now constituted 60 percent of the population due to the high death rates of men in war and out-migration over more than two decades. Female literacy was estimated at only 10–20 percent, with men's literacy at 40–52 percent. Life expectancy for women was 44 years, with death in childbirth being the biggest cause of women's deaths. Depression and suicide of women continued to be major mental health issues (Physicians for Human Rights 2001).

In summary, between 1978 and 2004 Afghans experienced a traumatic transition from a revolution launching the Democratic Republic of Afghanistan to a counter-revolution that culminated in the Islamic Republic of Afghanistan.

PEOPLE AND ORGANIZATIONS

Amin, Hafizullah (1929–1979)

Member of the radical Khalgh faction of the PDPA who became vice president following the April 1978 coup. In power, he rejected any and all dissidence and filled Kabul's prisons. Among those imprisoned were his own comrades from the Parcham wing of the PDPA. Amin's killing of Noor Mohammad Taraki triggered the Soviet intervention, and Amin was himself killed.

Central Intelligence Agency (CIA)

The Central Intelligence Agency of the United States worked with the Pakistani ISI to undermine the PDPA and DRA and strengthen the tribal-Islamist rebellion. Throughout the 1980s, the CIA provided the ISI with funds and arms for the Mujahidin

concentrated in Peshawar, Pakistan. The CIA and ISI also established training camps for the Afghan Mujahidin and for Arab volunteers who joined the anti-communist crusade/*jihad.*

Democratic Republic of Afghanistan (DRA)

The Democratic Republic of Afghanistan was established in April 1978, following a coup that brought to power the People's Democratic Party of Afghanistan (PDPA). In 1987 the name changed to the Republic of Afghanistan.

Hekmatyar, Gulbeddin (Born 1947?)

One of the Mujahidin commanders, he was a favorite of the CIA and ISI and received the lion's share of funds and arms. In the 1970s he became notorious for throwing acid at young women who were not wearing the *burqa.* He helped to launch the civil conflict of the post-Najibullah period.

Inter-Service Intelligence (ISI)

Pakistan's Inter-Service Intelligence agency worked with the CIA to undermine the PDPA and DRA and strengthen the tribal-Islamist rebellion. The CIA provided the ISI with funds and arms for the Mujahidin concentrated in Peshawar, Pakistan. The CIA and ISI also established training camps for the Afghan Mujahidin and for Arab volunteers who joined the anti-Communist crusade/*jihad.*

Karmal, Babrak (1929–1996)

A member of the Parcham faction of the PDPA, he became president of Afghanistan following the Soviet intervention and the death of Hafizullah Amin. He launched the "second phase" (*marhale-ye dovvom*) of the Saur Revolution and tried to continue the reform program while also trying to undo its more radical and provocative aspects. His other main preoccupation was the growing tribal-Islamist rebellion, then openly aided by the governments of the United States, Pakistan, Saudi Arabia, the Islamic Republic of Iran, and China. He resigned in 1986 for medical reasons and stayed in Moscow for treatment. He was succeeded by Dr. Najibullah.

Massoud, Ahmad Shah (1953–2001)

One of the Mujahidin commanders, he was very popular in France (he was conversant in French) but a thorn in the side of the Kabul government's army. After the Mujahidin came to power in late April 1992, he helped to launch an internecine battle with former allies.

Mujahidin

Formed when seven tribal-Islamist groups fighting the DRA united, encouraged by Pakistan's secret service (ISI) and the U.S. government's CIA. As they claimed to be launching a *jihad* (holy war) against Communists, they were also known as *jihadis*. They took power in late April 1992, after which Dr. Najibullah, president of Afghanistan from 1986, took refuge in the United Nations compound.

Najibullah, Mohammad (1947–1996)

An ethnically Pashtun medical doctor who in 1986 succeeded Babrak Karmal as head of the PDPA and president of Afghanistan. Previously he had been a functionary in the Khad, or political police. He sought to de-radicalize the revolution by dropping the "Democratic" from Republic of Afghanistan and later changing the PDPA to a more inclusive nationalist front organization. These measures proved futile as the United States and Pakistan were determined to ensure the downfall of the leftist government through strengthening the tribal-Islamist Mujahidin.

People's Democratic Party of Afghanistan (PDPA)

The People's Democratic Party of Afghanistan, formed in 1965 and aligned to the Soviet Union, broke into two factions defined by ethnic and political differences: the Pashtun-dominated and more militant Khalgh (masses) faction, and the Persian-speaking Parcham (banner) faction, which favored gradualism. The PDPA came to power following a coup in April 1978, which led to the dominance of Khalgh. After the Soviet intervention in December 1979, the Persian-speaking Parcham faction dominated. The PDPA ruled Afghanistan during the 1980s, with both Pashtun-speakers and Persian-speakers in government posts. As part of the effort to end the civil conflict and seek reconciliation, the PDPA was dissolved in 1990 and morphed into the National Homeland Front.

Ratebzad, Anahita (Born 1928)

A member of the Parcham faction of the PDPA, she also helped to found the Democratic Organization of Afghan Women (DOAW) in 1965 and was one of four female members of parliament in the 1970s. In 1976 she was elected to the central committee of the PDPA. Following the Saur Revolution, she was elected to the Revolutionary Council of the DRA and appointed Minister of Social Affairs. She was a principal agent in the reform program to raise the status of Afghan women and girls and to expand schooling. A charismatic figure who was active through most of the 1980s, she withdrew when her daughter was paralyzed in a Mujahidin rocket attack. She currently lives in Berlin.

Revolutionary Association of the Women of Afghanistan (RAWA)

RAWA was founded in Kabul in 1977 as an organization of Afghan women working for human rights and social justice. Its members advocate the establishment of a secular democracy in Afghanistan and expanded opportunities for women and work running schools, literacy programs, medical clinics, orphanages, and in providing assistance to Afghan refugees in Pakistan.

Taliban

The Peshawar "religious students" who mobilized in 1994 because of Mujahidin fighting, corruption, kidnappings, and rapes. They ousted the Mujahidin in September 1996, hanged Dr. Najibullah, and established a conservative Islamist regime until ousted by the 2001 U.S. invasion.

Taraki, Noor Mohammad (1917–1979)

Leader of the radical Khalgh faction of the PDPA, he became president following the April 1978 coup and launched the eight-point revolutionary program. He sought Soviet assistance as the tribal-Islamic resistance gained ground in 1979 and was killed in a palace coup by his deputy, Hafizullah Amin, an event which triggered the Soviet intervention.

Women's Alliance for Peace and Human Rights in Afghanistan (WAPHA)

WAPHA is an organization that works for human rights for Afghan women and girls. They support full equality for women and for participaton in every aspect of life, including the country's political, economic, educational, and medical systems.

Valentine M. Moghadam

See Also Cinema of Revolution; Documentaries of Revolution; Islamic Fundamentalist Revolutionary Movement; Russian Revolution of 1991 and the Dissolution of the U.S.S.R; Transnational Revolutionary Movements

References and Further Readings

Beattie, Hugh. 1984. "Effects of the Saur Revolution in Nahrin." Pp. 184–207 in *Revolutions and Rebellions in Afghanistan,* edited by Nazif Shahrani and Robert Canfield. Berkeley: University of California International Studies Institute.

Brzezinski, Zbigniew. 1998. "Les Révélations d'un Ancien Conseiller de Carter: 'Oui, la CIA est Entrée en Afghanistan avant les Russes . . ." *Le Nouvel Observateur* (Paris, January 15–21): 76.

Canfield, Robert. 1989. "Afghanistan: The Trajectory of Internal Alignments." *Middle East Journal* 42 (4) (Autumn): 635–648.

Centlivres-Demont, Micheline. 1994. "Afghan Women in Peace, War, and Exile." Pp. 333–365 in *The Politics of Social Transformation in Afghanistan, Iran, and Pakistan,* edited by Myron Weiner and Ali Banuazizi. Syracuse, NY: Syracuse University Press.

Coll, Steve. 2004. *Ghost Wars: The Secret History of the CIA, Afghanistan, and Bin Laden, from the Soviet Invasion to September 10, 2001.* New York: Penguin Books.

Cordovez, Diego, and Selig Harrison. 1995. *Out of Afghanistan: The Inside Story of the Soviet Withdrawal.* Oxford: Oxford University Press.

Gankovsky, Yuri. 1985. *A History of Afghanistan.* Moscow: Progress Publishers.

Gibbs, David. 1986. "The Peasant as Counterrevolutionary: The Rural Origins of the Afghan Insurgency." *Studies in Comparative International Development* 21 (1): 36–95.

———. 2000. "Afghanistan: The Soviet Invasion in Retrospect." Review Essay. *International Politics* 37 (June): 233–246.

Gregorian, Vartan. 1969. *The Emergence of Modern Afghanistan.* Stanford, CA: Stanford University Press.

Griffiths, John. 1981. *Afghanistan.* Boulder, CO: Westview Press.

Halliday, Fred. 1978. "Revolution in Afghanistan." *New Left Review* 112 (November/December): 3–44.

Hyman, Anthony. 2002. "Nationalism in Afghanistan." *International Journal of Middle East Studies* 34: 299–315.

Kamali, Mohammad Hashim. 1985. *Law in Afghanistan: A Study of the Constitutions, Matrimonial Law and the Judiciary.* Leiden, Netherlands: E. J. Brill.

Katsikas, Suzanne Jolicoeur. 1982. *The Arc of Socialist Revolutions: Angola to Afghanistan.* Cambridge, MA: Schenkman Publishers.

Moghadam, Valentine M. 1994. "Building Human Resources and Women's Capabilities in Afghanistan: A Retrospect and Prospects." *World Development* 22 (6): 859–875.

———. 2003. *Modernizing Women: Gender and Social Change in the Middle East.* 2nd ed. Boulder, CO: Westview Press.

Nawid, Senzil. 1999. *Religious Response to Social Change in Afghanistan 1919–29.* Costa Mesa, CA: Mazda Publishers.

Nyrop, Richard, and Donald Seekins. 1986. *Afghanistan: A Country Study.* Washington, DC: The American University. Foreign Area Studies.

Physicians for Human Rights. 2001. *Women's Health and Human Rights in Afghanistan: A Population-Based Assessment* (Boston: PHR).

Pilger, John. 2003. "What Good Friends Left Behind." *The Guardian* (September 20): 43–49.

Rahimi, Wali. 1991. *Status of Women in Afghanistan.* Bangkok: UNESCO Regional Office.

Rubin, Barnett. 1995. *The Fragmentation of Afghanistan: State Formation and Collapse in the International System.* New Haven: Yale University Press.

Tapper, Nancy. 1984. "Causes and Consequences of the Abolition of Bride Price in Afghanistan." Pp. 291–305 in *Revolutions and Rebellions in Afghanistan: Anthropological Perspective,* edited by Nazif Shahrani and Robert Canfield. Berkeley: University of California International Studies Institute.

Urban, Mark. 1988. *War in Afghanistan.* New York: St. Martin's Press.

UNIFEM. 2003. *Afghanistan: Women in the News* [a compilation of articles published in the media about women]. No. 11 (13–18 December). Kabul: UNIFEM.

Afghanistan Government Web Site www.afghangovernment.com/AfghanAgreementBonn.htm accessed Nov. 28, 2004.

Afghansite.Com www.afghansite.com accessed Nov. 28, 2004.

African American Freedom Struggle

CHRONOLOGY

1776	African slaves in North America are encouraged to demand rights after British colonists issue Declaration of Independence insisting that "all men are created equal, that they are endowed by their Creator with certain unalienable Rights, that among these are Life, Liberty, and the pursuit of Happiness."
1788	Former colonies ratify the Constitution of the United States, which protects the institution of slavery and defers decision on ending the slave trade until 1808.
1791	French Revolution sparks slave revolt in French Caribbean colony of Saint-Domingue, and slave rebels under the leadership of Toussaint-Louverture repeatedly repulse forces sent to suppress them.
1800	Virginia slaveholders execute participants in planned slave insurrection inspired by Saint-Domingue revolt and instigated by a slave blacksmith named Gabriel.
1804	Saint-Domingue becomes the republic of Haiti.

1822   Slave conspiracy in South Carolina led by Denmark Vesey, a free black carpenter who had traveled extensively in the Caribbean, is crushed by white authorities.

1829   Free black Bostonian David Walker publishes *Appeal to the Coloured Citizens of the World,* calling upon African Americans to join in a movement toward "the entire emancipation of your enslaved brethren all over the world."

1830   American Society of Free People of Colour, the first national meeting of African Americans, convenes in Philadelphia.

1831   Nat Turner leads slave revolt in Virginia resulting in death of fifty-five whites before militia forces capture and execute rebels.

1833   American Anti-Slavery Society formed in Philadelphia.

1840   Breaking with the gradualism of the American Anti-Slavery Society, black and white activists form the American and Foreign Anti-Slavery Society to support political candidates opposed to slavery.

1850   Seeking to heal sectional conflicts over the expansion of slavery into the western territories of the United States, Congress passes the Compromise of 1850, which includes a Fugitive Slave Act requiring private citizens to help capture runaway slaves.

1857   In *Dred Scott v. Sandford,* the Supreme Court rules that slaves and their descendants cannot acquire citizenship by moving to free states and that Congress's Missouri Compromise of 1820 was unconstitutional in limiting slavery in American territories.

1859   White abolitionist John Brown and black allies attack a federal armory in Harper's Ferry, Virginia, in an unsuccessful effort to spark a slave rebellion.

1861   Eleven southern slave states react to election of Republican Abraham Lincoln by seceding from Union to form the Confederate States of America, igniting Civil War.

1863   President Lincoln issues Emancipation Proclamation freeing slaves within the Confederate states.

1865   Following Confederate defeat, the Thirteenth Amendment is ratified, abolishing slavery in the United States.

1868   Fourteenth Amendment, protecting the citizenship rights of African Americans, is ratified.

1870   Fifteenth Amendment, prohibiting denial of voting rights "on account of race, color, or previous condition of servitude," is ratified.

1883   The Supreme Court declares that the Fourteenth Amendment prohibits racial discrimination by states but not by individuals.

1895   In a major speech in Atlanta, black educator Booker T. Washington urges African Americans to accommodate to southern racial segregation.

1896   In *Plessy v. Ferguson,* the Supreme Court concludes that laws requiring black Americans to use "separate but equal" facilities—such as trains and schools—do not violate the Thirteenth or Fourteenth Amendments.

        National Association of Colored Women founded with motto "lifting as we climb."

1905   Niagara Movement organized by W. E. B. Du Bois and other critics of Booker T. Washington's policy of accommodating to segregation.

1909   Reacting to Springfield, Illinois, race riot, black and white reformers establish the National Association for the Advancement of Colored People (NAACP).

1911   The National Urban League is formed to help black migrants to cities.

1916   Jamaican immigrant and black nationalist Marcus Garvey arrives in Harlem and soon recruits thousands of members for his Universal Negro Improvement Association (UNIA).

1919   Following the great migration of black southerners to northern cities, deadly racial rioting erupts in Chicago, Washington, and Omaha.

1921   Destruction of Tulsa's black community by a white mob results in more than fifty deaths.

1931   After nine black teenagers charged with rape are sentenced to death in Alabama, a Communist-led campaign results in new trials and Supreme Court rulings that defendants were denied adequate legal counsel and that black jurors were systematically excluded.

1938   In a case argued by NAACP lawyers, the Supreme Court rules that states must provide equal, even if separate, educational facilities for African Americans.

1940   The NAACP Legal Defense and Education Fund, Inc., is established under the leadership of Thurgood Marshall.

1941   A. Philip Randolph uses threat of a march on Washington to prod President Franklin D. Roosevelt to issue an executive order banning employment discrimination in defense industries.

1943   The National Federation of Committees of Racial Equality—later the Congress of Racial Equality (CORE)—launches protest campaign against segregated restaurants and other facilities in Chicago and other northern cities.

1947   In *Morgan v. Commonwealth of Virginia,* the U.S. Supreme Court bans segregation in interstate transportation, but this has little effect on southern practices.

The President's Committee on Civil Rights calls for federal action on behalf of civil rights.

W. E. B. Du Bois presents to the United Nations an "Appeal to the World" urging international intervention against racial discrimination in the United States.

1948   The Supreme Court rules that racially restrictive housing covenants are unenforceable

and, in *Sipuel v. Oklahoma State Board of Regents,* that states must admit qualified African Americans to previously all-white graduate schools when no comparable black institution is available.

President Harry S. Truman issues an executive order banning segregation in the military.

1950   Supreme Court rules that segregated graduate schools do not provide equal educational opportunities for black students.

1951   Barbara Johns leads a student strike at a segregated high school in Farmville, Virginia, stimulating a major NAACP desegregation lawsuit.

1954   Ruling on the Virginia case and four related NAACP lawsuits, the Supreme Court declares in *Brown v. Board of Education* that public school segregation was "inherently unequal" and thus unconstitutional under the Fourteenth Amendment.

1955   At the Bandung (Indonesia) Conference, African and Asian nations decide to remain unaligned in Cold War.

Black residents of Montgomery, Alabama, initiate a 381-day boycott of segregated buses under the leadership of Martin Luther King, Jr., that culminates in Supreme Court ruling against segregation policy.

1957   Activist black ministers establish the Southern Christian Leadership Conference (SCLC) under King's leadership.

NAACP and allies succeed in gaining congressional passage of Civil Rights Act of 1957, enhancing the attorney general's power to protect black voting rights.

1959   Youth March for Integrated Schools held in Washington, D.C.

1960   Protest by four black college students in Greensboro, North Carolina, ignites wave of student-led sit-ins at segregated lunch counters.

Student sit-in leaders form the Student Non-violent Coordinating Committee (SNCC).

1961   Following mob violence in Alabama, CORE calls off Freedom Ride to desegregate interstate bus stations, but black students continue campaign.

1962   Despite mob violence, James Meredith desegregates the University of Mississippi.

1963   With support from King's SCLC, thousands of black demonstrators in Birmingham, Alabama, confront police using dogs and fire hoses, attracting international news coverage and forcing white leaders to make civil rights concessions.

More than 200,000 demonstrators attend March on Washington for Jobs and Freedom, climaxed by King's "I Have a Dream" speech.

1964   Three civil rights workers are killed at start of Mississippi Summer Project intended to draw widespread attention to the Mississippi Freedom Democratic Party's effort to displace the all-white "regular" delegation at the Democratic National Convention.

President Lyndon B. Johnson signs the Civil Rights Act of 1964 outlawing segregation in public accommodations as well as banning racial discrimination in employment and in programs receiving federal funding.

Martin Luther King, Jr., accepts Nobel Peace Prize on behalf of the African American freedom struggle.

1965   Despite a violent police assault in Selma, Alabama, civil rights demonstrators achieve their goal of prodding President Johnson to introduce the bill that becomes the Voting Rights Act of 1965.

1966   After James Meredith is wounded at the start of his March against Fear in Mississippi, civil rights proponents continue march and debate the "Black Power" slogan promulgated by SNCC leader Stokely Carmichael.

Huey Newton and Bobby Seale form the Black Panther Party for Self-Defense in Oakland, California.

1967   Martin Luther King, Jr., provokes controversy by condemning U.S. military intervention in Vietnam.

After extensive racial violence in Newark, Detroit, and dozens of other American cities, the FBI secretly initiates a counterintelligence program (COINTELPRO) against black militants.

U.S. Supreme Court strikes down state laws prohibiting interracial marriage.

1968   National Advisory Commission on Civil Disorders attributes urban racial violence to longstanding racial inequality and discrimination.

Nationwide wave of urban racial violence erupts after Martin Luther King, Jr., is assassinated while aiding strike of sanitation workers in Memphis.

President Lyndon Johnson signs Civil Rights Act of 1968, which bans racial discrimination in housing.

1971   The newly founded Congressional Black Caucus boycotts President Nixon's state of the union address after Nixon refuses to meet with them.

In *Swann v. Charlotte-Mecklenburg,* the U.S. Supreme Court rules that busing schoolchildren to achieve racial integration is constitutional.

Forty-three guards and prisoners are killed when state troops crush revolt at New York's Attica Correctional Facility stemming from prisoners' demands for religious freedom, more educational programs, and an alleviation of overcrowding.

1972   The Equal Employment Opportunity Act is passed prohibiting employment discrimination based on race, sex, or religion.

1973   Marian Edelman forms the Children's Defense Fund.

The National Black Feminist Organization is founded.

1974   In *Milliken v. Bradley,* the U.S. Supreme Court rules against busing students between districts to eliminate de facto segregation in public schools.

1976   The U.S. Supreme Court rules that private schools cannot exclude African-American applicants.

1978   In *University of California Regents v. Bakke,* the U.S. Supreme Court rules against a policy admitting a set number of black students but allows colleges and universities to seek racial diversity in student admissions.

1979   Ku Klux Klan members kill five protesters at anti-Klan rally in Greensboro, North Carolina.

1981   Reagan administration announces it will not back mandatory busing plans to achieve school integration or affirmative action plans involving quotas or "reverse discrimination" against whites.

1982   Voting Rights Act of 1965 is extended for twenty-five years.

1986   National holiday honoring Martin Luther King, Jr., is celebrated for first time.

1988   Congress overrides President Reagan's veto to pass the Civil Rights Restoration Act, expanding reach of anti-discrimination laws.

1989   U.S. Supreme Court rules against "set-aside" programs enabling cities to give a portion of public contracts to minority contractors.

1990   International campaign leads to the release of South African anti-apartheid leader Nelson Mandela after twenty-eight years of imprisonment.

1992   An all-white jury acquits police officers involved in the beating of black motorist Rodney King, sparking a three-day uprising in Los Angeles that results in more than fifty deaths.

1995   The Million Man March, initiated by Nation of Islam leader Louis Farrakhan, is held in Washington, D.C.

1996   U.S. Supreme Court rules race cannot be used as a factor in the creation of congressional districts.

1997   President Bill Clinton establishes Commission on Race Relations.

2003   U.S. Supreme Court upholds the University of Michigan's program for encouraging minority applicants but rules against policy of awarding points to such applicants.

INTRODUCTION

Varied forms of collective resistance by the millions of African slaves taken to the Western Hemisphere culminated in the nineteenth century in a largely successful global effort to eliminate slavery. The anti-slavery campaign in the United States drew inspiration from the success of comparable campaigns in French and British Caribbean colonies, but white Americans resisted emancipation in part because they saw freed slaves as threats to white supremacy. Thus the nineteenth-century movement to extend citizenship rights to white men without property was often associated with efforts to bar African Americans from such rights. Nevertheless, popular support for the anti-slavery movement was sufficient to exacerbate North-South conflicts and to precipitate a civil war, which in turn led to the passage of the Thirteenth Amendment ending slavery and the Fourteenth and Fifteenth Amendments affirming the civil rights of former slaves.

Because the end of slavery did not prevent the imposition of new forms of systematic racial oppression, a century of protests and litigation were required to give substance to these constitutional provisions. During the years following the removal of Union troops from the South, African Americans in the region were suppressed under a new regime of racial supremacy, often called the Jim Crow system. Meanwhile, the United States and European nations expanded their economic and political domination of the world. By the end of the nineteenth century, most Asians and Africans were colonized or dominated by European settlers, and most descendants of African slaves in the Western Hemisphere were subject to systematic forms of racial subordination. Nearly all women and most men in the world lacked basic political rights, such as the right to vote.

During the twentieth century, the African American freedom struggle drew inspiration from anti-colonial movements and, to a much lesser extent, from the successful campaigns for women's suffrage in the United States and elsewhere. The range of ideological perspectives—from revolutionary Communism to liberal reformism to pro-capitalist conservatism—in the African American struggle somewhat reflected that of anti-colonial struggles, but the oldest and most enduring group devoted to African American advancement—the National Association for the Advancement of Colored People, or NAACP—focused mainly on implementing the Fourteenth and Fifteenth Amendments rather than seeking additional constitutional guarantees. The NAACP especially targeted lynching, segregation, and disenfranchisement, making effective use of litigation, lobbying, and anti-racist propaganda.

During the Cold War era following World War II, the NAACP adopted an anti-communist stance and achieved significant civil rights gains, most notably the 1954 Supreme Court ruling against public school segregation in the *Brown v. Board of Education* case. This victory was followed, however, by an upsurge of protest activity by African Americans who were dissatisfied with the pace of change. NAACP leaders had little control over the massive protests and sustained organizing efforts that mobilized large numbers of black southerners during the decade after black residents of Montgomery, Alabama, launched a bus boycott in December 1955. Even with the emergence of Montgomery minister Martin Luther King, Jr., as the best-known African American protest spokesman, the African American freedom struggle displayed considerable diversity in leadership, tactics, and ideology, shifting its focus from southern segregation and disenfranchisement toward broader racial goals. By the mid 1960s, this struggle had achieved major reforms, notably the Civil Rights Act of 1964 and the Voting Rights Act of 1965. But widespread black discontent in the United States continued to be fueled by the examples of anti-colonial movements in Asia and Africa.

Although the African American freedom struggle remained evident after the passage of landmark civil rights activism, it was increasingly split over its goals, reflecting the divisions that existed abroad within anti-colonial struggles and within former colonies. Civil rights reform had been achieved with the support of the United States government, but subsequent African American struggles to acquire economic and political power received far less governmental support. Moreover, the determination of the United States to oppose Communist-backed anti-colonial movements in Asia and Africa was paralleled by its determination to suppress African American militancy deemed to be subversive. In part because of the Cold War, extensive violence accompanied the transition to black majority rule in Portugal's African colonies and in South Africa. But by the time of the disintegration of the Soviet Union in 1991, South African apartheid was also ending due to international pressure as well as internal resistance. The election of Nelson Mandela as South Africa's first black president signaled the end of a centuries-long era of institutionalized racial supremacy on a global scale. By the end of the twentieth century, African Americans, like the descendants of African slaves elsewhere in the Western Hemisphere, were free from bondage and institutionalized racial discrimination but still victimized by racial disabilities resulting from the long history of racial oppression.

BACKGROUND: CULTURE AND HISTORY

Since Europeans began transporting large numbers of slaves from Africa to the Americas during the sixteenth century, African slaves and their descendants have struggled persistently and sometimes effectively to resist capture in Africa, transport on slave ships, and forced labor in the Western Hemisphere. Because slavery evolved in distinctive ways in different parts of the Americas, these struggles were varied in character. Large-scale slave rebellions were more common in Brazil and the Caribbean than in North America, but major rebellions took place in the British colonies of Virginia (1730) and South Carolina (1739) and in the French colony of Louisiana (1729); smaller-scale revolts occurred in various parts of North America, including cities such as Charleston and New York. Individual resistance—intransigence, running away, and efforts to secure better manumission or better treatment—was common everywhere slavery existed. Slavery was maintained through violence, legal codes, and racist ideologies of white supremacy, and slaves both resisted and accommodated to their conditions. By the nineteenth century, this resistance evolved into an effective international campaign against the institution of slavery.

The common experience of enslavement transformed Africans from different cultural and religious backgrounds into Afro-Europeans speaking European languages and often practicing distinctive forms of Christianity. In the region that became the United States, Africans gradually became a distinctive people as ever-smaller proportions of slaves were born in Africa. By the time of the founding of the United States, African Americans constituted roughly one fifth of the nation's population, although in southern states such as Virginia and South Carolina, the percentage was considerably higher. To a greater degree than in the Caribbean and Brazil, African Americans struggled for freedom by adopting egalitarian ideas from

Christianity and from the revolutionary movement for independence. During the 1770s, the American war for independence encouraged the first collective efforts by African Americans to protest and petition for rights as citizens.

These initial efforts made little headway, however, since the institution of slavery was protected by constitutional provisions that counted slaves in the allocation of representation in the House of Representatives, forbade states from emancipating fugitive slaves, and prohibited Congress from banning slave importation until 1808. With the invention of the cotton gin in the late eighteenth century and the subsequent expansion of slavery into Alabama, Mississippi, and Texas, the southern states used their political power to protect the institution of slavery. Although freed blacks in the North and sympathetic whites established antislavery organizations during the 1830s and 1840s, slavery became even more entrenched in the South during this period. There were major aborted slave conspiracies in Virginia (1800) and South Carolina (1822), but the only major slave revolt to occur in the South during the nineteenth century was the Nat Turner rebellion in Virginia (1831). After the strengthening of the federal fugitive slave law in 1850, the conflict between pro-slavery and abolitionist forces became increasingly violent. An abolitionist network known as the Underground Railroad assisted in the escape of thousands of slaves before the Supreme Court ruled in the 1857 *Dred Scott* case that neither slaves nor their descendants could ever become citizens entitled to use the courts to protect their rights.

The inability of white political leaders to resolve North-South conflicts led to the Civil War and ultimately to the defeat of the Confederacy in 1865. The Union victory led to passage of the Thirteenth Amendment (1865) abolishing slavery, the Fourteenth Amendment (1868) protecting the citizenship rights of African Americans, and the Fifteenth Amendment (1870) barring the denial of voting rights on the basis of color, race, or previous slave status. The abolition of slavery in the United States was a result of particular historical circumstances. However, it was also a consequence of the broad trend toward industrialism and the expansion of political rights that had encouraged earlier successful anti-slavery movements in the French and British colonial possessions and that would later spur a successful anti-slavery movement in Brazil, the world's last major slave society.

However, once the period of Union occupation of the South ended in 1875, whites were able to reinstitute racial political domination through the passage of Black Codes and through southern white terrorist activity against African Americans exercising their new constitutional rights, often with the collusion of local law enforcement officers. U.S. Supreme Court rulings basically abandoned African Americans to the states'-rights forms of post-slavery institutionalized racism. These included the 1883 Supreme Court ruling

declaring that the 1875 Civil Rights Law was unconstitutional and the subsequent ruling in the *Plessy v. Ferguson* (1896) case that it was constitutional for state governments to require racially segregated public facilities.

African Americans resisted the imposition of the southern Jim Crow system of segregation, but they were not able to overcome lynching and other forms of mob violence by whites. During the early decades of the twentieth century, however, African American protest and militancy became increasingly evident in northern urban areas, where the lure of expanding employment opportunities attracted thousands of black migrants from the rural South. Although black residents of northern cities faced racial discrimination in employment and housing, they had sufficient freedom to establish the black-led groups that instigated the modern African American freedom struggle. Black educator Booker T. Washington was the most prominent African-American leader at the beginning of the twentieth century. But opposition to Washington's policy of accommodation to segregation grew rapidly following the publication of W. E. B. Du Bois's influential book of essays, *The Souls of Black Folk* (1903), and crystallized with the formation of the Niagara Movement in 1905 and the National Association for the Advancement of Colored People (NAACP) in 1909.

Although the NAACP became the nation's largest and most well-funded civil rights organization, African Americans adopted increasingly varied ideologies and strategies in their struggles for collective advancement. During and after World War I, large numbers of African Americans were attracted to the Universal Negro Improvement Association (UNIA), a black nationalist organization founded by Jamaican immigrant Marcus Garvey. The UNIA eclectically drew inspiration from a variety of sources, including Washington's stress on self-help and economic development and the Irish cultural nationalist movements such as Sinn Féin. Black nationalists inspired by the 1917 Bolshevik Revolution in Russia formed the African Blood Brotherhood, and a small number of African Americans affiliated with the Communist Party of the United States (CPUSA). African American support for the CPUSA increased during the early years of the Great Depression, largely as a result of its fervent support for an international campaign for the "Scottsboro Boys," nine black teenagers who had been charged with rape in Alabama. During the 1920s and 1930s, African American discontent stemming from their racial subordination was increasingly expressed in literature, music, and other forms of popular culture, notably by the writers associated with the Harlem Renaissance.

As black Americans benefited from President Franklin Delano Roosevelt's New Deal relief and employment programs, however, most turned away from Communist radicalism in favor of Democratic Party liberalism. Subsequent black militancy often took the form of protests and lobbying designed to bring about more forceful federal action on behalf of civil rights reform. Roosevelt and subsequent Democratic presidents faced a delicate balancing act: keeping black discontent at bay through black appointments to government positions and modest concessions on civil rights issues and at the same time retaining the support of southern white segregationists.

During the early 1940s, as American leaders considered whether to enter the widening war in Europe, A. Philip Randolph threatened a massive march on Washington, D.C., to force President Roosevelt to ban racial discrimination in defense industries and racial segregation in the military. Roosevelt headed off this threat by issuing an executive order banning racial discrimination in the defense industries and establishing a presidential Fair Employment Practices Committee (FEPC). But despite continued black complaints and small-scale protests, the U.S. armed forces remained largely segregated during the war. Nonetheless, the NAACP's increasingly effective legal affiliate, the Legal Defense and Education Fund, Inc., achieved an important breakthrough when the Supreme Court ruled in *Smith v. Allwright* (1944) that black voters could not be excluded from state primary elections.

Following the war, Harry S. Truman, who become president after Roosevelt's death in 1945, established a Committee on Civil Rights that issued a report calling for "great leadership" by the federal government in the area of civil rights. Truman faced pressure from the leftist Civil Rights Congress and from Randolph, who spearheaded a campaign for military desegregation. In 1948 Truman sought to head off mass protests and to solidify his support from black voters by issuing Executive Order 9981 calling for "equality of treatment and opportunity" in the military. Although black leftists and liberal Democrats had often joined forces on behalf of racial reform during World War II, in subsequent freedom struggles, as in Asian and African anti-colonial movements, such alliances became less frequent after the post-war split between the United States and the Soviet Union. Although this East-West Cold War provided some leverage to civil rights proponents who insisted that the United States should end the southern racist practices that undermined the nation's international prestige, the anti-communist campaign also led to persecutions of black leftist activists such as Du Bois and entertainer Paul Robeson. These persecutions and the subsequent precipitous decline of the black Left lessened competition for NAACP leaders such as Thurgood Marshall, head of the Legal Defense and Education Fund, and the group's executive director, Roy Wilkins.

During the 1950s, the long-term African American freedom struggle became narrower in scope as NAACP litigation and black activism focused on the goal of civil rights reform, initially through civil rights legislation at the state level and through court decisions that expanded federal power by broadening the application of the Fourteenth Amendment and the interstate commerce clauses of the Constitution. Nevertheless, NAACP leaders were prodded by local black activists who took the initiative in challenging the demeaning practices associated with the southern Jim Crow system of segregation. For example, a high school walkout in 1951 led by fifteen-year-old Barbara Johns culminated in a NAACP legal challenge to the *Plessy* principle of "separate but equal" facilities in the field of education. In 1954 the NAACP legal staff won a major victory when the U.S. Supreme Court ruled in the case of *Brown v. Topeka Board of Education* that racial segregation in public schools was unconstitutional. The court did not, however, set a fixed time limit by which states had to desegregate their school systems; instead, it decided in 1955 to call for desegregation "with all deliberate speed," thereby helping to set the stage for future civil battles over public school desegregation.

CONTEXT AND PROCESS OF REVOLUTION

In the years after the *Brown* decision, other civil rights organizations departed from the NAACP's reform strategy and placed more emphasis on protest and mass mobilization. Starting with the Montgomery bus boycott of 1955–1956, southern blacks, aided by northern allies, successfully used boycotts, mass meetings, marches, rallies, sit-ins, and other insurgent tactics to speed the pace of civil rights reform. The Southern Christian Leadership Conference (SCLC), founded in 1957 and led for many years by Martin Luther King, Jr. (1929–1968), and the Student Nonviolent Coordinating Committee (SNCC), founded in 1960, spearheaded a series of mass struggles against white supremacy in the South. Many of the participants in these struggles were NAACP members and benefited from the legal support of this group. The predominantly white Congress of Racial Equality (CORE) contributed activists and expertise in the use of Gandhian nonviolent tactics. Although subsequent studies of this movement usually stressed its civil rights goals and national leadership, it was directed toward a broad range of economic and political changes and generated its own local leadership and institutions. Indeed, participants often called their movement a freedom struggle in order to express its far-reaching and sometimes radical goals, which went beyond the legislation and legal reforms sought by the major civil rights organizations. Rather than simply continuing the long-term civil rights efforts spearheaded by the National Association for the Advancement of Colored People (NAACP) and other national reform organizations,

African American men of the Detroit NAACP march in the 1940s with a casket symbolizing the imminent dismantling and "death" of discriminatory and segregationist "Jim Crow" laws. (Library of Congress)

the southern black struggle was a tactical and, ultimately, an ideological departure characterized by unconventional and increasingly militant tactics, locally initiated protest activity, decentralized direction, and a growing sense of racial consciousness among participants. Years of activism and vigorous debate within the black struggle resulted in a profound transformation of the racial values that permeated black communities throughout the nation.

Rosa Parks's unplanned refusal on December 1, 1955, to give up her seat on a Montgomery city bus to a white man stimulated a sustained bus boycott that soon inspired mass protests in other southern communities. On December 5 a group of local leaders established the Montgomery Improvement Association (MIA) to coordinate the boycott and chose as its leader Martin Luther King, a Baptist minister who had come to the city in 1954 after receiving his divinity doctorate from Boston University. King was one of many new leaders who would reflect the increasing confidence and militancy of

the movement. His oratory—increasingly filled with references to Christian and Gandhian concepts of nonviolent resistance—attracted widespread publicity and support. Despite the bombing of King's house and other acts of intimidation, the boycott continued until December 1956, when white officials in Montgomery reluctantly obeyed a Supreme Court order to desegregate the bus system. The Montgomery bus boycott served as a model for black protest movements in other cities, for it demonstrated the ability of black communities to struggle collectively and resolutely for common civil rights goals. In 1957 King and his supporters founded the Southern Christian Leadership Conference (SCLC) to provide an institutional framework supporting local movements that departed from the NAACP's strategy of litigation and lobbying. King moved cautiously, however, and SCLC did not initiate any mass protests during the next five years. Nevertheless, King's frequent speeches in various southern communities soon made him the most influential

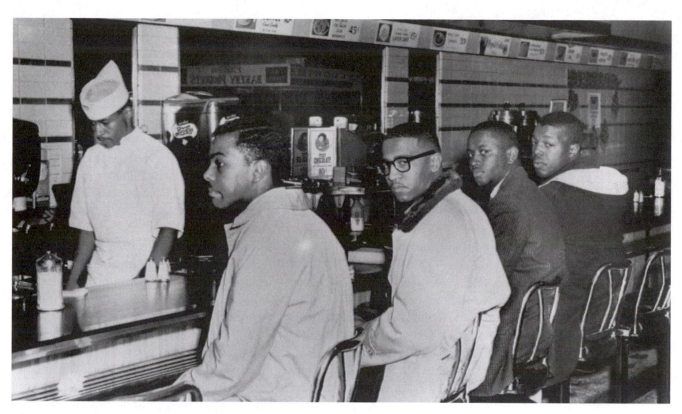

African American college students pose after their historic sit-in at a whites-only lunch counter in February, 1960. (Library of Congress)

African American leader and popularized King's vision of "social gospel" Christianity.

The second major phase of the southern black struggle began on February 1, 1960, when four black college students in Greensboro, North Carolina, sat at a lunch counter reserved for whites. Although affiliated with NAACP youth chapters, the students acted without consulting adult leaders. Thousands of students in at least sixty communities, mostly in the upper South, joined the sit-in movement during the winter and spring of 1960. In a few instances, violent clashes between protesters and white hecklers occurred, but student leaders usually succeeded in maintaining nonviolent discipline while also displaying greater militancy than most older black leaders. Despite efforts of the NAACP, SCLC, and the Congress of Racial Equality (CORE) to impose some control over the sit-in movement, the student protesters typically insisted on their independence of adult control. Even when student leaders formed the Student Nonviolent Coordinating Committee (SNCC) to coordinate the new movement, they retained authority to set policy for its constituent local groups. SNCC would remain the most decentralized, anti-authoritarian, and militant of the major civil rights organizations.

The third phase of the southern struggle, the freedom rides of 1961, was initiated by a civil rights organization—CORE. But this new form of protest activity did not have much impact on the broader southern movement until CORE abandoned its initial campaign after white mobs in Alabama viciously attacked two contingents of freedom riders. Student activists in Nashville, Tennessee, many of whom had participated in the sit-ins, promptly announced their determination to continue the rides. After encountering further mob violence in Montgomery, a group of riders traveled to Jackson, Mississippi, where they were promptly arrested for disobeying Jim Crow racial segregation rules. Despite Attorney General Robert Kennedy's plea for a "cooling-off" period, other young activists also rode buses to Jackson to join the students already in jail. The freedom rides into Mississippi encouraged similar protests elsewhere against segregated transportation facilities during the remaining months of 1961. Participation in freedom rides enabled students to become part of a community of activists who self-consciously saw themselves as the spearhead of the southern movement. This was particularly the case among students who spent part of the summer of 1961 in Mississippi jails and emerged from the experience as self-confident, racially conscious movement leaders.

These freedom riders played important roles in the fourth phase of the southern struggle that began in the fall of 1961, when they joined forces with older grassroots leaders to mobilize sustained mass movements in various places where white supremacy was maintained through terror. Especially in the Black Belt areas of Georgia, Alabama, and Mississippi, community organizers—most of them associated with SNCC and SCLC—sought support among poor and working-class blacks who had rarely been involved in previous protests. During the following two years, they were able to increase dramatically the size of the southern struggle. "Freedom songs," often based on traditional religious music, strengthened feelings of racial solidarity and fostered the emergence of a distinctive movement culture.

Learning from SCLC's largely unsuccessful Albany campaign of 1961 and 1962, King and other SCLC leaders initiated a tumultuous protest campaign in Birmingham, Alabama, during the spring of 1963. The campaign's goal was to prod the federal government to intervene in the South on behalf of civil rights reform. SCLC leaders worked with Baptist minister Fred Shuttlesworth to orchestrate confrontations between nonviolent demonstrators and the often brutal law enforcement personnel directed by Eugene T. "Bull" Conner. The international news coverage of these clashes disturbed many white Americans and prompted President John Kennedy to introduce legislation that became the Civil Rights Act of 1964.

Similar highly publicized mass protests in dozens of cities prompted a white "backlash" against black militancy but also made whites more aware of southern racial inequities, particularly the antiquated Jim Crow system. The protests during the spring and summer of 1963 culminated in the March on Washington for Jobs and Freedom, which attracted over 200,000 participants. As the southern struggle's best-known spokesperson, King used his concluding speech at the march as an opportunity to link black civil rights aspirations with traditional American political values, insisting that the Declaration of Independence and the Constitution constituted "a promissory note" guaranteeing all Americans "the unalienable rights of life, liberty, and the pursuit of happiness."

While media attention was concentrated on the urban demonstrations in Birmingham and elsewhere, a voter registration campaign in the rural deep South achieved a breakthrough that had a profound effect on the attitudes of blacks in the region. During the first half of the 1960s, SNCC spearheaded an effort to achieve voting rights for southern blacks and federal protection for civil rights workers. Although only a small proportion of eligible black voters in the segregationist stronghold of Mississippi had been registered by the end of 1963, the voter rights effort conducted through an umbrella group called the Council of Federal Organizations (COFO) stimulated the emergence of resilient indigenous leadership and new black-led organizations such as the Mississippi Freedom Democratic Party (MFDP) and the Lowndes County (Alabama) Freedom Organization, under local black leadership. Under the leadership of COFO director

Robert Moses, hundreds of northern white volunteers took part in a summer project in 1964 that attracted national attention to the Mississippi effort. Although the MFDP failed in its attempt to unseat the regular delegation at the 1964 national Democratic convention, the summer project and the series of protests the following year in the Alabama cities of Selma and Montgomery led President Lyndon Johnson to introduce voting rights legislation that was enacted during the summer of 1965.

The Selma to Montgomery march in March 1965 was the last mass protest in the South to secure widespread support among whites outside the region. The passage of voting rights legislation, the upsurge in northern urban racial violence, and the increasing white resentment of black militancy lessened the effectiveness of nonviolent protests as a means of advancing African American interests. In addition, the growing militancy of black activists made some of them less interested in working for civil rights reforms and more determined to achieve political power and cultural autonomy through building black-controlled institutions. Ideological conflict between proponents of "black power," such as SNCC chairman Stokely Carmichael, and more conventional civil rights leaders such as King came to a head during the Mississippi march held in June 1966 after the wounding of James Meredith, who had desegregated the University of Mississippi in 1962. The "black power" slogan, popularized by SNCC's chair Stokely Carmichael, summarized that group's emerging idea of a struggle seeking political, economic, and cultural objectives beyond narrowly defined civil rights reforms.

By the late 1960s, not only the NAACP and SCLC, but even SNCC and CORE faced increasingly strong challenges from black nationalist leaders and new militant organizations such as the Black Panther Party. Often influenced by Malcolm X (1925–1965) and by Pan-African ideologies, proponents of "black liberation" saw civil rights reforms as insufficient because they did not address the problems of poor blacks. They also questioned American citizenship and identity as goals for African Americans because these had resulted from the involuntary circumstances of enslavement. In addition, racial liberation proponents often saw the African American freedom struggle in international terms as a movement for "human rights" and national "self-determination" rather than merely for civil rights.

The twentieth-century African American freedom struggle occurred in the context of the broader political, economic, and cultural changes associated with modernization. Although the abolition of slavery and the end of legalized racial segregation and discrimination required sustained mass movements, these forms of racial domination also gave way to urbanization and the wage labor systems associated with the industrialization of the United States and Western Europe. Responding to the rapidly expanding demand for industrial workers that fueled mass migrations of agricultural laborers to urban areas, rural African Americans, like farm workers elsewhere in the world, sought greater freedom through urbanization as well as political militancy. Although some elements in the African American freedom struggle sought a revolutionary transformation of the American political and economic system, its main achievement was to overcome the southern system of white supremacy by prodding the federal government to impose on the South the urban-industrial patterns of race relations that prevailed in the rest of the nation.

Because urbanization and industrialization were global trends, the African American freedom struggle followed a historical course similar to that of other freedom struggles involving racially subordinated people in Asia, Africa, and the Caribbean. In these areas, various forms of white racial supremacy continued after the end of slavery, but these also gradually gave way to the global trend toward urbanization and industrialization, which strengthened efforts to expand the basic rights of nonwhite people. During the twentieth century, increasing immigration and travel as well as new communication technologies contributed to the exchange of tactical and strategic ideas among the African American freedom movement, anti-colonial movements, and the anti-apartheid movement in South Africa. Although many freedom movements drew inspiration from the emergence of Socialist and Communist parties, especially during the Great Depression and World War II, ties to such parties and their ideologies were also liabilities, especially during the Cold War era. Non-Communist nationalist movements generally achieved independence more rapidly and with far less violence than did Socialist- or Communist-backed nationalist movements, which often faced protracted civil wars, even after independence. In the United States, leftist civil rights activism was of minor importance during the two decades after World War II when major civil rights reforms were achieved largely within the context of the global movement away from colonialism and state-supported systems of racial supremacy.

IMPACTS

The most significant pieces of legislation to result from the mass struggles of the 1960s were the Civil Rights Act of 1964 and the Voting Rights Act of 1965 (Congress also passed notable civil rights bills in 1968, 1972, and 1990). Taken together, these laws greatly enhanced the civic status of blacks, women, and other groups and placed greater responsibility on the federal government to protect them from discriminatory treatment. Although the 1964 and 1965 legislation were in some respects simply restatements of the civil rights protections specified in the Reconstruction Amendments (the Thirteenth, Fourteenth, and Fifteenth Amendments), the impact of the new legislation was greater because of the coincident expanded scope of federal regulatory powers and continued militancy by victims of discrimination.

Since the mid 1960s, national civil rights policies have evinced awareness that anti-discrimination legislation was not sufficient to achieve tangible improvements in the living conditions of many blacks or to bring about equalization of the distribution of resources and services among racial groups in the United States. In 1968, the National Advisory Commission on Civil Disorders (also known as the Kerner Commission) concluded that, despite civil rights reforms, the nation was moving "toward two societies (one black, one white), separate and unequal" (National Advisory Commission on Civil Disorders 1968, 396). By the time of this report, the political coalition that had supported passage of the major civil rights legislation had become divided over the role, if any, government should play in eliminating these persistent racial inequities. A "white backlash" against black militancy and claims that black gains had resulted in "reverse discrimination" against whites further prevented significant new civil rights legislation during the 1970s and 1980s.

Although militant protest activity declined after the 1960s, the subsequent impact of the civil rights legislation of the decade was considerable. The increased black participation in the American political system that resulted from previous struggles lessened black reliance on extra-legal tactics, but civil rights issues continued to stimulate protest, particularly when previous gains appeared to be threatened. Furthermore, women, homosexuals, disabled people, and other groups suffering discriminatory treatment have mobilized civil rights movements and organizations of their own and thereby contributed to the continuing national dialogue about the scope of civil rights and the role of government.

During the 1970s and 1980s, debate continued over the appropriateness of employment affirmative action programs and court-ordered compensatory remedies for historically rooted patterns of discrimination. Nevertheless, despite contention over these issues and the conservative political climate of the period, most national civil rights policies established during the 1960s have survived. Moreover, civil rights advocates have continued to press, with limited success, toward implementation of policies seeking group advancement rather than simply individual rights, tangible gains rather than civil status, and equality of social outcomes rather than simply equality of opportunity. It is therefore accurate to conclude that the modern African American freedom and liberation struggles of the 1960s produced a major, though still controversial, shift in prevailing norms regarding the nature of civil rights in the United States.

At the same time, the global trends that contributed to the civil rights reforms in the United States constrained the African American freedom struggle in its attempt to achieve its far-reaching economic and political goals. For the most part, the universalization of basic political rights during the twentieth century reflected the globalization of social patterns associated with modern American capitalism. Thus the American and South African campaigns for equal rights and the anti-colonial movements in Asia and Africa were mostly evolutionary rather than revolutionary in their consequences. But at the end of the twentieth century, most Asians, Africans, and black Americans had gained basic political rights and were no longer racially segregated, yet they also typically continued to have fewer opportunities than white Americans and Europeans as workers and consumers in a global capitalist economy.

PEOPLE AND ORGANIZATIONS

Black Panther Party

In October 1966, Huey Newton and Bobby Seale, inspired by Malcolm X, drafted the program of a new urban-based black militant group initially called the Black Panther Party for Self-Defense. Their list of ten demands combined basic needs—full employment and decent housing—with more radical objectives, such as exemption of black men from military service. The last of the ten demands summarized their goals: "We want land, bread, housing, education, clothing, justice, and peace. And as our major political objective, a United Nations–supervised plebiscite to be held throughout the black colony in which only black colonial subjects will be allowed to participate for the purpose of determining the will of black people as to their national destiny" (Foner 1995, 3–4).

Assuming the posts of defense minister and chairman, respectively, Newton and Seale directed the group's rapid growth. The party's considerable appeal among young African Americans was based less on its program or its leaders' Marxist rhetoric than on its willingness to confront police. Among those attracted was Eldridge Cleaver, a former convict and author whose autobiographical essays were later collected in the bestseller *Soul on Ice* (1968).

On October 28, 1967, Newton was arrested after an altercation ending in the death of an Oakland police officer. The Panthers mobilized to free Newton. Stokely Carmichael of SNCC agreed to join in "Free Huey" rallies in Los Angeles and Oakland, which increased the national visibility of the Black Panther Party. But ideological and personal tensions increasingly divided Carmichael and Panther leaders, signaling the beginning of a period of pervasive, vicious infighting within the black militant community, exacerbated by constant confrontations with police and the covert disruptive activities of the FBI's counterintelligence program (COINTELPRO).

In 1970, when Newton's manslaughter conviction was reversed, he returned to find the party in disarray. He sought to revive it by de-emphasizing police confrontations in favor of survival programs that would meet the everyday needs of black communities while also educating people. Such programs attracted new members, allowed Panthers to interact with diverse segments of black communities, and helped to counter the party's negative image in the media. But Newton's efforts did not prevent further external attacks and internal conflicts from plaguing the group. After the mid 1970s, the party never regained its former prominence.

Congress of Racial Equality (CORE)

Founded in 1942 as the Committee of Racial Equality by an interracial group of students in Chicago, CORE evolved into a national civil rights organization devoted to using Gandhi's nonviolent tactics to achieve civil rights reform. Many of its early members were involved in protests against segregated restaurants and other public facilities.

The organization was initially co-led by white University of Chicago student George Houser and black student James Farmer. Farmer and fellow activist Bayard Rustin traveled throughout the United States recruiting members, most of them white middle-class college students from the Midwest. In 1953, Farmer became the first national director of CORE.

In April of 1947 CORE sent eight white and eight black men into the upper South to test a Supreme Court ruling that declared segregation in interstate travel unconstitutional and gained national attention when four of the riders were arrested in North Carolina and three, including Bayard Rustin, were forced to work on a chain gang.

CORE's direct action tactics gained favor with black student protesters in the South during the 1960s. In May of 1961 CORE organized the Freedom Rides. Near Birmingham, Alabama, a bus was firebombed and riders were beaten by a white mob, but CORE continued to locate field secretaries in key areas of the South to provide support for the riders. By 1963 CORE had already shifted attention to segregation in the North and West, where two-thirds of the organization's chapters were located. In an effort to build credibility as a black-protest organization, leadership in these northern chapters had become almost entirely black.

Roy Innis, chairman of the Harlem chapter of CORE, became national director in 1968. Under Innis's leadership, CORE embraced an ideology of pragmatic nationalism and lent its support to black economic development and community self-determination.

Du Bois, William Edward Burghardt (1868–1963)

W. E. B. Du Bois was a brilliant African American sociologist and historian, and a pioneering leader of the African American freedom struggle. Born in Great Barrington, Massachusetts, and educated at Fisk College and Harvard, he carried out several major studies of the sociology, culture, and history of African Americans. His book of essays titled *Souls of Black Folk* (1903) stimulated the emergence of African American militancy. As a social activist, he helped organize the Niagara Movement and then helped found the NAACP in 1909. For several decades he edited the NAACP's journal, *The Crisis,* until his increasingly controversial views led to his resignation during the 1930s. During the 1940s, his move toward the left and his increasing emphasis on pan-African unity led Du Bois to oppose the Cold War policies of the United States. He was acquitted when government officials sought to prosecute him as an agent of the Soviet Union, but his political influence was largely supplanted during the 1950s by anti-Communist NAACP leaders and by the emerging new protest leaders of the southern freedom struggle. During the early 1960s, he joined the Communist Party and left the United States to live in Ghana, where he died in 1963 on the eve of the March on Washington for Jobs and Freedom.

King, Martin Luther, Jr. (1929–1968)

Michael King, Jr., was born in Atlanta, Georgia, the son and grandson of Baptist ministers who had served as pastors of Atlanta's Ebenezer Baptist Church. King's formative experiences introduced him to the African American social gospel tradition exemplified by his father and grandfather, both of whom were leaders of the Atlanta branch of the National Association for the Advancement of Colored People. In 1934 the elder King, following his own father's request, changed his name and that of his son to Martin Luther King.

After graduating from Morehouse College, King attended Crozer Theological Seminary from 1948 to 1951, graduating at the top of his class. By the time he completed his doctoral studies at Boston University in 1955, King had refined his exceptional ability to draw upon a wide range of theological and philosophical texts to express his views with force and precision. His ability became evident in his preaching in Boston-area churches and at Ebenezer during school vacations. While in Boston, King also met and courted Coretta Scott, an Antioch College graduate who was then a student at the New England Conservatory of Music. On June 18, 1953, the two students were married in Marion, Alabama, where Scott's family lived.

King became pastor of Dexter Avenue Baptist Church in Montgomery, Alabama. In December 1955, when Montgomery black leaders formed the Montgomery Improvement Association to protest the arrest of NAACP official Rosa Parks for refusing to give up her bus seat to a white man, they selected King to head the new group. King utilized the leadership abilities he had gained from his religious background and academic training and gradually forged a distinctive protest strategy that involved the mobilization of black churches and skillful appeals for white support. With the encouragement of Bayard Rustin and other veteran pacifists, King also became a firm advocate of Gandhi's precepts of nonviolence, which he combined with Christian principles.

After the Supreme Court outlawed Alabama bus segregation laws in late 1956, King sought to expand the nonviolent civil rights movement throughout the South. In 1957 he became the founding president of the Southern Christian Leadership Conference (SCLC), formed to coordinate civil rights activities throughout the region. Publication of *Stride toward Freedom: The Montgomery Story* (1958) further contributed to King's rapid emergence as a national civil rights leader. He moved his family to Atlanta in order to be nearer SCLC headquarters in that city and to become co-pastor, with his father, of Ebenezer Baptist Church.

The southern civil rights movement gained new impetus from the student-led lunch counter sit-in movement during 1960. The sit-ins brought into existence a new protest group, the Student Nonviolent Coordinating Committee (SNCC), which would often push King toward greater militancy.

During 1963 King reasserted his preeminence within the African American freedom struggle through his leadership of the SCLC Birmingham campaign, the most massive civil rights protest demonstrations that had yet occurred. SCLC officials, with local black leaders, were able to orchestrate the Birmingham protests to achieve maximum national impact. King's decision to allow himself to be arrested for leading a demonstration on April 12 prodded the Kennedy administration to intervene. A widely quoted letter that King wrote while jailed displayed his ability to influence public opinion by appropriating ideas from the Bible and the Constitution. During May, televised pictures of police using dogs and fire hoses against demonstrators generated a national outcry. The brutality of Birmingham officials and Alabama governor George Wallace's refusal to allow black students into the University of Alabama prompted President Kennedy to introduce major civil rights legislation.

King's speech at the August 28, 1963, March on Washington, attended by more than 200,000 people, was notable for his extemporaneous concluding remarks: "So I say to you, my friends, that even though we must face the difficulties of today and tomorrow, I still have a dream. It is a dream deeply rooted in the American dream that one day this nation will rise up and live out the true meaning of its creed—we hold these truths to be self-evident, that all men are created equal."

King's ability to focus national attention on confrontations with racist authorities, combined with his oration at the 1963 March on Washington, made him the most influential African American spokesperson of the first half of the 1960s. Named *Time* magazine's man of the year of 1963, he was awarded the Nobel Peace Prize in 1964. The African American struggle expanded from desegregation protests to mass movements seeking economic and political gains in the North as well as the South. King's active involvement in a major series of voting rights protests secured popular support for passage of the national Civil Rights Act of 1964.

Early in 1966 King launched a major campaign against poverty and other urban problems, moving into an apartment in the black ghetto of Chicago. He was stoned by angry whites in the Chicago suburb of Cicero when he led a march against racial discrimination in housing. But the Chicago campaign resulted in no significant gains and black militants increasingly turned away from King's Gandhian precepts toward the black nationalism of Malcolm X.

King spoke out strongly against American involvement in the Vietnam War, making his position public in an address on April 4, 1967, at New York's Riverside Church. King's involvement in the anti-war movement reduced his ability to influence national racial policies and made him a target of further FBI investigations.

In November 1967, King announced formation of the Poor People's Campaign, designed to prod the federal government to strengthen anti-poverty efforts. The campaign was in its early stages when King became involved in a sanitation workers' strike in Memphis, Tennessee. King traveled to Memphis for the last time in early April 1968. On April 4, he was assassinated as he stood on a balcony of the Lorraine Motel. A white segregationist, James Earl Ray, later pleaded guilty to the crime. The Poor People's Campaign continued for a few months after his death but did not achieve its objectives. (*See* photo, p. 720.)

Malcolm X [born Malcolm Little; also known as el-Hajj Malik el-Shabazz (1925–1965)

Born in Omaha, Nebraska, to activists in the Universal Negro Improvement Association established by Marcus Garvey, Malcolm Little grew up in poverty after the death of his father (the victim of white racists, he believed) and his mother's subsequent mental deterioration.

Although Malcolm excelled academically and was popular among classmates at the predominantly white schools, he became embittered toward white authority figures. In 1941 he left Michigan to live in Boston with his half-sister, Ella Collins. While in Boston and New York during the early 1940s, he held a variety of railroad jobs while also becoming increasingly involved in criminal activities such as peddling illegal drugs and numbers running. Arrested in 1946 for larceny and breaking and entering, he was sent to prison in February 1946 and released in August 1952.

While in Concord Reformatory in Massachusetts, Malcolm X responded to the urgings of his brother Reginald and became a follower of Elijah Muhammad, leader of the Temple of Islam (later Nation of Islam—often called the Black Muslims), a small black nationalist Islamic sect that had previously attracted his brothers. After he was paroled, he became Minister Malcolm X, using the surname assigned to him in place of the African name that had been taken from his slave ancestors.

Malcolm X quickly became Elijah Muhammad's most effective minister, bringing large numbers of new recruits. In his speeches, he urged black people to separate from whites and win their freedom "by any means necessary." A 1959 television documentary on the Nation of Islam called *The Hate That Hate Produced* further increased Malcolm's notoriety. By 1963 he had become a frequent guest on radio and television programs and was the best-known figure in the Nation of Islam.

Malcolm X was particularly harsh in his criticisms of Martin Luther King, Jr.'s nonviolent strategy. But he nevertheless identified himself with grassroots southern civil rights leaders. His desire to move from rhetorical to political militancy led him to become increasingly dissatisfied with Elijah Muhammad's apolitical stance. When Malcolm X remarked that President John Kennedy's assassination in November 1963 was a case of the "chickens coming home to roost," Muhammad used the opportunity to ban his increasingly popular minister from speaking in public.

Malcolm X counseled boxer Cassius Clay, who publicly announced, shortly after winning the heavyweight boxing title, that he had become a member of the Nation of Islam and adopted the name Muhammad Ali. In March 1964 Malcolm announced that he was breaking with the Nation of Islam to form his own group, Muslim Mosque, Inc. The theological and ideological gulf between Malcolm and Muhammad widened during a month-long trip to Africa and the Middle East. After returning to the United States on May 21, Malcolm announced that he had adopted a Muslim name, el-Hajj Malik el-Shabazz, and that he was forming a new political group, the Organization of Afro-American Unity (OAAU), to bring together all elements of the African American freedom struggle.

But Malcolm had acquired many enemies, and the Federal Bureau of Investigation attempted to undermine his influence. In addition, some of his former Nation of Islam colleagues, including Louis X (later Louis Farrakhan), condemned him for publicly criticizing Elijah Muhammad. On February 21, 1965, members of the Nation of Islam shot and killed Malcolm as he was beginning a speech at the Audubon Ballroom in New York City.

After his death, Malcolm's views reached an even larger audience than during his life. *The Autobiography of Malcolm X*, written with the assistance of Alex Haley and published in 1965, became a best-seller. Other books appeared containing texts of many of his speeches, including *Malcolm X Speaks* (1965), *The End of White World Supremacy: Four Speeches* (1971), and *February 1965: The Final Speeches* (1992).

National Association for the Advancement of Colored People (NAACP)

Founded in 1909 by an interracial group of reformers, the NAACP became the largest national civil rights organization in the United States. NAACP founder W. E. B. Du Bois attracted considerable support through the articles he wrote for the group's journal, *The Crisis*. Although Du Bois favored the use of mass protest to achieve civil rights gains, the NAACP increasingly emphasized litigation and legislative lobbying.

During the 1930s the NAACP launched a concerted campaign to force state governments to provide equal educational opportunities for black residents. NAACP lawyers successfully challenged policies that barred black students from graduate and professional programs for which comparable black institutions did not exist. In 1954 Thurgood Marshall's legal staff achieved a major victory over public school segregation when the Supreme Court overturned its *Plessy* decision in *Brown v. Board of Education*.

During the 1950s and 1960s, the NAACP faced competition from other civil rights groups that favored mass protests. When Roy Wilkins became head of the NAACP, the organization commanded more financial resources than any other civil rights group. Many of those involved in the Montgomery bus boycott of the mid 1950s and the sit-ins of the early 1960s were NAACP members, but new organizations such as the SCLC and SNCC attracted considerable black support, especially among college students and local activists who were impatient with the pace of racial change. Wilkins and Marshall insisted that the NAACP's behind-the-scenes activities were vital to transforming mass protests into lasting civil rights reforms. Both men were strong critics of black power proponents in SNCC and CORE and of anti-war statements by Martin Luther King and Stokely Carmichael.

Randolph, Asa Philip (1889–1979)

A. Philip Randolph was a major African American labor organizer and leader in the struggle for African American freedom. Born in Crescent City, Florida, he attended the City College of New York. For years he worked to organize The Brotherhood of Sleeping Car Porters working for the Pullman Company and eventually succeeded. In the early 1940s, by threatening a march on Washington, he convinced the Roosevelt administration to ban discrimination in defense industries during World War II and later helped pressure President Truman to integrate the U.S. armed forces in 1948. As a leader within the American Federation of Labor-Congress of Industrial Organizations (AFL-CIO), Randolph worked for racial equality within the labor movement.

Southern Christian Leadership Conference (SCLC)

Based in Atlanta, the Southern Christian Leadership Conference was established in 1957 by activist black ministers. SCLC's main objective was to coordinate nonviolent protests throughout the South. Martin Luther King, Jr., served as president of SCLC from its founding until his death in 1968. The organization's strength derived from the power and independence of black churches.

The SCLC differed from organizations such as SNCC and NAACP in that it operated as an umbrella organization, coordinating the activities of local groups and training them in the philosophy of Christian nonviolence, opening citizenship schools, and registering voters.

In 1963, King and the SCLC collaborated with the Alabama Christian Movement for Human Rights (ACMHR) in mobilizing mass protest campaigns in Birmingham. They concentrated on desegregating just the downtown area, rather than overturning all segregation, which had been the aim in an earlier unsuccessful effort in Albany, Georgia. Clashes between nonviolent protesters and brutal law enforcement personnel generated national headlines and sparked massive demonstrations throughout the South. The SCLC won a desegregation settlement, and the Birmingham campaign laid the groundwork for the passage of the Civil Rights Act of 1964.

In 1965, the SCLC launched a voting rights campaign in Selma, Alabama. In some southern counties, less than 5 percent of the eligible black population was registered. In March, SCLC and SNCC organized a fifty-mile march from Selma to Montgomery. Not long after 600 marchers began their walk, state troopers, under orders from Governor George Wallace, attacked them with clubs and tear gas. Later that year, Congress passed the Voting Rights Act of 1965.

In the late 1960s, SCLC began to shift its attention toward economic inequality. Seeing poverty as the root of inner-city violence, SCLC planned the Poor People's Campaign to push for federal legislation that would guarantee employment, income, and housing for economically marginalized blacks. The assassination of Martin Luther King, Jr., on April 4, 1968, however, undermined the campaign. Under the leadership of Martin Luther King III, SCLC continues to organize around issues such as racial profiling, police brutality, hate crimes, and discrimination.

Student Nonviolent Coordinating Committee (SNCC)

Formed in April 1960 by college student activists who had gathered at Shaw University in Raleigh, North Carolina, SNCC became the most dynamic and influential civil rights group of the 1960s southern freedom struggles.

At first coordinating localized protests of students involved in the lunch counter sit-ins of 1960, SNCC gradually evolved into an organization initiating protests and community organizing efforts in the South. SNCC's emergence as a significant force in the civil rights movement came largely through the involvement of students in the 1961 Freedom Ride campaign designed to desegregate eating facilities at southern bus terminals. Hundreds of student freedom riders were jailed in Mississippi, and later many became full-time SNCC workers.

SNCC established major projects in areas of the Deep South where segregationist resistance was strongest. SNCC's Freedom Summer campaign of 1964, which involved hundreds of white college students from the North, proved instrumental in attracting national attention to the issues of black voting rights in the South.

The Alabama voting rights campaign of 1965 stimulated bitter ideological debates as some SNCC members openly challenged the group's previous commitment to nonviolent tactics and its willingness to allow the participation of white activists. Stokely Carmichael, who rose to chairmanship of SNCC, identified with the trend away from nonviolence and interracialism. Carmichael publicly expressed SNCC's new political orientation when he began calling for "Black Power" during a voting rights march through Mississippi.

At the May 1967 meeting where staff members elected Hubert "Rap" Brown chairperson, they also announced that they would "encourage and support liberation struggles against colonialism, racism, and economic exploitation" around the world. SNCC's Carmichael traveled extensively to build ties with revolutionary movements in Africa and Asia, and portrayed Afro-American urban rebellions as part of the international Socialist movement.

Although individual SNCC activists played significant roles in African American politics during the period after 1968 and many of the controversial ideas that once had defined SNCC's radicalism became widely accepted among blacks, the organization disintegrated.

Clayborne Carson

See Also Documentaries of Revolution (See U.S. Civil Rights Movement); Elites, Intellectuals, and Revolutionary Leadership; Haitian Independence Revolution; Slave Rebellions in the United States; South African Revolution; Student and Youth Movements, Activism and Revolution; U.S. Southern Secessionist Rebellion and Civil War; Women's Movement of the United States

References and Further Readings
Anderson, Carol. 2003. *Eyes Off the Prize: The United Nations and the African-American Struggle for Human Rights, 1944–1955.* New York: Cambridge University Press.
Borstelmann, Thomas. 2002. *The Cold War and the Color Line: American Race Relations in the Global Arena.* Cambridge, MA: Harvard University Press.
Branch, Taylor. 1988. *Parting the Waters: America in the King Years, 1954–63.* New York: Simon and Schuster.
_____. 1988. *Pillar of Fire: America in the King Years, 1963–1965.* New York: Simon and Schuster.
Carmichael, Stokely, with Ekwueme Michael Thelwell. 2003. *Ready for Revolution: The Life and Struggles of Stokely Carmichael [Kwame Ture].* New York: Scribner.
Carson, Clayborne. 1981. *In Struggle: SNCC and the Black Awakening of the 1960s.* Cambridge, MA: Harvard University Press.
_____, ed. 1998. *The Autobiography of Martin Luther King, Jr.* New York: Warner Books.
Collins, Patricia Hill. 1990. *Black Feminist Thought: Knowledge, Consciousness, and the Politics of Empowerment.* Boston: Unwin Hyman.
Dawson, Michael C. 1994. *Behind the Mule: Race and Class in African American Politics.* Princeton, NJ: Princeton University Press.
D'Emilio, John. 2004. *Lost Prophet: The Life and Times of Bayard Rustin.* New York: Free Press.
Dittmer, John. 2002. *Local People: The Struggle for Civil Rights in Mississippi.* Urbana: University of Illinois Press.
Foner, Philip S., ed. 1995. *The Black Panthers Speak.* New York: Da Capo Press.
Graham, Hugh Davis. 1990. *The Civil Rights Era: Origins and Development of National Policy, 1960–1972.* New York: Oxford University Press.
Horne, Gerald. 1986. *W. E. B. Du Bois and the Afro-American Response to the Cold War, 1944–1963.* Albany: State University of New York Press.
Jonas, Gilbert. 2005. *Freedom's Sword: The NAACP and the Struggle against Racism in America, 1909–1969.* New York: Routledge University Press.
Kennedy, Randall. 1998. *Race, Crime, and the Law.* New York: Vintage.
Klarman, Michael J. 2004. *From Jim Crow to Civil Rights: The Supreme Court and the Struggle for Racial Equality.* New York: Oxford University Press.
Kluger, Richard. 1975. *Simple Justice: The History of Brown v. Board of Education and Black America's Struggle for Equality.* New York: Knopf.

Lawson, Steven F. 1985. *In Pursuit of Power: Southern Blacks and Electoral Politics, 1965–1982.* New York: Columbia University Press.

Marable, Manning. 1991. *Race, Reform, and Rebellion: The Second Reconstruction in Black America, 1945–1990.* Jackson: University Press of Mississippi.

National Advisory Commission on Civil Disorders. 1968. *U.S. Riot Commission Report.* New York: Bantam Books.

Norrell, Robert J. 2005. *The House I Live In: Race in the American Century.* New York: Oxford University Press.

O'Reilly, Kenneth. *"Racial Matters": The FBI's Secret File on Black America, 1960–1972.* New York: Free Press.

Payne, Charles M. 1995. *I've Got the Light of Freedom: The Organizing Tradition and the Mississippi Freedom Struggle.* Berkeley: University of California Press.

Ransby, Barbara. 2005. *Ella Baker and the Black Freedom Movement: A Radical Democratic Vision.* Chapel Hill: University of North Carolina.

Van Deburg, William. 1992. *New Day in Babylon: The Black Power Movement and American Culture, 1965–1975.* Chicago: University of Chicago Press.

Von Eschen, Penny. 1997. *Race against Empire: Black Americans and Anticolonialism, 1937–1957.* Ithaca, NY: Cornell University Press.

Walters, Ronald W. 2003. *White Nationalism, Black Interests: Conservative Public Policy and the Black Community.* Detroit, MI: Wayne State University Press.

Williams, Juan. 1998. *Thurgood Marshall: American Revolutionary.* New York: Crown.

Wilson, William J. 1980. *The Declining Significance of Race: Blacks and Changing American Institutions.* Chicago: University of Chicago Press.

Woodward, Komozi. 1999. *A Nation within a Nation: Amiri Baraka (LeRoi Jones) and Black Power Politics.* Chapel Hill: University of North Carolina Press.

Algerian Islamic Revolt

CHRONOLOGY

7th century	Spread of Islam in North Africa.
8th–15th centuries	Independent Islamic caliphates rule North Africa.
16th century	Establishment of Ottoman control in North Africa.
1830	French conquest of Algiers.
1831–1847	War between Muslim tribes led by Emir Abdelkader and the French armies.
1848	Algeria becomes a French colony.
1926	Messali Hadj creates the proto-nationalist movement Étoile Nord-Africaine.
1931	Abdelhamid Ben Badis creates the reformist Islamic movement Association of Ulama.
1954	Creation of the National Liberation Front (FLN) and beginning of the Algerian war of de-colonization.
1962	Algeria becomes independent. The FLN becomes a state party, and Ahmed Ben Bella becomes the country's first president.
1965	Colonel Houari Boumediène stages a successful coup d'état.
1971	Oil and gas sector nationalized; land reform enacted.
1978	Death of President Boumediène.
1979	Colonel Chadli Benjedid is nominated president.
1980	Violent anti-government protest by the Berber population of Kabylia ("Berber Spring").
1986	Food riots in Constantine and Setif.
1988	October Riots—nationwide anti-governmental protests. Beginning of the Algerian democratic transition.
1989	Adoption of a new Algerian constitution allowing multipartism. Abassi Madani and Ali Belhadj create the Islamic Salvation Front (FIS).
1990	Victory of the FIS in local elections.
1991	An FIS-led general strike provokes the intervention of army. The two FIS leaders are jailed. Six months later, the FIS takes a commanding lead in the parliamentary elections.
1992	Forced resignation of President Chadli Benjedid between the two rounds of

parliamentary elections. The high security council, led by General Khaled Nezzar, declares a state of emergency and suspends the electoral process. The FIS is officially banned. Islamist insurrection in Algeria begins.

1993   Guerrilla warfare by Islamist groups becomes widespread throughout the country.

1994   General Liamine Zeroual is nominated head of state. Algeria signs structural adjustment package with the International Monetary Fund.

1995   Zeroual is elected president in an election boycotted by all the main opposition political parties.

1996   The nationalists of the National Liberation Front (FLN) and the moderate Islamists of Hamas (Harakat Al Mujtamaa Al Islami, Movement for an Islamic Society) enter a coalition government.

1997   Massacres of civilians by the guerrillas of the Armed Islamic Groups (GIA). The other main Islamic guerrilla organization, the Islamic Salvation Army (AIS), declares a ceasefire. Zeroual's party wins parliamentary elections amid widespread fraud.

1998   Wave of anti-governmental riots in Kabylia. Zeroual resigns from the presidency.

1999   Backed by the military led by Mohamed Lamari, Abdelaziz Bouteflika wins the presidential election after all the other candidates withdraw from the race. The AIS agrees to disband in exchange for a general amnesty.

2003   The leaders of the FIS, Madani and Belhadj, are freed.

2004   President Bouteflika is re-elected to second term.

INTRODUCTION

In 1988, Algeria was one of the first countries in the Muslim world to witness the arrival of the "third wave" of democratic transitions. This was the international trend toward democ-

ratization in place of authoritarian regimes which started in the 1970s. The first wave started with the American Revolution and lasted into the 1920s and the second wave commenced in the later stages of World War II and lasted into the early 1960s. However, the Algerian transition quickly took an unexpected turn when a pro-Islamic party took the lead in the elections. An even more dramatic political turn of events occurred in 1992 when the Algerian military organized a coup d'état to prevent the Islamists from gaining power. The military intervention paved the way for a popular insurrection and the emergence of a radical Islamist guerrilla movement. A vicious civil conflict pitting the supporters of the Islamists against those of the regime raged in the country between 1992 and 1999, and residual violence still persists today.

BACKGROUND: CULTURE AND HISTORY

The one feature of Algerian history that must not be underestimated when trying to comprehend Algerian politics and conflict in the late twentieth century is the French colonization of the country and the subsequent defeat of France by the National Liberation Front (*Front de Libération Nationale*—FLN) during a brutal war of de-colonization. Between 1830 and 1962, Algeria was the scene of a process of state formation that was probably the most systematic and drastic in the modern Middle East and North Africa. After defeating Emir Abdelkader, Algeria's main military, political, and religious power, in 1847, the French began to build a state and a nation—according to their idea of France's "civilizing mission." This thorough social, economic, and political transformation was an important homogenizing factor for the Muslim communities of the region, which had only been united until then by a loose formal political and religious allegiance to the Ottoman sultan. It is in response to this intensive process of French colonization that the Algerian indigenous elite tried to reaffirm themselves and their Arab-Muslim heritage in the aftermath of the First World War.

Two distinct movements led this revival in the inter-war period. First was the Étoile Nord-Africaine (North African Star), a proto-nationalist leftist movement that found support in the new Algerian working class and lower middle class. Then there was the Association of Ulama, a movement of Islamic revival spearheaded by urban intellectuals and local notables. Confronted by growing French censorship of the Arabic media as well as new policies for vetting imam and Islamic schools, the two movements joined forces in the 1940s. By the 1950s, however, the leadership of the movement had slipped away from the Islamic reformers into the hands of the nationalist elite of the National Liberation Front (FLN). Although Islamic rhetoric was repeatedly used during the war of de-colonization, it was more a means of galvanizing the masses than a reflection of the nationalist movement's ideological orientation.

The vicious war of de-colonization that lasted from 1954 to 1962 was another key event in the process of forging Algerian national identity. This long-drawn struggle against the French, which resulted in an estimated one million casualties, was the founding stone of the Algerian republic. Unsurprisingly, after gaining independence in 1962, the new Algerian government set about to Arabicize and Islamicize society in order to counter any remaining French influence in the country. It also proposed an ambitious program of social development for the country inspired by Arab Socialism. Finally, on the international scene, Algeria also promoted itself as a champion of Pan-Arabism and a leader of the Non-Aligned Movement.

From the time of its independence to the late 1980s, Algeria was thus ruled by a mildly authoritarian Arab Socialist regime led by Colonel Houari Boumediène until 1978, and then by Colonel Chadli Benjedid. In the early 1980s, however, Algeria's Socialist economy began to unravel. After the end of the second oil boom in particular, the policy of Soviet-style industrialization financed by the country's oil and gas resources was increasingly becoming unworkable, principally because of inadequate central planning. As a result, national growth stagnated and social development leveled off. The quickly patched together program of economic liberalization introduced by the Chadli administration in order to tackle these problems was ineffective, primarily because it was undermined by the patronage networks that had been built during the Socialist years. In effect, economic liberalization increased the inequalities between rich and poor, as well as between town and country. Furthermore, since these reforms allowed Algerians access to imported consumption goods, they spelled disaster for Algeria's domestic industry and seriously increased the country's debt burden. In its turn, this growing debt crisis forced the state to cut its subsidies to the state-owned industries, which went into recession and fueled a growing unemployment crisis. The slump in domestic production, in conjunction with rising inflation, also led to shortages of consumption goods (including staple foods), which hit the poor hardest. Popular unrest was on the rise, as evidenced by a spate of food riots in the summer of 1986. In the following years, as the economic situation continued to worsen, popular discontent with the regime mounted, but without finding an effective institutional means to voice its opposition to the existing policies. After another period of food shortages in the summer of 1988, popular anger finally exploded during the October Riots.

International developments like the spread of the "third wave" of democratic transitions and the collapse of Communism also had a significant impact on Algeria. In the late 1970s and throughout the 1980s, the number of transitions to democracy increased significantly around the world. Although Muslim countries were, by and large, not part of this wave of democratic transitions, they were aware that many authoritarian regimes in Latin America, Southern Europe, and then Eastern Europe, both leftist and rightist, had been forced to introduce democratic reforms. This demand for political liberalization followed an earlier "wave" of economic liberalization that affected Algeria in the mid 1980s. In these circumstances, some policy makers in the Algerian regime began to think that political liberalization was the next logical step in the development of the country.

Finally, throughout the 1980s, there was also a slow, mostly unnoticed but pervasive rise of the Islamic associative movement in Algeria. In contrast to other places in the Middle East where the Iranian Revolution directly fueled a revival of political Islam, in Algeria the Iranian example had limited direct impact outside the Islamist intelligentsia. The reason for the growth of Islamic associations in Algerian civil society was far more pragmatic: the process was connected to the erosion of the welfare provisions of Algeria's socialist state system and the slow meltdown of Algeria's domestic economy. As the state administration became increasingly unable to meet first the expectations of the population vis-à-vis social development and, later, their actual needs, Islamic charities stepped into the vacuum created by a retreating state. The Islamic associations provided basic social services like education and an alternative welfare system for the poor. Over time, the synergy between the rise of a more articulate Islamic discourse about social and cultural reform and the growth of Islamic social activism in civil society provided the foundation for the development of political Islam as an alternative to a nationalist political order and regime.

CONTEXT AND PROCESS OF REVOLUTION

Two very distinct Islamic-led rebellions occurred within the Algerian Islamic revolt. The first started and ended in October 1988—even though its political implications lasted much longer. This revolt forced the government of the day to agree to implement democratic reforms and to organize free elections in the country. The second Islamist revolt, more militaristic in outlook, began shortly after the January 1992 coup d'état, when the Algerian military canceled the electoral process and banned the Islamic Salvation Front (FIS). These actions created the conditions for a wave of Islamist-led civil disobedience and armed resistance by Islamist guerrillas that threatened the survival of the Algerian regime until the late 1990s.

This entire series of events started in October 1988, when the worsening of the economic situation in Algeria triggered a spate of food riots that seriously challenged the authority of the regime. Initially, the political objectives of the rioters were not well articulated. Soon, however, at Friday prayer, Islamist preachers began to organize demonstrations and to put forward a set of "Islamic" demands for reforming the political system. At the same time, liberal and democratic opposition figures demanded democratization of the political system according to a liberal-democratic model. Confronted by a nationwide wave of rioting, the Algerian president offered an olive branch to the demonstrators in the form of a democratic opportunity that would allow both Islamic and liberal players to have a formal say in Algerian politics.

In February 1989 a new, pluralist Algerian constitution was approved by referendum, and both previously banned political parties and new parties arrived on the political scene. Foremost among them was the Islamic Salvation Front (FIS). This pro-Islamic party grew out of a coalition of religious leaders formed during the October Riots, and it succeeded in developing institutional linkages with previously apolitical Islamic associations. The rise of the FIS rapidly overshadowed that of all other political parties. In June 1990, the pro-Islamic party scored its first major electoral success in the local and regional elections by coming in first in nearly all the main urban centers. Again in December 1991, the FIS was also poised to win an absolute majority in the National Assembly, nearly having obtained a straight majority in the first round of the parliamentary elections.

In January 1992, however, between the two rounds of the parliamentary elections a coalition of military officers led by General Khaled Nezzar staged a coup d'état to prevent the FIS from gaining power. Distrustful of the Islamist project and fearful of losing their privileges under the new regime, the military forced the president to resign and postponed elections indefinitely. The more secular and conservative Algerian political players supported the military intervention and the postponement of the democratic experiment so that a pro-Islamic government would not be swept into power. In contrast, the supporters of the FIS as well as the more liberal democratic parties took to the street in protest against the military intervention. In February 1992, as clashes escalated between the supporters of the FIS and the security forces, the military banned the FIS and arrested its cadres and thousands of its members. This increased repression had two distinct consequences. First it ensured that the pro-Islamic camp could not organize itself into an effective institutional opposition to the military-backed regime. Second, it convinced the more radical Islamists to abandon the political debate altogether and to challenge the new regime by means of armed struggle.

The Islamic Armed Movement (MIA) was the first important Islamist guerrilla group to arise in Algeria in March 1992. It began to mobilize Islamist sympathizers, particularly the youth disappointed by the failure of the democratic transition and alienated by the indiscriminate repression of the military forces. However, because the MIA leadership chose to wage traditional guerrilla warfare—establishing bases in the countryside and slowly progressing toward the town—it was not able to capitalize fully on the reservoirs of Islamist supporters living in most major urban centers. After less than a year of very slow progress, the leadership of the guerrilla movement split over tactics, and many guerrilla fighters chose to retreat into towns, where they started an urban guerrilla campaign.

Thus in 1993 the Armed Islamic Groups (GIA) came into existence in some of the poorer suburbs of the Algerian capital, Algiers. The GIA quickly acquired notoriety by targeting governmental officials and civil servants. Building on this early success achieved by multiple attacks on soft targets—including foreign nationals perceived to be helping the regime—the GIA rapidly grew in strength and began to expand throughout the country, supplanting the MIA as the country's main Islamist guerrilla organization. In 1994, the FIS, which had been mostly absent from the guerrilla scene, began to support its own guerrilla group, the Islamic Salvation Army (AIS), in order to keep in check the younger and more radical leadership of the GIA. Politically, the FIS also joined forces with the main Algerian opposition parties, the FLN and the Socialist Front (FFS), to propose a cross-parties political platform (the Sant Egidio agreements) to restart the democratic transition. Ultimately, however, both initiatives failed. On the political front, the Algerian regime simply ignored this proposal and any international remonstrance. On the war front, the disagreements between the various Islamist guerrilla groups led to frequent infighting and reduced the impact of their combined efforts against the military forces.

By late 1995 it had become clear that the armed struggle between the guerrilla groups and the Algerian military had reached a stalemate. The Islamists could not overthrow the Algerian regime by the force of arms, and the Algerian regime could not fully eliminate the guerrilla groups. Faced with these circumstances, a part of the guerrilla movement led by the AIS sought to find a negotiated exit to the conflict. Early in 1997, the AIS organized a cease-fire with the Algerian military. Another part of the guerrilla movement led by the GIA tried, instead, to escalate the conflict, which led to a series of massacres of the civilian population in 1997 and 1998. This strategy of radicalization of the conflict also failed to destabilize the Algerian regime, and it cost the GIA dearly in terms of popular support.

Electoral campaign in Algiers. Meeting of the Islamic Salvation Front (FIS) on Abdelkader Square, January 9, 1992. (Gyori Antoine/Corbis Sygma)

In 1999, the AIS successfully negotiated a formal amnesty for its members with the newly elected Algerian president, Abdelaziz Bouteflika. The GIA, weakened by its strategy of radicalization, split into various factions, some of which became indistinguishable from organized crime. Only the less radical faction, the Salafist Group for Combat and Preaching (GSPC), led by Hassan Hattab, retained a recognizable politico-military strategy of targeting the Algerian security forces. By that time, however, the Algerian regime had successfully survived the brunt of the Algerian Islamist insurrection. Although residual violence still mars the country today, and is likely to do so for many more years, the Islamic-led revolt that began in 1992 ran out of steam by the end of the decade.

IMPACTS

Domestically, the two phases of the Algerian Islamic revolt have had a profound impact on the organization of social and political life in the country. The first phase of the rebellion paved the way for the first democratic transition of the "third wave" in the Middle East and North African region. It also created propitious conditions for the establishment of a democratically endorsed pro-Islamic party, and for the first-ever transition to an "Islamic democracy." The second phase of the rebellion consisted of the fierce struggle for power between the Islamist guerrillas and the Algerian military that followed the 1992 coup d'état. Its pervasive violence profoundly marked Algerian society. Although political violence did not lead to a popular rejection of political Islam as a model of governance, it seriously undermined the prospects for a genuine return to a democratic process involving moderate Islamists in the short-to-medium term. In addition, the abuse of power by the military-backed regime seriously undermined the confidence of the population in the institutions of the state.

At the regional level, the impact of the Algerian democratic transition and the ensuing Algerian civil conflict cannot be underestimated. Most authoritarian regimes as well as most Islamist movements in the Middle East and North Africa analyzed carefully the progress of this democratic experiment to see which lessons could be applied to their own countries. After the coup d'état and the beginning of the civil conflict, however, the lessons appeared to be mostly negative, encouraging other regimes in the region not to go the route of democratization. Some governments, such as those of Egypt and Tunisia, used the events in Algeria as an excuse to increase the repression against their domestic political opposition, be it pro-Islamic or pro-democratic. The violent Islamist insurrection that raged in Algeria throughout most of the 1990s also had destabilizing impacts on its neighbors, particularly Morocco, where guerrilla groups often sought refuge, and on European countries because of the wave of refugees that fled across the Mediterranean. In addition, the practice of targeting the citizens of European countries in retaliation for their government's support of the Algerian regime—a tactic used by some of the Islamist guerrillas—was a significant foreign policy development. It was particularly important in the case of France, where the GIA organized a bombing campaign in 1994–1995.

Internationally, the Islamist success in the democratic transition in Algeria confirmed the fear of many Western policy makers that democratization in the Middle East and North Africa would be a troublesome matter. The military ending to the democratic transition and the growth of the Islamist insurgency in the country posed additional practical difficulties for liberal democracies. Western democracies did not fully understand (nor like) the way the process of democratization facilitated the institutionalization of a pro-Islamic movement as the dominant player in Algerian politics. But because the Islamists were playing by the rules of the democratic political game and because they were supported by a large part of the population, Western governments could not formally object to these developments simply because of ideological differences. This dilemma reached its critical stage in 1992, with the intervention of the Algerian military and the suspension of the democratic transition. Officially, liberal democracies could not condone a military putsch. Yet, because the Algerian military claimed to be saving Algerian democracy from a potentially threatening Islamic fundamentalist regime, Western governments voiced only muted criticism and implemented limited sanctions against the new military-backed Algerian regime. This state of affairs led many people in the Muslim world to believe that the Western discourse on democracy was mere rhetoric; and that Western powers were still willing to support authoritarian regimes if this prevented an Islamic movement from coming to power via the ballot box. Subsequently, this argument was also used to excuse some of the excesses of the Algerian Islamist guerrillas during the civil conflict.

PEOPLE AND ORGANIZATIONS

Armed Islamic Groups (Groupements Islamiques Armés—GIA)

The GIA came into existence in March 1993, when a loose association of small guerrilla groups was reorganized by the local commanders and ideologues of the Algiers area: Moh Levelley, Abdelhak Layada, Omar al-Eulmi, and Djaffar al-Afghani. The GIA gained its notoriety by organizing attacks against civil servants and members of the government. It also gained recognition on the international scene when it organized a campaign against foreign interests and foreign nationals perceived to be helping the Algerian government. The core GIA groups, first under Djamel Zitouni, then under Antar Zouabri, proposed increasingly radical interpretations of Islam to justify their guerrilla tactics. After the 1995 Algerian presidential elections, the GIA leadership declared apostate all the Algerian citizens who voted in the elections and made them legitimate targets for the guerrillas. The GIA targeting of civilians who were perceived to be supportive of the regime led them to commit large-scale massacres in 1997 and 1998, during the holy month of Ramadan. In 1999, the prospect of a general amnesty induced several GIA-affiliated groups to rally behind the AIS. Other factions, like Hassan Hattab's Group for Preaching and Combat (GSPC), challenged the GIA's radical strategy and reverted to more conventional guerrilla tactics in the Algiers and Kabyle regions. The GIA ceased to be a credible challenger to the regime at the end of the 1990s. (In 2001, after the al-Qaeda attacks on the United States, the GIA and the GSPC were nonetheless placed on the U.S. State Department's list of terrorist organizations linked to bin Laden's network).

Armed Islamic Movement (Mouvement Islamique Armé—MIA)

Under the leadership of Abdelkader Chebouti, the MIA was the first important guerrilla organization to challenge the new military-backed Algerian regime in 1992. This group staged attacks on military installations from its bases in the hills surrounding Algiers. Confronted by the unexpected resilience of the military, the core of the MIA withdrew from the Algiers region in 1993 and moved into the rural areas of the east and west of the country, where they tried to establish steadier guerrilla bases. At the same time, splinter groups retreated into the towns, where they provided the impetus for an urban guerrilla movement, the GIA, that eventually overshadowed the efforts of the MIA.

Islamic Salvation Army (Armée Islamique du Salut—AIS)

The AIS was created in 1994 from the remnants on the MIA and from independent guerrilla groups. Under the leadership of Madani Mezrag, the AIS presented itself as the "official" armed wing of the FIS. Quickly proving unable to defeat militarily the Algerian regime, the FIS-AIS association decided to reorganize the guerrilla movement in view of a negotiated solution to the Islamic insurrection. In 1997, the AIS negotiated an unofficial cease-fire with the Algerian military. In 1999, the AIS negotiated a formal general amnesty for its organization and its members with the newly elected Algerian president, Abdelaziz Bouteflika.

Islamic Salvation Front (Front Islamique du Salut—FIS)

The FIS was officially created in March 1989 under the leadership of Abassi Madani and Ali Belhadj. This pro-Islamic party rapidly grew in strength and numbers by proposing an Islamic alternative to the ruling party, and won the 1990 local elections. However, its political challenge ended at the beginning of 1992, when the Algerian military staged a coup d'état. The FIS was then banned, and the state security forces systematically arrested its cadres and imprisoned thousands of its supporters in detention camps in the Sahara desert. The FIS remained an important political player in the following years by going underground and by participating with other opposition parties in initiatives to restart the democratic transition. The issue of the re-legalization of the FIS remained a hot topic in Algerian politics, but despite the release from prison of Madani and Belhadj in 2003, it is unlikely to occur in the near-to-medium term.

Movement for a Society of Peace (MSP)—formerly Hamas

The MSP/Hamas is a moderate Islamist party linked to the Muslim Brotherhood created by Mahfoud Nahnah in 1990 and led by him until his death in 2003. It repeatedly cooperated with Algeria's military-backed regime and opposed the FIS.

National Liberation Army (Armée de Liberation Nationale—ALN)

The ALN was the military wing of the FLN and a key player during the war of de-colonization. After Algeria gained its independence, the military imposed its stamp on the country as Colonel Houari Boumediène, the strongman of the ALN and the country's defense minister, seized power from President Ben Bella in a coup d'état in 1965. In 1978, after Boumediène's death, another brief struggle for influence between the FLN cadres and the ALN officers turned to the advantage of the military, which selected Colonel Chadli Benjedid as the country's new president. In 1988, as divisions appeared inside the military leadership over the treatment of the Islamist challenge and the popular insurrection, Chadli tried to reorganize the military hierarchy by pushing aside older ALN commanders and promoting younger officers like General Khaled Nezzar, General Liamine Zeroual, and Colonel Mohamed Lamari. In 1992, as the democratic transition escaped the president's control, Chadli was forced to resign by a coalition of ALN officers led by Nezzar. In 1994, when the growth of the Islamist guerrilla forces put the military on the defensive, Nezzar was evicted by Zeroual and Lamari. Zeroual was then elected president in 1995 and remained in power until his eviction (attributed to Lamari) in 1998. Lamari then became the main power behind the throne, and he supported Abdelaziz Bouteflika's successful bid for the Algerian presidency in 1999.

National Liberation Front (Front de Libération—FLN; Jabhat al-TaHrir al-Watani)

The FLN was the hegemonic player in Algerian politics from the time it became a state party in 1963 until the beginning of the democratic transition in 1989. Then, under the leadership of Abdelhamid Mehri, the FLN sought to take advantage of the democratic opening to redefine itself as a democratic nationalist party and to cut its ties with the military establishment. This strategy of the FLN was not entirely successful because the party retained a divided loyalty. For several years it was able to act as a genuine opposition party, but after Mehri's eviction in 1996, the FLN was inclined to cooperate again with the military elite, and it subsequently entered several coalition governments.

Rally for Culture and Democracy (RCD)

The RCD of Said Sadi was created in 1989 on a regionalist (Berber) and liberal democratic platform. In 1992, it was one of the first parties to support the military intervention, and it subsequently spearheaded the anti-Islamist opposition.

Socialist Front (Front des Forces Socialistes—FFS)

The FFS of Hocine Ait Ahmed was created in the aftermath of the Algerian war of de-colonization in opposition to the state party system. Legalized in 1989, this regionalist party representing the Berber minority embodied the principal liberal-democratic forces in Algeria.

Frédéric Volpi

See Also Algerian Revolution; Cinema of Revolution; Documentaries of Revolution; Islamic Fundamentalist Revolutionary Movement

References and Further Readings

Burgat, François, and William Dowell. 1993. *The Islamic Movement in North Africa.* Austin: University of Texas Press.

Entelis, John P. 1999. "State-Society Relations: Algeria as a Case Study." Pp. 11–29 in *Area Studies and Social Sciences: Strategies for Understanding Middle East Politics,* edited by Mark A. Tessler, Jodi Nachtwey, and Anne Banda. Bloomington: Indiana University Press.

Martinez, Luis. 2000. *The Algerian Civil War 1990–1998.* Translated from the French by Jonathan Derrick. New York: Columbia University Press.

Mortimer, Robert A. 1996. "Islamists, Soldiers and Democrats: The Second Algerian War," *The Middle East Journal* 50 (1): 18–39.

Quandt, William B. 1998. *Between Ballots and Bullets: Algeria's Transition from Authoritarianism.* Washington, DC: Brookings Institution Press.

———. 2002. "Algeria's Uneasy Peace," *Journal of Democracy* 13 (2): 15–23.

Ruedy, John. 1992. *Modern Algeria: The Origins and Development of a Nation.* Bloomington: Indiana University Press.

Takeyh, Ray. 2003. "Islamism in Algeria: A Struggle between Hope and Agony." *Middle East Policy* 10 (2): 62–75.

Volpi, Frédéric. 2003. *Islam and Democracy: The Failure of Dialogue in Algeria.* London: Pluto Press.

Willis, Michael. 1999. *The Islamist Challenge in Algeria: A Political History.* New York: New York University Press.

Algerian Revolution

CHRONOLOGY

106 B.C.	Kingdom of Numidia is annexed by the Roman empire.
7th century	Led by Umayyad Khalif, the Arab tribes sweep through North Africa and Algeria becomes part of the empire.
1518	The power of the Ottoman sultan is formally established, although real control remains in the hands of the regional governor (*dey*).
1711	The tenth governor of Algiers obtains the title of *pasha,* implying the achievement of semi-independence from the Ottoman empire.
1830–1871	The process of French colonization begins with the taking of Algiers. The defeat of Algerian leader Abdelkader in 1847 accelerates French penetration. By 1871, the French occupy most of Algeria and 245,000 white settlers have arrived.
1871–1930s	The policy of assimilation is launched, but its contradictions awaken Algerian nationalism.
1936	The Popular Front wins the French elections, sparking enthusiasm among Algerians who believe that the new government will grant them full citizenship rights. Hopes are shattered when the settlers' movement boycotts any attempt at reform.
1943	A new Algerian nationalist spirit finds expression in the publication of a manifesto signed by twenty-eight prominent national figures and submitted to the French authorities. In the document the policy of assimilation is rejected in favor of the creation of a politically autonomous Algeria "associated" with, but not formally independent from, France. The French authorities reject the idea and remain committed to the policy of assimilation.
1945	In response to the dismissive attitudes of the French, the Algerians take to the streets in protest in May 1945. Cries for independence begin to be heard at demonstrations. Spontaneous upheavals occur, violence breaks out, and the crack down is swift and bloody. French repression results in the killing of between 10,000 and 45,000 people (Calchi Novati 1998, 62).
1954	On October 10, a number of leaders of the nationalist movement meet in Algiers to launch a campaign of armed insurrection with the goal of gaining independence. The National Liberation Front (FLN) is set up as the party representing all Algerians in their revolution.

| 1954–1962 | On November 1, the war of liberation officially begins with a series of attacks against French institutions. The French authorities proclaim martial law the following year to face down the "terrorists," but the revolutionary army raises its profile through spectacular offensives. |

1956   The first FLN party congress takes place in Soumann in August 1956, reaffirming the goal of political independence. The French government, blackmailed by the settlers' movement, gives General Massu carte blanche in Algiers to defeat the resistance in the capital city. The general temporarily succeeds and his victory emboldens the French army and the settlers who plot to overthrow the weak civilian government of France in an effort to arrive at a final solution against the insurgents.

1958   In June 1958 General de Gaulle is asked to "save the country" and becomes head of the French government, assuming special powers to deal with the crisis. While the war continues, de Gaulle begins to look for a negotiated way out of Algeria.

1961–1962   The peace process between France and the FLN begins in 1961 and, despite a number of attempts by radical settlers and some members of the armed forces to derail it, the war is officially over in March 1962 with the signing of the Evian Accords. The French approve by referendum de Gaulle's choice to let Algeria's residents vote on whether they want to become independent and then for France to honor the result. The settlers begin to leave. Algeria becomes independent in July 1962.

1963–1965   Internal strife plagues the FLN over the direction of the revolution. Ben Bella emerges victorious and is elected president. Under his leadership, Algeria formally espouses Socialism within an Islamic-values framework. One-party rule is consolidated.

1965–1978   Colonel Houari Boumediène deposes Ben Bella in June 1965 and assumes control of the country. Under his leadership Algeria begins its economic development based on the exploitation of hydrocarbons. He dies in 1978.

1979–1992   Colonel Chadli Benjedid is "chosen" by the army as the new president. By the mid 1980s difficult economic circumstances force him to introduce market reforms. These lead to the sudden pauperization of the population and to anti-government demonstrations. After a violent crackdown in October 1988, a transition to democracy begins. For almost three years Algeria experiences "democracy," but the victory of the Islamic Party (FIS) at the first round of legislative elections of 1991 triggers a military coup.

1992–2004   The second round of the legislative elections due to be held in January 1992 is called off, as the Algerian army takes direct control to stop the FIS from winning power through the ballot box. A bloody civil war ensues between security forces and Islamic resistance. By the end of the 1990s the war is virtually over, although violence sporadically continues. The army is victorious and it slowly reintroduces minor democratic reforms.

INTRODUCTION

The Algerian independence revolution of 1954 to 1962 provided a model for many national liberation struggles to follow. The conflict was characterized by a wide range of violent and nonviolent actions and strategies by all parties involved. The determination with which the Algerians strove for independence, coupled with the human, moral, and economic costs of the war, convinced most French citizens to allow the Algerians to vote in a referendum. Close to the entire population voted for independence. Yet the legacy of this truly popular and legitimate revolution has been one of political authoritarianism and economic failure. The contested "ideological" and political significance of the Algerian Revolution unfortunately served in the 1990s as the backdrop for a brutal civil war between the military and Islamic insurgents.

BACKGROUND: CULTURE AND HISTORY

The People's Democratic Republic of Algeria has had two defining moments during its long history. The first one came in the seventh century, when the Arab tribes swept through

North Africa and established themselves in the region, bringing Islam with them. The Berber indigenous population attempted to resist the Islamic expansion, but to little avail, given the military might they faced. Eventually, the local Berber population embraced Islam, although it continued to hold fast to some of its traditions and practiced the "new" religion by adapting it to local customs. Today, more than 99 percent of Algerians follow Sunni Islam. Understanding the role that Islam would play in Algerian history from that moment on is fundamental to understanding future developments. The divide between Arabs and, in particular, indigenous Kabyles living in a remote mountainous region became a permanent feature of Algerian political and cultural life. Although linguistic and ethnic differences were overshadowed at times by common concerns and struggles, at other times divisions emerged forcefully. To this day, the ethnic and linguistic composition of Algeria represents significant divisions in the population, even though they are not always officially recognized by authorities.

The second defining moment of Algerian history was French colonization, which began in 1830 and lasted until 1962, when national independence was finally achieved. This period, more that any other in Algerian history, forged the national character of modern Algeria. The effects of colonization are still deeply felt to this day.

Resistance to French occupation began almost immediately after the French made it clear that Algeria would not become a colony in the traditional sense. Instead, it would be a colony for white settlers to move to, and the indigenous Muslim population would be assimilated into this French national project. Abdelkader became the leader of the resistance in the early 1830s and has been credited later on with the title of the founder of the Algerian nation. His ability consisted in uniting the local populations against the French under the banner of Islam, which was the common denominator for all the Algerian tribes. This theme of Islam as a unifying factor would become a lesson for the future generations of resistance leaders. According to Calchi Novati (1998, 23), "Islam and independence will become inseparable elements for many Algerians in their manifestations of resistance to colonial rule." Despite his military abilities and his charisma, Abdelkader was defeated and exiled.

The military success of the French was not translated into political success when it came to the policy of assimilation of the Muslim population. In the name of the values of the French Republic born of the revolution of 1789, the policy was built on the premise of equality of all French citizens, but it excluded the "colonized" people because of their religion. Being Muslim trumped being a full citizen, and assimilation meant, for ordinary Algerians, the suppression of their cultural and political identity. To become French citizens with full civil and political rights they had to renounce their personal status as Muslims. The contradiction in the policy of assimilation was also evident in white settlers' political and economic rights. The French authorities solved the crucial issue of land ownership by expropriating "tribal" lands and giving them to white settlers. The resentment at the contradiction between an egalitarian policy of assimilation (the rights of all citizens) with the practical exclusion of all Muslims from the benefits of such citizenship mounted, over the course of the years, as a number of wealthy Algerians benefited from a French "republican" education. Whenever individual ministers in subsequent French governments proposed reforms to allow the participation of Muslims in the political process on more equal terms, the political power of settlers opposed to any concession always prevailed, leaving the emerging Algerian nationalist movement increasingly frustrated. It is worth noting that in the period between 1866 and 1934 only 2,500 Algerians became French citizens despite the Muslims' services to France in World War I (Calchi Novati 1998, 32).

The goal of early Algerian political movements until the mid 1920s was to solve the assimilation contradiction by campaigning from within French institutions for the inclusion of Muslims into the French nation without discrimination. The reluctance of successive French governments to meet at least some of these demands for inclusion meant that the original Algerian political groups were soon outflanked by more overtly nationalist movements that placed considerable importance on the egalitarian values of Islam and on political autonomy. Ahmed Messali Hadj became the father of this militant Algerian nationalism, in contrast with Ferhat Abbas, who wanted to keep working within "colonial legality." The religious *ulema* (clergy) sided with the more moderate wing to avoid the outbreak of violence. The moderates seemed to be vindicated in their approach when the Popular Front won the 1936 French national elections, and the new government set out to accept many of the demands made by Abbas. But the settlers boycotted all plans for reform, to the immense frustration of the moderate Algerians. The failure of the Popular Front to carry out the necessary reforms showed the vast majority of Algerians that political autonomy for the Algerian nation was the only viable solution to their status as second-class citizens.

The anti-colonial international environment after the end of World War II emboldened the nationalist movement, and the few changes that the French government made to the institutional set-up of Algeria to satisfy nationalist demands was a case of too little, too late. It is worth noting that this nationalist struggle saw all Algerians, Kabyles included, as protagonists, despite attempts made by the colonial authorities to play on ethnic and linguistic differences.

Together with the rise of militant nationalism, the post–World War II period confirmed the prominent political role that the settlers played in French politics and demonstrated once again French society's "psychological" attachment to Algeria, given its status as formal French *department.* The bloody repression of anti-colonial demonstrations and the extensive use of violence to quell anti-French dissent proved to all Algerian nationalists that armed insurrection to achieve formal political independence was the only means to obtain recognition and save the "national Algerian identity." Thus in October 1954, nine nationalist leaders (the so-called *chefs historiques,* historical leaders) met in Algiers to launch the Algerian Revolution. Significantly, Messali and Abbas did not participate in the meeting: a new generation of nationalists had arrived on the scene. The armed struggle officially began on November 1, 1954. It did not deviate from its ultimate goal of independence, although it was open to a political solution and not necessarily committed to a military victory over the French.

CONTEXT AND PROCESS OF REVOLUTION

The Algerian Revolution was the inevitable outcome of the policies implemented by the colonial power and of the unwavering allegiance of ordinary Algerians to their identity. The marginalization of indigenous Algerians in all aspects of life in a context where the "civilizing mission" (*mission civilisatrice*) of France was built around the concepts of equality, liberty, and brotherhood exposed the fundamental flaws behind the colonial project. By the end of World War II it had become evident that Muslims would not be allowed to become part of the French nation as equals because of social and economic impediments. The nationalist movement had tried to become a legitimate protagonist in French political life by working within colonial legality to change a discriminatory system, but French rejections and the inability of the French elites to correctly assess the degree of misery and desperation of the vast majority of Algerians paved the way for a new generation of "patriots."

It is in this context that the FLN (National Liberation Front) was formed: it was an attempt by nine young nationalists, known as the *chefs historiques,* to interpret the true anti-colonial sentiments of ordinary Algerians and, by implication, to become the vanguard that would finally achieve the objective of national liberation. The younger generation was a mixed group in terms of ethnicity and social background. Some of them were Kabyles (such as Belkacem Krim, Hocine Ait Ahmed, and Ben Boulaid) and some Arabs (the leading Arabs were Mohammed Boudiaf and Ahmed Ben Bella), pointing to the fact that the elites of the two largest ethnic groups in Algerian society were against colonial rule and committed to the idea of an Algerian nation. Some of the *chefs*

were of middle class and urban extraction (Mohammed Khider and Ben Bella), some were members of important rural families (Mohammed Boudiaf, Larbi Ben M'Hidi, and Hocine Ait Ahmed) who had been dispossessed of their lands by the French, and one was a mill worker (Ben Boulaid). The marginalization of older nationalist leaders like Abbas and Messali was a clear sign that the *chefs historiques* believed in the path of armed struggle as opposed to the peaceful methods employed until then. The nine founders of the FLN quickly discovered that their interpretation was the correct one: the Algerian people were indeed ready to move to a new phase of the struggle and understood that only a coordinated armed insurrection would rid them of colonial rule.

Thus, in November 1954 a true revolution began, aimed at subverting the colonial order through the use of violence and with the goal of finally making those who had been the "objects" of history into sovereign political subjects. The ultimate goal of the revolution was national independence, so the appeal to participate called on all Algerians regardless of their social status. In this respect the revolution concerned the entire Muslim population of Algeria. In a statement by the FLN, published soon after the launch of the armed insurrection, three goals stand out: political sovereignty, economic development, and reaffirmation of the Sunni Arab-Muslim identity threatened by colonialism (Calchi Novati 1998, 77). These very wide objectives and the decision by collegial consensus of nine chiefs to form a National Front to pursue them are evidence of the intent of the historical leaders to involve all sectors of Algerian society in the struggle, irrespective of political creed, social status, and tribal or ethnic affiliation. It is no coincidence that political analyses of the situation based, for instance, on Marxism were not part of the discourse of the FLN during the war of independence. It should also be emphasized that its intention to be the only leader of the revolution meant that the FLN conducted a policy of brutal repression against Algerian competitors, such as the *Mouvement National Algérien* created in December 1954 and led by Messali.

The lack of a specific political direction beyond that of sovereignty allowed all Algerians to join the war of liberation on their own terms and for their own reasons, giving the movement a true nationwide appeal. As a result, the ranks of the revolutionary army swelled until they constituted a drain on French resources of an unprecedented scale and eventually achieved an Algerian victory. But the absence of clear revolutionary goals meant that the movement was subject to internal divisions. These would become even more apparent after independence, when bitter disputes plagued the FLN and led to purges, arrests, and assassinations.

A number of dividing lines emerged within the FLN. The first important one was between political and military leadership. The first party congress of 1956, held in Soumann,

Muslim supporters of the National Liberation Front (FLN) demonstrate in the Casbah, Algiers, in front of a cordon of French troops, December 14, 1960. (Keystone/Getty Images)

established that the political leadership should have preeminence over the military commanders of the National Liberation Army in determining the political objectives and methods of the struggle. Abbane Ramdane emerged as the leading political figure at the time. The congress also established that the leadership operating within Algeria would be more important in terms of decision making than the FLN leaders operating outside the country and in charge of supplying weapons and maintaining contacts with potential allies. By 1957 these two decisions were overturned, and the FLN began to operate according the rule of equal authority between insiders and outsiders and between political and military leaderships. The military commanders soon began to gather increasing power and ruled over their districts as they pleased, marginalizing the political wing of the FLN. These commanders viewed with skepticism the Algerian army that was being formed outside Algeria under the command of officers who had defected from the French army. Among them was a commander of the outside Algerian army, Houari Boumediène. The political leadership, divided between those

outside and those inside the country, was also torn over the role Islam should play in the revolution. Abbane Ramdane was against the use of religious terminology to mobilize the masses and had opted for a nationalist discourse within which Islam was only one element. Ben Bella believed instead that Islam could be used in a stronger manner to further mobilize the population. Ben Bella's instrumental use of religion was effective in the short term because it guaranteed the support of the religious establishment; in the long term, it would be detrimental for the future of the country. The assassination of Ramdane by his comrades within the FLN who opposed his point of view signaled that the party was not immune to internal strife. Finally, it should be noted that many of the actual fighters were farmers and factory workers who had mobilized because of economic reasons. Their objectives were contrasted starkly with the objectives of a leadership that was largely of middle-class urban background. All these divisions were hidden behind the mask of "unanimity" in decision making, but they returned with a vengeance at the end of the war.

In spite of the divisions, the French found themselves unable to come to terms with the rebellion. In particular, the Battle of Algiers demonstrated the ability of the revolutionary army to carry out attacks at the heart of the country. Between September 1956 and September 1957, Algiers became the principal theater of the war. Ultimately, the French were able to defeat the revolutionary commandos, but the political gains for the FLN were tremendous. Just as the reaction to the FLN bombing campaign and the declaration of martial law had done in 1955, harsh French repression in the capital city provoked even further resistance among ordinary Algerians. More importantly from a political point of view, the high political and economic costs of the war began to undermine French domestic support for it. Finally, the fanaticism of the settlers in their quest to hold on to their privileges further weakened France's legitimacy domestically and internationally.

The French military victories of 1957 had emboldened both the settlers and the army, which wanted to continue its repressive campaign with even fewer constraints from the French government. To this end, a secret army-settler conspiracy brought down the government of France and resulted in General Charles de Gaulle coming to power in 1958 to save the unity of the French nation. Contrary to the expectations of sectors of the army and the settlers, de Gaulle did not support them. He understood that to "save France" a negotiated settlement was needed to get France out of the Algerian quagmire. Counting on his prestige and influence, he began to look for a political solution, which was finally found in March 1962. The revolution obtained what it had set out to achieve: national independence. In April 1962, 90.7 percent of mainland French approved by referendum de Gaulle's proposal regarding Algeria's right to self-determination (www.charles-de-gaulle.org/article.php3?id_article=164), and in July 1962, 6 million Algerians voted "yes" to independence from France while only 16,534 people voted against it (Calchi Novati 1998, 311). After the two referendums formalizing independence, Algeria was, however, on the verge of domestic collapse. Commanders of the internal resistance fought Boumediène's army, collaborationists who assisted the French were tracked down and executed, and the FLN was rife with other divisions and personal vendettas. Ben Bella, with the backing of Boumediène, emerged as the winner of all these struggles, and for a brief moment it seemed he was able to unite the country under the banner of Socialism. But he was replaced in June 1965 by Boumediène, the man who controlled the guns. The Algerian Revolution was over and dictatorship began.

IMPACTS

The revolution had tremendous impact both domestically and internationally. Toward the end of the war of liberation, it had emerged quite clearly that most of the political leaders of the Revolution wanted to introduce Socialist reforms to steer the country out of colonialism and underdevelopment. Ben Bella emerged as the leader of this faction within the FLN. After becoming president, he initiated a series of reforms that profoundly changed the Algerian society, which had suffered considerably during the revolution. According to Aggoun and Rivoire (2004, 52), "hundreds of thousands of Algerians had been killed and over two millions were internally displaced," and the economy was in dire straits. The "agrarian reform" was the first problem that Ben Bella tackled. The massive departure of the French settlers (almost a million fled in the three months following independence) facilitated his work, in the sense that vast amounts of land suddenly became available for redistribution. Against the advice and desires of others within the party Ben Bella did not proceed to full nationalization; instead he built on the traditional cooperative arrangements of Algerian peasants to introduce self-management Yugoslavian style. This particular reform was strongly opposed by the traditional land-owning Arab bourgeoisie, which remained in control of vast properties. Ben Bella also took advantage of the departure of the settlers to distribute abandoned houses and posts in the administration. During his short period in power, Ben Bella also began to transform Algerian society quite radically through his far-reaching social reforms, which included increasing educational opportunities, provision of other services including health care, and the beginning of domestic industrial activity. Once in power, Boumediène built on these improvements, thanks in particular to the revenues from the expanding hydrocarbon sector.

The positive social changes that took place shortly after the victory were not accompanied by equally positive political changes. In the political arena, the revolution failed to live up to the expectations it had generated. As it has following many other revolutions, political activity remained confined at the top, without any real democratic consultation with the population. Many opportunists also jumped on the bandwagon and carved out niches of power and influence, to the detriment of many who had truly contributed to the victory against the French. Just as the revolutionary enterprise itself involved a top-down approach, the post-victory period remained the domain of selected leaders, all vying for personal power and for the implementation of their own version of a new Algerian society. Divisions and squabbles plagued the FLN and contributed to undermining Ben Bella's presidency. Thus, it was no surprise that the army became the real wielder of power behind the scenes, since it seemed to be the only unifying institution in post-revolutionary Algeria. Ultimately, the "Socialist" revolution failed to deliver, both in terms of political democracy and of sustainable economic progress. Politically, Algeria remained a one-party dictatorship, although the army was the real power broker. Economically, after an initial period of solid growth, the country quickly stagnated in a quagmire of failed investments, corruption, and endless bureaucracy.

Nevertheless, the revolution had a tremendous international impact. To many countries still under direct colonial rule or indirect neo-colonial influence, the Algerian struggle demonstrated the possibility of emancipation and final victory over foreign domination. The Algerians supported other liberation movements, notably the Polisario Front, which had proclaimed the independence of the Saharoui Republic after the departure of the Spaniards and in the face of Moroccan desires of annexation. The victory in the war against the French also increased the appeal of Pan-Arabism, given that one of its goals was the reassertion of the Arab-Muslim identity of the country. The Socialist character of the revolutionary order also meant that the Socialist camp could count on a prestigious and powerful ally, although Algeria never joined any formal alliance with the Soviet Union. It became instead a leader of the non-aligned camp, but its anti-imperialist rhetoric obviously meant that the United States and its policies were consistently opposed. The launch by Algeria of the idea of a New International Economic Order, where the rights of weaker and less-developed nations would be upheld against economic imperialism, made Boumediène a leading figure for the Third World, and some of the issues raised at the time are still important in today's world.

Finally, in spite of the bitter war, Algeria and France maintained very significant links, particularly in the fields of economic and military cooperation—even though the official rhetoric in both countries never recognized the depth and importance of such ties.

The revolution did not fulfill many of the promises it had made, and its disputed legacy is still a matter of contention in today's political arena. It is worth noting, for instance, that the Islamic party banned in 1992, the Islamic Salvation Front (see Algerian Islamic Rebellion), claimed that the "revolution" had been stolen by a foreign ideology (Socialism) while many of those who died had fought in the name of Islam and the creation of an Islamic state. The contested nature of the revolution is directly linked to the nebulous character of its ideology and the inconsistencies in the implementation of post-revolution policies.

PEOPLE AND ORGANIZATIONS

Abbane, Ramdane (1920–1957)

According to journalists Aggoun and Rivoire (2004), he was one of the principal leaders of the revolution and the real "political" man. His intellectual abilities made him the true thinking man of the FLN, and he attempted to give the FLN viable democratic political structures, a clear political program, including political control over the National Liberation Army, and an ideological linkage with the population. His rising influence, his political abilities, and his opposition to the formation of localized commanders' powers, which had led to numerous abuses to the detriment of FLN centralized authority, posed a threat to the military wing of the movement. For this reason he was assassinated by other members of the FLN. To many, his assassination was the FLN foundational crime and the party never recovered from it. Elimination of political adversaries became the rule within the movement.

Abbas, Ferhat (1899–1985)

Although he became the first president of the provisional government, Abbas represents the failure of moderate nationalism in Algeria. Abbas had believed for a long time that Algerians could obtain their rights by "playing the colonial game." While his insistence on progressive change within the French establishment was seen by many as an illusion, Abbas represented a wide movement of young, educated Algerians who believed in the positive aspects of France's republican values and thus became supporters for political reforms and assimilation. The post–World War II repression undermined his personal beliefs, and he later joined the insurrection.

Abdelkader (1808–1883)

Military and religious leader who first fought the French. He was able to unite many of the Algerian tribes to fight the colonial power under the banner of Islam and in defense of their lands. He was eventually defeated, imprisoned, and then exiled. His struggle provided the modern national movement with a figure to revere and to point to for the legitimization of the existence of an Algerian national identity.

Ben Bella, Ahmed (Born 1916)

He is one of the nine historical leaders of the FLN; Ben Bella is considered by many the father of the Algerian nation, although he was one of the "outsiders" at the time of the revolution. He was very close to Egyptian leader Gamel Abdel Nasser. Imprisoned by the French for most of the war, he was able to outmaneuver his FLN rivals. With the backing of the army, he became the first president of Algeria (1963–1965), initiating a number of Socialist-oriented reforms. He was ousted by Colonel Boumediène in 1965, arrested, and then exiled. He came back to Algeria during the democratic transition, but his political impact was very limited. Ben Bella suggested mobilizing Islamic support during the revolution, and this strategy proved to be a success. But it left a long-term legacy that would be exploited by the Islamic movement in the early 1990s.

Boumediène, Houari (1932–1978)

Despite his youth, Boumediène was the leader of the "borders' army," pressuring the French from outside Algeria. At the end of the war, his forces clashed with those of the regional commanders of the revolutionary armed forces inside Algeria for control of the country. The strength of his army was far superior, and Boumediène became the real wielder of power behind Ben Bella. After securing his position even further, Boumediène decided to take control of the country directly and ousted Ben Bella in 1965. He supervised Algeria's golden age—at least in terms of economic and social advancements—thanks to the revenues from the hydrocarbon sector. However, the short-sighted policy choices made during his leadership were among the reasons for Algeria's social, political, and economic collapse during the 1980s.

Gaulle, Charles de (1890–1970)

After leading "Free France" to victory against Germany in World War II, de Gaulle's political career ended abruptly in 1953, when he retired from politics. Nevertheless, due to his personal prestige, he was elected president during the Algerian crisis in 1958 to lead France out of a dangerous political impasse. De Gaulle's appointment initially pleased the settlers and the army engaged in Algeria, but the president had already come to the conclusion that if France wanted to regain its status as a serious international player, it had to leave Algeria. It took de Gaulle almost four years to negotiate France's way out of Algeria, but he was ultimately successful. Algeria achieved independence, but the general had secured "good terms" of exit, and the French maintained some bases in Algeria, including a nuclear-bombs testing facility. Furthermore, the general made sure that economic links between France and independent Algeria remained very strong, particularly in the hydrocarbon sector.

National Liberation Front (Front de Libération Nationale—FLN, Jabhat al-TaHrir al-Watani)

The National Liberation Front was created as the political party at the helm of the revolution. The original leaders of its predecessor, the Committee for Revolutionary Action and Unity (CRUA), are the nine historical leaders who called the Algerians to rise up in arms against the colonial power. To persuade all Algerians to fight the French, it was necessary to create a political movement that would be able to hold together many different ideologies and social groups in the name of revolutionary liberation. This was the concept of the Front. The notion of the existence of the nine original leaders has been denied by some, but official history holds that they met in the summer of 1954 to decide the future course of action of the nationalist movement and opted for the creation of a united political front that would direct the revolution. The leaders were Ben M'Hidi, Ben Boulaid, Mohammed Boudiaf, Rabah Bitat, Belkacem Krim, Ahmed Ben Bella, Hocine Ait Ahmed, Mohammed Khider, and Didouche Mourad. The National Liberation Front led the Algerians to victory in the war against the French through its National Liberation Army and became the only party recognized in Algeria after independence. But because it was a front rather than a cohesive political party, it was plagued by internal strife and divisions over policies, personalities, and ideological direction.

Messali Hadji, Ahmed (1898–1974)

The political competitor to Abbas, Messali embodied a much more militant nationalism and very quickly dismissed the attitudes of those Algerians who thought that they could make the French political system more inclusive. Unlike Abbas, Messali, a real revolutionary nationalist leader, spent most of his life advocating independence and organized a number of political movements campaigning for that objective. But at the crucial time he was sidelined by a younger and more decisive generation of leaders. He formed a movement that attempted to provide an alternative to the FLN, but his Mouvement National Algérien was violently repressed by the FLN.

Organisation Armée Secrète—OAS, Secret Army Organization (1961–1963)

The Organisation Armeé Secrète was a right-wing terrorist group formed in 1961 by hard-line French settlers and some members of the French armed forces to boycott the negotiated independence. The settlers had traditionally been opposed to any concessions toward Muslim Algerians, and their hard stances had, over time, always thwarted reforms that could have avoided the 1954 uprising. The creation of the OAS was, for some of the settlers, the last attempt to hold on to their privileges. With their bombing campaign of early 1962, they tried to force the FLN to resume violence and therefore abandon the Evian Accords, but they ultimately failed. The departure of settlers in the aftermath of independence signaled the total defeat of OAS and of 120 years of political, social, and economic marginalization of Algerians.

Francesco Cavatorta

See Also Algerian Islamic Revolt; Cinema of Revolution; Colonialism, Anti-Colonialism and Neo-Colonialism; Documentaries of Revolution; Terrorism

References and Further Readings
Aggoun, Lounis, and Jean-Baptiste Rivoire. 2004. *Francalgerie.* Paris: La Découverte.
Aissaoui, Ali. 2001. *Algeria. The Political Economy of Oil and Gas.* New York: Oxford University Press.
Brett, Michael, and Elizabeth Fentress, eds. 1996. *The Berbers.* London: Blackwell Publishing.
Calchi Novati, Giampaolo. 1998. *Storia dell'Algeria Indipendente.* Milan: Edizioni Bompiani.
Ciment, James. 1997. *Algeria: The Fundamentalist Challenge.* New York: Facts on File.
Entelis, John. 1986. *Algeria: The Revolution Institutionalized.* Boulder, CO: Westview Press.
Entelis, John, and Philip Naylor, eds. 1992. *State and Society in Algeria.* Boulder, CO: Westview Press.
Gerber, Haim. 1988. *Islam, Guerrilla War, and Revolution.* London: Lynne Rienner.
Harbi, Mohammed. 1975. *Aux origines du FLN: le populism révolutionnaire en Algérie.* Paris: Francois Bourgois.
Humbaraci, Arslan. 1996. *Algeria: A Revolution That Failed.* London: Pall Mall.
Munson Junior, Henri. 1988. *Islam and Revolution in the Middle East.* New Haven CT: Yale University Press.
Ruedy, John. 1992. *Modern Algeria. The Origins and Development of a Nation.* Bloomington: Indiana University Press.
Quandt, William. 1969. *Revolution and Political Leadership: Algeria 1954–1968.* Cambridge MA: MIT Press.
———. 1998. *Between Ballots and Bullets.* Washington DC: Brookings Institute Press.
www.charles-de-gaulle.org/article.php3?id_article=164 accessed Feb. 4, 2005.

American Revolution

CHRONOLOGY

1754	As a young militia officer, George Washington skirmishes with the French near the forks of the Ohio River (modern Pittsburgh), beginning the conflict called in North America the French and Indian War, which ends in 1763.
1760	Anglo-American forces capture Montreal, the last bastion of French power in Canada, eliminating the French threat in North America. King George III ascends the throne in England. The British tighten up customs enforcement in North America.
1761	Writs of Assistance case makes it legal to use these warrants to curb smuggling.
1763	Treaty of Paris cedes Canada to Great Britain. Pontiac, an Ottawa Indian, leads a rebellion against the British in the west. Paxton Boys murder peaceful Indians and march on Philadelphia. The British government decides to station 10,000 troops to protect North America. King George III issues a proclamation prohibiting settlement west of the Appalachian Mountains.
1764	Parliament passes the Currency Act, prohibiting all colonies from printing paper money, and the Sugar Act, which lowers the duty on imported sugar but provides for more effective enforcement.
1765	Parliament passes the Quartering Act compelling colonists to provide barracks and supplies for soldiers. Parliament also passes the Stamp Act, which puts a small tax on all legal documents. Colonists protest the measure in pamphlets and resolutions. A Stamp Act Congress meets in New York to show united opposition. Sons of Liberty organize resistance and non-importation on the local level. Scores of riots and demonstrations break out throughout the colonies, making the Stamp Act unenforceable.
1766	A change of administration in Great Britain leads to a change in imperial policy. Parliament repeals the Stamp Act but passes the Declaratory Act stating that Parliament can legislate for the colonies. Land riots by tenants in New York's Hudson River Valley.
1767	Parliament passes the Townshend Duties, a tax on imported glass, lead, paint, and tea. Colonists protest this measure with resolutions and petitions. They also organize a non-importation movement. Opposition is less effective and not as concerted as against the Stamp Act. Regulators (vigilantes) in South Carolina act against back country criminals and marginal settlers.

1769   Regulator movement begins in North Carolina in the backcountry against an unfair court system within the colony.

1770   Local tension between soldiers and civilians leads to the Boston Massacre, where four civilians are killed (one other casualty later died from his wounds). New administration under Lord North repeals the Townshend Duties on all items except tea, which is left in place as a symbol of parliamentary supremacy.

1771   Battle at Almance Creek in North Carolina between forces led by Governor Tryon and Regulators.

1773   Parliament passes the Tea Act to help save the British East India Company from bankruptcy. Colonists object to the Tea Act and prevent the landing of tea in all colonies except Boston. Bostonians destroy tea on the night of December 16 by dumping it into the harbor.

1774   The British government passes the Coercive Acts to punish Boston and compel the city to pay for the destroyed tea. Since the Coercive Acts altered the charter of Massachusetts, other colonists believe that the laws set a dangerous precedent. The colonists send representatives to the First Continental Congress, which petitions the king for a redress of grievances but also resolves upon further resistance, including non-importation and non-consumption agreements. Crown authority begins to disintegrate in the countryside as committees of correspondence gain in power. Local militias begin to train in preparation for armed conflict.

1775   On April 19 British troops fight local militia at Lexington and Concord, Massachusetts, beginning the Revolutionary War. Thousands of Americans march to Boston, laying siege to the city. The British capture Breed's and Bunker hills overlooking Boston. The Second Continental Congress assumes the role of a government. The king declares the colonies to be in a state of rebellion. The new Continental army under the command of George Washington captures Dorchester Heights overlooking Boston Harbor. The British evacuate Boston. Revolutionaries organize local administration throughout the colonies. Governor Dunmore of Virginia offers freedom to any slave who fights for the king. Americans invade Canada, but fail to take Quebec in a snowstorm on New Year's Eve.

1776   Thomas Paine publishes *Common Sense*, urging independence. The Second Continental Congress opens American ports to all nations, declares independence, and drafts the Articles of Confederation. A massive British force captures New York, defeats Washington in a succession of battles, and compels the Continental army to retreat across New Jersey and into Pennsylvania. Washington attacks Hessians (German mercenaries hired by the British) at Trenton, capturing a thousand prisoners.

1777   The British march on Philadelphia from the Chesapeake Bay. They defeat Washington at the Battle of Brandywine and capture Philadelphia. Washington withdraws to Valley Forge. An invasion of New York from Canada fails and General John Burgoyne surrenders 5,000 British and Hessian troops at Saratoga.

1778   France signs an alliance with the United States. The British shift the locus of the war to the South, where they hope loyalist support will help them regain control of several colonies. They withdraw from Philadelphia. Washington fights an inconclusive battle with the British at Monmouth Court House in New Jersey. The British hold New York City and Newport, Rhode Island. They capture Savannah as part of their southern strategy.

1780   The British capture Charleston, where 5,000 Americans surrender. The British defeat the remainder of the Continental forces in the South at the Battle of Camden. A brutal guerilla war breaks out in South Carolina between loyalist and revolutionary forces. Pennsylvania passes gradual emancipation law.

1781   Maryland finally ratifies the Articles of Confederation, making it the official form of government for the United States. New Continental troops organize in the South under Nathanael Greene. A portion of this army defeats the British at the Battle of Cowpens. General Cornwallis pursues the Americans into North Carolina and gains a pyrrhic victory at Guilford Courthouse. He joins other British forces in Virginia, concentrating at a small Chesapeake port called Yorktown. A British relief fleet is beaten back by the French at the Battle of the Capes. Cornwallis surrenders to the Americans and French at Yorktown. This is the last major battle of the war.

1782   Negotiators agree to a preliminary peace treaty in Paris.

1783   Treaty of Paris is signed granting independence to the United States and providing extended boundaries to the new nation.

1786   Annapolis Convention calls for a convention to meet in Philadelphia to revise the Articles of Confederation. Shays' Rebellion begins as western Massachusetts farmers object to high taxes and foreclosures on property.

1787   Massachusetts militia suppress Shays' Rebellion. Congress passes Northwest Ordinance to organize territory north of the Ohio River. The measure provides for the full integration of territories to equal status as states. Philadelphia Convention meets and creates a new government with a strong executive, two houses of legislature, an independent judiciary, and the power to tax. Ratification process begins. The first of the *Federalist Papers* defending the Constitution is published.

1788   Nine states ratify the Constitution, putting the new form of government into effect. Eleven states ratify the document by the end of the year. Washington is elected president.

1790   Hamilton's Report on the Public Credit begins political debate that will lead to the development of the Federalist political party (supporters of Hamilton) and the Republican political party (supporters of Thomas Jefferson and James Madison).

1791   Bill of Rights ratified.

1793   War between Great Britain and France creates great economic opportunity for American trade. The political division between Hamilton (Federalists) and Jefferson (Republicans) deepens as the Federalists support Great Britain and the Republicans support France.

1794   Whiskey Rebellion in western Pennsylvania against excise tax. Jay Treaty agreed to, granting Great Britain most-favored-nation status while not fully opening up the British West Indies to American trade.

1795   Pinckney Treaty with Spain allows free navigation of the Mississippi and the right of deposit in New Orleans, and grants a generous boundary with Spanish-held Florida.

1798–1800   The United States fights the Quasi War with France.

1800   Thomas Jefferson is elected president, marking a change in national policy. Republicans will emphasize a smaller national government.

1803   Louisiana Territory is purchased from France, doubling the size of the United States.

1807–1809   Because of trouble over neutral trade and impressments (the British practice of forcing Americans to serve in their navy), the United States establishes an embargo stopping almost all trade. American economy is devastated.

1812–1815   United States goes to war with Great Britain.

1814   War ended with the Treaty of Ghent.

INTRODUCTION

The American Revolution can be viewed on three different levels. First, it was simply the movement and war for independence that covered the period from 1765 to 1783. Second, in addition to independence, the American revolution included the creation of new representative government on the state and national levels, covering the writing of state constitutions, the creation of the United States under the Articles of Confederation, and the writing and ratification of the Constitution in 1787 and 1788. Third, a much more comprehensive definition of the American Revolution encompasses the first two definitions. It extends the political coverage to include the successful establishment of a national government during the early republic and embraces a host of social and economic changes that continued until well into the nineteenth century, as a hierarchical worldview gave way to a society marked by egalitarianism, individualism, capitalism, and democracy.

BACKGROUND: CULTURE AND HISTORY

As colonial Americans faced the second half of the eighteenth century, many of them should have been among the most content people in the world. (This observation excludes a half million African American slaves and several hundred thousand Native Americans; most colonial women whose legal identities were subsumed under those of men.) The vast majority of British North Americans were farmers working rich agricultural land. Their tax burden was extremely light, as little as one-quarter to one-fifth the taxes paid in England. Their government was not just benign, but more democratic than any other government anywhere in the eighteenth century. In most colonies adult white male property holders could vote for local administrators and representatives to colonial assemblies. True, the king chose the governor in most colonies and could exert a veto over any legislation, but the colonists did not object to this procedure. Rather, they tended to view the king as a benevolent, father-like figure who protected their welfare. After 1760, moreover, the largest threats to this Arcadian paradise had been eliminated—the French had been driven from the continent and the Native Americans had been all but pushed back to the other side of the Appalachian Mountains. So to understand the background for the American Revolution we must go beyond material conditions and the nature of government to the society and the sources of tension that led to crisis.

Colonial American society was hierarchical. Colonial Americans shared with their British cousins a belief that social distinctions were not only appropriate, but were the best means to ensure stability and provide happiness for the greatest number. Crucial to the acceptance of hierarchy were three key concepts: corporatism, deference, and paternalism. Corporatism was the belief that society was an organic whole. Like the human body, where each part of the anatomy contributed to the well-being of the entire corpus, everyone within the society shared the same interest. Some parts of corporate society reflected the head, others the torso, legs, and hands. All had to be in agreement and follow the lead of the head for the body to move, survive, and thrive. Connected to this concept was a belief that those on the bottom of society (the torso, legs, and hands) had to defer to those at the head of society. Likewise, those at the top of this hierarchy were expected paternalistically to protect the interest of the greater corpus. Colonial Americans had brought these ideals with them when they arrived in North America. If anything, as colonial America became wealthier and distinctions within society greater, these ideas became more deeply rooted—at least at the top of society. American social ideals, in other words, reflected their Anglo-American background.

Those social ideals, however, were being challenged in a variety of areas. There emerged an ongoing revolt against patriarchy in the mid eighteenth century. One source of this attack on hierarchy came from the intellectual movement called the Enlightenment, which asserted that all elements of the world should be based in nature and reason instead of theology which was the norm. Enlightened thinkers held that nature and reason would lead to the perfectability of mankind. In particular, the philosophers of the Enlightenment believed that all men should be educated so that they could naturally and reasonably fulfill their greatest potential. Among the elite, these ideas were exciting and seemed innocent enough. But when they were applied to the common man, their implications were revolutionary. If people could improve themselves through education, then the hereditary nature of hierarchy—the basis of all previous authority—would be threatened. Another source of attack on patriarchy came from below in thousands of individual actions. Sometimes it manifested itself in the simple belief that a man and woman should marry for love instead of money or fulfilling their parents' wishes. In many New England towns in the mid eighteenth century, as many as one-third of all brides were pregnant, suggesting that they were making their own decisions about their mates. This revolt against patriarchy, in other words, was manifested every time the younger generation challenged the authority of the older generation. It also occurred in a host of other conflicts within society.

Although there was supposed to be a single corporate interest in society, differences among colonists were growing. Ethnic distinctions increased in the eighteenth century, as more Germans and Scotch-Irish arrived in the colonies. Simultaneously, religious differences grew, born out of these ethnic distinctions and the religious revival known as the Great Awakening. The same expanding economic distinctions that made the social elite more attached to the ideal of hierarchy convinced some colonial Americans that the elite were not always protecting the interests of everyone in society. When men like George Washington used their political connections to acquire thousands of acres of undeveloped land, it became difficult to see how he was working for the greater good. In North Carolina, men who lived on the frontier began to complain about the multiple officeholders who seemed to control a court system that favored the rich.

Discontent about this issue contributed to the Regulator (vigilantes) movement of the later 1760s and early 1770s. In 1771, backcountry Regulators fought a battle with the governor and his supporters from the coastal regions at Alamance Creek that led to over a score of fatalities. Regulators also appeared in South Carolina, but these Regulators were less concerned with reforming the court system than in meting out vigilante justice for frontier criminals and marginal settlers who were not behaving themselves. Similar social divisions motivated the settlers in Massachusetts who pushed for a land bank that would lend farmers printed money to facilitate their paying debts to eastern merchants and encouraged land riots in New York, New Jersey, and the future state of Vermont. In 1763, Scotch-Irish settlers in Pennsylvania became convinced that the Quakers and Germans who dominated the province were not protecting their interests in the wars against the Indians. Frontiersmen known as the Paxton Boys massacred two groups of peaceful Indians and then marched on Philadelphia seeking a redress of grievances. Only the persuasive powers of Benjamin Franklin convinced them to return home.

Contributing to these difficulties was a dramatic increase in population. The British North American colonies had about 200,000 people in 1700. By 1750 that number had grown to about one million. In the next twenty-five years the population doubled again, from both immigration and natural increase. This demographic boom created pressures on the land. A two-hundred-acre farm that would be more than enough to support a family became a scant patrimony when divided among a dozen children. The solution was for some of the family to seek a living elsewhere, either in the small colonial cities, or on the frontier. Both moves further challenged the authority of the older generation. The solution also led to other problems, as conflicts erupted in the backcountry between colonies claiming the same land and with the Native Americans who resided there. The French and Indian War (1754–1763) was triggered by George Washington traveling to the frontier to solidify Virginia's claim on the Ohio country. Victory in that conflict, it was hoped, would ease the shortage of land experienced by many living closer to the Atlantic coast.

There were also some long-term and short-term economic problems in the decades before the Revolutionary War. In the immediate aftermath of the Anglo-American conquest of French Canada, there was a post-war depression. During the conflict the British had recruited Americans to fight and devoured vast quantities of supplies, creating an artificial economic boom. Victory meant that military expenditures would be cut. Men had trouble finding work, especially in the colonial seaports. During the resistance movement of the 1760s and 1770s there were plenty of sailors and other men hanging around the waterfront, eager to join the mobs that became so instrumental in opposing British imperial policy. The more long-term economic problem revolved around colonial debt. As producers of raw materials and agricultural products—tobacco, rice, indigo, wheat, and naval supplies—and importers of manufactured goods—textiles, tableware, iron products—the colonies had a negative balance of trade that drained coin money (precious metal) to Great Britain. This difficulty was in the aggregate. On the individual level, this situation led to the increase of personal debt, especially among the large property holders, who spent increasing amounts on luxury goods like fine cabinetry, carriages, dinnerware, etc. Between 1760 and 1772 personal debt among colonists doubled from £2,000,000 to £4,000,000 (Wood 2002, 15).

After 1760 these conditions, taken together, created a highly charged atmosphere. What brought all of these various currents together was a political crisis in Great Britain combined with an effort to reorganize the British American empire. The political crisis began with the ascension of George III to the throne. The two previous Georges had both been more German in their orientation than British and allowed Parliament and its leaders to guide the country relatively unmolested. George III, the grandson of George II, came to the throne determined to reassert the role of the king in government. He did not intend to usurp the liberty of either his English or his North American subjects; he simply believed that he should take a more active role in government than his immediate predecessors. He therefore insisted that he should determine who his chief minister would be. The result was a highly unstable political situation in Great Britain between 1760 and 1770, with seven different administrations.

In the meantime, the British attempted to overhaul their overseas empire. Bureaucratically, the North American colonies were a mess. A hodgepodge of different governments and conflicting jurisdictions made them difficult to rule. Militia from one colony would sometimes refuse to go to another colony for a military operation. Colonial governments had difficulty raising extra taxes to fight the war against the French. And smuggling was rampant. In 1760 the British government did a survey of the customs service in North America and discovered that it cost more money to run than was being raised in revenue. Something had to be done, especially with the acquisition of new territory in Canada and Florida, to rationalize the imperial system.

In addition, the British government decided that it needed to keep a ten-thousand-man army in North America to respond to three areas of potential conflict. First, the British wanted to protect the colonists and their new Indian subjects from each other. Pontiac's Rebellion in 1763 and 1764 had devastated the frontier. Indians captured every outpost west of the Appalachian Mountains except Forts Detroit and Pitt. A military presence would, they hoped, prevent a similar outbreak and limit contact between European Americans and Native Americans. Second, the French remained a threat. They still controlled several islands in the West Indies from which to launch an attack against North America, and there were 60,000 Frenchmen in the newly acquired province in Canada. Third, an army in North America could help enforce any new regulations passed by Parliament in its efforts to reorganize the empire. The efforts at imperial reform, the placement of an army in North America, an unstable government in Great Britain, and colonies undergoing social and economic change together created an explosive situation that led to rebellion and revolution.

CONTEXT AND PROCESS OF REVOLUTION

The imperial crisis began when the British tightened customs enforcement before the end of the French and Indian War. Smugglers had operated almost with impunity; now the British navy and army would aid in customs enforcement. The Writs of Assistance facilitated the customs officer by allowing immediate search and seizure of a smuggling vessel and its cargo. Previously, by the time an official obtained a warrant the smugglers would have unloaded the illicit goods. The British government also passed other measures to ensure the rule of law. The king issued the Proclamation of 1763, forbidding settlement west of the Appalachian Mountains, to avoid conflict with Indians and guarantee that colonial speculators did not take unfair advantage of Native Americans. The measure also organized colonies in Canada and Florida and encouraged settlement of these regions. The Currency Act (1764) prevented the colonies from printing the inflationary paper money that had been used to pay off debts to British merchants. Parliament passed a Quartering Act in 1765, which made the colonies provide appropriate shelter for the soldiers stationed in North America.

Parliament also enacted two revenue-generating laws. The Sugar Act of 1764 lowered the duty on sugar and molasses from six pence to three pence (later it was lowered to one pence) per gallon. The idea was to have a lower duty, but also to have more rigorous enforcement. The Stamp Act of 1765 exacted a small tax on every legal document and each copy of every newspaper and pamphlet (dice and playing cards were also taxed). Great Britain already had a similar law, and it was considered self-enforceable, since no legal process would be official without the stamp. These two laws were expected to generate about £100,000 annually (Middlekauff 1982, 58), or about half the money required to pay for the troops stationed in British North America. The rest of the money was to come from British coffers. These taxes were not intended to pay the British debt from a century of war. That debt stood at £135 million, and the interest alone was over £5 million per year (Wood 2002, 17–18). Previous efforts to have the colonists raise money on their own had failed, so Parliament was now legislating for its colonies. The British believed that what they were doing was reasonable.

The colonists found all of the new regulations objectionable. However, concerted resistance only began with the passage of the Stamp Act. In opposition to the Stamp Act, colonial Americans developed a pattern of resistance that would be used throughout the imperial crisis. First, constitutional and legal arguments were articulated through newspapers and pamphlets. Based upon a republican ideology that held that government had been instituted to protect the public good, the authors of these works took a rhetorical high ground and asserted that the British imperial measures violated the ideal of English liberty. Second, colonists used official and quasi-official channels to petition for a redress of grievances and organize resistance. Colonial assemblies such as the Virginia House of Burgesses passed resolves (resolutions) against the Stamp Act. Nine colonies sent representatives to a Stamp Act Congress that met in New York in October 1765 to send a petition to the king and Parliament. Most important were the committees called the Sons of Liberty, which organized opposition on the local level. These committees worked to ensure the success of a non-importation movement intended to put pressure on Great Britain to repeal the law. Third, there was mob action to intimidate anyone who would comply with the Stamp Act. Without people shouting in the street, parading with effigies, and at times destroying property of government officials, the resistance movement would have been ineffective. All of this opposition made the Stamp Act unenforceable in the colonies but it took a change in British administration not directly connected to colonial efforts to repeal the tax in 1766. Simultaneously, Parliament passed the Declaratory Act, which asserted that Parliament had the right to legislate for the colonies in all cases whatsoever.

The same pattern of resistance that emerged in 1765 and 1766—constitutional arguments, organizational efforts, and mob action—was repeated in reaction to the Townshend Duties of 1767 and the Tea Act of 1773, with somewhat different results. Another new ministry in 1767 led to the passage of the Townshend Act, which established taxes on imported paint, glass, paper, and tea to help defray the costs of colonial administration. Again, pamphlets and newspaper articles decried the unconstitutionality of taxation without representation, petitions were sent to Great Britain, a non-importation movement was organized by Sons of Liberty, and mob action intimidated customs officials. But this resistance was not as concerted or as intense as the anti–Stamp Act movement and was beginning to weaken in 1770, despite the confrontation called the Boston Massacre on March 5, 1770, where a handful of soldiers fired on a mob and killed five civilians (the riot was more about local civilian-military tensions than imperial considerations). A new administration in Great Britain under Lord North removed all of the taxes except for the one on tea, which was kept as a symbol of parliamentary authority.

More explosive was the situation that developed in 1773. Parliament passed the Tea Act to help the British East India Company, which was on the brink of bankruptcy. The Tea Act would allow the British East India Company to import tea directly to the colonies, avoiding extra charges of shipping through Great Britain and thus increasing its revenues while lowering the price of tea in the colonies. Colonists saw this law as an effort to gain acceptance of the one remaining Townshend duty and establish a monopoly. Most tea in the colonies was smuggled. Under the Tea Act, British tea would be sold by agents of the British East India Company (selected from only a handful of colonial merchants) at a low enough price to drive the smugglers out of business. Again, colonists published constitutional arguments against the Tea Act, formed committees to organize resistance, and used mob violence. In the Boston Tea Party on December 16, 1773, a Boston crowd destroyed about £10,000 (Middlekauff 1982, 226) worth of tea by dumping it into the harbor rather than allowing it to be unloaded and sold in the colony.

Parliament in 1774 decided that it had enough of colonial insolence and passed the Coercive Acts to punish Boston until the city paid for the destroyed tea. These measures closed the port of Boston, altered the Massachusetts charter, limited local government, and established royal control over the judiciary. The Coercive Acts convinced many colonists to push resistance even further. In 1774 the First Continental Congress met and endorsed a non-importation and even a non-consumption agreement. Committees of Correspondence also organized throughout the colonies to coordinate resistance. Militia began training for a potential military confrontation. In mid April, General Thomas Gage determined to send a raiding party into the countryside outside Boston to seize weapons and opposition leaders. On April 19, 1775, British troops fired on local militia on Lexington Green, beginning the Revolutionary War.

On the surface, the colonial response to imperial regulation appears blown out of all proportion. The British were not out to destroy American liberty, but somehow many colonial Americans, despite their good life, became convinced that their freedom as Englishmen was being threatened. The key to comprehending the colonial reaction is in understanding the social conditions that existed in the years leading up to the outbreak of war. Colonial Americans understood that their world was changing. The ideal of a corporate society was becoming more difficult to sustain, and paternalism and deference seemed to be breaking down. Rather than blame themselves for their own problems, colonial Americans saw in the imperial crisis an effort to corrupt their world. If Americans seemed to be less virtuous and less willing to sacrifice for the common good—the key elements in their republican ideology—then it had be the king's fault. But colonial Americans only reluctantly came to this final conclusion. They began the war still hoping that the king would see their side of the story. Within a year they changed their minds. Thomas Paine's *Common Sense,* a pamphlet which sold over 100,000 copies in 1776, was crucial to this development. In plain language Tom Paine lambasted not only George III, but the idea of having a king and hereditary monarchy. It therefore became easy to assert the ideal of equality and blame the entire crisis on the king in the Declaration of Independence on July 4, 1776.

The war for independence lasted from 1775 to 1783. One aspect of the war centered on the battles. This contest was crucial to the outcome, since the Continental army and the need to gain allies (the French joined the conflict in 1778) sustained a national organization even as thirteen separate states emerged out of the revolution. George Washington wanted to create a professional army just like the British army. At first he struggled in this effort. During the summer of 1776 he experienced a series of defeats that drove him out of New York and across New Jersey. Even his mid-winter victories at Trenton (December 26, 1776) and Princeton (January 3, 1777) did little more than enable the conflict to continue. In 1777 the British defeated Washington at Brandywine (September 11) and Germantown (October 4), capturing the U.S. capital of Philadelphia. The British, however, suffered a major defeat at Saratoga in New York, when General John Burgoyne surrendered an entire army (October 17). Over the winter of 1777–1778 at Valley Forge, the Continental army became a more professional force and fought the British to a draw at the Battle of Monmouth (June 28) in New Jersey. While holding on to New York City, the British shifted the war to the South, capturing Charleston (May 12, 1780) and defeating the Americans at the Battle of Camden (August 16, 1780). However, after battles at the Cowpens (January 17, 1781) in South Carolina and Guilford Courthouse (March 15, 1781) in North Carolina, Lord Charles Cornwallis moved his British troops to Virginia. There, the French alliance and the professionalization of the Continental army finally paid off when Cornwallis was isolated at Yorktown by a combined French and American force. After a French fleet beat back a British relief force

A poster exhorts young men to join General George Washington's Continental army in the fight for American independence from Great Britain. (North Wind Picture Archives)

(September, 10, 1781), Cornwallis surrendered at Yorktown (October 18, 1781), ending major hostilities.

Alongside this war of armies and larger strategy was a more local conflict for the hearts and minds of Americans. The revolution was a civil war that pitted Americans against each other. Many Americans refused to fight against their king and became loyalists. In this war of loyalties, local militias were crucial, and the forces supporting independence had the advantage. Years of local organizational work in the Sons of Liberty and various committees prepared the revolutionaries for seizing the reins of local government and coercing their opposition. Loyalist militias appeared, but they relied on the reg-

ular channels of government, which disintegrated as the conflict gained momentum. The ability to compel adherence to the new revolutionary committees and state governments contributed significantly to the revolutionaries' victory.

IMPACTS

The Treaty of Paris of 1783 that ended the Revolutionary War was highly favorable to the Americans. It not only recognized independence, it granted generous boundaries, extending the United States to the Mississippi River in the west, to the

Great Lakes in the north, and to Florida (which was granted to Spain) in the South.

Independence also meant that the American states had to establish their own governments. This process began in 1776 with the writing of state constitutions and the creation of the Articles of Confederation. Each state considered itself a sovereign entity and experimented with different formulas to realize the republican dream of representative government that would guarantee the public good. Fearing executive power, the Pennsylvania Constitution of 1776 did away with a governor and created an executive council with a president heading a committee to execute the laws. A single house of legislators was elected every year with a franchise that included all white male taxpayers and their adult sons. Other states sought a greater balance between different branches of government. The Massachusetts Constitution of 1780 not only had a Senate and lower house, but also a powerful executive who could veto legislation (which could be overridden by a two-thirds majority), appoint many state officials, and command the state's armed forces. The Confederation government provided for the future full integration of its western territories as new states with the Northwest Ordinance of 1787. The Articles of Confederation was more like an alliance among independent states than a strong national government. Exercising any of its powers, such as declaring war or signing a treaty, required the consent of a minimum of nine of the thirteen states. But that was exactly what the revolutionaries wanted. The imperial crisis had taught Americans to fear a powerful central government with a strong executive.

During the 1780s some Americans began to criticize the Articles of Confederation. James Madison argued that the state governments reflected the whim of the people, creating the "mutability" or "malleability" of the laws. These nationalists decided that the United States needed a central authority that would enlist "the purest and noblest characters" (Madison's words) in government. The Annapolis Convention in 1786 was supposed to discuss interstate trade; instead it issued a call for a convention in Philadelphia in the summer of 1787 to revise the Articles of Confederation. Once the delegates met in Philadelphia, they determined to write a new form of government, sidestepping the amendment process under the Articles because it entailed unanimous action. The Constitution created a strong central government with a powerful executive and two houses of legislature and an independent judiciary. The founders believed it was possible to vest the president with so much authority because, unlike a king, he directly represented the people. Similarly, it was possible to have a Senate with six-year terms selected by state legislatures because it did not represent an aristocracy; it was considered another representation of the people. Even the judiciary could be seen as an expression of the public will. Likewise, neither the federal government nor the state governments were sovereign; both derived their power from the sovereign people.

Page one of the Articles of Confederation, which called for a loose organization of states with a weak central authority. (National Archives)

The writing and ratification of the U.S. Constitution established the format for the new American government. But during the 1790s and early 1800s, Americans debated the exact nature of that government as well as the contours of the new society and economy. Two political parties emerged. The leaders of the Federalist Party did not fully understand the democratic changes wrought by the revolution. Led by Alexander Hamilton, they hoped to put into place a government of the elite. As secretary of treasury under President George Washington, Hamilton successfully instituted an economic program that tied the business leaders to the national government by fully funding the national debt, assuming the state debts, and creating a national bank. Hamilton also wanted to encourage manufacturing through government intervention. Thomas Jefferson and James Madison led the Republican Party in opposing these measures, believing that the individual should be independent from government influence. Although their ideas centered around the importance of agriculture, ultimately their approach helped to foster the laissez faire capitalism that became such an essential part of nineteenth-century America. The Federalists dominated the 1790s, but after Jefferson's election in 1800, the ideals of equality and democracy gained greater force, and American society came to trumpet the common man.

The United States also had difficulty in gaining the respect of foreign nations. This problem became especially acute after the outbreak of hostilities between Great Britain and France in 1793 as a result of the French Revolution. The Republicans supported the French Revolution, hoping that egalitarian ideas would spread throughout the Atlantic world. The Federalists favored Great Britain, which had a navy and was the main trading partner for the United States. Foreign policy veered first one way and then another. As long as the United States maintained its neutrality, its merchants reaped great profits from neutral trade in a time of war. The U.S. role in neutral trade almost led to war with Great Britain in 1794. Then the United States fought an undeclared war with France from 1798 to 1800 over the same question. War threatened with Great Britain again in 1807. The United States fought a war with Great Britain from 1812 to 1815. The Treaty of Ghent that ended the war settled none of the outstanding issues between the two countries but signaled a final acceptance of the United States as an independent power. War in Europe had benefits besides neutral trade by presenting opportunities for expansion. Spain was weakened by the conflict, allowing the United States to take advantage with a treaty in 1795 that conceded a favorable southern boundary with Florida, free navigation of the Mississippi, and the right of deposit in New Orleans (the right to ship goods through the port of New Orleans, which remained under Spanish control). By 1819 the Spanish weakness led to the U.S. acquisition of all of Florida. Similarly, Napoléon's preoccupation with the conflict with Great Britain, and his inability to subdue the Haitian Revolution, convinced him to sell the Louisiana Territory to the United States in 1803, doubling the size of the country.

The revolution also had an important impact on Americans who were not white men. Most Native Americans had sided with the British and felt betrayed by the Treaty of Paris of 1783. Indians therefore resisted the incursion of European Americans onto their land. In the 1790s and in the early 1800s, Native Americans formed massive confederacies in a vain effort to stem the tide of European American immigration into the Mississippi Valley. The revolution also had a significant impact on African Americans. Many blacks seized opportunities provided by the upheaval of the war to gain their freedom by either joining an army (the British were the first to offer freedom for military service) or running away in the confusion of the conflict. White Americans also questioned the institution of slavery. Northern states began to take legal action freeing their slaves. Some of these measures, like the Pennsylvania law of 1780, set up a process of gradual emancipation. Even southern states considered similar measures, and many made it easier for masters to manumit their slaves if they so chose. By 1800, however, states in the South began to rededicate themselves to slavery with the expansion of cotton production. This development initiated the process that separated a slave South from a free North and contributed to the origins of the Civil War. Women gained few legal rights as a result of the revolution. Many women had supported the boycotts and non-importation movements during the 1760s and 1770s and sacrificed dearly during the war for independence. As a result, some women became more interested in politics. Elite women identified themselves as the repositories of virtue and believed that as republican mothers and wives they had a special role in society: to insure the proper upbringing of the next generation of republican citizens. It remains unclear how far down in society these ideas reached. But it was not unusual for even a female house servant to assert her identity as a republican citizen, even though she could not vote or, if married, own property. In 1848, one of the opening salvos of the women's rights movement was the Declaration of Sentiments and Resolutions at Seneca Falls, New York, which used the Declaration of Independence as its model. It began "we hold these truths to be self evident, all men and women are created equal."

By establishing a new nation, asserting the ideal of equality, and emphasizing the independence of the individual, the American Revolution provided a model for other countries around the world and set the terms of debate for almost every major issue in American history from 1776 to today. It also represents the first successful effort by European overseas colonists to gain independence.

PEOPLE AND ORGANIZATIONS

Adams, John (1735–1826)

John Adams was a Harvard-trained lawyer who became a leading revolutionary, an important diplomat, and the second president of the United States. Adams attended both the First and Second Continental Congress. In the First Continental Congress he was instrumental in gaining support for opposition to the Coercive Acts. In the Second he became an early advocate for independence. He was one of the hardest-working members of Congress, serving on over ninety committees and chairing twenty-five. He was also the principal author of the Massachusetts Constitution and was sent to Europe as a diplomat in 1780.

He negotiated recognition of the United States and a loan in the Netherlands. He also participated in the talks that led to the Treaty of Paris of 1783. From 1785 to 1788 he was America's first ambassador to Great Britain. He then returned to the United States to become its first vice president. He was elected president in 1796. During his contentious administration, the United States fought the quasi war with France. Adams insisted on a negotiated settlement to this conflict and avoided the expense of a declared war. This act of statesmanship probably cost him the election in 1800, since many in his own Federalist Party did not support him. Adams retired to his home in Braintree, Massachusetts, where he died on July 4, 1826—the fiftieth anniversary of American independence.

Committees of Correspondence

These committees were local organizations that oversaw the implementation of the non-importation movements in opposition to imperial regulation. These organizations continued after the war broke out and became effective agencies of revolution on the community level.

Continental Congress

There were two Continental Congresses. The first met in 1774 and provided a pan-colonial endorsement for the resistance to the Coercive Acts. In particular it supported a non-importation movement and then a non-consumption movement to compel Great Britain to relent in its efforts to legislate for the colonies. It also petitioned the king, asking for a redress of grievance, and agreed to reconvene as the Second Continental Congress in June 1776. By that date, hostilities had broken out. Although the Second Continental Congress again petitioned the king, it called for each colony to organize its own state government, opened North American ports to trade from all nations, and in July 1776 declared independence from Great Britain. The Continental Congress took on the administrative and legislative functions of a national government, including the support of the Continental army. It also wrote the Articles of Confederation, which was finally implemented in 1781.

Federalists

Federalists were initially those who supported the ratification of the U.S. Constitution in 1787 and 1788. They labeled their opponents "Anti-federalists." During the 1790s, a political party emerged also called the Federalists who supported the Hamiltonian program, strong government, and the British in their war against the French.

Franklin, Benjamin (1706–1790)

Benjamin Franklin began his career as a printer and retired at the age of forty-two to devote himself to science and public service. By the time of his death he had become a statesman, diplomat, and a world-renowned celebrity. His experiments with electricity brought him many honors, including membership as a Fellow of the Royal Society of London. He became an important provincial leader in Pennsylvania in the 1750s, was appointed joint postmaster of the colonies, and was sent to Great Britain in 1757 as colonial agent. While in England he hoped to obtain land grants in North America and high office for himself. He also articulated many colonial concerns to the British government, including opposition to the Stamp Tax. As relations with Britain soured in the 1770s, Franklin's position became untenable. He returned to North America in 1775 and quickly joined the revolutionary movement. He attended the Second Continental Congress and was on the committee that wrote the Declaration of Independence. Franklin went to France in late 1776 to obtain supplies and seek recognition. He negotiated the alliance of 1778, secured foreign aid, and served as a symbol of the American republic in France. He participated in the talks that led to the Treaty of Paris of 1783. When he returned to the United States in 1785 he was hailed as a hero of the revolution and was elected president of Pennsylvania's executive council. He was a member of the Constitutional Convention but was not particularly active due to age and illness.

George III (1738–1820)

As the ruler of Great Britain during the imperial crisis and the Revolutionary War, George III has been blamed for the conflict that broke up the British empire. But George III had not set out to attack American liberty. He had wanted to have a greater say in the British government than his predecessors, and he wanted his government to run more efficiently. However, he would not tolerate any insolence and determined to punish the colonies for disobedience after the Boston Tea Party. He declared the colonies to be in a state of rebellion in August 1775 and only reluctantly came to accept the British defeat at the end of the war.

Hamilton, Alexander (1755–1804)

Alexander Hamilton was a Revolutionary War officer, a leading nationalist in the 1780s, and the mastermind behind the Federalist Party program in the 1790s. Hamilton was born in the West Indies and was attending King's College (later Columbia College) in New York at the outbreak of the Revolutionary War. He joined the Continental army in 1776 and became General Washington's aide-de-camp in 1777. At the end of the war he spent a brief term in Congress and began a lucrative law career. He also married into one of the richest families in New York. Hamilton attended both the Annapolis and Philadelphia Conventions. He was one of the key authors of the *Federalist Papers,* an articulate defense of the U.S. Constitution during the debates over ratification. George Washington appointed him secretary of the treasury, a position Hamilton viewed as akin to the British prime minister. He outlined a sweeping economic plan that led to the institution of national taxes, the full funding of the national debt, the assumption of state debts, and the creation of the Bank of the United States. After he returned to his law practice, he remained active in politics as the unofficial head of the Federalist Party. He opposed the election of his fellow Federalist John Adams in 1800, contributing to the Federalist loss in that year. Aaron Burr killed him in a duel in 1804.

Jefferson, Thomas (1743–1826)

Thomas Jefferson was a leading revolutionary, diplomat, secretary of state, and president. Jefferson grew up in relative affluence in Virginia, was educated at William and Mary, and trained as a lawyer. In 1774 Jefferson brilliantly articulated the American position against British imperial regulation in *A Summary View of the Rights of British America.* With a reputation as clear thinker and gifted stylist, he became the main author of the Declaration of Independence in the Second Continental Congress. During the war he also wrote the first draft of the Virginia Constitution and a bill to establish religious freedom in Virginia. He also served as a wartime governor of Virginia. After the Revolutionary War he went to France to replace Benjamin Franklin as America's minister in Paris. He returned in 1789 to become the first secretary of state. In the cabinet he opposed Hamilton's economic plan and, along with James Madison, organized the Republican Party during the 1790s. He resigned from the cabinet in 1793, supposedly to retire to his plantation at Monticello. But he ran for president in 1796, coming in second, and became John Adams's vice president. Despite a long friendship and collaboration, he opposed many of Adams's policies and was elected president in 1800. As president he had a successful first term marked by the purchase of the Louisiana Territory. His second term was marred by the difficulty of maintaining free trade while Great Britain and France were at war. Jefferson's embargo almost ruined the economy. Jefferson retired to Monticello, where he died on July 4, 1826, the same day as John Adams. Jefferson was full of contradictions, especially when it came to slavery and race. He opposed slavery yet owned slaves until the day he died. He did not believe that the white and black races could live peaceably together, yet he had children with his slave mistress, Sally Hemmings.

Loyalists

Loyalists, also called Tories and refugees, were Americans who opposed the revolutionary movement. As much as one-third of the population may have been loyalists. Coming from all levels of society, tens of thousands of these Americans left the United States at the end of the war.

Madison, James (1751–1836)

James Madison, a Virginian who was crucial to the creation of the U. S. Constitution, served as secretary of state and as the fourth president of the United States. Educated at Princeton, Madison became involved in Virginia politics just as the Revolutionary War broke out. During the war he participated in the writing of the Virginia Constitution and served on the state's executive council and in the Continental Congress from 1780 to 1783. During the 1780s he became concerned with the weakness of the national government under the Articles of Confederation and was one of the leaders of the movement for the Constitutional Convention in Philadelphia in 1787. His draft of the "Virginia Plan" became the basis for the Constitution. He wrote several of the *Federalist Papers* during the ratification debate. During the 1790s he was a Congressional leader and helped to organize the Republican Party. He was Jefferson's secretary of state and was elected president in 1808. He led the nation during the War of 1812.

Morris, Robert (1734–1806)

Robert Morris played a major role in running the finances of the United States during the Revolutionary War. A well-known merchant in Philadelphia, Morris was a leading figure in the Continental Congress throughout the war but was especially important from 1781 to 1784, when he was superintendent of finances. At one point near the end of the conflict, Morris even used his own personal credit to support the government. During the 1790s Morris became involved in massive land speculations that ultimately drove him to bankruptcy and debtors' prison.

Paine, Thomas (1737–1809)

Thomas Paine was a publicist of revolution. Trained as a corset maker, Paine also worked as a customs collector in

England before heading to North America in 1774. He quickly became a supporter of the resistance movement and in 1775 wrote *Common Sense,* advocating independence. This pamphlet not only attacked King George III, but also the idea of a hereditary aristocracy. It also outlined plans for a new and more democratic form of government. The pamphlet sold over 100,000 copies in a few months. Paine also served in the army in 1776 and wrote a series of essays called *The American Crisis,* which was intended to bolster support for the revolution despite several military reverses. Paine was involved in Pennsylvania politics in a minor way until 1787, when he returned to England. In 1791 and 1792 he published in two parts his *Rights of Man,* which defended the French revolution. He also went to France and served in the National Convention in 1793. He wrote *The Age of Reason,* a deist tract, and *Agrarian Justice,* supporting a tax on hereditary wealth, while in France during the 1790s. He died in obscure poverty in 1809 in the United States.

Republican Party

The Republicans were the party of Jefferson and Madison. They believed in a weak central government, equality, and supported the French against the British. They are also called Democratic-Republicans. This party should not be confused with the Republican Party of Abraham Lincoln founded in the 1850s. In fact, the Republican Party of the early national period evolved into the Democratic Party of Andrew Jackson.

Sons of Liberty

The Sons of Liberty became a generic term to describe any of the supporters of the revolution. During the Stamp Act controversy, the Sons of Liberty referred to the specific committees that organized local resistance.

Washington, George (1732–1799)

George Washington commanded the American forces during the Revolutionary War, presided over the Constitutional Convention in 1787, and was the nation's first president from 1789 to 1797. Washington was the younger son of an affluent and rising Virginia family. While in his twenties he hoped to earn military glory. His actions on the frontier in 1754 and 1755 in attempting to assert Virginia's claim to the Ohio Valley helped to trigger the French and Indian War. He gained military experience as an officer with Virginia troops during the war. He also inherited his older brother's estate and married a rich widow, Martha Custis Washington. Dur-

ing the 1760s and early 1770s he enjoyed life as a Virginia gentleman, dabbling in politics while managing and expanding his estates. He supported the resistance movement to imperial regulation and attended the Second Continental Congress, where he was selected commander of the Continental army on the basis of his previous military experience and the fact that he was a Virginian. Although he endured many defeats throughout the war, he was an inspirational leader who held the Continental army together and forged it into a powerful fighting unit. At the end of the war, when some Americans would have made him king, he resigned his commission and returned to his plantation at Mount Vernon. He came out of retirement in 1787 to preside over the Constitutional Convention and was the unanimous choice of all 69 electors for president in 1789. By the end of his second term he had become frustrated with partisan politics and advocated an avoidance of political parties. He died at Mount Vernon in 1799.

Paul Gilje

See Also Colonialism, Anti-Colonialism, and Neo-Colonialism; Documentaries of Revolution; French Revolution; Slave Rebellions in the United States; Spanish American Revolutions of Independence

References and Further Readings

Bailyn, Bernard. 1967. *The Ideological Origins of the American Revolution.* Cambridge, MA: Harvard University Press.
———. 1974. *The Ordeal of Thomas Hutchinson.* Cambridge, MA: Harvard University Press.
Breen, T. H. 2004. *The Marketplace of Revolution: How Consumer Politics Shaped American Independence.* New York: Oxford University Press.
Calloway, Colin G. 1995. *The American Revolution in Indian Country: Crisis and Diversity in Native American Communities.* New York: Cambridge University Press.
Elkins, Stanley, and Eric McKitrick. 1993. *The Age of Federalism.* New York: Oxford University Press.
Ellis, Joseph J. 2004. *His Excellency: George Washington.* New York: Alfred A. Knopf.
Ferguson, E. James. 1960. *The Power of the Purse: A History of American Public Finance, 1776–1790.* Chapel Hill: University of North Carolina Press.
Frey, Sylvia R. 1991. *Water from the Rock: Black Resistance in a Revolutionary Age.* Princeton, NJ: Princeton University Press.
Gilje, Paul A. 1987. *The Road to Mobocracy: Popular Disorder in New York City, 1763–1834.* Chapel Hill: University of North Carolina Press.
Gross, Robert A. 1976. *The Minutemen and Their World.* New York: Hill and Wang.
Higginbotham, Don. 1971. *The War of American Independence: Military Attitudes, Polices, and Practice, 1763–1789.* New York: Macmillan.
Kerber, Linda K. 1980. *Women of the Republic: Intellect and Ideology in Revolutionary America.* Chapel Hill: University of North Carolina Press.
Maier, Pauline. 1997. *American Scripture: Making the Declaration of Independence.* New York: Alfred A. Knopf.

Middlekauff, Robert. 1982. *The Glorious Cause: The American Revolution, 1763–1789.* New York: Oxford University Press.

Morgan, Edmund S., and Helen M. Morgan. 1952. *The Stamp Act Crisis: Prologue to Revolution.* Chapel Hill: University of North Carolina Press.

Wood, Gordon S. 1969. *The Creation of the American Republic, 1776–1787.* Chapel Hill: University of North Carolina Press.

———. 1993. *The Radicalism of the American Revolution.* New York: Random House.

———. 2002. *The American Revolution: A History.* New York: The Modern Library.

Anarchism, Communism, and Socialism

MODERN EMERGENCE OF SOCIALIST IDEOLOGIES

Anarchism, Communism, and Socialism, like most political ideologies, are not static terms with a single definition. Rather, many anarchisms, Communisms, and Socialisms have come to exist, and the definitions for these terms are often hotly contested. Since most variants of anarchism, Communism, and Socialism arose from the post-Enlightenment aspiration to create the most rational and beneficial societal organization possible for the largest number of people, most scholars begin their histories with the early Utopian theorists. Their ideologies were often seen as the products of similar efforts to formulate a future society based on cooperation rather than competition, and all rose in response to the early stages of the development of modern capitalism.

Out of the meetings, discussions, and writings of the early Utopians, a vision of a future cooperative society began to emerge. Often referred to as "Socialists," writers including the Compte de Saint-Simon (Claude de Rouvroy), Charles Fourier, and Robert Owen argued for a wide range of views centered around the collective or social, rather than individual, ownership of property. One of the major pioneers was the French author and revolutionary Pierre-Josef Proudhon. In his seminal work, *What Is Property?* (1840), Proudhon answered the question by saying "Property is theft!" His argument was that private ownership of such property as agricultural land or an industrial factory actually steals its use from the rest of the people in a given community. This work had a profound influence on the German social scientist and revolutionary Karl Marx, although Marx rejected Proudhon's anarchist conclusions concerning the immediate need to abolish all strong central governments.

Marx differed from the Utopians in that he disagreed with the view that Socialism could result primarily from the application of rationalism and moral arguments. He proposed that certain historically determined circumstances were necessary for Socialist society to exist. Marx formulated a theory of historical materialism which predicted that technological progress would eventually lead to the creation of the material conditions for the advent of Socialism and that class conflict would precede the transition from capitalism to Socialism. The apparently more scientific Marxist explanation for how Socialism would be achieved appealed to many intellectuals, workers, and future revolutionaries.

Nevertheless, the idea of a utopian Socialist future that developed in this tumultuous period took hold of large swaths of workers and intellectuals. Their efforts eventually culminated in the creation of the First International in 1864–1872, an international congress of workers and radical intellectuals from around the world. With the creation of this political body, however, a struggle began to ensue between two opposing factions of the Socialist labor movement. Leading the libertarian side, which advocated the concept of total individual freedom from government control or intervention, was the anarchist revolutionary Mikhail Bakunin. Anarchism is an expression derived from the Greek language meaning being without a leader or governing head. Bakunin, a Russian, argued that workers should not attempt to seize the state; rather, their task should be to destroy it in the process of collectivizing property. According to Bakunin and other anarchists, morally valid and just social organization can only be based on free agreements among free individuals. Bakunin maintained that the state was a coercive and dominating apparatus, and that a "Socialist" revolution that seized the state but preserved its repressive functions for its own use would create a new class of domineering and exploitative bureaucrats rather than the classless society envisaged by the revolutionaries of the time. Bakunin argued instead for mutual agreements made between autonomous and federated collectives of industrial and agricultural workers. Criminal behavior would be attended to by addressing the social conditions that shaped these behaviors through the eradication of poverty, the elimination of institutionalized coercion and violence, and the destruction of the nation-state. This libertarian strand of Socialism became widely known as anarchism.

Bakunin's most outspoken critic was the young German firebrand Karl Marx. Marx argued that any revolutionary period is followed by a period of counter-revolutionary attempts to restore the old order. In order to protect the revolution against these attacks (and in order to smooth the transition to Socialism), the workers should seize the state apparatus and use state power to squash any attempts by counter-revolutionists to return society to a capitalist

Portrait of nineteenth-century Russian anarchist Mikhail Bakunin. Bakunin traveled far and wide disseminating the doctrine of anarchism and engaging in revolutionary activities throughout Europe. (Library of Congress)

economic system. Marx further argued that the state, like the machines and factories that created material wealth, was a tool, and that it was not an inherently flawed institution. Rather, the social class that controls the state determines its uses. The Marxist view of the revolutionary Socialist movement later diverged into a democratic Socialist version in which control of the state was to be achieved through elections; what became viewed as an authoritarian Socialist version was advocated by Lenin in the context of the Russian Revolution of 1917, in which control of the state was to be seized and a one-party-state system created. This later Leninist form of revolutionary Socialism became known as *Communism*. (The use of the term here is different than how Marx used it. According to his theory of history, Communism referred a higher stage of social development to follow the Socialist stage of post-capitalist society.)

For good or ill, Marx's camp emerged victorious from the debate in the First International; as a result, Bakunin and many anarchists were later expelled at the Hague con-

gress of 1872. This expulsion, many have argued, set the stage for a Marxist hegemony over radical discourse and the marginalization of anarchist ideas within the radical/ Socialist milieu. In the more contemporary context, however, following the failures of Marxist/Leninist governments in Eastern Europe and the U.S.S.R. and disappointment with repressive one-party rule in China and Cuba, anarchism has made a resurgence among radicals, particularly in the movements against globalization, neo-liberalism, and environmental destruction. Among radical Socialist activists in the twenty-first century, the "anarchist" strain is often referred to as the leftist (or libertarian) wing of the movement. "Communist," then, is used to describe the more rightist (or authoritarian) wing of the Socialist movement, though many anarchists still refer to themselves as Communists as well.

SOCIALISM AND THE RUSSIAN REVOLUTION

The revolutions in Russia in 1905 and 1917 were somewhat spontaneous and relatively unplanned upheavals. The potential for revolutionary change that these uprisings demonstrated, however, encouraged some members of the radical intelligentsia to attempt to direct the revolutionary activities of the working masses. These revolutionary leaders generally agreed that it was necessary to bring down the Tsarist regime in favor of a more democratic system, and most also believed in some kind of Socialist alternative for economic organization. Within the Socialist camps, two groups eventually emerged from a split in the Russian Social Democratic Party as major contestants for the leadership of the working class: the Bolsheviks (or "majority men") and the Mensheviks (or "minority men").

According to Marx, a Socialist revolution should occur after a period of capitalist development and bourgeois (capitalist class) rule in a given country or region. It is an irony of history that the first "Marxist" revolution happened in Russia, a country with a largely agrarian economy and a Tsarist political structure. This was a major point of debate between the Menshevik and Bolshevik camps of radical Russia.

The Mensheviks argued that fighting for political reforms, including through democratic means, was an appropriate step in the development of the Russian revolutionary effort. They held that the labor movement should align itself with the liberal bourgeoisie and attempt to expedite the process of capitalist expansion in order to eventually bring about a Socialist revolution. To the Mensheviks, it was of utmost importance to create the necessary economic base for a Socialist society before the Socialist revolution could occur and be successful in fulfilling its vision.

The Bolsheviks (named by the astute propagandist, Lenin) accused the Mensheviks of class-collaborationism and liberal reformism. They argued that the Socialist movement in Russia should focus not only on the overthrow of the czarist regime, but also on the immediate replacement of the capitalist economy with a Socialist economic system. They rejected the Menshevik position that the working class in Russia should form an alliance with the Russian bourgeoisie and argued that electoral gains should not be the focus of the working class. Instead, the Bolsheviks insisted that it was necessary to seize power and rapidly achieve revolutionary change. Lenin skillfully manipulated the divisions among the Russian Socialists (partly because after the fall of the czar in early 1917 the Mensheviks continued to support the increasingly unpopular policy of keeping Russia in the disastrous war against Germany), and the Mensheviks lost their political battle with the Bolsheviks.

The Bolsheviks seized power in the fall of 1917. The next year they adopted the name Communist Party and established a one-party government. Many Socialists around the world debated the issues that divided the Bolsheviks and the Mensheviks in Russia. Those who sided with Lenin and the Bolsheviks often formed Communist parties in their own countries, while Socialists who favored the more democratic principles of the Mensheviks continued to call their political organizations Socialist parties, from which were descended the generally less-radical social democratic parties, such as the British Labor Party and the German Socialist Party.

ANARCHISM AND THE SPANISH CIVIL WAR

Perhaps one of the most dynamic examples of the revolutionary anarchist movement is that of the anarchists before and during the civil war in Spain. In the late nineteenth century and the three decades preceding the Spanish Civil War, the anarchists were probably best known for the sensational minority of terrorists within their ranks. Inspired by what they described as "Propaganda by the Deed," this vocal minority was credited for a bombing that killed twenty-one visitors to a theater, another bombing at the Corpus Christi procession that killed ten participants, and the assassination of Spanish prime minister Antonio Cánovas in 1897 (Carr 1982, 441).

After the arguments about the utility of Propaganda by the Deed and the brutal police repression that followed these attacks, the Spanish anarchist movement began to take on a more syndicalist character (that is, they tended to use the union or collective as the instrument for political action and relied on strikes and popular militancy rather than individual acts of violence to air their grievances with the state and

the bourgeoisie). This strategy culminated in the creation of the CNT (the National Confederation of Labor) in 1908, an anarcho-syndicalist union with strong popular support in Andalusia, Aragon, Levante, and Catalonia, as well as the secretive group within the CNT known as the FAI (Federation of Iberian Anarchists). Despite the creation of this union, sporadic resurgences in terrorist activities continued (even during the civil war), especially after waves of brutal police repression. Not surprisingly, the anarchists of Spain often had bitter disputes with their Marxist contemporaries, and the CNT was no exception. They competed for membership with the Socialist UGT (General Worker's Union) and had ideological struggles with its leaders and rank and file because of the UGT's objective to create a workers' state with a strong central government—as opposed to the CNT's advocacy of a loose confederation of worker and peasant communities.

The UGT was successful in industrial areas, especially in Madrid, and attracted workers who were suspicious of anarchist goals and tactics. Lacking a theoretical method of dealing with agrarian issues, however, the UGT could not compete with the various anarchist groups in Spain's countryside. Thus, by the time of the creation of the CNT, there was already a large base of support for anarchist goals in the agrarian regions of Catalonia and Andalusia. The CNT and the anarchists had substantial support in some industrial centers as well. Indeed, Barcelona proved to be an excellent example of anarchist organization in an urban setting, and the CNT flourished there.

During the Spanish Civil War (1936–1939), the groups that opposed Francisco Franco's right-wing military rebellion against the Second Republic were far from united. While the CNT argued for arming the workers and peasants and allowing them to organize without a militaristic hierarchy, and the POUM (Worker's Party of Marxist Unification) seemed willing to accept that, the Stalinist PSUC (Unified Socialist Party of Catalonia) and the fledgling bourgeois Republican government resisted this approach. Furthermore, the peasantry of Aragon and Catalonia had been successfully collectivizing the land and putting councils into place to mirror the functioning of the Republican authorities. This was seen as a mistake by the Republican government, because the councils usurped its authority. The leaders of the PSUC, for their part, argued against radically altering the sociopolitical system of Spain during the war. They accepted the doctrinal Marxist assumption that a given region must undergo a period of capitalist expansion before a successful Socialist revolution can be mounted, and they did not want to drive all property owners into opposing the elected government of the Republic and instead supporting Franco. As a result, the PSUC and the Republican government became odd allies in their fight against immediate Socialist revolution in Spain while at the same time trying to defeat Franco's Spanish military forces and those of his Fascist Italian and German Nazi allies.

This split concluded in the "May Events" of 1937. On May 3, police officers under PSUC control attempted to take over Barcelona's telephone exchange building, which had been controlled by the CNT since the beginning of the civil war. This signaled the end of the revolutionary period of the Spanish Civil War. The Republican government then maintained largely liberal capitalist policies. The POUM was outlawed and accused of serving Fascist interests, while the CNT was tolerated for a time. With both the liberal bourgeoisie and the Spanish Stalinists aligned against their revolutionary methods and goals, the Spanish anarchists slowly lost the autonomy and collectivization that they had gained during the first ten months of the Spanish Civil War. Some felt that the end of the social revolution contributed to a significant loss of popular support for the Republican cause, which, coupled with the internal conflicts among the Republic's supporters, contributed to its defeat in the civil war. Nevertheless, the CNT continues to exist, and the anarchist movement in Spain in the twenty-first century is still largely syndicalist, though its influence is a fraction of what it was in the years preceding and during the Spanish Civil War.

COMMUNISM AND MARXISM-LENINISM

Following the struggles between the Bolsheviks and the Mensheviks in Russia, the Bolsheviks, as noted earlier, began to refer to themselves as "Communists" and in 1918 adopted the title "Communist Party." Their ideology was framed around a Marxist critique of capitalism, but it also relied heavily on the writings of the Bolshevik leader Vladimir Lenin. Lenin interpreted Marx's notion of the "Dictatorship of the Proletariat" to mean the one-party rule of the Communist Party in post-revolutionary "workers' states." He also theorized the necessity of the "vanguard party" to awaken and organize the working people for revolution. The Communist parties were to play this role around the world and lead the masses to revolt against capitalism. Despite Lenin's desire for a powerful and centralized government in post-revolutionary states, he still argued that eventually under the economic conditions of Socialism, which would in time produce enormous technological advances and material abundance, the state would begin to "wither away" to only the smallest and most basic of functions as the stage of Communist society was achieved. This theoretical model, coupled with certain other important elements—such as Lenin's view of the functions of capitalist imperialism and the role of revolutions in lesser developed societies in bringing about world revolution—became known as Marxism/Leninism.

After the Russian Revolution, many Socialists began to think that Marxism/Leninism was vindicated. That is, since the working class revolution looked to be a success in Russia, they believed the same model for revolution and post-revolution, which included state ownership of all productive property and agricultural land and a centrally planned economy, would be successful elsewhere. Much less apparent to most of the outside world until the 1950s was the extent of persecution and government terror that characterized Joseph Stalin's rule of the U.S.S.R. Stalin's leadership and the actions of his supporters perverted the Leninist one-party system into a brutal personal dictatorship. Since the Stalinist system had emerged from the revolution Marxism/Leninism inspired, millions of people were alienated from this ideological perspective.

Perhaps some of the best examples of Marxism/Leninism at work in other countries and how revolutionary leaders there modified Lenin's theories to fit their own circumstances, agendas, and needs can be found in the Chinese and Cuban revolutions.

Mao Zedong altered Marxism/Leninism to include the theoretical treatment of the peasantry as a key revolutionary class, along with the urban working class, a task which was crucial to waging a successful revolution in China's overwhelmingly agrarian society. Later, as post-revolutionary China began using the aid sent by the Soviet Union in ways that contradicted Soviet intentions and also began directing criticisms at the U.S.S.R., including aspects of its foreign policy, the "Sino-Soviet split" occurred. To the amazement and initial disbelief of some capitalist governments, the two Communist Party–governed giants became hostile to one another. Then the leaders of both countries claimed to be the primary revolutionary heirs to Marxism/Leninism, although the Chinese Communist Party began using the appellation "Maoism" to describe its particular brand of Marxism/Leninism.

In Cuba, Marxism/Leninism was not publicly espoused as the guiding ideology during the military phase of the revolution, which ended at the beginning of 1959. Fidel Castro did not announce that he was a Marxist/Leninist until December of 1961. The creation of a new Cuban Communist Party to control the post-revolution government was achieved by integrating the largest revolutionary organizations in Cuba into a single new organization called the ORI (Integrated Revolutionary Organizations). It consisted of Castro's revolutionary Movement of the 26th of July, the old Communist Party, and the Revolutionary Directorate. Cuba was extremely active for many years in attempts to bring Socialism to other parts of the world and provided inspiration, assistance, and training for Latin American and African revolutionaries. Interestingly, both Cuba in the 1990s and China more extensively and earlier, beginning in the late 1970s, adapted their forms of Marxism/Leninism to allow significant levels of private business activity and foreign capitalist investment in order to spur their economies to greater productivity while retaining exclusive Communist Party control of government.

CONTEMPORARY ANARCHISM, COMMUNISM, AND SOCIALISM

The contemporary anarchist movement has expanded beyond its doctrinaire Socialist roots. Though the largest part of the movement still tends towards collectivism and the various strains of classical anarcho-communism, new groups claim to have modified anarchist theory to meet the demands of late-modern, or in the opinion of some, post-modern society. Some anarchists have eschewed "organizationalism" altogether, sometimes in favor of attempting to "live anarchy"— trying to create autonomy in their daily lives rather than attempting to form a revolutionary movement to institute anarchism. Still others, the anarcho-primitivists, expand anarchist critiques of the state and capitalism to civilization itself and argue for a revolt against the "Totality" or what they describe as the modern "megalopolis." Some anarchists have also called for a split with traditional leftism, which they argue has been too obsessed with work and workers, and the creation of a new, "post-left" anarchism. Nevertheless, the libertarian Communism of the classical anarchists still remains the majority component within the larger anarchist movement.

Despite the variations in ideology and methodology among those self-described as Marxist/Leninists, there have usually been some basic ideas in common. Armed struggle was central to Marxist/Leninist ideology, as was the concept of the vanguard party, the dictatorship of the proletariat interpreted to mean one-party rule, and resistance to liberal collaboration and power-seeking through electoral means. In recent years, however, some political parties whose leaders claimed to embrace at least certain aspects of Marxism/Leninism, such as the Russian Communist Party and the South African Communist Party, have participated in democratic elections and held seats in their countries' parliaments. While Marxism/Leninism has been on the wane in radical movements around the globe, its strength in Cuba, China, North Korea, Vietnam, and a number of revolutionary movements and political parties around the world points to its continuing significance in the development of modern Socialist thought.

The term *Socialism* is now usually used to describe the liberal "Socialist" parties of Western Europe and other industrialized regions. These groups have eschewed revolutionary methodology and invariably seek power through the democratic political process. They also tend to advocate a large welfare state, with policies such as universal health care, large subsidies to the poor, employment protectionism, longer vacations, and sometimes shorter workweeks and workdays. Despite their Socialist history, most of these parties have stopped arguing for the collective ownership of property that their forebears espoused in favor of capitalist economies that are heavily taxed in order to provide for social programs.

The rise of globalization and neo-liberal economics has provoked rancorous debate about the state of the class struggle. While many economists argue that capitalism has been vindicated as the best economic system and that Socialism is dying or dead, workers, intellectuals, and self-described revolutionaries in a number of countries argue that the fight for collective ownership is now more important than ever. Movements for a world organized cooperatively rather than competitively seem far from over. Expansions and revisions are constantly made to the classical theorists in attempts to effectively continue the struggle for this vision. Revolutionary and radical perspectives still have a prominent place in social theory.

Deric Shannon

See Also Chinese Revolution; Cinema of Revolution; Cuban Revolution; Documentaries of Revolution; Inequality, Class, and Revolution; Russian Revolution of 1917; Spanish Revolution and Counter-Revolution; Transnational Revolutionary Movements; Vietnamese Revolution

References and Further Readings
Carr, Raymond. 1982. *Spain: 1808–1975.* Oxford: Oxford University Press.
Goldman, Emma. 1910. *Anarchism and Other Essays.* New York: Mother Earth Publishing.
Keeran, Roger, and Thomas Kenny. 2004. *Socialism Betrayed: Behind the Collapse of the Soviet Union.* New York: International Publishers.
Lazzerini, Edward J. 1999. *The Chinese Revolution.* Westport, CT: Greenwood Press.
Leonard, Thomas M. 1999. *Castro and the Cuban Revolution.* Westport, CT: Greenwood Press.
Marx, Karl, and Friedrich Engels. 1983. *Manifesto of the Communist Party.* New York: International Publishers.
Proudhon, P. J. 1994. (1840) *What Is Property?* New York: Cambridge University Press.
Treadgold, Donald W. 1964. *Twentieth Century Russia.* Chicago: Rand McNally.

Angolan Revolution

CHRONOLOGY

1st millennium A.D.	As result of the long-term and widespread Bantu migrations, scattered civilizations grow up and form the first centralized society in central Africa.

By the late 14th century	Foundation of small states mainly in the Angolan western and central highlands region.
By the early 15th century	Kingdom of Kongo (capital Mbanza Kongo) is founded along the Congo River.
1483	Portuguese ships, led by Diogo Cão, reach the mouth of the Congo River.
1491	Introduction of Christian missions.
1506–1543	King Afonso I of Kongo officially adopts Christianity and transforms Kongo into a Christian kingdom.
1576	Foundation of the city of Luanda and the colony of Angola by Portuguese Paulo Dias de Novais.
1617	Foundation of the city of Benguela, to become the main Angolan port for exporting slaves.
1624	Princess Nzinga Mbandi takes power in Ndongo kingdom.
1640–1648	Occupation of Angola (Luanda and surrounding regions) by the Dutch army.
1665	Battle of Ambuila; Kongolese army defeated. Civil war starts between factions of the Kongolese monarchy.
1704–1706	Antonians religious movement led by Beatriz Kimpa Vita seeks to reunify the Kongo kingdom.
1836	Portuguese government outlaws the slave trade.
1878	Slavery officially abolished in Angola.
1919–1921	Foundation of nationalist-oriented groups in Luanda.
1931	Foundation of the African National Movement (Movimento Nacionalista Africano).
1953–1960	Several modernist and radical nationalist organizations founded. Many are small, short-lived groups without political programs, but
	two will become particularly important: the UPNA/UPA, founded in 1957 (later called UPA), and the MPLA, founded in January 1960.
1960	Strike on the cotton plantations of Baixa de Cassanje (Malanje) in January. Severe reprisal with dozens of protesters killed.
	Nationalist revolt in Luanda in February. Attack on prisons.
	On March 15, a general uprising by UPA begins in the north.
	In June, Agostinho Neto and other nationalists are arrested in Luanda. Dozens of protesters killed in Catete (Bengo region, Neto's birthplace).
1962	Álvaro Holden Roberto forms FNLA (Frente Nacional de Libertação de Angola—National Front for the Liberation of Angola), and GRAE (Governo Revolucionário de Angola no Exilio —Angolan Revolutionary Government in Exile).
1963	MPLA expelled from Léopoldville. Moves to Brazzaville. Opens military front in Cabinda.
1964	Jonas Malheiros Savimbi resigns from FNLA.
1966	UNITA (Union for the Total Independence of Angola) founded.
1974	Military coup in Portugal on August 24. Salazarist regime leaves power.
1975	In January, Alvor agreement between FNLA, MPLA, UNITA, and the new Portuguese authorities, leading to independence.
	In July, MPLA wins Luanda battle against FNLA. FNLA and UNITA are expelled from Luanda. End of the transitional government.
	On November 11, MPLA declares the independence of Angola and the creation of the Peoples Republic of Angola. FNLA and UNITA create the Democratic Republic of Angola in Huambo.

1977   Coup d'état in May by the extreme leftist and pro-Soviet wing of MPLA led by Alves Bernardo Baptista, also known as Nito Alves. Nito and his companions are arrested weeks later and executed. Thousands who were believed to have been Nito supporters are killed.

In December MPLA holds first congress creating the MPLA-Labor Party (MPLA-Partido do Trabalho).

Declaration of "Scientific Socialism" and Marxism Leninism as the official ideology.

1991   In May, Bicesse (Portugal) Peace Agreement between Angolan government and UNITA rebellion.

1992   First democratic elections in September.

Civil War resumes in October.

2002   Jonas Savimbi is killed in combat on February 22.

Luena Agreement in April between Angolan government and UNITA. The civil war officially ends.

INTRODUCTION

The roots of the Angolan Revolution, along with its internal divisions and violence, can be found in the Portuguese colonial system. These internal divisions first emerged when the nationalist movement split into three separate movements, which never reunited during the fight against the colonial power. When the Salazar regime fell on April 25, 1974, the three movements came to an agreement with Portugal for the de-colonization of Angola, but later they confronted each other in a bloody battle for power. These divisions also explain why two new republics were proclaimed in newly independent Angola on November 11, 1975: the Popular Republic of Angola was proclaimed in Luanda by the MPLA (Popular Movement for the Liberation of Angola) and led by Agostinho Neto; the Democratic Republic of Angola was proclaimed in Huambo, a city located in the central highlands, under the dual leadership of Holden Roberto of the FNLA (National Front for the Liberation of Angola) and Jonas Savimbi of UNITA (Union for the Total Independence of Angola). This conflict among Angolans persisted until the end of the civil war in 2002.

BACKGROUND: CULTURE AND HISTORY

The territories and peoples who made up Angola as defined by the Portuguese colonial power are largely from the Bantu linguistic groups. Some non-Bantu African groups are concentrated in the extreme south, most notably the so-called Bushmen or !Kung, who are spread throughout southern Africa. In addition, within a few decades of their arrival in Angola, the Portuguese and other Europeans had mixed with the local population to create a new racial minority known as the *mestiços*. Add to this a white minority that descended from the colonists and chose to adopt Angolan nationality after independence. Thus, the newly independent Angola was a multiethnic and multiracial society.

The process of colonizing the vast Angolan territory evolved differently from one region to another and from one period to another. During the first centuries of the colonial era, the Portuguese were concentrated largely along the coast. The first direct contact between the African societies of the hinterland and the Europeans occurred during the seventeenth century through two means. On the one hand, during the wars of occupation of Ndongo, the Portuguese troops fought the Mbundu people. These confrontations, which continued throughout much of the seventeenth century, were led by the famous Queen Nzinga Mbandi and characterized by intervals of military action followed by intervals of peace achieved through negotiated treaties. During the same period, Portuguese traders known as *sertanejos* were gradually penetrating inland into the Ovimbundo territory in the central highlands region now known as the provinces of Huambo and Bié. The Portuguese traders created alliances with the Ovimbundo chiefs through marriages between the Europeans and the daughters of local families. This system of intermarriage enabled the Portuguese to penetrate to the heart of the inland trading system and to consolidate their role in the slave trade. The creation of the city of Benguela in 1617 solidified the commercial links between the coast and the central highland area, engaging this region in the Atlantic trade system and its various commercial and cultural dynamics.

In contrast, the East (Moxico and Kuando Kubango regions) and Northeast (northern and southern Lunda) would have no direct contacts with the Europeans until much later, starting in the eighteenth century, in some cases, and only in the twentieth century in others. In some of these areas, the European presence was limited to religious missions and commercial outposts. In the Kikongo territories of Angola, the Christian missions had a significant political and cultural impact on Kikongo society from 1491 onward. The Christian influence in this region led King Mbamba Nzika, best known by his Christian name, Afonso I, who reigned from 1506 to

1543, to transform the kingdom of Kongo into a Christian kingdom. From this point on, the Kongo territory served as a bridge, allowing the penetration of Christianity farther into the interior of this region. This Christian influence played an important role in developing the messianic ideology that characterized Kikongo nationalism in both modern Angola and the two modern Congos. The influence of the Christian missionaries gradually spread throughout the Angolan colony, making up for the lack of investment by the Portuguese colonial power in education for the Africans.

It was thanks only to the Christian missions that the first Africans received a modern education. This was the case with António Agostinho Neto, whose father (from the Mbundu ethnic group) was a Methodist pastor and who received a Methodist scholarship to study medicine in Portugal in 1947. Some of the other founders of the MPLA had been educated by the Catholic missions, which in turn impacted their intellectual development. In the Ovimbundu region, a number of different religious missions were influential. Some members of the elite that created UNITA, notably Jonas Malheiros Savimbi, were educated early on by an American Christian mission known as the American Board of Commissioners.

The precursors of modern Angolan nationalism come from two sources. One group came from among the old Euro-African families of the elite, whose social and economic links with the Portuguese colonists dated from the sixteenth century. By the nineteenth century, however, conflicts of interest had emerged between the Euro-Africans and the Portuguese. The independence of Brazil (1822) and the progressive abolition of slave labor in the Americas and in the West Indies made life difficult for the slave traders in Angola. Many, particularly the Europeans and Luso-Brazilians, were unable to adapt to this new economic context and left Angola and the surrounding region. From this point on, the Angolan economy was dominated by the Euro-Africans until the de facto end of the slave trade, officially abolished in 1836 but which continued illegally for four decades. This forty-year period was an economic boom period for the Euro-Africans. Not only did their businesses prosper, but their newly acquired wealth also enabled them to become politically and administratively prominent—a process aided by both the scarcity of skilled white men in the Portuguese colonial administration in Angola and the weak technological development of Portugal itself (Venâncio 1996). Later they reinvested the fortunes they had accumulated through the slave trade in the development of a plantation economy.

As a result of these developments, the re-establishment of full Portuguese control over Angola in the late nineteenth century led to conflicts of interest between the Euro-Africans and the newly arrived Portuguese colonists sent to secure the colonial presence. The renewed interest of the Portuguese in

their African colonies, and especially in Angola, was largely motivated by their unexpected and sudden loss of Brazil, the "jewel in the crown" of the Portuguese empire. The Portuguese involvement brought an end to the Euro-African reign. With the arrival of more Portuguese colonists, many of the once prosperous Euro-African families went into decline. They became marginalized economically, politically, and within the administrative management structures of the colony. This marginalization is one of the factors that explain the active involvement of the Euro-Africans or *mestiços* in nationalist activism.

The political organizations that had been formed in the 1920s and 1930s were reformist in nature and did not have the independence of Angola as an objective. The *mestiço* elite and a handful of blacks known as *assimilados*—those who had been assimilated into Portuguese culture—essentially dominated all of these organizations. Some of them had even been created by the colonial administration. That would change following World War II, when a radical nationalism emerged in Angola.

CONTEXT AND PROCESS OF REVOLUTION UNTIL THE LATE 1970S

With the rise of a wide range of political organizations in the 1950s, politics in Angola moved into a more radical period. While this new radicalism affected the entire Angolan territory, it was most evident in the coastal regions between Luanda and Benguela and also in a corridor that included the Mbundu lands of Malanje, the region that is now North and South Kwanza (an area that produced many of the prominent figures of the MPLA and Angolan nationalism), and the Central Highlands.

These developments were, in part, a consequence of the post–World War II era. Portugal sought to politically isolate its colonies, particularly Angola, from outside influences through the use of a political police force known as the PIDE (Polícia Internacional de Defesa e Segurança de Estado [International Police for State Defense and Security]). At the same time, however, the religious missions were giving educational scholarships to an increasing number of young people to study abroad in Portugal. These youth tended to come from the privileged social elite, the so-called *assimilados*. While studying abroad, these youth came into contact with people from other parts of the world and learned about nationalist movements in other colonies.

During the same period, other members of the *assimilado* group who remained in Angola began to organize themselves into a network of clandestine political organizations, which gradually grew. The Communist Party of Angola (Partido Comunista de Angola), founded in 1955 by Viriato da

Cruz, Mário António de Oliveira, António Jacinto, and Ilidio Machado, was the first of these organizations that was firmly radical in its thinking. This group had only a short life, however, and was followed by a series of other short-lived groups until the end of the 1950s. There were two main reasons so many of these nationalist groups were short-lived. On the one hand, Angolan colonized elites and nationalist groups were themselves deeply divided along racial, religious, and social lines—whites, *mestiços,* blacks, *assimilados* and non-*assimilados,* Catholics and Protestants, Methodists and Baptists, rural and urban elites. On the other hand, the Portuguese colonial police (PIDE) were extremely effective in infiltrating and aggressively repressing each new nationalist structure that arose, particularly from the 1950s onward. These factors undermined efforts to build a strong underground movement within Angola. Not surprisingly, then, the three long-lived liberation movements emerged from abroad, where the exiled elites could find better conditions for building strong and sustainable nationalist organizations.

From a geographical perspective, three types of Angolan nationalist groups emerged during the colonial process. These formed largely along ethnolinguistic lines: the Ovimbundu area, from which UNITA emerged; the Kimbundu area, from which the MPLA emerged; and the Kikongo area, from which the FNLA emerged. The founding group of the FNLA was largely but not entirely Kikongo. In the same way, UNITA was created by a group of Ovimbundo who drew a number of people of Kikongo, Chokwe, Lwena, and Luchazi origins. The MPLA emerged from an urban context, initially concentrated along the coast (Luanda), then spread south to Kwanza region and east to Malanje. The MPLA grew out of a middle class of *assimilados* that included, on the one hand, a *mestiço* elite, and on the other hand, a social elite of black *assimilados.*

The FNLA was created by Kikongo exiles who were influenced by the urban culture of the former Belgian Congo. The neglect of northern Angola after the end of the Atlantic slave trade system marked the second phase of the Portuguese presence in this region. During the twentieth century, people from the Angolan Kikongo region began migrating to the Belgian colony of Congo and to a lesser extent (particularly in the case of the Kikongo peoples from Cabinda) to the French Congo. The occupation and expropriation of ancestral African lands by the Portuguese exacerbated this migratory process, particularly during the coffee boom just after World War II. As a result of this migration, an Angolan community of Kikongo origin emerged over the decades in the Belgian Congo and later in the independent state of Congo. It was from within this community that the principal Angolan Kikongo nationalists emerged. The most important of these nationalist groups was the UPNA, which was founded in

1957. When it first emerged, this movement had a narrow regional-ethnic focus, but with time, it sought to become more inclusive. In 1959, the UPNA changed its name to UPA, which signaled its more inclusive perspective. In 1962, the UPA merged with another Kikongo nationalist group, the Democratic Party of Angola (PDA [Partido Democrático de Angola]), to become the FNLA, led from then on by Álvaro Holden Roberto.

These different regional experiences—political, social, and religious—created the divisions among the future national elites that eventually led to irreconcilable political differences among the three main groups that made up the armed nationalist movement in Angola: FNLA, MPLA, and UNITA. The lack of a common educational system during the colonial period also contributed to the difficulty of building a unified Angolan nationalist movement.

One aspect these new nationalist movements had in common was the belief that the Portuguese colonial system would not disappear without an armed struggle. The revolt on the Baixa de Cassanje cotton plantations in January 1961 was the work of various nationalist groups. It ignited the violence that would develop systematically after February 4, when the prisons in Luanda were attacked by nationalist groups. The intention of this uprising was to liberate nationalist detainees and to open a guerrilla front in the interior of Angola. But no prisoners were freed, and the attackers were either killed or arrested, with very few managing to escape. There are now several different historical interpretations of this event. The version promoted by the MPLA claims that its militants were behind the attacks on the prisons, but recent studies question that account. What is clear is that Father Manuel das Neves, a Catholic priest of the Luanda diocese, provided the moral leadership for this attack, which was carried out by an organization called the Angolan Liberation Army (Exército de Libertação de Angola [ELA]). On March 15, 1961, an insurrection followed in the North of Angola, led by the UPA, which crossed into Angola from its base in the Democratic Republic of Congo. In this uprising, both white farmers and assimilated blacks were indiscriminately massacred by the revolutionary army.

The liberation movement continued as a movement with two heads, the FNLA and MPLA, until 1966, when a third component, UNITA, emerged. This organization was created by Jonas Malheiros Savimbi, who held the position of minister of foreign affairs in the FNLA's Revolutionary Government of Angola in Exile (GRAE).

All efforts to create a common anti-colonialist revolutionary front were unsuccessful. Nonetheless, the armed struggle in the colonies debilitated the colonial power and contributed to the decision by the Portuguese military to lead a coup d'état that toppled the Salazar regime on April 25, 1974. The de-colonization process that followed was

Men wanting to join the MPLA in Angola attend weapons training at the Revolutionary Instruction Center at Cabinda, 1974. (Keystone Features/Getty Images)

negotiated by the three movements with the new Portuguese authorities, and it established November 11, 1975, as the date of independence. Shortly after making this agreement, the three movements re-engaged in their struggle for power. Because of its urban roots, particularly in Luanda, the MPLA was able to take control of the capital. The MPLA unilaterally declared independence in Luanda, while the two rival movements declared their independence in Huambo. This civil war became more complex when foreign armies intervened in support of each side. Cuban troops and Soviet weapons aided the MPLA. Two regional countries, South Africa and Zaire, invaded Angola in support of UNITA and the FNLA, respectively. The conflict was further complicated by the participation of mercenaries of various origins. The United States, still recovering from its defeat in Vietnam, avoided a frontal attack in Angola, choosing to provide support to the MPLA's adversaries through the CIA on the one hand and by supporting the South African invasion on

the other, making Angola the most significant proxy war battlefield in the post-Vietnam era. After a short interruption in 1991, the civil war resumed with fierce fighting in 1992, as UNITA rejected the results of the first democratic elections held in Angola.

IMPACTS

When the MPLA unilaterally declared the independence of Angola on November 11, 1975, it was recognized immediately by most African nations and shortly thereafter by the Organization of African Unity as the legitimate government. At that time, the MPLA espoused nothing more than a revolutionary nationalism. It was only during its first congress in December of 1977 that the MPLA adopted "scientific" socialism as its political system and Marxism-Leninism as the official ideology.

In the national plan, this choice meant a complete economic transformation that would entirely eliminate the market economy inherited from the colonial system. The MPLA made radical economic changes, nationalizing banks, private sector businesses, land, and the health and educational systems, and creating a new national currency—the Kwanza. On the ideological front, the choice to adopt Marxism-Leninism brought an end to the vast social alliance that had permitted the MPLA to win the political and military battle in Luanda without much difficulty. Religious groups and the moderate social sector now felt marginalized by the party.

At the same time it moved to the left, the MPLA was confronted by a more extreme left wing that emerged from its urban base of support. These youth organizations, which arose almost spontaneously after the fall of the Salazar regime, included student associations called Comités de Accão (Action Committees) which were organized at schools, but were also active at work sites, in villages and neighborhoods, and in local militias. The refusal by some of these organizations to affiliate with the MPLA party structures and, more importantly, their criticism of the ideological position of the MPLA at the time led to their systematic persecution and repression by the secret police of the MPLA regime, the DISA (Angolan Department of Information and Security).

From a regional and continental perspective, the success of a radical wing of Angolan nationalism, long allied with the victorious regimes in other former Portuguese colonies in Africa, such as Mozambique, and with the ANC of South Africa as well as with other nationalist movements in southern Africa, breathed new life into the struggle against the South African apartheid regime. Shortly after coming to power, the MPLA began receiving and training fighters from SWAPO (Namibia), the ANC (South Africa), and ZAPU (Zimbabwe African People's Union). To reaffirm what they considered to be their responsibility to support revolutionary movements abroad, the MPLA developed the slogan, "*Na Namibia, no Zimbabwe, e na África do Sul, está a continuação da nossa luta*" ("Whether in Namibia, Zimbabwe, or South Africa, our struggle continues").

In 1976–1977 the MPLA became internally divided when the most radical, pro-Soviet wing of the party, led by Major Alves Bernardo Baptista (also known as Nito Alves), a former guerrilla instructor responsible for political education and the minister of home affairs, attempted to carry out a coup d'état on May 27, 1977. Nito, a charismatic speaker, had developed a large following, particularly in the poorer neighborhoods of Luanda. He denounced rampant corruption and the social and economic supremacy of light-skinned peoples (whites and *mestiços*) in Angola. He advocated a radical Marxist-Leninist and pro-Soviet revolution, and his attempted coup had the indirect blessing of the U.S.S.R. Some high-ranking military and civilian members of the government were assassinated, supposedly by the insurgents. When the coup failed, Nito and his closest companions were arrested and executed. The MPLA cracked down hard in the aftermath of the coup, arresting thousands of people it believed to be Nito Alves followers, most of whom were subsequently executed.

In December 1977, the MPLA held its first congress, during which it transformed itself from a liberation movement into a labor party known as the MPLA-Partido do Trabalho (Labor Party). At this stage it formally adopted Marxism-Leninism as its ideology. In the late 1980s, pressured by the political changes in Eastern Europe, the MPLA renounced socialism, adopting a "market economy" approach.

After almost four decades of war, much of Angola's best agricultural land was unusable due to the heavy use of landmines by all sides involved in the fighting, making it the second most mined country after Cambodia. The country's economic infrastructure was also largely destroyed. By the end of the war, the economically viable areas of the country were limited to the coastal region and provincial capitals inland that remained under governmental control. The United Nations intervention in the 1990s did not end the war. The UN peacekeeping mission ended in the late 1990s, when both the Angolan government and UNITA had lost trust in the UN's mediation efforts. The end of the war came in February 2002, with the military victory of Angolan governmental forces over a much-debilitated UNITA.

PEOPLE AND ORGANIZATIONS

Alves, Nito (1945–1977)

Bernardo Baptista, aka Nito. A black politician from the Kimbundu ethnic group, he went to high school in Luanda before joining MPLA guerrillas in northern Angola (Dembos region) in 1966, where he became a political instructor. After the coup d'état in Portugal in April 25, 1974, Nito Alves played a crucial role in consolidating Agostinho Neto's leadership of the MPLA by mobilizing grassroots support for the party and by crushing internal critics and groups from the extreme left. Nito Alves was nominated minister of home affairs after independence. A charismatic populist speaker, he had widespread support in the slums as well as in part of the black middle class. Seeing himself as the true leader of the Angolan Revolution, he and his followers within the MPLA eventually clashed with—and challenged—Agostinho Neto's leadership, accusing Neto and other MPLA politburo members of being "social-democratic" and "Maoists." Nito Alves and his followers organized the May 27, 1977, attempted coup as a way of radicalizing the revolution after a long political crisis within the MPLA's leadership structures.

Andrade, Mário Coelho Pinto de (1928–1990)

A *mestiço,* Andrade was the intellectual figure who best symbolized modern Angolan nationalism. When he became the first president of the MPLA, he was the least ideological of the movement's leadership. He defined himself as "an intellectual who had been given on loan to politics." He was a sociologist by training, a writer who lived in exile in Paris in the 1950s and later in 1963, after breaking with Agostinho Neto. In 1974, he joined the so-called Revolta Activa (Active Revolt), a dissident movement led by intellectuals and militants from the MPLA. Mário de Andrade later joined the PAIGC (African Party of Independence for Guinea and Cape Verde) regime in independent Guinea-Bissau. He died in exile in London in August of 1990.

Christian Missions

These institutions played an important role in the training of the educated African elite who would otherwise have had few educational opportunities within the almost nonexistent Portuguese educational system. The protestant missions earned the reputation of inciting the Africans to develop nationalist ideas. All of the congregations helped develop important Angolan nationalist figures, who used their religious affiliations as a cover for their subversive nationalist activities.

Cruz, Viriato Clemente da (1928–1973)

A *mestiço* born in Porto Amboim (southern Kwanza), Viriato da Cruz was without doubt a revolutionary; even before the armed struggle began, he had evolved from a simple underground activist to one with a radical nationalist vision. He was a declared Communist as early as the 1950s. Cruz was the founder of the Angolan Communist Party (Partido Comunista Angolano) and was heavily influenced by Marxism in his analysis of Angolan society. The first secretary general of the movement, which at the time was led by Mário de Andrade, Cruz was a strategic thinker for the MPLA and the only declared Communist in the movement. He broke with the MPLA in 1963, after Agostinho Neto became the president of the movement in 1962, due to disagreements over strategy and a clash between two divergent political paths. He went into exile in China, where he died in 1973.

Lara, Lúcio Rodrigues Barreto de (Born 1929)

Son of a wealthy Portuguese colonist and a Luso-African woman who was the grandchild of a *soba,* or traditional chief, from Libolo (northern Kwanza), Lúcio Lara is closely associated with the history of the MPLA since its foundation. He first met Agostinho Neto as a student in Portugal. His affiliation with the MPLA signified a break with his class origins in favor of the revolutionary struggle. For many years he played the role of the party ideologue; he was also the de facto number two in the party during the first few years after independence, during Neto's reign. After the death of Agostinho Neto, Lara preferred to transfer power to a younger man of black origins: José Eduardo dos Santos, an oil engineer trained in the former U.S.S.R. In 2003, he voluntarily retired from political life. Lúcio Lara was a nationalist revolutionary heavily influenced by Marxist ideology.

National Front for the Liberation of Angola (Frente Nacional de Libertação de Angola—FNLA)

The FNLA was founded by Alvaro Holden Roberto in 1962 and developed in part as a successor to the UPNA/UPA. Ethnically it also drew its membership disproportionately from the Kikongo-speaking people. Although organized as an anti-colonial movement, in the 1970s it split with the more leftist MPLA and later received backing from President Mobutu's government in Zaire. In 1975 the FNLA along with UNITA tried to establish a government in the town of Huambo to rival the MPLA government in Angola's capital, Luanda. But other nations continued to recognize the MPLA government. MPLA forces were successful in militarily defeating the FNLA.

National Union for the Total Independence of Angola (União Nacional para a Independência Total de Angola—UNITA)

UNITA was founded in 1966 by Jonas Savimbi, once a member of the FNLA, largely among the Ovimbundu people in the south of Angola. In 1965 Savimbi received military training in China. Later China provided some assistance to his movement. After 1975, Savimbi's UNITA received help from the apartheid-era white South African Army. UNITA's conflict with the MPLA-led government in Luanda lasted at varying levels of intensity until Savimbi was killed in combat in 2002.

Neto, António Agostinho (1922–1979)

An assimilated black, poet, physician, and son of a Methodist pastor and primary school teacher, Agostinho Neto was the prototype of a radical nationalist revolutionary. His repeated arrests by the colonial authorities for his nationalist activities gave rise to his poetry of combat, most of which was written during his time in prison. His days as a member of Communist youth groups in the 1950s, when he was a student in Portugal, influenced his political and ideological choices. Agostinho Neto was undoubtedly a nationalist revolutionary, clearly inspired by Marxist-Leninist ideas. His dream was to create a Socialism along the lines of Tito's Yugoslavia, independent of the U.S.S.R.; yet the Soviet Union and Cuba's assistance, during the period of all-out war between 1975 and 1977 and later, became critical to keeping the MPLA regime afloat during the Cold War era. This explains the MPLA's unconditional alignment with Moscow, which was not consistent with Neto's early desire to preserve the MPLA as a non-aligned independence movement.

Neves, Manuel Joaquim das (1896–1966)

A *mestiço* born in Golungo Alto (northern Kwanza) and educated in the Catholic seminary in Luanda, Neves was ordained a priest in 1918. As priest of the diocese of Luanda and president of the National African League (Liga Nacional Africana) in the 1940s, he was an example of an ecumenical missionary with nationalist ideals, which included the use of armed violence as an option for opposing the Portuguese colonial system. It was he who hid the machetes that would later be used by nationalist activists during the assault on the prisons in Luanda at dawn on February 4, 1961. He was arrested and deported to Portugal, where he died in 1966.

Popular Movement for the Liberation of Angola (Movimento Popular de Libertação de Angola— MPLA)

The MPLA was founded as a pro-independence movement in Luanda in 1960 initially among *mestiços* (Angolans of mixed racial ancestry), other Angolans assimilated to Portuguese culture, and educated workers. Whereas the FNLA drew members largely from the northern Kikongo-speaking people and Unita was centered in the southern Ovimbundu region, the MPLA was initially most successful in recruiting among the Kimbundu ethnic group. The MPLA's members waged a long struggle against Portuguese colonial rule and adopted a leftist-oriented ideology under the leadership of Agostinho Neto. When the Portuguese agreed to give up their control of Angola in 1974, the MPLA eventually emerged as the victor in a struggle for control of Luanda against the rival liberation groups, the FNLA and UNITA. Later with the assistance of Cuban advisors and combat troops and weapons from the Soviet Union, the MPLA defeated the FNLA and

generally effectively countered UNITA forces and the white South African Army which repeatedly invaded Angola to attack the MPLA and assist UNITA.

Roberto, Álvaro Holden (Born 1923)

A black nationalist from the Kikongo ethnic group, Roberto was born in São Salvador (now again known as Mbanza-Kongo) in northern Angola. He emigrated with his family as a little boy to the Belgian colony of Congo, where he was educated in a Baptist missionary school in Léopoldville (now Kinshasa). A controversial and at times enigmatic figure, Roberto did not fully exploit the advantage he had by having his movement based outside Angola. He was first of all a promoter of an ethnic and regional nationalism, before embracing an Angolan nationalism. Compared to the leaders of the other Angolan liberation movements, Roberto was conservative, anti-Communist, and not a full-blown revolutionary.

Savimbi, Jonas Malheiros (1934–2002)

Savimbi, a charismatic Ovimbundu speaker and leader, was undoubtedly the most controversial and polemic figure of Angolan nationalism. After leaving the FNLA, Jonas Savimbi tried unsuccessfully to join the MPLA but was denied the high-ranking position he required as a condition for joining the movement. He was later trained as a guerrilla fighter in China and created UNITA in March of 1966, having launched his first armed attack during the same month. It is well documented that in the 1970s, Savimbi collaborated with the Portuguese military authorities against the other two movements. After the failure of the government of transition in 1975, Savimbi reinitiated his guerrilla activities, which only ended with his death in combat in February 2002, when he was killed by Angolan government troops. His controversial alliance with the South African regime during apartheid blurred the radical nationalistic character of his earlier years as a revolutionary fighter.

Union of the Peoples of Northern Angola (União das Populações do Norte de Angola, UPNA; later called UPA—Union of the Peoples of Angola—Unão das Populações de Angola)

An anti-colonial nationalist group founded in 1957 among the Kikongo-speaking Bakongo people in the northern section of Angola to in part protect and promote the interests of the Bakongo. Later the UPA merged with other northern

Angola groups to form the FNLA (National Front for the Liberation of Angola Frente Nacional de Libertação de Angola).

Jean-Michel Mabeko-Tali

See Also Cuban Revolution; Documentaries of Revolution; Guinea-Bissau: Revolution and Independence; Mozambique Revolution; South African Revolution

References and Further Readings
Birmingham, David. 1992. *Frontline Nationalism in Angola and Mozambique.* Trenton, NJ: African World Press.
Broadhead, Susan H. 1992. *Historical Dictionary of Angola,* 2nd ed. Metuchen, NJ, and London: Scarecrow Press.
Heimer, Frantz W. 1978. *O processo de descolonização em Angola 1974–1976.* Lisbon: A Regra do Jogo.
Mabeko-Tali, Jean-Michel. 2001. *Dissidências e Poder de Estado— O MPLA perante si próprio (1962–1977).* 2 vols. Luanda, Angola: Editorial Nzila.
Marcum, John A. 1969. *The Angolan Revolution.* Vol. 1, *The Anatomy of an Explosion (1950–1962).* Cambridge, MA: M.I.T Press.
Messiant, Christine. 1983. *L'Angola colonial, histoire et société, les prémisses du mouvement nacionaliste.* PhD diss, s/dir Georges Balandier. Paris: Ecoles des Hautes Études en Sciences Sociales.
Nunda, Geraldo Sachipengo. 2002. *A educação colonial e a construção da unidade nacional.* BA diss, s/dir Jean-Michel Mabeko-Tali. Luanda, Angola: ISCED, Universidade Agostinho Neto.
Pélissier, René. 1978. *La colonie du minautore: nationalisme et révoltes en Angola, 1926–1961.* Orgeval, France: Édition Pélissier.
Valentim, Alexandre. 2000. *Velho Brazil, novas Africas—Portugal e o Império (1808-1975).* Lisbon: Edições Afrontamentos, Biblioteca das Ciências Sociais.
Venâncio, José Carlos. 1996. *A Economia de Luanda e hinterland no século XVIII: Um estudo de Sociologia Histórica.* Lisbon: Editorial estampa.

Arab Revolt

CHRONOLOGY

1515–1918	The Ottoman empire conquers the Middle East and rules until the end of the First World War.
1893–1908	Hussein Ibn Ali and his sons live under surveillance in Istanbul.
1908	Sultan Abdul Hamid II appoints Hussein Ibn Ali as sharif (a title meaning "noble" and ap-

plied to descendants of the prophet Muhammad) of Mecca.

Official opening of the Hijaz railway linking Damascus to Medina. The Hijaz is the narrow western portion of the Arabian Peninsula bordering the Red Sea in which both Mecca and Medina are located. The railway was built by the Ottoman empire to transport pilgrims from Damascus to Medina, from where they could travel to Mecca for the Muslim pilgrimage. The railway was heavily damaged during World War I as a result of the Arab Revolt against Ottoman rule in Arabia.

Sultan Abdul Hamid II is forced to accede to the demands of the Young Turks' Committee of Union and Progress (CUP), which demands constitutional rule in Turkey. The CUP imposes the Turkish language and centralized government on what has hitherto been a multilingual and loosely governed empire, alienating the Arabic-speaking regions of the empire and causing an upsurge in Arab nationalism.

1914	In November, the Ottoman Turks enter World War I on the side of Germany. The Turks conspire with the Germans to attack Russia. Russia then declares war on Turkey, and Russia's allies, the British and the French, follow suit.
1915	In July, Hussein-McMahon correspondence begins regarding the terms under which Hussein would ally himself with the British against the Ottoman Turks in World War I in return for British recognition of Arab independence in territories ranging from Syria to Yemen.
	In December, a treaty of friendship between the British government and Abd al-Aziz abd al-Rahman al-Saud is signed.
1916	Hussein-McMahon correspondence concludes in March.
	The secretly negotiated Sykes-Picot agreement between Great Britain and France, with the consent of Russia, is signed in May. It provides for the dismemberment of the Ottoman empire. The agreement led to the division of Turkish-held Syria, Iraq,

Lebanon, and Palestine into various French- and British-administered areas.

On June 5, 1916, Sharif Hussein launches Arab Revolt against Ottoman Turks.

1917   On November 2, the British issue the Balfour Declaration pledging "the establishment in Palestine of a national home for the Jewish people with the understanding that nothing shall be done which may prejudice the religious and civil rights of existing non-Jewish communities in Palestine."

The Ottoman Turks in Palestine surrender to the British under General Allenby in December.

1918   Faisal enters Damascus in October and brings an end to the Arab Revolt.

World War I ends on November 11 with the declaration of an armistice.

INTRODUCTION

The Arab nationalist movement emerged as a literary movement whose major concern focused on the revival of Arab literature and the Arabic language and culture in the nineteenth century. In the early twentieth century, the movement became more active against the Ottoman Turks. With its own societies and organizations, its main concern centered on galvanizing and mobilizing efforts and resources for Arab independence from the Ottoman empire. As the second decade of the twentieth century developed, the idea of a new world based on the self-determination of national entities was promoted by Western Allied leaders, including the U.S. president, Woodrow Wilson. World War I (1914–1918) and the events surrounding it had aroused a desire among some Arabs for a change in their political status. In Arab North Africa, Algerian and Tunisian soldiers, many of them volunteers, had fought in the French army on the western front and desired changes that would recognize what they had done. Egyptians, who did not directly fight in the war, had suffered hardships and humiliations by the British army, which had occupied the country since 1882. In Ottoman-controlled Arab territories, the change was of a different kind. In the summer of 1916, Hussein Ibn Ali, sharif of Mecca, launched a revolt against the Ottoman Turks, and an Arab force, recruited partly from Bedouin of western Arabia and partly from prisoners and deserters from the Ottoman army, fought alongside the Allied forces and captured Palestine and Syria. In return for the revolt, Britain promised support for Arab independence after the war (Hourani 1991, 315–319).

The British government financed the revolt and supplied the necessary arms. Britain also sent military experts to advise and assist the Arabs in successfully carrying out their uprising, among them the legendary Lawrence of Arabia (Thomas Edward Lawrence). The British goal was to find an ally that could assist in defeating the Ottoman Turks and replacing their rule in the Middle East, as T. E. Lawrence wrote:

We [the British] could see a new factor was needed in the East, some power or race which would outweigh the Turks in numbers, in output and in mental activity. No encouragement was given us from history to think that these qualities could be supplied ready-made from Europe . . . Some of us judged that there was latent power enough and to spare in the Arabic peoples (the greatest component of the old Turkish empire), a prolific Semitic agglomeration, great in religious thought, reasonably industrious, mercantile, politic, yet solvent [comfortable with who they are] rather than dominant in character. (Lawrence 1961, 56)

The revolt launched on June 5, 1916, was preceded by an exchange of letters between Hussein and Sir Henry McMahon, the British high commissioner in Egypt, regarding the future political status of the Arab territories of the Middle East, where Britain was seeking to incite an armed revolt against Ottoman rule. Arab nationalists viewed McMahon's letters as a pledge of immediate Arab independence in the form of a unified state. Unfortunately, such a pledge was violated by the region's partition, in the 1920s, into British and French League of Nations mandates, fulfilling the secret Sykes-Picot agreement of May 1916. Particular controversy surrounded the status of Palestine, which McMahon later claimed was excluded from the discussions with Hussein. The British promised the Jews, in the November 1917 Balfour Declaration, a national home in Palestine. The ambiguity of British promises became the cause of post-war quarrels between Great Britain and Arab nationalists, particularly with regard to Palestine. The Arab Revolt was a significant event in the modern history of the Middle East. It helped hasten the end of Ottoman rule in the Arab Middle East and inspired a generation of Arab nationalists as they struggled against the French and British rule that followed in the aftermath of World War I.

BACKGROUND: CULTURE AND HISTORY

Arab opposition to Turkish rule over vast Arab territories started in the early 1500s and continued with the turn of the

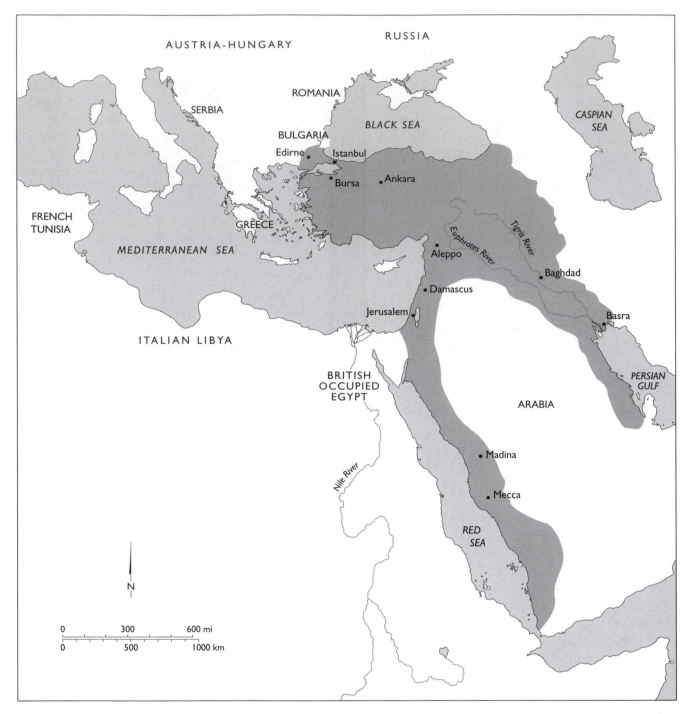

Ottoman empire at the beginning of World War I. Arab peoples within the empire rose in revolt against the Ottomans with the assistance of the British.

twentieth century. In the late nineteenth and early twentieth centuries, a number of Arab nationalists, organized in movements and secret cultural and political groups, demanded Arab independence from the Ottoman empire. Among the most frequently cited of these is the sharif of Mecca, Hussein Ibn Ali, a Hashemite descendant of the prophet Muhammad, and his four sons: Ali, Abdullah, Faisal, and Zayd. The Ottoman government questioned Hussein's loyalty, forcing

him and his sons to live in Istanbul from 1893–1908. When he was appointed sharif of Mecca by Sultan Abdul Hamid II, Hussein returned to Mecca. Once in Mecca, Hussein, who had long hoped for a state of his own, began to rally surrounding tribes against attempts to conscript Arabs into the Ottoman armed forces.

In February 1914, Hussein sent one of his sons, Abdullah, to meet with the British agent and consul general in Cairo,

Arab guerrillas and Englishman T. E. Lawrence ride through the desert in July 1917. The Arab uprising of 1916–1918 against the Ottoman empire during World War I failed to achieve true independence for Arab states in the Middle East. (Hulton Archive/Getty Images)

Lord H. Herbert Kitchener, to discuss the possibility of British aid against the Ottoman Turks. Kitchener did not offer a definitive answer. Instead, he contacted Ronald Storrs, oriental secretary at the British Agency in Cairo, and asked him to inform Hussein that in return for Arab assistance, the British government would defend the Arabs against external aggression and protect Hussein against internal threats. Storrs was also instructed to convey to Hussein that Britain would endorse an Arab caliphate in Mecca, presumably with Hussein at the helm.

As relations between the Arab provinces and Istanbul continued to deteriorate due to poor economic conditions, mass arrests of suspected Arab nationalists, and resentment against compulsory conscription, Hussein attempted to reestablish contact with the British. In 1915, he reopened negotiations through Lord Kitchener's successor in Cairo, Sir Henry McMahon. In an exchange of ten letters known as the Hussein-McMahon correspondence, Hussein offered assis-

tance to Britain against the Ottoman Turks in return for a British promise to recognize the independence of the Arab countries whose boundaries encompassed all of Greater Syria, including Palestine, Lebanon, Iraq, and the Arabia Peninsula, and British protection of the holy places against external aggression. In return, Hussein promised that the British would be guaranteed preference in all economic affairs in the Arab countries.

Following Hussein's exchange of correspondence with McMahon, Ottoman authorities initiated a massive crackdown on Arab nationalists. In May 1916, twenty-one leading Arab citizens of Damascus and Beirut were arrested and executed by public hanging. These events undermined what little loyalty remained among Arab inhabitants of the empire and sparked widespread support for open revolt (Antonius 1938, 188–190). Opposition to Ottoman rule further intensified, due to famine resulting from the destruction of crops by a locust plague in 1916. In retaliation for Arab opposition, the Turkish authorities refused to permit outside relief supplies into the region and, as a result, thousands of Arabs died of starvation.

In June 1916, Hussein ordered tribes in the Hijaz to strike at Ottoman garrisons and proclaimed Arab independence. The revolt ended in October 1918, when Faisal's forces captured Damascus and an Arab regime under the auspices of Allied forces was established.

CONTEXT AND PROCESS OF REVOLUTION

The existence of a strong nationalist movement among the Arabs of the Ottoman empire dates back to the late nineteenth century. The Arabs' desire for separation and independence from the Ottomans manifested itself through a series of nationalist agitations and conspiratorial activities among the educated in Syria and declaration of independence by chieftains of central and eastern Arabia. Aware of these developments, the British decided at the outset of World War I to negotiate with various Arab leaders in order to secure Arab military support against the Ottoman Turks. The British vision in the long term was to create an independent Arab state or confederation of states that would replace Ottoman rule.

The British had to decide which group of Arabs in the empire was representative enough to warrant the opening of negotiations. The Syrian nationalists were the most outspoken among Arab nationalists and the most politically conscious. However, the British could not reach them personally, because Damascus and Beirut, where most of these nationalists resided, continued under the firm and direct control of the Turkish authorities. The only area relatively free from Turkish control remained the Arabian Peninsula. There the British concentrated their efforts on two fronts. They negotiated and signed agreements with Abd al-Aziz abd al-Rahman al-Saud, ruler of the Najd and its dependencies, and with Sharif Hussein of Mecca.

In the case of al-Saud, the British colonial office in India conducted the negotiations and concluded that asking al-Saud to fight with the British in the war against the Ottomans risked alienating Indian Muslims: it would give the impression that British policy was hostile to an Ottoman sultan that a majority of Indian Muslims considered the caliph, or ruler, of the Faithful. Instead, British officials in India decided to recognize al-Saud as ruler of the Najd and its dependencies, and promised to defend him against aggression. In return, al-Saud pledged not to interfere with foreign power access (particularly that of Great Britain) to any portion of his domain, and to avoid attacking the British-protected territories along the Persian Gulf. During the nineteenth century the British colonial government of India had signed treaties and agreements with the rulers of Southern Arabia, Kuwait,

Bahrain, the United Arab Emirates, and Muscat and Oman during the nineteenth century, making these states essentially British protectorates. A similar arrangement with Asir, in the Red Sea coastal region north of Yemen, was concluded in 1915, and another with Qatar in 1916.

The agreement with al-Saud, signed in December 1915, contributed to favorable developments in Arabia. Al-Saud provided assistance to the Allies by continuing periodically to battle the powerful pro-Turkish clan of the Rashidis, and by not responding to the Sultan's appeal for a *jihad*. In addition, al-Saud prevented the Ottoman Turks from being supplied by sea via the Persian Gulf coast. He also refrained from attacking Sharif Hussein of Mecca. Overall, al-Saud's contribution to the British war effort was passive but not insignificant (Lenczowski 1987, 79–90).

While the British courted the goodwill of al-Saud in the interior of Arabia, they also conducted negotiations with Sharif Hussein of Mecca in the Hijaz. Hussein, who had spent many years in forced exile in Istanbul, had been appointed sharif of Mecca in 1908. By 1914 he had established himself as a powerful influence in the Arab world. Hussein had many ambitions, including the creation of an independent and unified Arab kingdom, and he believed that World War I provided an opportunity for him to fulfill his ambitions. When British officials in London and Cairo began to seriously consider his demands, his goals began to materialize. Kitchener, then secretary of war, advised both Sir Reginald Wingate, governor general of the Sudan, and Sir Henry McMahon, high commissioner in Egypt, to keep in touch with Sharif Hussein. Against this background, the British conducted full-scale negotiations, known as the Hussein-McMahon correspondence, from July 1915 to January 1916. The British initiated these negotiations when the Ottoman Turks entered the war on Germany's side in October 1914.

Hussein's strategy involved engaging the British by committing them to his cause, while giving the Ottomans in Istanbul the impression that his support of the Ottoman state remained steadfast. This dual strategy is evidenced by Hussein's decision to send his son Faisal to Damascus in the spring of 1915 on a mission to reassure the Turkish authorities of his loyalty. And even though Faisal originally felt pro-Turkish sentiments and did not share his father's enthusiasm for a British alliance, the visit to Damascus changed his position. There he became initiated into Arab nationalist secret societies where activists pushed for an Arab revolt against the Ottoman Turks. The activists fully stated their objectives in the so-called Damascus Protocol, which underlined the demand for Arab independence and unity under the leadership of Sharif Hussein of Mecca. The document called for British recognition of Arab independence, with boundaries specified to include the whole Arabian Peninsula (except for Aden, already under British rule) and the Fertile

Crescent extending north to embrace a narrow region of present-day Turkey, as far north as Adana and Mersin on the Mediterranean coast of Anatolia. In return, the Arab nationalists offered to conclude a defensive alliance with and grant economic concessions to Britain. The Arab nationalists handed over these conditions, knows as the Damascus Protocol, to Faisal for transmission to his father, whom they supported as a leader as long as their agenda for independence was fulfilled. Subsequently the conditions stated in the protocol constituted the basis of territorial demands during Sharif Hussein's negotiations with Great Britain. On the basis of these negotiations, Sharif Hussein launched the Arab Revolt on June 5, 1916 (Antonius 1938, 126–200).

It is important to note that the British believed that gaining allies was imperative if they were to win the war. Russia, Italy, France, and the Arabs were such allies. For example, McMahon was careful in his correspondence with Hussein to point to the close ties between Britain and France. The British also believed that an understanding with the Zionists would similarly produce a new ally in the form of world Jewry. Such an alliance could accomplish two goals: it might influence the United States to render greater assistance to or even enter the war on the side of Britain and France, and it might also persuade Russia, which after February 1917 was led by revolutionaries, some of whom were Jewish, to continue the war against Germany.

Zionists, under the leadership of Chaim Weizmann, remained active in England during the war. The Zionists in Britain focused on obtaining a guarantee from the Allies that, in the event of Turkey's defeat, Palestine would be recognized as a Jewish commonwealth and freely open to immigration. To this end, Weizmann secured the sympathy and actual collaboration of a number of public figures in Great Britain. Weizmann argued that an Allied pronouncement in favor of Zionism might win over German Jewry to the Allied cause and, indirectly, help create internal disaffection in the Central powers.

On November 2, 1917, following acceptance by the British cabinet of the major point of the draft submitted by the Zionists, Lord Balfour addressed the following letter to Lord Rothschild:

> His Majesty's Government view with favor the establishment in Palestine of a national home for the Jewish people, and will use their best endeavors to facilitate the achievement of this object, it being clearly understood that nothing shall be done which may prejudice the civil and religious rights of existing non-Jewish communities in Palestine, or the rights and political status enjoyed by Jews in any other country. (http://www.yale.edu/lawweb/avalon/mideast/balfour.htm)

When the news of the declaration reached Hussein, he requested clarification from the British authorities. In response, the British sent to Arabia D. G. Hogarth, staff member of the Arab Bureau in Cairo. On January 4, 1918, Hogarth assured Hussein that Britain's determination to assist the return of Jews to Palestine would not interfere with British promises to the Arabs.

These overlapping and conflicting claims came to full exposure at the Paris Peace Settlements in 1919, at which all parties presented their claims. Both the Zionists and the Arabs were represented by pro-British leaders: the Zionists by Chaim Weizmann, the Arabs by a Hijazi delegation headed by Faisal (Faisal Ibn Hussein). T. E. Lawrence acted at the conference as adviser to Faisal.

IMPACTS

The immediate impact of the Arab Revolt is that it aided the Allied war efforts by diverting and harassing the Ottoman Turkish troops in Arabia and later in Syria. The Arab Revolt played an important and controversial role in post-war negotiations and in the decisions taken by Great Britain and France about the territorial divisions of the former Arab provinces of the Ottoman empire. The princes heading the revolt became the principal and recognized spokesmen for the Arab national cause at the peace conferences and in the settlement following the dismemberment of the Ottoman empire. Although the princes' connection to the earlier Arab nationalists in the Middle East was at best only partial, the Arab Revolt is to this day seen as the golden age of Arab nationalism. Several of the leaders of the Arab Revolt became spokesmen and leaders in the Arab states in the 1920s and 1930s, and they continued to glorify the memory of the revolt.

The revolt represents a critical juncture in Arab-Anglo relations. Most of the evidence suggests that Britain was double-dealing with the Arabs, because at the same time that it negotiated with Hussein over the fate of the Ottoman Arab domain in the Middle East, it simultaneously discussed the same subject with France and Russia, keeping the two sets of negotiations separate. Arguably Britain, engaged in a deadly war with Germany, had to take into account the wishes of its principal allies. The secret Anglo-French-Russian agreement, known as the Sykes-Picot agreement, became a clear decision in principle to divide the whole of Iraq and Syria into spheres of British and French influence, leaving only Jerusalem and parts of Palestine (on Russian insistence) to some form of international administration. Further, the interpretations of the Hussein-McMahon correspondence and the Balfour Declaration have been disputed, partly because of deliberate vagueness by the British who, to obtain French, Arab, and Jewish support during the war, made conflicting promises they could not keep. Contributing to the confusion are partisan scholars who read into the correspondence interpretations that fit their ideological positions.

PEOPLE, ORGANIZATIONS, AND NEGOTIATIONS AND AGREEMENTS

Ali, Hussein ibn (1853–1931)

Also known as sharif of Mecca. He descended from the Hashemite family of Mecca. He was the sharif of Mecca (1908–1916), King of the Hijaz (1916–1924), and the father of Ali, Zayd, Faisal, and Abdullah. He is best known for launching the Arab Revolt in June 1916 against the Ottoman army.

al-Saud, Abd al-Aziz abd al-Rahman (1876–1953)

Founder of Saudi Arabia and its first king. Signed a friendship treaty with Britain in 1915 that recognized him as ruler of the Najd and its surroundings. In 1924–1925, al-Saud militarily defeated Hussein of Mecca and proclaimed himself king of Hijaz and Najd. After consolidating his power over most of the Arabian Peninsula, he changed (1932) the name of his kingdom to Saudi Arabia.

Balfour Declaration

A statement made on behalf of the British government by its foreign secretary, Arthur J. Balfour, on November 2, 1917, in a letter dispatched to the World Zionist Organization through Lord Rothschild. The Arabs condemned the declaration on the ground that Britain promised the Jews a land which had earlier been promised the Arabs (there exists a controversy over the background of this promise—see Hussein-McMahon correspondence).

Damascus Protocol

A document drawn by members of Arab nationalist organizations in 1915. This protocol underlined the demand for Arab independence and unity under the leadership of Sharif Hussein of Mecca. The document called for British recognition of Arab independence, with boundaries specified to include the whole Arabia Peninsula (except for Aden, already under British rule) and the Fertile Crescent extending north to embrace a narrow region of present-day Turkey as far north as Adana and Mersin, on the Mediterranean coast of Anatolia. In return, the Arab nationalists were willing to conclude a defensive alliance with and grant economic concessions to Britain. The Damascus Protocol, transmitted by Faisal to his father Sharif Hussein, constituted the basis for the Hussein-McMahon correspondence.

Hijaz Railway

Approximately an 800-mile-long railway connecting Damascus in Syria to Medina in Hijaz. Built between 1900–1908 at the initiative of Sultan Ab al-Hamid of the Ottoman empire, who hoped the railway would consolidate his central rule in the empire and prevent rebellion in the Arabian Peninsula. The official purpose of the railway centered on transporting pilgrims to Mecca. The guerillas of the Arab Revolt sabotaged the railway and destroyed many parts of it during the period 1916–1918.

Hussein, Faisal ibn (1885–1933)

Faisal was born in 1885, the third of four sons of Sharif Hussein. Educated in Istanbul and later sat in the Ottoman parliament as deputy for Jiddah, he became the leading figure in the Arab Revolt. He reigned as King of Iraq (1921–1933) and his brother, Abdullah, became prince and, later on, king of Trans-Jordan/Jordan (1921–1949) with British support.

Hussein-McMahon Correspondence

A 1915–1916 exchange of letters between Hussein Ibn Ali, sharif of Mecca, and Sir Henry McMahon, British high commisioner in Egypt, regarding the future political status of the Ottoman Arab domain in the Middle East, in which Britain supported an armed revolt against Ottoman rule. McMahon's promises were interpreted by Arab nationalists as a pledge of immediate Arab independence which was violated by the region's subsequent partition into British and French League of Nations mandates under the secret Sykes-Picot agreement of May 1916. The Arabs remained particularly interested in including the territory of Palestine, which McMahon later claimed was excluded from the discussions, and where Britain promised to endorse the creation of a Jewish national home in the Balfour Declaration of November 1917.

Kitchener, Horatio Herbert (1850–1916)

British field-marshal and administrator. He held a number of important posts, including commander of the Anglo/Egyptian army in 1892 and governor-general of the Sudan in

1899. He became British "Agent and Consul-General" in Egypt 1911–1914. He negotiated requested Arab assistance to fight against the Ottoman Turks in World War I. He indicated to Hussein that the British would consider, in return for Arab support in the war, recognition of a Hussein-led unified Arab state.

Lawrence, Thomas Edward (1888–1935)

British solider and author. He is better known as "Lawrence of Arabia." In 1916, he joined the Arab forces under Sharif Hussein's son Faisal and became a leader in the Arab revolt against the Ottoman Turks. He was a member of the British delegation at the peace conference in 1919 and acted as adviser to Faisal. His account of the revolt is chronicled in his classic books, *Seven Pillars of Wisdom: A Triumph* and *Revolt in the Desert*.

Sykes-Picot Agreement

A secret exchange of notes that culminated in an agreement in May 1916 among the chief Allies of World War I (Britain, France, and Russia), relating to the partition of the Ottoman empire after its defeat after the war. The agreement is named after its chief British and French negotiators, Sir Mark Sykes (an Orientalist then serving in the War Office) and Charles Francois George-Picot (a career diplomat and a former consul-general in Beirut). According to the agreement, the non-Turkish provinces of the Ottoman empire were to be divided between the British and the French. The provinces were envisaged as areas in which semi-independent Arab states or a confederation of Arab states might be established, while Britain and France were to supply advisers and to be accorded economic privileges. The agreement was approved by Russia in return for Britain and France's recognition of Russia's right to annex some territories in Anatolia. The agreement was published and repudiated in November 1917 by the Bolsheviks who found it in the Russian Imperial Foreign Office archives. Both Arabs and Zionists strongly criticized the agreement as being inconsistent with promises Britain had made to them (the McMahon-Hussein correspondence and the Balfour Declaration, respectively).

Ahmed H. Ibrahim

See Also Algerian Revolution; Colonialism, Anti-Colonialism, and Neo-Colonialism; Documentaries of Revolution; Egyptian Revolution of 1952; Iraq Revolution; Nationalism and Revolution; Palestinian Movement; Transnational Revolutionary Movements

References and Further Readings

Antonius, George. 1938. *The Arab Awakening: The Story of the Arab National Movement.* London: H. Hamilton.

Fromkin, David. 1989. *A Peace to End All Peace: The Fall of the Ottoman Empire and the Creation of the Modern Middle East.* New York: Avon Books.

Hourani, Albert. 1991. A *History of the Arab Peoples.* Cambridge, MA: Harvard University Press.

Kedourie, Elie. 1987. *England and the Middle East: The Destruction of the Ottoman Empire, 1914–1921.* Boulder, CO: Westview Press.

———. 2000. *In the Anglo-Arab Labyrinth: The McMahon-Hussein Correspondence and Its Interpretations, 1914–1939.* London: Frank Cass.

Khalidi, Rashid, Lisa Anderson, Muhammad Muslih, and Reeva S. Simon, eds. 1991. *The Origins of Arab Nationalism.* New York: Columbia University Press.

Lawrence, T. E. 1962. *The Seven Pillars of Wisdom: A Triumph.* New York: Penguin Books.

Lenczowski, George. 1987. *The Middle East in World Affairs.* Ithaca, NY: Cornell University Press.

Monroe, Elizabeth. 1981. *Britain's Moment in the Middle East.* Baltimore, MD: Johns Hopkins University Press.

Zeine, Zeine N. 1973. *The Emergence of Arab Nationalism with a Background Study of Arab-Turkish Relations in the Middle East.* New York: Caravan Books.

The Balfour Agreement (http://www.yale.edu/lawweb/avalon/mideast/balfour.htm accessed Nov. 15, 2004.)

Armed Forces, Revolution, and Counter-Revolution

ARMED FORCES AND OPPOSITION TO REVOLUTION

Anti-revolutionary regimes often depend on armed force as the ultimate basis of their power, and this can pose significant dilemmas during periods of social and political unrest. These states must ensure the loyalty of their military to the existing regime, defeating revolutionary plots both by soldiers recruited from the peasantry or working classes (as in France during the 1820s and the early 1830s) and by liberal or reformist officers (as in the Decembrist plot in Russia in 1825). Maintaining a reliable soldiery is doubly difficult in colonial situations where the majority of the regime forces are recruited from the local populace, which has been subordinated racially or ethnically as well as economically. Thus the French found Algerian troops effective in Vietnam (1945–1954) but not against their country people in Algeria (1954–1962). (Indeed, Algerians trained by the French provided valuable military expertise to the Front Liberation

Nationale.) Once engaged in actual counter-revolutionary military operations, anti-revolutionary military leaders must prevent the radicalization or politicization of their personnel, either in sympathy to the revolutionaries or in quest of harsher measures than the regime considers desirable. Once again, colonial cases show the most intense pressures and the most extreme outcomes: on the reactionary side, French officers in the OAS (Organisation Armée Secrète) attempted to overthrow the Fourth Republic and Charles de Gaulle in order to use more aggressive measures to hold on to Algeria; in contrast, Portuguese officers became revolutionaries themselves in 1974 when they revolted against both domestic Fascism and the colonial wars in Angola, Guinea-Bissau, and Mozambique.

As in Portugal, an anti-revolutionary regime may face the danger that its armed forces will become infected with revolutionary beliefs. This was especially likely in traditional societies undergoing the throes of modernization. The combination of economic change and the penetration of liberal or Marxist ideas affected all segments of society, including the supposedly distinctive (whether because of being isolated or elitist) military. Periods of crisis have often added more immediate spurs to military radicalization, especially among enlisted soldiers. This was the case in the collapse of the Tsarist Russian army from mass desertions in 1917 as soldier-peasants returned home in quest of "peace and bread," precluding the maintenance of an effective defense against the Germans no matter who controlled St. Petersburg. These former soldiers, and their comrades who had remained on the farms, constituted a revolutionary movement in themselves, independent of the urban revolutionaries ultimately dominated by the Bolsheviks. Indeed, most peasant veterans preferred a decentralized regime that would respect local autonomy and control over the food supply, and they often resisted control by Bolsheviks, White forces, and Germans alike. This essentially urban-rural clash over resources was aggravated by ethnic tensions in regions like Ukraine.

More characteristic of revolutionary influence in established military forces were the plots and attempted coups—by officers, noncommissioned officers, and enlisted soldiers who had been influenced by liberal ideas of reform and modernization—against the conservative French, Spanish, and Russian monarchies after 1815. In Spain in 1820, in Turkey in 1908, and throughout the "less-developed" world of Latin America, Africa, Asia, and the Middle East since independence, juntas of military officers have seized power declaring their superior devotion to the public good, their determination to sweep away corrupt civilian elites (whether of new or traditional origin and power), and to "get things done" in the name of the people and the nation. Examples include Bolivia in 1952, Nasser's coup in Egypt the same year, and much more recently, Hugo Chávez's attempted coup and then elec-

tion in Venezuela. Given the frequent weakness of civilian institutions in most of these nations, and the technological superiority and internal discipline of military forces, many of these coups have succeeded in gaining power. Faced with multiple problems, often with roots extending deep into society, their success as liberal or modernizing regimes has been limited; given their background in authoritarian command, many military leaders ultimately cut the Gordian knots of modernization through centralization at the expense of democracy.

Military forces have often been powerful agents of reaction, employing deadly force on their own initiative and seizing political power in the name of maintaining order during periods of social conflict, as in Spain in 1936, Iran in 1953, South Korea in 1960, South Vietnam in 1963, Greece in 1967, repeatedly in Turkey and Pakistan, and Chile in 1973. Reactionary military commanders assert their devotion to the nation and its modernization (albeit in different forms than do liberal commanders), but, as in liberal coups, they have proven very reluctant to return power to civilian politicians after the moment of immediate crisis that "precipitated" the coup.

In Western nations during the twentieth century, military forces unhappy with conservative or liberalizing political tendencies in the civilian government have been less likely to seek the overthrow of existing regimes than to resist their policies through obstruction or subversion. This has been due mainly to socialization to norms of accepting political and social democracy and military subordination to civilian control, and to the greater specialization, and thus segmentation, of the larger, more complexly articulated military organizations of the modern West. Under these circumstances, military elites have been more likely to seek favorable policy outcomes through alliances, usually informal and social as well as budgetary and economic, with civilian political and economic elites, and by doing so have preserved at least a claim to political nonpartisanship and functional autonomy within their professional sphere. An unusual exception, the product of a combination of domestic upheaval, a collapse of military discipline, and a proto-Fascist wartime mobilization, was the German Freikorps of 1919 and 1920. These veteran volunteers of the First World War, some of aristocratic origin, some motivated by extreme nationalism, and some simply by the prospect of unemployment and the camaraderie of war, battled revolutionary leftists to protect the moderate government at home while fighting Polish, Russian, and Baltic forces (composed of regular soldiers, guerrillas, and peasant rebels alike) to maintain continued ethnic and Junker class domination of the eastern borderlands of German settlement. An important source of early Nazi Party members, the Freikorps was also a significant model for Nazi visions of military forces as agents of political mobilization and racial struggle.

Members of the German Freikorps parade before Hitler, ca. 1923. (Hulton Archive/Getty Images)

Specific elements of Western military forces have sometimes taken more active political roles in revolutionary conflicts, however. This has been especially true in unconventional and colonial wars, in which some conventional military personnel became disillusioned with their duties. The most likely case is when draftees and conscripts lose faith in a cause and feel their sacrifices are unrecognized by the population at home, as among the French in Algeria or many American soldiers in Vietnam. Domestic social unrest, particularly among disenfranchised minorities like African Americans, and increased uncertainty and moral conflict about a colonial or anti-revolutionary war effort can lead to reluctance to serve in that cause. An example with great domestic political impact was the Portuguese military in Africa, whose disaffection contributed directly to the democratic coup and revolution against the Salazarist Fascist regime in Angola in 1974, which led immediately to de-colonization and the withdrawal of Portuguese armed forces from Africa.

Reactionary military personnel who come to believe that only more ruthless measures will defeat insurgents have proven more dangerous, both to established regimes and to democracy. Their most notorious tactic, often undertaken with the tacit complicity of reactionary regimes, has been the use of death squads whose members kill or "disappear" persons suspected of being rebels or their supporters. But the potential for divergence between conservative regimes and extremist military forces has been most significant, and complex, when military forces have been sent to defend settler colonies of their own ethnicity against the uprisings of colonized populations. Thus, while the Israeli Defense Forces (IDF) have had to deal with officers and soldiers refusing to serve for political reasons, either against the Palestinian *intifada* or in the removal of Jewish settlers from the West Bank and the Gaza Strip, the most dangerous assaults on Israeli democracy and the Israeli-Palestinian peace process have come from terrorists within the IDF, like the military reservists who massacred twenty-nine Palestinians at the Hebron Mosque in 1994 and assassinated Prime Minister Yitzhak Rabin the following year. In these cases, the very mass basis of the IDF made it vulnerable to extremities of public opinion. Northern Ireland provides further examples, from the Curragh Mutiny of 1914, in which top officers of the British army made it clear that they would not act to repress Unionist resistance to the introduction of Home Rule, to the often murky and perhaps illegal tactics of the British SAS (Special Air Services) against the insurgents of the Provisional IRA (Irish Republican Army) in Ulster during the 1970s and 1980s.

The ultimate specter of rogue military forces occurred in French Algeria, where the French government gave the army extraordinary powers of detention to clear Algiers of insurgents after a campaign of terrorist bombings in the summer of 1957, only to find that the extremes of deadly force that this authority tacitly condoned—the torture and "disappearances" of civilians as well as insurgents and terrorists—led elements of the army ever deeper into lawlessness and terror. This occurred at precisely the time that French public opinion began to turn against the cost of maintaining French Algeria and the excesses committed in the name of doing so. The consequence was a growing gap between French settlers in Algeria, along with elements of the French armed forces, and the people of France. Organized military resistance (the OAS) developed against Charles de Gaulle's decision to move toward Algerian independence. The April 1961 attempt by generals sympathizing with the OAS to overthrow the French government was the culmination to decades of politicization in the French armed forces, going back to the radical polarization of French society during the 1930s and the World War II Vichy regime. The defeat of the "putsch" (notably, a borrowing of the German term most often associated with Hitler's abortive uprising in Munich in 1923) and the repression of the OAS laid the foundations for final de-colonization and engendered the army's withdrawal from politics, ensuring the survival of the Fifth Republic without civil war then or during the widespread leftist protests in 1968 (as might have happened had the French army remained the reactionary, even proto-Fascist, force it had become between 1918 and 1961).

REVOLUTIONARY ARMED FORCES

Perhaps the most significant problem facing any successful revolution is the control of armed force. This is a political problem of the internal security of revolutionary policy direction against domestic counter-revolutionary resistance as well as a traditional "national security" problem of external defense against neighbors fearful of revolutionary infection or eager to take advantage of apparent weakness in the post-revolutionary state. Debates over the direction of post-revolutionary policy can also lead to civil war among the revolutionaries unless a clear monopoly of force is established, and doing so often fosters conflict between different elements of the revolutionary armed forces.

The most likely internal consequences of the struggle for control of a revolution's armed forces are *radicalization,* in which segments of the revolutionary armed forces push for greater change, often justified by their sacrifices, and *caudilloism,* in which the leaders of segments of the revolutionary armed forces establish local or regional fiefdoms, usually based on sectional social geographies, whether more radical or conservative than the revolutionary mainstream, as in Mexico after the revolutions of 1810–1821 and 1910–1920. Both are species of *praetorianism,* the forcible rise of military elites to political power. A third variant, the most dangerous to a revolution, is that in which military forces compel the nation to turn or return to a less socially revolutionary path, as in France under Napoléon.

The armed forces of revolutionary regimes or those engaged in revolutionary war can undergo intense but often contradictory politicization. Examples include the French army of the 1790s and the armed forces arrayed against the Soviet occupation of Afghanistan during the 1980s. In 1789 and 1790 the French army experienced infection by revolutionary fervor, while the flight of many noble and royalist officers soon compelled the promotion of new officers from the enlisted ranks. The onset of war in 1792 led to a more radical revolutionary regime and mass civil and military mobilization via the first law of national conscription in Western Europe, the *levee en masse* of 1793. Yet by the late 1790s the army felt a growing distance from a government that had reverted to moderation, was unable to hold power without resorting to military force against its domestic enemies, and was unable and perhaps unwilling to secure peace with the reactionary European monarchies. Whether from disappointed revolutionary fervor, a desire for greater recognition and reward, or, most likely, some combination of the two, the French army soon became the instrument of the most famous praetorian since Julius Caesar, Napoléon Bonaparte. A similar possibility occurred in the fledgling United States in the so-called Newburgh Conspiracy among Continental army officers in 1783 but was deflected by George Washington, the only possible candidate for the role of military dictator.

The international security environment is one of the principal sources of shifts between military professionalism and revolutionary fervor. The relative peace of 1789–1791 enabled the French Revolution to survive an army gutted by officer desertions and enlisted unrest, while the war years that followed forced a choice between (1) winning victory and national security primarily through ideological fervor and camaraderie, as in 1792, 1793, and 1794, and (2) relying instead on an infusion or revival of greater professionalism, training, and discipline, as in later years. The Russian Revolution went through a similar process, though the initial collapse of military discipline in 1917 forced the revolutionaries to make a humiliating peace with Germany in 1918. Following internecine struggles over the composition of the Red Army during the civil war, by 1921 Leon Trotsky was engaged in a debate over the philosophy of military operations and operational procedures with supposedly more radical Bolsheviks. While maintaining party political control through commissars attached to the Red Army (like the *representatives en mission* of the Committee of Public Safety during the French Revolution terror), Trotsky and Lenin—and eventually Stalin, throughout the course of his career—ultimately stressed professional experience and skill in traditional conventional tactics and operations over revolutionary fervor.

Particularly in modernizing countries, one of the most common variants of the trajectory from military professionalism to revolution—and back—is caudilloism. Amid the opportunities presented by revolution, enlisted soldiers or lower-ranking officers discover previously unknown talents; their success enables them to claim authority within the new revolutionary regime. The regional power bases of such men and the military units they lead distinguish this phenomenon from simple praetorianism. The best examples come from Mexico, where the varying social characteristics of different areas of the country compelled aspiring revolutionary regimes to depend for local authority on indigenous leaders like Vicente Guerrero circa 1820, or Emilio Zapata in the revolution of the 1910s. In some cases caudillos, like these two, have been social radicals, and in other cases, like that of Pancho Villa, true federalists (decentralizers). But many, if not most, have turned their revolutionary power bases into personal fiefdoms as notables in the new order. Indeed, one might view the more general diffusion of post-revolutionary authority in South and Central America in much this light, as creole (persons born in Spanish America rather than Spain) elites soon managed to secure control over the direction of most of the regional and all of the new national regimes that succeeded Simón Bolívar's *Gran Colombia* and the United Provinces of Central America. Whether radical, conservative, or reactionary, these successor regimes usually depended on military power as much or more than their predecessors: the radicals to fend off centralist coercion, the conservatives to repress a more politicized peasantry.

When a centralizing or nationalizing revolutionary force failed to win rapid control of the new government, the stage was often set for interregional conflict and even civil war among the revolutionaries. While existing civil society was strong enough to manage or repress regional divisions in the French and American revolutions, and Leninist repression eventually secured the revolution of the Soviets against all rivals, the extent and duration of Chinese warlordism after the beginning of the Republican Revolution of 1911 suggests the difficulties of controlling armed forces across large and diverse social geographies. Afghanistan during the 1980s and 1990s provides an example of a traditionally decentralized society engaged in a struggle for national independence, followed by an extended civil war between the ethnic, cultural, and religious factions of the various regions. The ultimate

victor, prior to the U.S. invasion of October 2001, was an extreme fundamentalist religious movement, the Taliban, rooted in the Pashtun ethnic group and supported by the military of neighboring Pakistan, which had emerged from the Islamist mobilization against the atheist Soviet invaders. The Taliban used its religious fervor to incorporate allies throughout much of the country and impose a new conformity in the late 1990s.

Wars of national liberation can easily become civil wars after the defeat of the foreign invaders as popular mobilization stirs demands for greater political participation in the post-liberation government and advocates of competing visions of post-revolution society come into conflict with one another. In China this occurred long before unified national sovereignty was regained, as the Guo Min Dang became more socially conservative (in part due to warlord influence), while the Communists pressed for peasant political mobilization in the late1920s. While the Chinese Communists held a number of important civilian, rather than sufficient military, positions during the Guo Min Dang–Communist Party alliance of 1924–1927, their error of underestimating the crucial importance of military leadership became painfully apparent when Chaing Kai Shek, former commandant of the Guo Min Dang's Whampoa Military Academy, achieved control of the Republican army and turned it against the Communists in 1927, beginning a campaign to annihilate them. Other examples include the struggle between Communists and Chetniks (led largely by former Yugoslav army officers) in Axis-occupied Yugoslavia, and that between Greek conservatives and Communist partisan veterans during and after World War II, and may also be extended to describe the strife between Filipino guerillas aligned with or against the Americans during the years following the wars against Spain (1898–1903) and Japan during the 1940s. Indeed, the divisions of Korea and Vietnam might well be interpreted in this light, though international pressure was at least equally significant.

Even when revolutionary regimes secure power against overtly counter-revolutionary alternatives, divisions within the revolutionary movement may emerge, particularly between those revolutionaries concerned with consolidating power by establishing a solid institutional and economic base and those eager to exploit openings for further revolutionary change by pursuing more radical decentralizations or more egalitarian distributions of culture, economic resources and opportunities, and political and military power. Apart from the use of revolutionary military forces by one faction or another to win dominance, this rift can be reflected in competition between different types of revolutionary military forces, rivalries that may be based on or expressed in contrasting philosophies of military action (as in Trotsky's conflicts with military radicals over Red Army doctrine), in manpower sources, especially local vs. national recruiting bases, or in disparate philosophies of military organization and discipline. The armies of the French Revolution, and to some extent the American Revolution, present cases in which officer veterans of previous royalist regimes clashed with subordinates who came of age under revolutionary auspices. But the twentieth century also provides good examples in which distinct military organizations competed, both philosophically and for dominance, over the direction of a revolution's organized armed force. These include the conflict during the Spanish Civil War of the 1930s between the anarchist militias and the regular forces of the Republic trained and sponsored by Stalinist Russia, and the contest in Khomeini's Iran during the early 1980s between the Islamic Revolutionary Guard and the professional forces inherited from the Shah. During the Chinese Cultural Revolution of the mid 1960s, the paramilitary strength and radical violence of the Red Guards led to a number of interventions by the PLA (People's Liberation Army), a force as well known for its politicization as for its substantial military effectiveness. In fact, the PLA stands as perhaps the most comprehensive synthesis of revolutionary fervor and military capability since the French army of the late 1790s, or the New Model Army of the English Civil War. The Cultural Revolution "to revive the revolution," initiated by Mao in 1966, was in accord with the PLA's Maoist doctrine of "people's war." But battles between Red Guard students and more moderate workers placed local politicians and administrators in an impossible position in which they had little alternative but to call on the military if order was to be restored. Indeed, the several roles played by the PLA—as "revolutionary vanguard" and tool for political mobilization in the war against Japanese aggression and in the Chinese Civil War, as "volunteers" against the threat of foreign intervention in the Korean War, as "vanguard workers" in the fields and factories during collectivization and the (disastrous) Great Leap Forward, and as a force for coercive stability during the Cultural Revolution and the Tiananmen Square protests—stand as perhaps the most illuminating example of the role of military forces in revolution and counter-revolution.

Samuel Watson

See Also Afghanistan: Conflict and Civil War; Algerian Islamic Revolt; Algerian Revolution; American Revolution; Chilean Socialist Revolution, Counter-Revolution, and the Restoration of Democracy; Chinese Revolution; Cinema of Revolution; Documentaries of Revolution; Egyptian Revolution of 1952; French Revolution; Greek Civil War; Guatemalan Democratic Revolution, Counter-Revolution, and Restoration of Democracy; Guerrilla Warfare and Revolution; Indonesian Counter-Revolution; Iranian Revolution; Iraq Revolution; Irish Revolution; Italian Fascist Revolution; Japanese New Order Movement; Korean Civil War; Libyan Revolution; Mexican Revolution; The Nazi Revolution: Politics and Racial Heirarchy; Philippine entries; Reform, Rebellion, Civil War, Coup D'etat, and Revolution; Russian Revolution of 1917; Salvadoran Revolution; South Korean Democracy Movement; Spanish Revolution and Counter-Revolution; Turkish Revolutions of 1908 and 1919–1923; U.S. Southern Secessionist Rebellion and Civil War; Venezuelan Bolivarian Revolution of Hugo Chávez; Vietnamese Revolution; War and Revolution

References and Further Readings

Bertaud, Jean-Paul. 1988. *The Army of the French Revolution: From Citizen-soldiers to Instrument of Power.* Trans. R. R. Palmer. Princeton, NJ: Princeton University Press.

Cann, John P. 1997. *Counterinsurgency in Africa: The Portuguese Way of War, 1961–1974.* Westport, CT: Greenwood Press.

Chorley, Katherine. 1973. *Armies and the Art of Revolution.* 2d edition (1st 1943). Boston: Beacon Press.

Davis, Diane E., and Anthony W. Pereira, eds. 2003. *Irregular Armed Forces and Their Role in Politics and State Formation.* Cambridge: Cambridge University Press.

Forrest, Alan. 1990. *Soldiers of the French Revolution.* Durham, NC: Duke University Press.

Hagen, Mark von. 1990. *Soldiers in the Proletarian Dictatorship: The Red Army and the Soviet Socialist State, 1917–1930.* Ithaca, NY: Cornell University Press.

Kelly, George Armstrong. 1965. *Lost Soldiers: The French Army and Empire in Crisis, 1947–1962.* Cambridge, MA: M.I.T Press.

Lartéguy, Jean. 1961. *The Centurions.* Trans. Xan Fielding. New York: Dutton.

Lee, Hong Yung. 1978. *The Politics of the Chinese Cultural Revolution: A Case Study.* Berkeley: University of California Press.

Mao Tse-Tung. 1967. *Selected Military Writings of Mao Tse-Tung.* 2nd edition. Peking: Foreign Languages Press.

Porch, Douglas. 1974. *Army and Revolution: France, 1815–1848.* London: Routledge and Kegan Paul.

———. 1977. *The Portuguese Armed Forces and the Revolution.* London: Croom Helm.

Scott, Samuel F. 1978. *The Response of the Royal Army to the French Revolution.* Clarendon: Oxford University Press.

Waite, Robert G. L. 1952. *Vanguard of Nazism: The Free Corps Movement in Postwar Germany, 1918–1923.* Cambridge, MA.: Harvard University Press.

Woodhouse, A. S. P., ed. 1992. *Puritanism and Liberty: Being the Army Debates (1647–1649) from the Clark Manuscripts.* London: J. M. Dent.

B

Bangladesh Revolution

CHRONOLOGY

ca. 1500 B.C.   Indo-Aryans arrive in the Indus valley.

ca. 1000 B.C.   Bang tribe arrives in the lower Ganges valley.

273–232 B.C.   Reign of Maurya emperor Asoka. Following his death the empire begins to break up, and local chieftains rule in Bengal.

320–510 A.D.   Gupta dynasty. Rule is extended into portions of Bengal.

750   Founding of the Pala dynasty, a Buddhist dynasty that extends its rule well beyond Bengal into northern India.

1095   Fall of Pala dynasty in Bengal to Sena dynasty and the restoration of Brahmanical Hinduism. Pala dynasty continues to rule in Bihar until 1155.

1202   Fall of Sena dynasty to army of the Muslim Ghurid dynasty in Delhi.

1608   Dhaka becomes the capital of the Mughal province of Bengal.

1690   Calcutta (Kolkata) founded by British.

1757   British, led by Robert Clive, defeat army of Bengal Nawab at Plassey and establish and later extend British control over northern India.

1857   Sepoy mutiny put down by British.

1885   Indian National Congress founded at Bombay (Mumbai).

1905   Partition of province of Bengal into the province of Bengal and the province of Eastern Bengal and Assam, of which Dhaka is capital.

1906   Muslim League founded in Dhaka.

1909   Separate electorates for Muslims and other minorities established by Morley-Minto Act of British Parliament.

1911   Partition of Bengal annulled. Indian capital transferred from Calcutta to New Delhi.

1917   British government declares that its ultimate goal is self-government for India (that is, the territory that is India, Pakistan, and Bangladesh today).

1937   Elections are held for provincial assemblies, giving provinces autonomy and responsibility for government in most matters. Fazlul Haq becomes premier of Bengal.

1940   Muslim League passes a resolution stating that the partition of India into Muslim and Hindu majority areas may be necessary. It is often called the Pakistan Resolution, although the word *Pakistan* does not appear in the resolution.

1937–1947   Muslim League–led ministries govern Bengal, except for a short period in 1945–1946, when the governor rules directly.

1947   Indian independence on August 14 results in partition of India into India and Pakistan. Pakistan comprises two wings, divided by India. Bengal is partitioned into Muslim-majority and Hindu-majority areas as East Bengal and West Bengal. Muslim League rules in East Bengal.

1952   Demonstrators demand that Bengali be declared a co-national language with Urdu, the language favored by the leaders in West Pakistan. Three students and several non-students are killed on February 21, a date that is commemorated as Language Martyrs' Day in Bangladesh.

1954   Muslim League is trounced in provincial assembly elections. United Front, comprising Awami League and Krishak Sramik Party, forms government.

1956   First constitution is passed. A key provision makes "parity" (equal representation of West and East Pakistan, despite population size differences) the basis for representation in the National Assembly. That provision deprives East Pakistan (the constitution's new name for East Bengal) of the benefit of its majority of the population of Pakistan.

1958   Government of Pakistan declares martial law on October 7.

   General Mohammad Ayub Khan assumes power on October 28.

1966   Sheikh Mujibur Rahman ("Mujib") announces Awami League Six-Point Program.

1969   Ayub Khan resigns on March 25 and is replaced by General Yahya Khan ("Yahya"), who promises elections and the end of parity.

1970   Elections are held for national and provincial assemblies. East Pakistan is allotted 162 seats in national body and West Pakistan 138, reflecting actual population figures. Of the 162, the Awami League wins 160, thereby gaining an absolute majority in the National Assembly without winning any seats in the west.

1971   Talks among Yahya, Mujib, and Zulfiqar Ali Bhutto of the Pakistan People's Party, winner of the largest number of seats in the west, fail to lead to an agreement on a national government.

   In the evening of March 25, Pakistan army troops move against Bangladeshis (as they now term themselves). Civil war ensues.

   India enters the conflict in late November.

   Pakistan forces surrender on December 16.

1972   Mujib, who had been arrested by the Pakistanis, returns to Dhaka and becomes prime minister on January 10.

   Constitution of Bangladesh is promulgated on December 16.

INTRODUCTION

The Bangladesh Revolution or, more accurately, the Bangladesh War of Independence, began in March 1971. It ended on December 16 of the same year with the surrender of the Pakistan army to the Indian army, which had entered the conflict to assist the Bangladeshis in their quest for independence. With the surrender, the former province of East Pakistan became the independent People's Republic of Bangladesh, although the title "People's Republic" was not intended to imply similarity to Communist regimes.

BACKGROUND: CULTURE AND HISTORY

Bengal was the most easterly of the provinces of British India but the center of British expansion in northern India. The Bengal city of Calcutta (now Kolkata) was the capital of British India until 1911, when the capital was moved to New Delhi.

Although the identity of the earliest settlers in Bengal has not been determined, it is believed that Dravidian and/or Mongoloid people inhabited the region. About 1000 B.C. the Indo-Aryan people who had entered India from the northwest extended their settlement to Bengal. The tribe that settled is known as the Vanga or Bang (hence Bengal). What government there was seems to have been local until the Mauryan empire, centered in Bihar, expanded its control over at least some portions of Bengal under the Emperor Asoka (273–232 B.C.). The emperor was Buddhist, and it is believed that the expansion of Buddhism to Burma, Ceylon, and the Malay Peninsula was accomplished by sea from the Bengal port of Tamluk. For a considerable time there was contact between Bengali Buddhist scholars and those elsewhere, especially in Tibet. Following the death of Asoka and, shortly thereafter, the collapse of the Mauryan empire, Bengal apparently reverted to local governments by Hindu rajas. Portions of Bengal were conquered by the Gupta empire and the revival of that empire by Harsha in the seventh century A.D.

It was not until 750 that Bengal was reunited under the staunchly Buddhist Pala dynasty, whose sculpture graces museums in Europe and America. The Palas established their capital first at Patna and then at Monghyr, both in Bihar, and extended their rule over much of northern India. Although the dynasty continued to rule in Bihar and beyond until 1155, its Bengali dominions fell to the Sena dynasty in 1095. Under the Senas, strict Brahmanical Hinduism was restored to Bengal.

The rule of Muslims began in 1202, when a general in the employ of the Ghurid dynasty in Delhi captured the Sena capital. Islam then spread rapidly, especially in the eastern portion of Bengal, and most of Bengal remained under Muslim rule, either under Delhi or under local Muslim dynasties, until 1757. In that year, the British, who had established trading posts or "factories" as early as 1650, defeated the nawab of Bengal in the battle of Plassey and established British rule, which would last until 1947.

Britain initiated and gradually expanded Indian participation in the governance of India through a series of laws passed by Parliament in 1894, 1909, and 1919, culminating in the 1935 Government of India Act that provided for provincial autonomy: local matters would thenceforth be handled by provincial assemblies and provincial ministries. The act also continued a system of separate electorates begun with the 1909 act, under which Hindus and Muslims would vote separately for assembly representatives. Seats were allotted roughly in proportion to the population adhering to each religion and allocated at the provincial level.

The demand for separate electorates had come from the Muslims, who formed the Muslim League in Dhaka in 1906. Mohammed Ali Jinnah (1876–1948) soon became its primary leader. The idea of separate electorates was strongly opposed by the Indian National Congress, founded in 1885 and led by Mohandas Gandhi.

Animosity between the congress and the league over the future of an independent India led to the partition of India on August 14, 1947, into India and Pakistan ("land of the pure," the latter divided into two wings, Bengal in the east and Punjab, Northwest Frontier, Sindh, and Balochistan in the west). Both Bengal and Punjab were themselves partitioned into Muslim and non-Muslim majority areas, the latter going to India.

Following independence, the government of Pakistan was dominated by refugees who had moved to the west wing (including Jinnah, who had been active in Bombay), supplemented to some degree by residents of the west wing. The east wing was all but left out of the government, in the cabinet, in the civil services, and in the military. Following the death of Jinnah in 1948, Khwaja Nazimuddin, a former premier of Bengal, replaced Jinnah as governor general of Pakistan (i.e., head of state), but power remained in the hands of westerners, especially in the civil service and military. After the assassination of the prime minister of Pakistan (i.e., head of government), Liaquat Ali Khan (1895–1951), Nazimuddin stepped down to become prime minister, but western control continued. He was dismissed from his post by the then governor general, Ghulam Muhammad, in 1953.

Elections for provincial assemblies were held in 1951 in the western provinces other than Balochistan (which did not have full provincial status) but were delayed in East Bengal (called East Pakistan after 1956) until 1954. The 1954 East Bengal election proved an almost total rout of the Muslim League by the United Front, which comprised several parties, principally the Awami (People's) League, led by Husain Shahid Suhrawardy, and the Krishak Sramik Party (Peasants and Workers Party), led by Fazlul Haq. (Both of these men had earlier served as premier of undivided Bengal.)

The 1954 election results were a clear statement that East Bengal opposed the central government of the Muslim League. The government's decision shortly after independence that Urdu would be the official language of Pakistan met with particularly strong resistance, since Bengali, the language of East Bengal, was actually the majority language for all of Pakistan. Urdu was not even the primary language of West Pakistan, but was widely spoken by Muslims in what would become India. But because many of the leaders of newly independent Pakistan were migrants from India, their view on the national language dominated. No other western languages, including Punjabi and Sindhi, were accorded special recognition. Agitation for equal status for Bengali was frequent in East Bengal and culminated in a student demonstration on February 21, 1952, when police fired on demonstrators and killed three students and several non-students. February 21 is now celebrated annually in Bangladesh as Language Martyrs' Day.

After nine years of debate, Pakistan finally adopted a constitution in 1956. The four provinces in the west wing were combined into West Pakistan, and East Bengal was renamed East Pakistan. The constitution was opposed by East Pakistanis on a number of points, but the essential disagreement was over parity in representation in parliament. Under parity, the eastern province would have the same number of seats in parliament as the western, thereby depriving East Pakistan of its 54 percent majority in population (Baxter and Rahman 2003, 164).

On October 7, 1958, the president, Iskander Mirza, in cooperation with General Mohammad Ayub Khan, dismissed the government and proclaimed martial law. On October 28, General Mohammad Ayub Khan dismissed the president and assumed control of Pakistan. He proclaimed a new constitution in 1962 that retained parity and the official language designation of Urdu. Elections would be held through an electoral college comprised of "basic democrats," persons chosen by local bodies. Ayub was elected in 1962 and again in 1967. His term also saw the September 1965 war between Pakistan and India (during which the Indians made no attack on East Pakistan).

In 1966, Mujibur Rahman ("Mujib"), who had succeeded Surhawardy as leader of the Awami League, issued a document that became known as the Six Points, which declared his and the league's concept of a future government for Pakistan. It provided for (1) federal parliamentary government with free and regular elections, (2) federal control of foreign affairs and defense only, (3) separate currency or fiscal accounts for East Pakistan to control the movement of capital from east to west, (4) all power of taxation at the provincial level, with the federal government subsisting on grants from the provinces, (5) the right of each federating unit to enter into foreign trade agreements on its own, and (6) the right of each unit to raise its own militia. Clearly these demands, if enacted, would reduce Pakistan to a confederation and perhaps destroy any semblance of unity altogether.

On March 25, 1969, Ayub Khan resigned the presidency and was replaced by General Agha Muhammad Yahya Khan, who reimposed martial law. Yahya, however, took a number of steps in an attempt to mollify the public. He abolished the system of basic electorates. To placate the west, he abolished the one unit of West Pakistan and restored the four separate provinces. For the east he ended parity and stated that elections would be conducted on the basis of population. He announced elections to parliament and the provincial assemblies for December 1970. The Awami League won 160 of the 162 parliamentary seats from East Pakistan—a clear majority of the 300 seats—but none of the 138 seats from West Pakistan (Baxter and Rahman 2003, 90). The largest party in West Pakistan was the Pakistan People's Party led by Zulfiqar Ali Bhutto. Yahya could not accept a government dominated by the Awami League. Talks among Yahya, Mujib, and Bhutto did not reach a solution acceptable to the Awami League.

CONTEXT AND PROCESS OF REVOLUTION

Following the breakdown of the talks among Yahya, Mujib, and Bhutto in the early months of 1971, demonstrations against the government broke out in Dhaka and other cities of East Pakistan. During the talks, Yahya had referred to Mujib as the future prime minister of Pakistan, and demonstrators demanded that this statement be carried out—that Mujib be made prime minister. When this did not happen, the demonstrators increasingly demanded that East Pakistan secede from Pakistan and become the new state of Bangladesh ("the land of the Bengalis"). Pakistan began to reinforce its rather small military establishment in East Pakistan but soon ran into difficulties. India refused to allow Pakistani aircraft to fly over Indian territory, which meant that they now had to refuel in Sri Lanka, and the route became much longer.

During the evening and night of March 25, Pakistani forces struck against the demonstrators, especially on the campus of Dhaka University. A large number of faculty members, administrators, and students were killed. Mujib was captured by the Pakistanis and sent to West Pakistan to stand trial. A few Awami League leaders who escaped capture fled to a village on the India–East Pakistan border, which they renamed Mujibnagar, and set up a government that was later relocated to Calcutta. A declaration of Bangladeshi independence was made over a radio station in Chittagong by Major Ziaur Rahman, a future president of Bangladesh and one of the heroes of the Bangladeshi conflict.

Resistance to the Pakistan army was led by Bangladeshi officers and defectors from the Pakistan army stationed in Bangladesh; by the East Pakistan Rifles, a border security force that was renamed the Bangladesh Rifles; by the police; and especially by individuals, often students, who assembled themselves into revolutionary formations. As the struggle continued, India began to supply equipment and provide training as well as giving hospitality in Calcutta to the interim government. India's involvement in the conflict was influenced by a number of factors. Many East Pakistanis had fled into India's West Bengal territory creating an enormous refugee problem likely to continue until the strife ended. Furthermore, the transformation of East Pakistan into the independent nation of Bangladesh, with the aid of India, would

A crowd cheers a truckload of guerrillas in Dhaka after the revolution which transformed East Pakistan into Bangladesh succeeded, December 18, 1971. (Bettmann/Corbis)

likely reduce the threat to India from the remainder of Pakistan and ensure India's dominance in the region. Finally, India's armed forces, equipped with weapons from the Soviet Union, was generally thought to be superior to Pakistan's both numerically and in terms of armament.

Opposing the Mukti Bahini ("Freedom Fighters"), as the forces against Pakistani rule became known, were not only the Pakistan army but a number of Urdu-speaking residents of East Pakistan known generally as Biharis, since many of them had fled eastward from the Indian state of Bihar at the independence of India in 1947. Many Biharis were organized by the Pakistan army into groups known as *razakars* ("volunteers"). According to some accounts, not fully verified, many of the most heinous atrocities against Bengali speakers were undertaken by *razakars*.

Except for India, international support was generally lacking. The United States and most of its allies called for an end to hostilities and a compromise solution to the problem. Initially, the United States continued to deliver contracted military goods to Pakistan, but no new contracts were made.

One reason for the position of the United States was undoubtedly the then well-kept secret of Kissinger's visit to China via Islamabad. The Soviet Union supported India's position, which culminated in the Indo-Soviet treaty of 1971 that brought the two states much closer together.

Indian troops entered East Pakistani territory in late November or early December (the exact date is uncertain, since Indian forces had probably entered initially to assist in training). The fate of the Pakistan army was then sealed, and it surrendered to Indian forces on December 16, 1971, at Dhaka. The independence of Bangladesh was complete.

IMPACTS

The secession of Bangladesh from Pakistan created a new state. Many of the Biharis fled to India and beyond to Pakistan. The population is described as 98 percent Bengali; the remaining 2 percent were Urdu-speaking Biharis and tribal groups (Baxter and Rahman 2003, 134).

In Pakistan, immediate changes followed the independence of Bangladesh. Yahya resigned as president and designated Bhutto as his replacement. Bhutto promised that elections would be scheduled and that a new constitution would be formulated.

Although India and countries of the Soviet Bloc quickly recognized the independence of Bangladesh, other states did not act rapidly. Observers in Bangladesh and elsewhere saw American policy during the conflict as "tilted" toward Pakistan. Although American relief aid came promptly after the conflict ended, formal recognition did not come until February 1972.

Recognition by Islamic states was also delayed. The Organization of the Islamic Conference, founded in 1972, held its second summit in Lahore, Pakistan, in February 1974. Bhutto did not invite Bangladesh to attend. When the summit was convened, other Muslim states, in deference to Pakistan, had not accorded recognition to Bangladesh. As the delegates (almost all heads of state or government) assembled, several objected to the absence of the third largest Muslim state (after Indonesia and Pakistan). Leading the objectors was King Hussein of Jordan. Bhutto yielded, and an aircraft was sent to Dhaka to bring Mujib and his delegation to Lahore. Pakistan and the other Muslim states then accorded diplomatic recognition to Bangladesh. (Earlier, Pakistan had declared that it would break diplomatic relations with any state that recognized Bangladesh as independent, but this threat obviously proved to be impractical and was not implemented.)

The close relations between Pakistan and China, both antagonistic toward India, permitted Pakistan to use the Chinese veto in the UN Security Council to deny Bangladesh membership in the United Nations, and China did use its veto in 1972 and 1973. Nevertheless, Bangladesh joined a number of the specialized agencies of the United Nations. Since Pakistan had recognized Bangladesh in February, China did not exercise its veto in 1974, and Bangladesh was admitted to the United Nations that year.

Thus by the end of 1974, Bangladesh was fully admitted into the community of nations. At the United Nations, it has been a member of the Security Council, elected in 1978 and 2000, and supplied a president of the General Assembly in 1986. Bangladesh has also regularly supplied forces to United Nations peacekeeping operations.

Since its independence, Bangladesh has been a major recipient of economic assistance and will remain so for many years to come. It is a member of the Group of 77 (now 132), a consortium of Third World countries seeking economic cooperation. It is also a member of all of the economic, technical, and cultural organizations associated with the United Nations.

Bangladesh spearheaded the founding of the South Asian Association for Regional Cooperation, a group designed to discuss and, if possible, implement policies that would tie the member countries more closely together in such varied matters as water, technology, trade, and agriculture. Political matters, such as the dispute between India and Pakistan over Kashmir, are excluded from consideration. Others members include India, Pakistan, Sri Lanka, Nepal, Bhutan, and the Maldives. The concept of cooperation was initiated by Bangladesh president Ziaur Rahman, but the treaty was not concluded until December 1985, after Rahman's death. Despite the exclusion of political issues, meetings were postponed, but not completely prevented, as a result of India-Pakistan animosity.

Following the termination of the Bangladesh independence conflict, a number of issues required immediate attention. Both Bengali and Pakistani citizens—including military and civil service personnel, business people, and students— were now stranded in the "other" country. Bangladesh and India both held Pakistani prisoners of war, and Bangladesh wanted to try the Pakistan military personnel it held for war crimes. India convened a tripartite meeting on these issues, and the parties agreed to permit the movement of the personnel held to their countries of origin. Bangladesh dropped its demand for trials. A dispute between India and Bangladesh over the division of the waters of the Ganges River remains, although a treaty was signed on the subject in 1996.

Bangladesh has requested an apology from Pakistan for the events of 1971, but successive governments in Pakistan refused to do so. But in July 2002, President Pervez Musharraf, visiting Dhaka, expressed his regret over the events of 1971.

PEOPLE AND ORGANIZATIONS

Awami League

Founded in 1949, it opened its membership to non-Muslims, contravening the membership policy of the Muslim League. Its principal founder was Husain Shahid Suhrawardy, but he was assisted by others, including Sheikh Mujibur Rahman. In the first post-independence election to the provincial assembly, the Awami League formed the United Front with the Krishak Praja Party and trounced the Muslim League. Although the United Front was not stable, segments of it ruled until the declaration of martial law by President Iskander Mirza in collaboration with General Mohammad Ayub Khan in 1958. When elections were again held in 1970, the Awami League took the majority of seats in East Pakistan but won none in West Pakistan. It then demanded that it be allowed to form the government of Pakistan. The demand was rejected and demonstrations erupted, resulting in an attack in 1971 by the Pakistan army. In independent Bangladesh, the Awami League formed the first government under Mujib, which ended with Mujib's assassination in 1975. The league did not take power again until 1996, under the leadership of Mujib's daughter, Hasina Wajid. She and the league were defeated in the 2001 election.

Ayub Khan, Mohammad (1907–1974)

Pakistani military officer who, as chief of the army staff, governed under martial law beginning in October 1958 and declared himself president. Opposition in the late 1960s to his authoritarian administration from a number of population sectors, coupled with growing popular unrest in East Pakistan, and his ill health, led to his resignation of the presidency in March 1969.

Bangladesh Nationalist Party (BNP)

Founded in 1978 as a political vehicle for President Ziaur Rahman ("Zia"). Following Zia's assassination in 1981, both the leadership of the party and the presidency were assumed by Abdus Sattar, who was overthrown by General Husain Muhammad Ershad in 1982. The leadership then fell to Zia's widow, Khaleda Zia. The party was key in the overthrow of Ershad in 1990 and won the 1991 election. The center-right BNP lost in 1996 to the Awami League but regained power in the election of 2001.

Biharis

Term used to describe Muslim Urdu-speaking refugees from India, most often from the state of Bihar, who fled to East Bengal (now Bangladesh). Some opposed the Mukti Bahini during 1971, some returned to India, and a few remain in Bangladesh. Those remaining are generally discriminated against, especially in employment.

East Bengal

The official name of what is now Bangladesh from the independence and partition of India in 1947 until 1955, when the name was changed to East Pakistan.

Ershad, Husain Muhammad (Born 1930)

President of Bangladesh through a coup, 1982–1990.

Hamoodur Rahman Commission

A group appointed in 1972 by the government of Pakistan to investigate the actions of the military during its 1971 attack on demonstrators. The commission sharply criticized the tactics and strategy of the military and its treatment of the East Pakistan citizenry. The secret report was leaked in December 2000.

Jama'at-i-Islam

A Muslim fundamentalist political party that opposed the Mukti Bahini. In post-independence elections it fared poorly until the 1996 election, when it allied with Khaleda Zia's BNP. In the 2001 elections it won 18 of the 300 parliamentary seats.

Khaleda Zia (Born 1945)

Widow of Ziaur Rahman, she assumed the leadership of the BNP on May 10, 1984. In the election in 1991 following the fall of Ershad, she became prime minister. Losing in 1996 to the Awami League, she returned to power in 2001.

Krishak Sramik Party (Peasants and Workers Party)

Headed by Fazlul Haq, it was a resurrection of the pre-Indian-independence Krishak Praja Party (Peasants and People's Party). It joined the Awami League in 1954 in the United Front to defeat the Muslim League, but it did not survive Haq's death in 1962.

Mujibur Rahman, Sheikh ("Mujib") (1920–1975)

A founding member of the Awami League, he led the party during the Ayub period and spelled out his Six Points before Ayub fell. He led the league to victory in the 1970 election. At the outbreak of the conflict of 1971, he was captured by the Pakistanis and held in West Pakistan. Released in December 1971, he returned to Dhaka as prime minister, then became president in 1975. He was assassinated August 15, 1975, by disgruntled army officers.

Mukti Bahini

The Bengali name for the freedom fighters in the 1971 conflict.

Razakars

Persons living in East Pakistan who opposed the break-up of Pakistan. The group comprised Urdu-speaking residents and some Bengalis who held that view. Among them were members of the Jama'at-i-Islam.

Sattar, Abdus (1906–1985)

The successor (1981–1982) to Ziaur Rahman as president of Bangladesh. He was overthrown by Husain Muhammad Ershad.

South Asian Association for Regional Cooperation (SAARC)

Founded in 1985 at the initiative of Ziaur Rahman, it brings together the seven South Asian states to discuss matters (other than political matters) that might tie the states more closely together.

Wajid, Sheikh Hasina (Born 1947)

Daughter of Sheikh Mujibur Rahman, she became leader of the Awami League in 1981 and served as prime minister from 1996 to 2001.

Yahya Khan, Agha Muhammad (1917–1980)

President of Pakistan who succeeded Ayub Khan in 1969. He held the office during the Bangladeshi rebellion. When it ended in 1971, he resigned the presidency to Zulfiqar Ali Bhutto.

Ziaur Rahman (1936–1981)

In the turmoil following the assassination of Mujibur Rahman, he emerged as the leader in November 1975. He assumed the title of president in April 1977 and held the post until his assassination on May 30, 1981. He was succeeded by Abdus Sattar.

Craig Baxter

See Also Indian Independence Movement; Pakistan Independence and the Partition of India; War and Revolution

References and Further Readings
Bangladesh Documents. 1971. New Delhi: Ministry of External Affairs.
Baxter, Craig. 1997. *Bangladesh: From a Nation to a State.* Boulder, CO: Westview Press.
———, and Syedur Rahman. 2003. *Historical Dictionary of Bangladesh,* 2nd edition. Lanham, MD: Scarecrow Press.
Eaton, Richard M. 1993. *The Rise of Islam and the Bengal Frontier, 1204 to 1760.* Berkeley: University of California Press.
Feldman, Herbert. 1975. *The End and the Beginning: Pakistan, 1969–1971.* London: Oxford University Press.
Imam, Jahanara. 1989. *Of Blood and Fire: The Untold Story of Bangladesh's War of Independence.* Trans. Mustafizur Rahman. New Delhi: Sterling Publishers.
Muhith, A. M. A. 1992. *Bangladesh: Emergence of a Nation.* Dhaka, Bangladesh: University Press.
Shelly [Shelley], Mizanur Rahman. 1979. *Emergence of a New Nation in a Multi-Polar World: Bangladesh.* Dhaka, Bangladesh: University Press.
Sisson, Richard, and Leo Rose. 1990. *War and Secession: Pakistan, India and the Creation of Bangladesh.* Berkeley: University of California Press.
Zaheer, Hasan. 1994. *The Separation of East Pakistan: The Rise and Realization of Bengali Muslim Nationalism.* New York: Oxford University Press.

C

Cambodian Revolution

CHRONOLOGY

9th–14th centuries	Khmer Angkor kingdom, centered in north-western Cambodia.
Late 14th century	Angkor occupied by Siam (Thailand), but Cambodia retains its independence.
Mid 19th century	Wars between Thailand and Vietnam, waged in Cambodia, severely weaken the small Buddhist kingdom.
1863	Cambodia's King Norodom permits Cambodia to become a French protectorate, later part of French Indochina.
1945	Japanese imprison French throughout Indochina and force King Norodom Sihanouk to declare independence. By the end of the year, however, French forces re-occupy Cambodia.
1953	Facing growing pressure from Sihanouk's normally friendly regime, France grants independence to Cambodia.
1955	Cambodia becomes a constitutional monarchy; Sihanouk abdicates the throne, and his new political movement wins all the seats in the national election.
1965	Scared that Vietnam War will spill into Cambodia, Sihanouk breaks off relations with the United States.
1969	Sihanouk re-establishes relations with the United States; the "secret" bombing of Cambodian border areas begins.
1970	General Lon Nol overthrows the Sihanouk government and forms an alliance with the United States against Communist-led Vietnamese and Cambodian forces. Sihanouk responds by joining a Khmer National United front with Lon Nol's enemies.
1975	On April 17, Communist-led Cambodian forces, the Khmer Rouge ("Red Khmer"), win the war and seize Phnom Penh. Within twenty-four hours they force all residents into the countryside and establish a repressive Maoist regime in Cambodia.
1976	Democratic Kampuchea promulgates a constitution, assumes Cambodia's seat at the United Nations.
1977	Border conflicts break out, followed by all-out war between Cambodia and Vietnam.

91

1978	Vietnamese forces invade Cambodia, capture Phnom Penh, oust the Khmer Rouge regime, and install a new government, the Peoples' Republic of Kampuchea, led by pro-Vietnamese Cambodian Communists under Heng Samrin.
1984	Hun Sen, 31, becomes prime minister of Cambodia and holds the office, with one brief exception, for the next twenty years and beyond.
1989	Vietnamese troops withdraw from Cambodia; the Cambodian Communist Party renounces Marxism-Leninism; the country is renamed the State of Cambodia.
1991	Paris Peace Accords establish framework for UN interregnum, UN-supervised elections.
1993	UN-sponsored democratic elections are held in Cambodia. Hun Sen's Cambodian Peoples' Party, formerly the Communist Party, loses election but forces the winners into a coalition dominated by the CPP. Sihanouk is crowned king again.
2004	Sihanouk abdicates.

INTRODUCTION

From 1945 until the late 1980s, Cambodia was a theater of war. From 1975 to 1979 the country was governed by a Marxist-Leninist regime whose fiercely utopian policies and actions led directly or indirectly to the deaths of over 1.5 million people— one in seven Cambodians. During these years, Cambodia made war against Vietnam on two occasions. Cambodia's Revolution, which arguably began in 1951, ended in 1990, when its ruling Communist Party abandoned Marxism-Leninism, but sporadic fighting continued into the end of the decade.

BACKGROUND: CULTURE AND HISTORY

The majority of Cambodia's people consider themselves to be Khmer. Their culture reflects both Hindu and Buddhist influences. The Khmer established the Angkor empire, which lasted from the ninth to the fourteenth centuries and included most of eastern Thailand and southern parts of present-day Vietnam. In 1863 a weakened Cambodian kingdom, following wars with neighboring Thailand and Vietnam, agreed to become a French "protectorate," in effect accepting colonial status in return for French military protection.

Concerned with generating profits by producing products for the world market, the French established rubber plantations in Cambodia and encouraged Cambodian farmers to grow rice for export. Vietnamese were brought into the country to work on the rubber plantations, because the French believed they were better workers than the Cambodians. Vietnamese often served as lower-level colonial officials while Chinese immigrants came to play significant roles in Cambodia's economy, some as money lenders, provoking resentment among many rural Khmer.

During World War II, the Japanese occupied Cambodia. In March 1945 they captured and locked up French forces throughout Indochina, forcing Prince Norodom Sihanouk, a member of the royal family whom the French had chosen to be king, to declare Cambodia independent. But after Japan's defeat in World War II a few months later, the French re-occupied the country and re-established their protectorate.

The struggle for Indochina's independence from France erupted into full-scale war in November 1946, spearheaded by the Vietnamese Communists. For the next eight years, most of the fighting took place in northern Vietnam, and very little spilled over into Cambodia. By 1948, however, the Vietnamese Communists, leading the Viet Minh (League for Vietnamese Independence), a coalition of pro-independence groups, dominated the struggle throughout Vietnam. They took command of the resistance in Cambodia and Laos without disclosing their Communist allegiance. The Indochina Communist Party (ICP) (at times known as the Vietnamese Communist Party) had announced its dissolution in 1945. Its leaders hoped by this stratagem to encourage Vietnamese, Lao, and Khmer to join a united, apparently non-Communist struggle. In fact, the Viet Minh maintained tight control of all three resistance movements. In 1951, the Vietnamese founded the Communist-led Khmer Peoples' Revolutionary Party (KPRP), based in eastern Cambodia. Its statutes, written in Vietnamese, were translated into Khmer. Its leaders were Cambodians who had been born and raised in southern Vietnam. The party's anti-French platform, its vague promises of empowerment, and its warlike agenda attracted considerable peasant support. Hundreds of young Cambodians received military and political training as the war dragged on. Their role was to provide logistical support to Viet Minh forces in southern Vietnam.

At the Geneva Conference in 1954, KPRP troops, unlike their counterparts in Laos and Vietnam, were awarded no regroupment zone. Fearing arrest, about a thousand party members and sympathizers sought asylum in North Vietnam. They expected to return home after the Communists won the elections called for at the Geneva Conference. These elections never took place, however, and most of the exiled cadre remained in Vietnam until the early 1970s. The year before the Geneva Conference, Cambodia was finally granted its independence. Then in 1955, Prince Sihanouk abdicated in favor of his father and transformed the country into a constitutional monarchy with an elected national assembly. He helped found the Buddhist-influenced Popular Socialist Community political party, which won a large majority of the popular vote in the election later that year, and Sihanouk became prime minister (Harff 1991, 220).

CONTEXT AND PROCESS OF REVOLUTION

Several middle-class Cambodians, while studying in France in the late 1940s, had joined the French Communist Party. Returning home, they began to work publicly as schoolteachers or as government officials and clandestinely for the Communist cause. Several of these men and women, including Saloth Sar (who later used the pseudonym Pol Pot), Khieu Samphan, Ieng Sary, and Son Sen, occupied powerful positions when the so-called Khmer Rouge or Red Khmers came to power in 1975. These men and women formed the nucleus of the clandestine urban Communist movement. The movement suffered from police harassment, poor morale, and a lack of guidance from its mentors in Hanoi. It was also hamstrung by Sihanouk's popularity and by its failure to articulate a revolutionary agenda.

At a secret meeting in September 1960 in Phnom Penh, two dozen Communist leaders hammered out a revolutionary program for the Cambodian Communist movement and gave the party a new name—the Workers' Party of Kampuchea (WPK). Two years later, the secretary of the WPK, Tou Samouth, was abducted and killed by Sihanouk's police. Saloth Sar took Tou Samouth's place. Fearing arrest, he fled the capital in 1963 with several colleagues and found refuge in a Vietnamese Communist encampment on the Vietnam-Cambodian border.

In mid 1965 he was summoned to Hanoi in North Vietnam. He traveled there on foot, in a journey that took several months. North Vietnamese authorities wanted to revive the networks of support that the KPRP had given the Viet Minh during the First Indochina War. When Sar arrived in Hanoi, his opposite number, Le Duan, criticized the manifesto that the WPK had drawn up in 1960. The document called for the liberation of Cambodia from "feudalism." It failed to mention Marxism-Leninism, solidarity among Communist parties, or the fighting elsewhere in Indochina. Le Duan chastised Sar for over an hour. He called the manifesto naive, inept, and theoretically unsound. A Vietnamese document reporting the encounter noted that at the conclusion of Le Duan's tirade, Saloth Sar said absolutely nothing. His concealed resentment is easy to imagine.

After several months in Hanoi, Saloth Sar traveled to China. His visit was kept secret, because the existence of the WPK was still concealed and because the Chinese were allied with Sihanouk's regime.

Saloth Sar's visit to China led him to loosen his dependence on Vietnam. In June 1966 he moved his headquarters into the forested northeastern province of Ratanakiri. Although Vietnamese Communist troops were stationed nearby, the Khmer Rouge leaders no longer lived in a Vietnamese military camp. Over the next four years, isolated from developments in Cambodia and elsewhere, they cobbled together a visionary, Chinese-inspired program that they hoped to set in motion when they came to power. They kept their existence secret and never publicized their plans for the country.

The Second Indochina War changed character after 1965. Hundreds of thousands of American troops landed in southern Vietnam, the North Vietnamese army became heavily involved in fighting there, and tens of thousands of Vietnamese Communist troops sought shelter in Cambodia with Sihanouk's tacit permission. As the war intensified, a Communist-backed uprising in northwestern Cambodia was brutally suppressed by government forces.

Conditions in Cambodia deteriorated in early 1968, when the Khmer Rouge inaugurated armed struggle against Sihanouk's regime. Students and intellectuals were already disillusioned with the prince, and many of them were more impressed by developments in China than by Sihanouk's ramshackle "Buddhist Socialism" or his ambiguous neutral stance. In the late 1960s, dozens of these young people trekked into northeastern Cambodia or to other secret bases to join the Khmer Rouge. Many of them were purged in 1977 when the WPK believed that its more educated members were plotting against it.

America's "secret" bombing of Vietnamese sanctuaries in Cambodia, which began in March 1969, pushed Vietnamese Communist troops deeper into Cambodia. Over the next fourteen months, the U.S. air force flew thousands of sorties over Cambodia and dropped over 100,000 tons of bombs on suspected Vietnamese troop concentrations, camps, and supply routes (Chandler 2000, 207).

By the end of 1969, as U.S. president Richard Nixon began withdrawing American troops from Vietnam, Cambodia's neutrality was in tatters and Sihanouk's reign was limping to a close. In March 1970, when the prince was traveling abroad, the National Assembly voted to remove him from office as chief of state. Sihanouk's cousin, Prince Sisowath Sirik Matak, a pro-Western entrepreneur, was a moving force behind the coup. U.S. support came swiftly, in part because

Matak persuaded Cambodia's military commander, the mystical patriot Lon Nol, to join the coup. Lon Nol brought the army officer corps along with him and took Cambodia into an ill-starred military alliance with the United States.

Sihanouk heard about the coup when he was visiting the U.S.S.R. Proceeding to Beijing, he was persuaded by China's premier, Zhou Enlai, to form a united front with the Vietnamese Communists and the Khmer Rouge. Sihanouk wanted to avenge the coup and remove the new, pro-American regime in Phnom Penh. The decisions reached in Beijing swept Cambodia into the Second Indochina War. In April 1970, four North Vietnamese divisions entered the country to secure supply routes and to fend off Cambodian forces. Lon Nol ordered all Vietnamese units to leave the country within forty-eight hours. None of them did.

Nixon was convinced that Cambodia was a key to America's withdrawal from Vietnam. He apparently believed that destroying Vietnamese bases and military supplies there would help protect the U.S. supported South Vietnamese regime and facilitate the withdrawal of U.S. forces. However, he overestimated Lon Nol's intelligence and military strength. He also underestimated Vietnam's staying power and the rapidly improving fighting capacities of the Khmer Rouge. By August the Lon Nol government and its army of 50,000 men controlled less than half the country, while Khmer Rouge forces were estimated to be almost as numerous. Two disastrous offensives in late 1970 and the middle of 1971 against Communist forces decimated Lon Nol's poorly led and badly trained army and its last offensives of the war.

In early 1972 the military situation stabilized somewhat because of continuous U.S. bombardment of Vietnamese supply lines and troop concentrations. In Phnom Penh, Lon Nol used his flagging energies to stay in power and keep his opponents off balance. His confidence in the United States and the confidence of the United States in his abilities as a wartime leader were both tragically misplaced.

In the meantime, behind the shield formed by the Vietnamese army, the Khmer Rouge gained battle experience, recruited new members, and trained leaders in a rough-and-ready, utopian form of Socialism. Some men and women joined the movement thinking that they could restore Sihanouk to power. Some joined because they were disillusioned with the corruption and incompetence of the Lon Nol regime. Others joined because U.S. bombing angered them, and still others because they were attracted by the Communists' social agenda, which promised to overturn centuries of injustice inflicted on the rural poor. The word *Communist* was never mentioned outside the party's inner circles, however, probably because Saloth Sar and his colleagues wanted to stress the nationalist fervor of their movement.

In 1971–1972, tensions developed between the Khmer Rouge and their Vietnamese allies. By this time several hundred Cambodian Communists had come down the Ho Chi Minh Trail from Hanoi, where they had been living since the 1950s, to fight alongside the Khmer Rouge. The so-called Hanoi Khmer were suspected of pro-Vietnamese bias. None of them was given large responsibilities, and many were secretly put to death. As the Khmer Rouge forces grew larger, better trained, and more independent, quarrels with the Vietnamese over commanders, tactics, and equipment often degenerated into pitched battles.

Vietnam withdrew most of its troops from Cambodia at the end of 1972 as part of the cease-fire agreements reached in Paris between Vietnam and the United States. Lon Nol agreed to the cease-fire. But the Khmer Rouge leadership refused to do so, probably because they feared that the Khmer Republic might strike a deal whereby Sihanouk could return to Cambodia to head an ostensibly neutral state. The Khmer Rouge leadership was now in the hands of those who, like Saloth Sar, had remained behind in Cambodia in the late 1950s. These men and women had their own Maoist-inspired revolutionary agenda. They were deeply hostile to Vietnam. They saw the cease-fire and the Vietnamese withdrawal as deliberate betrayals of the Cambodian Revolution and as part of a pattern on the part of the Vietnamese to undermine and destroy the Cambodian Revolution. In political meetings, Communist leaders began referring to Vietnam as Cambodia's "number one enemy." Freed at last from Vietnamese scrutiny and advice, the Khmer Rouge began in 1973 to introduce harsh measures, including forced labor and collectivization, in the areas under their control.

The war now pitted Khmer against Khmer and entered an agonizing phase. The Khmer Republic controlled a quarter of the country, but 60 percent of the population had sought refuge in government-controlled zones. In 1973 and 1974 the situation for everyone in the country grew steadily worse. Conditions for combatants were horrific. Fighting often took place at close quarters, and neither side allowed prisoners to survive. American carpet-bombing of the countryside around Phnom Penh postponed a Khmer Rouge assault on the capital. But the campaign inflicted thousands of civilian casualties in a country where hardly any U.S. military were at risk and where no U.S. economic interests were involved. Opposition to the bombing in the U.S. Congress led to its suspension in August 1973.

Khmer Rouge assaults on the capital in 1974 were beaten back, but conditions in the government-controlled area throughout Cambodia got worse and worse. Refugees and long-term residents alike suffered from runaway inflation, unemployment, malnutrition, and disease. They correctly perceived the government as corrupt and powerless. Many of them hoped that the invisible and mysterious Khmer Rouge would win the war quickly and deliver peace and social services to all Khmers, and allow the refugees to go home.

On January 1, 1975, the Khmer Rouge opened their final assault on Phnom Penh with a rocket and artillery barrage. Lon Nol left Cambodia in tears on April 1 and died in the United States nine years later. On April 17 Cambodian Communist forces entered Phnom Penh and ended the five-year war. Most residents of the city welcomed them, but the solemn-looking, heavily armed young men and women marching along the avenues were unresponsive and hostile. Few of them had ever seen a city, and they had been told Phnom Penh was filled with enemies of the revolution who deserved no mercy.

The residents of Phnom Penh and other cities received none. Within twenty-four hours, the entire population of the capital was ordered to leave and to take up residence in the countryside. Two million people headed out of town on foot in the hottest month of the year. In the exodus, perhaps as many as 20,000 died. By turning everyone into agricultural workers, the Khmer Rouge had solved the "urban problem." They had also abolished Cambodia's bourgeoisie with a suddenness that delighted Maoist sympathizers throughout the world.

Over the next few months, Communist leaders were hidden from view. They referred to themselves in public as the "Higher Organization" (angkar loeu). Working with trusted cadre and military commanders trained at frequent political meetings, angkar loeu set in motion a radical restructuring of Cambodia that had no precedent in Cambodia's past. Its leaders boasted that it followed no foreign models. Immediately private property, markets, and money were abolished. Schools, law courts, libraries, hospitals, and places of worship were closed. Overland communications with Laos, Thailand, and Vietnam were shut down. Extra-marital sex was prohibited. So were radios, jewelry, Western-style haircuts, and any printed material. Everyone was made to wear peasant dress. Urban life, Buddhism, and the visible apparatus of government ceased to exist overnight.

For the remainder of 1975, Cambodia had no name, no ministries, and no flag. In the first months of the new regime, thousands of former Lon Nol soldiers were put to death, and so were hundreds of men and women suspected of being "bourgeois" and therefore enemies of the state. The revolution was being waged, spokesmen asserted, to end centuries of exploitation. After April 17, 1975, there would be no more rich or poor, and no more exploiters or exploited people in the country.

Sharp differences continued to exist in the new society. Those who felt themselves to have been exploited in the past became exploiters. Men and women who had lived in areas under Khmer Rouge control before April 1975 were called "base people." Most of them were treated relatively well and were allowed to remain in their homes. Exiles from the cities, however, were called "April 17 people" or "new people."

They were considered hostile to revolutionary ideas and were treated harshly.

Saloth Sar and his colleagues took office under heavy guard in the abandoned capital. In January 1976, a constitution was promulgated and the state announced its new name: Democratic Kampuchea (DK). National elections took place three months later. Only "base people" were allowed to vote, and slates of candidates, named by angkar, were divided among "peasants," "soldiers," and "industrial workers." Among the candidates drawn from "rubber plantation workers" was someone called "Pol Pot," who was later named DK's prime minister. It was over a year before outside observers were able to identify "Pol Pot" as Saloth Sar. When the new government took power, Prince Sihanouk, who had returned home in mid 1975 and had been nominally in charge of the country, was placed under house arrest in Phnom Penh, where he remained until the last days of the DK regime.

IMPACTS

The constitution and the elections were public-relations exercises intended for overseas consumption. Cambodia's national assembly convened for a single day and then permanently adjourned. Instead, Pol Pot and his trusted colleagues wanted to set in motion a set of utopian policies aimed at achieving Socialism more rapidly and more thoroughly than it had been achieved anywhere in the world. In this headlong rush to collective action, perhaps as many as two million Cambodians died from malnutrition, overwork, untreated or mis-treated diseases, and executions.

The Khmer Rouge leadership believed, like Mao Zedong, that the energies released by the "liberation" of peasants and workers would overcome shortfalls in raw materials, modern equipment, rational planning, and expertise. Cambodia had just emerged from five years of grueling warfare. What remained of its agricultural workforce was exhausted. Its road network and irrigation works had been severely damaged. Hundreds of thousands of draft animals needed for plowing had been killed. Over a million city dwellers with no experience at farming had been thrown into the countryside without adequate food or shelter. Probably unaware that China's Great Leap Forward in the late 1950s and early 1960s had been a colossal failure, the Khmer Rouge chose the same name, some of the same goals, and much of the same methodology for their own revolutionary agenda.

The DK's "great leap" was enshrined in a slapdash four-year plan that sought to double Cambodia's output of rice in order to earn money from exports, which would pay for industrialization. The national goal of three tons of rice per hectare was nearly three times as high as average yields had been in pre-revolutionary times. The program was a disaster.

Surpluses of rice, where they existed, were siphoned off by the state; in other places, the rice needed to feed people was sent to government warehouses. The people who had grown the rice starved. Ill-conceived and poorly constructed dams and irrigation schemes claimed many lives through overwork and often wrought ecological havoc. Thousands of Khmer succumbed to amateur medical treatment meted out by untrained, self-confident adolescents. Perhaps 200,000 died in captivity or were executed as "enemies of the state," often on trumped up charges. Toward the end of 1976, a series of far-reaching purges began to burn through party ranks. The written "confessions" of over 5,000 of these men and women have survived and provide grim documentation of the regime's far-reaching paranoia.

As DK came under increasing internal pressure, its leaders became convinced that the Vietnamese were undermining the revolution and were working to overthrow the regime. In 1976–1977, DK launched punitive raids across the border into Vietnam and secretly executed the few Vietnamese who still remained in Cambodia. In October 1977, Pol Pot visited China and, for the first time, announced the existence of the Cambodian Communist Party. In Beijing he sought Chinese assistance for what he considered to be an inevitable war with Vietnam, which Chinese authorities considered to have entered the Soviet camp. China sent military equipment but no volunteers, and it did little to encourage DK's aggressive stance.

Soon after Pol Pot returned home, Vietnamese forces launched a major attack on the eastern part of Cambodia, inaugurating the Third Indochina War. The troops remained in the region until January 1978. When the Vietnamese withdrew, they took with them several thousand Khmer who feared the wrath of the DK regime. Some of these men were veterans of the Communist movement in the 1950s and were relatively friendly toward Vietnam. In February 1978 DK launched a purge of the Eastern Zone, accusing party leaders and soldiers there of failing to defeat the Vietnamese and of collaborating with them. Thousands of these people, most of them soldiers, were brought into a secret interrogation center in Phnom Penh and put to death. Fearing for their lives, a few high-ranking Eastern Zone Cambodian Communist leaders, and hundreds of their followers, defected to Vietnam, where they were formed into a "liberation front" by the Vietnamese, alongside previous refugees.

On Christmas eve 1978, Vietnamese forces launched a blitzkrieg attack into Cambodia on several fronts, using tanks, over 100,000 infantry, and a sustained aerial bombardment. They claimed publicly that the troops in the invasion were those of the newly formed liberation front. Although DK units fought bravely, they were no match for the Vietnamese. On January 5, Sihanouk was released from house arrest and flown to Beijing, along with the staff of the Chinese embassy. A day later, Pol Pot fled by helicopter to Thailand. Vietnamese troops and unarmed Khmer auxiliaries entered Phnom Penh on January 7. But tens of thousands DK troops retreated to the northwest and managed to regroup along the Thai border. There the Thai, with Chinese help, formed them into a guerrilla force. For another fifteen years they were a thorn in the side of successive Phnom Penh regimes.

DK officials, policies, and institutions disappeared almost overnight. The new regime installed by the Vietnamese called itself the Peoples' Republic of Kampuchea (PRK). Its leaders were Khmer Rouge defectors and Cambodians who had sought refuge in Vietnam in the 1950s. Over 100,000 Vietnamese troops remained in Cambodia for the remainder of the 1980s. They fought DK units along the Thai border, helped train a new Cambodian army, and probably kept the Khmer Rouge from regaining power.

Despite appealing social reforms, political controls in PRK were severe. For most of the decade, a single, Marxist-Leninist party governed the country. Vietnam's occupation of the country was part of a long-term strategic plan to join the components of French Indochina into a Vietnamese-dominated federation. Because the DK held on to Cambodia's seat at the UN—the only government in exile to do so—the PRK was cut off from international assistance aid except for what could be provided by the Soviet Bloc. In 1989, as the Cold War sputtered to a close, Vietnam withdrew its last troops from Cambodia. The country changed its name to the State of Cambodia, while keeping the same, largely Vietnamese-appointed leadership in place. The Communist Party renounced Marxism-Leninism but remained in place. A key figure in both the pre- and post-1989 regimes was Hun Sen (b. 1952), a former Khmer Rouge military commander who had fled to Vietnam in 1977. Hun Sen was dynamic, adaptable, brutal, and astute. He used his talents as a "strong man" to lead Cambodia into the twenty-first century.

In 1991, under agreements reached in Paris, Cambodia's foreign patrons withdrew their support from warring Cambodian factions and drafted a peace agreement that placed Cambodia under a UN protectorate while it prepared for pluralistic politics and acceptance by the international community. In effect, the powerful patrons who had kept Cambodia at war for almost half a century walked away from the country and decided that it should solve its own problems, aided in the process by massive infusions of foreign aid.

The UN protectorate in Cambodia was the most expensive UN operation to date, and it was a mixed success. On

Vietnamese soldiers leave Pursat, Cambodia, on September 22, 1989. The Vietnamese invasion and occupation of Cambodia from December 1978 to September 1989 drove out the genocidal Khmer Rouge regime, but temporarily isolated the Socialist Republic of Vietnam from the international community and led to a brief war with the People's Republic of China. (Reuters/Corbis)

the positive side, 300,000 Cambodians were resettled from refugee camps in Thailand, and local human rights organizations were allowed to flourish. Free and fair elections, arguably the first in Cambodian history, were conducted in 1993. Other elections followed in 1998 and 2004. On the other hand, the Khmer Rouge guerrillas in the northwest remained armed. The CPP and its leaders, many of whom were former Khmer Rouge, continued to dominate the political scene. In 1993 Cambodia became a kingdom again, and Sihanouk re-ascended the throne that he had first occupied in 1941.

The second half of the twentieth century showed how vulnerable Cambodia was to revolutionary rhetoric and international pressure. It also showed how its leaders often failed Cambodia's people, and how transient international commitments can be. More to the point, perhaps, the half-century also verified the Cambodian adage that "when elephants fight, the grass gets trampled." In 2004, Cambodia was still shadowed by its recent past, and the legacies of its

horrific revolution, none of them positive, continued to haunt the Cambodian people.

PEOPLE AND ORGANIZATIONS

Angkor loeu

The "upper organization"—a name used by the Communist Party of Kampuchea. The party's existence was concealed from nonmembers between its seizure of power in Cambodia 1975 until 1977, when the existence of the party was announced.

Democratic Kampuchea (DK)

Official name of the Marxist-Leninist regime that governed Cambodia between April 1975 and January 1979.

Hun Sen (Born 1952)

Former Khmer Rouge military commander in Cambodia who defected to Vietnam in 1977, returning two years later as minister of foreign affairs in the newly installed, pro-Vietnamese government. He was named prime minister by the Vietnamese in 1984 and has held on to the position more or less continuously ever since.

Indochinese Communist Party (ICP)

Formed in Hong Kong in 1930 by Vietnamese exiles. Very few non-Vietnamese members joined the party before World War II. In the 1940s, although it had supposedly been dissolved, the party spearheaded resistance to the French colonial power in Cambodia, Laos, and Vietnam.

Khmer People's Revolutionary Party (KPRP)

A Communist-style party established by the Vietnamese in Cambodia in 1951. Its role was to aid Vietnamese forces fighting against the French in neighboring southern Vietnam, then known as Cochin China.

Khmer Rouge

Popular name given to the Cambodian Communist movement by Cambodia's charismatic chief of state Norodom Sihanouk in the 1960s. Western journalists used the name in the 1960s and 1970s.

Lon Nol (1911–1984)

Commander of Cambodia's army who overthrew the Sihanouk government in March 1970 and allied with the United States against Communist-led Vietnamese and Cambodian forces. Lon Nol suffered a stroke in 1971. The Khmer Rouge defeated his regime in April 1975, forcing him to flee the country. He died in Fullerton, California, never regaining full health.

Norodom Sihanouk (Born 1922)

Crowned King of Cambodia by the French in 1941. Abdicated the throne in 1955, when he founded a national political movement that dominated Cambodian politics until 1970, when he was overthrown in a bloodless coup. The prince allied himself with Cambodian Communists, hoping to regain the throne, but when the Communists defeated the new rulers in Phnom Penh in 1975 Sihanouk was brushed aside and placed under house arrest. He spent most of the 1980s in exile in China and North Korea, then returned to Cambodia in 1992. He was crowned king again in 1993 but, lacking political power, spent much of the next decade and a half away from Cambodia. He abdicated in 2004.

Saloth Sar (Pol Pot) (1925–1998)

Born into a wealthy peasant family with connections to the Cambodian throne, Saloth Sar was educated in French-language schools and in France, where he joined the French Communist Party. In the late 1950s, working as a schoolteacher in Phnom Penh, he helped to organize a clandestine Communist movement. He took charge of the movement in 1962 and fled to Vietnam to avoid arrest in 1963. After traveling to Hanoi and Beijing in 1965–1966, Sar established his headquarters in northeastern Cambodia and plotted to seize power. His Khmer Rouge forces joined with Vietnamese Communist units to defeat the regime that replaced Norodom Sihanouk in 1970. In 1975, the Communist Party of Kampuchea took power in Phnom Penh. Saloth Sar, using the pseudonym Pol Pot, presided over a regime under which more than 1.5 million Cambodians—one in seven—were executed or died of overwork or malnutrition. Driven into exile by the Vietnamese invasion in 1979, Pol Pot retained control of the Khmer Rouge movement until 1997, when he was deposed by less radical colleagues. He died on the Thai border in 1998.

David Chandler

See Also Documentaries of Revolution; Elites, Intellectuals, and Revolutionary Leadership; Human Rights, Morality, Social Justice, and Revolution; Lao Communist Revolution; Terrorism; Vietnamese Revolution; War and Revolution

References and Further Readings
Becker, Elizabeth. 1986. *When the War Was Over.* New York: Simon and Schuster.
Chandler, David. 1999. *Brother Number One: A Political Biography of Pol Pot.* Boulder, CO: Westview Press.
———. 2000. *A History of Cambodia,* 3rd edition. Boulder, CO: Westview Press.
Chandler, D., B. Kiernan, and C. Boua, eds. 1988. *Pol Pot Plans the Future.* New Haven, CT: Yale University Southeast Asia Program.
Etcheson, Craig. 1984. *The Rise and Demise of Democratic Kampuchea.* Boulder, CO: Westview Press.
Harff, Barbara. 1991. "Cambodia: Revolution, Genocide, Intervention." Pp. 218–234 in *Revolutions of the Late Twentieth Century,* edited by Jack A. Goldstone, Ted Robert Gurr, and Farrokh Moshiri. Boulder, CO: Westview Press.

Jackson, Karl, ed. 1989. *Cambodia l975–1979: Rendez-vous with Death.* Princeton, NJ: Princeton University Press.

Kiernan, Ben. 1981. "Origins of Khmer Communism." *Southeast Asian Affairs 1981.* Singapore: Hieneman Educational Books.

_____. 1987. *How Pol Pot Came to Power.* Thetford, England: Thetford Press.

_____. 1995. *The Pol Pot Regime.* New Haven, CT: Yale University Press.

Ponchaud, Francois. 1978. *Cambodia Year Zero.* New York: Holt, Rinehart and Winston.

Vickery, Michael. 1984. *Cambodia: 1975–1982.* Boston: South End Press.

Chechen Revolt against Russia

CHRONOLOGY

1859	Imam Shamil surrenders to Russian forces. Chechnya is incorporated into Russian empire.
1922	Chechnya is incorporated by force into the Soviet Union.
1934	Checheno-Ingushetia becomes an autonomous republic of the Russian Federation.
1944	After revolts against Soviet rule, Stalin deports entire Chechen population to Central Asia, alleging collaboration with German forces.
1957	Khrushchev allows Chechens and others to return home.
1991	National revolt led by General Dzhokhar Dudayev. Independence of Chechnya from Russian Federation is proclaimed.
1993	Leading Chechen figures revolt against Dudayev's rule, citing his growing autocracy, and ally themselves with Moscow.
1994	In December, following a failed attempt by the Chechen opposition to take Grozny, Russian forces invade Chechnya. Much of Grozny is destroyed in the fighting that follows. International radical Islamist fighters led by a Jordanian, Abdurrahman ibn-ul-Khattab, move to Chechnya to fight the Russians.
1995	In June, Chechen rebels led by Shamil Basayev seize hundreds of hostages at a hospital in the Russian town of Budyonnovsk.
1996	Dudayev is killed by Russian rocket in April.
	In August, Chechen fighters recapture much of Grozny.
	The Russian government signs a peace agreement with Chechen chief of staff Aslan Maskhadov providing for the withdrawal of Russian forces from Chechnya and negotiations on Chechnya's long-term status.
1997	In February, Maskhadov is elected president of Chechnya with 65 percent of the vote to Basayev's 23 percent.
1998	Chechnya falls into anarchy. Criminal groups and Islamist extremists launch raids into Russia, kidnapping some 1,300 people. Two Russian envoys to Chechnya are kidnapped and murdered, along with a number of Westerners. In June, Maskhadov orders a state of emergency. He later announces that Chechnya will become a Sharia-ruled Islamic republic.
1999	Radical commanders, including Shamil Basayev and Arbi Barayev, declare Maskhadov deposed in the name of Sharia Islamic law. They form an alliance with the radical Islamists and create a council for the liberation of the neighboring Russian autonomous republic of Daghestan and its union with Chechnya in one Islamic republic.
	In August, in the name of this program, Chechen, Islamist, and Daghestani fighters launch an incursion into Daghestan, which is repelled by Russian forces. Maskhadov denounces the invasion of Daghestan but is unable to prevent it.
	In September, terrorist attacks in Moscow and elsewhere kill more than 300 people. The Kremlin blames them on Chechen radicals.
	In October, Moscow withdraws its recognition from Maskhadov's government and recognizes instead a group of dissident Chechen parliamentarians. Russian forces once again invade Chechnya.

2000   In February, Russian forces capture Grozny.

In June, Moscow appoints the previously pro-independence Chechen religious leader Ahmed Kadyrov as head of the government in Chechnya.

2001   Heavy fighting continues in Chechnya, with numerous casualties among Russian troops, Chechen fighters, and the civilian population. Western human rights groups allege severe human rights abuses by Russian troops. Hundreds of thousands of Chechen refugees flee from Chechnya, some 6,000 moving to the Pankisi Gorge of neighboring Georgia, which becomes a base for attacks on Russian forces and for a plot by international Islamist terrorists to carry out a poison attack on London.

2002   In October, Chechen terrorists led by a member of the Barayev clan, linked to the radical Islamists, seize the Dubrovka Theater in Moscow along with some 800 hostages. All the rebels and some 120 hostages are killed when Russian forces storm the building.

2003   In March, a referendum in Chechnya confirms Chechnya's status as an autonomous republic of the Russian Federation, but the validity of the vote is widely contested.

In October, Ahmed Kadyrov is elected president of Chechnya.

2004   In February, former Chechen vice president Zelimkhan Yandarbiyev is assassinated by Russian agents in Qatar.

In May, Ahmed Kadyrov and other leading members of his administration are killed in a bomb blast in Grozny.

In June, Chechen and Ingush fighters briefly seize much of Nazran, capital of the neighboring republic of Ingushetia, killing dozens of policemen and officials.

In August, fresh Russian-organized elections are held, and the former Chechen interior minister Alu Alkhanov is elected president. Other candidates are barred from standing.

In September, Chechen terrorists seize a school in the town of Beslan in northern Ossetia. More than 300 people, mainly children, are killed when the terrorists detonate bombs. Shamil Basayev takes responsibility for the attack. Maskhadov condemns it and offers fresh talks with the Kremlin, which Moscow rejects.

2005   In March, Aslan Maskhadov, a leader of the Chechen rebels and a former Chechen president, is killed by Russian forces.

Chechen parliamentary elections were held in November.

INTRODUCTION

Chechnya is a tiny territory of the northern Caucasus that, at the start of the twenty-first century, achieved an importance out of all proportion to its size. Unfortunately, this importance has developed for tragic reasons: the two conflicts between Chechen separatists and the Russian state. These conflicts have spawned terrorism and extremism on the Chechen side, and brutality and chauvinism on the Russian. By 2004, Chechnya had been sucked into the wider struggle between Islamist extremism and a number of states around the world, and the Chechen conflict was doing much to undermine the remains of democracy in Russia.

BACKGROUND: CULTURE AND HISTORY

The Chechens are a people of the northeastern Caucasus who have been settled in this region since before the dawn of recorded history. Thanks to the Chechens' isolation and the natural protection of their mountains and forests, they remained—right up until the early modern period and even, to a limited extent, until the present—a clan-based society of a strikingly archaic and egalitarian cast, without rulers, feudal lords, a military or merchant caste, or a formal clergy, and fiercely resistant to outside rule and indeed to government in general. Their language is unaffiliated with any of the other languages of the region except for the closely related Ingush. Chechens were converted to a superficial form of Islam beginning in the twelfth century, but it was only with the arrival of Sufi missionaries in the later eighteenth century, and mobilization in the name of Islam for the struggle against Russian conquest, that deeper forms of Islamic faith and observance became central to Chechen life.

Chechnya, showing major cities including the capital, Grozny, the site of intense fighting during the conflict.

In the later eighteenth century, the Ingush and the lowland Chechen clans fell under Russian rule. They were, therefore, insulated from the Islamic revival that swept the Chechen mountains and Daghestan. This history explains to a considerable degree the important cultural differences that continue to exist between the Chechens and Ingush, and between different regions of Chechnya—differences that also help explain different levels of nationalist and religious radicalism in the region after 1990. The Chechen mountain clans fiercely resisted Russian rule, in alliance with other Muslim peoples of the region. They were led by a series of leaders—mostly from neighboring Daghestan—of whom the most famous was Imam Shamil. The Russian conquest of the Caucasus, and the resistance to it, closely resembled other colonial wars of the period, most notably the Algerian resistance to French conquest led by Imam Abd-el-Qadir.

In 1921 the Soviet government, with Stalin as its local representative, set up a Soviet Mountain Republic embracing the Chechens, Ingush, Ossetes, Karachai, and Balkars. In 1924 this republic was broken up and separate autonomous regions organized. In 1936, the Chechen-Ingush region was raised to the status of Autonomous Republic, but unfortunately Chechnya was kept as part of the Russian Federation rather than given status as a full Union Republic like Azerbaijan or Georgia.

In the middle and late 1920s, Chechnya once again experienced a period of uneasy peace as part of the Soviet Union

and under the rule of Chechen Communists. This peace was shattered by Stalin's forced collectivization of agriculture after 1929. His savage assault on the rural economy and traditions was opposed by the Chechen Communist leadership, which, like most of the other national leaderships in the Soviet Union, was then ferociously purged by Stalin. The consequence was another series of Chechen revolts.

In January 1940, a former leading Chechen Communist intellectual, Hassan Israilov, led a rising in the Chechen mountains that gathered pace after the German invasion of the Soviet Union in June 1941. The German surrender at Stalingrad in February 1943 began the German withdrawal from the North Caucasus; eight months later Stalin launched the operation to deport the entire Chechen, Ingush, Kalmyk, Karachai, and Balkar peoples to Central Asia. According to the most credible figures, 478,479 Chechens and Ingush were loaded onto trains in February 1944. Under Khrushchev, 400,478 were later officially reported as having been deported, which suggests that the other 78,000—around one-fifth of the total Chechen population—died or were killed during the operation. In several mountain villages the NKVD troops massacred all the inhabitants.

In 1957, following massive pressure from the deported peoples, the Soviet government of Nikita Khrushchev allowed them to return (with the exception of the Meskhetian Turks and the Crimean Tatars). The last three decades of Soviet rule saw considerable tension between the Chechens and local Russians, who had either settled on confiscated Chechen land or had come to Chechnya to work in the oil industry. Gradually, the Chechens gained the upper hand, in part due to a birthrate much higher than that of the Russians. However, it was not until 1989 that a Chechen, Doku Zavgayev, became leader (first secretary) of the Communist Party of the Chechen-Ingush autonomous republic.

In the 1970s and 1980s, the Chechen birthrate per thousand was between 31 and 40, while the Russian had dropped to 12. The Chechen proportion of the urban population in Chechnya increased from a mere 9 percent in 1959 to 42.1 percent in 1989. By the census of 1989 there were 775,980 Chechens living in the Chechen-Ingush autonomous republic (58 percent of the population), with more than 300,000 living elsewhere in the then Soviet Union. This birthrate generated large numbers of unemployed young men, many of whom moved to other parts of the Soviet Union to seek work, frequently in the world of organized crime. Those who remained in Chechnya eventually helped swell the ranks of the pro-independence fighters.

For much of the Soviet period, Grozny was second only to Baku as a center of oil production. After the 1960s, however, production fell steeply as reserves were exhausted. Furthermore, the nature of Soviet rule and the monopolization of positions in the industry by ethnic Russians for most of the Soviet period meant that most Chechens gained very little profit from this oil. Chechnya on the eve of the Soviet collapse remained one of the poorest areas of the Russian Federation. Today, oil is of political and military importance as a source of funding for some of the Chechen rebel groups and a source of corruption for Russian forces in Chechnya and their Chechen allies, but it no longer makes Chechnya a major strategic prize.

CONTEXT AND PROCESS OF REVOLUTION

Due to their history of resistance and their sufferings under Soviet rule, many Chechens retained a fierce resentment at rule from Moscow, especially at the domination of local government structures by Russians. During 1990, as Soviet rule weakened, Chechen nationalists formed a national congress to call for Chechnya to be raised from the status of an autonomous republic of the Russian Soviet Socialist Republic to a full republic of the Soviet Union (like Georgia or Azerbaijan). This would have meant that Chechnya would have received international recognition as an international state when the Soviet Union collapsed the next year. However, the demand was rejected by the Soviet government.

In August 1991, Soviet loyalists in the Communist Party, KGB, and army commands launched a coup in Moscow, which collapsed within three days in the face of mass opposition and the refusal of most of the military to support it. In Chechnya, armed radicals led by Dzhokhar Dudayev seized this opportunity to launch a coup of their own against the local Communist leadership under Doku Zavgayev. Official buildings were seized and the Russian deputy chief of the local party was murdered. The jails were opened, and numerous criminals serving time in Chechnya were released to join the Chechen fighters.

In October 1991, Dudayev held presidential and parliamentary elections in Chechnya, winning the presidency with an overwhelming majority. On November 2, the Chechen parliament declared full independence from Russia. An attempt by Moscow to intervene militarily collapsed when Russian forces were surrounded at Grozny airport and persuaded to leave again. In the following months, Russian forces were withdrawn from Chechnya as a result of both a mixture of pressure and bribes from the Chechen side, and the chaos attendant on the collapse of the Soviet Union and armed forces.

Over the next two years, government and state services in Chechnya largely collapsed. Despite subsidies from Moscow, wages and pensions were no longer paid, and schools and hospitals became dependent on private charity. In consequence of these developments and Dudayev's own increasingly autocratic and erratic behavior, in 1993 a majority of the Chechen parliament began to question his rule. Dudayev then suppressed the parliament by force, and several Chechen leaders fled from Grozny to northern Chechnya, where they established an armed base under Russian protection.

In 1994, after Tatarstan signed a union treaty with Russia, Chechnya was left as the only autonomous republic of the Russian Federation still asserting its full independence from Moscow. As a result of this situation and exasperation at the role of Chechnya as a base for criminality and smuggling, in the summer of 1994 the Yeltsin administration decided to increase pressure on Chechnya to accept autonomous status. Initially, Moscow exerted this pressure through armed support for the Chechen opposition. When an opposition attack on Grozny was humiliatingly defeated in December 1994, the Kremlin ordered an improvised invasion of Chechnya with Russian forces.

The war that followed was a disaster for both Russia and Chechnya. The Russian forces suffered numerous defeats, and Russia's collapse as a military superpower was humiliatingly revealed. In August 1996, Chechen fighters actually succeeded in recapturing most of Grozny. The Chechens suffered tens of thousands of casualties among fighters as well as civilians, and the city of Grozny, along with much of the Chechen economy, were destroyed. Most damaging of all were the effects on Chechen society. The war created a large number of brutalized, heavily armed, unemployed fighters, led by commanders like Shamil Basayev and Arbi Barayev—men with no experience of government and no program except for continued war against Russia in the name of a mixture of Chechen nationalism and radical Islam.

In August 1996, President Boris Yeltsin deputed General Alexander Lebed, then head of the security council, to negotiate an agreement with the Chechen chief of staff, General Aslan Maskhadov (Dudayev had been killed earlier in the year). In the Khasavyurt Accords, Moscow agreed to withdraw all its forces from Chechnya. Maskhadov agreed that negotiation on the constitutional status of Chechnya should be delayed for five years.

In February 1997, Maskhadov was elected president. But he faced a shattered economy, and he lacked an army, police, and a state bureaucracy. He was also confronted with numerous independent commanders and their heavily armed followers, along with a small but well-funded group of Arab Islamist militants. As a result, he was never able to consolidate his authority. Instead, he was forced to give senior positions to warlords like Shamil Basayev, who was prime minister for six months in 1998, and Vaqa Arsanov, who served as Maskhadov's vice president while simultaneously protecting the kidnapping and radical Islamist group commanded by his relative, Arbi Barayev. Moscow could have given more support to Maskhadov but was alienated by his insistence on immediate talks on Chechen independence, which Moscow thought had been deferred to a later date.

Chechen fighters ride a captured Russian tank through the ruins of Grozny on August 16, 1994. The demand for independence in Chechnya, proclaimed by Muslim separatists, was only one of many such movements that arose following the dissolution of the Soviet Union in 1991. Russian president Boris Yeltsin's 1994 decision to quell the Chechen uprising with force greatly underestimated the strength of the independence fighters. (Hulton Archive/Getty Images)

The result of all this was an explosion of kidnapping, banditry, and terrorism throughout the period from 1997 to 1999. Kidnapping alone claimed in all some 1,300 Russian victims and a number of Westerners. These included four British telecom engineers kidnapped and beheaded by the Islamist group led by Arbi Barayev—one of the first instances in recent times of beheading being used in this way. After two Russian envoys were kidnapped while under Maskhadov's personal protection, the Kremlin's faith in Maskhadov vanished. The great majority of the Chechen people, despite their exasperation with the activity of many of the warlords, have not been able to mobilize to support their president or create new institutions at the grassroots level.

In 1999, the radical Islamists and their Chechen allies restarted war with Russia by invading the Russian republic of Daghestan. The Russian occupation of Chechnya that followed in October led to tens of thousands more Russian and Chechen casualties. Russian fury at Chechen behavior from 1997 to 1999 meant that in the first three years of this war, there was an even higher incidence of human rights abuses by Russian soldiers than in earlier periods of the conflict, with almost 3,000 "disappearances" of arrested Chechens documented by Human Rights Watch.

Gradually, however, the Russian army gained control of the situation in Chechnya, and by late 2004, violence within the republic was much reduced. For the nine months of that year, the Russian opposition civil rights group Memorial documented only 98 civilian deaths in Chechnya, with 81 soldiers and policemen killed, and 278 kidnappings (many of them, it is suspected, by Russian troops or Chechen allies).

However, the waning of the guerrilla war within Chechnya only led radical sections of the Chechen militants, led by Basayev and others and allied to the Islamists, to launch a wave of terrorist attacks on Russian territory. These attacks, in turn, lent support to the long-standing Russian portrayal of the Chechen rebel movement as "terrorist." Maskhadov, driven underground, denounced these terrorist attacks but was unable to prevent them.

At the end of 2004, a form of stalemate had been reached, in which the Chechen militants were unable to drive the Russians from Chechnya, but the Russians were unable to stop ferocious acts of Chechen terrorism. Barring some very unlikely form of international intervention, it seems that the Chechen Rebellion will become one of the world's long-running, low-level conflicts, a principle effect of which would be to further undermine democracy in Russia.

IMPACTS

The Chechen Revolt against Russian rule beginning in 1991 must be considered a rebellion rather than a revolution, because unlike either the Communist or the Islamist revolutions of the past century, it did not succeed in creating new structures of government or society. For that matter, the Chechens have never even succeeded in creating a modern political-military organization to conduct the independence struggle, such as the FLN in Algeria, the Irish Republican Army (IRA) in Northern Ireland, or the Tamil Tigers in Sri Lanka. Instead, the Chechen resistance has always been a matter of diffuse groups under a range of different commanders—more akin to the historic patterns of resistance to conquest among segmentary tribal peoples like the Berbers or Pashtuns.

This diffuse organization has been a grave drawback to the Chechen side in organizing a united resistance to Russia, but it has been an equally grave drawback in negotiating with Russia. A tightly disciplined nationalist organization like the IRA or Tamil Tigers, if its leadership decides that it is time to negotiate peace or even just a truce, is in a position to make most of its followers obey. That has never been true on the Chechen side, and the lack of such an organization, or acknowledged supreme leader, has led many Russian officials to conclude that there is no point in negotiating with the relatively moderate Chechen rebel leadership under Maskhadov, because that leadership does not control most of the fighters and will be unable to make any agreement stick. The most disastrous period from this point of view was that of Maskhadov's presidency (1997–1999), when in the absence of Russian forces, Chechnya slipped into anarchy and became a base for very serious and closely linked criminal, terrorist, and Islamist attacks on Russia.

The roots of this political and military tendency of the Chechens to fragment into warring groups, striking in such a small and ethnically homogenous people, must be sought in three factors. The first is the Chechens' own ancient social traditions. In the past, the segmentary clan, or *teip*, was of central importance to Chechen society. However, clan loyalty was always cut across by other allegiances. In recent decades it has been severely qualified by the impact of Soviet rule, deportation, modernization, and most recently by the shattering effects of the wars after 1994 on Chechen society and tradition. The result is a loose, overlapping, ambiguous, and often contradictory set of simultaneous allegiances to different clan, familial, political, regional, and religious identities, together with personal loyalties to particular politicians, warlords, or criminal bosses.

The nature of Soviet totalitarian rule also prevented the Chechens from developing even the rudiments of a modern civil society or a capacity for spontaneous political organization. This, of course, was also true for all the other regions of the Soviet Union. But the effects were even more dangerous among the Chechens because of that people's history of extreme individualism and resistance to government. Stemming from a mixture of the Soviet system with the Chechen experience of that system and Chechen cultural tradition has been the third factor preventing Chechen national organization: the role of organized crime. The disproportionately prominent role played by Chechen groups in this area of the Soviet and post-Soviet economies has been helped by the Chechens' intense traditions of familial and ethnic loyalty, akin to the Sicilian mafia code of *omerta;* by ethnic traditions of legitimate raiding and banditry; and by savage resentment at the Soviet and Russian systems for their deportation and oppression of the Chechens. In the words of John Baddeley, a British observer who visited the North Caucasus in the 1890s, when the memory of the old days was still very much alive:

> Cattle-lifting, highway robbery, and murder were, in this strange code, counted deeds of honor; they were openly instigated by the village maiden . . . who scorned any pretender having no such claims to her favor; and these, together with fighting against any foe, but especially the hated Russian, were the only pursuits deemed worthy of a grown man. (Baddeley 1969: xvii)

Organized criminal groups have played a central and disastrous role in Chechen developments since 1990. But Chechen mafia power in Moscow has reportedly diminished greatly in the course of the recent wars, with the police backing other criminal groups in cutting them down to size.

Within Chechnya, every single political or military grouping that has emerged since 1990 has either originated in a criminal body or has turned into one. This was true after 1991 of both the armed groups that remained loyal to the independence camp and those that eventually sided with Russia. After 1996, the warlord groups that formed an alliance with the international Islamists were deeply involved in criminality, above all, hostage-taking for ransom. After the Russian reconquest of 1999–2000, all the Chechen groups that the Russians have backed have also become heavily involved in kidnapping, extortion, and corruption.

The one force in Chechnya that has represented a genuinely revolutionary program has been the radical Islamists, inspired by modern radical Sunni Islamist ideology (known in the former Soviet Union, not wholly accurately, as "Wahabism," after the official faith of Saudi Arabia, which provided the original inspiration for Osama bin Laden and al-Qaeda). Their program of Islamic Revolution, though contrary to all generally accepted ideas of modern progress, is nonetheless internally coherent and capable of inspiring absolute devotion in men who have seen every other ideology and moral support fail. Furthermore, the mobilization of the Chechen ethnonationalist struggle under the banner and discipline of radical Islam has a long lineage in Chechnya.

The radical Islamists, however, also face formidable obstacles in Chechnya. Their foreign origins and radical ideology make them deeply distrusted by many Chechens. In particular, they have earned the undying hatred of what is left of both the educated Chechen classes and the old Sufi orders. Although Shamil Basayev and other commanders have forged an alliance with the Islamists and adopted their rhetoric, it has also never been entirely clear whether this represented a wholly sincere conversion or was to some extent a tactical measure intended to provide ideological and moral justification for the overthrow of Maskhadov and a continuation of the war against Russia. Finally and most importantly, of course, the Russian invasion of 1999 aborted any further moves in the direction of making Chechnya into an Islamic republic.

The impact of the Islamists has nonetheless been important and disastrous. Their alliance with Basayev and Barayev behind a program of *jihad* against Russia was chiefly responsible for the renewed Russian invasion of 1999. They have contributed greatly to radicalizing the Chechen struggle and turning their allies toward terrorism. Dreadful incidents like the hostage-taking at Beslan have lost the Chechen cause much support in the West and provided the justification for growing authoritarianism on the part of the administration of Vladimir Putin. The Islamists have also increased Russian hostility not only to the Chechens, but to the Muslim world in general, and thereby increased the possibility of wider ethnoreligious tension and even conflict in the Russian Federation and the former Soviet Union. Rather than a force for the creation of a new state or a new social and moral order, the Chechen Rebellion to date must be judged to have been almost entirely negative in its effects.

PEOPLE AND ORGANIZATIONS

As noted above, organizations as such have played little role in the Chechen Rebellion and have not been generated by that rebellion. A leading role has, however, been played by certain individuals, of whom the following are the most important:

Alkhanov, General Alu (Born 1957)

Born in Kazakhstan in 1957, Alkhanov joined the Soviet police in 1983, after leaving the army. He served mainly in the transport department of the North Caucasus region. He has supported Russia in both Chechen wars. In 2003 he was made Chechen interior minister in the government of Ahmed Kadyrov. After Kadyrov's assassination, he was appointed by Moscow as president-designate, an appointment confirmed in a highly flawed election in August 2004. Alkhanov is widely regarded as brave and dedicated, but has no real following within Chechnya.

Aslakhanov, General Aslanbek (Born 1942)

Aslakhanov was born in Chechnya in 1942 and deported to Kazakhstan with his family. In 1967 he joined the Soviet Interior Ministry, eventually rising to the rank of general. Aslakhanov has always favored Chechnya remaining part of the Russian Federation and is now one of the most prominent of the pro-Russian figures in Chechnya. From 2000 to 2003 he served as a deputy in the Russian parliament, and since 2003 he has been a senior adviser to President Putin. However, there have been tensions between him and the Russian government over Moscow's favoring of the Kadyrov clan and its refusal to hold free elections in Chechnya and allow candidates to run against Russia's chosen leaders. General Aslakhanov has always been strongly critical of human rights abuses and corruption by Russian forces in Chechnya. He can be considered one of the figures whom Moscow is holding in reserve and who could be given new prominence in the future.

Basayev, Shamil (Born 1965)

Basayev is the best-known Chechen commander and has become the most notorious Chechen terrorist leader. Born in the mountain district of Vedeno, Basayev first came to prominence by hijacking an Aeroflot passenger plane in 1991 in support of Chechen independence. The plane landed in Turkey, and Basayev was allowed to go free. In 1992–1993, he led a Chechen force that fought for Abkhaz independence from Georgia—paradoxically, with Russian support. On the strength of this experience, when Russian forces invaded Chechnya in December 1994, Basayev quickly emerged as one of the most successful Chechen military leaders, inflicting a series of shattering reverses on the Russian army.

Basayev stood for election as president in February 1997 but was crushingly defeated by Maskhadov, winning only 23 percent of the vote. In January 1998, he was appointed prime minister by Maskhadov. After six months he resigned and formed an alliance with the Arab Islamist leader Khattab and other field commanders to overthrow Maskhadov, make Chechnya an Islamic state, and launch a *jihad* to drive Russia from the whole North Caucasus. In pursuit of this program, Basayev, Khattab, and others launched an armed incursion into neighboring Daghestan in August 1999.

After Russian forces entered Chechnya again later that year, Basayev lost a leg when his fighters escaped from the Russian siege of Grozny. Thereafter, he has become an increasingly elusive figure. He has taken responsibility for a number of terrorist attacks on Russia, most notably the hostage-taking at the school in Beslan in September 2004, which caused more than 300 deaths and led to worldwide condemnation. He is now regarded as a terrorist by both the West and Russia, and Western governments have insisted that Maskhadov break off relations with him. He has been named Commander of the Faithful by his followers and their backers in the Muslim world, implying leadership of a *jihad* against the infidel.

Dudayev, General Dzhokhar (1944–1996)

Dudayev grew up in exile in Central Asia. He served in the Soviet air force, rising to the rank of major general. In November 1990, the newly formed Chechen National Congress elected him as its leader. The following year, he led the overthrow of the Communist authorities in Chechnya, and proclaimed Chechen independence. Dudayev himself always declared that he was a Soviet loyalist, and that he really would have liked the Soviet Union to have survived as a free union of peoples with Chechnya a constituent republic.

During his period as president, Dudayev's anti-Russian rhetoric became increasingly extreme and even wild. Without this, it is possible that Boris Yeltsin would have agreed to meet with him and that a compromise could have been negotiated that would have given Chechnya enhanced autonomy within the Russian Federation, along the lines of

Tatarstan, and avoided the later conflicts. Dudayev's nationalist extremism reflected his personal opinion and character, but also the fact that as his popularity within Chechnya waned, he became more and more dependent for support on armed Chechen militants. Having initially declared Chechnya a secular republic, Dudayev also began to use more religious symbolism in his propaganda. However, he himself remained at heart a secular figure, as reflected by his continued marriage to a Russian woman.

In April 1996 Dudayev was killed by a Russian rocket. During the period of Chechen quasi-independence from 1997–1999 he was given the status of official national hero, and Grozny was renamed Dzhokhar-yurt in his honor.

Maskhadov, Aslan (1951–2005)

Maskhadov was born in exile in Kazakhstan. After he finished school, he joined the Soviet army, serving in the artillery and rising to the rank of colonel. In 1991 he returned to Chechnya and became the chief of staff before and during the war of 1994–1996, in which role he was widely seen as the chief organizer of Chechen victory. After negotiating the Khasavyurt Accords of 1996, which provided for Russian withdrawal from Chechnya, Maskhadov was elected president in February 1997 with 65 percent of the vote. He was never able to consolidate his authority, and from 1998 faced rebellion by different Chechen commanders allied to radical Islamists from the Middle East. His efforts to suppress these groups failed, and Moscow lost confidence in him as a partner. After the Russian invasion of 1999 he was driven underground, and he and his supporters were denounced by the Russian authorities as terrorists. However, as a man formerly elected by an overwhelming vote, he retained a measure of prestige, both among ordinary Chechens and in the West.

Kadyrov, Ahmed (1951–2004)

Kadyrov was born in Kazakhstan. From 1982 to 1986 he studied to be a Muslim cleric at a Soviet-approved religious university in Tashkent. In 1990, he studied at the Islamic University of Amman, Jordan. In the early and mid 1990s he was a strong supporter of Chechen independence, and in 1995, during the first war, he was elected by other clerics as the chief mufti of Chechnya.

After 1996, Kadyrov became deeply worried by the growing anarchy under Maskhadov and the growing power of the radical Wahabi Islamists and their Arab backers in Chechnya. He therefore broke with President Maskhadov and supported the Russian military intervention of 1999, though he also repeatedly denounced atrocities by the Russian troops.

In June 2000 Moscow appointed him head of the Chechen government, and in June 2003 he was elected president in a widely criticized vote. In May 2004 he was assassinated by a bomb planted in Grozny's sports stadium. Leadership of his political, military, and criminal coalitions passed to his son, Ramzan Kadyrov, who was appointed deputy prime minister by Moscow following his father's death.

Khattab (1969–2002)

Abdurrahman ibn-ul-Khattab was born in Saudi Arabia and fought in Afghanistan against Soviet forces in the 1980s. After the Russian invasion of Chechnya in 1994, Khattab led a group of Afghan veterans and other international Islamist volunteers to Chechnya and became a leading Chechen commander. With the help of copious amounts of money from radical Middle Eastern funding sources like the Egypt-based organization Al Karamein (banned by the United States after September 11, 2001, for its links to al-Qaeda), Khattab was able to forge an alliance with leading Chechen commanders like Shamil Basayev and Arbi Barayev, and win them over to his radical Islamist philosophy. This strategy dictated, among other things, a *jihad* against Russia for the liberation of the North Caucasus and its union with Chechnya in one Islamic republic.

In 2002, Khattab was poisoned by agents of the Russian secret service. His chief successor is believed to be Abd-al-Azis al Ghamidi, who uses the nom de guerre of Abu al-Walid. The latter is also a native of Saudi Arabia who fought in Afghanistan and Bosnia before moving to Chechnya with Khattab in 1995. Walid has since been reported killed, but there has been no confirmation of this.

Anatol Lieven

See Also Documentaries of Revolution; Ethnic and Racial Conflict: From Bargaining to Violence; Islamic Fundamentalist Revolutionary Movement; Nationalism and Revolution; Russian Revolution of 1991 and the Dissolution of the U.S.S.R.; Terrorism; Transnational Revolutionary Movements

References and Further Readings

Baddeley, John F. 1969. *The Russian Conquest of the Caucasus.* New York: Russell and Russell.

Baiev, Khassan. 2005. *The Oath: A Surgeon under Fire in Chechnya.* New York: Walker.

Lieven, Anatol. 1998. *Chechnya: Tombstone of Russian Power.* New Haven, CT: Yale University Press.

———. 2004. *America Right or Wrong: An Anatomy of American Nationalism.* Oxford: Oxford University Press.

Meier, Andrew. 2004. *Chechnya: To the Heart of a Conflict.* New York: W. W. Norton.

Orr, Michael. 2005. *Russia's Wars with Chechnya, 1994–2003.* Oxford, UK: Osprey Publishing.

Tishkov, Valery. 2004. *Chechnya: Life in a War-Torn Society.* Berkeley: University of California Press.

Trenin, Dmitri, and Alexei Malashenko. 2004. *Russia's Restless Frontier: The Chechnya Factor in Post-Soviet Russia.* Washington, DC: Carnegie Endowment. http://www.AltChechnya.com.

Jamestown's Chechnya Weekly: http://www.jamestown.org/ publications_view.php?publication_id=1.

Chilean Socialist Revolution, Counter-Revolution, and the Restoration of Democracy

CHRONOLOGY

1970   Salvador Allende is the presidential candidate of Popular Unity, a coalition of parties of the Left dominated by the Communist Party and his own Socialist Party.

On September 4, in a three-way race, Allende receives 36.2 percent of popular vote, a plurality of 1.3 percent over Jorge Alessandri, the candidate of the Right; Radomiro Tomic, the candidate of the centrist Christian Democrats, receives 27 percent. The Chilean constitution provides that if no candidate received a majority, the Chilean Congress should decide between the top two candidates 50 days after the popular election.

Since Allende has promised to nationalize most of the larger businesses, an economic panic ensues. During September and October, the period before the congressional vote, the United States government tries to prevent Allende's victory by subsidizing opposition groups and promoting a military coup.

On October 22, Rene Schneider, army commander who opposes any military interference with the constitutional process, is murdered during a kidnapping attempt by a group of officers who opposed Allende's election.

Following Allende's endorsement of a series of constitutional guarantees demanded by the Christian Democrats, in November he is elected by Congress and becomes president of Chile. In his inaugural address he quotes Marx on the possibility of a peaceful transition to Socialism and promises a *via chilena* that will carry out the revolution by democratic means.

1971   Allende's first year in office is a qualified success. His initial targets for nationalization are the large, American-owned copper mines, partial ownership of which had already been purchased—with an international loan—by the previous Christian Democratic government.

In April, Popular Unity wins about 50 percent of the popular vote in municipal elections.

Since the Christian Democrats had come to accept the need for full nationalization of the industry, in July Allende is able to secure a large majority for a constitutional amendment in favor of the takeover. Allende hires a French firm to come up with a compensation figure, instructing them to deduct from the compensation "excess profits" of the foreign copper companies since 1955. The result is that except for one new mine, none of the companies are to receive compensation. This leads to problems with the U.S. government, including a threatened cutoff of U.S. aid. The copper companies also sue to secure compensation from copper shipments to foreign countries.

In November, Fidel Castro visits Chile and President Allende, exacerbating political tensions.

Allende imposes price controls on many items, while allowing wages to rise. The resulting increase in consumption gives the economy a boost, but private and foreign investment plummet. At the end of his first year in office, shortages begin to appear.

On December 1, The opposition to the Allende government organize a right-wing women's "march of the empty pots" in protest.

1972   Early in his second year in office, two by-elections lead the Center and Right parties to form an opposition coalition, which makes it difficult to adopt government-proposed legislation. An attempt is made to negotiate an agreement between Popular Unity and the Christian Democrats, but the left wing of the Allende coalition and the right wing of the Christian Democrats scuttle the negotiations. Inflation takes off. There are violent takeovers in the countryside and strikes in the factories, some of which are nationalized by invoking a 1932 law permitting the "temporary" government takeover of companies that provide articles of "basic necessity."

A strike initiated by private owner-truckers in October and November spreads to many sectors of the economy, and leads to the appointment of the army commander, General Carlos Prats, as interior minister to negotiate a settlement.

1973   Allende's third year in office begins with the run-up to the March 1973 congressional elections, in which the opposition hopes to secure a two-thirds majority to impeach the president. (Congress already impeached several cabinet ministers, which only requires a simple majority, but Allende simply appoints them to other cabinet posts.)

The congressional elections in March produce an opposition vote of 56 percent to 44 percent (omitting abstentions) against the Allende coalition, continuing the government stalemate. Just after the vote, the government introduces a proposal for a compulsory National Unified School curriculum, which would teach all Chilean children, whether in private or public schools, the principles of "humanist socialism." The private schools and the Catholic Church oppose the proposal, and riots and demonstrations follow.

The proposal also leads the military to meet to express their opposition and to begin to consider the possibility of an armed takeover. Their concern is intensified by the emergence of armed groups who challenge their monopoly of the instruments of coercion. The army also begins to carry out arms searches in accordance with an arms control law that is adopted after it is discovered that Cuban arms are being shipped clandestinely into the country.

June

A rebellion in June by a tank regiment is put down by General Prats. Inflation is out of control, and there are shortages of basic necessities and a flourishing black market. Worker groups take over many more factories and there are violent seizures of rural property.

Another nationwide strike in July involving not only the truck owners but many other groups, and partly financed, it is later revealed, by the U.S. Central Intelligence Agency, paralyzes the economy.

In August the supreme court accuses the government of systematic violation of the constitution and the Chamber of Deputies passes a similar resolution, which appears to be an invitation for military intervention. By now the navy and air force generals favor a coup, but General Prats, the army commander, continues to support the constitution.

The army generals meet in August and pass a vote of no confidence in Prats, leading to his resignation. He recommends to Allende that he appoint Augusto Pinochet as his successor.

On September 9 Pinochet joins the coup plotters after he is told that the coup will take place with or without him.

On September 11, the armed forces and national police carry out a coup that includes the bombing of the presidential palace. Allende commits suicide.

Within a few hours the armed forces have taken control of the entire country. The members of the military junta appear on television and make it clear that they intend to remain in power until they have eradicated what one of them calls "the cancer of Marxism." Leftists, intellectuals, and trade union leaders are rounded up in the National Stadium and other detention centers.

Many of them are brutally tortured, "disappeared," and murdered.

1974–1980

By the end of the first year of military rule, it is clear that General Pinochet has consolidated his power and is determined to maintain control for an indefinite period. The coup and the repression that follow produce worldwide protests. In Europe there are large demonstrations, and many countries organize large programs to receive Chileans who have taken shelter in foreign embassies. In the United States, congressional investigations produce calls for greater control of Central Intelligence Agency (CIA) covert actions, and a special report on the CIA's activities in Chile is published by the Senate Special Committee on Intelligence Activities, headed by Senator Frank Church. The leaders of the Allende government who had not fled the country or taken refuge in friendly embassies are detained on Dawson Island in the south of Chile and later permitted to leave the country. The newly created Directorate of National Intelligence (DINA) systematically hunts down and kills the leaders of the Castroite Movement of the Revolutionary Left (MIR) and of the Socialist and Communist parties. According to investigating commission reports in 1991 and 2004, during the seventeen years of the dictatorship nearly 3,200 Chileans are killed (Rettig 1991), and 28,000 held in detention centers, subject to brutal interrogations and torture (Valech 2004; www.commisiontortura .cl/inicio/index.php; Valech Report 2004; www.ipsnews.net/ 2004; www.state.gov/g/ drl/rls/hrrpt/2001/wha/831.8.htm 2001).

1976

Operation Condor, an international campaign against opponents of the military regime, leads to the September 21, 1976, murder in Washington of Allende's former foreign minister, fellow-Socialist Orlando Letelier.

The Chilean exiles and the Socialist and Communist parties in Europe debate the lessons of the coup. Fidel Castro and the left wing of the Socialists argue that Allende's mistake was not to prepare for the inevitable armed confrontation with "the forces of reaction." The Italian Communist Party, on the other hand, blames the Allende government for not making greater compromises with the Christian Democrats. The Chilean exiles who belonged to the Socialist and related parties split into many groups that debate whether or not to continue to pursue a revolutionary line. Their relations with the Communists deteriorate, particularly after 1980, when the Communists adopt a policy of support for "all forms of struggle" including violence—a departure from their earlier endorsement of the *via pacifica*.

1980–1988   In the 1980s the "renovated" Socialists who argued for renewed support of electoral democracy and for alliances with "bourgeois" parties become the dominant group, particularly after a partial opening in Chile leads to the formation of opposition alliances between the Left and Center against the Pinochet regime.

The electoral alternative—which also involves mass demonstrations and street protests—becomes more attractive, because Chile adopts a constitution in 1980, written (and rewritten) by Pinochet's henchmen, that provides for a plebiscite in 1988 on whether Pinochet should remain in office for another eight years. The Socialists, the Christian Democrats, and other centrist and center-left groups form the Coalition (*Concertacion*) for the No, against the extension of Pinochet's term. The "No" wins the plebiscite, 55 percent to 43 percent.

1989–2000   Following a lengthy transition prescribed by the constitution, the now-renamed Coalition for Democracy wins the 1989 elections.

In March 1990, Patricio Aylwin of the Christian Democratic Party becomes president. He has promised to pay "the social debt" incurred by the Pinochet government by increasing government spending on education, health care, and basic human services while maintaining the export-oriented and investor-friendly economic policies of the previous administration.

The Communist Party, legalized after the return to democracy, receives only 4–6 percent of the vote and has no representation in the Congress, because the electoral system excludes small parties that are not part of larger party alliances. The Christian Democrats are the largest party, and the parties in the Coalition (*Concertacion*) for Democracy name Christian Democrats Patricio Aylwin and Eduardo Frei Montalva (the son of the former president) as their presidential candidates in 1989 and 1993. They win absolute majorities in the first round of voting.

In 1999, Ricardo Lagos, a Socialist, wins the coalition's internal primary. The candidate of the Right, Joaquin Lavin, campaigns against him as the candidate of change. Profiting from the lingering suspicion of Socialists on the part of middle-class voters, Lavin comes within 1.5 percent of winning in the first round. In the runoff between the top two candidates, Lagos wins by a slightly larger margin, 2.6 percent, partly with the aid of Communist votes.

2000–2004   Ricardo Lagos had worked with the Allende government and had been nominated to be ambassador to the Soviet Union at the time of the 1973 coup. After a period of exile in the United States he had returned to Chile in the early 1980s and had been a prominent leader in the anti-Pinochet movement, and he was the first opposition leader to appear on television when this was permitted during the plebiscite. He had served in several ministries in earlier governments and was committed to democracy and social reform.

The Lagos government concludes free trade agreements with the United States and the European Union, substantially increases foreign investment, and extends medical coverage to lower-income groups. During his term and those of his two *Concertacion* predecessors, the Chilean economy grows by 5–7 percent per year, and the percentage of Chileans living in poverty drops from about 42 percent to around 18 percent (web.worldbank.org/ WBSITE/EXTERNAL/TOPICS/ EXTPOVERTY/EXTPA/0, 2004).

Revolutionary Socialism has promoted social justice at the cost of economic growth; the military counter-revolution has promoted economic growth at the cost of democracy and social spending. The coalition made up of both former supporters and opponents of the Allende Socialist Revolution seems to have found a combination of the two goals that works.

INTRODUCTION

Salvador Allende, a member of the Chilean Socialist Party, was elected president of Chile in 1970. During the next three years he attempted to carry out "the Chilean way to Socialism," a "revolutionary" transition from capitalism using constitutional and quasi-constitutional methods. Facing a hostile Congress and judiciary, he nevertheless was able to carry out many changes in the Chilean economy. But runaway inflation, political polarization, and increasing violence finally led to a bloody military coup on September 11, 1973. General Augusto Pinochet, who headed the military junta that succeeded Allende, reversed most of the Allende measures and opened the Chilean economy to the global economy. Using a combination of repression and legalistic devices, he was able to stay in power until 1990, and thereafter to continue as military commander until 1998. Full civilian control of the military was only re-established in the early years of the twenty-first century, when the courts began to prosecute Pinochet and others for violations of human rights, and the Congress amended the provisions of the 1980 constitution that granted the military a privileged position and provided for appointed senators who supported the Right.

BACKGROUND:
CULTURE AND HISTORY

The Left in Chile has a long history. It began as an organized force in the mining sectors of the north in the early twentieth century. Numerous strikes in the foreign-owned copper and nitrate mining areas, some of them put down with great ferocity, were carried out by the workers, who had been organized by the Chilean Workers Federation and the Socialist Workers Party. Following World War I, the examples of the Mexican and Soviet revolutions and the collapse of the international price of nitrate led to increased mine-worker militancy and the spread of Marxist ideology. In 1920 the Socialist Workers Party affiliated with the Soviet-sponsored Third International, and two years later it became the Communist Party of Chile. From the beginning the Communists were closely tied to the Soviet Union, a link that provided external support but produced ideological rigidity that limited its appeal.

In the early 1930s, when the Great Depression produced massive unemployment and economic paralysis, new So-

cialist groups emerged. In 1932, when left-leaning military men seized power, there was even a twelve-day Socialist Republic. In October 1933, the Socialist Party of Chile was founded by the fusion of several small groups that included, among others, a young doctor named Salvador Allende. The party's principles, while critical of international Communism, combined Marxist-influenced anti-imperialism and emphasis on the class struggle with a populist nationalism that called for an alliance of workers, peasants, and lower-middle-class ("petit bourgeois") groups against the domination of domestic and international economic elites.

Throughout the party's history, its relationship with the Communists has been ambivalent. On the one hand, the Marxist sectors of the Socialists advocated cooperation; on the other, the two parties competed for the same electoral groups, and the Socialists tried to appeal to both workers and middle-class groups. In 1938 they joined the Communists in supporting the Radical Party–dominated Popular Front. However, they left the coalition two years later when it became apparent that it would not carry out the revolutionary reforms that the Socialists proposed. They supported the Radical government of Gabriel Gonzalez Videla in 1946 but opposed it when it outlawed the Communist Party in 1948. After the legalization of the Communists in 1956, the Socialists formed a coalition with them, the Front for Popular Action (FRAP), that nominated Salvador Allende as its candidate in the 1958 presidential elections. In a five-candidate race, Allende came within 30,000 votes of winning against the Conservative candidate, Jorge Alessandri. In 1964, Allende ran again as the Communist-Socialist candidate but was defeated by the centrist Christian Democratic candidate, Eduardo Frei Montalva. Frei won an absolute majority, because the Liberal and Conservative parties, fearing an Allende victory, had thrown their support to him.

The Frei administration attempted to carry out what it called "a Revolution in Liberty" involving land redistribution and reforms in the areas of education, health, taxation, and housing, as well as "Chileanization"—that is, the partial purchase—of the large American-owned copper mines. Lacking a majority in the senate, Frei secured the support of the Left for land reform and of the centrist Radical Party for the Chileanization program. After initial success, the Frei government began to experience a worsening of inflation and a general radicalization of demands for change. In 1967, influenced by the Cuban Revolution and the spread of guerrilla movements in Latin America, the Socialist Party at its congress declared its opposition to bourgeois democracy and its support for proletarian revolution. On the far left, a Castroite revolutionary group, the Movement of the Revolutionary Left (MIR), carried out land seizures and called for an armed uprising. The Radical Party split into left and right factions, with the Left in control of the party apparatus. The Christian Democrats also split with the secession of the

Movement for United Popular Action, a small but influential left sector. On the right, the Liberal and Conservative parties, weakened by a Christian Democratic vote that had reduced them to an historic low, combined to create the National Party, which fiercely opposed the land reform law passed in 1967.

As the parties nominated their candidates in 1969, it was clear that the 1964 scenario would not be repeated. The Right was opposed to the agrarian reform, and its candidate was the popular former president Jorge Alessandri. President Frei, who was much more popular than his party, was prohibited by the constitution from running for a successive second term. The Christian Democratic candidate, Radomiro Tomic, called for radicalization of the social reforms and possible alliances with the Left. The Left, in turn, had broadened its base of Socialists and Communists to include in the new Popular Unity coalition, the main body of the Radical Party, the ex–Christian Democrats of the Unitary Popular Action Movement (MAPU), and several smaller groups.

The Allende program was strongly influenced by the Communists and was specific about the measures that it would take. It did not propose a wholesale takeover of industry but listed specific areas, giving priority to the nationalization of the copper mines and of other foreign-owned sectors. There was a distinct lack of enthusiasm for Allende's candidacy in his own Socialist Party, since he had lost in three previous elections. Furthermore, despite his close connections with Fidel Castro, he was not regarded as sufficiently revolutionary for a party that was now situated, in terms of advocating rapid transformation of society and greater willingness to use violence to overcome resistance to change, well to the left of the Communists.

On the eve of the election it was evident that Chile was divided into what some called "the three thirds"—the Left, the Center, and the Right. The supporters of Alessandri appealed to the Christian Democrats to imitate their own conduct in 1964 and support their more popular candidate in an effort to prevent an Allende victory. However, the Tomic forces argued that the revolutionary program of the Christian Democrats would be betrayed by a vote of their constituents in the 1970 election for the *mumios* (mummies) of the Right. The United States did not openly take sides in the election, as it had done in 1964, but engaged in an anti-Communist "spoiling" program that funneled covert funds into Chile for anti-Allende propaganda. Most polls showed that Alessandri would win, but in a country and a world that had become radicalized by the Cuban Revolution, opposition to the Vietnam War, and the revolt of students and young people, Allende triumphed by a narrow margin.

But this was a revolution with two months notice, since the constitution mandated a congressional runoff between the two top candidates fifty days after the popular election.

In the intervening period, the economy contracted as domestic and foreign capital fled the country. The Right tried unsuccessfully to persuade the Christian Democrats to vote for Alessandri, promising that he would resign after his election, thus making it possible for Frei to run and win in another presidential vote. The United States supported this option; when it failed, President Nixon ordered the CIA to organize a military coup. When the coup organizers failed to get military support, principally because of the opposition of the army commander, General Rene Schneider, a rightist group attempted to kidnap Schneider and killed him in the process, producing a wave of popular support for the observation of the constitutional process and a congressional victory for Allende.

CONTEXT AND PROCESS OF REVOLUTION

Why did Allende take office as president in what was basically a conservative country? Part of the explanation was Chilean respect for constitutionalism and legality, which made it possible for him to reach the presidency with only 36 percent of the vote, and with a legislature and judiciary strongly opposed to him. In addition, he had threatened violent action in the streets if the Congress did not respect its traditional practice (not required by the constitution) of electing the candidate who had an electoral plurality. The general radicalization of opinion in Chile and the world also had something to do with it. The example of the Cuban Revolution seemed to argue that a Marxist government would produce greater equality and social justice, and Allende had promised that this would take place within the constitutional framework. The Communists had for many years been committed to the peaceful road (*via pacifica*) to Socialism, and Allende represented the more moderate faction in what had become a Socialist Party committed to revolution. The fact that his coalition included segments of the parties that represented the middle classes also broadened his appeal.

The Christian Democratic program of agrarian reform also made it impossible for the Right to support their candidate as they had in 1964. The agrarian reform law adopted in 1967 set an upper limit on landholdings and provided compensation in bonds that were only partially adjustable for inflation. Moreover, the Christian Democratic ideology, which was based on neo-Thomism (the application of the principles of Saint Thomas Aquinas to modern political, social, and economic conditions) and the papal social encyclicals, supported a "communitarian" alternative to both capitalism and Socialism. When the party did not move in the direction of what its *rebelde* Left called "a non-capitalist way to development," they seceded from the party and helped to form the

Allende coalition. The Radical Party, which, despite its name, represented moderate small-town and middle-class groups and had supported the 1958–1964 Alessandri government, was taken over by its left wing, mostly young people, and had shifted its support to the Left.

On the right, the Alessandri forces were radicalized in a different direction. A student takeover of the Catholic University in 1967 had produced an alliance between the newly formed *gremalistas,* who resisted the politicization of the university by the Left, and the so-called Chicago Boys, the conservative professors of the School of Economics trained at the University of Chicago, who favored free enterprise and opposed both Marxism and what they regarded as the state interventionism of the economic policies of the Christian Democrats.

Once in power, the Allende government was divided on ideological lines between the "go slow" policies of the Communists and the Socialists most closely allied to Allende, and the commitment to revolution of the rest of the coalition. In addition, the Castroist Movement of the Revolutionary Left promoted land seizures and acceleration of the agrarian reform at the same time that on the shop floor young Catholic and Marxist radicals supported plant takeovers and economic democracy. When Allende tried to engage the Christian Democrats in negotiations, he was opposed by his own party at the same time that the Christian Democratic right wing became more and more intransigent.

Christian Democratic opposition was intensified in June 1971 by the assassination of Frei's former interior minister, Eduardo Perez Zucovic, by a member of a revolutionary group. By early 1972, the Christian Democrats and the Right had formed an opposition alliance that worked together in the Congress and in the 1973 congressional elections to oppose the Allende government. By 1973, the country had become deeply polarized, and groups on both sides began to arm themselves for an anticipated civil war. In July 1973, as inflation reached 500 percent, the economy was paralyzed by a second anti-Allende nationwide strike as well as pro-Allende worker takeovers of factories and peasant seizures of farms. The stage was set for the bloody coup d'état that followed on September 11. (A photograph of the Chilean military attack on September 11, 1973 can be found in the entry Reform, Rebellion, Civil War, Coup D'état, and Revolution on page 718).

Before the coup, most Chileans expected that the military would intervene, outlaw the Communist and Socialist parties, and call new elections, which ex-President Frei would win handily. This view underestimated the hostility of the military leaders to the Christian Democrats, whom they blamed for radicalizing the country and allowing Allende to come to power. They needed an alternative, however, and that was provided by the Chicago Boys in the form of a detailed program to open the economy and create an export-oriented Chilean Hong Kong, removing the elaborate program of state-controlled subsidies and spending for social welfare that had been built up since the 1930s.

They faced initial opposition from business groups that had been protected by high tariff walls, as well as from Catholic integralists who wished to establish a corporatist state. But when copper prices dropped and the economy ran into deep trouble, the Chicago Boys took control. They remained in power for most of the Pinochet period, except for a short time after a deep recession in 1982–1983. After a slow start, their programs were so successful economically that even after Pinochet left power, the opposition continued to support the opening to a globalized economy and the anti-inflationary fiscal policy they had promoted.

The continuities in economic policy were possible because the Socialists and the Christian Democrats now accepted an open market economy and the encouragement of private and foreign investment as necessary to finance the social programs they favored. The Communists continued to oppose the economic opening, however, and the remnants of a leftist guerrilla group, the Manuel Rodriguez Patriotic Front, engaged, for a time, in violent actions against the elected government, which they viewed as an instrument of bourgeois capitalism.

IMPACTS

Within and outside Chile, the Chilean Revolution was seen as a morality play, but each ideological group drew different moral lessons. The Right saw the Allende Revolution as part of the worldwide Communist conspiracy that would have established a Cuban-style "popular democracy," destroying religion, political pluralism, and economic freedom. The rapid escalation of violence and extremism they viewed as a consequence of the utopianism of the Left and the radicalization of the Center. On the left, the fact that Allende's overthrow was aided and abetted by the United States (there is no evidence that the United States was directly involved in the coup itself) was interpreted as yet another example of the determination of "imperialism" to dominate the world. The repression that followed and Pinochet's dictatorial rule were regarded as a typical response to the threat to capitalism posed by any popular democratic revolution that challenges economic privilege. For the Center, it was, in ex-President Frei's words, a "Greek tragedy" made inevitable by the willingness of both Left and Right to abandon democracy and compromise in defense of ideological purity and violent solutions (Personal interview, 1978).

The Allende experience was a learning process for each of the ideological groups. The Right largely abandoned its earlier reliance on state subsidies and tariff protection as well as its economic nationalism. It reorganized its activities to profit from increasing globalization, the creation of market-driven alternatives to government social policies, and the privatization of state enterprises. The Center realized that deficit spending, even for worthy social purposes, led to inflation that hurt low-income groups, and it largely abandoned its search for a "third way" as an alternative to capitalism and Socialism. The Left concluded that violent revolution was not the way to achieve social justice, and that "bourgeois" democracy and civil liberties were values to which the Left should be committed.

Internationally, the overthrow of Allende led to an intense debate on the place of revolution in the thought of the Left and encouraged the development of the "Eurocommunist" alternative to the Soviet model. This moderate approach to social reform, which involved commitment to change through legal, democratic means, was adopted by certain Western European Communist parties, including those in Italy and France. In Latin America and Europe, Chilean exiles led the fight against the Pinochet dictatorship, and Chileans participated in the Sandinista Revolution that overthrew the Somoza government in 1979. In 1980, partly because of the Sandinista success, the Chilean Communists abandoned the peaceful road to Socialism in favor of "all forms of struggle," including violence.

The economic success of the Pinochet reforms also encouraged other Latin American countries to adopt policies of privatization of state industries and social services, although the debt crisis and revenue problems also had much to do with those measures. In the United States, the Chilean case led to investigations of the covert operations of the Central Intelligence Agency and increased congressional supervision of its activities. The repression that followed the coup also was directly linked to the adoption of legislation by the U.S. Congress promoting human rights, and to the formal incorporation of democracy and human rights as goals of U.S. foreign policy.

PEOPLE AND ORGANIZATIONS

Alessandri, Jorge (1896–1986)

President of Chile from 1958 until 1964. A member of a prominent political family, his father had been president in the 1920s at the time of the adoption of the 1925 constitution and again from 1932 to 1938. He considered himself a businessman rather than a politician and was noted for his abstemiousness and modesty. He was supported by the Liberal, Conservative, and Radical parties. He ran again in 1970 as the candidate of the National Party, which had been formed by a fusion of the Liberals and Conservatives. He received 34.9 percent of the popular vote and came in second, forcing a congressional runoff that, following a period of tumult, resulted in the election of Salvador Allende, the candidate of the Left.

Allende, Salvador (1908–1973)

President of Chile from 1970 until his overthrow and death in a coup in 1973. One of the founders of the Socialist Party of Chile in 1933, he was trained as a doctor but spent his life as a professional politician. A self-declared Marxist, he pursued policies that wavered between a determination to carry out a full-scale Socialist revolution and a politician's willingness to compromise in order to secure agreement. During the September 1973 coup, he broadcast a moving farewell speech to the Chilean people and committed suicide as the military were entering the presidential palace.

Bachelet, Michelle (Born 1951)

A member Chile's Socialist Party and candidate of Concertación Coalition which included the Socialist and Christian Democrat Parties, was elected president of Chile on January 15 of 2006. Bachelet's father, an air force general, opposed the 1973 coup that violently overthrew the elected government of Salvador Allende. He was tortured by the Pinochet regime and died in prison. Later Michelle Bachelet and her mother were imprisoned for being members of the then-illegal Socialist Party. In 1975 they were exiled to Australia and later Bachelet lived in East Germany where she resumed her medical studies. In 1979 she returned to Chile and completed her medical training at the University of Chile in 1982. She joined the movement to re-establish democracy and worked to help the children of tortured or disappeared persons. In the 1990s, she took advanced courses at the National Security Academy in Chile and the Interamerican Defense College in Washington, D.C. During the administration of President Lagos, Bachelet first served as minister of health and then as the defense minister.

Christian Democratic Party of Chile

Founded in 1956 as fusion of the Falange, a progressive Catholic party, and the Social Christian wing of the Conservative Party. It supports democracy, human rights, and social welfare on the basis of Christian and humanist principles.

President Michelle Bachelet of Chile, elected on January 15, 2006, is a medical doctor and a Socialist Party member like President Salvador Allende, overthrown in the violent military coup on September 11, 1973. (Nancy Coste/Corbis)

Communist Party of Chile

Founded in 1922, it incorporated earlier Socialist groups based principally in the mining sectors. From the outset the party had close links to the Soviet Union, following its foreign policies and receiving subsidies from it. It had a major role in forming the Popular Unity coalition that elected Salvador Allende, and many of its leaders were murdered by the Pinochet regime. In 1980 it abandoned its earlier policy advocating a peaceful transition to Socialism in favor of the use of violence against dictatorial regimes. Outlawed by Pinochet, the party was legalized again after the transition to democracy and received 4–6 percent of the vote in the elections that followed.

Conservative Party of Chile

The oldest party in Chile, generally identified with the defense of the landed interests and the Catholic Church. It was dissolved in 1966 when it joined the Liberal Party to form the National Party.

Frei Montalva, Eduardo (1911–1982)

President of Chile from 1964 until 1970. A founder of the Christian Democratic Party of Chile, he led the party as it became the largest party in Chile during the 1960s. Committed to what he called "The Revolution in Liberty," a program of democratic reform based on Christian and humanist principles, he carried out an agrarian reform program, modernized education, health care, and fiscal policies, and directed the partial purchase of the American-owned copper mines in Chile. In the last period of the Allende administration, he led the opposition to Allende. Following a brief period of support for the coup, he was the principal opponent of the Pinochet dictatorship until his death in 1982.

Kissinger, Henry (Born 1923)

National security advisor and secretary of state during the presidencies of Richard Nixon and Gerald Ford, Kissinger was the principal and controversial architect of U.S. policy toward the Allende and Pinochet governments. He approved a program of economic pressures and covert assistance against the Allende government, which he regarded as a threat to U.S. interests in the Cold War.

Lagos, Ricardo (Born 1938)

President of Chile from 2000 until 2006. Originally a member of the Radical Party, he later became a Socialist and participated in the government of Salvador Allende. Returning from exile in the United States in the 1980s, he was one of the principal leaders of the Coalition (*Concertacion*) for Democracy that defeated Pinochet in the 1988 plebiscite and has won every Chilean election since then. Defeated as a candidate for the Chilean Senate in the 1989 elections as a result of a quirk in the electoral system, he was a cabinet minister in the Christian Democratic governments of the 1990s, and was elected president in 2000. During his administration, many of the legal and constitutional limits on Chilean democracy contained in the 1980 constitution were repealed, and the Chilean judiciary began to prosecute more vigorously the human rights violations that took place under Pinochet.

Liberal Party of Chile

With roots going back to the beginning of Chile, it represented business and urban interests, and joined with the Conservatives in forming the National Party in 1966.

Manuel Rodriguez Patriotic Front

A guerrilla group formed in the 1980s and drawn from the Communist Party youth. It carried out bombings and assassinations against the Pinochet regime, including an attempt on the dictator's life. For a time after the return to democracy, it continued to function and was responsible for the murder of a rightist senator in 1991. Most of its leaders are now in exile or in prison.

Movement of the Revolutionary Left

A pro-Castro guerrilla group established in 1967. It gave critical support to Allende but was not part of his Popular Unity coalition. Its members were systematically hunted down and killed by the Pinochet regime.

National Party of Chile

A party created to replace the Liberal and Conservative parties in 1966. It nominated Jorge Alessandri in the 1970 presidential election and was dissolved after the 1973 coup. An attempt was made to revive it during the 1980s, but it was replaced by new rightist parties.

Pinochet, Augusto (Born 1915)

Leader of the military coup that overthrew Allende and president of Chile from 1973 until 1990. Pinochet was appointed commander in chief of the Chilean army in August 1973, after the army generals forced Carlos Prats out of office. He joined the coup at the last minute, implementing a plan to seize control that had been developed earlier. His government engaged in a systematic program of torture, disappearances, and murder of members of the Chilean Left, especially in the early years after the coup. He promoted an economic opening to the global market and a reduction of state influence, while delaying political liberalization until the 1980s. In October 1988 he lost a plebiscite to extend his term that had been mandated by the 1980 constitution written under his auspices. He continued as commander in chief of the army until 1998. In October of that year he was placed under house arrest in Britain as a result of a Spanish extradition request for human rights violations. Returned to Chile for reasons of health, he continued to be subject to judicial actions for human rights abuses carried out during his presidency.

Popular Unity

The coalition of left parties and groups that nominated Salvador Allende as its candidate in 1969. It included the Communists, Socialists, Radicals, and other small groupings, including the Unitary Popular Action Movement (MAPU), that had seceded from the Christian Democratic Party.

Radical Party

Founded in the 1860s and strongly influenced by the Masonic order, it represented the middle class and government employees. It dominated the political Center in Chile in the mid twentieth century, until it was overtaken by the Christian Democratic Party. In 1967, it moved to the left and later joined the Popular Unity coalition behind Salvador Allende. After the return to democracy, it took the name of the Radical Social Democratic Party and became a relatively minor member of the Coalition for Democracy that has been in power in Chile since 1990.

Socialist Party of Chile

Founded in 1933, the party of Salvador Allende. The party ideology was originally a mixture of Marxism, populism, and nationalism. Strongly influenced by the Cuban Revolution, the party took a more radical position in the late 1960s. After the coup the Socialists were divided, but during the 1980s they were reunited, adopting a "renovated" position that rejected Marxism and promoted alliances with other parties to restore democracy to Chile. After the transition to democracy in 1990, they shared power with the Christian Democrats and other parties in the Coalition (Concertacion) for Democracy. Socialists Ricardo Lagos and Michelle Bachelet were elected presidents of Chile in 2000 and 2006 respectively.

Paul Sigmund

See Also Armed Forces, Revolution, and Counter-Revolution; Cuban Revolution; Democracy, Dictatorship, and Fascism; Documentaries of Revolution; Guatemalan Democratic Revolution, Counter-Revolution, and Restoration of Democracy; Human Rights, Morality, Social Justice, and Revolution; Literature and Modern Revolution; Reform, Rebellion, Civil War, Coup D'état, and Revolution; Terrorism

References and Further Readings
Cockcroft, James D., ed. 2000. *A Salvador Allende Reader.* New York: Ocean Press.
Davis, Nathaniel. 1985. *The Last Two Years of Salvador Allende.* Ithaca, NY: Cornell University Press.
Debray, Regis. 1971. *Conversations with Allende.* London: N.L.B.
Dinges, John. 2004. *The Condor Years.* New York: W. W. Norton.

Dinges, John. 2004. *The Condor Years.* New York: W. W. Norton.

Dinges, John, and Saul Landau 1980. *Assassination on Embassy Row.* New York: Pantheon Books.

Drake, Paul W. 1978. *Socialism and Populism in Chile, 1932–52.* Urbana: University of Illinois Press.

Faundez, Julio. 1988. *Marxism and Democracy in Chile, from 1932 to the Fall of Allende.* New Haven, CT: Yale University Press.

Furci, Carmelo. 1984. *The Chilean Communist Party and the Road to Socialism.* London: Zed Books.

Gil, Federico G., Ricardo Lagos, and Henry A. Landsberger, eds. 1979. *Chile at the Turning Point, Lessons of the Socialist Years, 1970–73.* Philadelphia: Institute for the Study of Human Values.

Oppenheim, Lois Hecht. 1999. *Politics in Chile,* 2nd edition. Boulder, CO: Westview Press.

Pollack, Benny, and Herman Rosenkranz. 1986. *Revolutionary Social Democracy, The Chilean Socialist Party.* London: Frances Pinter.

Rettig, Raul. 1991. *The Rettig Report: The National Commission for Truth and Reconciliation Report.* Santiago: National Commission for Truth and Reconciliation.

Sigmund, Paul E. 1977. *The Overthrow of Allende and the Politics of Chile.* Pittsburgh, PA: University of Pittsburgh Press.

Valech, Bishop Sergio. 2004. *The Valech Report: National Commission on Political Imprisonment and Torture Report.* Santiago: National Commission on Political Imprisonment and Torture.

Valenzuela, Arturo. 1978. *Chile: The Breakdown of Democratic Regimes.* Baltimore, MD: Johns Hopkins University Press.

Walker, Ignacio. 1988. *Socialism and Democracy: Chile in Comparative Perspective.* PhD diss. Princeton, NJ: Princeton University.

"Chile, Country Reports on Human Rights Practices—2001." 2001. www.state.gov/g/drl/rls/hrrpt/2001/wha/8318.htm accessed January 21, 2005.

Gonzalez, Gustavo. 2004. "Reparations, but Not Justice, for Torture Victims." 2004. www.ipsnews.net/interna.asp?idnews=26468 accessed January 21, 2005.

"Poverty and Income Distribution in a High Growth Economy—The Case of Chile 1987–98." 2004. http://poverty2.forumone.com/library/view/11513: accessed on December 2, 2005

Valech Report. 2004. www.commisiontortura.cl/inicio/index.php accessed January 24, 2005.

Chinese 1989 Democracy Movement

CHRONOLOGY

1976	In January, reformist Chinese Communist Party (CCP) leader Zhou Enlai dies. In April, crowds mourning Zhou and supporting CCP pragmatist Deng Xiaoping are violently dispersed.
	In September, Mao Zedong, the leader of the Chinese Communist Party (CCP) since 1935, dies.
1978	Deng Xiaoping becomes the top leader of the CCP. Economic modernization is declared the key goal of the party, and ideological controls are loosened.
1978–1980	The "Democracy Wall Movement" emerges. Posters, unofficial "people's periodicals," and petitioners call for political reform and the redress of grievances arising from the period of Maoist rule. Beginning in late 1979, major participants are arrested and given lengthy prison terms.
1981	Hu Yaobang is appointed to the top post in the CCP, yet Deng Xiaoping remains the most powerful decision maker within the party.
1983	Deng Xiaoping begins the "Anti-Spiritual Pollution" campaign, opposing wholesale westernization.
1986–1987	Student demonstrations call for campus autonomy and political reform. Due to his support of the protestors, Hu Yaobang is forced to resign. Zhao Ziyang replaces him in the top CCP post. The "Anti-Bourgeois Liberalization" campaign condemns wholesale westernization.
1987–1988	Beijing University students form various reform-oriented discussion groups.
1989	
April 15	Hu Yaobang dies. Posters of mourning appear on Beijing campuses.
April 17	Beijing students march to Tiananmen Square to memorialize Hu.
April 18	Students begin a sit-in at Tiananmen Square.
April 19	The Beijing University Autonomous Union (BUAU) forms.
April 20	The Beijing Normal University Autonomous Union (BNUAU) forms.
April 21	BNUAU leaders initiate the formation of the Temporary All-Beijing Student Autonomous Federation.

April 24   Representatives of all Beijing universities formally establish the All-Beijing Student Autonomous Federation (BSAF).

April 25   The text of the April 26 *People's Daily* editorial is broadcast, accusing the demonstrators of "creating turmoil" and branding the new organizations "illegal." The BSAF agrees to hold a march on April 27.

April 27   Over 100,000 students march to Tiananmen Square, passing peacefully through numerous police blockades and attracting huge crowds of onlookers and supporters.

April 29   Government and student leaders hold an inconclusive dialogue.

May 4   Hundreds of thousands of students gather at Tiananmen Square.

May 13   Approximately 800 students march to Tiananmen Square, formally initiating a hunger strike.

May 14   Government and student leaders hold a second inconclusive dialogue.

May 15   The student occupation of Tiananmen Square forces the cancellation of the planned welcoming ceremony for Soviet president Mikhail Gorbachev.

Hunger-striking students form the Hunger Strike Command (HSC).

May 16–19   Thousands of students from outside Beijing arrive in Tiananmen Square; hundreds of new students join the hunger strike. The Outside Students Autonomous Federation (OSAF) and Beijing Workers Autonomous Federation (BWAF) are formed.

May 18   Government and student leaders hold a third inconclusive dialogue.

May 19   Zhao Ziyang and CCP premier Li Peng visit the square. Li Peng announces the imposition of martial law. The army is blocked when hundreds of thousands of citizens spontaneously fill the streets.

May 27   Representatives of all major factions and groups agree to withdraw from the square on May 30. Hunger-strike participants vow to remain at the square until June 20.

May 29   Prominent student leaders Wu'er Kaixi and Wang Dan publicly suggest that the students withdraw from the square. Approximately 5,000 hunger-striking students remain.

June 1   News of an impending army takeover reaches the square.

June 3   Violent clashes erupt between soldiers and citizens as the army closes in on the square.

June 4   Minutes before the army reaches the square, the remaining students agree to withdraw. They are soon escorted by a contingent of soldiers. None are harmed. Up to 2,000 others, mostly ordinary citizens, are killed. Thousands more are injured. Official pronouncements describe the movement as a "counterrevolutionary rebellion." A "Twenty-One Most Wanted" list is circulated, and major movement leaders go into hiding, flee the country, or face arrest and lengthy prison terms. Zhao Ziyang is purged from his party posts and placed under house arrest. Jiang Zemin is appointed to the top CCP post.

1992   Deng Xiaoping tours the free-enterprise zones of southern China, calling for rapid economic liberalization and international opening.

1992–1996   Newly freed political prisoners secretly network.

1997–1998   China signs the UN covenants on Economic, Social, and Cultural Rights, and on Civil and Political Rights.

1998   In June, the China Democracy Party (CDP) is established. Local party committees appear in twenty-four provinces and cities, and a national preparatory committee is formed. In December, top CDP leaders are imprisoned.

1999   Second-tier CDP leaders are arrested. Public CDP activities cease.

| 2004 | CDP leaders Wang Youcai and Xu Wenli are paroled and forcibly exiled to the United States. Zhao Ziyang dies. |
| 2005 | Xu Wenli establishes the Overseas Exile Headquarters of the China Democracy Party. |

INTRODUCTION

The Chinese People's Movement of 1989 was the largest and most sustained opposition movement to appear in Communist China. Even so, it was not a successful "revolution." Not only was it violently crushed by Communist Party authorities before it achieved any substantial change, but the protestors themselves did not seek to overthrow the existing regime. Nonetheless, the movement was branded a "counter-revolutionary rebellion" (Yuan 1989, 12) by the Communist Party and is widely viewed as a "failed" revolution, especially in contrast to the fall of Communist regimes in Russia and Eastern Europe during the same period. Moreover, the movement and its repression continue to influence China's domestic and international politics through the present.

BACKGROUND: CULTURE AND HISTORY

The Chinese Communist Party (CCP) has ruled China since 1949. Through 1976, Mao Zedong led the country according to his vision of ideological purity over pragmatism. This vision resulted in policies of radical land redistribution, the liberation of women, the creation of massive agricultural collectives, and a tumultuous internal "Cultural Revolution" against feudal and capitalist ideas. When other top CCP leaders opposed Mao's policies, they typically were purged from their party positions. One such person, Deng Xiaoping, was stripped of his party posts in 1966 and branded a "capitalist-roader" due to his pragmatic views. Still, in the early 1970s another relatively pragmatic top CCP leader, Zhou Enlai, was designated the successor to Mao. From this position, Zhou pursued détente with the United States and announced his commitment to the "Four Modernizations"—agriculture, industry, science/technology, and defense.

In 1976, the deaths of Zhou Enlai and Mao Zedong led to great conflict and transformation. In January, Zhou passed away, dashing the hopes of many who had hoped for a less ideologically driven polity. As part of the annual April festival in memory of the dead, huge crowds gathered in Beijing's central Tiananmen Square, carrying wreaths mourning Zhou's passing, but also displaying symbols of support for Deng Xiaoping. On April 5, the crowds were forcibly dispersed, and dozens were injured, killed, or arrested. The pro-Mao "Gang of Four," which remained in control of the media, branded the demonstrations "counter-revolutionary" and reiterated earlier charges that Deng Xiaoping was a "capitalist-roader." Meanwhile, the relatively unknown and powerless Hua Guofeng was appointed as Mao's successor. In September, Mao died. One month later, the Gang of Four were arrested, and the Cultural Revolution formally came to an end.

At this point, Deng Xiaoping made a comeback. After being restored to his former posts in 1977, he was appointed general secretary in 1978. Simultaneously, the earlier verdict on the "April 5 Movement" was reversed, and economic modernization was declared the key goal of the party. Ideological controls were loosened, private enterprise was tolerated, and joint investment with foreign companies was encouraged, especially in newly designated Special Enterprise Zones (SEZs) on the southeastern coast of China.

In this context, in late 1978, citizens began to put up posters, distribute unofficial "people's periodicals," and speak at a wall near Tiananmen Square. Most expressed grievances for suffering endured during the Cultural Revolution, but some also called for political reform. Initially, Deng voiced support for the sentiments expressed at "Democracy Wall," but as the movement spread to other major cities, and as the appeals became critical of Deng and his policies, Deng's attitude turned. Well-known participants, including Wei Jingsheng (author of the "Fifth Modernization"—democracy) and Xu Wenli were arrested and given extended prison sentences. By 1980, the wall had been shut down and the political environment had become constricted. It was clear that although Deng was a pragmatist who favored economic privatization and marketization, he was no democrat. The "Anti-Spiritual Pollution" campaign of 1983 further displayed Deng's concern about checking full-scale westernization.

Meanwhile, in 1981 Hu Yaobang was appointed to the top CCP post. Although Hu evidenced greater openness to political reform than Deng Xiaoping, Deng still held the real reins of power. Nonetheless, Deng's desire for economic modernization soon led him to consider further reform. In 1986, largely under the prodding of Hu, the University of Science and Technology (UST) was designated to lead educational reform. As university administrators, faculty, and students discussed the content and pace of reforms, some began to call for larger political reforms, and some even ran for political office as non-CCP candidates. By the winter of 1986, student demonstrations had erupted at the UST and other major campuses. In early 1987, under the direction of Deng, CCP authorities successfully pressured the demonstrators to cease.

The UST president was expelled from the party, and Hu Yaobang was dismissed from his post. To re-instill the "proper" attitude among the citizenry, Deng launched the "Anti-Bourgeois Liberalization" campaign. Another round of political loosening and restriction had come to pass. The same process—albeit on a much larger scale—would repeat itself in the spring of 1989.

CONTEXT AND PROCESS OF REVOLUTION

In 1987–1988, CCP leaders disagreed over reform, and public discontent ran high. In 1987, Zhao Ziyang replaced Hu Yaobang in the top CCP post, yet the elder Deng Xiaoping remained the final arbiter of all major decisions. In October of 1987, Zhao called for hastened economic reform and "emancipation of thought." But by the summer of 1988, inflation had spiraled out of control. Moreover, most ordinary citizens believed that corruption was rampant within the CCP.

In this context, Beijing University (BU) students established various informal discussion and reform groups that skirted the required CCP oversight. On April 15, 1989, a public announcement roused these and other students to more overt public action: Hu Yaobang was dead. Immediately, posters began to appear on Beijing campuses to mourn the students' beloved leader. On April 17, students marched to Tiananmen Square. Following another march on April 18, some students began a sit-in at the square.

During the week of April 19–26, more formal movement organizations began to emerge. On April 19, hundreds of Beijing University students gathered on campus to discuss the formation of a campus-wide non–Chinese Communist Party student organization. Nine students came forward to form the Beijing University Autonomous Union (BUAU). On April 20, three Beijing Normal University (BNU) students, led by Wu'er Kaixi, formed a similar organization. Instead of holding a meeting, these BNU students simply drew up a poster announcing the group's establishment and naming themselves as the group's leaders. After the poster appeared, virtually every department on campus sent a student representative to register with the group. In this way, the BNU Autonomous Union (BNUAU) was established. Subsequently, the initiators of the BNUAU circulated a flyer announcing that on April 21 a city-wide student autonomous federation would be formed at the BNU soccer field. On the appointed date, approximately 60,000 students from every Beijing institution of higher learning gathered. They agreed to send representatives to a more formal meeting on April 24. On that date, the All-Beijing Student Autonomous Federation (BSAF) was formally established.

Yet continued organization was threatened by a strongly negative official editorial that aired the following evening. Entitled "It Is Necessary to Take a Clear-Cut Stand against Turmoil," the statement accused the demonstrators of "creating turmoil" and branded the new organizations "illegal" (Oksenberg, Sullivan, and Lambert 1990, 207–208). The BSAF meeting that followed this broadcast was tense and heated. Student representatives feared the consequences of further provoking the authorities, yet were outraged at the government's fierce response to their actions. In the end, they agreed to hold a march April 27, but to chant "Long Live the Communist Party" and to march only partway to Tiananmen Square before returning to their campuses. When April 27 arrived, over 100,000 students from every higher education institution in Beijing joined the march. Moreover, hundreds of thousands of city folk lined the streets to watch and express their support. The students' confidence was so high that when they approached various police blockades, they simply marched peacefully through. And when they reached their designated return point, they spontaneously continued on to the square. Public support for the students swelled.

Although the students were jubilant from their success, events over the next few days displayed the precarious position of the protestors and the new organizations. On April 28, the BSAF decided to hold a second march on May 4. This date marked the seventieth anniversary of the May 4th Movement of 1919, which had called for democracy and science during China's period of warlord rule and had been a formative experience for the original founders of the CCP. Meanwhile, divisions over the student movement were becoming more apparent within the top ranks of the CCP. On April 29, the government called for a dialogue. When the talks were held, student representatives grilled the government officials with questions regarding the legitimacy of the official CCP-led student government, political corruption, education reform, and constitutional provisions regarding freedom of expression. The government representatives provided only vague and rambling replies, and abruptly ended the meeting after alleging that the demonstrations had included some "bad elements," "idlers," and "perverts" (Oksenberg, Sullivan, and Lambert 1990, 218–244). No agreement was reached, and the students were outraged. Yet Zhao Ziyang seemed sympathetic to the students' concerns. For example, when hundreds of thousands of students converged on Tiananmen Square for the May 4 demonstration, Zhao declared that the movement did not present a serious threat to political stability and should "be handled through legal and democratic means" (Oksenberg, Sullivan, and Lambert 1990, 255). Nevertheless, students were unable to make any clear progress. Frustrated, some students began to call for more provocative measures to elicit a satisfactory government response. On May 11, six BU and BNU students met to discuss a possible hunger strike.

On May 12, these students presented the idea to the BUAU, BNUAU, and BSAF. When some members of the BUAU and BSAF expressed opposition to the hunger strike, proponents insisted that they would begin the strike regardless of the organizations' positions. On May 13, approximately 800 students from BU and BNU marched to Tiananmen Square. After formally announcing the initiation of the hunger strike, they commenced a continuous occupation of the square.

Meanwhile, on May 15 Soviet president Mikhail Gorbachev was due to arrive in Beijing for the first meeting of Chinese and Soviet leaders in forty years. As international media converged on Beijing for this momentous event, CCP elites attempted to convince the students to evacuate the square. Thus, on May 14, a second dialogue was held. Yet, like the first, it ended abruptly before any compromise was reached. Consequently, hundreds of hunger-striking students remained in the square on May 15. The planned gala welcoming ceremony for Gorbachev was cancelled, and images of China's hunger-striking students were broadcast around the globe.

This series of events convinced Deng Xiaoping that the demonstrations had to be ended. While Gorbachev was in town, however, the party's hands were tied. Meanwhile, during this brief period the number of students and citizens at the square had increased exponentially. With the expanded media coverage, tens of thousands of students from outside Beijing flocked to the square, and hundreds more joined in the hunger strike. To help organize the hunger-striking students, a new organization was formed—the Hunger Strike Command, led by Chai Ling, Feng Congde, and Li Lu. In addition, an Outside [Beijing] Students Autonomous Federation was established. At the same time, ordinary workers began to join the demonstrations and organize, ultimately forming the Beijing Workers Autonomous Federation. By the time of Gorbachev's departure, the movement had swelled enormously.

This only hardened Deng's resolve to put an end to the movement. On May 18, the government made one last-ditch effort to stop the demonstrations peacefully. Early that morning, BSAF leaders were notified that the government would hold another dialogue. Unlike the previous meetings, this dialogue was televised nationally. However, the result was the same: intransigence and condescending statements on the part of government representatives (in this case, including Premier Li Peng himself), and frustration and anger on the part of the students. Around dawn on May 19, Li Peng and Zhao Ziyang made a surprise appearance at the square. Li uttered only a few words of greeting, but Zhao wept and said, "We have come too late. I am sorry, fellow students. You have the right to criticize us. It is proper for you to do so" (*Data from the Chinese People's Movement of 1989* 1991, 295). Later that day, Li Peng announced the imposition of martial law, and the army began to enter the city. To every-one's surprise, however, hundreds of thousands of ordinary citizens spontaneously went into the streets to block the army's movement toward the square. With no clear orders in anticipation of this occurrence, the army retreated.

The demonstrators were heartened by this turn of events, yet remained extremely fearful, as martial law remained in place. On May 27 representatives met from all of the major groups that had formed since the movement's start. They agreed to withdraw from the square on May 30. On May 29, Wang Dan, Wu'er Kaixi, and Chai Ling were to announce the withdrawal. But when Chai Ling reported the decision to the hunger-striking students, many were outraged. In the end, the hunger strikers agreed that they would remain at the square until June 20. When Wang Dan and Wu'er Kaixi arrived at the square on May 29, Chai Ling informed them of the hunger strikers' change in plan. Given this, Wang and Wu'er publicly "suggested" that the students withdraw. Most did, yet about 5,000 hunger-striking students remained at the square.

Shortly thereafter, the army again moved to assert control over the city. On June 1, news of an impending army takeover reached the hunger-striking students. Late at night on June 3, the army began to move toward the square. Once again, citizens came into the streets to block them. Yet this time, the soldiers had clear orders to advance at any cost. Consequently, thousands of citizens, and dozens of soldiers, were killed or injured.

Hearing reports of violent confrontations, and aware that the army was fast approaching, the students who remained at the square held a final meeting where they decided to retreat. Led by Chai Ling, Feng Congde, and Li Lu, the students formed an orderly line and marched out of the square. They were soon met by a contingent of soldiers. But rather than harming the students, the soldiers escorted them; none of the students who had remained at the square until the end were harmed.

In the days and months that followed, Deng sought to reestablish control. Official pronouncements called the movement "a shocking counter-revolutionary rebellion" (Yuan 1989, 12) that had fomented "a struggle involving the life and death of the Party and state" (Chen 1989, 3). To facilitate the arrest of major movement leaders, a "Twenty-One Most Wanted List" was circulated widely. Those on the list went into hiding, fled the country, or were arrested and sentenced to lengthy prison terms. Within the top ranks of the CCP, Zhao Ziyang was purged from his party posts and placed under house arrest. In his stead, Jiang Zemin, the party secretary in Shanghai, was appointed to the top CCP post. Ideological education was stepped up in universities and schools, study-abroad programs were curtailed, and lower-level movement leaders faced varying degrees of official surveillance and difficulties in finding desirable employment.

A Chinese man stands alone to block a line of tanks after the pro-democracy demonstration in Tiananmen Square. (AP/Wide World Photos)

Thus, while Communist Party rule fell in Eastern Europe and the Soviet Union, in China it remained. Though the student and citizen demonstrators in China had only called for dialogue and reform, they had been branded "counter-revolutionaries" and severely punished. No concrete gains had been achieved by the protestors, and in the end, the ruling regime had only strengthened its hand.

IMPACTS

Although the movement of 1989 did not result in a revolution, it continues to influence China's domestic and international politics. In the short term, the CCP's brutal repression of the protests precipitated a souring of relations with major world powers. Within a few years, normal relations largely resumed, yet CCP elites still face regular international criticism for their role in the massacre.

Domestically, for the millions who participated in the demonstrations in some way, the movement's repression and continued official condemnation have left a deep feel-

ing of bitterness that detracts from the legitimacy of the ruling Communist Party. In fact, the movement is so well known that the simple mention of "6–4" ("*liu-si*") instantaneously evokes the memory of the regime's violence against ordinary citizens. Consequently, as each anniversary of the June 4 massacre approaches, the government tightly cracks down to ensure that no memorials are held. Known dissidents are placed under heavy surveillance or detained, and security forces ensure that Tiananmen Square and other public gathering places remain clear. Meanwhile, in Hong Kong, tens of thousands gather yearly to memorialize the movement.

As the 1990s progressed, CCP elites reaffirmed their commitment to economic reform and gave some indications of political loosening. In 1992, Deng Xiaoping toured the free-enterprise zones in southern China, calling for rapid economic liberalization and international opening. In the years that followed, a number of prominent 1989 leaders, as well as earlier dissidents, were released from prison. Some fled the country, but others, including 1989 leader Wang Youcai and Democracy Wall leaders Xu Wenli and Qin Yongmin, remained. These newly released dissidents cautiously began to network. In 1997–1998, they were emboldened by some seemingly promising official signs. Most importantly, China signed the United Nations covenants on Economic, Social, and Cultural Rights, and on Civil and Political Rights.

With this apparent political loosening, some former 1989 and Democracy Wall leaders decided to make a public move. On the eve of U.S. president Bill Clinton's visit to China in June of 1998, Wang Youcai announced the establishment of a local preparatory committee of the China Democracy Party (CDP). This was the first true opposition party formed in China since 1949. Wang and his companions attempted to form and then register their group with the local government and called on other citizens to do the same. Surprised by this action, CCP elites appeared unsure of how to respond. Meanwhile, local CDP organizations proliferated, with Democracy Wall activists Xu Wenli and Qin Yongmin joining the CDP's leading ranks. By the end of 1998, local party committees had appeared in twenty-four cities and provinces, and a national preparatory committee had formed.

Yet, reflecting the CCP's desire to maintain its monopoly on political power even while pursuing economic reform, public CDP actions were forcibly ended after only a few months. In December of 1998, Wang Youcai, Xu Wenli, and Qin Yongmin each were sentenced to more than ten years in prison. When second-tier CDP leaders persisted in their activities, they, too, were arrested. By 2000, virtually all public CDP activities had ceased. In 2004–2005, Xu Wenli and Wang Youcai were released on medical parole and forcibly exiled to the United States. In 2005, Xu established the Overseas Exile Headquarters of the China Democracy Party, which coordinates the efforts of pro-democracy activists overseas and also works with domestic activists who remain underground in China.

The influence of the movement of 1989 on the CDP is apparent. Its founder, Wang Youcai, helped lead the BSAF in 1989 and was punished with six years in prison. This experience is typical. In fact, more than one of four CDP leaders played a leadership role in the spring of 1989. Moreover, 60–70 percent of all CDP members participated in the 1989 protests in some way (Wright 2002, 921–922; Wright 2004, 172).

Nonetheless, China's pro-democracy activists face an uphill battle. In early 2004, former CCP general secretary Zhao Ziyang passed away, erasing the presence of the last top CCP leader to sympathize with the protests of 1989. Zhao's death was quietly mentioned only days after the event, and no public funeral was held. CCP elites carefully prevented any potential public outpouring of mourning that might develop into a movement similar to that which resulted from the death of Hu Yaobang in 1989. Security remained tight as the

April festival to memorialize the dead passed, and no sign of public dissent emerged. Still, as long as CCP leaders refuse to acknowledge the peaceful intent of the 1989 protestors or apologize for their brutal repression, the party's legitimacy will be weak, and it will be vulnerable to calls for political change.

PEOPLE AND ORGANIZATIONS

All-Beijing Student Autonomous Federation (BSAF)

The BSAF formed out of an open-air meeting called by the BNUAU's founders on April 21, 1989. During the movement of 1989, it represented every higher education institution in Beijing.

Beijing Normal University Autonomous Union (BNUAU)

Formed by three students, the BNUAU was the second student movement group to emerge in the spring of 1989. Immediately following its formation, the BNUAU's founders initiated the establishment of the BSAF.

Beijing University Autonomous Union (BUAU)

The BUAU was the first student movement group to be formed in the spring of 1989. It was established following an open-air meeting at Beijing University on April 19.

Beijing Workers' Autonomous Federation (BWAF)

The BWAF was formally established in mid May of 1989. By early June, Workers' Autonomous Federations had appeared in twenty other major Chinese cities, with a total membership of roughly 20,000. The BWAF's leaders were among the first arrested in the crackdown on the movement.

Chai Ling (Born 1966)

One of the key initiators of the hunger strike and the HSC, Beijing University student Chai Ling was one of the last students to remain at the square. She was married to Feng Congde, though they later divorced. After appearing on the "Twenty-One Most Wanted List," Chai fled to the United States.

Chang Jing (Born 1967)

In 1988, Chang Jing formed a reform-oriented student group at Beijing University. In the spring of 1989, Chang was a founding member of the BUAU. Following the movement's repression, he fled to the United States.

China Democracy Party (CDP)

In June of 1998 many 1989 activists helped to form the CDP, which was the first true opposition party in Communist China. The CDP quickly expanded to twenty-four cities and provinces across China. Beginning in December of 1998, top CDP leaders were arrested; by 2000 its public activities ceased.

Deng Xiaoping (1904–1997)

Although he did not always hold a formal position, Deng Xiaoping was the most powerful leader of the CCP from 1978 to 1997. He pursued economic privatization and marketization, but also ordered the violent repression of the 1989 protests.

Feng Congde (Born 1967)

Married to Chai Ling (but later divorced), Beijing University student Feng Congde was a founding member of the BUAU and the HSC. He was one of the last students to remain at the square. After appearing on the "Twenty-One Most Wanted" list, he fled to France.

Hu Yaobang (1915–1989)

Hu Yaobang served in the top CCP post from 1981–1987. Due to his support of the student demonstrations of 1986–1987, Hu was forced to resign. His death in April of 1989 sparked the protests that culminated in the June 4 massacre.

Hunger Strike Command (HSC)

The Hunger Strike Command was formed on May 15, 1989, to help support and organize the hunger-striking students at the square. The HSC rejected the May 27 agreement to withdraw from the square on May 30. Consequently, the group was the last to remain at the square.

Li Lu (Born 1966)

In late April 1989, Nanjing University student Li Lu joined the student demonstrations. He helped to form the Hunger Strike Command and was one of the last students to remain at the square. After appearing on the "Twenty-One Most Wanted" list, Li fled to the United States.

Li Peng (Born 1928)

As premier in 1989, Li Peng took a hard-line stance against the demonstrations. He remains a top CCP leader.

Mao Zedong (1893–1976)

A founding member of the CCP, Mao Zedong led the party from 1935–1976.

Outside Students Autonomous Federation (OSAF)

The OSAF was established on May 18, 1989, to organize and support the thousands of students from outside Beijing who had come to Tiananmen Square.

Qin Yongmin (Born 1953)

For his role in the Democracy Wall Movement, Qin Yongmin was sentenced to seven years in prison in 1980. He became a major leader of the China Democracy Party in 1998, for which he was re-arrested and sentenced to eleven years in prison.

Shen Tong (Born 1968)

In 1988, Shen Tong helped form two reform-oriented student groups at Beijing University. In the spring of 1989, Shen helped lead the BUAU and the BSAF. He later fled to the United States.

Wang Dan (Born 1969)

In 1987–1988, Wang Dan formed three reform-oriented student groups at Beijing University. In April of 1989, Wang was a founding member of the BUAU. Subsequently, he became a prominent "freelance" leader of the movement. After appearing on the government's "Twenty-One Most Wanted" list, Wang was arrested and sentenced to four years in prison. He was paroled in 1993, but arrested again in 1995 for petitioning for the release of 1989-related political prisoners and sentenced to eleven years in prison. In 1998, he was forcibly exiled to the United States.

Wang Youcai (Born 1966)

Beijing University student Wang Youcai helped lead the BSAF. After appearing on the "Twenty-One Most Wanted" list, he was jailed for three years. In 1998, he was sentenced to eleven years in prison for founding the China Democracy Party. In 2004, he was forcibly exiled to the United States.

Wu'er Kaixi (Born 1968)

Wu'er Kaixi was the key founder of the BNUAU and the BSAF who later became a prominent "freelance" leader of the movement. During the student-government dialogue of May 18, Wu'er confronted CCP premier Li Peng on national television. After appearing on the "Twenty-One Most Wanted List," Wu'er fled to the United States. He later moved to Taiwan.

Xu Wenli (Born 1943)

For his role in the Democracy Wall Movement, in 1980 Xu Wenli was sentenced to fifteen years in prison. He became a major leader of the China Democracy Party in 1998, for which he was re-arrested and sentenced to thirteen years. He was forcibly exiled to the United States in 2004. In 2005, he established the Overseas Exile Headquarters of the China Democracy Party.

Yang Tao (Born 1970)

In 1987–1888, Yang Tao helped establish three reform-oriented student groups at Beijing University. In the spring of 1989, he helped lead the BUAU. After appearing on the government's "Twenty-One Most Wanted" list, he was detained for thirteen months. In 1998, he petitioned the CCP for the release of CDP leader Wang Youcai. In 1999, he was detained for petitioning to commemorate the tenth anniversary of June 4, 1989. In 2003, he was sentenced to four years in prison but was released within a few months.

Zhao Ziyang (1919–2004)

Zhao Ziyang served in the top CCP post from 1987 to 1989. In the spring of 1989, Zhao expressed support for the demonstrations. Consequently, he was removed from the top party post and placed under house arrest, where he remained until his death in 2004.

Zhou Enlai (1898–1976)

From 1972 until his death in 1976, Zhou Enlai was the designated successor to Mao Zedong. Following Zhou's death in 1976, huge crowds were forcibly dispersed after gathering at Tiananmen Square in mourning, and in support of Deng Xiaoping.

Teresa Wright

See Also Chinese Revolution; Cinema of Revolution; Democracy, Dictatorship, and Fascism; Documentaries of Revolution; Elites, Intellectuals, and Revolutionary Leadership; Human Rights, Morality, Social Justice, and Revolution; South Korean Democracy Movement; Student and Youth Movements, Activism and Revolution

References and Further Readings
Black, George, and Robin Munro. 1993. *Black Hands of Beijing: Lives of Defiance in China's Democracy Movement.* New York: John Wiley and Sons.
Calhoun, Craig. 1994. *Neither Gods nor Emperors: Students and the Struggle for Democracy in China.* Berkeley: University of California Press.
Chen Xitong. 1989. *Report on Checking the Turmoil and Quelling the Counter-Revolutionary Rebellion.* Beijing: New Star Publishers.
Data from the Chinese People's Movement of 1989 (Bajiu Zhongguo Minyun Ziliao). 1991. Hong Kong: Hong Kong Chinese Language University Student Union.
Han Minzhu and Hua Sheng, eds. 1990. *Cries for Democracy: Writings and Speeches from the 1989 Chinese Democracy Movement.* Princeton, NJ: Princeton University Press.
Hartford, Kathleen, Lawrence Sullivan, Suzanne Ogden, and David Zweig, eds. 1992. *China's Search for Democracy: The Student and Mass Movement of 1989.* Armonk, NY: M. E. Sharpe.
Nathan, Andrew, and Perry Link, eds. 2001. *The Tiananmen Papers.* New York: Public Affairs.
New China News Agency (Xinhua) (Beijing; in English). May 4, 1989. P. 255 in *Beijing Spring, 1989; Confrontation and Conflict; The Basic Documents*, edited by Michel Oksenberg, Lawrence R. Sullivan, and Marc Lambert. Armonk, NY: M. E. Sharpe.
New China News Agency (Xinhua). May 19, 1989. P. 295 in *Data from the Chinese People's Movement of 1989.* Hong Kong: Hong Kong Chinese Language University Student Union.
Oksenberg, Michel, Lawrence R. Sullivan, and Marc Lambert, eds. 1990. *Beijing Spring, 1989; Confrontation and Conflict; The Basic Documents.* Armonk, NY: M. E. Sharpe.
Saich, Tony, ed. 1990. *Perspectives on the Chinese People's Movement: Spring 1989.* Armonk, NY: M. E. Sharpe.

Schell, Orville. 1994. *Mandate of Heaven.* New York: Simon and Schuster.

Shen Tong. 1990. *Almost a Revolution.* Boston: Houghton-Mifflin.

Unger, Jonathan, ed. 1991. *The Pro-Democracy Protests in China: Reports from the Provinces.* Armonk, NY: M. E. Sharpe.

Walder, Andrew, and Gong Xiaoxia. 1993. "Workers in the Tiananmen Protests: The Politics of the Beijing Workers' Autonomous Federation." *The Australian Journal of Chinese Affairs* 29: 1–29.

Wright, Teresa. 2001. *The Perils of Protest: State Repression and Student Activism in China and Taiwan.* Honolulu: University of Hawaii Press.

———. 2002. "The China Democracy Party and the Politics of Protest in the 1980s–1990s," *China Quarterly* 172 (December): 906–926.

———. 2004. "Intellectuals and the Politics of Protest: The Case of the China Democracy Party." Pp. 158–180 in *Chinese Intellectuals between State and Market,* edited by Edward Gu and Merle Goldman. New York: Routledge.

Yuan Mu (news conference). Beijing Television Service. June 6, 1989. FBIS (Foreign Broadcast Information Service) June 7, 1989, p. 12.

———. 1990. "Text of Student Dialogue with Yuan Mu." Pp. 218–244 in *Beijing Spring, 1989; Confrontation and Conflict; The Basic Documents,* edited by Michel Oksenberg, Lawrence R. Sullivan, and Marc Lambert. Armonk, NY: M. E. Sharpe.

Zhao Dingxin. 2004. *The Power of Tiananmen: State-Society Relations and the 1989 Beijing Student Movement.* Chicago: University of Chicago Press.

Chinese Revolution

CHRONOLOGY

551–479 B.C.   Confucius develops a social and political philosophy that shapes China's culture for hundreds of years.

1644–1911   The Manchu (Qing) dynasty rules China. This Manchurian family's rule brings an extended period of peace, allowing the population to greatly expand. But the Manchus' inability to resist invaders and foreign economic exploitation of China weaken their hold on power and turn many Chinese against the monarchy, eventually giving rise to the Republican Revolutionary Movement.

1839–1842   Great Britain defeats China in the Opium Wars, forcing China to allow British merchants to expand the sale of opium and other products, to permit European Christian missionaries freedom to preach and convert Chinese, to pay war indemnities or reparations to Britain, and to give Britain possession of certain Chinese territories, such as Hong Kong and sections of other Chinese cities.

1851–1864   The Taiping Rebellion occurs, inspired in part by Christian concepts and advocating a more egalitarian society with greater rights and freedoms for women. It is crushed by the Chinese Manchu–controlled army. The rebellion and its suppression are thought to have resulted in the loss of approximately 20 million lives.

1898–1900   The anti-foreign, anti-Christian Boxer Uprising takes place but is defeated by the combined military forces of several foreign powers.

1911   The Republican Revolution, inspired by Dr. Sun Yat-sen, begins in several central and southern provinces.

1912   Manchu dynasty ends through abdication. General Yuan Shikai, former commander of the Manchu Imperial Army, becomes president of the new republic after Sun resigns in Yuan's favor, hoping to prevent a civil war. Dr. Sun and his supporters organize the Guo Min Dang (National People's Party).

1916   After dismissing China's parliament and declaring himself the new emperor, Yuan dies, leaving China divided into individual regions controlled by different military leaders or warlords and their allies.

1919   The victorious World War I Allies confirm Japan's right to control territory in China formerly held by defeated Germany rather than returning it to China. This act is viewed as a betrayal of the widely publicized claim that World War I was a war for worldwide democracy. Many young Chinese intellectuals believe Japan had been invited by the United States, Britain, France, and other nations to become a partner in the economic exploitation of China. Lenin's theory of capitalist imperialism offers an explanation for this and

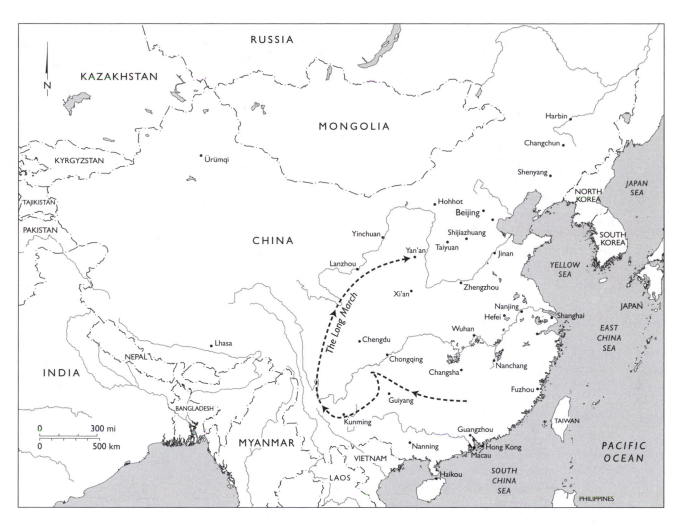

Contemporary China and neighboring countries showing the route of the 1934–1935 Long March during which Communist-led revolutionary forces survived a grueling year-long fighting retreat covering approximately six thousand miles.

attracts many young people to Marxist ideas, leading to the formation of the Chinese Communist Party.

| 1921 | Young Chinese revolutionaries, including Mao Zedong, found the Chinese Communist Party in Shanghai. |

1924 Sun's Guo Min Dang Party (GMD) forms an alliance with the rapidly expanding Chinese Communist Party.

1925 Sun dies, leaving his Republican Movement and Guo Min Dang Party deeply divided between leftists who desire to unify China, free it from foreign control, and bring about a sweeping social revolution to benefit China's poor majority, and rightists, who, while generally supporting the leftists' other goals, have little or no desire for a social revolution.

1926 Guo Min Dang Republican Army, led by General Chiang Kai Shek, marches north to subdue the warlords and unite China.

1926–1927 General Chiang Kai Shek seizes control of both the Guo Min Dang Republican Army and the GMD Party.

1927 General Chiang Kai Shek turns against the Communists and attacks them in Shanghai, causing a new civil war.

1931–1934 Communist forces, led by Mao and Zhu De, establish a rural base area, primarily in southern Jiangxi Province.

1934–1935 Communist forces retreat in the 6,000-mile "Long March." Mao, advocate of peasant-based revolution and mobile warfare, becomes the dominant Communist leader.

1937	The Communists and the Guo Min Dang temporarily halt the civil war in order to form an alliance to fight the invading Japanese.
1947–1949	After World War II, the civil war resumes and the Communists win.
1950–1953	The Korean Civil War breaks out. China enters the war on the side of North Korea and, despite heavy losses, fights the United States and its allies to a virtual stalemate. Many Chinese view this as a great achievement, since China had been continuously badly defeated by Western forces throughout its previous history.
1958–1960	The Great Leap Forward occurs. It is intended to accelerate economic development, but instead it temporarily disrupts both agriculture and industry.
1960–1961	Soviets disagree with Chinese policies and withdraw advisers: Sino-Soviet split.
1966–1968	The Great Proletarian Cultural Revolution takes place. This extreme leftist movement, supported by Mao, was intended to renew the egalitarian ideals of the revolution and remove self-seeking Communist Party leaders and other officials from power. Instead, it resulted in the physical and psychological abuse of thousands, caused intense and even violent social conflict, and impeded China's economic progress for years. The ideological impact of the Cultural Revolution lasted until Mao's death.
1976	Mao dies. With his death, Communist support for extreme leftist policies declines.
1978	Communist leaders launch new economic policies, such as permitting farming for private profit, the establishment of private businesses, and expanded foreign investment. China begins accelerated economic growth.
1989	The pro-democracy movement develops, but is suppressed.

INTRODUCTION

About the same time that revolutionary movements and organizations were being created in czarist Russia, they were also developing in China. But for the Chinese, the social basis and the geographic pattern of revolution were different. Russian revolutionaries recruited urban industrial workers to serve as the core of their revolution and, taking advantage of the unique historical circumstances near the end of World War I, were first victorious in European Russia's major cities and then later achieved control of rural areas. But when Chinese revolutionaries attempted to follow the Russian example, they failed. The eventual success of the Chinese Revolution was the result of adjusting Marxist ideas to China's culture and social characteristics and basing the revolution not primarily on urban workers, but instead on the huge mass of impoverished peasants in the countryside. Thus in China the revolution would achieve victory first in rural areas and only later in the cities.

BACKGROUND: CULTURE AND HISTORY

Early in the twentieth century, only about 10 percent of China's people, including groups such as administrators, craftsmen, and merchants, along with their employees and servants, lived in cities, while 90 percent were peasants living in the countryside and working the land (DeFronzo 1996, 74). The political culture of pre-revolutionary China was based on Confucianism. Confucius (551–479 B.C.) was a brilliant thinker who compiled much of the wisdom developed by earlier Chinese scholars, added his own modifications and innovations, and created a political and social philosophy that dominated China for the next 2,500 years. Confucius believed that social order and harmony were rooted in respect for one's family and ancestors, obedience to one's parents, and observance of other key hierarchal relationships in society. These included the obedience of wives to husbands, younger brothers to older brothers, and the people to the emperor. The emperor was viewed, in a sense, as a father figure to the national family who ruled because he enjoyed the mandate of heaven. But Confucian political culture included the concept that an emperor enjoyed the mandate only as long as he ruled fairly and competently. The right to rule was not unconditional. Heaven could withdraw the mandate when an emperor behaved immorally or foolishly. Throughout China's history there were some twenty-four different dynasties, since periodically rebellions and wars ousted ruling family lines.

To rule vast China, thousands of imperial government administrators were selected through a series of examinations that required years of study to pass. Many of the items on the exams were designed to test a person's knowledge of Confucian classical writings, reflecting the belief that knowledge of Confucian wisdom would make a person a good and competent administrator. During the late nineteenth century, there were approximately 40,000 top government administrators or mandarins running the various parts of China on behalf of the emperor (DeFronzo 1996, 75). There were also many lower-ranking officials. Almost all of the thousands of top government administrators came from China's landlord-gentry class, about 2 percent to 4 percent of China's pre-revolutionary population (DeFronzo 1996, 74). Members of this class owned large tracts of land that they rented in sections to poorer people to farm, charging up to 50 percent of the crop the renter produced (Skocpol 1979, 148). Members of the landlord-gentry class also derived income from interest they charged on loans to other people. The families in this class often had income levels that permitted them to do without the productive labor of one or more male children and to pay for the years of tutoring necessary to prepare for the exams.

During the nineteenth century, the Qing or Manchu dynasty ruled China. The Manchus, a distinct ethnic group in northeast China constituting only about 0.5 percent of the country's population, established the Qing dynasty (1644–1912) after a Manchu army took advantage of conflict within China to sweep down and capture the capital and oust the Ming dynasty (DeFronzo 1996, 77). Many Chinese accepted the Qing dynasty on the assumption that the Manchu army could not have been victorious unless heaven had withdrawn the mandate from the Ming and bestowed it on the Qing. But many other Chinese, particularly in China's southern regions, continued to resent and even resist Manchu rule. However, two Manchu emperors had unusually long reigns, covering 1683–1796, during which China was relatively free from war. Stable government and peace during this period helped bring about an enormous increase in the size of China's population.

Among the peasants—the approximately 90 percent of China's people who obtained all or much of their livelihood through farming the land—there were four major categories: rich, middle, poor, and landless (DeFronzo 1996, 74–75). About one in ten peasant households was "rich," generally meaning that the family possessed not only enough land to grow the food necessary to feed household members, but also additional land to rent to others to cultivate. "Middle" peasants, perhaps three in ten peasants, owned sufficient land to meet the needs of the household but no excess land to rent to others. About half of the peasants were "poor" peasants. Poor peasants owned some land but not enough to yield the food necessary to support their families. Members of poor peasant households, in addition to working their own land, had to engage in other work, such as farming land rented from landlords or rich peasants. One in ten peasants was landless and survived by renting land from others or working as a laborer.

Because so many of China's people were poor or landless peasants who barely lived at minimal subsistence levels when crops were good, any events that disrupted agriculture—wars, droughts, or floods—could quickly cause widespread famine. Some starving peasants would resort to desperate measures to survive, such as selling the small amount of land they might own, or to more drastic acts such as selling a child, prostitution, or banditry in order to steal from landlords or rich peasants. Occasionally hard times would drive large numbers of peasants to rebellion. Some large peasant rebellions even played roles in toppling ruling dynasties.

Chinese peasants were prone to rebellion against perceived injustice but not to revolution (changing social institutions). The traditional peasant rebellion throughout Chinese history typically pursued the goal of "bringing back the good old days"—that is, returning to some idealized period in China's past when the Confucianist system worked the way it was supposed to. Leaders of traditional Chinese peasant rebellions did not generally view the Confucianist political, social, and economic systems as the cause of problems but rather blamed the bad or incompetent people who were temporarily in charge of these systems. If these persons could be replaced with good and competent people, the systems would work fine once again. A central aim and major achievement of China's twentieth century revolutionaries was to convince the poor and landless peasants that by changing China's social, political, and economic systems or institutions, rather than just replacing rulers or administrators, major problems and sources of misery would be eliminated. The modern revolutionary leaders succeeded in great part because they were able to couple the tradition of peasant rebelliousness with the revolutionary goal of creating a new and better society.

China was greatly affected by contact with European nations during the nineteenth century. Great Britain's trade, economic policies, and military actions were of particular importance. In the 1830s, British merchants were trading for certain Chinese products including silk, tea, and porcelains. But both these businessmen and the British government were troubled by the Chinese demand that these goods be paid for in hard currency. The British hoped to, in effect, pay for the products they desired from China through vastly expanding the marketing of British goods in China, in particular the opium that was produced in parts of Britain's colonial territories. The Chinese government objected to an expansion of the opium trade and burned a shipment of British opium, leading to outbreak of war between Britain and China in 1839.

Britain's superior armaments forced the Chinese to agree to its demands in 1842 in order to end the so-called Opium Wars. The Chinese were required to allow British merchants to sell both opium and manufactured goods, a policy that would later be blamed for an enormous expansion in the number of Chinese opium addicts. The terms also allowed European Christian missionaries to freely preach Christianity. China was required to pay large sums of money to Britain as war indemnities for the damage done to British persons and property during the war. The Chinese had to relinquish control of Hong Kong to Britain (which China was only able to retrieve in 1997) and to provide the British with certain other territories within China. Following the British example, other nations, such as France and Japan, later went to war with China and won similar rights and indemnities. The benefits foreigners enjoyed in China were not only economic. In the foreign-controlled districts of Chinese cities such as Shanghai, hundreds of brothels filled with young Chinese women catered to ten of thousands of foreign customers, both civilian and military.

The series of defeats by Britain and other foreign powers had major economic, psychological, and political consequences. China's government had to raise enormous sums to pay indemnities to foreign powers and to cope with unfavorable trade relationships structured by the victorious powers. The Chinese government attempted to deal with its financial problems by raising taxes. To pay taxes, the landlords and rich peasants had the option of increasing the rents they earned and the interest rates on loans they made to the country's less fortunate residents. Thus the economic impact of foreign victories over China fell most heavily on the shoulders of the country's relatively powerless and already impoverished peasant masses.

Foreign control of much of China's territory, discrimination by foreigners against Chinese in their own land, and the many Chinese girls and women driven to prostitution for the benefit of foreign troops, businessmen, and tourists caused the development of intense feelings of humiliation among many Chinese, along with widespread hatred of foreigners. Many Chinese began to blame the Manchu ruling dynasty for China's inability to resist foreign military attacks and economic exploitation, and eventually blamed the institution of the monarchy itself.

Increasing peasant distress resulted in the outbreak of major peasant rebellions in China, including the Nian Rebellion (1853–1868) in central China and the huge Taiping Rebellion (1851–1864), which originated in southern China but spread to other parts of the country. The Taiping Rebellion was unique in that its leaders did not propose to simply replace the Manchu dynasty with a new ruling family line. The Taiping leaders proposed to drastically transform virtually all of the institutions in China, including the political structure and the country's economic and social systems as well as much of its religious culture. The founder of the Taiping movement was Hong Xiuquan (1814–1864) who was born into a peasant family in a village outside of Guangzhou (Canton). Hong was a member of south China's Hakka minority group, which had cultural traditions of relative gender equality and property sharing. Hong would combine Hakka traits with certain Christian concepts to produce the unique ideology of the Taiping rebels.

Hong's family sent him to Canton in an effort to help him get a job as a teacher. While there, Hong read pamphlets about Christianity and was influenced by Christian missionaries, such as American Baptist preacher Issachar Roberts from Tennessee. At one point, Hong became very ill and for about a week suffered from bouts of delirium during which he had a strange dream. After he recovered he eventually came to believe that he had experienced a vision in which he was visited by God the Father and his son Jesus and was told that he, Hong, was in fact also the Son of God, the younger brother of Jesus. Hong also came to believe that God intended him to rid the earth of demons, which included the Confucianist social, economic, and political systems, the landlord class, and the emperor and his mandarins, and establish a kingdom of heavenly peace.

Hong began to preach that all land should be owned collectively by the people as a whole and that status in society be based on individual merit rather than on the family or the class a person was born into. Hong also taught that women should have much greater freedom and responsibility than that permitted in Confucianist society. The Taiping Movement banned the selling of women, prostitution, and the footbinding of female children (women with very small feet were sexually attractive to some men). Marriage was to be monogamous and based on mutual attraction rather than arranged for financial or social reasons. Women were allowed to serve as soldiers in the Taiping armies and to hold administrative positions. Hong also preached there was only one God.

Many poor peasants, oppressed by the Manchu government and the landlord-gentry class and suffering from economic hardship, were attracted to Hong's movement and its vision of a much fairer and equalitarian society. After Manchu armed forces attempted to suppress the growing Taiping Movement in south China, Taiping supporters formed an army and began to conquer one part of China after another. Taiping forces captured Nanjing in 1853 and established their capital there. However, with the aid of weapons and military advisers provided by foreign powers whose leaders feared that their economic and territorial arrangements with the Manchus would be sabotaged if the Taiping Movement succeeded throughout China, the Manchu army defeated the Taiping forces at Nanjing in 1864 and executed surviving Taiping leaders. But in areas of China where support for the Taipings had been strong, the ideals of the Taiping rebels were passed down to later generations of peasants, many of whom would be sympathetic to the similar goals of twentieth-century Chinese revolutionaries.

The inability of the Manchu dynasty to defend China from foreign invasion and exploitation, coupled with the widespread hardships suffered by the large majority of the people, caused a new generation of young Chinese intellectuals to turn against not only the ruling dynasty but also against the monarchy system of government and much of the Confucianist political culture that supported it. This new generation of rebels concluded that China would not be strong enough to free itself from foreign control until China was a republic.

CONTEXT AND PROCESS OF REVOLUTION

The central leader of the Chinese Republican Revolution was Dr. Sun Yat-Sen (1866–1925). Dr. Sun, like the Taiping leader Hong, was born into a peasant family in a village not far from Guangzhou. Sun claimed that one of his village schoolteachers was a surviving soldier of the Taiping army who told his students about the ideals of the Taipings. When Sun was about five years old, an older brother left China to live and work in Hawaii. After saving some of his wages to start a small store, Sun's older brother brought Sun to Hawaii in 1879 and enrolled him in a protestant Anglican school there. Sun learned about Western societies, their advancing technologies, and their more democratic political systems, and he eventually converted to Christianity. He came to feel that China's weakness and poverty were due to a combination of China's incompetent Manchu rulers, an outmoded monarchal political system, and a traditional culture that fostered superstition, polytheism, and backwardness and constituted an impediment to modernization.

Sun and his associates worked, often among Chinese exiles in Japan and Hawaii, to create the United Revolutionary League, a revolutionary organization for the overthrow of the Manchu dynasty and the establishment of a republic form of government in China. Sun developed a broad ideology for his movement called The Three Principles of the People: Nationalism, Democracy, and People's Livelihood (which he sometimes called Socialism). Nationalism meant freeing China from foreign control, ousting the corrupt Manchu dynasty that had prostituted the country to foreign interests, and unifying China under a republic. Democracy meant establishing a government of, by, and for the people. However, he suggested that China might have to undergo a period of development in which only one revolutionary party controlled the government. Once China had a strong economy and government and was relatively free from foreign threats, a fuller democracy could be established. People's Livelihood meant providing all of China's people with equality of opportunity and the basic necessities of a happy and meaningful life, including education, medical care, food, shelter, and employment. Sun wanted to reduce the gap between the rich and the mass of China's population. He hoped, optimistically, that these changes could be brought about peacefully.

In October 1911, hundreds of Chinese soldiers in south China who had secretly joined the illegal republican movement became alarmed that their involvement was about to be revealed. Rather than submit to arrest and possible execution, these troops rebelled against the Manchu government. The rebellion spread to several other southern and central Chinese provinces. In the south of China, the Republic of China was proclaimed, with Sun as president.

But northern China was still in the hands of the Manchu army under the command of General Yuan Shikai. The general persuaded the Manchu royal family to give up the throne in February 1912, and return to Manchuria. In an effort to prevent further civil war, Sun agreed that if General Yuan would support the formation of a republic in China, Sun would resign and allow General Yuan Shikai to become president. General Yuan agreed. Sun's movement then founded a new revolutionary political party, the Guo Min Dang or National People's Party, in 1912, and male voters were allowed to elect a parliament. But within months, the general, now President Yuan Shikai, betrayed Sun and the other republican revolutionaries when the parliament refused to let him rule in a dictatorial way. Yuan Shikai supporters assassinated the Guo Min Dang parliamentary leader, and parliament was disbanded. In 1915, Yuan declared himself the new emperor, but he died the next year, apparently of natural causes. This left China without any strong central government. Military leaders, including generals of the former Manchu army, ruled as warlords in individual provinces or groups of provinces almost as if they were separate countries. In the south, Sun's forces controlled a limited area.

Sun concluded that he and his supporters had to build a strong Republican army in the south of China that would one day have the strength to march north to subdue the warlords and unify China under the republican government. To build a powerful Republican army, Sun needed weapons and military advisers. But most major nations appeared to prefer China weak and divided in order to protect their profitable trade and other economic operations there. Only the newly established and avowedly anti-imperialist government of the U.S.S.R. agreed to send assistance, including military advisers, to south China to help prepare Sun's Republican army.

Sun's Guo Min Dang included a wide range of social, economic, and political groups—workers, peasants, landlords, merchants, anti-Manchu secret societies, and others with often opposing interests or visions of the future—allied under Sun's charismatic leadership in the goal of achieving a united, independent China. The right wing of Sun's movement advocated the nationalist goal of freeing China from foreign control but did not support the concept of a sweeping, rapid redistribution of resources to benefit China's poor. A major rightist figure in Sun's Guo Min Dang was General Chiang Kai Shek. Chiang went to Tokyo in 1907 to attend a Japanese military school and while in Japan met Sun. Chiang joined Sun's Republican Movement and returned to China when the 1911 rebellion occurred to fight against the Manchu dynasty. Later Sun sent him to the U.S.S.R. in 1923 to study the Bolshevik Revolution and its developing new military, political, and social systems. But Chiang did not seem to support the sweeping social revolution that he witnessed in the U.S.S.R. and that was implicit in Sun's concept of People's Livelihood. Chiang gained significantly greater military influence when he was put in charge of Sun's Whampoa Military Academy in 1924, where many future officers of the Guo Min Dang Republican Army were trained.

The left wing of Sun's movement, especially the Chinese Communist Party, aimed not only to free China from foreign exploitation but also to accomplish a socioeconomic revolution to greatly improve the lives of China's impoverished majority. The Chinese Communist Party emerged in part from the 1915–1919 New Youth (New Culture) Movement, which rejected traditional Chinese culture and looked to the West for new institutions and values to modernize and strengthen China. Its slogan was "Democracy and Science!" But when the victorious World War I Allies consented to Japan's takeover of German colonial territory in China instead of returning it to China, many young Chinese intellectuals felt betrayed by the capitalist nations, who seemed intent on reserving democracy for themselves while dictating policies to the peoples of less-developed societies. They turned to Lenin's theory of imperialism for an explanation of the Allies' seeming hypocrisy regarding their promise of self-determination and democracy for all the peoples of the world.

Lenin argued that the advanced capitalist nations sought to control the resources of the less-developed countries in order to not only increase the wealth of their ruling elites, but also improve the lifestyles of their own working classes, in effect making them partners in the exploitation of much of Asia, Africa, and Latin America. This protected the ruling classes of the advanced nations because it reduced the lower classes' motivation for revolution. Lenin predicted, therefore, that revolutions to Socialism would tend to occur first in less-developed countries like China, and that the success of these revolutions would end the pattern of international exploitation. Eventually economic conditions would deteriorate for the majority of the people in the advanced capitalist societies. This would cause increased internal economic conflict, which would result in the advanced capitalist nations transforming to more equalitarian Socialist economic systems. These concepts inspired many young Chinese intellectuals, such as Mao Zedong (1893–1976), son of a rich peasant, to found the Chinese Communist Party in Shanghai in 1921.

Dominated generally by Russian-influenced or -trained Chinese revolutionaries through the 1920s, the Chinese Communist Party focused initially on recruiting urban workers as the vanguard of a Chinese Revolution. But Mao, a student of the role of China's often rebellious peasantry in the country's history, felt that the key to revolutionary victory in China would be to propagate a Socialist revolutionary ideology among the mass of China's impoverished peasant class. After the outbreak of violent conflict between Chiang Kai Shek's army and Communist forces in 1927, Mao also helped develop a revolutionary strategy that put primacy on preserving and increasing the size of the revolutionary army rather than trying to hold territory or seize cities against superior enemy forces.

In 1924, Sun allowed the Chinese Communist Party to merge into his Guo Min Dang Party. Then in 1925, with the republic still confined to a few provinces in south China, Sun Yat-Sen, the charismatic hero and leader of the Republican Revolution, died of cancer. Within a year of Sun's death, General Chiang Kai Shek had used his military position to gain control of most of the growing Guo Min Dang armed forces and then the party itself. He began to limit the influence of its Communist leaders.

In July of 1926, General Chiang Kai Shek commanded the Republican military forces to march north and unify China. Hundreds of young revolutionary activists typically infiltrated ahead into villages and cities in warlord territory to rouse popular support and assistance for the Republican army, often by promising reforms to help the poor once the warlords were defeated. The type of assistance people rendered depended on the opportunities available. In some cases, it was simply information about the movement, deployment, size, armament or morale of warlord forces. In other cases, workers might be able to stage a work strike, bringing the economy of a region to a near standstill until the local warlord agreed to surrender and support the Guo Min Dang. In several instances, little fighting took place and warlord generals simply placed their units under General Chiang Kai Shek's command in return for high-ranking positions in his army. Steadily the Republican army made progress in unifying China.

But Chiang apparently felt threatened by the more radical goals of the rapidly growing Chinese Communist Party. He decided to attempt to destroy the Communist movement, beginning with a surprise attack on the Shanghai Communist Party and allied labor unions and workers' militias on the morning of April 12, 1927. The plan apparently involved an offer of financial aid for Chiang's army from Shanghai businessmen, who desired a cheap and tame labor force and wanted Chiang's army to help crush the Communist Party and the city's militant workers' movement. Chiang's associates enrolled the support of Shanghai's notorious secret society, the Green Gang, which was reportedly involved in much of the city's drug trade and prostitution. Green Gang members, familiar with working-class neighborhoods, aided Chiang's military units in identifying, attacking, killing, or capturing thousands of known or suspected Communists or other leftist activists. These events in Shanghai marked a turning point for the Chinese Republican Revolution. The right wing of the movement, which dominated the Republican military, sought through massive violence in Shanghai and elsewhere, to effectively neutralize the Guo Min Dang's left wing, particularly the Chinese Communist Party. This attempt was possible partly because the Communist leaders underestimated both Chiang and the importance of having more Communist leaders in top military positions in the Republican army.

In response, the Chinese Communist Party's leadership, still dominated by Russian-trained Chinese Communists and several foreign advisers from the Stalin-dominated Soviet Union, at first pursued a fruitless, often disastrous urban-focused strategy of attacking and attempting to hold towns and cities or to stage uprisings there. The Communist-led units were almost invariably routed or even totally destroyed by Chiang's typically better-armed and numerically superior divisions. Mao Zedong, a young Communist Party leader and former Guo Min Dang official from a rich peasant family in Hunan Province, began to employ a different approach. Among the central elements of Mao's strategy, which eventually would play a major role in the Communist victory, were the following: (1) develop the revolutionary potential of China's mostly impoverished peasants, transforming their traditional rebelliousness into peasant revolution by giving the peasants a vision of a new, more socially just society worth fighting for. In the process, make them China's key revolutionary class and wage primarily rural warfare; (2) fight a People's War, in which the majority of the nation's people strongly support the Communist-led revolution and aid the revolutionary army; (3) use the tactic of mobile warfare, in which preservation of the existence of the revolutionary army is a primary strategy.

Mobile warfare meant maneuvering to avoid clashing with superior enemy forces while trying to strike only inferior enemy units. The advantage of this approach was that it could preserve the revolutionary army; the disadvantage was that because the revolutionary army did not hold territory, the mobile warfare strategy rendered the people who supported the revolutionary armed forces vulnerable to abuse and terror from Chiang's army. But since attempting to hold territory against vastly superior enemy forces could not succeed and could only result in the destruction of the Communist-led armed forces while they were still relatively weak, mobile warfare made sense.

By definition, the strategy of People's War meant that winning the support of the majority of the people was a necessity for the Communist-led forces to win. This involved educating the poor peasants to the beneficial goals of the revolution so that most people would aid revolutionary forces and many would even join the revolutionary army. A key element in gaining the support of the people was recruiting or creating revolutionary soldiers who were morally dedicated to the cause for which they were fighting. Not only would they fight much harder and sacrifice more than the enemy soldiers, they would also treat the people better than the enemy troops and, by their example and dedication, win greater popular support for the revolution. Employing the peasant strategy, and People's War, and mobile warfare, Mao's soldiers developed a large rural base in Jiangxi Province in south China. The apparent success of Mao's concepts would raise his status in the Communist leadership. But not until mid January 1935, at the meeting of top Communist leaders at the town of Zunyi, would Mao emerge as the dominant figure in the Communist Party.

General Chiang Kai Shek launched repeated military attacks to crush Mao's forces from 1930 through 1933. Finally, he ordered a huge 700,000-man army to surround and destroy them in 1934. By constructing and manning concrete forts along roads in Jiangxi Province, Chiang's units began to limit the Communists' freedom of movement and to close in for a final battle. To avoid annihilation, the main Communist army of some 100,000 people broke out of the encirclement and began an arduous retreat on foot, often marked by desperate battles, which ultimately covered 6,000 miles— a journey that became known the Long March. Less than one-third of Mao's Communist army finally reached the relative safety of Shensi Province in north central China in 1935. In the summer of 1937, the Red Army moved its headquarters from Mao'an sixty miles east to the town of Yan'an, which would serve as its main base from then until after the end of World War II.

The events of World War II in Asia played a major role in the course of the Chinese Revolution. In 1931, Japanese forces had entered the Chinese province of Manchuria seeking to exploit its mineral resources. They supported a pro-Japanese Manchurian emperor there. Those Manchurian military forces that resisted the Japanese were forced to withdraw into north China, where General Chiang Kai Shek assigned them the task not of retaking their home territory, but of wiping out Mao's Communist army. The leader of the Guo Min Dang's Manchurian forces, Marshal Zhang Xueliang, refused to fight fellow Chinese and instead formed an alliance with the Communists to together fight the Japanese. When General Chiang Kai Shek, apparently unaware of this development, visited north China, he was kidnapped by Zhang's soldiers and forced to sign a truce with the Communist army and agree to ally with the Communists to form a United Anti-Japanese Front (1937–1945). Technically, the Communist forces were put under General Chiang's command as China's Eighth

Route Army. In reality, the Communist army and Chiang's forces fought separate campaigns against the Japanese and occasionally clashed with each other.

The Communists employed the strategy of People's War and the tactic of mobile warfare against the Japanese with relative success primarily in the northern sections of China. The Japanese held many cities, but the Communists controlled most of the countryside around them. The size of the Communist forces grew to an estimated 900,000 by the end of the war (Short 2000, 400). U.S. military advisers, intelligence agents, and newspaper reporters visited and evaluated both Chiang Kai Shek's and the Communist armies and generally had far more positive views of the morale, integrity, and fighting ability of the Communist-led forces. In contrast, Chiang's army was often characterized as led by corrupt officers whose behavior contributed to low morale. Furthermore, the Americans criticized Chiang for not using his best U.S.-armed and -trained divisions to combat the Japanese. They suspected he was holding them in reserve to be used against the Communist-led forces after the Japanese had been defeated by the United States. Chiang resented the American criticisms, but because of the greater effort and success of the Communist-led forces against the Japanese, an increasing number of China's people came to view the Communist-led army as China's true national army. In addition, Chiang's regime carried out few reforms to benefit the poor in the areas his government controlled.

As World War II came to an end, representatives of the U.S. government attempted to negotiate the creation of a unified government in China including both the Communist leaders and Chiang's GMD officials. Americans who visited the Communist-held base areas—members of the so-called Dixie Mission—even suggested that the United States consider cooperating with the Communists, since they considered Chiang's regime incompetent and corrupt by comparison. The possibility of Mao visiting Washington to meet with U.S. leaders was even discussed. But conservative U.S. political and military figures overruled or sabotaged these suggestions and later accused members of the U.S. Dixie Mission of being soft on Communism or even pro-Communist.

Attempts to prevent the resumption of the civil war failed, and by 1947 a full-scale conflict was under way. Major elements of Chiang's army became cut off in cities, surrounded by millions of peasants sympathetic to the Communists. One by one, they surrendered or were defeated, and whole divisions, along with hundreds of millions of dollars worth of U.S. military equipment, fell into the hands of the Communist-led forces.

On October 1, 1949, Mao addressed a huge crowd in Beijing and proclaimed the creation of the Communist-dominated People's Republic of China. Fighting in the south-

Chairman Mao shown reading a proclamation of the founding of the People's Republic of China on the Tiananmen Gate rostrum, October 1, 1949. (Bettmann/Corbis)

ern parts of China continued for several more months, with steady Communist victories. Chiang Kai Shek and some 500,000 of his supporters and army crossed the Formosa Strait to the island of Taiwan, proclaiming that Taiwan was now the seat of the only legitimate government of China, the Republic of China. The United States and many of its allies refused to recognize the legitimacy of the new government on mainland China for many years. Until the 1970s, China's permanent seat on the United Nations Security Council was held by Chiang's Republic of China government on Taiwan.

U.S. policy changed abruptly in the early 1970s, when the Nixon administration re-established U.S. relations with China. There appeared to be three major motives for this radical shift: first, the change would allow U.S. corporations to do business in China and eventually reap large profits; second, aware of the conflicts that had developed between China and the U.S.S.R., friendly relations between the U.S. and China would force the U.S.S.R. leaders to be concerned about the possibility of war with both the U.S. and China and commit large military forces to defend its long border with China; and third, by establishing ties with China, the Nixon administration hoped to obtain China's assistance in persuading the Vietnamese to accept U.S. terms for an end to the Vietnam conflict.

IMPACTS

The victory of Mao's forces resulted in China's Communist Party gaining control of the most populous nation in the world and embarking on what some have called the greatest social revolution in history. Land was taken from the landlord class and divided among millions of peasants. But instead of owning the land as individuals, peasants were soon required to pool their land and animals and to farm the land collectively. This system persisted, for the most part, until the late 1970s when, in order to increase productivity, China's leaders allowed peasants to lease parcels of land and, after selling a part of their crop at set prices to the state, market the rest for personal profit. After the revolution, many businesses, factories, and banks were seized by the state. But in the late 1970s, after the death of Mao, the government allowed for the creation of many privately owned businesses to operate alongside state-owned enterprises and also for the creation of many manufacturing and other business enterprises operated jointly by foreign corporations and the Chinese government or by foreign companies under conditions set by the Chinese government.

In 1950, shortly after the Chinese Revolution ended, the Korean Conflict broke out, and China sided with Communist-led North Korea. China suffered hundreds of thousands of casualties but fought the U.S. and its allies to a stalemate. Since this was a far superior military outcome than China had ever achieved before against a powerful Western nation, the result seemed to increase nationalist support for the Communist-led government.

However, the Korean Conflict further alienated the United States and other Western nations and left the U.S.S.R. as China's only source of significant foreign assistance, similar to the situation in the early 1920s for President Sun Yat-Sen's Republic in south China. The Soviets, still recovering from the devastation of World War II, sent technicians and some machinery and construction plans to China. The Soviet advisers favored the type of centralized planning that had rapidly developed Soviet industry in urban areas during the 1930s, and China's economy grew at a significant pace during the early 1950s.

Mao, however, was not satisfied with the speed of economic growth or with what he and some of his associates viewed as the concentration of development in urban areas while neglecting the rural areas, where the revolution had essentially been won. Mao proposed drastically accelerating and redirecting the modernization process, primarily by making use of China's enormous pool of untapped potential industrial labor, including many millions of Chinese women. The effort was called the Great Leap Forward (1958–1960). Many factories were built in small cities, towns, and even rural areas. This dispersal of industry was not economically efficient, but the process was intended partly as a way of increasing income for China's rural population and also as a defense against a possible nuclear conflict in which China's major cities might be destroyed.

Despite some significant achievements, the Great Leap, instead of advancing, set back economic development and helped alienate the Soviet Union. Much of the production from the new small factories was of poor quality, and the rural industrial drive contributed to disrupting agriculture. This, coupled with poor weather conditions and insufficient material incentives for farmers, contributed to famines in which approximately 20 million people died (Short 2000, 505), which in turn damaged the industrial labor force. Furthermore, Soviet leaders were unhappy. Convinced that much of their aid to China was being wasted, upset with Chinese criticisms of Soviet leaders as elitist and too quick to appease the United States, and irritated with China's decision to develop its own atomic bomb, the Soviets withdrew technical and material assistance. China's industrial productivity dropped by over 38 percent in 1961 (DeFronzo 1996, 99).

These consequences of the Great Leap temporarily weakened Mao's authority. More pragmatic Chinese leaders attempted to revive the economy in part by allowing peasants once again to farm some land for private profit and to reorganize China's industrial development through more centrally planned and efficient policies. But Mao frowned on what he and some similarly minded associates viewed as "capitalist tendencies." He formulated a new theory of social conflict, in which he claimed that "capitalist tendencies" were bound to arise in any society in which power differentiation occurred, regardless of whether the country was relatively equalitarian in an economic sense. That is, if some people were allowed to accumulate a disproportionate share of power, they also would tend to acquire economic and other privileges for themselves and their families. Therefore, the people must always be ready to mobilize against the tendency to concentrate power in the hands of a few leaders.

Mao employed this point of view and his still enormous prestige as leader of the victorious revolution to mobilize a mass movement against much of the Communist Party leadership during the Great Proletarian Cultural Revolution (1966–1968). A stated purpose of the Cultural Revolution was to return power to the people and remove from major positions of authority persons who supposedly were using their power to enrich themselves and to subvert the equalitarian goals of the revolution. Without a mass movement to restore revolutionary fervor and practice, China faced the danger, Mao argued, of developing self-serving institutional elites like those that existed in capitalist nations like the United States and in the version of Socialism that had developed in the U.S.S.R. Furthermore, the Cultural Revolution would sweep away many capitalistic and feudalistic cultural norms and values that persisted among many people even after the Communist-led revolution.

Many supporters of the Cultural Revolution accepted Mao's view that it is possible to create Communist norms, values, and psychology, even in the absence of the advanced technological development and the superproductive economy that earlier Marxist theory seemed to assume constituted necessary objective conditions for the creation of Communist culture. Mao seemed to promote the notion that a conscious effort, particularly on the part of young people, could create the relatively "selfless" psychology of the "new" women and men who would then build a technologically advanced Socialist economy.

Movement leaders mobilized millions of young people, self-proclaimed Red Guards, in huge demonstrations and confrontations around the country in which hundreds of leading party members, government officials, factory managers, and others thought guilty of misusing their power were forced to submit to public ridicule and were then often relieved of their positions and instead given manual labor jobs. Many educational institutions shut down for extended periods as students participated in the movement. Because the purges of high-ranking officials were carried out directly by mobs of young people, often under the guidance of local leaders, rather than in a more organized fashion, excesses were common. Some people were beaten to death, while others were so distressed and humiliated that they committed suicide. Disagreements frequently arose regarding whether a particular person should be criticized and ousted from his or her position. In some places, violent conflicts broke out between Red Guard units and other groups of citizens or even between Red Guard factions. In the summer of 1968, Mao called on the one major institution relatively untouched by the Red Guard purges, the People's Liberation Army, to stop the fighting. In many parts of the country, military units restored order and military officers often stepped into governmental posts whose former occupants had been removed by Red Guard militants. By the end of the mass-mobilization stage of the Cultural Revolution, many local government administrations were staffed by military personnel. Although the turbulent phase of the Cultural Revolution was over by the end of 1968, the ideals of the movement tended to dominate Chinese society until the death of Mao in 1976.

Shortly after Mao's death, several leaders of the Cultural Revolution blamed for some of its excesses, the so-called Gang of Four, including Mao's third wife, Jiang Qing, were arrested and imprisoned. Leadership of the party soon fell into the hands of some of the very officials, such as Deng Xiaoping, whom the movement had forced for years into relative obscurity and often into manual labor jobs. China's new leaders viewed the Cultural Revolution as largely a social and economic disaster for China and reversed a number of Mao's policies. In so doing, they set the stage for a huge expansion of China's economy. Among the changes instituted after 1978 were a return to material incentives through measures such as allowing the establishment of many privately owned businesses and permitting farmers to sell at least part of their crops for profit. Foreign companies were allowed to establish manufacturing enterprises in China, under terms set by the Chinese government, and to take advantage of the country's plentiful supply of relatively cheap labor.

The increased freedom and private initiative in China's economic system, greater contact with societies with more democratic political systems, discontent with corruption among some of China's leaders and officials, and resentment over mistakes made by major Communist leaders in the past spurred a movement for greater governmental accountability and political freedom. Reforms toward a more democratic political system in the U.S.S.R. during the 1980s likely also encouraged demands for similar changes in China.

On April 17, 1989, thousands of young people took to the streets, initially to show admiration for a former Communist Party leader, Hu Yaobang, an advocate of greater freedom of expression, who had recently died. March participants chanted demands for more democracy and the right to more openly criticize government leaders and the Communist Party, many with the motivation of forcing reforms within the Party. On May 4, tens of thousands of young people participated in demonstrations in Beijing and other cities on the anniversary of what was widely regarded as China's first major student protest, which had taken place on May 4, 1919. The students' demands for greater democracy and accountability of leadership to the people enjoyed wide popular support, including that of many within the Communist Party. However, the majority of top leaders in the party were apparently not inclined to agree to all of the protestors' demands and grew angry at the demonstrators' continued occupation of Beijing's Tiananmen Square. Unarmed police and soldiers were ordered to clear the square, but were turned back by the crowd. Then on June 3, heavily armed soldiers, some apparently believing that other soldiers had been killed at the square, were ordered in. Military units meeting resistance on the streets leading to the square resorted to violence. Reports indicated that at least several hundred people were killed. Later thousands of people involved in the protests around the country were arrested. A number of officials thought supportive of the demonstrators were demoted from their positions.

The dominant Communist Party leadership tended to portray the demonstrations as at least partly foreign inspired and many of the participants as privileged young people seeking reforms that would give them further advantages over the majority of the people and lead to greater internal social conflict. They argued that this would make the country easy prey for the foreign capitalist nations seeking to once again dominate China and exploit it as had been the case before the revolution. Among the changes instituted was a policy requiring students to work at least one year at a manual labor job so as to identify more closely with the country's industrial working and peasant classes.

The Chinese Revolution is generally viewed as the most sweeping social revolution in world history. It brought about major changes in China's political, economic, social, and cultural systems, including an enormous redistribution of land, opportunity, and other resources to the majority of the country's people. It also brought about a dramatic increase in the rights and freedoms of Chinese women. The revolution unified China and freed it from previous foreign military occupation and economic exploitation.

At the same time, however, the new order introduced measures that resulted in the deaths of hundreds of thousands of former members of the landlord class and others at the hands of outraged poor peasants. After the revolutionary victory, inadequately planned policies and extreme leftist movements, such as the Great Leap Forward and the Great Proletarian Cultural Revolution, disrupted the economy, contributed to famines in which millions are thought to have perished, and brought about the physical or psychological abuse of many others.

The success of China's rural-based revolution provided encouragement for many other revolutionaries around the world, including those in neighboring Vietnam. As its leaders fell into conflict with the leaders of the Soviet Union, China eventually became a partial ally of the United States, contributing to the end of Communist Party rule in the Soviet Union and Eastern Europe and to the dissolution of the U.S.S.R. China's decades of impaired relations with the Soviet Union also seemed to prove that there was no unified international Communist movement and that Communist-led countries could become hostile towards one another over nationalist or other concerns.

After 1978, China's less ideological and more pragmatic leaders set the nation on the path to becoming an economic superpower. In the early part of the twenty-first century, China's economy, enjoying increasing international trade, continued to grow at a rapid pace while its government remained under the control of the Communist Party.

PEOPLE AND ORGANIZATIONS

Chiang Kai Shek (1887–1975)

Japanese-trained Chinese army officer who joined Sun Yat-Sen's Republican Revolution. He became head of Sun's Whampoa Military Academy, where many future Republican army officers were trained in the 1920s, and rose in prominence. After Sun's death in 1925, Chiang assumed control of the Guo Min Dang army and then the party. In 1926 he marched north to subdue warlord generals and unite China. But in 1927 he turned against the left wing of the GMD, in particular the Communist Party, precipitating a new civil war eventually won by the Communists.

Chinese Communist Party (CCP)

The Chinese Communist Party was founded in 1921 by young Chinese intellectuals and activists inspired by Marxist ideas, particularly by Lenin's theory of imperialism, and disillusioned by the perceived aggression and exploitation of capitalist nations. The party first pursued an urban strategy but eventually adopted a rural approach to revolution based on gaining the support of millions of impoverished peasants by providing them with hope for a new and better society. During the fight against the Japanese invaders in World War II, the Communist Party and army grew rapidly. When the civil war resumed after the war, the Communists won a rapid victory over Chiang Kai Shek's GMD army and established a one-party government in the new People's Republic of China.

Deng Xiaoping (1904–1997)

A top Communist Party leader, Deng Xiaoping was accused of being a "capitalist roader" during the early phase of the Great Proletarian Cultural Revolution. He was removed from his important positions but allowed to retain his party membership. He was eventually politically "rehabilitated" and was China's top leader from 1978 until his death. He helped bring about the "reforms" that reintroduced many capitalistic economic activities to China. Some criticized the reforms as a betrayal of Mao's principles, but others praised him for greatly accelerating China's economic growth and technological progress, and in so doing, strengthening China and preserving Communist Party domination of the government.

Guo Min Dang (National People's Party—GMD)

This was Sun Yat-Sen's political party, which was formed from his United Revolutionary League and other republican revolutionary organizations. In 1924 Sun incorporated the small but rapidly growing Chinese Communist Party into the GMD. But after Sun's death in 1925, General Chiang Kai Shek seized control of the GMD army and then the party, and began shifting its policies in a conservative direction. In April of 1927, Chiang turned against the Communist movement and attempted to annihilate it, precipitating a new civil war which, after World War II, the Communists won.

Hong Xiuquan (1814–1864)

Hong was the leader of the huge but ultimately unsuccessful Taiping Rebellion (1851–1864), which shared certain goals with those of the later Communist-led revolution, such as redistribution and sharing of resources, including land, and greater equality for women. A member of the Hakka minority group, he was born into a peasant family near Guangzhou. After being exposed to Christian teachings, he formulated an ideology for the Taiping movement that appeared to combine aspects of Christianity with certain Hakka cultural traits.

Mao Zedong (1893–1976)

Mao was the primary leader of the successful Chinese Communist Revolution and later of China from 1949 until his death. Along with Karl Marx and Vladimir Lenin, he is widely regarded as one of the three great theoreticians of Marxist Communist ideology. He was born into a rich peasant family in Hunan Province and joined the Republican movement. Later, influenced by Marxist and Leninist ideas, he helped found the Chinese Communist Party in 1921. He served as a Communist official in the Guo Min Dang before General Chiang moved to crush the Communist movement. Mao began to question the policies of the initial Russian-inspired Chinese Communist leadership and eventually proved that his strategies of developing a peasant-based revolution and employing mobile warfare were correct. His enormous prestige as the main architect of the victorious revolution allowed him to convince millions of Chinese to embark on huge, ambitious, but ultimately disruptive post-revolution social movements, such as the Great Leap Forward (1958–1960) and the Great Proletarian Cultural Revolution (1966–1968), the later of which attacked and at least temporarily removed from power major leaders of the Communist Party and the Chinese government. After his death, Mao was officially viewed as a great leader whose contributions to China significantly outweighed his mistakes, including the serious damage caused by the movements he inspired after the victorious revolution.

People's Liberation Army (PLA)

The revolutionary army formed by the Chinese Communist Party to fight against General Chiang's forces and the Japanese invaders. After World War II, the PLA, led by Mao and his associates, won the civil war and became China's new national army.

Red Guards

Bands of young people, for the most part, who were inspired by Mao's calls to cleanse China of harmful cultural traits left over from pre-revolutionary Chinese society and of Communist leaders and other officials allegedly betraying the ideals of the revolution. They participated in the Great Proletarian Cultural Revolution (1966–1968).

Sun Yat-Sen (1866–1925)

Sun was the great leader of the Chinese Republican Revolution. He was born into a peasant family near Guangzhou but, with the aid of an older brother, was educated at a Christian school in Hawaii. Later he earned a medical degree. Sun became convinced that China was weak and dominated by foreign powers and corrupt officials, due to the rule of the Manchu Qing dynasty and the monarchy system of government. He helped organize Republican revolutionary groups, such as his United Revolutionary League, often among Chinese exiles in Japan and Hawaii.

After the Republican Revolution began in 1911, Sun became the leader of the new Chinese Republic, initially composed of several southern Chinese provinces. Sun received help from the Soviet Union to build a powerful Republican army that would eventually march north to unify China. In 1924 he allied his Guo Min Dang Party with the rapidly growing Chinese Communist Party. However, in 1925 Sun died, and his GMD was soon taken over by a rightist military officer, General Chiang Kai Shek, who turned against the Communists in 1927.

United Revolutionary Society

Sun's Republican Revolutionary organization which, with other revolutionary groups, formed the Guo Min Dang in 1912.

Yuan Shikai (1854–1916)

Commander of the Manchu imperial armies who, when confronted with the Republican Rebellion in south China, convinced the Manchu family to abdicate in February 1912. General Yuan agreed to support the establishment of a republic in China as long as Sun would resign as president and allow Yuan to take his place. But as president, Yuan asserted that his authority was greater than that of China's new parliament. In 1914, Yuan attempted to outlaw Sun's GMD and dismissed parliament. The following year Yuan further betrayed the Republican Revolution by declaring himself the new emperor—only to die, apparently of natural causes, in 1916.

Zhou Enlai (1898–1976)

A top Communist Party leader who, after initially opposing Mao, became one of his most loyal supporters. Zhou, a skillful politician and diplomat, served as China's prime minister from 1949 until his death.

Zhu De (1886–1976)

A participant in the Republican Revolution in 1911, Zhu joined the Chinese Communist Party. He became commander of the Communist-led army and a top party and government leader.

James DeFronzo

See Also Anarchism, Communism, and Socialism; Armed Forces, Revolution, and Counter-Revolution; Chinese 1989 Democracy Movement; Cinema of Revolution; Colonialism, Anti-Colonialism and Neo-Colonialism; Democracy, Dictatorship, and Fascism; Documentaries of Revolution; Elites, Intellectuals, and Revolutionary Leadership; Guerilla Warfare and Revolution; Human Rights, Morality, Social Justice, and Revolution; Ideology, Propaganda, and Revolution; Inequality, Class, and Revolution; Japanese New Order Movement; Korean Civil War; Music and Revolution; Nationalism and Revolution; Population, Economic Development, and Revolution; Russian Revolution of 1917; Student and Youth Movements, Activism and Revolution; Taiping Revolution; Transnational Revolutionary Movements; Vietnamese Revolution; War and Revolution

References and Further Readings
Bianco, Lucien. 1971. *Origins of the Chinese Revolution*. Stanford, CA: Stanford University Press.
Blecher, Marc. 1986. *China: Politics, Economics and Society*. London: Printer.
Bottomore, Tom. 1983. *A Dictionary of Marxist Thought*. Cambridge, MA: Harvard University Press.
Cheng, Chgu-yuan, ed. 1989. *Sun Yat-sen's Doctrine in the Modern World*. Boulder, CO: Westview.
Chesneaux, Jean. 1972. *Popular Movements and Secret Societies in China, 1840–1950*. Stanford, CA: Stanford University Press.
Clubb, O. Edmund. 1978. *20th Century China*. New York: Columbia University Press.
DeFronzo, James. 1996, 2007. *Revolutions and Revolutionary Movements*. Boulder, CO: Westview.
Dittmer, Lowell. 1994. *China under Reform*. Boulder, CO: Westview.
Domes, Jurgen. 1985. *The Government and Politics of the PRC*. Boulder, CO: Westview.
Fairbairn, Geoffrey. 1974. *Revolutionary Guerrilla Warfare*. Middlesex, UK: Penguin.
Feuerwerker, Albert, ed. 1964. *Modern China*. Englewood Cliffs, NJ: Prentice-Hall.
Jordan, Donald A. 1976. *The Northern Expedition*. Honolulu: University Press of Hawaii.
Mackerras, Collin, and Nick Knight. 1985. *Marxism in Asia*. New York: St. Martin's.
Mao Zedung. 1967. *Selected Readings from the Work of Mao*. Beijing: Foreign Languages Press.
Meisner, Maurice. 1986. *Mao's China and After*. New York: Free Press.
Overholt, William. 1993. *The Rise of China*. New York: Norton.
Payne, Robert. 1969. *Chiang Kai-shek*. New York: Weybright and Talley.
Salisbury, Harrison E. 1985. *The Long March: The Untold Story*. New York: McGraw-Hill.
Short, Philip. 2000. *Mao: A Life*. New York: Henry Holt.
Skocpol, Theda. 1979. *States and Revolutions*. Cambridge: Cambridge University Press.
Thaxton, Ralph. 1983. *China Turned Rightside Up*. New Haven, CT: Yale University Press.
Tucker, Robert, ed. 1975. *The Lenin Anthology*. New York: Norton.
Wasserstrom, Jeffrey N., and Elizabeth J. Perry. 1994. *Popular Protest and Political Culture in Modern China*. Boulder, CO: Westview.
Wolf, Eric. 1969. *Peasant Wars of the Twentieth Century*. New York: Harper and Row.
Yabuki, Susumu. 1995. *China's New Political Economy*. Boulder, CO: Westview.

Cinema of Revolution

The cinema of revolution partakes of the problematic of historical film. The relation of historical film to history has engaged a number of historians for a generation. Rosenstone (1995) for one has developed a perspective that moves beyond the traditional critique of historical films. He spells out that film is not only different from written discourse, and necessarily so, but that this very difference constitutes an important contribution; he posits historical film as a history sui generis. The transmission of history may be argued to be undergoing a profound change, to enter an age where the History of the Film stands alongside the History of the Book, providing a more comprehensive view of the past. There is, of course, precedent for such a major change in the transmission of history: the History of the Book was preceded by the History of Orature. Filmed history diverges from written history of necessity. If both construct a historical world, if neither offers the "truth," film is dependent on outright invention. Film creates fictional people, and its historical characters are impersonated by actors who show them in more detail than can be documented. Likewise film must invent historical settings in all their specifics. Even more importantly, the dramatic impact of film is contingent on presenting visually a coherent story. That story tends to be self-contained, rather isolated from the flow of history—historical films often are much longer than the norm because of the difficulty of such compression; it very rarely allows significant space for alternative interpretations; and it nearly always focuses on individuals. While films usually eschew the controversy that enriches written history—and that signals the problematic nature of historical reconstruction—they integrate in individual experiences multiple aspects of history, aspects that tend to be compartmentalized in written discourse.

Whatever the drawbacks of historical films, they have increasingly come to shape popular views of historical events. *Gone with the Wind* has inflected many Americans' perception of the American Civil War for generations. Feature films are unrivaled in their impact on viewers. Cinema—with its images, its sounds, and a setting that blocks out all other stimuli—provides an immediacy of experience rarely found in documentaries and that the written word cannot match. It brings history alive in images, and sound, and characters, and story. The dramatic story elicits emotional response, the individual characters engage empathy. The empathy elicited by films becomes particularly important where they reach audiences who start out with negative views of particular historical events. Such is the case of most revolutions, for contemporary U.S. audiences in particular.

Historians are members of an established discipline, they have trained to join the discipline, and they are held to professional standards. Filmmakers have no such training, and they are not held to any specific standards concerning the production of historical films. Their films are thus akin to popular history written outside the academic realm. They are quite unfettered in their approach to an historical event. Apart from issues of censorship, their primary concerns are public response, the box office, and the critics who influence public response and shape the directors' reputations. Under these circumstances it is not surprising that the historical context of a film's production tends to profoundly shape its re-creation of the past.

Still, the historical film, like the history book, cannot ignore what we already know. Historical films are expected to reconstruct the past, to create plausible scenarios, characters and dialogue, to invent inner thoughts, to show dreams and hallucinations, but, as Rosenstone (1995, 72) puts it, "like any work of history, a film must be judged in terms of the knowledge of the past we already possess." If outright distortions of the historical record are common, a more pervasive problem arises from the tendency of historical films to adopt specific perspectives on historical events. Apart from the requirements of the dramatic story that allow little space for contesting views, many historical films have been brought forth by the political commitment of directors and sponsors who have little use for alternative readings of the past. Thus the role of the critic becomes crucial. Film critics, however, are more expert on questions of film history and on aesthetic approaches in cinema rather than on history per se; they are usually ill equipped to critically evaluate a representation of the past. If at times they repeat as fact what the film has invented, they more commonly accept uncritically the film's perspective on the past. Historical films can be extraordinarily powerful, but they demand a critical approach that is well informed about the past.

The cinema of revolution may be taken to encompass a large body of films. The following discussion is limited to selected feature films relating to revolutions and national wars of liberation in the twentieth century. Its primary aim is to contextualize them. While proceeding roughly in the chronological order of these historical events, it compromises that order at times to present them within their regional contexts.

The Soviet leadership embraced cinema for its political potential. Generously funded and inspired by revolutionary commitment, Soviet cinema established itself as a world leader in cinematography. A number of remarkable films focused on the Soviet Revolution. If they were the work of several major directors, it is Sergei Eisenstein who to this day is lionized for his contribution to the development of cinematography. *The Battleship Potemkin* (1925) is most commonly cited for its montage technique as well as its revolutionary story. Commissioned for the twentieth anniversary of the failed 1905 revolution, it focuses on the episode of mutineers taking over the Potemkin, dramatizing the utter disregard of the officers for their men and the wholesale slaughter of civilians sympathizing with the mutineers. The sequence of civilians being shot on the steps leading down to the Odessa landing is among the most famous in all cinema history. If the incident is not based on actual events, it may be taken as artistic license to dramatize the cruelty of czarist repression. More troublesome for the historian, however, is the liberty Eisenstein took with the outcome of the mutiny—rather than have it spoil his celebration of the revolution.

Eisenstein was commissioned to produce *October* (1927) for the tenth anniversary of the Soviet Revolution. He is said to have studied closely John Reed's eyewitness account, *Ten Days that Shook the World,* and the film was initially released under that title outside the U.S.S.R. That title, however, is somewhat misleading, since the film presents key events from the deposition of the czar in February 1917 to the Bolshevik Revolution in October of the same year uncritically. It does so in documentary fashion. In addition to the intertitles, a rich assortment of symbols are mustered to interpret these episodes, prominent among them statues of Napoléon that are made to represent Alexander Kerensky as well as Lavr Kornilov. The film drew on a cast of—literally—thousands and was shot in local settings, the Winter Palace in particular, that had little changed. An approach that focused on mass actions and allowed only for brief interludes with various individual characters fit the collectivist ideology, but it leaves viewers bereft of individuals to engage with, putting them at a distance from the drama of those truly dramatic times. For those already familiar with the events, the film provides the opportunity to visualize them, an opportunity all the more welcome given the lack of documentary material on the revolution. But if Soviet citizens were familiar with their recent revolutionary history, the film's montage style and its rich symbolism obscured the story for many, and Eisenstein was severely criticized for his failure to reach "the masses."

Viewers who are not familiar with the course of the Bolshevik Revolution may appreciate Eisenstein's intellectual cinema, but they are likely to find themselves detached observers of a bewildering array of episodes, a rather dry—illustrated—history lesson. That lesson was rewritten in the political context in which the film was produced. The historical revision involved the course of events and the depiction of those opposing the Bolsheviks. As the film was about to be released in time for the celebration of the tenth anniversary of the revolution, Stalin intervened personally to order massive cuts and some scenes to be shot afresh. His revision served his struggle to put himself in full control of the Communist Party: a number of scenes involving Lenin were omitted, Stalin was featured prominently, and Trotsky all but disappeared. For the fiftieth anniversary of the revolution, Eisenstein's collaborator Grigori Aleksandrov produced what is claimed to be a full restoration. *October* does not carry the viewer along with a powerful story—it may be taken to reflect a collectivist ideology that holds little regard for individuals, a mind-set that presaged the transformation of the Communist dream into tyranny. But *October* achieved its purpose to the extent that it was mistaken for a documentary that respects the historical record and became part of that record.

Vsevolod Pudovkin's *The End of St. Petersburg* (1927) avoided most of the pitfalls of *October* with a story of anonymous individuals. The film starts out with a depiction of pervasive poverty in czarist Russia. When there is one more mouth to feed, a young peasant has to leave the countryside to find work in the city. He is introduced to a co-villager in St. Petersburg, but that family is desperately poor and they have no food to share. The co-villager is a Communist worker, and they are both arrested in turn. When World War I breaks out, the peasant is taken out of prison and enlisted as a "volunteer." Three years later, when the "Communist" exhorts troops to support the workers' Soviets rather than Kerensky's Coalition Government, the "village lad"-turned-soldier joins him. Eventually they both take part in the storming of the Winter Palace that brings the Bolsheviks to power. Along the way, Pudovkin puts in an appearance as a German officer.

The simple story is transformed into a powerful film by Pudovkin's craft and the soundtrack added in 1969 effectively dramatizes it. The viewer comes to understand intellectually and to feel emotionally how urban workers and soldiers were drawn into the revolution. Pudovkin creates striking images of poverty and affluence, of trench warfare and stock market speculation, of crowds and the Winter Palace they attack; he dramatically juxtaposes them in repetitious montage that drives the message home. A major part of the film features some of the most powerful anti-war imagery ever, a prelude to anti-war classics to come. Beyond that, viewers are introduced to class analysis, and they are carried along as they feel the suffering of the characters and become involved in their struggles. On further reflection viewers may also come to understand that the peasant's attack on the factory owner and his manager demonstrates the futility of individual action, however heroic, and that only collective action can create a better world. They may appreciate the significance of the pact between peasant/soldier and worker. And they may perceive the dawn of a new—Communist—age when the film ends with the Communist's wife handing out her potatoes, precious potatoes she had previously refused to share, among the revolutionary fighters. With hindsight, this ending may prompt the conclusion that its melodrama was indicative of the utopian character of the Communist dream. *The End of St. Petersburg* stands as a masterwork of the silent era.

The Bolshevik Revolution inspired several notable films produced outside the U.S.S.R. David Lean's *Doctor Zhivago* (1965), based on Boris Pasternak's epic novel, which won the Nobel Prize, is a spectacular Hollywood production that was showered with Oscars and became a huge success—Lara's theme, a melody of yearning, has joined the canon of popular music. In Hollywood fashion the film employs Western actors who communicate in English. And the story is conventional, a man's affectionate love for one woman and his impetuous love for another. But it is set in an extraordinary historical context, taking viewers all the way from the days of the czar through World War I and the Soviet Revolution to the civil war. The film denounces the brutal repression of the czarist regime—the murderous cavalry charge at peaceful demonstrators rivals the famous Odessa steps sequence in *Potemkin* for emotional impact, while adopting a humanistic stance incarnated in the protagonist, Dr. Zhivago. Repelled by czarist repression, he is sympathetic to the revolutionaries, but he is not one of them—cold-hearted revolutionaries stand in stark contrast to the doctor dedicated to healing. Zhivago readily accepts the revolutionary changes, but he is too independent minded to fit into the authoritarian new order and eventually withdraws into family life. The story is framed by a meeting in the 1930s between Zhivago's half-brother and a young woman he presumes to be Zhivago's daughter. She and her engineer friend may be seen to embody the success of the revolution, the more so given the setting: they work at an electric power generation station—a ready reminder of Lenin's dictum, "Socialism is Soviet power plus the electrification of the whole country." The significance of that setting, however, is likely to escape most viewers, who are more likely to come away deploring the violent pursuit of revolutionary goals.

Warren Beatty's *Reds* (1981), winner of numerous awards, is also a story of personal relationships, those of two American "reds," John Reed and Louise Bryant, whose lives were closely interwoven with the early years of the Soviet Union. Reed established his reputation reporting from the Mexican Revolution; he became famous with his eyewitness account of the Bolshevik Revolution, *Ten Days that Shook the World*. Even though Reed's records were impounded for a while by U.S. Customs when he returned to the United States in 1918, he had the book published the following year, with a brief introduction by Lenin. It created a sensation. Beyond the couple's stormy relationship, the film provides impressions of the American labor movement in the early twentieth century, showcasing leading figures of the day. Of the revolutionary transformation in the Soviet Union and the civil war, *Reds* offers only glimpses.

The revolutionary agitation among European intellectuals in the years preceding the Soviet Revolution is dramatically conveyed in Margarethe von Trotta's *Rosa Luxemburg* (1986). The film offers vignettes of a large cast of the leading left-wing intellectuals beyond the most distinguished woman in their midst, Rosa Luxemburg, and her close collaborator Karl Liebknecht. It presupposes some familiarity with those leaders and the historical setting. Thus many viewers are confused by a flashback from a German prison where Rosa Luxemburg was detained during World War I to a Polish prison a decade earlier, in a part of Poland where the Russian empire held sway at the time. They miss the excitement of recognizing celebrated historical figures such as August Bebel, Jean Jaurès, Karl Kautsky, and Clara Zetkin as they hold forth. Still, any viewer can get a sense of Europe's largest Socialist party, which had gained respectability as the German emperor's loyal opposition by the end of the nineteenth century

and held out the promise of a social-democratic future; of Socialist politicians confronting each other over theory and policy; of a minority desperately struggling to raise popular resistance to the preparations for World War I; and of an extraordinary woman who established herself as a prominent radical intellectual. The film facilitates empathy with "Red Rosa" by dwelling on her personal life, her loves, her friendships, her love of nature. Luxemburg exemplified the transnational character of the revolutionary milieu: a Polish Jew, she had been a cofounder of the Polish Socialist Party, proceeded to become one of the leading figures in the German Social Democratic Party, participated in Poland in the failed revolution against the czarist regime in 1905, and finally left the German Social Democratic Party in 1916 to establish the Spartacus League with Liebknecht and agitate for an end to the war. After the war the Spartacus League evolved into the Communist Party, but the attempt to bring the Soviet Revolution to Germany in 1919 was doomed. Luxemburg, who had cautioned that the Communist revolt was premature, was arrested and murdered along with Liebknecht. The film does not touch on Luxemburg's disagreements with Lenin and her warnings that his dictatorship over the proletariat, rather than the dictatorship of the proletariat, would become permanent.

The revolutionaries' vision of the Socialist revolution spreading across Europe remained a dream. Instead Fascists took power in a number of countries, most prominently Italy in 1922, Germany in 1933, and Spain in 1939. Only in Spain did they encounter determined resistance, and the outcome hung in the balance through a long civil war. The Spanish Civil War gave rise to a large number of films, though Spanish directors could not explicitly deviate from the dictatorship's version of events until more than a generation later, when democracy was restored. An outstanding film is *Libertarias* (1996), by the prominent Spanish director Vicente Aranda. Its extravagant premise—in 1936 a nun finds refuge in a bordello and ends up fighting with the anarchists and quoting Mikhail Bakunin and Pyotr Kropotkin—would seem risky, but Aranda succeeded in creating characters that are convincing and remain memorable. The *libertarias,* the women libertarians, are involved in a threefold battle: they are fighting Franco's insurrectional army, they are threatened by other factions on their own side that oppose the anarchists, and they confront male chauvinism. Along the way the famous anarchist leader Buenaventura Durruti puts in an appearance. Aranda offers a complex portrayal of these conflicts, of divided loyalties, of brutality and humanity.

The Bolshevik Revolution of 1917 was followed two generations later by revolutions against the client regimes that the Soviet Union had installed in Eastern Europe after World War II. They were "proletarian revolutions" insofar as workers often played the foremost role. Most striking in that respect were the repeated revolts against the Polish regime that eventually led to the establishment of an independent labor union, Solidarity. Andrzej Wajda created two masterworks denouncing the Communist regime and celebrating workers' resistance. He details the construction of public discourse under a totalitarian regime, from selective reporting to scripted interviews, to arbitrary accusations, to coerced confessions. Wajda used a documentary style, partly by employing black-and-white documentary, which seamlessly integrates both genuine documentary material and fictional documentary. A particularly telling technique for exposing the falsehood of government documentaries contrasts them with takeouts, footage discarded for "technical reasons."

Andrzej Wajda's *Man of Marble* (1976) tells of Agnieszka, a student graduating from the film academy who is making a film about Matheuz Birkut, a young worker who had become a national hero in the 1950s by achieving extraordinary feats of production. She gradually uncovers how the authorities had picked out Birkut to work under artificial circumstances that made such feats possible. Eventually he had fallen afoul of workers as well as the authorities: Birkut was sabotaged by workers who resented the use of his performance to increase their work quotas; and when he sought to help his teammate and friend who had been detained on suspicion of having been involved in the sabotage, he ended up in prison. As Agnieszka seeks to reconstruct Birkut's past, she runs into resistance; even twenty years later some of Poland's Stalinist past has to remain shrouded in mystery. When Agnieszka finally finds Birkut's son Maciek at the Lenin Shipyards in Gdansk, she learns that Birkut has died. The ending appears disjointed and inconclusive—for a peculiar reason. If Wajda had seized the opportunities that presented themselves in the 1970s, at a time when the regime became somewhat less repressive, he had stretched the newly found leeway beyond its limits: the conclusion of *Man of Marble* was cut by the censors—validating the film's recurrent theme of censorship. Viewers had to wait for *Man of Iron* to learn how Birkut had come to his death and what had happened to Agnieszka's film. Even today, *Man of Marble* ends in suspense: the censored ending has not been restored.

Man of Iron (1981) includes documentary footage Andrzej Wajda shot himself during the strike at the Gdansk shipyards in 1980 that brought the establishment of Solidarity, the independent labor union that gained legal status. Now the fictional story of *Man of Marble* could be brought to its proper end: Birkut was shot during the 1970s strike at the very same shipyards. His son Maciek is the principal protagonist in *Man of Iron*. He had been a participant in the student protests of 1968—which workers in general, and his father in particular, had refused to support. He and his fellow students in turn had failed to join the striking workers in 1970. After the death of his father, Maciek had discontinued his studies and, after the compulsory army service, come to work in the shipyards. Now, ten years after his father's death, Maciek has become one of the strike leaders. Lech Walesa, the legendary leader of Solidarity, appears in *Man of Iron* not only in news clips but also in the fictional narrative. Particularly touching is his role as one of the witnesses at the wedding of Maciek and Agnieszka. *Man of Iron* was released early in 1981. It went on to earn the Palme d'Or at the Cannes Film Festival that spring. Proclaiming to the world at large the feat of the workers who had established Solidarity, *Man of Iron* rallied international support to their cause. At the end of 1981, however, martial law was declared in Poland, Solidarity was banned and its representatives arrested. Wajda, facing persecution, went into exile. Finally, in 1989, free elections were held, and Walesa became president of Poland, Wajda a senator.

The Communist Party that came to power in China in 1949 took control of the film industry as the Bolsheviks had done three decades earlier. Like their Soviet counterparts they sought to use film for propaganda purposes. But in the U.S.S.R. political pressure to produce only films readily accessible to the masses did not arise until a decade after the revolution; in China, it impacted the film industry as soon as the Communists came to power. Perhaps the most popular film of that period was Xie Jin's *The Red Detachment of Women* (1961), where young peasant women battle Nan Batian, "the tyrant of the South," in the 1930s. The film's popularity played a major part in the decision to turn it into a ballet as well as an opera—one of the very few theatrical performances officially sanctioned during the Cultural Revolution—filmed in the early 1970s.

Political pressure combined with the vagaries of regime politics to delay the introduction of films of note for more than three decades. Only in the 1980s did Chinese cinema come into its own with a new generation of filmmakers who had trained after the Maoist excesses and, for the first time, had access to foreign films. Born after the victory of the revolution, they produced films on the revolutionary period that touched only marginally on the revolutionary struggle. Chen Kaige's *Yellow Earth* (1984) and Zhang Yimou's *Red Sorghum* (1987), set in the 1930s, told of traditional rural societies characterized by inequality and patriarchy; they were revolutionary insofar as they reminded viewers of the changes Communism had accomplished. These films gained a measure of international recognition and allowed their directors to obtain major funding outside the People's Republic. Several directors of this "fifth generation" of Chinese filmmakers became world famous in the 1990s, when they found a greater measure of independence from the regime. Films such as Zhang Yimou's *To Live* and Tian Zhuangzhuang's *The Blue*

Kite did not extol the Communist Revolution but instead denounced the exactions of the Communist regime, exactions they had experienced themselves.

To Live (1994), which earned the Grand Jury Prize at Cannes, tells the story of an urban family who endures the three cataclysms that befell the Chinese people after the horrors of the Japanese invasion: the civil war that resumed after World War II and lasted until the Communist victory in 1949, the Great Leap Forward 1958–1960, and the Cultural Revolution 1966–1976. Zhang Yimou shows the upheavals and destruction wrought on ordinary people by war and the edicts of the party, with Mao Zedong very much in the lead launching the disasters of the Great Leap and the Cultural Revolution. In stark contrast, and in a somewhat melodramatic fashion, individuals are invariably depicted as good and caring, whether they are family members, or friends, or even local party officials. Confronted with outside forces beyond their control, they just want *to live.*

Tian Zhuangzhuang's *The Blue Kite* (1992) similarly follows the fortunes, or rather the misfortunes, of a family in Beijing from the early 1950s to the Cultural Revolution. Dramatic changes such as the collectivization of private property, sudden reversals in party policy such as that from the liberalizing Let a Hundred Flowers Bloom Campaign to the Anti-Rightist Campaign in 1958, the Great Leap Forward, the Rustication Movement that sent millions to the countryside, the Cultural Revolution, all in turn bring upheavals, sorrow, and even death. And there is the abuse of power: a soldier who refuses the advances of "leaders" finds herself arrested for "counter-revolutionary crimes." Within the close-knit, caring family there are disagreements between the oldest sister, a veteran of the 1930s who unquestioningly endorses the party line of the day, and her siblings, who harbor reservations they only very rarely express. While individuals are well intentioned, politics profoundly affects their relationships: a man is made to falsely denounce his friends; another forsakes his betrothed from a "bad" class background for a poor peasant bride.

Both films roundly condemn Communist Party rule. Neither allows for any suggestion of Communist achievements. Such was perhaps the only forthright position possible a few years after the bloody repression of the democracy movement at Tiananmen Square in 1989. It certainly was a courageous position. Tian and Zhang managed to produce these films to foreign acclaim, but in China *To Live* had only a very limited release, *The Blue Kite* none at all. And the directors paid a price in restrictions put on their subsequent work—Tian was not to release another film for a decade. Still, they were able to denounce the horrors of life under Mao Zedong, even as the Communist Party continued to revere the Great Leader. As yet they cannot tell of Tiananmen.

A Single Spark (1995) is the story of a martyr in the prolonged struggle against repressive military rule in South Korea. The film is directed by Park Kwang-su, considered the leader of the New Korean Cinema movement and the first Korean filmmaker to found his own independent production company. Part of the film, in black and white, tells the story of Jeon (Chun) Tae-il, who denounced harsh and dangerous working conditions in the rapidly industrializing country in the 1960s—conditions the film graphically depicts. Jeon attracted worldwide attention when he immolated himself in 1970 to protest the failure of the Park Chung Hee regime to enforce existing labor laws. His story is interwoven with a second story, in color, set in 1975, when the fictional Kim Yong-su is researching and writing a book about Jeon. By now Park has declared martial law. Students organize impressive protests, but they are quickly broken up by force. Kim, an academic who used to teach labor law, is in hiding. His pregnant girlfriend, who is trying to establish a union at her workplace, is threatened, beaten, jailed. Other dissidents are executed. Jeon's story ends with him engulfed in flames. The fictional story concludes with Kim watching a passerby carrying a copy of his book *The Life and Death of Jeon Tae-il.* Jeon's biography was indeed written in the mid 1970s by a lawyer on the run because of his political activities, Cho Young-rae. When a publisher took the risk to put it into print in 1983, the author had to remain anonymous. Even though parts of the manuscript had been omitted, and some phrasing changed, the book was quickly suppressed by the authorities. In 1991 the original text was restored in a second Korean edition, which could now carry the author's name and on which the film is based.

Vietnamese films telling of the thirty-year war are not readily available in the West. The French and American invaders, however, produced a series of striking films. Oliver Stone's *Platoon* (1986) is particularly effective in describing the experience of American draftees. Shot in the Philippines with young actors who had been put through two weeks of grueling boot camp in the jungle, the film conveys the reality of fighting an elusive enemy. *Platoon* establishes striking contrasts in men's responses to fighting a war they did not believe in. The film opens with Chris Taylor arriving in Vietnam in 1967, as did Stone on his twenty-first birthday, a volunteer for the infantry. Stone himself puts in a brief appearance as the battalion major whose bunker gets blown up by a lone Vietnamese sapper. The film's platoon is a composite of men Stone came to know in two different units. He gives Sergeant Elias the memorable line: "We been kickin' other people's asses so long, I guess it's time we got our own kicked." Stone (2001) details how closely events in the film reflect his own experiences during a one-year tour in Vietnam that included being wounded twice. He tells of being on the verge of killing a civilian himself, of preventing rape.

Scene still from Gillo Pontecorvo's *The Battle of Algiers* (1966). (Casbah/Igor/The Kobal Collection)

Occasionally the film dramatizes and exaggerates, especially toward the end. Elias and Chris mowing down enemy soldiers partakes of exploits that lack credibility, and the quasi-crucifixion of Elias strikes a false chord. Stone had spent ten years trying to get funding for *Platoon,* but Hollywood was not interested in his story. Eventually it was a British producer that funded both *Platoon* and *Salvador.* The Philippine army provided full support for the production—the U.S. army had refused to do so because the film was "unrealistic." Unlike *Salvador,* released a few months earlier, *Platoon* was well received; it won four Oscars, including Best Picture and Best Director, as well as many other awards, became the top-grossing film in the United States, and established Stone as a major Hollywood director.

The government of newly independent Algeria produced a number of films about the colonial experience and the guerrilla war against the French. Best known is the epic *Chronicle of the Years of Embers* (1975), which takes viewers from about 1940 to the outbreak of the war; it won the

Palme d'Or at Cannes. But the most extraordinary film arose out of an Algerian-Italian coproduction, Gillo Pontecorvo's *The Battle of Algiers* (1966), which focuses on the war waged in Algiers by the FLN, the National Liberation Front, from summer 1956 to fall 1957. The film presents in detail the methods used by the FLN to erode French commitment to maintaining colonial rule and to gain international recognition, as well as the response by European settlers and the colonial authorities. This was asymmetrical warfare, to use a term that has recently found widespread use. As the captured FNL leader Larbi Ben M'Hidi puts it in the film in response to a journalist questioning the attacks on civilians with explosive devices hidden in baskets: "Isn't it even more cowardly to attack defenseless villages with napalm bombs that kill many thousands of times more? Obviously, planes would make things easier for us. Give us your bombers, sir, and you can have our baskets." The film displays harrowing pictures of the atrocities committed by both sides, of shootings, bombings, and torture. At the same time, it invites viewers to embrace the nationalist cause. They are led to sympathize with the nationalist struggle as well as the victims, whoever they are.

The Battle of Algiers presents its story in a most unlikely manner—or so thought the Italian producers, who refused to finance this particular film by a director they were eager to work with. Pontecorvo perfected a newsreel style he had used before to such effect that the film appears to be an historical documentary based on newsreel footage—he found it necessary to precede the film with a disclaimer that it does not use any such footage. The historical reconstruction took on newsreel style through image, setting, and story. Pontecorvo used film stock and processing that approached the grainy look of newsreel, in black and white as newsreel was then. He shot in the actual locations in Algiers where events had taken place a decade earlier. And he gave major play to crowd scenes, crowds mourning innocent victims, crowds screaming their protest. The film remains the story of events rather than individuals, even when it does spend time with individual characters, the historical three FLN leaders in Algiers in particular—among them Ali La Pointe, whose real-life transformation from criminal to guerrilla leader, enacted by a peasant recently arrived in Algiers, illustrates the powerful appeal of the nationalist cause. None of the characters were played by professional actors except for the French officer leading the fight against the rebels, Colonel Mathieu. The dramatic developments ensure emotional impact, but the stance remains that of the distanced newsreel camera. The music constitutes a departure from newsreel style—subtly it plays a major role in moving viewers to side with the rebels. Pontecorvo succeeded in creating a work of fiction that gives viewers a sense of observing historical events, a powerful film that won the Golden Lion at the Venice Film Festival but could not be shown in France for many years.

The portrayal of guerrilla warfare in *The Battle of Algiers* is without peer, not just in terms of urban guerrillas, but of guerrillas anywhere. Pontecorvo worked closely with his long-time scriptwriter Franco Solinas, studying historical records and interviewing participants in Algeria and France. They could draw on the experience of Saadi Yacef, the FLN commander who had led the battle and published his own account, whose company coproduced the film, and who took on his own role under the name of El-hadi Jaffar. Beyond the depiction of the methods employed by both sides, the film's particular achievement lies in portraying the rebels as well as the French military as rational actors who cast aside the law and humanity in pursuit of their mission. Only the European settlers appear propelled by emotion to engage in random retribution, which will contribute to their eventually having to depart from what they considered their homeland. Pontecorvo's surgical detachment was presumably shaped by his Marxist background and his own experiences leading partisans against the German occupation in northern Italy in the last stages of World War II.

The Battle of Algiers shows how the French won the battle: systematic torture enabled them to dismantle the FLN network. It does not show how the FLN moved from such defeat to eventual victory. The very background of the conflict—over a century of colonial exploitation, revolts, and repression—is only briefly touched upon. The film concludes with a brief coda of mass demonstrations in Algiers in 1960 and a voiceover announcing independence in 1962. But the jump from the destruction of the FLN network in Algiers to independence omits more than four years of bitter struggle. Such ellipses presumably arise from the need for compression in a film that runs already well beyond the length customary for a feature film. The character of Colonel Mathieu, who represents a composite of several of the leading French army officers, may be seen in the same light. Other omissions may be understood in terms of the political context in which the film was shot in Algeria in 1965, in coproduction with an FLN leader who played a key role in the film and ensured government support. Most distorting is a pattern of describing both sides in the conflict as monoliths. The probing questions of journalists express concerns over the methods used in the war, but there is no indication of French opposition to the war. The only reference to the international context is a debate at the United Nations that remained inconsequential. On the Arab side, the film touches on the crucial issue of rallying public support for the FLN only to the extent that it shows how French repression alienated the Arab majority. The only dissent is that of the owner of a brothel who refuses to endorse the FLN campaign against drugs and prostitution. And there are no collaborators—only through torture can the French exact assistance. The film shows teeming multitudes of poor people but gives no hint of the established Arab bourgeoisie—in fact, the three women bombers had a bourgeois background that allowed two of them to pass for French. There is certainly no mention of the deadly conflicts between different nationalist groupings and even within the FLN leadership.

The lasting contribution of *The Battle of Algiers* is its powerful demonstration of the rationality of torture and its suggestion of the limitations of such barbarism. The film confronts its viewers with the reality of torture, demonstrates its effectiveness in extracting secrets from its victims, and suggests how it alienates its victims and their sympathizers. It barely touches on the role that torture played in fueling opposition to the war in France and provoking international condemnation. Without torture the French could not have won the battle, but its very use undermined their position and contributed to their eventual defeat. The continuing relevance of the film was demonstrated when the Pentagon scheduled an in-house screening in August 2003 as the United States in its turn faced urban guerrilla warfare—and resorted to torture. As for the aftermath of independence, Mohamed Chouikh's *Youcef* (1994) presents a searing indictment of the betrayal of the ideals men and women had fought and died for.

The history of the Iranian Revolution is paradigmatically represented by the biography of Mohsen Makhmalbaf, one of the foremost directors of an Iranian cinema that has come to enjoy worldwide recognition. In 1972 the fifteen-year-old established an underground group that distributed anti-shah leaflets. Two years later Makhmalbaf attacked a police officer. The story is retold in his film *A Moment of Innocence* (1996), which disowns his revolutionary past, depicting himself and a woman accomplice as idealistic dreamers living in a world of fantasy, and makes amends of sorts: Makhmalbaf had his victim participate in the film. Makhmalbaf was injured in the attack, arrested, and jailed, until he was freed with the advent of the revolution in 1978. The first films made by the autodidact in the early 1980s reflected his religious morality; they were even screened in mosques. Soon, however, Makhmalbaf became critical of the religious regime that had entrenched itself in power and produced films denouncing social injustice under the new dispensation. *Marriage of the Blessed* (1989) presents a reckoning with the revolution ten years after its victory. At the end of the devastating Iran-Iraq War, it contrasts the suffering of the war's victims with flourishing profiteering. The protagonist, a shell-shocked photo reporter, "wants to work for Islam," but his photos of urban poverty are censored by the newspaper. Eventually, at the lavish wedding his rich father-in-law has put on, he screams, "Robbed food tastes delicious!" All the while the religious leaders' egalitarian slogans on city walls are contradicted by graffiti: "Volunteer combatant, a lion in battle fields, a victim in town." Tahmineh Milani in turn denounced the violent repression of the secular Left in the early days of the revolution in her riveting *The Hidden Half* (2001)—which earned her a time in jail.

Viva Zapata! (1952) has been perhaps the most successful film on the Mexican Revolution. The film portrays Emiliano Zapata sympathetically and conveys key turning points in the protracted conflict. But even though the film was written by John Steinbeck and directed by Elia Kazan, it fails to transcend the Hollywood conventions of the day. American film stars are inserted among the Mexican peasantry. Distortions abound, incidents are dramatized. Throughout, the film studiously avoids showing the actual fighting, the dead, the wounded, so that when characters occasionally tell of men killed, of being tired of the fighting, their words are hollow. Instead, romance is duly introduced, featuring Zapata's courtship as caricature. The melodrama is matched by the rather intrusive music, which alternates between martial themes and sentimental folklore. *Reed: Insurgent Mexico* (1973) does convey the exhausting grind of fighting that went on for years. The Mexican production, directed by Paul Leduc, is based on the reporting that first established John Reed's reputation. It does not so much tell a story as present a series of vignettes illustrating what Reed wrote in 1913–1914. *Que Viva Mexico!*, Sergei Eisenstein's grand monument to Mexican history, was to conclude with the Mexican Revolution, but that part was never shot.

The revolutionary regime that took power in Cuba in 1959 assumed control of film production like its predecessors in the Soviet Union and China. The Instituto Cubano de Arte y Industria Cinematográficos (ICAIC) released its first feature film the following year. Films such as *Stories of the Revolution* (1960) and *The Young Rebel* (1961) were huge successes with the Cuban audiences for which they were intended: each had about a million admissions (Chanan 2004, 357)—from a population that numbered about seven million at the time. They were, however, rather didactic and provided little of the context foreign viewers needed. Of greater interest is a Soviet-Cuban coproduction, *I Am Cuba*.

I Am Cuba (1964) was directed by Mikhail Kalatozov, a long-established Soviet director of international renown. The film recalls Sergei Eisenstein's unfinished magnum opus on Mexican history, *Que Viva Mexico!* There are similarities in style as well as structure. Both films are strikingly lyrical. Like Eisenstein, Kalatozov starts out with a lush tropical landscape and glimpses of a languid "indigenous" life, then proceeds to tell four distinct stories. The peaceful introduction contrasts with the first story, which shows the Havana tourist scene of aging men and scantily clad beauties and concludes in a Havana shantytown. Rural poverty is the theme of the next story of an indebted peasant who loses his sugar cane and his house when the landowner sells his ranch to the United Fruit Company. The third story tells of Havana students protesting against the Batista dictatorship, burning the screen at a drive-in cinema, getting killed by the police. The final story features a peace-loving peasant who is persuaded by the army's indiscriminate bombing to join the rebels, where we witness a broadcast of the famous *Radio Rebelde*. All along, the mythical voice of Cuba, "I am Cuba," comments on the action. Episodes are drawn out in long continuity shots and repetitions. If the stories are grim, they are told in a lyrical mode, the images at times expressionistic; Kalatozov and his cinematographer Serguey Urusevsky infused agitprop with poetry. Their approach was poorly received in both Cuba and the U.S.S.R., and the film all but disappeared until it was rediscovered in the 1990s for its aesthetic qualities.

Cuban film production quickly came into its own with films that gained wide international recognition. If Cuban cinema echoed the glorious 1920s in the Soviet Union, it differed in that it retained a degree of artistic freedom for nearly half a century, up to the present. And while it did not engage in outright regime critique like Chinese films of the 1990s, it critically engaged with the problems of the revolutionary transformation. *Death of a Bureaucrat* (1966) by Tomás Gutiérrez Alea, Cuba's most distinguished director, is a remarkable example. It is a classic screwball comedy that draws on half a century of cinematic gags, stunts, and symbolism. The hilarious opening credits, in bureaucratese, acknowledge Alea's debt to a dozen American, European, and Japanese directors and actors, beginning with Luis Buñuel and Stan Laurel. Many of Alea's variations on their work are obvious, even to those only vaguely familiar with film classics. Alea thus establishes his cinema in Western traditions (and that of Kurosawa)—but he does not mention a single Soviet director or actor. The film, released in 1966 toward the end of Cuba's "Year of the Struggle against Bureaucracy," is a biting satire of bureaucratic red tape, rigidity, and outright obstruction. The endless complications surrounding the recovery of a document take on a morbid dimension as they involve the corpse of an "exemplary worker" who needs to be exhumed and then cannot be reburied. Three graveyard workers are the only people prepared to do what needs to be done. Along the way Alea takes potshots at "revolutionary" rhetoric, mechanistic hero worship, blind belief in machines, and the routinization of the very campaign against bureaucracy which was under way when the film was shot. *Death of a Bureaucrat* concludes with the funeral procession of the bureaucrat responsible for much of the mayhem. But there is no suggestion that bureaucracy has been buried with him. In Cuba, the film attracted 1.4 million viewers, making it the most popular Cuban film in 1966. Alea's own comments on his film illustrate his political purpose alongside his playfulness. In an interview in 1977 he affirmed that the film had revitalized the entire discussion about the risks of bureaucratization in an incipient Socialist society—and he told American film critics in 1978 that at least two things had gone wrong with the movie: "unfortunately, we killed only one bureaucrat," and the bureaucrats themselves enjoyed the movie (Burton 1977; Stone 1997, 123).

Up to a Certain Point (1983), also directed by Tomás Gutiérrez Alea, combines fiction with documentary and is constructed in three layers: the film is about the making of a film, which in turn relates to a play—an actual play based on an idea by Alea, *La Permuta* by Juan Carlos Tabío. Alea manages to make his complex film quite accessible to viewers. In spontaneous, unscripted interviews Alea and Oscar Alvarez, the actor who plays the male protagonist, a writer, in both films, talked with dock workers about their attitudes to women. *Up to a Certain Point* is about fictitious filmmakers conducting these interviews in preparation for a film about *machismo*. It soon becomes obvious that *machismo* is not an issue at the workplace—the revolution has been successful in that respect. Rather, *machismo* lives on in the domestic context. The film's poignancy derives from the fact that the writer and the director of the film in the film turn out to be old-fashioned machos themselves. The intellectuals are shown to be hypocrites, setting out to denounce in others what they practice themselves; their assumptions reveal the persistence of class prejudice and thus present an implicit critique of several earlier Cuban films focusing on *machismo*. The film is poetic, drawing on a Basque song:

> *If I wished,*
> *I could clip her wings,*
> *and she would be mine.*
> *But then she couldn't fly,*
> *And it's the bird that I love.*

But the film's message goes beyond such noble sentiment. While the song assumes men in control, Lena, the dock clerk the writer has fallen for, won't have her wings clipped by any man—like the woman protagonist of the play, who refuses to follow the script and throws it at the audience. *Up to a Certain Point* is a denunciation of the all-pervading double standard and of lingering class divisions, but it introduces a further dimension. Documentary footage from workers' meetings and a couple of interviews focus on productivity. The speakers are "exemplary workers," all concerned with raising productivity. Their comments turn out to be a litany of complaints about repairs that have not been carried out, about replacements that have not been made for months or even years. They amount to a critique of bureaucracy Socialist-style—echoes of *Death of a Bureaucrat*.

A decade later Tomás Gutiérrez Alea launched an all-encompassing, trenchant critique of the Cuban political system—and a passionate defense of the recognition of all sexual orientations—in his penultimate film, *Strawberry and Chocolate* (1995), supposedly set in 1979. The film's principal protagonist, Diego, joined the Literacy Campaign as a fourteen-year-old and still considers himself a supporter of the revolution. But he has found that the party tolerates neither his independent mind nor his homosexuality, and he has become highly critical. A man of great culture, he may be seen as Alea's alter ego as he takes the regime to task in his confrontations with David, a student whose naive enthusiasm for the revolution is matched by an education that has been narrowly circumscribed. When they get to Diego's place, Diego puts on a Maria Callas recording and exclaims:

> *God, what a voice! Why can't this island produce*
> *another voice like that? We need another voice*
> *so badly!*
> *We have had enough of Maria Remolá!*
> *Come out neighbors!*
> *Onions have finally arrived to the market.*

Scene still from Oliver Stone's *Salvador* (1986). (Hemdale/The Kobal Collection)

If the mockery of artists who chant the praises of the revolution is obvious, Cuban viewers will hear it as Diego protecting himself, perhaps the directors protecting themselves as well, from the accusation that "We need another voice so badly" was referring to Fidel Castro, the great orator.

On their next meeting an exchange goes:

DAVID: I'll show you we Communists are not savages.
DIEGO: That sounds marvelous.
SOON AFTER DIEGO TOASTS: Long live democratic
   communism!

Eventually Diego loses his job when he publicly denounces the party's interference with the exhibition of a sculptor friend. Exile becomes his only option. Alea, suffering from terminal cancer, would not have been able to produce *Strawberry and Chocolate* but for the help of his long-time collaborator Juan Carlos Tabío. Unfortunately the result of their collaboration created characters that fail to convince and some rather conventional plot developments.

Whatever its shortcomings, *Strawberry and Chocolate* stands as a powerful critique of Castro's rule—a critique that was in part financed by the Cuban government and released to attract the largest audience ever (Chanan, 2004, 472).

The most powerful film devoted to the guerrilla movements challenging oppressive regimes in Latin America, and denouncing American complicity and outright involvement in the brutal repression of all dissent, is Oliver Stone's *Salvador* (1986). The film is based on the experiences of Richard Boyle, a twenty-year photojournalist veteran of wars around the globe, who had made seven trips to El Salvador between 1979 and 1982. Events that took place over several years are compressed into a few weeks in 1980–1981. They include two outrages that impacted public consciousness in the United States: the killing of Archbishop Oscar Romero by a gunman, and the recovery of the bodies of four Americans, three nuns and a lay missioner, who had been raped and killed by National Guardsmen. Stone took liberties with the historical record, exaggerating and inventing outright. The number of corpses strewn around the film's version of El Payon, the notorious site where right-wing death squads dumped the bodies of their victims, is dramatically increased; the guerrillas did not use horses in combat, and they certainly would have been a hindrance in an urban setting; the circumstances of the killing of Archbishop Romero were different; U.S. ambassador Robert White never acceded to demands for the resumption of assistance to the military; and the real-life Newsweek photographer was killed in cross fire. While there were thus numerous deviations from the historical record, they may be argued to have little changed the historical significance of events. They certainly greatly enhanced dramatic effect.

Hollywood had not been prepared to back Stone on either *Salvador* or *Platoon,* but British and Mexican funding allowed *Salvador* to be released while war was raging in El Salvador and elsewhere in Central America, and the United States was backing, often covertly, brutal repression. The film had to be shot in Mexico. Initial critical reaction was mixed, and the film had only a limited run. It may be argued that Stone violated the cinematic conventions of Hollywood and that the general public in the United States was not particularly concerned with the goings-on next door. The success of the video release, however, suggests otherwise. The difficulties the film encountered were in large part due to Stone violating the political conventions of Hollywood. At the time, Hollywood was fearful of producing films critical of major U.S. foreign policy actions while they were still ongoing. In this case it was U.S. support for the brutal El Salvadoran government and military blamed for torturing and murdering tens of thousands of people. The film depicts this brutality and the U.S. government aid to the side in the conflict most responsible for it. They clearly played a part in the refusal of Hollywood to back *Salvador.* Limited foreign funding forced Stone to produce *Salvador* under financial constraints so severe that the very completion of the film was in doubt. Foreign sales were substantial, but rebuffs from U.S. distributors led the British producer, Hemdale, to venture into distribution, for the first time ever, with very limited resources. The response of some U.S. critics to the film appear not to have been altogether unrelated to its politics. *Under Fire* (1983), directed by Roger Spottiswoode and shot in Mexico, is set in Nicaragua in spring 1979, as the regime of Anastasio Somoza Debayle comes to its end. The film conforms to the Hollywood pattern by not having a single Nicaraguan among the protagonists. Thus the climactic event is the death of an American journalist—an event that had its real-life counterpart in the execution of ABC News correspondent Bill Stewart by members of Somoza's National Guard, which was similarly caught on film and shown on U.S. television. The film emphasizes the importance of the media, and images in particular, in civil war. It touches on the U.S. government support that the Somoza dictatorship enjoyed and the involvement of the CIA. And it conveys the confusing

character of urban guerrilla warfare, offering up scenes of street fighting, of a daring guerrilla attack on soldiers established on a church roof, of soldiers killing civilians. But as in an action movie, the deaths remain at a distance, soliciting little emotional involvement from the viewer. Too many elements of the story are from the realm of fantasy, while their melodramatic conclusions remain altogether predictable.

Four Days in September by Bruno Barreto, the distinguished Brazilian director, provides a guerrilla perspective. This is the story of the kidnapping of U.S. ambassador Charles Elbrick in 1969 by members of two guerrilla movements operating together, the October 8th Revolutionary Movement and the National Liberation Group—an event that brought worldwide attention to the Brazilian guerrilla. It is set in the context of the usurpation of power by the military in 1964 and their brutal repression of all opposition. Barreto tells a gripping story of grand strategy, of tactical brilliance, and of little mistakes with big consequences. He presents the story in shades of gray, avoiding easy clichés. He draws a range of differentiated characters among the seven men and women who carried out the kidnapping, from the wizened veteran of the Spanish Civil War to the battle-hardened man in charge of fresh student recruits whose reactions to their prisoner and the stark choices facing them range widely. The ambassador is portrayed sympathetically. The Secret Service agent who is hot on the heels of the kidnappers, a man who routinely uses torture, appears as a troubled human being. Barreto uses this cast of characters to unobtrusively present arguments about opposition and repression, about the use of violence. Fernando, alias Paulo, is the guerrilla we come to know best—for a good reason: he wrote the book on which the film is based. Fernando Gaberia went on to become a journalist, a prolific author, and a Green Party member of the Brazilian Congress.

Space limitations preclude discussion of films on a number of other conflicts, so brief comments will have to suffice. Two fine films on rural guerrilla warfare were produced in Africa. Flora Gomes's *Mortu Nega* (1988) tells of guerrillas and the civilians supplying them in the war against Portuguese colonial rule in what is now Guinea-Bissau. Ingrid Sinclair's *Flame* (1996) is the story of two girls who join the struggle against the white minority regime that usurped power in what became Zimbabwe and find themselves fighting male chauvinism as well.

On the struggle against apartheid in South Africa, Euzhan Palcy's powerful *A Dry White Season* (1989), based on the novel of the distinguished Afrikaner writer André Brink, reenacts the 1976 Soweto Uprising and brings home the repression in the police state that the white minority regime had established in South Africa. The remarkable *Mapantsula* (1988), filmed surreptitiously by Oliver Schmitz during a state of emergency, effectively conveys the reality of the unarmed urban struggle in the 1980s that played a major role in the eventual demise of apartheid.

On the Israel-Palestine conflict, *Kedma* (2002), by the Israeli director Amos Gitai, set in 1948, gives voice to both Jewish survivors of the Holocaust disembarking in the promised land and Arabs fleeing their ancestral homes. *Hitchhikers* (1998), by the Israeli director Asher Tlalim, presents political commentary as well as comedy as four strangers—a family man, a hippie woman, an orthodox soldier, and an Arab Israeli—travel together in a car. If such Israeli films offer dialogue, the asymmetry of power between Israelis and Palestinians is reflected by the fact that the few Palestinian filmmakers are single-mindedly dedicated to advancing the cause of their people. Two remarkable films are Michel Kleifi's *Tale of the Three Jewels* (1995), a story of children living and dreaming amid violence in Ghaza, and Hany Abu-Assad's *Rana's Wedding* (2002), the story of a would-be bride confronting the hurdles of Israeli roadblocks between Israel and the Occupied Territories as she tries to make the deadline her father imposed for her marriage. These films' choices of protagonists and touches of humor allow them to reach a wider audience. *Tale of the Three Jewels* and *Hitchhikers* further soften their message by offering up two endings: each concludes in a tragedy that reflects the violence of the conflict, but then the action briefly resumes to provide a happy end.

Islamic fundamentalism has been the focus of a number of films in recent years. Siddiq Barmak's *Osama* (2003) is a searing indictment of Taliban ideology and of brutality and corruption under Taliban rule in Afghanistan. Yamina Bachir-Chouikh's *Rachida* (2002) presents a dramatic denunciation of the atrocities committed in the name of fundamentalism in Algeria; women are portrayed as resilient victims by the female director. Merzak Allouache's *The Other World* (2001) also conveys the horror of terrorism in 1990s Algeria. These are powerful films, but they remain denunciatory; they do not attempt to provide an understanding of the broad appeal of Islamic fundamentalism. That task is undertaken by Atef Hetata in *Closed Doors* (1999), where an adolescent in Cairo, abandoned by his father, acutely aware of the corruption around him, of glaring inequalities, and of the disparities that draw Egyptians to oil-rich countries, falls under the spell of fundamentalists. Youssef Chahine gives historical depth to the conflict between liberals and fundamentalists in his extraordinary epic *Destiny* (1997), telling the story of a Muslim philosopher confronting the fundamentalists of his day. Averroës had a major influence on Jewish and Christian thought, on St. Thomas Aquinas in particular, and Chahine presents Muslim Andalusia in the twelfth century in all its splendor—its learning, its architecture, its arts—all the while entertaining his viewers.

Josef Gugler

Acknowledgements I would like to thank, without implicating, Joseph Cary, James DeFronzo, Robert Lang, and Freya Schiwy for helpful suggestions.

Filmography

The Battle of Algiers. 1966. Film directed by Gillo Pontecorvo, written by Franco Solinas and Gillo Pontecorvo, based on a true story by Saadi Yacef. Produced by Casbah Films (Algeria) and Igor Film (Italy). Distributed in the U.S. by Rialto. 121 minutes.

Battleship Potemkin / Bronenosets Potyomkin. 1925. Film directed by Sergei Eisenstein, written by Nune Agadzhanove-Shutka. Restored with a soundtrack in 1976 by Mosfilm Studios (U.S.S.R.). Distributed in the U.S. by Corinth Films. 74 minutes.

The Blue Kite / Lan fengzheng. 1992. Film directed by Tian Zhuangzhuang, written by Xia Mao. Produced by Longwick Production (Hong Kong) and Beijing Film Studio (China). Distributed in the U.S. by Kino International. 138 minutes.

Chronicle of the Years of Embers / Chronicle of the Smoldering Years / Waqai Sanawat Al-Djamr / Chronique des années de braise. 1975. Film directed by Mohammed Lakhdar-Hamina, written by Mohammed Lakhdar-Hamina, Tewfik Fares, and B. Boudjedra. Produced by the Office National pour le Commerce et l'Industrie Cinématographique. Distributed by in the U.S. by Arab Film Distribution. 175 minutes.

Closed Doors / Al Abwab al-Moghlaka. 1999. Film written and directed by Atef Hetata. Produced by Misr International Films, Médiane Production (France) and Arte France Cinéma (France). Distributed in the U.S. by Arab Film Distribution. 110 minutes.

Death of a Bureaucrat / La Muerte de un burócrata. 1966. Film directed by Tomás Gutiérrez Alea, written by Alfredo L. Del Cueto, Ramón F. Suárez, and Tomás Gutiérrez Alea. Produced by Instituto Cubano de Arte y Industria Cinematográficos (Cuba). Distributed in the U.S. by New Yorker. 87 minutes.

Destiny / al-Massir. 1997. Film directed by Youssef Chahine, written by Youssef Chahine with the collaboration of Khaled Youssef. Produced by Ognon Pictures (France), France 2 Cinema (France), and Misr International Films (Egypt). Distributed in the U.S by Leisure Time Features. 135 minutes.

Doctor Zhivago. 1965. Film directed by David Lean, written by Robert Bolt. Produced by Metro Goldwyn Mayer (USA). 197 minutes.

A Dry White Season. 1989. Film directed by Euzhan Palcy, written by Colin Welland and Euzhan Palcy. Produced by Metro Goldwyn Mayer (USA) in association with Star Partners II (Britain). 106 minutes.

The End of St. Petersburg / Konets Sankt-Peterburga. 1927. Film directed by Vsevolod Pudovkin and Mikhail Doller, written by Nathan Zarkhi. Produced by Mezhrabpom-Rus Studio (U.S.S.R.). Restored with a soundtrack in 1969 by Mosfilm Studios (U.S.S.R.). Distributed in the U.S. by Image Entertainment. 87 minutes.

Flame. 1996. Film directed by Ingrid Sinclair, written by Ingrid Sinclair with Barbara Jago and Philip Roberts. Produced by Black and White Film (Zimbabwe), JBA Production (France), and Onland Productions (Namibia). Distributed in the U.S. by California Newsreel. 85 minutes.

Four Days in September / O que é isso, companheiro? 1997. Film directed by Bruno Barreto, written by Leopoldo Serran, based on Fernando Gabeira's *O que é isso, companheiro?* Produced by Produções Cinematográficas L.C. Barreto (Brazil) and Filmes do Equandor (Brazil). Distributed in the U.S. by Miramax Films. 106 minutes.

The Hidden Half / Nimeh-ye Penhan. 2001. Film written and directed by Tahmineh Milani. Distributed in the U.S. by Irmovies. 108 minutes.

Hitchhikers / Trempistim. 1998. Film directed and edited by Asher Tlalim, written by Dudu Topaz. Produced by POV Productions (Israel). Distributed in the U.S. by Ergo. 47 minutes.

I am Cuba / Ya Kuba / Soy Cuba. 1964. Film directed by Mikhail Kalatozov, written by Yevgeny Yevtushenko and Enrique Pineda Barnet. Produced by Mosfilm (U.S.S.R.) and Instituto Cubano de Arte y Industria Cinematográficos (Cuba). Distributed in the U.S. by Milestone. 141 minutes.

Kedma. 2002. Film directed by Amos Gitai, written by Amos Gitai and Marie Jose Sanselme. Produced by Agav Hafakot (Israel), Arte France Cinéma (France), Agav Films (Israel), M.P. Productions (France), and BIM Distribuzione (Italy). Distributed in the U.S. by Kino International. 100 minutes.

Libertarias. 1996. Film directed by Vicente Aranda, written by Antonio Rabinad, José Luis Guarner, and Vicente Aranda. Produced by Sogetel (Spain) and Lolafilms (Spain). Distributed in the U.S. by Ventura. 125 minutes.

Man of Iron / Czlowiek z Zelaza. 1981. Film directed by Andrzej Wajda, written by Aleksander Scibor-Rylski. Produced by Film Polski (Poland). Distributed in the U.S. by Metro Goldwyn Mayer. 140 minutes.

Man of Marble / Czlowiek z Marmuru. 1976. Film directed by Andrzej Wajda, written by Aleksander Scibor-Rylski. Produced by Film Polski (Poland). Distributed in the U.S. by Vanguard. 160 minutes.

Mapantsula. 1988. Film directed by Oliver Schmitz, written by Oliver Schmitz and Thomas Mogotlane. Produced by One Look (South Africa), David Hannay Productions (Australia), and Haverbeam (Britain). Distributed in the U.S. by California Newsreel. 104 minutes.

Marriage of the Blessed / Wedding of the Blessed / Arousi-ye Khouban. 1989. Film written, directed, and edited by Mohsen Makhmalbaf. Distributed in the U.S. by Facets Video. 70 minutes.

A Moment of Innocence / Nun va Goldoon. 1996. Film written, directed, and edited by Mohsen Makhmalbaf. Produced by Paksh (Iran). Distributed in the U.S. by New Yorker. 78 minutes.

Mortu Nega / Those Whom Death Refused. 1988. Film directed by Flora Gomes, written by Flora Gomes, Manuel Rambout Barcelos, and David Lang. Produced by Instituto Nacional de Cinema (Guinea-Bissau). Distributed in the U.S. by California Newsreel. 93 minutes.

October / Ten Days that Shook the World / Oktyabr. 1927. Written and directed by Sergei Eisenstein and Grigori Aleksandrov. Restored with a soundtrack in 1967 by Mosfilm Studios (U.S.S.R.). Distributed in the U.S. by Corinth Films. 103 minutes.

Osama. 2003. Film written and directed by Siddiq Barmak. Produced by Barmak Films (Afghanistan), NHK (Japan), and leBrocquyFraser (Ireland). Distributed in the U.S. by United Artists. 82 minutes.

The Other World / L'Autre Monde. 2001. Film written and directed by Merzak Allouache. Produced by Lancelot Films (France) and Baya Films (Algeria) in coproduction with Arte France Cinéma, Canal+ Horizons (France), We Aime El Djazaïr (Algeria), and E.N.T.V. (Algeria). Distributed in the U.S. by ArtMattan. 97 minutes.

Platoon. 1986. Film written and directed by Oliver Stone. Produced by Hemdale (Britain). Distributed in the U.S. by Orion. 113 minutes.

Rachida. 2002. Film written and directed by Yamina Bachir-Chouikh. Produced by Ciné Sud Promotion (France), La Fondation Gan (France), and ARTE France Cinéma (France). Distributed by Les Films du Paradox. 100 minutes.

Rana's Wedding / Jerusalem, Another Day / Al Quods Fee Yom Akhar. 2002. Film directed by Hany Abu-Assad. Based on a story by Liana Badr. Written by Ihab Lamez and Liana Badr. Distributed in the U.S. by Arab Film Distribution. 90 minutes.

The Red Detachment of Women / Hongse niangzijun. 1961. Film directed by Xie Jin, written by Liang Xin. Produced by Tianma Studio (China). 105 minutes.

Red Sorghum / Hong gaoliang. 1987. Film directed by Zhang Yimou, written by Chen Jianyu, Mo Yan, and Zhu Wei, based on Mo Yan's *Red Sorghum* and *Sorghum Wine.* Produced by X'ian Film Studio (China). Distributed in the U.S. by New Yorker. 91 minutes.

Reds. 1981. Film directed by Warren Beatty, written by Warren Beatty and Trevor Griffiths. Produced by Paramount (USA). 195 minutes.

Reed: Insurgent Mexico / Reed, México Insurgente. 1973. Film directed by Paul Leduc, written by Juan Tovar and Paul Leduc, based on John Reed's *Insurgent Mexico.* 104 minutes.

Rosa Luxemburg. 1986. Written and directed by Margarethe von Trotta. Produced by Bioskop-Film, Pro-Ject Film im Filmverlag der Autoren, Regina Ziegler Filmproduktion, Bärenfilm, and Westdeutscher Rundfunk (all Germany). Distributed in the U.S. by New Yorker. 122 minutes.

Salvador. 1986. Film directed by Oliver Stone, written by Oliver Stone and Richard Boyle. Produced by Hemdale (Britain) and Pasta Producciones (Mexico). Distributed in the U.S. by Hemdale. 122 minutes.

A Single Spark / Jeon Tae-il. 1995. Film directed by Park Kwang-su, written by Lee Chang-dong, Kim Chung-kwan, Lee Hyo-in, Hur Jin-ho, and Park Kwang-su, based on Cho Young-rae's *A Single Spark: The Biography of Chun Tae-il.* Produced by Cine 2000, Daewoo Cinema, and Jeon Tae-il Commemorative Association (all South Korea). Distributed by Fortissimo Film. 93 minutes.

Stories of the Revolution / Historias de la Revolución. 1960. Film directed by Tomás Gutiérrez Alea, written by Humberto Arenal, Tomás Gutiérrez Alea, and José Hernández. Produced by Instituto Cubano de Arte y Industria Cinematográficos (Cuba). 81 minutes.

Strawberry and Chocolate / Fresa y chocolate. 1995. Film directed by Tomás Gutiérrez Alea and Juan Carlos Tabío, written by Senel Paz, based on his short story *El lobo, el bosque y el hombre nuevo.* Produced by Instituto Cubano de Arte y Industria Cinematográficos (Cuba), Instituto Mexicano de Cinematográfica (Mexico), Tele Madrid (Spain), La Sociedad General de Autores de España the Movement of the 26th of July, M-26-7 (Spain), and Tabasco Film (Mexico). Distributed in the U.S. by Miramax. 104 minutes.

Tale of the Three Jewels / Hikayat al-Jawahir Thalath. 1995. Film written and directed by Michel Khleifi. Produced by Sindebad Films (Britain) and Sourat Films (Belgium). Distributed in the U.S. by Arab Film Distribution. 107 minutes.

To Live / Living / Lifetimes/ Huozhe. 1994. Film directed by Zhang Yimou, written by Yu Hua and Lu Wei, based on Yu Hua's *To Live.* Produced by ERA International (Hong Kong) in association with Shanghai Film Studio (China) for Century Communications (Hong Kong). Distributed in the U.S. by Samuel Goldwyn. 133 minutes.

Under Fire. 1983. Film directed by Roger Spottiswoode, written by Clayton Frohman and Ron Shelton. Produced by Metro Goldwyn Mayer (USA). 128 minutes.

Up to a Certain Point / Hasta cierto punto. 1983. Film directed by Tomás Gutiérrez Alea, written by Serafín Qiñones, Juan Carlos Tabío, and Tomás Gutiérrez Alea. Produced by Instituto Cubano de Arte y Industria Cinematográficos (Cuba). Distributed in the U.S. by New Yorker. 68 minutes.

Viva Zapata! 1952. Film directed by Elia Kazan, written by John Steinbeck, based on Edgcumb Pinchon's *Zapata the Unconquered.* Produced by Twentieth Century Fox (USA). 112 minutes.

Yellow Earth / Huang tudi. 1984. Film directed by Chen Kaige, written by Zhang Ziliang. Produced by Guangxi Film Studio (China). 86 minutes.

Youcef. 1994. Film written and directed by Mohamed Chouikh. Produced by CAAIC (Algeria), ENPA, and Ministère de la Communication et de la Culture (Algeria). Distributed by Médiathèque des Trois Mondes. 105 minutes.

The Young Rebel / El joven rebelde. 1961. Film directed by Julio García Espinosa. Produced by Instituto Cubano de Arte y Industria Cinematográficos (Cuba).

References and Further Readings

Burton, Julianne. 1977. "Individual Fulfillment and Collective Achievement." Interview with Tomas Gutierrez Alea. *Cineaste* 8 (1): 8–21, 58.

Chanan, Michael. 2004. *Cuban Cinema.* Cultural Studies of the Americas 14 (series). Minneapolis/London: University of Minnesota Press.

Clark, Paul. 1987. *Chinese Cinema: Culture and Politics since 1949.* Cambridge Studies in Film (series). Cambridge: Cambridge University Press.

Dabashi, Hamid. 2001. *Close Up: Iranian Cinema, Past, Present and Future.* London/New York: Verso.

Georgakas, Dan, and Lenny Rubenstein, eds. 1983. *The Cineaste Interviews: On the Art and Politics of Cinema.* Chicago: Lake View Press.

Gugler, Josef. 2003. *African Film: Re-Imagining a Continent.* Oxford: James Currey; Bloomington: Indiana University Press; Cape Town: David Philip.

Lu, Sheldon Hsiao-peng. 1997. "National Cinema, Cultural Critique, Transnational Capital: The Films of Zhang Yimou." Pp. 105–136 in *Transnational Chinese Cinemas: Identity, Nationhood, Gender,* edited by Sheldon Hsiao-peng Lu. Honolulu: University of Hawaii Press.

Lu, Tonglin. 2002. *Confronting Modernity in the Cinemas of Taiwan and Mainland China.* Cambridge: Cambridge University Press.

Mellen, Joan.1973. *Filmguide to The Battle of Algiers.* Bloomington: Indiana University Press.

Riordan, James. 1995. *Stone: The Controversies, Excesses, and Exploits of a Radical Filmmaker.* New York: Hyperion.

Rosenstone, Robert A. 1995. *Visions of the Past: The Challenge of Film to Our Idea of History.* Cambridge, MA: Harvard University Press.

Solinas, PierNico, ed. 1973. *Pontecorvo's* The Battle of Algiers: *A Film Written by Franco Solinas.* New York: Charles Scribner's Sons.

Stone, Judy. 1997. *Eye on the World: Conversations with International Filmmakers.* Los Angeles: Silman-James Press.

Stone, Oliver. 2001. Running commentary on *Platoon* on DVD release.

Taylor, Richard. 1979. *The Politics of the Soviet Cinema.* Cambridge: Cambridge University Press.

Zhang, Yingjin. 2004. *Chinese National Cinema.* New York/London: Routledge.

Colombian Armed Conflict

CHRONOLOGY

1819	Colombia gains its independence from Spain.
1839–1895	The country experiences eight generalized civil wars, in addition to a series of regional conflicts between the country's two political parties, Liberals and Conservatives.
1899–1902	Colombia endures a larger-scale civil war, the War of One Thousand Days, in which approximately 120,000 people die. Panama separates from Colombia and becomes an independent state.
1910	Relatively free and fair elections are formalized.
1948–1953	The country endures *La Violencia,* a prolonged civil war in which the Conservative government persecutes members of the Liberal Party throughout Colombia. The Liberals respond by creating self-defense guerrilla groups. The violence between Conservatives and Liberals leaves nearly 200,000 people dead.
1953	General Gustavo Rojas Pinilla carries out a coup d'état, stops state-sponsored violence, and establishes a short-lived dictatorship. Rojas also offers an amnesty to Liberal guerrillas, but many demobilized rebels are killed after turning in their weapons.
1957	A restricted form of democracy is reinstated with the National Front, a power-sharing agreement between Liberals and Conservatives that is intended to stabilize the political situation by eliminating inter-party conflict.

1964–1966   The guerrilla organizations FARC (Revolutionary Armed Forces of Colombia), ELN (National Liberation Army), and EPL (Popular Liberation Army) are founded. While the FARC is an orthodox Marxist-Leninist guerrilla group, the EPL embraces Maoism, and the ELN espouses a Cuban style of revolutionary practice.

1970   General Rojas Pinilla participates in Colombia's presidential elections as the candidate of a populist party, Popular National Alliance (ANAPO), and is defeated in seemingly fraudulent elections by Conservative candidate Misael Pastrana Borrero.

1974   The guerrilla group April 19 Movement (M-19) is created by disaffected ANAPO members and former guerrillas expelled from FARC.

The National Front is gradually dismantled. This process culminates in the 1991 constitutional reform. Production of marijuana and later cocaine increases dramatically during the 1970s and 1980s.

1978–1982   Liberal president Julio César Turbay Ayala adopts a repressive strategy to contain insurgency that eventually fails. The rebel groups grow in numbers and the M-19 gains popularity in urban centers.

1982–1986   Conservative president Belisario Betancur carries out an unsuccessful peace process with the rebel groups FARC, M-19, and EPL. In 1985, eleven supreme court judges and approximately ninety other civilians are killed as a result of the M-19 raid on the Colombian Palace of Justice. Toward the end of Betancur's administration, drug-financed right-wing paramilitary groups begin to engage in the systematic murder of left-wing militants. These paramilitary groups would form an umbrella organization, the United Self-Defense Forces of Colombia (AUC) in 1997.

1986–1990   Liberal president Virgilio Barco leads the only successful peace process in Colombia that ends in the demobilization of the M-19, EPL, CRS (a splinter faction of the ELN), and other minor rebel groups. The M-19 and EPL form political parties and participate in the 1990 elections. Three presidential candidates, Carlos Pizarro of the M-19, Bernardo Jaramillo of the Patriotic Union (a political party created by FARC), and Liberal Luis Carlos Galán are assassinated. Notwithstanding the murder of its presidential candidate, the M-19 undergoes a successful (albeit short-lived) transformation from rebel group into an active political party.

1990–1994   President César Gaviria attempts to reach a peaceful settlement with the FARC and ELN in meetings held in Caracas, Venezuela, and Tlaxcala, Mexico, but no agreement is achieved. War intensifies once again in the country. The 1991 constitution introduces mechanisms designed to increase the participatory nature of Colombian democracy.

1994–1998   Ernesto Samper Pizano is elected president in controversial elections in which the Cali drug-trafficking cartel contributes funding to his campaign. Given Samper's lack of legitimacy, the rebel groups refuse to engage in peace talks with his administration. Ironically, the two largest drug-trafficking organizations, the Medellín and Cali cartels, are dismantled during this period. Armed groups, in particular the FARC and AUC, begin to participate more actively in drug-related activities.

1998   Conservative president Andrés Pastrana announces the demilitarization of five municipalities in southern Colombia in order to start peace talks with the FARC. Preliminary talks are also initiated with the ELN. Pastrana fails to rein in paramilitary group activities, and the AUC grows and is strengthened between 1998 and 2002.

2000   United States funding for Plan Colombia is approved by the U.S. Congress. Colombia becomes the third largest recipient of U.S. military assistance in the world. A massive drug eradication and counterinsurgency campaign is begun in the southern part of the country.

2002	In February, President Pastrana formally ends the peace negotiations with the FARC, alleging that this organization has taken advantage of the demilitarized zone to harbor kidnapping victims, rearm itself, and engage in drug-trafficking activities. The FARC are labelled terrorist actors, and the war intensifies. Right-wing candidate Álvaro Uribe Vélez is elected president after pledging to defeat the FARC and the ELN militarily.
2003	Members of the AUC agree to disarm and to begin peace talks with the Colombian government. Formal talks begin in July 2004.

INTRODUCTION

Since the late 1940s, Colombia has endured two different but interrelated waves of insurgency. Even today, rebel groups, namely the FARC (Revolutionary Armed Forces of Colombia) and the ELN (National Liberation Army), continue to challenge the Colombian state in many rural and urban areas. Although Colombian rebels have never come close to triggering revolution, they have not been militarily defeated either. Their survival may be explained by factors such as Colombia's vast and rugged territory, the presence of a variety of natural resources that have been looted by the rebel groups, periodic repressive state policies that have worked to radicalize some peasant communities, and the failure of the Colombian state to adequately address the needs of the underprivileged. In turn, the rebels' inability to gain mass support and topple the government is mainly explained by their increasing recourse to criminal tactics, and the fact that Colombian democracy has been interrupted only once and for a very short period of time.

BACKGROUND: CULTURE AND HISTORY

Following over 300 years of Spanish colonial rule, a series of popular rebellions led to Colombian independence in 1819. During the period of colonial rule, the country was renowned for its gold resources, which were appropriated by Spanish settlers. In the post-independence period, Colombia became an exporter of tobacco, cotton, and leather. In the late 1800s the country started producing coffee, which became Colombia's main export crop during most of the twentieth century. The country is rich in other natural resources as well, and presently is one of the world's leading exporters of emeralds, bananas, and flowers. The legal economy has been mirrored by the existence of an illegal one centered on the cultivation, processing, and export of coca leaf, poppy, cocaine, and heroin. Today, Colombia produces approximately 80 percent of the cocaine sold in the world and a large percentage of the heroin consumed in the United States.

Although the 1991 constitution defines Colombia as a "multiethnic and pluricultural country," the country displays relative homogeneity compared to others that are deeply divided along ethnic or religious lines. In fact, a great majority of the population (about 60 percent) consists of mestizos, that is, persons of mixed white and indigenous parentage. Indigenous and black minorities do exist, but together they represent no more than 8 percent of the population. In addition, due to its Spanish heritage, Colombia is a predominantly Catholic country, despite the existence of a few religious minorities. The Colombian conflict has seldom (if ever) been framed along ethnic or religious divisions, which is indicative of the primacy of politics as one of its root causes.

However, the ways in which politics and armed conflict mix in Colombia has produced a great deal of debate. The country is one of the oldest democracies in Latin America. Democracy was established in the early twentieth century and only interrupted once and for a very short time during the dictatorship of General Gustavo Rojas Pinilla (1953–1957). Since the late 1940s, Colombia has also experienced endemic insurgency. The country has endured two different but interconnected cycles of violence. The first, lasting from late 1940s until the early 1960s, consisted of an armed confrontation between Liberals and Conservatives that resulted in approximately 200,000 casualties. A second cycle began in the mid 1960s; it has been a war of attrition between the state and a number of predominantly Communist-inspired rebel groups, and has produced over 100,000 deaths.

The fact that Colombia is a democratic regime that also displays a high propensity for internal warfare constitutes a major puzzle. In general, rebellion tends to be the outcome of political systems that prevent participation by all groups in society, leaving few options other than armed forms of opposition. Although no revolutionary organization has been able to overthrow the Colombian government, political and economic exclusion, the existence of lucrative drug-related resources, and some of the country's rugged geographic conditions have offered fertile soil for the reproduction of political violence.

Between 1910 and 1949, the Colombian polity underwent a transition from a competitive oligarchy, in which powerful elites struggled with each other for control of the government, to an oligarchic democracy, in which the larger populace was able to play a limited role in selecting members of the elites for governmental positions through the vote. During the early decades of the twentieth century, significant levels of coercion and fraud influenced electoral outcomes but never jeopardized the occurrence of regular elections. Such practices diminished in the 1930s and 1940s as a result of rapid urbanization and increasing levels of political participation. Although not every election was truly competitive, no single party was forcibly prevented from taking part in the elections—though on occasion a party refused to participate in electoral contests as a way to conceal its own political weakness and/or to delegitimize the regime.

From the mid nineteenth century onward, the Liberal and Conservative parties became the principal vehicles for generating national political identities. Neither party was predominantly rural or urban, bourgeois or proletarian, nor did they display significant ideological differences. Instead, the two largely resembled each other: they both consisted primarily of patronage networks that sought office as a way to obtain political and economic privilege and to distribute favors to their respective clienteles.

Partisan identities became so strong that they were considered an ascriptive trait inherited from generation to generation. As early as the mid nineteenth century, party elites became effective at mobilizing their mostly rural clienteles against members of the opposite party during electoral contests and in a series of violent regional clashes and civil wars. Personal, vertical, clientelistic relations nurtured party loyalties, but violence played an equally important role in forging partisan identities. Bipartisan conflict alternated with periods in which Liberal and Conservative elites moderated the tone of their confrontation. To a large degree, party elites agreed to reduce inter-party conflict whenever such animosity endangered their dominance over the lower classes.

The conflict between Liberals and Conservatives escalated considerably during the 1940s. Political turbulence played in favor of the populist Liberal politician Jorge Eliécer Gaitán, a radical party insider who occasionally flirted with Socialist ideas. Gaitán gained popular support by using an inflammatory rhetoric that blamed the bipartisan oligarchy for the dire conditions of the poor. His populist style and massive support made the bipartisan elites fear that they could no longer control a radicalized popular movement through patronage and clientelism.

In 1947, Gaitán was elected to lead the Liberal party, and the following year he headed a massive silent demonstration to denounce president Ospina's Conservative government for complicity in acts of violence against Liberals. Shortly afterward, on April 9, 1948, Gaitán was murdered in Bogotá. Apparently the conspiracy involved a group of radical Conservatives, but no one was ever indicted for masterminding the assassination. Gaitán's murder provoked the "Bogotazo," a massive urban insurrection backed by the police that partly destroyed the capital city and spread to other regions. After several days, the uprising was violently suppressed by

the military, but it is considered the single occasion in which Colombia has approached the brink of popular revolution.

In the midst of escalating violence, and absent a proper electoral contest, Conservative candidate Laureano Gómez won the presidency in 1949. Gómez promoted an all-out anti-Liberal, anti-Communist crusade, resorting to the army and the police to persecute Liberals in various regions of the country. Such violence "cleansed" entire regions of Liberal party presence and allowed Conservative factions to appropriate land in these areas. Faced with the dilemma of resisting or being killed, some Liberals joined forces with Communist militants and in 1949 formed the first peasant self-defense organizations in Tolima department and the region of Sumapaz. By 1952, approximately 6,500 Liberal guerrillas operated in the countryside, although other estimates suggest the existence of as many as 20,000 armed men. The rebels responded to state terrorism with more terrorism, mainly by engaging in massacres of Conservatives.

President Laureano Gómez's authoritarian style alienated many political sectors that also became increasingly concerned by the escalation of violence in the country. In 1953, various Conservative factions, the Catholic Church, the private sector, and the military backed a coup d'état by General Gustavo Rojas Pinilla. Rojas installed a military dictatorship, stopped the war, and offered an immediate amnesty to the rebels. The amnesty, coupled with the decision of Liberal politicians to stop supporting the guerrilla fighters, led to the disarmament of 3,540 combatants in 1953.

When Rojas attempted to extend his tenure by forming a direct alliance between the armed forces and "the people," Liberal and Conservative politicians decided to end bipartisan hostilities. Liberal and Conservative leaders Alberto Lleras Camargo and Laureano Gómez crafted a power-sharing agreement known as the National Front that took effect in 1958. Under the National Front, the two parties divided all political posts at the levels of public service and cabinet and excluded the participation of third parties in the congress. While it was initially intended to last sixteen years (1958–1974), this arrangement was extended into the mid 1980s through formal mechanisms and informal understandings.

Bipartisan violence gradually decreased during the National Front, as party elites shared power and averted practices that could foster social polarization. However, following Rojas' amnesty, over 100 armed groups were still operating in the countryside. Various rebel leaders refused to disarm, suspicious of the sudden goodwill of the army and the conciliatory tone adopted by Liberal politicians regarding their foes in the Conservative Party. Lacking political support from the Liberal Party, most of these groups turned to common delinquency and were subsequently eliminated by the military. But some of them survived, and along with a few new (predominantly Communist) rebel groups, continued to wage a guerrilla war.

These groups were the seeds of various rebel organizations that emerged in the 1960s. Remnants of the Liberal and Communist guerrillas and self-defense organizations established links with the Communist Party and in 1964 formed the FARC (Revolutionary Armed Forces of Colombia). The Sino-Soviet split in the mid 1960s also gave rise to the Maoist guerrilla organization EPL (Popular Liberation Army). And in 1964, after returning from a trip to Cuba, a group of students formed the rebel group ELN (National Liberation Army), aimed at replicating Castro's revolution in Colombia.

Several factors explain the formation of these groups. To begin with, the Cuban Revolution helped to radicalize many university students and union members. Some of them joined rebel organizations believing that persistent backward social structures and growing levels of popular mobilization made revolution in Colombia inevitable. Colombia's vast territory, rugged terrain, inaccessible mountains, and thick forests also facilitated guerrilla activity.

Most rebel groups settled in peripheral areas that remained outside the reach of the administrative and coercive apparatus of the state. In many ways, the rebel groups actually became state surrogates in the regions they occupied. Although their military strength was marginal throughout the 1970s, they began to expand in the following decades.

In 1974, a new urban rebel organization, the M-19 (April 19 Movement), was formed. General Rojas Pinilla had participated in the 1970 presidential elections, held on April 19, as the National Popular Alliance (ANAPO) candidate, but he was defeated in seemingly fraudulent elections by Conservative candidate Misael Pastrana. This led disaffected members of ANAPO, in alliance with a group of Communists expelled from the FARC, to create the M-19. Between the 1980s and 1990s, other new (though minor) rebel groups were formed. Some were splinter factions of already existing guerrilla organizations, as in the case of the CRS (Socialist Renovation Movement) and PRT (Revolutionary Workers' Party), both outgrowths of the ELN. Others, such as the indigenous MAQL (Quintin Lame Armed Movement) resulted from regional conflicts over land.

President Belisario Betancur (1982–1986) made the first systematic attempt to reach a negotiated settlement between the government and the rebel groups. Betancur was elected on a platform that held that insurgency was a by-product of poverty, injustice, and lack of opportunity, and his government sought to redress such objective causes of the conflict. However, procedural mistakes and bad faith on behalf of the armed factions jeopardized Betancur's efforts. The Colombian president appointed peace commissions comprised of individuals lacking decision-making authority and initiated the peace process without creating credible verification mechanisms. Both factors allowed for systematic cheating by the rebel groups. In addition, civil-military relations were handled poorly, providing the army with incentives to torpedo the peace process. Not surprisingly, the accords collapsed in the midst of violations and mutual recriminations.

Betancur's successor, Virgilio Barco (1986–1990), resumed negotiations with the rebel groups. Barco corrected many mistakes committed during the previous administration by mending fences with the army and establishing clear procedures, rules, and verification mechanisms. Additional factors guaranteed the success of this effort. Barco's tenure coincided with the waning of the Cold War, which made various guerrilla organizations question the relevance of real-world Socialism. In addition, most rebel groups had incurred high military and political costs during this period. A popularly elected National Constituent Assembly also offered them a unique opportunity to participate in the transformation of the Colombian political regime. This last factor was a powerful incentive for various guerrilla organizations to lay down their arms and take part in the constitutional reform. The experience of the M-19, the first rebel group to demobilize and to obtain an important political victory, led to the disarmament of other guerrilla organizations. President Barco and his successor, César Gaviria, signed peace agreements with five different rebel organizations. Between 1990 and 1994, 791 M-19, 2,149 EPL, 433 CRS, 205 PRT, and 148 MAQL guerrillas disarmed (Comisión de Superación de la Violencia 1992, 266).

Although not formally part of the peace negotiations, the National Constituent Assembly was included as a topic of debate on institutional transformation, and it became linked to the peace process with other guerrilla organizations. The assembly introduced several measures to benefit previously excluded political groups, including greater representation of minorities in the Senate, the creation of special districts for indigenous people and other ethnic minorities in the House of Representatives, and restrictions aimed at reducing traditional political party influence. Three judicial institutions, the General Prosecutor's Office, the Ombdusman's Office, and the Constitutional Court, combined with new legal procedures such as the *tutela,* were designed to assure better protection of individual rights.

Notwithstanding its positive attributes, the assembly also exhibited serious limitations. It helped introduce neo-liberal reform in Colombia, which tended to increase inequality, contradicting the spirit of the constitution in terms of the distribution of political power and, to a lesser degree, wealth. In addition, as the war continued, and as the country's involvement grew in the production of and trafficking in illegal drugs, debates on demilitarization remained off-limits. For example, the Assembly made no attempt to modify the budget, structure, and operations of the armed forces.

Neither the FARC nor the ELN, the two largest rebel groups, signed peace accords with the government. Although the FARC began preliminary peace talks with the government, the parties did not trust one another and never sat down at the bargaining table. The case of the ELN was different, since it was the most radical of all the armed groups and did not even consider sitting down to negotiate.

During the second half of 1991, President Gaviria made a last-ditch effort to reach an agreement with the FARC and ELN by sending negotiators to meet with spokespersons of the rebels in Caracas (Venezuela) and then in Tlaxcala (Mexico). However, the parties failed to achieve any type of settlement. While the FARC and the ELN viewed the talks as a means of solving the country's main problems, the government only sought to make the rebel groups disarm. Since the National Constituent Assembly had recently undertaken significant institutional reforms, the government was in no position to negotiate the rules of the game all over again.

During Liberal president Ernesto Samper's tenure (1994–1998), the armed conflict escalated. The rebel groups refused to engage in any peace negotiations with Samper, given revelations that the Cali cartel had provided funding for his presidential campaign. The legitimacy crisis faced by the government was so deep that the rebel groups believed that the government would be unable to assume any credible peace-related commitments.

The most recent attempt to seek a negotiated solution to the armed conflict in Colombia was undertaken by Andrés Pastrana (1998–2002). Upon assuming office in August 1998, Pastrana began negotiations with the FARC. Following a series of violent incidents and lack of progress at the bargaining table, the peace process broke down in February 2002. In 1999, Pastrana also started negotiations with the militarily weaker ELN, but the government failed to make any progress due to the disruptive effects of the ongoing war.

CONTEXT AND PROCESS OF REVOLUTION

Between the early 1960s and the mid 1970s, the FARC, ELN, and EPL rebel groups had little offensive capacity, operated only in remote rural areas, and were heavily repressed by the state. These three rebel organizations differed in strategies, in location, and in the social origins of their members. While the FARC was originally a self-defense organization, the ELN embraced Che Guevara's *foquismo,* and the EPL embraced the Maoist "prolonged popular war." *Foquismo* is a revolutionary strategy based upon the deployment of small groups of rebel troops, or revolutionary focal points whose attacks on government forces and installations would theoretically

Rebels of the Revolutionary Armed Forces of Colombia (FARC) patrol in the Cundinamarca mountains. (Reuters/Corbis)

attract the attention and support of the masses in order to rapidly undermine and overcome the pre-revolutionary regime. This strategy can be contrasted with the prolonged war approach, which stresses the importance of mass mobilization of the population and anticipates a long, drawn-out struggle to achieve victory. Over time, all the rebel groups converged in a strategy of "prolonged popular war."

In terms of their areas of operation, the FARC took root in the southern plains, the ELN in the northeastern department of Santander, and the EPL in the northwestern coastal region of Urabá, Antioquia, and Córdoba. The FARC was the only truly peasant guerrilla organization, while ELN and EPL militants were drawn, for the most part, from student movements and dissidents of the Liberal Party, as well as urban, middle-class professionals.

During the mid 1970s, the M-19 obtained unprecedented levels of support among the urban middle classes. The group's popular appeal derived from its nationalist rhetoric and the employment of highly visible, populist actions, including the distribution among the poor of milk stolen from milk trucks, and the theft of Simón Bolívar's sword as a symbol of its commitment to lead Colombia in its political renovation. By this point the National Front system had prompted increasing social unrest, since it had failed to provide an adequate response to social demands outside the network of patronage politics controlled by the Liberal and Conservative parties. Rather than undertake reforms to contain the turmoil, successive governments opted to repress social movements, criminalize social protest, and install a quasi-permanent state of siege.

The rural-based guerrilla organizations did not garner as much support as the M-19 during this period. The expansion of these rural insurgencies was partly contained by policies like the DRI (Rural Integrated Development), which channeled important resources to peasants engaging in small-scale agriculture starting in 1976. Between 1971 and 1978, Colombia also experienced rapid economic growth and decreasing levels of income inequality, with rural wages rising above the average national income.

While this situation may have temporarily contained the appeal of revolutionary groups among the peasantry, the situation changed in the following decades. Rebel organizations expanded considerably in terms of their number of men, fronts, and areas of operation. In 1978, the guerrilla organizations had only 17 fronts operating in remote rural areas; in 1994 the number had increased to 105 fronts operating in 569 municipalities. In spite of such phenomenal expansion, the rebel groups were unable to achieve mass mobilization of the peasantry and the working classes through the use of nationalist and anti-authoritarian discourse, largely because democratic procedures, although deficient, were consistently maintained in the country.

What factors explain insurgency growth? Political exclusion partly explains guerrilla warfare. Between 1910 and 1949, the Colombian political regime was labeled an "oligarchic democracy," meaning that only a small elite pertaining to the Liberal and the Conservative parties enjoyed a de facto right to rule. When the National Front was established in 1958, only the Liberal and Conservative parties benefited from this power-sharing agreement, while any emerging third political force had no access to the state.

These factors are insufficient for labeling Colombia a mere democratic façade. Even during the National Front, elected incumbents reflected popular preferences as expressed by a majority of votes. There may have been important pockets of corruption, especially in rural areas, but these rarely (if ever) thwarted electoral results at the national level. Furthermore, Colombia moved from formal mechanisms of exclusion during the National Front, to informal exclusion after 1974, to a dismantling of this system altogether during the mid 1980s. Such a trend does not explain why political violence has risen constantly since the late 1970s.

Highlighting the rules of the game in order to explain the nature of political exclusion is insufficient. Political violence has operated as a permanent informal barrier, preventing the empowerment of third political forces and the imple-

mentation of democratic outcomes. This has been one of the central limitations of the Colombian polity and a factor that partly explains why Colombia has experienced chronic insurrection.

Colombia has a long history of political violence directed against opposition parties. Following the amnesty granted by General Rojas Pinilla, many Liberal guerrillas who turned their weapons in were killed. During the truce between President Betancur and the FARC in the 1980s, the Patriotic Union (UP), the political party of the FARC, was virtually annihilated. Although drug-trafficking organizations were partly responsible for these murders, state security agencies are also considered major culprits in the systematic killing of UP militants. The EPL suffered heavy casualties in the aftermath of its demobilization: nearly 400 of its 2,500 members were murdered between 1991 and 2001. However, a significant percentage of the killings were attributed to FARC guerrillas and to a dissident faction of the EPL that continued waging war, and that accused its comrades who had signed peace accords of betraying the revolution. In the case of the M-19, although its first presidential candidate, Carlos Pizarro, was murdered in 1990 (as well as nearly twenty former rebels), the great majority of the key figures in this organization survived the aftermath of their demobilization.

Economic exclusion also explains the relentless expansion of guerrilla warfare in Colombia. According to the National Department of Statistics (DANE), in 2003 approximately 66 percent of the national population (nearly 29 million people) and an even higher percentage of the rural population failed to meet their basic consumption needs. Economically, the country is one of the most unequal in Latin America and the world (Karl 2000, 149–156). Taken together, these factors suggest that Colombia has not approached a threshold of social welfare that would make the underprivileged deaf to revolutionary appeals.

But even these seemingly obvious statements are contestable. An anomaly that remains to be explained, for example, is why the rebel organizations expanded militarily in the 1970s and 1980s, precisely when poverty and inequality reportedly decreased. In fact, most economic trends were positive during both decades. Colombia's semiorthodox economic policies helped to avert painful adjustment measures at a time when the debt crisis hit most of the Latin American economies extremely hard. Between 1980 and 1992, Colombia reduced poverty and inequality, while the real income of all social classes improved. During the 1980s, the living standards of rural dwellers improved due to diminishing levels of inequality and a substantial reduction of poverty, with the percentage of rural families living in poverty decreasing from 80 percent to 62 percent (Karl 2000, 149–156).

Studies comparing patterns of violence in different municipalities conclude that poverty does not explain the territorial expansion of guerrilla warfare during the period 1978–1995. In fact, the rebel groups opened new fronts in strategic areas characterized by dynamic economic activity, while some of the poorest municipalities, those with the largest percentages of people with incomes below the poverty level, remained relatively peaceful. Inequality, however, does seem to be associated with political violence. The Economic Planning Department of the Colombian government found that the most unequal municipalities were also the most violent ones, regardless of their high rates of economic growth. Rebel organizations have taken root especially in areas where inhabitants have resented the rapid generation of wealth that benefits only a few.

Perhaps the clearest economic cause of political violence has to do with land concentration. Colombia has a particularly bad record of failed agrarian reforms as well as successive episodes in which peasants have been forcefully evicted from their plots. In the mid 1930s, Liberal president Alfonso López Pumarejo attempted to implement an agrarian reform, Law 200 of 1936, but it failed to change the structure of property in the countryside, due to opposition from large landowners. A subsequent agrarian law, Law 100 of 1944, which benefited the landed classes, only increased the peasants' frustration. An agrarian reform undertaken by President Lleras Restrepo (1966–1970) distributed land in targeted hotspots of radicalism and partially contained the spread of the revolutionary groups. However, the implementation of the reform was too limited to have any significant economic effect. It also suffered an additional setback during the government of President Misael Pastrana Borrero (1970–1974).

A more recent attempt at land distribution occurred during the Barco administration (1986–1990). This was another moderate agrarian reform that ultimately failed, mainly due to the fact that drug traffickers bought up much of the land in hundreds of municipalities, especially in areas characterized by agrarian and guerrilla conflicts. An even higher concentration of land property resulted, as well as the forceful displacement of many peasants from their land. Additionally, the newly acquired lands were mainly reserved for cattle-raising, an activity that has been tied to agrarian conflict in Colombia over the past three decades due to its concentration on the country's most fertile soils.

The results of these agrarian reform laws have been marginal at best. However, Colombia is a large country with an extensive agricultural frontier, so pressure over land resources has been partly offset by rural-to-urban migration and rural-to-rural migration as well. At the same time, though, a percentage of forcefully evicted landless peasants has been willing to support the armed insurgency. Rural unemployment allowed the guerrilla organizations to recruit many militants in the 1980s and 1990s.

Another explanation for the multiplication of both guerrillas and rebel fronts is the upsurge of the cocaine trade in the 1980s, given that the insurgencies have benefited from added resources obtained from taxing coca cultivators and drug traffickers. While the rebel groups do in fact derive significant resources from their participation in the drug trade, it would be a mistake to simply identify them as drug trafficking organizations. The tremendous expansion of insurrection indicates that the rebels are not as politically isolated as some might suggest: many underprivileged sectors are receptive to the guerrillas' discourse on injustice, exclusion, and inequality, regardless of how cynical, terrorist, or nonideological the rebels are accused of being.

IMPACTS

Colombia has experienced chronic insurgency and armed conflict but no revolution. Most experts agree that the prospects of a successful revolutionary effort in the country are quite dim. To a large extent, the growing involvement of the FARC (and the paramilitary AUC) in drug-related activities explains this group's survival as an irregular armed force but also the distortion of its revolutionary ideals. The civilian population is targeted by armed actors on the right and the left, and in a milieu of pervasive violence the general quality of democracy has deteriorated considerably.

The terrorist attacks of September 11, 2001, in the United States, in combination with the intractable nature of the armed conflict in Colombia, have also changed the ways the war is viewed by the governments of both countries. Increasingly, the armed conflict is described as a war against terrorism, which precludes any possibility of peaceful negotiations with the rebel groups. As a result, Colombia has experienced growing levels of militarization and polarization. U.S. involvement, too, has risen noticeably. Between 2000 and 2004, for example, Colombia received $3.5 billion for its war against drugs and terrorism (Latin American Working Group, CIP and WOLA 2004, 11).

The intensification of the drug and anti-terrorist war in the country has led to the regionalization of the Colombian security crisis. Armed actors regularly cross over into neighboring countries, especially Venezuela and Ecuador; growing numbers of displaced persons seek refuge in Colombia's border regions; and intensive fumigation of coca crops in the southern part of the country has started to push drug production to other parts of the Andean region. Colombia's neighbors have responded by militarizing their borders.

PEOPLE AND ORGANIZATIONS

United Self-Defense Forces of Colombia (Autodefensas Unidas de Colombia—AUC)

The growth of private right-wing self-defense groups coincided with the expansion of the drug trade in Colombia during the 1980s. Wealthy drug trafficking organizations financed private armies to defend their land holdings from the guerrillas. Paramilitary activities, which are largely responsible for human rights violations in Colombia, have often been carried out in collaboration with members of the armed forces. In 1997, AUC, led by Carlos Castaño until 2001, was created as an umbrella organization to join disparate paramilitary groups operating throughout Colombia. The AUC's sources of funding include contributions from wealthy landholders and drug trafficking organizations as well as direct participation in the drug trade. At present, the group operates in 35 percent of Colombian national territory. The AUC have approximately 13,500 members (see Center for International Policy Colombia Program website, http://www.ciponline.org/colombia/infocombat.htm, for information on numbers of troops of different armed forces and areas of operation).

Bush, George W. (Born 1946)

Former governor of the state of Texas and forty-third president of the United States, George W. Bush led the country through the terrorist attacks of September 11, 2001, as well as two wars, in Afghanistan and Iraq. Bush inaugurated a new national security strategy whose cornerstone was the idea of preemptive war against potential terrorist threats to the United States. United States foreign policy during the Bush administration has been characterized by a unilateral style, as evidenced by the decision to withdraw from several multilateral agreements, including the Kyoto treaty, a biological weapons agreement, the International Criminal Court, and the Anti-Ballistic Missile Treaty. In 2002, the Bush government sought and received support for lifting restrictions on United States counternarcotics assistance to Colombia in order for it to be used in the fight against armed actors considered terrorists.

Conservative Party

One of two traditional political parties in Colombia, the Conservative Party was created in 1849. Although few ideological differences are discernable between this party and its Liberal counterpart, historically the Conservative Party has favored a close cooperation between the state and the Catholic Church, strong central government, and protectionism.

National Liberation Army (Ejército de Liberación Nacional—ELN)

Created in 1964 by students who received training in Cuba, the National Liberation Army (ELN) applied a "foco" or *foquismo* model of rural revolution in Colombia. Historically, its primary area of operations was the northeastern department of Santander. The ELN's primary sources of funding have included extortion, largely related to the country's oil industry, and kidnapping, but the group has never been actively involved in the drug trade. The group numbers approximately 3,500 members.

Revolutionary Armed Forces of Colombia (Fuerzas Armadas Revolucionarias de Colombia—FARC)

Remnants of the Liberal and Communist guerrillas and self-defense organizations established links with the Communist Party and in 1964 formed the Armed Revolutionary Forces of Colombia (FARC). The FARC took root in the southern plains of Colombia, and is the only true peasant guerrilla organization in the country. At present, the group operates in 40–60 percent of Colombian national territory. Its primary sources of financing include kidnapping and extortion, and it is involved in the early stages of the drug production chain. The FARC has as many as 18,000 members.

Liberal Party

One of two traditional political parties in Colombia, the Liberal Party was created in 1851. Although few ideological differences are discernable between this party and its Conservative counterpart, historically the Liberal Party advocated a separation between church and state, free-trade-based economic policies, and federalism, a type of political system that grants relatively strong powers to state or provincial governments relative to the central government.

Marulanda Vélez, Manuel (Born 1930)

A peasant guerrilla who fought in the Colombian Violence since 1948, Manuel Marulanda was one of the survivors of a surprise military attack on a peasant cooperative called the "independent republic of Marquetalia," located in Tolima. In 1964, following the attack, he led the creation of the FARC and continues to be the organization's undisputed leader in 2004.

Navarro Wolf, Antonio (Born 1948)

Former top commander of the M-19 armed group, Navarro ran unsuccessfully for the presidency in 1990 and went on to hold several public offices, including minister of health, mayor of Pasto, and congressman. He is currently a senator of the Republic.

Organization of American States (OAS)

In February 2004, the OAS was granted authority by the Permanent Council to provide technical support for the verification of the cease-fire, ending of hostilities, demobilization, and disarmament of members of the AUC. Its role has since been limited to the monitoring of the Uribe administration's negotiation process with the paramilitaries.

Pastrana, Andrés (Born 1954)

A member of the Conservative Party and former mayor of Bogotá, Andrés Pastrana was the elected president of Colombia between 1998 and 2002. Pastrana assumed leadership of a country plagued by a deep economic recession and ravaged by war, high levels of corruption, and a flourishing drug trade. Pastrana pledged to put an end to the armed conflict by negotiating with the FARC and ELN guerrillas while also actively seeking out international aid. During the Pastrana administration, U.S. assistance to Colombia skyrocketed to approximately $500 million annually. Following the end of the peace process with the FARC in early 2002, Pastrana took measures to portray this organization as a terrorist group; with that act, the Colombian Conflict was successfully inserted into the global war against terrorism. Consequently, the United States lifted restrictions associated with its aid package to Colombia in order for this money and equipment to be employed in counterinsurgency efforts.

United Nations

The importance of international participation in the Colombian armed conflict is a relatively new concept. During the Samper administration (1994–1998), the UN High Commissioner for Human Rights was invited to set up an office in the country in order to monitor the human rights situation. In addition, in 2001, the UN Secretary General appointed a special adviser on Colombia to offer UN assistance with the peace process that the Pastrana administration was undertaking with the FARC. The UN special adviser was particularly active in the final stage of the negotiations with the FARC and attempted to mediate between the government and the insurgency to avoid the termination of the process.

United States Southern Command

The United States Southern Command is responsible for all U.S. military activities in Latin America south of Mexico, operating in nineteen countries in Central and South America and twelve countries in the Caribbean. Its mission is to conduct military operations and promote security cooperation to achieve the strategic objectives of the United States. To this end, the South Com is actively involved in military training related to counternarcotics and counterinsurgency operatives in Colombia, where the United States has provided over $3 billion in military assistance between 2000 and 2004.

Uribe, Álvaro (Born 1952)

A member of the Liberal Party and former governor of Antioquia, Álvaro Uribe (2002–2006) was the first presidential candidate in Colombian history to win a majority vote in the first round of elections. Uribe won the elections on a "get tough" platform in which he promised to win the war against the FARC insurgents and terrorism in general. A cornerstone of his security strategy has been the Defense and Democratic Security Policy, through which he has declared an all-out war against terrorism and has sought to legitimize the use of force in doing so. His foreign policy has been characterized by close relations with the United States and a strong anti-terrorist discourse.

Carlo Nasi
Arlene B. Tickner

See Also Documentaries of Revolution; Guerrilla Warfare and Revolution; Inequality, Class, and Revolution; Transnational Revolutionary Movements

References and Further Readings
Arnson, Cynthia, and Robin Kirk. 1998. *State of War: Political Violence and Counterinsurgency in Colombia.* New York: Human Rights Watch.
Bejarano, Jesus A. 1995. *Una agenda para la paz.* Santa Fe de Bogotá: Tercer Mundo.
Boudon, Lawrence. 1996. "Guerrillas and the State: The Role of the State in Colombia Peace Process." *Journal of Latin American Studies* 28: 279–297.

Braun, Herbert. 1994. *Our Guerrillas, Our Sidewalks: A Journey into the Violence of Colombia.* Niwot: University Press of Colorado.

Chernick, Marc. 1999. "Negotiating Peace amid Multiple Forms of Violence: The Protracted Search for a Settlement to the Armed Conflicts in Colombia." Pp. 159–195 in *Comparative Peace Processes in Latin America,* edited by C. Arnson. Washington, D.C. and Stanford, CA: Woodrow Wilson Center Press and Stanford University Press.

Comisión de Superación de la Violencia. 1992. *Pacificar la paz.* Bogotá: IEPRI, CINEP, Comisión Andina de Juristas Seccional Colombia, CECOIN.

Garcia, Mauricio. 1992. *De la Uribe a Tlaxcala: procesos de paz.* Bogotá: CINEP.

Hartlyn, Jonathan. 1988. *The Politics of Coalition Rule in Colombia.* New York: Cambridge University Press.

Karl, Terry. 2000. "Economic Inequality and Democratic Instability." *Journal of Democracy* 11 (1): 149–156.

Kline, Harvey F. 1999. *State Building and Conflict Resolution in Colombia, 1986–1994.* Tuscaloosa: University of Alabama Press.

Latin American Working Group, Center for International Policy (CIP), and Washington Office on Latin America (WOLA). 2004. "Blurring the Lines. Trends in U.S. Military Programs with Latin America." Working Report, Washington D.C., October. The Washington Office on Latin America (WOLA).

Oquist, Paul H. 1980. *Violence, Conflict, and Politics in Colombia.* New York: Academic Press.

Pizarro Leongomez, Eduardo. 1996. *Insurgencia sin revolucion: la guerrilla en Colombia en una perspectiva comparada.* Bogota: IEPRI-TM Editores.

Richani, Nazih. 2002. *Systems of Violence: The Political Economy of War and Peace in Colombia.* New York: State University of New York Press.

Safford, Frank, and Marco Palacios. 2001. *Colombia: Fragmented Land, Divided Society.* New York: Oxford University Press.

Sanchez G., Gonzalo. 2001. *Bandits, Peasants, and Politics: The Case of "La Violencia" in Colombia.* Austin: University of Texas Press.

Villamizar, D. 1997. *Un adiós a la guerra.* Santa Fe de Bogotá: Planeta.

Wilde, Alexander. 1978. "Conversations among Gentlemen: Oligarchical Democracy in Colombia." Pp. 28–81 in *The Breakdown of Democratic Regimes,* edited by J. L. A. Stepan. Baltimore, MD: Johns Hopkins University Press.

Colonialism, Anti-Colonialism, and Neo-Colonialism

COLONIALISM

The process of colonialism is intimately linked with the rise of the nation-state in Western Europe and the strengthening of nationalism as the "glue" to hold citizens within state borders together. One of the most deleterious aspects of the nation-state as the primary actor of international relations has been its drive to compete with other similar entities for territories and power. As part of this competition, European states began to look beyond the continent for opportunities to increase their comparative advantage over potential rivals. The so-called geographic Great Discoveries of the late fifteenth century were a significant factor in triggering a colonial "race," and although conquest of foreign territory was hardly a novelty in world politics, "the colonial conquests of Spain and Portugal in the Americas constituted a great break in human history" (Waites 1999, 24). These two states represented the most dynamic economies at the time and utilized the territories they conquered in the Americas to strengthen their position on the European continent, while at the same time maintaining the newly acquired territories and peoples in a dependent and inferior position with respect to the parent state. This state of dependence is one of the significant factors that distinguished colonialism from previous types of conquest.

This first phase of colonialism was also characterized by other important themes that would have tremendous repercussions on the development of world politics. First of all, the conquest emerged from the economic theory of mercantilism, which held that a strong state needed to have a favorable balance of trade and needed to accumulate gold. The economic advantages of conquering territory where gold was abundant and that could produce goods to serve the financial interests of the parent state were substantial and underpinned this first phase of pre-industrial colonialism. Secondly, the colonial powers had the support of the Catholic Church in their mission, which became an opportunity to gain "converts" to Catholicism and to perform God's will by exporting the universal values of Christianity to lands inhabited by "ignorant savages." The Pope even involved himself personally in colonial affairs by solving disputes that were arising between Portugal and Spain over the conquest of territory in Latin America in order for the colonial enterprise to be continued cooperatively in the name of God and the Catholic Church. Later on, both France and Britain launched their own colonial enterprises in North America and, with the decline of Spain and Portugal, became the most expansive colonial powers.

The second phase of colonialism began in the 1800s, involved a greater number of states, and penetrated all the continents of the world. A number of reasons have been offered to explain this surge. First, central to the colonial enterprise was certainly the idea of economic gains through the expansion of territory that gave the colonizer the opportunity to extract the natural resources necessary to "feed" the growing industrial needs of the homeland. In turn, the colonies were considered exclusive new markets for the products of the parent state. Second, although European countries were locked in a competitive struggle with each other, they tended to look abroad for conquests rather than triggering conflicts in Europe, which would be mutually detrimental. A third very important factor that made colonization a project embraced with much enthusiasm by European societies was the widely held concept of European racial, moral, and cultural supremacy. There was, without doubt, a pervasive sense of the superiority of European civilization, which was viewed as somewhat entitled to export its values, norms, and technologies to other lands for the perceived benefit of peoples of inferior societies. There were different strands within this camp of civilizational enthusiasts. Some supported the idea of eliminating the local populations because the conquered territory was needed for surplus European populations. Others believed indigenous people could be assimilated into European civilization. Still others were imbued with the same religious drive that characterized the first phase of colonialism and were preoccupied with spreading Christianity.

The administration of colonies varied as greatly as the reasons for securing them. The fundamental objective of the Spanish *conquista* of the Americas with respect to the indigenous population was to conquer them, convert them to Catholicism, and transform them, so far as possible, into the vassals of the Spaniards, who were granted temporary lordship and tributary rights over specified Indian communities. Later imperialists preferred other methods of control. British colonial rule was, for instance, much more reliant on native surrogates. The British ruled indirectly through friendly indigenous elites kept in power through British support. The French preferred, instead, to espouse a policy of assimilation, whereby natives would be part of the shared French construction of national identity and republican values. The Belgian experience in the Congo was much closer to the Spanish one, since the African territory was formally the private property of the king and was managed as such.

However, irrespective of the method of rule, colonized societies and most colonized peoples suffered immensely, and the impact of colonialism was considerable in a number of ways. From a demographic point of view, both repression and diseases wiped out or generally decreased indigenous populations. Some colonial expeditions even had the declared objective of eliminating the natives' presence, as the early campaigns of the French troops in Algeria demonstrated in the 1830s and 1840s. In addition, the widespread use of slave labor meant that the harsh conditions of slavery further reduced the number of indigenous people. From a psychological point of view, the trauma of colonialism was substantial, as indigenous peoples realized that their traditional cultures, religions, governments, and social systems were incapable of preventing their being subjugated and exploited by Europeans. The experience of colonialism also affected the colonizers by encouraging feelings of superiority. In describing the Spanish *conquista,* Ansprenger (1989, 2) argues that "the Europeans, with their white skin, their horses and muskets, seemed like gods. So they began to feel like supermen themselves." From a purely political point of view, colonialism often undermined the pillars of traditional authority in many societies by introducing indigenous peoples to very European concepts such as nationalism and statehood. This would have tremendous repercussions for post-colonial societies. The restructuring of territorial boundaries, the artificial drawing of borders, and the limited privileges accorded to one group to the detriment of another would all affect post-colonial life. Generally, it has often been argued that conquered peoples who were colonized tended to develop shared feelings of humiliation, manipulation, and exploitation. Simultaneously, members of indigenous elites were groomed by the colonizing power to become assimilated to the culture of the colonial power, typically converted to its religion, and transformed into a new colonial elite, ethnically like the mass of the indigenous people, but culturally and psychologically more like the upper-class residents of the colonizing power and economically dependent on the maintenance of the previously structured exploitive relationship between the imperialistic power and the colony.

ANTI-COLONIALISM

Contrary to conventional wisdom, the vast majority of colonized societies resisted quite strongly the penetration of European powers from the very beginning and did not accept external domination. In spite of these efforts, the power differential between European *conquistadores* and indigenous populations was very substantial and, ultimately, led to establishment of colonial control.

Over the long period though, colonized societies developed a discourse and practice of resistance that led to anti-colonial political struggles. Anti-colonialism presents a number of different facets that make it a much more varied phenomenon than usually believed. For instance there is a substantial difference between the anti-colonial struggles that occurred in the Americas and the ones that took place in other parts of the world almost two centuries later. The anti-colonial struggle in the Americas (both North and South) waged against Britain, France, Spain, and Portugal was the outcome of changing power relations between the home country elites and the newly established settlers' elites in the colonized territories. The settlers' refusal to submit to faraway rulers was at the heart of the wars of independence fought in North and South America. Issues of taxation, privileges, and control of trade and natural resources were the real bones of contention. This early anti-colonial movement did not originate with the indigenous population but was the domain of the descendants of the early white settlers. While the issues emphasized by this struggle had substantial political implications (for instance, the very revolutionary idea of "no taxation without representation"), the newly independent nation still pursued policies based on the continued exploitation of indigenous peoples.

The second phase of de-colonization was quite different. It was rooted in the increasing ability of some sectors of the indigenous elites to exploit the political and ideological contradictions that the home countries presented. The international events of the early twentieth century greatly contributed to the anti-colonial struggles of the following decades. First and foremost, the contribution of colonized people to the war effort of their respective "home country" during World War I made them aware both of the injustice at the root of their subordinate role and of their "indispensability." Also important was the concept that an Allied victory in World War I would result in the granting of self-determination to peoples without a state. According to early leaders of the anti-colonial struggle, this should apply not only to Europeans, but also to non-European peoples as well. At this stage, however, the goal of many nationalist and anti-colonial movements was not full political independence and autonomy from the home country but the full recognition of the rights of colonial peoples as individuals of equal worth with the Europeans and of their lands as separate entities within the empires. The main demands of Algerian nationalists at the time, for instance, were the granting of equal citizenship rights that would recognize their Muslim character and the establishment of true channels of political representation. It was only after World War II that most nationalist movements took up the demand for full political independence. The French empire had been weakened by the fact that France itself was occupied and exploited by the Nazi Germans. Britain's tremendous economic burden from financing its armed forces during World War II and its mobilization of and reliance on many soldiers from its colonies undermined its imperial system. Many Asian and African nationalists had been encouraged by the ability of the armed forces of a non-European people, the Japanese, to initially defeat those of the previously invincible British and Dutch empires. Both superpowers supported the the anti-colonial stance of their post–World War I leaders, President Woodrow Wilson of the United States and Vladimir Lenin of the Soviet Union, and the Charter of the new United Nations called for national self-determination and human rights. The international context had radically changed, and the process of de-colonization became irreversible.

It is interesting to note that the anti-colonial discourse through which political independence was achieved had much to do with ideas that the colonial powers had introduced to the colonies and that were subsequently taken up by a small section of the indigenous elites, popularized among the masses, and used as a justification for getting rid of colonial rule. Concepts such as nationalism, self-determination, and progress in the name of Socialism were all European constructs. The great anti-colonial leaders such as the Algerian Ben Bella, the Indian Gandhi, and the Vietnamese Ho Chi Minh had all acquired European humanistic knowledge and adapted this to local beliefs and practices to suit their anti-colonial struggles, turning the hypocrisy of colonial powers to the cause of anti-colonialism. Given that the two superpowers were generally supportive of anti-colonialism for both ideological and self-interested material reasons, the process of de-colonization took place in a relatively benign international environment. It should be emphasized, however, that the masses who fought in the name of anti-colonialism were fighting for a better life that they thought could only be achieved through independence. Victory and the creation of an independent state would be followed by tackling fundamental issues such as land re-distribution or access to basic services.

The methods used to attain the political goal of independence varied across countries and across time. Most anti-colonial movements began in a rather peaceful manner, with indigenous political movements demanding profound changes in the economic and political relationship with the home country and eventually turning into armed struggles and wars of liberation in response to the repression of the early demands. At the beginning of the process of de-colonization, which was in full swing by the early 1950s, the French and the British governments were extremely reluctant to concede political independence to the many territories they controlled and found themselves engulfed in a number of conflicts. At the same time, the two governments also realized that certain territories could be "given up" or had to be abandoned if they were to hold on to more important ones. In the end, this strategy dragged colonialism on for no apparent gain. In any case, France fought vicious wars both in Indochina (the French left Vietnam in 1954 after their comprehensive defeat at Dien Bien Phu) and Algeria (the French left after an eight-year war), while Britain fought quite harshly to retain possession of Kenya. India is a particularly interesting case, because it is one of the few countries that was able to achieve independence without resorting to armed struggle. It managed to gain political autonomy by 1948 through a very well-conceived and well-led campaign of civil disobedience. Other colonial powers attempted to hold on to their possessions

Under the guard of Communist-led Viet Minh troops, French and Vietnamese prisoners of war march from the battlefields of Dien Bien Phu. The victory of the Vietnamese nationalist Viet Minh at the 1954 battle of Dien Bien Phu marked the fall of French Indochina. (Bettmann/Corbis)

but failed to do so. The Dutch were eventually forced out of Indonesia and the Portuguese out of Angola and Mozambique in the mid 1970s.

Anti-colonial struggle was largely very successful, and by the mid 1970s the process of de-colonization was completed; most nationalist movements were able to secure political independence and set about the task of organizing governments and nation building. But after the early years of enthusiastic mobilization, this task proved to be riddled with problems and conflicts. The legacy of colonial subjugation still affects the social, economic, and political landscape of a number of post-colonial societies. In this context, many students of colonialism asserted that the end of active colonial rule was simply transformed into a more legitimate and "softer" method of domination of the strong over the weak. The end of colonialism and the success of anti-colonialism did not translate into an effective redistribution of power and resources at the global level. The adoption of Socialism as a model of economic development by many of the new nation-states did little to enhance their prospects in the long term, and adapting to the require-

ments of the new globalized economy has been the main preoccupation of many post-colonial societies over the last two decades.

NEO-COLONIALISM

Far from a fresh start for colonized societies, according to some, the end of colonialism simply represented a shift in the patterns and methods of domination and exploitation. It is thus argued that when the colonial rulers departed, they largely left the power relations between the home country and the newly created entities intact through a variety of means.

First, colonial powers such as Britain overlooked local ethnic differences as well as similarities to artificially create nation-states that were formally independent but really still very dependent upon the former colonial power economically, and often politically and militarily. This was the case when the British set the borders for certain Middle Eastern territories they controlled. Apparently to serve its interests, Britain created a number of oil-rich states with small ruling elites who appeared quite loyal to the British Crown. This policy had tremendous repercussions with ruling elites in the area, often still enjoying very little real domestic legitimacy but able to survive as autonomous entities simply due to their links with larger Western powers. According to some, with the waning of British power, the United States became the "substitute" imperialist in the region. The same phenomenon occurred in the former French colonies, particularly in Africa, where the continued existence of many regimes has been dependent on good relations with the former colonial power. The many French interventions in the region during the last three decades bear witness to that.

Second, elite selection in the former colonies has been a complicated affair. Colonial powers ensured that they left behind elites they could do business with and, with a few exceptions, this has been the case. Post-colonial elites were as much part, intellectually and socially, of the old order as they were representative of the colonized people. This meant that their programs and ideas of modernization coincided with the interests of the former colonial elites, leading them to form either open or more secretive alliances that would benefit both camps. For instance, while the new Algerian elites paid lip service to anti-imperialism and accused France of the worst atrocities, they entertained very solid economic links and deep military cooperation.

Finally, the problem of economic restructuring emerged quite forcefully and further undermined the formal achievement of political independence. For decades or even centuries, the economies of the colonial territories were geared toward satisfying the requirements of the home country, with little or no regard for the welfare of the local populations. This meant that, upon independence, there was the need to redress this imbalance in order to give independence some substantive meaning. But this restructuring did not take place in many of the former colonies, which remained in a subordinate position in the international economic system. For instance, colonies that had been exploited for the production of one natural resource without the significant development of any other type of economic activity continued to function economically along the same lines even after independence, often to the detriment of the local populations and to the benefit of stronger economic actors residing in the former colonial power. These relationships are well captured by Immanuel Wallerstein's categories of core (Western countries) and periphery (largely comprising former colonies).

Further compounding the problems of these societies were domestic divisions that had been used or even intensified by the colonial power to "divide and rule" the indigenous populations (the 1994 genocide in Rwanda was viewed by many as the product of the Belgian policy of divide and rule, privileging one group over another during colonial times to better secure the colonial power's interests). Tribes, ethnic groups, and clans were either divided in different nation-states or grouped into the same nation-state despite creating societies that would have to overcome enormous difficulties in the process of nation building. Scholars of neo-colonialism would argue that this was quite intentional to keep post-colonial societies weak and divided and therefore in need of outside intervention and guidance.

Dependence has not withered away with colonialism, possibly quite the opposite has happened.

Francesco Cavatorta

See Also Algerian Revolution; American Revolution; Angolan Revolution; Arab Revolt 1916–1918; Chinese Revolution; Cinema of Revolution; Congo Revolution; Cuban Revolution; Documentaries of Revolution; Egyptian Revolution of 1952; Ghana's Independence Revolution: Decolonizing the Model Colony; Guerilla Warfare and Revolution; Guinea-Bissau: Revolution and Independence; Ideology, Propaganda, and Revolution; Indian Independence Movement; Indonesian Independence Revolution; Iranian Revolution; Iraq Revolution; Kenyan Mau Mau Rebellion; Libyan Revolution; Mozambique Revolution; Nationalism and Revolution; Pakistan Independence and the Partition of India; Palestinian Movement; Philippine Independence Revolution and Wars; South African Revolution; Spanish American Revolutions of Independence; Student and Youth Movements, Activism, and Revolution; Terrorism; Transnational Revolutionary Movements; Vietnamese Revolution; War and Revolution; Zimbabwean Revolution; Zionist Revolution and the State of Israel

References and Further Readings
Ansprenger, Franz. 1989. *The Dissolution of Colonial Empires.* London: Routledge.
Chamberlein, Muriel. 1998. *European Decolonization in the Twentieth Century.* London: Longman.
Fanon, Frantz. 1967. *Black Skin White Masks.* New York: Grove Weidenfeld.
Pieterse, Jan Nederveen, and Bikhu Parekh, eds. 1995. *The Decolonization of Imagination: Culture, Knowledge and Power.* London: Zed Books.
Schulze, Reinhard. 2002. *A Modern History of the Islamic World.* New York: New York University Press.
Waites, Bernard. 1999. *Europe and the Third World: From Colonization to Decolonization, c. 1500–1998.* New York: St. Martin's Press.
Wallerstein, Immanuel. 1974. *The Modern World-System: Capitalist Agriculture and the Origins of the European World-Economy in the Sixteenth Century.* New York: Academic Press.
———. 1980. *The Modern World System II: Mercantilism and the Consolidation of the European World-Economy, 1600–1750.* New York: Academic Press.
———. 1988. *The Modern World System III: The Second Era of Great Expansion of the Capitalist World-Economy, 1730s–1840s.* New York: Academic Press.

Congo Revolution

CHRONOLOGY

1492	The Portuguese visit Kongo kingdom on Atlantic Coast. In the sixteenth century, Kongo adopts Christianity and is drawn into Atlantic slave trade.
1700	Kimpa Vita leads prophetic movement to restore unity of Kongo kingdom.
18th–19th centuries	Congo is drawn into three slave-trade networks: Luso-African or Angolan, Arab-Swahili, and Arab network of Sudan.
	(The name *Congo* comes from the Congo River and the Kongo people, but the Congo colony included more peoples than the Kongo people. The region was referred to as "Congo" by Europeans since the end of the 15th century.)
1860s	Arab-Swahili trader Tippu Tib, Scottish missionary David Livingstone reach Congo.
1870s	H. M. Stanley visits Congo, is hired by Leopold II, king of Belgium, to explore the country and sign treaties with local rulers
1882	Tippu Tib begins constructing state in eastern Congo.
1884–1885	Leopold II wins international recognition of his Congo Free State.
1893	Ngongo Lutete (Leteta), former agent of Tippu Tib who had joined the Free State, is executed by Free State officer.
1895, 1897, 1900	So-called Batetela mutinies of Tetela and others, including many former soldiers of Ngongo.
1900–1916	Resistance of Shi (Bashi).
1904	Congo Reform Association opens campaign against Free State atrocities.
1903–1904, 1910	Uprisings of Boa (Babua).
1903–1905	Uprising of Mbuja (Budja).
1907–1917	Resistance of Luba-Katanga.
1908	Belgium takes over former Free State, which becomes Belgian Congo.
1921	Simon Kimbangu begins preaching, healing the sick. He is sentenced to death for sedition by Belgium authorities fearing that his religious teachings would inspire Congolese resistance to Belgium's colonial rule, but his sentence is commuted to life in prison.
1923	Kitawala movement begins spreading across eastern Congo.
1931	Pende revolt in Kwilu against colonial state and companies.
1941	UMHK (Union Minière du Haut-Katanga) workers strike in Likasi and Lubumbashi, many killed.
1944	Kitawala revolt in Kivu; Force Publique mutiny in Lubumbashi.
1945	Dockworkers strike and demonstrate in Matadi.
1950	ABAKO (Alliance des Bakongo) established as cultural association.
1951	Simon Kimbangu dies in prison in Lubumbashi.
1956	ABAKO responds to Van Bilsen's thirty-year plan for Congo self-rule.
1957	Municipal elections at Kinshasa, Lubumbashi, Likasi. Joseph Kasavubu elected to a local position at Kinshasa.
1958	Patrice Lumumba becomes leader of MNC-Lumumba.

1959   Kinshasa (Leopoldville) riots in January, followed by Belgian government announcement of transition to independence.

1960   Round Table meeting in January, Brussels.

Electoral victory of MNC-Lumumba in May.

Independence in June.

Mutiny of army (ex–Force Publique) in July; Katanga secedes.

Lumumba ousted in first Mobutu coup in September.

1961   In January, Lumumba is murdered in Katanga.

1963   UN troops end Katanga secession in January.

1964   In January, Mulele launches attacks in Kwilu.

Simbas (Lumumbists) take Uvira (South Kivu) in May.

On November 24, 1964, Belgo-American parachute drop decapitates People's Republic of the Congo.

1965   On November 24, Mobutu stages coup d'état, ushering in Second Republic.

1967   In May, Mobutu launches Mouvement Populaire de la Révolution (MPR).

1968   In October, Mulele is killed in government custody, Kinshasa.

1971   Congo is rebaptized "Zaire" in October.

1973   Zairianization of foreign business.

1974   Mobutu intervenes in Angola. Defeat followed by purge of military officers.

1977   First Shaba war ended by Moroccan troops with French support.

1978   Second Shaba war ended by French and Belgian paratroopers.

1982   Thirty parliamentarians including Tshisekedi defy Mobutu; their movement later becomes Union for Democracy and Social Progress (Union pour la Démocratie et le Progrès Social (UDPS)

1990   Mobutu announces multipartyism in April.

1992   In August, National Sovereign Conference (CNS) votes to change name from "Zaire" to "Congo," elects Tshisekedi prime minister.

Tshisekedi is ousted by Mobutu in December.

1994   Genocide in Rwanda, flood of Hutu refugees into Zaire/Congo.

1996   Rwanda-Uganda sponsor invasion of Congo under AFDL (Alliance of Democratic Forces for the Liberation of the Congo) (spokesman Laurent Kabila).

1997   In May, AFDL enters Kinshasa, Laurent Kabila proclaims himself president, and restores the name "Democratic Republic of Congo."

1998   Rwanda-Uganda-People's Democratic Rally (RCD) launches second war.

2001   Laurent Kabila assassinated; his son Joseph succeeds him.

2003   End of second war, formation of 1 + 4 government (one president, four vice presidents).

2004   Joseph Kabila praises "pioneers" of Belgian colonialism in speech to Belgian senate.

INTRODUCTION

Congo won its independence from Belgium in 1960, having given the greatest number of votes to a party headed by Patrice Lumumba. Lumumba had promised a revolutionary transformation of Congolese society but was murdered before he could fulfill this promise. Cold War politics led to the establishment of a Western-backed, single-party dictatorship headed by General Mobutu Sese Seko. In the early 1990s, a broad-based democratic movement failed to dislodge

Mobutu. In 1996 and 1998, Congo's neighbors intervened to oust first Mobutu, and then his successor Laurent Kabila. But transformation of Congo society seemed as far off as ever.

BACKGROUND: CULTURE AND HISTORY

Congo takes its name from the Congo River and from the Kongo people who live at the mouth of the river. It has been known successively as the Congo Free State, Belgian Congo, Republic of Congo, Democratic Republic of Congo, Republic of Zaire, and once again, the Democratic Republic of Congo.

From the beginning, Congo has been seen as possessing enormous riches and an enormous potential on the one hand, and on the other, as a country whose people suffer enormously, in part because of foreigners attempting to seize those riches.

There are more than 200 peoples ("tribes") in Congo. Perhaps 75 or 80 percent of these peoples and of the Congolese population speak Bantu languages. Three of the four major ethnic clusters are Bantu: the Kongo, Luba, and Mongo. The fourth is the Mangbetu-Zande cluster of northeastern Congo, speakers of Sudanic languages. Together, the major clusters account for about 45 percent of the Congolese population. However, these ethnic clusters are not the most relevant political actors. Often they are divided—Luba-Kasai vs. Luba-Katanga, or Tetela (Mongo of Kasai) vs. Mongo-Equateur.

The majority of Congolese are Christians. The Roman Catholic Church has the largest number of adherents. Protestants of various denominations are numerous, as are Kimbanguists (members of the Church of Jesus Christ on Earth by the Prophet Simon Kimbangu). The Muslim and Orthodox Christian communities also enjoy official recognition. In addition, there is a flock of religious movements, often combining Christian and traditional values, and offering earthly success rather than salvation.

Congo began to come under external influence at the end of the fifteenth century. Since then, Congolese have shown themselves to be quite open to foreign culture and ready to take advantage of new economic opportunities as well. In the political sphere however, Congolese have struggled to restore their independence and to get a better life for themselves and their children. Again and again, their revolutionary efforts have failed.

In Congolese thinking, these three spheres—political, economic, and cultural—are closely linked. MacGaffey (1983), an anthropologist, argues that to the Kongo people, political power and religion are inextricably linked. This is true of most other Congolese. In some Congolese languages, the words for *chief* (political leader) and *rich man* are the same or closely related. For many Congolese, to be successful in politics or in business, one must possess magico-religious power.

Pre-colonial Congo included major states in the northern and southern savannas and in the eastern highlands. Major states of the southern savanna included Kongo, on the Atlantic coast, and Luba and Lunda, farther east. In the north, the Zande and Mangbetu states were very important. In the east, the Shi and Nande kingdoms were important. A major state, Luba for example, had a central core where the monarch ruled directly and a periphery of semiautonomous states whose rulers paid tribute to the central monarch. Beyond the semi-autonomous states lay others where the central monarch was prestigious but did not rule. A monarch was more than a political ruler; typically he served also as a high priest, responsible for bringing rain to ensure success in agriculture.

In the equatorial rainforest, small, segmentary systems prevailed. These were organized on a family model, with the chief of one segment considered the older brother of the chiefs of other segments. Typically, however, this genealogical model was fictional, as many people in the community were not members of the "family."

From the sixteenth to the nineteenth centuries, the peoples of Congo came under foreign influence. Portuguese visited the Kongo kingdom in 1492, and over the next century, the Kongo state adopted Catholicism. It also was drawn into the Atlantic slave trade. In 1665, Kongo's defeat at the hands of the Portuguese of Angola in the Battle of Ambuila weakened the kingdom, which eventually broke up into autonomous chiefdoms. In 1700, a young woman, Kimpa Vita, led a prophetic movement to restore unity and strength of the Kongo kingdom. (Nzongola 2002; Thornton 1998)

By the nineteenth century, Congolese were being drawn into three networks of trade in slaves and other goods: the Luso-African network (based in Angola), the Arab-Swahili network (based in Tanzania), and the Sudanese Arab network. Europeans began arriving in the 1860s (Livingstone, Stanley). In the 1880s, Belgium's Leopold II won international recognition for his private colony, the Congo Free State, and set about eliminating the rival networks. In order to finance its colonization and generate immediate profits for international investors, the Free State used forced labor and violent expropriation of land, ivory, and wild rubber. Many Congolese perished. Following an international scandal over these abuses, Belgium annexed the Free State in 1908, making it the Belgian Congo. Belgium eliminated the more brutal aspects of the Free State but continued to treat Africans as children. Congo's vast mineral wealth was exploited through state-private partnerships. In areas lacking minerals, requirements to grow cotton and other crops were imposed on villagers. The Catholic Church, responsible for education, was the third element of what some call "the colonial trinity," along with the administration and the companies.

Congolese efforts to free themselves fall into five overlapping categories: (1) primary resistance and revolt, (2) religious movements, (3) urban strikes and uprisings, (4) prepolitical modern associations, and (5) political parties.

Primary resistance—armed opposition to conquest, usually led by traditional rulers—was widespread. It was most frequent when Free State agents encountered well-structured traditional states in areas remote from the initial state bases. Examples of periods of resistance include the Shi (1900–1916) and Luba-Katanga (1907–1917).

The uprisings of the Boa in 1903–1904 and 1910 and the Mbuja in 1903–1905, both segmentary systems of the forest zone, represent a second type of primary resistance. Both peoples felt the impact of harshly enforced rubber and ivory deliveries of the "red rubber" era. "Red rubber" refers to the rubber obtained through the brutal and bloody practices of the King Leopold of Belgium regime in forcing Congolese people to search for and bring in quotas of wild rubber. These uprisings represent the reaction of the entire society to Free State atrocities.

Once primary resistance was over (not until the 1930s in some remote areas), the stage of millenarian movements began, described by Young (1965, 28), a political scientist, as an era "when no secular remedy to the frustrations engendered by the colonial situation seemed available. The disequilibria introduced in traditional communities by colonial contact found temporary remedy through the millennial dream." However, if by "no secular remedy," Young means no political remedy, this point is debatable. Nzongola, also a political scientist, argues (2002, 30) that the Kongo prophet Kimbangu preached both the millennial dream (salvation for the soul) and also freedom from Belgian rule. The other major millenarian movement was Kitawala, an Africanized version of the Jehovah's Witnesses. It inherited from the Witnesses their aversion to state authority, but harsh repression by the Belgians led to radicalization. Kitawalists revolted in 1944 in Kivu.

As Congo became more industrialized and urbanized, new forms of resistance arose. In Lubumbashi in 1941 and in Matadi in 1945, demonstrations by African workers led to large-scale loss of life. In 1944, a mutiny of the Force Publique (colonial army) led to a night of rioting and looting in Lubumbashi. This mutiny was part of a larger plot that failed to materialize, due both to the gap between *évolués* and less-educated Congolese, and that between Congolese of various ethnic backgrounds.

Évolués, Congolese whose education and life style distinguished them from the masses, were encouraged to form associations that would operate under the supervision of the colonial administration. Prominent among them were associations of men having studied in the same school or school network (e.g., Jesuits or Marist Brothers). In the towns, people from the same administrative subdivision or ethnic background were allowed to form associations. Eventually, Congolese were allowed to form trade unions or professional associations. An important example was APIC, the Association of Native Personnel of the Colony, representing clerks and other Congolese working for the state. These organizations were not political. Their importance comes mainly from the occasions that they provided for Congolese to meet one another and to gain experience in organization. The *évolués* began by insisting on their rights to equal pay for equal work; only after they had been frustrated in such demands did they turn to anti-colonial nationalism.

In 1955 a Belgian professor published a thirty-year plan for emancipation of Belgian Africa. Catholic *évolués* associated with the organization *Conscience Africaine* supported the proposal. In response, *évolués* of the Kongo ethnic group demanded "immediate" emancipation. The Kongo group ABAKO (Alliance des Bakongo) was Congo's first political party, under the leadership of Joseph Kasavubu. The Congolese National Movement (MNC), which grew out of the *Conscience Africaine* group, became the first Congo-wide nationalist movement under the leadership of Patrice Lumumba.

On January 4, 1959, Kinshasa's population rioted when an ABAKO meeting was postponed, resulting in the death of many Africans at the hands of colonial security forces. On January 13, the Belgian government recognized independence as its ultimate goal, to be reached "without fatal procrastination, yet without fatal haste." However, the colonial administration lost the initiative to the nationalists and to the masses. The Belgian government responded by convening a Round Table conference of Congolese parties in Brussels in January 1960. The aim was to define conditions for a viable transfer of power, but the result was hasty de-colonization. Congo became independent six months later.

CONTEXT AND PROCESS OF REVOLUTION

Since formal independence in 1960, there has been repeated failure to achieve the nationalist objectives of radical transformation of society. Lumumba had campaigned for office on the basis of such a transformation. His party was the only one that was both national (Congo-wide, as opposed to regional or ethnic) and radical (calling for immediate independence and a transformation of the colonial economy, starting with an end to compulsory growing of cotton). The MNC-Lumumba did better than any other party in preindependence elections, winning thirty-three seats in the

137-seat lower house of parliament. The country attained independence on June 30, with Lumumba as prime minister, despite Belgian attempts to find an alternative, and his rival, Joseph Kasavubu, as president. Lumumba's government was a coalition of contradictory political forces, with several key ministers sharply opposed to his nationalist ideas.

Within a week of independence the army mutinied and the Katanga Province seceded. Belgium sent troops, ostensibly to protect its nationals, and Kasavubu and Lumumba invited in the United Nations to defend Congo against Belgian "aggression." Both Belgium and the United States began plotting to eliminate Lumumba. Within a few months his former personal secretary, Joseph-Désiré Mobutu, whom he had named army chief of staff after the mutiny, ousted Lumumba from power at the behest of Belgium or the Americans.

Kasavubu, leader of the Kongo ethnic party ABAKO, had been intransigent on the question of immediate self-rule. He now showed himself to be much more moderate and pro-Western than Lumumba, the turbulent prime minister. Mobutu, a former army clerk turned journalist, had his base among the Ngbandi of the far north and more generally among the "Bangala" cluster of Equateur Province, heavily represented in the army. Recruited first by Belgian intelligence, then by the American CIA before becoming an aide to Lumumba, Mobutu remained open to guidance from both his foreign paymasters.

The army mutiny set off the "Congo Crisis," the conflict over control of the Congo among different leaders and groups. It included the murder of Patrice Lumumba and civil war. The "Congo Crisis" also refers to the international Cold War conflict over the Congo among the United States, France, the Soviet Union, and the United Nations. Nzongola sees the mutiny as the response to a provocation by the Belgian army commander Janssens. Whether or not this is so, there was resentment on the part of the Congolese soldiers who retained their pre-independence ranks while civilian clerks became ministers.

Katanga Province was "an integral part of the multinational corporate empire established in Southern Africa before the First World War under British hegemony" (Nzongola 2002: 99). At the same time, its mines provided the Belgian Congo with most of its tax revenues. The secession was organized by top officials of the UMHK (Union Minière du Haut-Katanga) and other Belgian companies in the province, in collaboration with white settlers. Some Katangan Africans, notably Moise Tshombe and Godefroid Munongo, served as "front men" for the secession. Munongo, whose grandfather had come from the present Tanzania to establish a state in Katanga in the nineteenth century, was the most intransigent opponent of Lumumba, of a united Congo, and of the pres-

His arms roped behind him, ousted Congolese premier Patrice Lumumba (center) is captured by troops of strongman Colonel Mobutu Sese Seko in 1960. Lumumba was killed in early 1961 under mysterious circumstances, exacerbating the violence that began shortly after independence and continued for years under Mobutu's dictatorship. (Bettmann/Corbis)

ence in Katanga of Congolese from other provinces. Tshombe, son of a princess of the Lunda royal house, had a less rigid ideological stance. After suppression of the Katanga secession, he was able to recycle himself as a Congolese and even become prime minister.

In the face of considerable Western support for the Katanga secession and UN reluctance to use force to end it, Lumumba requested and received some military aid from the Soviet Union in August 1960. This led to the CIA requesting and receiving President Eisenhower's authorization to eliminate Lumumba. However, Belgium had decided much earlier to get rid of Lumumba. His Congolese adversaries, acting in connivance with the former colonial ruler, Belgium, and the United States, murdered Lumumba. Lumumbist revolutionaries took over nearly half the country in 1964–1965 but were crushed by the central government's army, decisively backed by the United States and Belgium.

In 1965, before victory over the rebels had been assured, Colonel Mobutu seized power in the name of the Army High Command. Rather than handing power back to civilians, he established a single-party regime that lasted until the early 1990s. Mobutu's single party was the Mouvement Populaire de la Révolution, but the promise of a revolutionary transformation of Congolese society was not fulfilled. Mobutu attempted to strengthen the state at the expense of the other two members of the "colonial trinity" and to weaken ties to Belgium. Politically, he stole the clothes of Lumumba, attempting to build a reputation as a nationalist. In the cultural domain, he promoted the doctrine of authenticity, meaning that Congo (renamed Zaire to signify a break with the past) would be true to itself. This brought him into conflict with the Catholic Church, which had implemented the cultural dimension of colonial rule. Nationalization of the universities deprived the Catholic Church of its control of the country's primary institution of higher education, Lovanium University. The party-state was declared a religion and Mobutu its "Messiah." The Church was undergoing its own struggle for authenticity—to conform to Congolese ways of thinking, it spoke of "the God of our ancestors." Thus reformed the Church was able to constitute a major force of opposition to Mobutu's dictatorship. The Protestants and the Kimbanguists, granted formal equality with the Catholics, tended to align themselves with the regime or at least to pose fewer problems. (On Mobutism as a religion, see Schatzberg 2001.)

In the economic sphere, Mobutu's activities were first to attack the Belgian-dominated corporations that had constituted one of the members of the "colonial trinity" and second to form a new Zairian capitalist class centering on himself. His efforts were somewhat successful in the short term but catastrophic in the long term, leaving Congo/Zaire poorer and more dependent than ever. Tshombe supposedly had settled the *"contentieux belgo-congolais"* (the bundle of disputes concerning the former colony's assets and debts) during his brief tenure at the head of the central government. Accusing Tshombe of treason for accepting a settlement too favorable to the Belgians, Mobutu reopened the *"contentieux"* but was unable to do much better. He nationalized the Union Minière du Haut-Katanga and created a Congolese corporation, the Générale des Carrières et de Mines or Gécamines. This company managed the holdings of the former UMHK within Congo but was unable to find an alternative to the "downstream" refining and marketing arrangements in Belgium. Subsequently, a second state enterprise, SOZACOM (Société de Commercialisation des Minerais), was entrusted with marketing the production of Gécamines and other Zairian producers. The company built a spectacular building on Boulevard du 30 juin in Kinshasa—hailed in a propaganda song as Zaire's Eiffel Tower—but still did not greatly improve Zaire's leverage in the sale of its copper and other minerals. Instead, SOZACOM proved a conduit for transfer of Zaire's mineral revenues into the hands of Mobutu and other politicians; it was dissolved in the 1980s, under pressure from the international financial institutions.

In 1974, Mobutu carried out Zairianization, by which most foreign-owned businesses were handed over to local owners, generally drawn from the ranks of politicians rather than businessmen. This had the effect of disorganizing the distribution of goods, as many of the "Zairianized" businesses went bankrupt.

An internal opposition movement began in 1982, when thirteen members of parliament submitted a letter to Mobutu calling for democratic reforms. The "group of 13" evolved into the Union for Democracy and Social Progress (UDPS) under the leadership of Etienne Tshisekedi. In 1990, as the Soviet Union collapsed and France pushed for democracy in its former colonies, Mobutu was forced to allow multiparty competition. Congo/Zaire adopted the model of the "sovereign national conference," pioneered in the former French colony of Benin. However, Mobutu and his allies thwarted the efforts of the conference (CNS) to lead a transition to democracy. Tshisekedi, named prime minister three times, was unable to consolidate his position.

In 1997, Mobutu was chased from power by Laurent Kabila, front man for Rwanda and Uganda. He died in exile soon thereafter. Mobutu's overthrow, wished for so long by Congolese, failed to lead to improved living conditions. Instead, they suffered from a civil war generated and sustained by foreign intervention, especially from Rwanda and Uganda. The ex-Lumumbist rebel, Kabila, headed the central government that replaced Mobutu. After his assassination, his son Joseph took his place. Joseph Kabila has presided over the reunification of the national territory. A residue of revolutionary rhetoric remains and Congolese national identity has been reinforced, but revolutionary transformation seems no closer than before.

IMPACTS

Democratic Republic of Congo borders on nine other states. Events and processes in Congo have influenced neighboring states and vice versa. The Kongo kingdom was divided between the three colonies of Belgian Congo, French Congo, and (Portuguese) Angola, but Kongo people and movements, notably Kimbanguism, interacted across borders. This is true for other divided populations, including the Lunda and Cokwe (divided between Congo, Angola, and Zambia) and the Rwanda (divided between Congo, Uganda, and Rwanda). Kinshasa and Brazzaville, capital cities of the two Congos, are sister cities, sharing the same language. In the years after World War II, reforms in French Equatorial Africa contributed to nationalist ferment in Belgian Congo, as did events in British-ruled Central Africa.

Since 1959–1960, these reciprocal influences have continued, particularly in regard to Rwanda and Burundi, also former Belgian colonies. The MNC-Lumumba established an alliance with the Union Nationale Rwandaise (Rwandan National Union, UNAR), which also was calling for immediate independence. After the murder of Lumumba, Burundi served as a base for Lumumbist forces seeking to combat the pro-Western regimes in Congo and Rwanda. After leftist revolutionaries seized power in Congo-Brazzaville, they provided shelter to Lumumbists.

The independence of the Congo put it on the front line of the struggle between independent "Black Africa" and the white-ruled territories to the south. This was true in 1960, when Rhodesia supported the Katanga secession. It was true at the beginning of 1963, when Katanga gendarmes took refuge in Portuguese Angola, then returned to help their leader, Tshombe, combat the Lumumbists. In 1975, when Angola underwent its own precipitous de-colonization and civil war, Mobutu intervened in support of the U.S.- and South African–backed forces against the Popular Movement for the Liberation of Angola (MPLA), supported by Cuba and the Soviet Union. Following the MPLA victory, Mobutu provided continuing support to Jonas Savimbi's UNITA (National Union for the Total Independence of Angola), while the MPLA regime in Angola supported the Congo National Liberation Front (FLNC) and its "Tigers," a militia of Katangans and others. The FLNC invaded Katanga (then called Shaba) twice in the 1970s.

Mobutu's government cooperated with Rwanda and Burundi in the framework of the Economic Community of Great Lakes Countries (CEPGL), and his party-state served as a model to the Hutu regime of General Juvénal Habyarimana in Rwanda. When the Tutsi-led Rwandese Patriotic Front (RPF) threatened Habyarimana, Mobutu's Zaire was there to help, along with France. The Rwanda genocide and the victory of the RPF led to the flight of two million Rwandans, mostly Hutu, into Congo. The presence in Congo of armed Hutu, including many genocide suspects, was the main reason Rwanda cooperated with Uganda and other neighbors to recruit Laurent Kabila and install him as Mobutu's successor, in 1997.

Kabila's inability to serve as a useful ally led to the second war, 1998–2003. A Congolese bodyguard assassinated Kabila in 2001, but foreign involvement was suspected. Eventually, an internationally brokered agreement led to an unwieldy transitional government, headed by Kabila's young son Joseph. There were four vice presidents, including one each from the Rwanda-backed and Uganda-backed rebel movements. Early in 2004, Joseph Kabila addressed the Belgian senate and paid tribute to the "pioneers" of Belgian colonialism in Congo.

Neo-colonialism can be understood, in Nzongola's words (2002, 126–127), as involving "the uninterrupted exploitation of the country's resources, but this time in collaboration with national ruling classes. The primary mission of the national ruling classes is to maintain the order, stability and labour discipline required for meeting the country's obligations to the international market." Joseph Kabila seemed to be promising the Belgians a neo-colonial policy, if only their businesses would return to Congo. When revolutionary forces are on the ascendancy in Congo, as in the days of Lumumba and his followers (including Mulele and Laurent Kabila), the entire region is affected. When neo-colonial forces are on the ascendancy, as in the days of Mobutu and perhaps again now, this too affects all of Central Africa.

PEOPLE AND ORGANIZATIONS

Alliance des Bakongo (ABAKO)

The first Congolese political party, founded in 1950 as the Association of the Bakongo for the Unification, the Preservation, and the Expansion of the Kikongo Language. In 1956, the ABAKO published a manifesto calling for immediate self-government. Under Kasavubu's leadership, ABAKO became the leading party at Kinshasa (Leopoldville) and in Kongo regions of Leopoldville Province. ABAKO won twelve seats in the parliamentary elections of May 1960 and at the provincial level finished second to the PSA (African Solidarity Party). ABAKO won recognition of its province of Kongo Central, which survives today as Bas Congo Province.

Confederation of Tribal Associations of Katanga (Confédération des Associations Tribales du Katanga—Conakat)

A grouping of ethnic associations of Katanga, including the Union Katangaise, an association of white settlers. Conakat finished in a virtual tie in the May 1960 election at the province level in Katanga with Balubakat and allies but was able to form the provincial government, thanks to the votes of unelected chiefs. Led the secession of Katanga in July 1960.

Congolese Democratic Rally (Rassemblement Démocratique Congolais—RCD)

Congolese group assembled by Rwanda and Uganda to provide cover for their second invasion of Congo in 1998. The RCD split on several occasions. Its former president Wamba dia Wamba formed his own RCD-Kisangani, only to be abandoned by his vice president Mbusa Nyamwisi, who formed the RCD-ML (Mouvement de Libération).

General Quarry and Mining Company (Générale des Carrières et des Mines— GECAMINES)

This state-owned company was created by Mobutu in 1967 to take over operations of Union Minière du Haut-Katanga.

Kabila, Joseph (Born 1971)

President of the Democratic Republic of Congo from 2001 onward. Son of Laurent Kabila (although his opponents claim he is not the biological son). Put in power by the ruling clique in Kinshasa following the assassination of Laurent Kabila.

Kabila, Laurent-Désiré (1939–2001)

President of the Democratic Republic of Congo, 1997–2001. A leader of the 1964 Simba rebellion in North Katanga, he headed a pocket of armed resistance to the Mobutu regime in South Kivu hills until 1980s. Kabila was chosen by Rwanda and Uganda to head the Alliance of Democratic Forces for the Liberation of the Congo (Alliance des Forces Démocratiques pour la Libération du Congo—AFDL). He declared himself president of the Democratic Republic of Congo in 1997 and was assassinated by a bodyguard in 2001.

Kasavubu (or Kasa-Vubu), Joseph (1910?–1969)

A seminary-educated civil servant, Joseph Kasavubu took over the ABAKO presidency in 1954. He was responsible for the ABAKO manifesto of 1956 calling for immediate self-government. Elected burgomaster of one of Kinshasa's communes in the first Congolese elections in 1957, he was chosen chief of state in 1960, with Lumumba as his prime minister. He dismissed Lumumba in September 1960, then was deposed as president by Mobutu in November 1965.

Lumumba, Patrice-Emery (1925–1961)

Lumumba received his primary education in schools run by the Passionist Fathers and Methodists in Kasai, then completed a short course for postal clerks. He was the founder of Lumumba wing of Mouvement National Congolais (MNC-L) and the first prime minister of independent Congo from June to September 1960. He was murdered in Katanga in January 1961.

Mining Union of Upper Katanga (Union Minière du Haut-Katanga—UMHK)

The most important capitalist enterprise in Belgian Congo and part of the family of companies owned by the Société Générale de Belgique, UMHK dominated copper mining in Katanga, Congo's richest province. It provided strong backing to the secession of Katanga in 1960. In 1967, Mobutu nationalized UMHK but failed to break the grip of the SGB companies on marketing of Congo's copper.

MNC-L, MNC-Lumumba

Lumumba wing of Congolese National Movement (Mouvement National Congolais). The MNC grew out of *Conscience Africaine*, a Catholic organization and was politically very moderate. Patrice Lumumba was elected president in 1958. His leadership led to a split between moderates and radicals, the moderate wing becoming the MNC-Kalonji, a de facto ethnic party of the Luba-Kasai. The MNC-L won thirty-three seats in the national elections of May 1960, more than any other party, and its leader became the country's first prime minister. Following the murder of Lumumba, the party split. During the 1990s, a dozen parties claimed the title MNC-Lumumba, one of them headed by François Lumumba, son of Patrice.

Mobutu, Joseph-Désiré (aka Mobutu Sese Seko) (1930–1997)

Born into the Ngbandi, a non-Bantu community in the far north, divided by the border with the Central African Republic, Mobutu was expelled from secondary school and inducted into Force Publique (the colonial army). In 1957 he began working as a journalist. Recruited by the Belgian intelligence service, he was sent to Belgium for intelligence training. In Brussels, he was recruited by the CIA in Brussels. In 1959, he met Lumumba and was invited to become the Brussels representative of MNC-L. When Lumumba became prime minister, he named Mobutu as junior minister in the prime minister's office. When the army mutinied, he named Mobutu number two man in the army. Mobutu ousted Lumumba in September 1960 and was among those responsible for sending him to Katanga, where he was murdered.

Mobutu was a leading member of the "Binza Group" by which Americans ruled indirectly in Congo, 1960–1965. He seized power in a second coup in November 1965 and ruled until 1997, when he was ousted by Laurent Kabila and his Rwandan and Ugandan backers. He died in Morocco shortly thereafter.

Mulele, Pierre (1929–1968)

Mulele was one of several ministers from the radical wing of the African Solidarity Party (Parti Solidaire Africain—PSA). When Lumumba fell, Mulele went to China for political and military training. He returned to Kwilu in 1963 and spent six months doing political education before launching his insurrection. He went to Congo-Brazzaville in 1968 but was lured back by a promise of amnesty, then murdered by Mobutu's generals.

Ngongo Lutete (or Leteta) (?–1895)

War leader of Tetela or Songye origin. Conducted slave raids, especially among Luba-Kasai, on behalf of the Arabs, then changed sides and fought the Arabs on behalf of the Congo Free State. Suspected of plotting against the Free State, he was executed in 1895. Some of his men revolted against the Free State, leading to the first of the so-called Batetela mutinies.

Popular Revolutionary Movement (Mouvement Populair de la Revolution—MPR)

Mobutu founded this party in 1967 following the model of the single governing party then in vogue in Africa. Later the MPR was to be one of three parties, according to Mobutu's announcement of multiparty competition in 1990. It survives as one of many political parties in the Kabila era.

Sovereign National Conference (Conférence Nationale Souveraine—CNS)

This meeting of delegates of political parties and nongovernmental organizations and high-level state functionaries took place between August 1991 and December 1992. It failed to lead the country to a new constitution and to democracy, due to the obstructionism of Mobutu and allies.

Tshisekedi, Etienne (Born 1932)

Leader of the democratic opposition to Mobutu, he was briefly prime minister in the 1990s. Tshisekedi was a student leader and member of the College of Commissioners (government) set up by Mobutu after his ouster of Lumumba in September 1960. He represented his home area of Kasai Oriental in the national legislature under Mobutu. In 1980, he was one of thirteen members of parliament to send a letter to Mobutu, demanding democratic reforms. This "group of 13" evolved into the UDPS. In 1991, Tshisekedi was named prime minister by Mobutu, only to have his acceptance "vetoed" by mass demonstrations in Kinshasa. After military riots, Tshisekedi again was named prime minister but only served for a few days. In August 1992, the Sovereign National Conference elected Tshisekedi prime minister. He served until December, when Mobutu ousted his government. Tshisekedi later allied himself to the Rwanda-backed RCD but was unable to translate this support into a major post in the government of national unity.

Tshombe, Moise-Kapenda (1919–1969)

Tshombe served first as prime minister of the secessionist state of Katanga, then as prime minister of the Congo, from which Katanga had attempted to secede. Tshombe's father was a successful Congolese businessman, his mother a member of the royal house of the Lunda state. Tshombe headed a Lunda ethnic association, and when electoral politics began in 1959, he became president of the Confederation of Tribal Associations of Katanga (Conakat). Conakat, supported by European settlers and the UMHK, favored continued close relations with Belgium. When the Congo became independent in 1960, Tshombe announced the secession of Katanga. Lumumba was murdered in Katanga in 1961, with Tshombe's complicity. When the United Nations forcibly ended the secession in 1963, Tshombe fled to exile in Spain. Tshombe was recalled from exile and named premier in 1964 to help President Kasavubu put down a Lumumbist rebellion. Dismissed the following year, he returned to Spain. In 1967, after his return to the Congo was rumored, he was kidnapped and taken to Algeria where he died in 1969.

Union for Democracy and Social Progress (Union pour la Démocratie et le Progrès Social—UDPS)

The UDPS developed from the "group of 13," a group of deputies in the Congo parliament who wrote to President Mobutu in 1982 demanding political reforms. It became the most important opposition group, with strong support in most regions of the country. UDPS leader Etienne Tshisekedi briefly became prime minister in the early 1990s but failed to consolidate power. When Laurent Kabila became president, he ignored the UDPS and its leader. The UDPS remains an important party, especially in Kinshasa and in Tshisekedi's home province of Kasai Oriental.

Tom Turner

See Also Colonialism, Anti-Colonialism, and Neo-Colonialism; Documentaries of Revolution; Ethnic and Racial Conflict: From Bargaining to Violence; Rwanda Civil Wars

References and Further Readings

De Witte, L. 2001. *The Assassination of Lumumba.* London/New York: Verso.

Gérard-Libois, J. 1966. *The Katanga Secession.* Madison: University of Wisconsin Press.

Harms, R. 1981. *River of Wealth, River of Sorrow: The Central Zaire Basin in the Era of the Slavery and Ivory Trade, 1500–1891.* New Haven, CT: Yale University Press.

Lemarchand, R. 1964. *Political Awakening in the Belgian Congo.* Berkeley: University of California Press.

Likaka, O. 1991. *Forced Cotton Production in the Belgian Congo, 1917–1960:* Minneapolis: University of Minnesota.

Lumumba, P. 1972. *Lumumba Speaks: The Speeches and Writings of Patrice Lumumba, 1958–1961.* Boston: Little, Brown.

MacGaffey, W. 1983. *Modern Kongo Prophets: Religion in a Plural Society.* Bloomington: Indiana University Press.

Nzongola-Ntalaja, G. 2002. *The Congo from Leopold to Kabila: A People's History.* London/New York, Zed Books.

Schatzberg, M. G. 2001. *Political Legitimacy in Middle Africa: Father, Family, Food.* Bloomington: Indiana University Press.

Thornton, J. 1992. *Africa and Africans in the Making of the Atlantic World, 1400–1680.* Cambridge: Cambridge University Press.

———. 1998. *The Kongolese Saint Anthony: Dona Beatriz Kimpa Vita and the Antonian Movement, 1684–1706.* Cambridge: Cambridge University Press.

Turner, T. 1997. *Zaire: Flying High above the Toads: Mobutu and Stalemated Democracy.* Pp. 246–264 in *Political Reform in Francophone Africa,* edited by D. E. Gardinier and J. F. Clark. Boulder, CO: Westview Press.

Weissman, S. R. 1974. *American Foreign Policy in the Congo, 1960–64.* Ithaca, NY: Cornell University Press.

Young, M. C. 1965. *Politics in the Congo.* Princeton, NJ: Princeton University Press.

Cuban Revolution

CHRONOLOGY

1868–1878	The First War of Cuban Independence ends in a stalemate.
1881–1895	Jose Marti lives and writes in the United States. His works encourage a new generation to fight for Cuban independence and inspire Cuban reformers and revolutionaries later in Cuba's history.
1886	Slavery abolished in Cuba.
1895–1898	Second War of Cuban Independence; Jose Marti returns to Cuba and is killed by Spanish forces. The war ends in Spanish withdrawal but occupation by U.S. military.
1902	Cuba is granted independence severely limited by the Platt Amendment, which restricts the financial relations and treaties Cuba can have with other nations, allows U.S. forces to be stationed at Guantanamo, and permits the U.S. the right to intervene in Cuba.
1906, 1912, 1917	U.S. military interventions in Cuba.
1924	General Gerardo Machado elected president.
1933	Revolution ends Machado regime; Fulgencio Batista, an army sergeant, becomes leader of the Cuban armed forces.
1940–1944	Bastista, supported by four political parties, elected president.
1944–1952	Elected governments plagued by extensive corruption.
1947	In response to widespread corruption, Cuban senator Eduardo Chibas and several other politicians and businessmen found the Orthodox reform party. Law school student Fidel Castro is a member.
1952	General Fulgencio Batista stages a military takeover, preventing scheduled national elections. A dictatorship is established until the victory of the revolution on January 1, 1959.
1953	Fidel and Raul Castro and associates carry out the unsuccessful Moncada attack on July 26.
1954	The U.S. CIA helps overthrow the elected reform government in Guatemala. A brutal right-wing dictatorship friendly to U.S. economic interests is established there. Ernesto "Che" Guevara is present in the country at the time. The CIA operation in Guatemala will provide a model for the agency's 1961 Bay of Pigs operation in Cuba.
1953–1955	The Castro brothers and other Moncada survivors serve prison sentences on the Isle of Pines.
1955	Responding to public protests, Batista releases the Moncada survivors on May 15.

In June and July, the Castro brothers, along with others, organize the Movement of the 26th of July, M-26-7. Under surveillance and fearing assassination, they go to Mexico.

1955–1956   In Mexico, Fidel and Raul Castro meet Ernesto "Che" Guevara, an Argentine who joins their effort. Members of M-26–7 prepare for months to return to Cuba and launch an armed revolutionary effort to overthrow the Batista regime.

1956   On November 25, eighty-two men, including the Castro brothers and Guevara, leave Mexico on a thirty-eight foot boat, the *Granma,* and land in eastern Cuba. Within days, they are attacked by Batista's troops and many rebels are killed or imprisoned. Sixteen survivors, including Fidel and Raul Castro and Che Guevara, make their way into the mountains of Oriente Province, the Sierra Maestra, to establish a base for the revolutionary struggle.

1957–1958   Celia Sanchez and other rebels send scores of recruits from Santiago and and other cities and towns to join Castro's forces in the mountains. U.S. reporters interview Castro and portray him as a revolutionary fighting for democracy and social justice against cruel tyranny and corruption.

Hundreds of anti-Batista rebels in urban areas, often young people from middle- or upper-middle-class families, are tortured and killed by Batista's forces.

Responding to stories of atrocities committed by Batista's army and police, the Eisenhower administration stops providing assistance to Batista's armed forces in March, 1958. Faced with loss of aid and growing popular resistance, their morale deteriorates rapidly.

In August, Castro's forces move down from the mountains.

In late December, revolutionary units led by Che Guevara defeat Batista's army at the central Cuban city of Santa Clara.

1959   In January, Batista flees Cuba. Santiago and Havana garrisons surrender. Castro establishes a provisional revolutionary government.

Fidel Castro visits the U.S. in April and has a meeting with Vice President Richard Nixon. Later the U.S. administration decides to oppose Castro's revolution and the Castro government begins to seek trade with and aid from the Soviet Union.

In May and June, large landholdings are broken up and land is distributed to poor rural workers.

1960   The U.S. CIA arms and trains approximately 1,400 anti-Castro Cubans in preparation for invading Cuba.

In June, U.S. oil refineries in Cuba refuse to refine Russian oil. Within a short time, Cuba expropriates the refineries and U.S. big business holdings, while the U.S. refuses to buy Cuban sugar. The Soviet Union agrees to purchase much of the sugar previously bought by the U.S. and to start supplying Cuba with weapons. Attempts to kill Castro apparently begin, involving alleged U.S. Mafia figures John Roselli and Sam Giancana (Szulc 1986, 523–524). Tens of thousands of Cubans who disagree with the new government's policies leave the country.

In October, the U.S. begins an economic trade embargo against Cuba, which it broadens in 1962.

1961   In January, John F. Kennedy is inaugurated as U.S. president, informed of the CIA-organized invasion of Cuba, and is persuaded to allow the invasion to take place.

In April, after the invasion air force only partially destroys the planes of the Cuban air force on the ground, about 1,400 men of the CIA-sponsored invasion force land in Cuba at the Bay of Pigs. Local Cuban militia resist the assault. Within hours they are reinforced by tens of thousands more militia. The Cuban air force destroys or drives off the invasion aircraft and sinks or forces the withdrawal of invasion ships. President Kennedy refuses to permit direct U.S. military intervention. The invasion force surrenders.

In December, Fidel Castro declares that he is a Marxist-Leninist.

1962   The U.S.S.R.'s and Cuba's leaders agree to deploying Soviet nuclear missiles in Cuba in part as a deterrent to a U.S. invasion. In October the U.S. establishes a naval blockade of Cuba and threatens further military actions. The U.S.S.R. agrees to remove the missiles in return for the U.S. pledge not to invade Cuba and to remove similar U.S. nuclear missiles from Turkey near the Soviet border. Later the U.S. and U.S.S.R. agree to establish a "hotline" or direct communications between the U.S. and Soviet leaders in case of future emergencies.

1966   In January, hundreds of activists and revolutionaries from around the world attend the Tricontinental Conference in Havana.

1967   Che Guevara, pursuing his "guerrilla foco strategy," is captured and executed in Bolivia in October.

1970   Cuba recognizes alternate paths to social revolution, including the democratic system in Chile that results in the election of Marxist Salvador Allende as president.

1973   On September 11, the Chilean military overthrows the Allende government, resulting in many deaths, including that of Allende, and the establishment of a pro-U.S. right-wing dictatorship.

1975–1989   Cuban troops arrive in Angola and help the forces of the leftist Popular Movement for the Liberation of Angola (MPLA) halt invading South African apartheid military units.

1975–1976   Alleged mafia figures Giancana and Roselli, called to testify on topics such as plots to kill Castro and the assassination of President Kennedy, are murdered separately.

1976   On October 6, a Cuban airliner is destroyed by a bomb, killing all seventy-three persons on board. Anti-Castro Cuban exiles blamed.

1980   Over 100,000 Cubans leave from the port of Mariel for the United States.

1987–1988   Cuban, MPLA, and ANC (African National Congress of South Africa) forces defeat South African apartheid military units at the Battle of Cuito Cuanavale in Angola.

1991   The U.S.S.R. disintegrates and Cuba loses valuable financial assistance.

1993   Cuba allows limited small private business activity.

1994   Private farmers' markets are permitted to counter food shortages.

1996   U.S. Helms-Burton Act attempts to force companies in other nations not to invest in or conduct business with Cuba. Many nations of the World Trade Organization oppose the act and some threaten economic retaliation against U.S. companies if the act is used against their companies.

1997   Che Guevara's remains are retrieved from Bolivia and re-buried at Santa Clara, Cuba, the site of Guevara's greatest victory during the Cuban Revolution.

1998   Pope John Paul II visits Cuba calling for freedom of expression and an end to the U.S. economic embargo against Cuba.

2000   Elected leftist president of Venezuela, Hugo Chavez, an admirer of Fidel Castro's social revolution and a proponent of similar goals to help Venezuela's poor through democratic means, arranges to sell oil to Cuba.

2002   Former U.S. president Jimmy Carter visits Cuba and calls for an end to the U.S. economic embargo against Cuba.

2004   On October 28, for the thirteenth consecutive year the UN votes overwhelmingly for the

U.S. to end its economic embargo against Cuba.

2005   Cuba and Venezuela further integrate aspects of their economies. Venezuela continues to ship oil to Cuba and Cuba sends thousands of doctors to Venezuela. The governments of Cuba and Venezuela support the Bolivarian Alternative for the Americas (ALBA) socially beneficial trade system.

INTRODUCTION

The Cuban Revolution of the 1950s resulted in the establishment of the first revolutionary Socialist system in the Western Hemisphere and brought Cuba world attention and influence far beyond its relatively small size and population. Radical redistribution of resources and the rapid expansion of medical services and educational opportunities to the large proportion of poor people, particularly in the rural areas of the island, won the enthusiastic support of the majority of Cuba's population. But the coercive measures through which some of the changes were brought about outraged many Cubans, especially those who looked forward to the revolution establishing a multiparty democratic political system and those who lost property. The Cuban Revolution inspired many young people to take up arms to bring similar transformations to their own peoples, and some who participated in the Cuban conflict, such as Ernesto "Che" Guevara, lost their lives trying to help them succeed. The U.S. government feared the spread of Cuban-style revolutions and provided training and other assistance to the armed forces of many countries to defeat revolutions. After the fall of the U.S.S.R., Cuba maintained its Communist Party government, and the United States not only continued but attempted to intensify, in the face of overwhelming international opposition, its economic embargo against Cuba.

BACKGROUND: HISTORY AND CULTURE

Cuba was "discovered" by Columbus in 1492, and the Spanish soon began to colonize and develop the island as a naval refreshment station for ships traveling between the Americas and Spain. The local Indian population was forced to work mining for gold and clearing land for agriculture. Harsh treatment and susceptibility to diseases brought by the Spanish virtually eliminated the Indian population as a separate cultural group. When large sugar plantations were established in Cuba in the late eighteenth and early nineteenth centuries, the labor force included 250,000 African slaves brought in legally and another estimated 60,000 illegally between 1792 and 1821 (Wolf 1969, 253). More than half of the population, which was about six million at the time of the 1950s revolution and a little over eleven million in 2005, was of at least partial African ancestry.

Cuba experienced unsuccessful slave rebellions in 1810, 1812, and 1844. As the peoples of South and Central America rose to end Spanish rule, many Cubans, fearing slave rebellion, relied on Spanish military garrisons for protection. But eventually Cubans, discontented with what they viewed as Spanish economic discrimination against them, limited freedom of speech, lack of sufficient representation in the Spanish Cortes (parliament), and some of them desiring to end slavery, launched the First War of Cuban Independence, which lasted from 1868–1878. Divisions among the rebels and Spanish military strength resulted in a stalemate after tens of thousands had perished. Spain continued to hold the island, although slavery was abolished in 1886.

The Second War of Cuban Independence was led by Cuban patriots inspired by the writings of Jose Marti. Marti was born in Havana in 1853, the son of Spanish immigrants. In 1870 he was imprisoned for pro-independence activities and then exiled to Spain, where he earned university degrees in literature, philosophy, and law. After the war ended, he returned to Cuba but was soon expelled again when he resumed pro-independence activism. He spent from 1881 to 1895 living in New York City, working for the *New York Sun* as an art critic, and writing. He argued that Spanish control of Cuba helped perpetuate exploitation and great inequality. Marti criticized the Cuban Catholic clergy, many of whom were Spanish, for opposing independence and doing too little to help the poor. He optimistically predicted that it was within the power of human beings to eliminate poverty and racism, and he opposed the economic and social institutions which supported these evils. As the war started in 1895, Marti returned to Cuba to participate in the struggle but was soon killed by Spanish forces. Later Fidel Castro would assert repeatedly that his revolution was inspired by Marti's nationalism and concern for the poor and that his policies were intended to fulfill Marti's aspirations for Cuba and its people.

During the second independence war, the Spanish forcibly relocated much of the rural population to deprive independence fighters of support and recruits. But after three years of brutal warfare, the rebels controlled much of the countryside. In the United States, some of whose citizens and businesses had significant investments in Cuba, many people sympathized with the independence struggle, and some helped smuggle weapons and ammunition to independence forces. On February 15, 1898, the U.S. battleship *Maine,* which was visiting Havana harbor, suddenly blew up

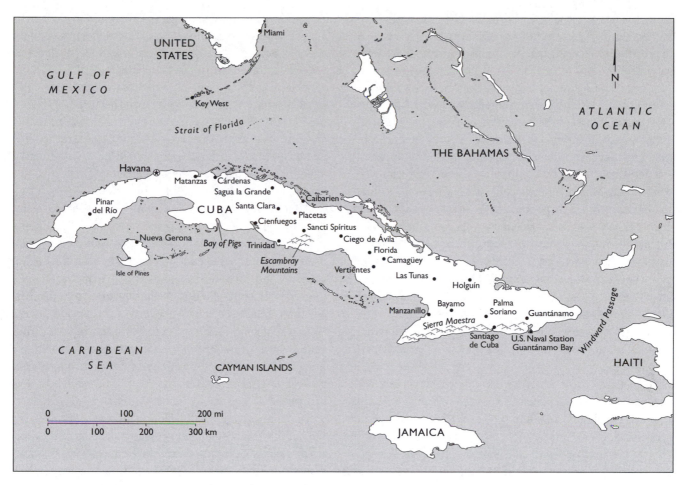

Cuba, showing Havana, Santiago, the Sierra Maestra, Santa Clara, and the Bay of Pigs. Che Guevara's success at Santa Clara in late December 1958 was one of the important battles leading to the final victory of the revolution.

and sank, with the loss of hundreds of lives. Modern scientific investigations indicate that the explosion was an accident. But at the time many people in the United States suspected a Spanish plot to discourage U.S. involvement. In response to mounting popular pressure, the U.S. government issued an ultimatum for Spain to free Cuba. When the Spanish refused, U.S. naval forces proceeded to destroy Spanish fleets in the Caribbean and in the Philippines. Cut off from resupply and under attack by both the U.S. army and Cuban independence fighters, the Spanish military in Cuba was forced to surrender.

After the war, U.S. forces occupied the island until a Cuban constitution and government could be organized. Some U.S. political leaders, however, were concerned that a fully independent Cuba could pose a threat to U.S. investments there. Their solution was the so-called Platt Amendment, which Cubans were forced to accept as part of their constitution. The Platt Amendment, named after U.S. senator Orville Platt, limited the amount of money Cuba could borrow from other nations, declared that Cuba could make

no treaties with other countries that impaired its independence, and gave the United States the right to buy or lease Cuban territory for U.S. naval bases, including Guantanamo. Most importantly, the Platt Amendment gave the United States the right to intervene in Cuba to preserve Cuban independence and provide for a Cuban government capable of protecting life, property, and liberty. U.S. military forces intervened in Cuba in 1906, 1912, and 1917. Although some Cubans supported U.S. involvement and growing investment in Cuba in areas such as mining and utilities, many believed that their struggle for independence had been betrayed and that Cuba was transformed from a colony of Spain to a possession of the United States entrusted to the local oversight of corrupt puppet governments.

After the formal declaration of Cuban independence in 1902, sugar continued to be the island's major export, much of it sold to the United States. U.S. companies invested hundreds of millions of dollars in manufacturing, mining, oil refineries, utilities, agriculture, sugar growing and milling, and tourism. Eventually organized criminals based in the

United States became involved in resort hotels and gambling casinos. Tens of thousands of Cuban women engaged in prostitution catering to tourists and visiting military personnel. Although Cuba was far from the poorest Latin American nation, the country was characterized by tremendous inequality. Rural Cubans, about 45 percent of the population at the time of the revolution, suffered from lack of medical and educational facilities and high illiteracy rates. Many members of Cuba's upper and middle classes were strongly attracted to U.S. culture and concerned with becoming rich. Medical doctors could not make much income selling their services to poor peasants, so many opted to live and work in urban areas. Cuban lawyers and other professionals, desiring to achieve great wealth, sometimes found that the only opportunity available to them was to become politicians and achieve government positions, which would give them access to public funds and bribes. Historically, Cuba's pre-revolution governments were plagued by extreme levels of corruption which, like perceived foreign domination and exploitation, was a recurring motive for revolution.

As in many other Latin American countries, the army existed not so much to defend the nation from foreign aggression as to maintain order and protect the government and property. For many poor people, joining the army provided opportunity and an island of economic security in a sea of poverty. Racism was a powerful social force in pre-revolutionary Cuba. Before 1933, only persons of European ancestry could become officers in the army. Non-whites were limited to the enlisted ranks.

Because of inequality and racism, some Afro-Cubans joined the Communist Party. The Cuban Communist Party was founded in 1925 by a group of militant union activists and students at Havana University. The party's first secretary general was a popular student leader, Antonio Mella. The Machado regime soon outlawed the party and apparently paid assassins to murder Mella. But the party continued to grow, and some of its members became important organizers of Cuban workers' unions, such as Afro-Cuban Communist labor leaders Lazaro Pena, Blas Roca Calderio, and Jesus Menedez Larrondo, head of the Sugar Workers' Federation.

In 1924, Gerardo Machado, a then-popular former general in the independence army, promising to end governmental corruption and persuade the United States to agree to eliminate the Platt Amendment, was elected president, supposedly to serve only a single four-year term. But Machado's government was accused of extensive corruption, the Platt Amendment stayed in place, and the regime cooperated with foreign business interests. Since Machado gained control of both the Liberal and Conservative parties,

he had the constitution changed to allow him to win a new six-year presidential term in 1928. His supporters and police were accused of using torture and murder to suppress opponents. Machado's increasingly dictatorial and brutal ways provoked popular anger and hatred and this emotional response increased over time and led to the 1933 Revolution. Discontent was increased by the hardships of the early 1930s Great Depression. With Cuba wracked by demonstrations and fighting, the United States withdrew its support for Machado, and he was forced to leave the country. Mobs killed scores of his henchmen.

Although Machado was gone, many Cubans felt that main aims of the 1933 revolutionaries went unfulfilled. Many people who had opposed and helped overthrow the Machado dictatorship wanted to end foreign control over the Cuban economy and government and to greatly reduce economic inequality. But after the 1933 revolution, foreign companies still dominated the economy, poverty was still widespread, government continued to be enormously corrupt, and Havana became a hemispheric vice capital and center for prostitution. Outrage at these conditions motivated a new generation of Cuban revolutionaries, including the Castro brothers.

One phase of the 1933 Revolution involved a rebellion by the multiracial enlisted men of the Cuban army. They were led by a charismatic mixed-race sergeant, Fulgencio Batista, who became the new leader of the army. Batista temporarily supported Havana University professor Ramon Grau San Martin as the new president of Cuba, but Grau's proposed reforms—establishing an eight-hour workday, limiting the ability of foreign companies to import cheaper non-Cuban labor, land redistribution, and lowering utility rates—provoked opposition from U.S. companies and the U.S. government. Batista was persuaded to replace Grau with a president more acceptable to the United States and U.S. businesses operating in Cuba.

After Grau left the presidency, the United States agreed to abrogate the Platt Amendment in 1934. Batista supported a number of other temporary presidents until he himself ran for and won the presidency in 1940 under Cuba's new constitution. He instituted some reforms that benefited the poor, including allowing non-whites to become officers in the Cuban army, but did not seriously threaten the interests of the Cuban upper class or U.S. business interests. Batista was accused of becoming a long-time friend of U.S. gangsters, such as Meyer Lansky, and helping mobsters set up gambling and other lucrative businesses in Havana. According to the 1940 constitution, a president could not immediately run for a second term. After serving his four years as president, Batista remained involved in Cuban politics but spent some of his time in Florida.

After Batista, two presidents followed from the Autentico Party, pledging to be true to the "authentic" principles of Jose Marti: Ramon Grau (1944–1948) and Carlos Prio (1948–1952). Their governments enacted some reforms but were repeatedly accused of corruption. Cuba's social ills, gangster-infested resorts, and the seemingly endless parade of corrupt government officials inspired the charismatic Cuban senator Eduardo Chibas, promising to promote the true or orthodox principles of Jose Marti, to leave the Autentico Party and found the new reform Orthodox Party in 1947. Fidel Castro, a student activist at Havana University Law School, was reportedly present at the party's founding. As the party gained support, Chibas attempted to expose corruption on his radio show. In August 1951, he promised to present his listeners evidence about a situation of corruption on his next broadcast. But whoever was to deliver the evidence failed to do so. Ashamed at disappointing his listeners and perhaps distressed at being betrayed, Chibas shot himself at the radio station and soon died of the wound. Despite this tragedy, the Orthodox Party presented a significant threat to corrupt officials in the 1952 election. Rather than allow the election, Batista commanded military units to seize control.

CONTEXT AND PROCESS OF REVOLUTION

By 1952 many Cubans had come to view Fulgencio Batista as a corrupt politician who served foreign interests, all the more dangerous because of his military background. When he used army units to prevent the election of 1952 and create a dictatorship, some, including Fidel Castro and his associates, decided to resort to violent insurrection.

Castro was born into a wealthy land-owning family in Oriente Province. His father was a self-made affluent landowner who had risen from relative poverty. Castro's family sent him to Jesuit-run schools, including prestigious Belen College, where he was a good student, a charismatic speaker, and a very good athlete in several sports. Fidel claimed that he first learned Marxist Socialist concepts at Havana University, where he earned a law degree. Outraged at social injustice, dishonest politicians, and foreign exploitation, Fidel believed that by participating in electoral politics he could eventually become Cuba's leader and then bring about a socioeconomic revolution to benefit the poor. But he felt that the Communist Party did not have the popular appeal to win an election. Instead, he joined Eduardo Chibas's Orthodox reform party. Fidel worked as a lawyer in Havana and planned to run as an Orthodox candidate for the Cuban leg-

Fidel Castro, the leader of a group of middle- and working-class rebels known as the July 26 Movement, sits in the guerrilla stronghold in the Sierra Maestra Mountains of southeast Cuba on March 14, 1957. On January 1, 1959, the rebel movement successfully toppled the corrupt presidency of Fulgencio Batista, ushering in a revolutionary government led by the charismatic Castro. (AP/Wide World Photos)

islature in the 1952 elections, which Batista's seizure of power prevented from taking place.

On July 26, 1953, Castro led approximately 120 of his friends, including two women, in a doomed attack on the Santiago Moncada military base. The plan apparently had been to seize the base's weapons, distribute them to opponents of the Batista regime in Santiago, take the city, and call for island-wide uprisings against the dictatorship. Eight of the attackers were killed in fighting, and sixty-one more were captured and executed (Szulc 1986, 264–265, 273). Archbishop Perez Serantes called for the surviving Moncada attackers to be brought in alive to stand trial. The Castro brothers had the good fortune to be apprehended later by an army unit commanded by Afro-Cuban lieutenant Pedro Manuel Sarria, a professional officer, who refused to allow his soldiers to execute the captives.

At his trial Castro gave his two-hour-long "History Will Absolve Me" speech describing the injustices in Cuba and the reasons for the Moncada attack. After serving about one year and seven months of a fifteen-year sentence, Castro and his associates were given amnesty on May 15, 1955, in response to public protests on their behalf. A secret National Directorate for their revolutionary organization, the Movement of the 26th of July, or M-26–7 (named after the date of the Moncada attack, which was viewed as the beginning of the revolution), was established on June 12. The Castro brothers, under surveillance and fearing assassination in Cuba, left for Mexico, Raul on June 24 and Fidel on July 7. In Mexico, Alberto Bayo, the Cuban-born guerrilla-warfare expert who had served on the Republican side in the Spanish Civil War, agreed to train Castro's force. The Cuban revolutionaries also met a young Argentine leftist physician, Ernesto Guevara. Since Guevara used the Argentine expression "che" for gaining one's attention, meaning "you" or roughly "Hey, you!," his non-Argentine friends gave him this nickname. Che joined Castro's M-26–7 and played a major role in the victory of the Cuban Revolution.

Guevara was a specialist in allergies (he suffered from asthma). He had ridden a motorcycle with a friend through much of South America and was appalled at the tremendous poverty of many of the people. Guevara was present in Guatemala in 1954, when an elected reform government, pursuing policies to redistribute land to the poor and reduce inequality, was overthrown by a CIA-organized counter-revolution. In place of democracy, a brutal right-wing dictatorship was established that protected the interests of the wealthy and foreign companies while terrorizing and killing thousands who craved social justice and democracy. To Guevara, the U.S. government had proven willing to betray its own democratic principles to protect the property and profitability of its corporations doing business in Guatemala, even if this meant subjecting generations of Guatemalans to economic misery and oppression. Guevara became committed to violent revolution, to insuring that the post-revolution armed forces were firmly under the control of revolutionary leaders, and that the post-revolutionary political system would be immune from bribery or other schemes of counter-revolutionaries and anti-revolutionary foreign interests. He, along with Raul Castro, is thought to have swayed Fidel in the direction of adopting Marxist-Leninist policies.

Fidel traveled to the United States to raise money from anti-Batista Cubans to buy weapons and a thirty-eight-foot hurricane-damaged yacht, the *Granma,* to transport him, Raul, Guevara, and seventy-nine others to eastern Cuba. They left on November 25, 1956, but due to bad weather and mechanical problems did not arrive until December 2. Within days they were attacked by Cuban army troops. Many

were killed, but Fidel and others made their way into the mountains. With aid and recruits from nearby Santiago, organized and sent by Celia Sanchez, Frank Pais, and others, Castro's guerrillas began to pose a significant threat to the Batista regime, in part by inspiring through their example rebels in the cities and other parts of Cuba to attack or resist the dictatorship.

The National Directorate of M-26–7 included representatives from both urban and rural units acknowledging Fidel Castro as the overall leader. Anti-Batistia resistance groups outside of M-26–7 were also active, such as the Revolutionary Directorate (DR), many of whose members were university students from middle-class families. Dozens of DR members attacked the National Palace in Havana on March 13, 1957, in an unsuccessful attempt to kill Batista (Quirk 1993, 135). Many DR participants died at the scene, and others were hunted down and killed later. Urban assaults on the dictatorship during 1957–1958 failed, and in the process many of the more moderate revolutionary opponents of Batista died in combat or were captured, tortured, and executed. Their defeat left no significant revolutionary alternative to Castro's M-26–7 in the countryside. Furthermore, the brutal repression against young middle-class opponents of the dictatorship turned much of the middle class against Batista's regime. The brutality of the dictator's army, perception of widespread and increasing opposition to Batista, and the apparent impression in the United States that Fidel Castro was not a Communist contributed to the Eisenhower administration's decision to halt arms shipments to Batista's army in March 1958. (However, according to Szulc (1986, 448–449), evidence has surfaced that Batista's planes were being refueled and rearmed with bombs at the U.S. base at Guantanamo during fighting that summer).

Faced with the cut-off of weapons from the United States and increasing popular support for the rebels, the morale of the Cuban army deteriorated. On May 20, 1958, Batista launched a "summer" offensive; it was decisively defeated after seventy-six days of combat (Szulc 1986). In the third week of August, Castro sent two groups of guerrillas, one under the command of Che Guevara and the other led by Camilo Cienfuegos, down out of the mountains to head east toward central Cuba. Other M-26–7 rebels moved toward Santiago. As civilians joined in to help Castro's units, Batista's army kept retreating. At the end of December 1958, Che's forces advanced into the city of Santa Clara. On hearing of Guevara's victory, Batista fled Cuba on January 1, 1959. Regular Cuban army units that had not already given up the fight then surrendered to Castro's forces.

A provisional revolutionary government, established under Castro's leadership, quickly began a series of reforms. Rents and utility rates were lowered. Private clubs and beaches were opened to the entire population. A land-reform program broke up many of the large agricultural estates and turned the land over to the use of tens of thousands of poor people in rural areas. A great literacy campaign was launched in which tens of thousands of young people went to temporarily live in the countryside and teach illiterate rural workers and farmers and their families to read and write. Within a short time hundreds of schools and clinics were built in the countryside where few existed before.

In April, Fidel Castro traveled to the United States to meet with U.S. officials and discuss plans for the future development of Cuba. Although President Eisenhower would not meet with him, he was allowed a short visit with Vice President Richard Nixon. Based on what happened later regarding Cuban and U.S. policies, the meeting was apparently less than successful. In the United States, government leaders concluded that Castro's plans were not acceptable and decided that he should be removed from power. Castro and his associates soon came to believe that the U.S. government would try to prevent many of the changes they wanted to bring about and would in fact intervene to alter the outcome of the revolution. They decided to counter U.S. opposition and potential aggression by creating a one-party state. Such a system would theoretically be able to more quickly bring about the changes the revolutionaries thought were necessary to improve the lives of most of Cuba's people. Also, from their point of view, there would be no multiparty elections in which candidates could be bribed by U.S. officials or political campaigns distorted by the infusion of millions of dollars to promote the election of politicians willing to serve foreign interests. Furthermore, establishing a government in which the Communist Party alone controlled the state could attract assistance from the Soviet Union to compensate for the anticipated cut-off of trade and aid from the United States.

However, Castro viewed the pre-revolution Communist Party as flawed. Some of its members had collaborated with Batista. Corrupt persons or opportunists were to be removed and the rest of the old Communist Party merged with M-26–7 to create a new Communist Party. In addition, the Cuban army had to be cleansed of conservative or corrupt personnel, and most importantly of Batista henchmen. The new Cuban army was to be completely loyal to the revolution.

As had occurred during and after the 1933 Revolution against Machado, thousands of Cubans called for the execution of those in Batista's service who had tortured and murdered their friends and relatives. Rather than allow mob vengeance as had occurred in 1933, the new revolutionaries attempted to provide a semblance of legal proceedings in the form of short trials of the accused. Although the brief trials were later cited in the United States as evidence of injustice on the part of Castro and other revolutionary leaders, a pub-

lic opinion poll at the time indicated that a large majority of the Cuban public supported the executions (Quirk 1993, 229).

The developing establishment of Communist Party rule offended many Cubans, including some who had fought as members or allies of Castro's M-26–7. Thousands began leaving Cuba, many heading to the United States. Some started their own rebellion in the Escambray Mountains in central Cuba but were eventually overwhelmed and defeated by tens of thousands who supported Castro's policies. In March of 1960 the Eisenhower administration began organizing a plan for a CIA-sponsored invasion of Cuba by anti-Castro Cubans. This was to be modeled after the successful CIA-assisted overthrow of the elected reform government in Guatemala in 1954. Anti-Castro Cubans were provided with weapons and trained at a base in Guatemala. An invasion air force composed of World War II–vintage twin-engine B-26 bombers was formed to bomb and destroy the Cuban air force on the ground and then support the invasion. Some of the pilots were U.S. citizens, four of whom were shot down and killed during the invasion. In addition, according to Szulc (1986, 523–524), in September 1960 "a CIA plot to assassinate him [Castro] was formally set in motion." If Castro could be eliminated, it was thought that a rebellion against the revolutionary government would have a better chance of success. The plan reportedly involved alleged Mafia figure John Roselli and U.S. mobsters who had lost money when their businesses in Cuba were shut down by Castro's revolution.

While these preparations were under way, Cuba and the United States clashed openly over the issue of oil Cuba had purchased from Russia. In June 1960, U.S. refineries in Cuba, apparently at the request of the Eisenhower administration, refused to refine the oil. In response, the Cuban government seized the refineries. In a sequence of reciprocal actions, the United States cut its purchases of Cuban sugar and then imposed an economic embargo while Cuba expropriated other foreign-owned businesses.

After John F. Kennedy was inaugurated president in January of 1961, he was informed of the invasion plan and convinced, apparently partly based on false information that most Cubans had turned against Castro, to permit the invasion to take place. The CIA invasion air force attempted to destroy the Cuban air force during bombing raids on April 15, but most Cuban planes survived. On April 17, the invasion force of approximately 1,400 landed on Cuba's south coast at the Bay of Pigs, meeting resistance from the vastly outnumbered local militia. But quickly the Cuban air force sank two of the invasion's freighters and the rest fled. It also shot down or drove off the CIA planes. Then tens of thousands of Cuban militia joined the battle against the invasion. Within 72 hours the surviving invaders, approximately 1,200, were forced to surrender (Quirk 1993, 374). Instead of overthrowing the Castro government, the invasion strengthened its popular support by seeming to show that for the first time in its history, Cuba had been able to defeat foreign intervention.

The Cubans, however, anticipated that the U.S. government would eventually launch another, bigger invasion with U.S. troops and so were receptive when the U.S.S.R., under Nikita Khrushchev's leadership, offered to deploy intermediate-range nuclear missiles in Cuba. Presumably the U.S. government would not dare to invade Cuba if it had thirty-six missiles, each with a warhead fifty times the power of the Hiroshima bomb and capable of reaching most of the United States. Both the Russians and the Cubans felt this move was justified by the fact that the Turks had allowed similar U.S. missiles aimed at the Soviet Union to be placed on their territory close to the U.S.S.R. border. But the U.S. population had never faced such a threat, and President Kennedy demanded that the missiles be removed. U.S. leaders considered carrying out an invasion not realizing that in addition to the missiles that could reach U.S territory, Russian forces in Cuba possessed dozens of short-range tactical nuclear weapons for use against such an invasion. Fortunately an agreement was reached, and the U.S.S.R. withdrew its missiles in return for a promise by the U.S. government not to invade Cuba and a secret understanding that the United States would remove its own missiles from Turkey.

In the following years, Cuba trained revolutionaries from countries in Latin America, Africa, and the Middle East. In January 1966 Cuba hosted the Tricontinental Conference of hundreds of activists and revolutionary leaders from around the world. Attempting to combat revolution, the U.S. trained special units of existing governments' armies in counter-insurgency warfare. Che Guevara and Cuban volunteers in 1965 fought on the side of revolutionaries in the Congo. In November 1966, Guevara and a number of Cubans infiltrated Bolivia to commence what they hoped would be a revolutionary effort that would spread to neighboring countries and bring about a continental revolution. But his "guerrilla foco" achieved little local support, and most of Guevara's forces were destroyed by U.S.-assisted Bolivian troops. (See the Guevara biography in the People and Organizations section for an explanation of his "guerrilla foco" theory.) In October 1967 Guevara was wounded, captured, and secretly executed under the pretence that he was killed in battle.

In 1970, Cuba announced its recognition of alternate paths to Socialism, in particular the efforts of the leftist Popular Unity alliance under Salvador Allende's leadership in Chile to win power through elections and bring about a social revolution through democratic means. These hopes were dashed when the Chilean military overthrew the elected government and democracy on September 11, 1973, resulting in the deaths of President Allende and many others, and established a brutal right-wing dictatorship.

In the 1970s and 1980s Cuba continued to assist revolutionary movements in other nations. Units of its armed forces fought for governments it supported in Africa. Cuba's educational system produced many doctors, nurses, and teachers, thousands of whom brought medical services and education to places around the world where people had little or no access to them.

The destruction of the Soviet Union meant an end to the financial assistance that Cuba had received for years from the U.S.S.R. The Cuban economy suffered greatly from fuel shortages and other scarcities, and in reaction its economic policies changed to permit small-scale private enterprises and encourage foreign investment and business operations. Gradually the Cuban economy began to improve. The Republican-controlled U.S. Congress passed the Helms-Burton Act in 1996. This law was an attempt to pressure other nations' companies to stop investing in or doing business with Cuba. The most controversial aspect of the Helms-Burton Act, Title III, would permit U.S. companies or citizens the right to sue in U.S. courts foreign companies using property in Cuba that once belonged to them. If they won their suits, U.S. courts could provide them with compensation from the U.S. assets of the accused foreign companies. Many nations strongly objected to the Helms-Burton Act, and some threatened economic retaliation against the United States if the act was fully implemented. U.S. presidents Bill Clinton and George W. Bush repeatedly postponed activation of Titile III of the Helms-Burton Act, apparently out of concern with provoking international economic warfare (*New York Times,* Feb. 21, 1997, A1; *PBS NewsHour Update,* July 17, 2001). World opinion regarding U.S. policy toward Cuba was reflected in part through the overwhelming international opposition to the U.S. economic embargo. On October 28, 2004, the UN voted 179–4 to condemn the U.S. embargo against Cuba. Only Israel, the Marshall Islands, and Palau supported the United States. The 2004 vote was the thirteenth year in a row that the UN voted against the embargo.

IMPACTS

The Cuban Revolution had major impacts domestically and internationally, including on the internal politics of the United States. The social transformation brought by the revolution expanded health care and educational opportunities, including higher education, to hundreds of thousands of Cubans, some of whom brought these services to people in other nations. The revolution inspired the formation of a number of movements in Latin America and other parts of the world, and Cuba often provided revolutionaries with military training and other forms of assistance. This aid was used to justify a continuation of the U.S. economic embargo, U.S. counter-insurgency training for Latin American armies, and apparent toleration of or support for anti-Communist authoritarian regimes. The threat of Cuban-style revolution also motivated major U.S. assistance programs to Latin American countries, such as the Alliance for Progress, intended to increase the size of the middle classes and reduce poverty so that people would be less inclined to create or join revolutionary movements.

Cuban forces played significant military roles in Africa in the 1970s and 1980s, particularly in Angola, where they helped turn back the invading apartheid South African army. While most of the revolutionary movements aided by Cuba were defeated, a few were successful, such as the Nicaraguan Sandinista Movement, the Popular Movement for the Liberation of Angola, and the African National Congress (ANC) of South Africa. After the first post-apartheid elections in South Africa, which resulted in the selection of the ANC's Nelson Mandela as president, the victorious ANC addressed the Cuban people on Cuba's National Day, July 26, 1995:

> The ANC wishes to salute the Cuban people for the immense role they have played in the national liberation struggle both in South Africa and in the Southern African region as a whole. . . . The Cuban government selflessly sacrificed their own precious physical, financial and human resources to ensure that our members in exile were fed, provided with basic necessities, as well as opportunities to further their education. The people and government of Cuba remain a shining example of practical solidarity to oppressed peoples of our continent. (http://www.hartford-hwp.com/archives/43b/025.html)

But many Cubans who lost property after the revolution or preferred a multiparty democratic political system left the island, often settling in Florida. There they formed a fairly conservative voting block, probably swinging the state and the presidential electoral college in 2000 to George W. Bush, with all the resulting consequences. The hostility between the United States and Cuba contributed to disagreements between the United States and other nations that opposed the U.S. trade embargo. In 2005, Venezuela in particular, under president Hugo Chavez, criticized U.S. policy and continued to ship oil to Cuba while Cuba sent thousands of doctors and nurses to Venezuela.

The civil war that began in Cuba in the 1950s affected the peoples of many nations in various ways. What will happen to Cuba after the passing of Fidel Castro seems uncertain, but the ideals that drove Cuban revolutionaries to take up arms will likely also continue to motivate the young men and women who will determine their nation's future.

PEOPLE, ORGANIZATIONS, AND CENTRAL EVENTS

Autentico Party

The Autentico Party was a major political party in Cuba during the 1940s whose leaders claimed they would be true to the "authentic" principles of Jose Marti. Candidates of the Autentico Party won the presidency of Cuba in 1944 and 1948, but members of their administrations were accused of corruption and theft of public funds. In response, Eduardo Chibas and others founded a new reform party in 1947, the Orthodox Party, pledging that they would be true to the real or "orthodox" principles of Jose Marti.

Batista, Fulgencio (1901–1973)

Fulgencio Batista seized power through a military takeover in 1952 and established a brutal dictatorship until he fled the island on January 1, 1959, in the face of the revolution led by Fidel Castro. Batista's parents were sugar plantation workers who were believed to be of African, Chinese, Indian, and European ancestry. In 1921 he joined the army and by 1933 had risen to the rank of sergeant. At that time, only men of European ancestry were allowed to become officers. As the effects of the Great Depression hit Cuba, the repressive and corrupt regime of Gerardo Machado became unbearable for most Cubans, who rose in revolt. Many enlisted soldiers in the Cuban army also rebelled, led by the charismatic Sergeant Batista, who became the new leader of the army. He temporarily supported Havana University professor Ramon Grau San Martin as the new president of Cuba, but Grau's proposed reforms, such as establishing an eight-hour workday and land redistribution, provoked opposition from U.S. companies and the U.S. government. Batista was persuaded to replace Grau with a president acceptable to U.S. businesses.

Batista supported a number of other temporary presidents until he himself ran for and won the presidency in 1940 under Cuba's new constitution. Batista was accused of helping U.S. mobsters set up gambling and other lucrative businesses in Havana. After serving his four-year presidential term, he remained involved in Cuban politics but spent much of his time in Florida. He planned to run for president again in 1952, but polls showed him in last place. Instead he used the army to prevent the elections and set up a military-backed dictatorship. In response to rebellions and assassination attempts, torture and murder were used against opponents of Batista by members of his military and police, hundreds of whom were executed by the revolutionaries after Batista left Cuba on January 1, 1959.

Bay of Pigs Invasion

The Bay of Pigs invasion was the unsuccessful CIA-sponsored attempt to overthrow Castro's revolution and government in April of 1961. It was patterned in part after the CIA's successful effort in 1954 to overthrow the democratically elected reform government in Guatemala whose policies had provoked anger from U.S. businesses operating there. Approximately 1,400 anti-Castro Cubans were trained and armed by the CIA at bases in Central America for the assault. The CIA also provided a small air force of World War II B-26 bombers for the invaders, some with U.S. pilots, of whom four were shot down and killed in the invasion. Instead of welcoming the invaders, the vast majority of Cubans rallied to overwhelm them and forced their surrender within 72 hours. By seeming to show that Cuba could for the first time in its history defeat foreign intervention, the Bay of Pigs invasion was thought to have increased popular support for Castro and his government.

Castro, Fidel (Born 1926)

Fidel Castro was the charismatic and main leader of the Cuban Revolution. He was born into a wealthy land-owning family in Oriente Province. His father was a self-made affluent landowner who had risen from relative poverty. His mother, Lina, at least twenty-five years younger than his father, was his father's second wife and had once worked as a servant in the household. Fidel was the third of their five children, and they reportedly were not legally married until several years after Fidel's birth. As a young child Fidel briefly attended a local school with children from very poor families. Later he said that his youthful realization that his first classmates would soon have to leave school to work and that most would live lives of relative ignorance and poverty set him on the path to becoming a revolutionary.

Castro's family sent him to Jesuit-run schools, including Belen College, considered perhaps the best in the country. He was a fairly good student, a charismatic speaker, and a very good athlete in several sports. He went to Havana University Law School, where he claims he first learned Marxist Socialist concepts, and became a student activist. Fidel believed that by participating in electoral politics he could eventually be elected Cuba's leader and then bring about a socioeconomic revolution to benefit the poor. But he felt the Communist Party did not have the popular appeal to win an election. Instead he joined Eduardo Chibas's Orthodox reform party. Fidel worked as a lawyer in Havana and planned to run as an Orthodox candidate for the Cuban legislature in the 1952 elections, which Batista's seizure of power prevented from taking place. On July 26, 1953, Castro led more than a hundred of his friends in the disastrous attack on the Santiago Moncada military base, which resulted in the deaths of about half of the participants. After serving one year and seven months of a fifteen-year sentence, Castro was given amnesty.

The Castro brothers, along with others, founded a new revolutionary organization, the Movement of the 26th of July, M-26–7, and quickly left Cuba for Mexico. After preparing for many months, the Castro brothers and eighty others arrived on December 2, 1956, in eastern Cuba by boat. Within days many were killed or captured, but Fidel and other survivors made their way into the mountains. With aid and recruits from nearby Santiago and local peasants, and the aid of actions by rebels in various cities, popular support swung decisively in favor of the revolutionaries. After the victory, Castro went to the United States, apparently to seek help. But he quickly came to believe that the United States would oppose the socioeconomic revolution he and his associates planned to carry out. He instructed his M-26–7 to merge with the old Communist Party to create a new Cuban Communist Party that would exclusively control the government and carry out radical transformations of Cuban society. In a series of confrontations with the United States in 1960, Cuba nationalized foreign businesses while the United States imposed an economic embargo and organized a plan to land CIA-armed and -trained anti-Castro Cubans at the Bay of Pigs to overthrow Castro's government. Popular support for Castro and his policies, however, led to the defeat of the invasion within 72 hours and to even greater nationalist enthusiasm for Castro. To prevent a future invasion and aid the Soviet Union, a major source of financial and military assistance, Castro permitted the deployment of Soviet nuclear missiles in Cuba, which led to the October 1962 Cuban Missile Crisis.

Castro's government provided assistance and training to many revolutionaries from other lands. Although some political leaders in the United States expected the Communist government in Cuba to fall after the loss of aid from the Soviet Union in the early 1990s, Cuba endured hardships to maintain its Socialist system. In the mid 1990s, with increased tourism, economic reforms, and foreign investment, the Cuban economy began to revive. Castro won support from the vast majority of the world's nations and Pope John Paul II to end the U.S. embargo.

Castro, Raul (Born 1931)

Raul Castro is a younger brother of Fidel Castro. Raul also attended excellent schools, but, unlike Fidel, supported the Communist movement as a student. Raul is thought, along with Che Guevara, to have exerted influence on Fidel to adopt Marxist-Leninist ideology and seek help from the Soviet

Union. Raul took part in the 1953 Moncada attack and traveled with his brother back to Cuba in December 1956 to renew the revolutionary struggle. After the revolution, he became a major political and military leader.

Chibas, Eduardo (1907–1951)

Chibas, a Cuban senator and radio program host, was the founder of the Orthodox reform party in 1947, through which he hoped to combat government corruption in Cuba. Fidel Castro joined the Orthodox Party at its inception and was a candidate for the Cuban legislature on the party's ticket for the 1952 election, which never took place because of Batista's seizure of power. Chibas used his popular radio program in attempts to call attention to corruption. After he promised that he would describe a major case of corruption on his next broadcast, Chibas felt betrayed when the evidence did not arrive and distressed at disappointing his listeners. He shot himself at the radio station and died shortly thereafter, mourned by Castro and other party members.

Cienfuegos, Camilo (1932–1959)

Camilo Cienfuegos was considered one of the key male leaders of the Cuban Revolution along with Fidel and Raul Castro and Che Guevara. He was active in resistance activities against the Batista regime and eventually assumed command of a major group of Castro's revolutionary guerrillas. After the victory he was extremely popular. He played a major leadership role in the new army and fought counter-revolutionaries. He also helped carry out the land-reform program. The light plane he was flying from Camaguey to Havana disappeared over the sea on October 28, 1959.

Cuban Communist Party

The Cuban Communist Party was founded in 1925 by some militant union activists and students at Havana University. The party's first secretary general was a popular student leader, Antonio Mella. The Machado regime outlawed the party and apparently paid assassins to murder Mella. The party grew, and its members became important organizers of Cuban workers' unions. The party gained up to 10 percent of the popular vote in elections and in 1940 was part of the four-party coalition that supported Batista's victorious campaign for the Cuban presidency. After Batista's military takeover in 1952, some Communist politicians collaborated with Batista and criticized Fidel Castro and his resort to armed revolution, which they thought was doomed to fail-

ure. The party began to support Castro's effort in 1958, when it appeared that it might succeed. After the revolution, Castro's supporters merged the M-26–7 organization with the old Communist Party to create a new Communist Party that would control the Cuban government.

Cuban Missile Crisis of October 1962

Following the failed Bay of Pigs invasion, many Cubans expected the humiliated U.S. government to launch a new, more powerful invasion. The Soviet leader Nikita Khrushchev, hoping to bring his nation closer to a balance of nuclear capability with the United States, which had nuclear missiles in Turkey near the Soviet border, offered to station intermediate-range ballistic missiles with nuclear warheads in Cuba to deter a future U.S. invasion of the island. The Cuban leaders accepted this proposal, and thousands of Soviet troops with three dozen intermediate-range missiles were secretly brought to Cuba during 1962. Soviet and Cuban leaders hoped that the missiles would not be immediately detected. In order to avoid affecting the November U.S. congressional voting, the presence of the missiles and warheads was not to be announced until after the elections had taken place. However, spy-plane flights detected the missiles in October, and the U.S. government decided to demand removal of the missiles and all offensive weapons from Cuba or resort to military action up to and including an invasion of the island. The Kennedy administration instituted a naval blockade of Cuba to turn back any Russian ships carrying missiles or warheads or other offensive weapons. Apparently all or almost all of the missiles had been made operational. But these could not be launched without permission from Moscow. Unknown to the U.S. government, however, was the presence of scores of small tactical nuclear warheads with relatively short-range delivery systems. These were to be directed against a U.S. invasion, and the local Russian commander could use them without having to wait for permission from Moscow. Fortunately, rather than facing nuclear war the Soviets agreed to withdraw their missiles and warheads in return for a public U.S. promise not to invade Cuba and a secret understanding that the United States would remove its nuclear missiles from Turkey. The 1962 missile crisis is generally thought to have been the closest the world came to nuclear war.

Cuban Revolution of 1933

The Cuban Revolution of 1933 was a massive explosion of popular anger and hatred for the regime of Gerardo Machado, his associates, and elements of his military and police, intensified by the hardships of the Great Depression of the early 1930s. Machado, who had been elected in 1924, had had the constitution changed to remain in power. He was blamed for stealing millions of dollars from the Cuban treasury, and his military and police were accused of torture and murder. After Machado fled Cuba, mobs killed scores of his supporters. One phase of the 1933 Revolution involved a rebellion by the enlisted men of the Cuban army against officers. The enlisted men were led by a mixed-race sergeant, Fulgencio Batista, who became the new leader of the army and allowed non-whites to become officers. But many Cubans felt that major aims of the 1933 revolutionaries went unfulfilled, since foreign companies still dominated the economy, poverty was widespread, and the government continued to be enormously corrupt.

Guevara de la Serna, Ernesto "Che" (1928–1967)

Guevara was a young Argentine medical doctor, a specialist in allergies (he suffered from asthma) who joined Castro's M-26–7 revolution in Mexico and played a major role in the victory of the Cuban Revolution. He was born into a leftist upper-middle-class family. Guevara had ridden a motorcycle with a friend throughout much of South America. He was appalled at the tremendous injustice of social systems that permitted a small minority of families to enjoy enormous wealth and privilege while millions were left illiterate, and to experience the tragedy of seeing their children die from malnutrition or from diseases easily prevented if basic medical treatment was available.

Guevara was present in Guatemala in 1954 when an elected reform government, pursuing policies to redistribute land to the poor and otherwise reduce inequality, was overthrown by a CIA-organized counter-revolution. In place of Guatemalan democracy, a brutal right-wing dictatorship was established that protected the interests of the rich and foreign corporations. To Guevara, the U.S. government had proven willing to betray its democratic principles to safeguard the property and profitability of its corporations doing business in Guatemala, even if this meant surrendering generations of Guatemalans to economic misery and oppression. Guevara became committed to violent revolution, to ensuring that the post-revolution armed forces were firmly under the control of revolutionary leaders, and that the post-revolutionary political system would be immune from bribery or other schemes of counter-revolutionaries and anti-revolutionary foreign interests.

During the Cuban Revolution, Guevara was known for bravery and for enforcing discipline among revolutionary soldiers. He, along with Raul Castro, who first met him and introduced him to Fidel, is thought to have swayed Fidel in the direction of adopting Marxist-Leninist ideas. Following the revolution, Guevara attempted to aid revolutionaries in other lands, including in Africa and South America. He formulated the so-called Theory of the Guerrilla Foco, which held that the injection of a small band of armed, dedicated revolutionaries, perhaps thirty to fifty (Guevara 1969b, 112), into a society characterized by extreme inequality and injustice, could eventually mobilize mass support for revolution. By attacking the ruling elements and their repressive army, the revolutionary foco (focus) would attract the attention of the people and wake them from their apathy and despair, show them that the oppressors were vulnerable, propagate the vision of a new society, and thus win the popular support necessary for the revolution to succeed.

Guevara attempted to bring revolution to South America by secretly entering Bolivia in 1966 with Cuban volunteers to create a guerrilla foco there and use Bolivian territory to support revolution in the South American countries that bordered it. However, he and his associates never gained significant local support, and Bolivian military units, provided with U.S. assistance and CIA personnel, destroyed most of Guevara's forces and wounded, captured, and secretly executed him in October 1967. Guevara continues to be an inspirational figure for revolutionaries around the world.

Machado, Gerardo (1871–1939)

Machado had been one of the leaders of pro-independence forces during the Second War of Cuban Independence. When he ran for the presidency, he promised to end corruption and convince the United States to abandon the Platt Amendment, which gave the United States the right to intervene in Cuba. Instead, Machado's government was accused of enormous corruption. Machado came to control both the Liberal and Conservative parties. He had the constitution changed to allow him to win a new six-year presidential term in 1928. His supporters and police were accused of using torture and murder to suppress opponents. When mass uprisings erupted in 1933 and the United States withdrew support for his government, Machado fled the island.

Marti, Jose (1853–1895)

Jose Marti was an advocate of Cuban liberation whose writings inspired the Second War of Cuban Independence. As the war started, Marti was killed by Spanish forces. As a teenager he had been imprisoned for writing in support of independence and then later expelled from Cuba. He spent from 1881 to 1895 living, working, and writing in New York City. He argued that Spanish control of Cuba helped perpetuate exploitation and great inequality. He optimistically predicted that it was within the power of human beings to eliminate poverty and racism. Fidel Castro claimed his revolution was inspired by Marti's nationalism and concern for the poor and that his policies were intended to fulfill Marti's aspirations for Cuba. Critics of the Cuban Revolution argue that Castro betrayed at least some of Marti's ideals.

Movement of the 26th of July (M-26–7)

Named after the date of the 1953 Moncada attack, this revolutionary organization was founded by Fidel Castro and others in June of 1955 and eventually succeeded in defeating the Batista dictatorship. In late 1959 and 1960, M-26–7 combined with the old Cuban Communist Party to create a new Communist Party, which then had exclusive control over the Cuban government.

Orthodox Party

The Orthodox Party was a reform party organized in 1947 by Eduardo Chibas and others, including Havana University law student Fidel Castro. Party leaders promised they would be true to the real or "orthodox" principles of Jose Marti. The party gained major popular support, and Castro intended to run on the Orthodox ticket for a seat in the Cuban legislature in the 1952 elections. These elections never took place because Fulgencio Batista staged a military takeover and established a dictatorship from 1952–1958, until it was overthrown by the Cuban Revolution.

Sanchez, Celia (1920–1980)

Celia Sanchez was a major participant and leader of the Cuban Revolution. One of her crucial tasks was to organize supplies and new volunteers from the Santiago area for Castro's guerrilla force in the nearby mountains. Later she joined Castro in the Sierra Maestra. After the revolution she became secretary to the presidency of the Council of Ministers and one of the key advisers and trusted friends of Fidel Castro for the rest of her life. Her death from cancer in 1980 was a major emotional blow to Fidel Castro and other leaders of the revolution, and may have contributed to the suicide of her friend and fellow revolutionary Haydee Santamaria later the same year.

Santamaria, Haydee (1922–1980)

Haydee Santamaria was an important participant in and leader of the revolution. After its victory she established and directed the Casa de las Americas, which provided a home and support for writers and artists fleeing the repression of right-wing dictatorships in their homelands. She participated in the July 26, 1953, attack on the Moncada barracks along with her brother Abel and her lover Boris, who were both tortured and executed. She and Celia Sanchez help bring journalists to Fidel Castro's mountain base to interview him and win international support for the revolution.

James DeFronzo

See Also Anarchism, Communism, and Socialism; Angolan Revolution; Chilean Socialist Revolution, Counter-Revolution, and the Restoration of Democracy; Cinema of Revolution; Colonialism, Anti-Colonialism, and Neo-Colonialism; Documentaries of Revolution; Guatemalan Democratic Revolution, Counter-Revolution, and Restoration of Democracy; Guerrilla Warfare and Revolution; Music and Revolution; Nationalism and Revolution; Nicaraguan Revolution; Salvadoran Revolution; South African Revolution; Student and Youth Movements, Activism and Revolution; Transnational Revolutionary Movements; Venezuelan Bolivarian Revolution of Hugo Chavez; Women and Revolution

References and Further Readings

Aguila, Juan M. 1988, 1994. *Cuba: Dilemmas of a Revolution.* Boulder, CO: Westview.

ANC. 1995. *Statement on Cuba's National Day by the African National Congress, 26, July, 1995.* Johannesburg: Department of Information and Publicity. http://www.hartford-hwp.com/archives/43b/025.html accessed June 12, 2005.

Anderson, Jon Lee. 1998. *Che Guevara: A Revolutionary Life.* New York: Grove/Atlantic.

Arreaza, Teresa. 2004. *ALBA: Bolivarian Alternative for Latin America and the Caribbean.* http://www.venezuelanalysis.com/docs.php?dno=1010 accessed June 19, 2005.

Brenner, Philip. 1988. *From Confrontation to Negotiation.* Boulder, CO: Westview.

Castro, Fidel. 1953. *History Will Absolve Me.* New York: Center for Cuban Studies.

Congressional Quarterly Researcher. 1991. "Cuba in Crisis." *Congressional Quarterly Researcher* 28: 897–920.

Debray, Regis. 1967. *Revolution in the Revolution.* New York: Monthly Review Press.

DeFronzo, James. 1991, 1996. *Revolutions and Revolutionary Movements.* Boulder, CO: Westview.

Dominguez, Jorge I. 1978. *Cuba: Order and Revolution.* Cambridge, MA: Harvard University Press.

Eckstein, Susan. 1986. "The Impact of the Cuban Revolution: A Comparative Perspective." *Contemporary Studies in Society and History* 28 (July): 502–534.

Feinsilver, Julie. 1993. "Can Biotechnology Save the Revolution?" *NACLA Report on the Americas* 26 (May): 7–10.

Flakus, Greg. 2005. *Chavez Establishes Oil Office in Havana.* http://www.voanews.com/english/2005–04–29-voa9 .cfm?renderforprint=1&textonly=&& accessed June 19, 2005.

Gleijeses, Piro. 1991. *Shattered Hope: The Guatemalan Revolution and the United States, 1944–1945,* Princeton, NJ: Princeton University Press.

Gott, Richard. 2000. *In the Shadow of the Liberator: Hugo Chavez and the Transformation of Venezuela.* London: Verso.

Guevara, Ernesto Che. 1968a. *Episodes of the Revolutionary War.* New York: International Publishers.

———. 1968b. *The Diary of Che Guevara.* New York: Bantam Books.

———. 1969a. *Guerilla Warfare.* New York: Vintage Press.

———. 1969b. *Che: Selected Works of Ernesto Guevara.* Edited by Roland E. Bonachea and Nelson P. Valdes. Cambridge, MA: M.I.T Press.

———. 2000. *The African Dream: The Diaries of the Revolutionary War in the Congo.* New York: Grove Press.

"On the Street Cubans Fondly Embrace Capitalism." *New York Times,* February 3, 1994, p. A4.

Oppenheim, Lois Hecht. 1993. *Politics in Chile.* Boulder, CO: Westview.

PBS Online News Hour Update. 2001, July 17, 3:10 p.m. EST. *Bush Renews Waiver of Helms-Burton Provision.*

PBS (Public Broadcasting Service). 1985. *Frontline: Crisis in Central America: Castro's Challenge.* http://www.pbs.org/ newshour/updates/july01/cuba_7–17.html accessed June 15, 2005.

Perez-Sable, Marifeli. 1993. *The Cuban Revolution.* New York: Oxford University Press.

Petras, James, and Fernando Ignacio Leiva. 1994. *Democracy and Poverty in Chile.* Boulder, CO: Westview.

Quirk, Robert. 1993. *Fidel Castro.* New York: Norton.

Rosset, Peter. 1994. "The Greening of Cuba." *NACLA Report on the Americas* 28 (November/December): 37–41.

Ruiz, Ramon Eduardo. 1968. *Cuba: The Making of a Revolution.* New York: Norton.

Schlesinger, Stephen, and Stephen Kinzer. 1982. *Bitter Fruit: The Untold Story of the American Coup in Guatemala.* Garden City, NY: Doubleday.

Siegelbaum, Portia. 2004. "UN Condemns U.S. Cuba Embargo." cbsnews.com www.cbsnews.com/stories/2004/11/30/world/main658417.sh tml accessed June 14, 2005.

Szulc, Tad. 1986. *Fidel: A Critical Portrait.* New York: Morrow.

Thomas, Hugh. 1977. *The Cuban Revolution.* New York: Harper and Row.

"U.N. Urges U.S. to End Ban on Cuba." *New York Times,* November 3, 1995, p. A8.

"U.S. Rejects Role for World Court in Trade Dispute." *New York Times,* February 21, 1997, p. A1.

Wolf, Eric R. 1969. *Peasant Wars of the Twentieth Century.* New York: Harper and Row.

Wyden, Peter. 1979. *Bay of Pigs: The Untold Story.* New York: Simon and Schuster.

D

Democracy, Dictatorship, and Fascism

Democracy, dictatorship, and Fascism are interrelated terms. The understanding of each contributes something to the understanding of the others.

DEMOCRACY

Democracy is a compendium of ideas as well as a system of governance. Characteristic democratic ideas include the belief in the importance and value of the individual and the enabling role of government in the pursuit of individual aspirations. Freedom, equality, the rule of law, government by popular consent with leaders responsible to the people—all these are characteristic watchwords of political democracy. Although many names are associated with all these notions in modern times—John Locke, Jean Jacques Rousseau, John Stuart Mill, among them—probably the most famous and important single sentence about the meaning of democracy comes from the pen of Thomas Jefferson in the 1776 American Declaration of Independence:

> We hold these Truths to be self-evident, that all Men are created equal, that they are endowed by their Creator with certain unalienable Rights, that among these are Life, Liberty and the Pursuit of Happiness—That to secure these Rights, Governments are instituted among Men, deriving their just Powers from the Consent of the Governed, that whenever any Form of Government becomes destructive of these Ends, it is the Right of the People to alter or to abolish it, and to institute new Government, laying its Foundation on such Principles, and organizing its Powers in such Form, as to them shall seem most likely to effect their Safety and Happiness.

As a system of governance, democracy traces its roots to the Greek city-states, several hundred years before the Christian era. In the relatively small communities of ancient Greece, democratic rule was carried out by assemblies of the people who all gathered in one place—a city square or field—and made whatever decisions they wished about the policies and rules to be followed by the whole community. Even in those earlier times, however, there were certain important qualifications on this seemingly simple and direct "rule by the people."

First of all, there was the issue of who was really part of the "people" for purposes of political decision making. Among those generally excluded were women, resident foreigners, persons held as slaves, and also children. The latter category always required—as it does to this day—an arbitrary definition of when it is that a person ceases to be a child. Furthermore, all the members of the "people" could not carry out all the possible duties that the government of the whole community—even then—might require. Older persons, or individuals with some disabilities, might be able to vote in an assembly, but they might not be able to serve as soldiers or guards, for example. Even in the small, ancient city-state there had to be some delegation of power from the "people" to designated executive agents, whose work would

Portrait of Thomas Jefferson, third president of the United States. Jefferson authored the Declaration of Independence and Virginia Statute of Religious Freedom. (Library of Congress)

be more continuous and who would exercise a degree of expertise not shared by everyone.

Finally, although each member of the people's assembly might possess a vote equal to that of every other member, this did not mean that each possessed an influence equal to that of any other. Persons who possessed oratorical skills, for example, were likely to be more influential with respect to what an assembly of the people might actually decide to do as opposed to people who lacked such skills. Reputation, appearance, wealth, and famous family connections gave some people far more influence than others. The qualifications on "democracy" in its simplest and oldest settings continue to be important for the modern, representative democracies of the twenty-first century.

Modern states such as the United States, Britain, Germany, Brazil, and India are much too large and complex to be governed by an assembly of all their citizens. They depend on representation, delegation, and accountability. Modern democracies typically operate through national elections in which citizens, through secret ballot and under conditions of personal freedom and security, periodically choose, either directly or through representatives, who shall constitute their government. This government makes policies, enacts laws, and oversees the day-to-day administration of the country.

Those who are elected by the people are held accountable, in part by (1) elections; if the voters are dissatisfied with the performance of those elected, they may punish them at the polls by denying them re-election. Democratic accountability also rests upon (2) the "rule of law," which means that all citizens, regardless of station, may be held responsible for whatever crimes or legal wrongs they may commit. (3) Oversight by the legislature is another important aspect of government accountability. In all the democracies, the power to dismiss the executive on a continuing—as opposed to periodic—basis is ultimately vested in the representatives of the people (legislature). This is most apparent in the so-called parliamentary systems where the vote of the legislature may remove the prime minister and his or her cabinet for whatever cause is deemed sufficient by the parliamentarians. In so-called presidential systems, however, like those of the United States and most states in Latin America, analogous legislative power is exercised, although with more procedural difficulty under more narrowly drawn provisions for impeachment.

Legislative oversight also includes the power of investigation and disclosure. Parliamentary or congressional inquiries and hearings, supported by the power of official subpoena and open to public revelation, are formidable weapons against actual or potential government misconduct. (Depending on their proximity to the election cycle, they can be especially troublesome to governments.)

Governments may also be held accountable in less dramatic ways by the degree of cooperation—or opposition—the legislature may display toward the executive's budgets, appointments, and legislative programs. For all practical purposes, a recalcitrant legislature may make an executive ineffectual.

An important way in which the power of government may be opposed and diminished in a democracy is by the simple expedient of (4) sustained public criticism. Prolonged, massive criticism and public attacks in the media, by word of mouth, and in public gatherings certainly have the potential of undermining public confidence in and support for government. They may also influence the outcome of upcoming elections. Democratic governments are naturally motivated to minimize such attacks on themselves. They much prefer praise to censure. This leads them to attempt to satisfy, so far as they can, demands emanating from their political environments—they try to be "responsive."

Unfortunately, this strategy does not necessarily and always make everyone happy. People sometimes strongly disagree on what it is that they value. Practically speaking, the meaning of *justice* and *fairness* is not self-evident. Giving A what he wants may make B quite dissatisfied, and vice versa.

DICTATORSHIP

Dictatorship is an alternative to democracy. In relatively pure or severe form, dictatorship is the negation of democracy in virtually every sense in which this term is defined above. Dictatorship connotes not the diffusion or dispersal of power to the whole body of a state's citizens, but rather its concentration in the hands of one or a few top leaders; the power of dictatorship is based on exclusion, rather than on inclusion; political decisions are made not only by a relative handful of people, but they are generally made in secrecy, often in an arbitrary fashion, without regard for law, due process, or widespread public consultation with those whom the policy might affect. Very importantly, dictatorship is based on the denial of a legally permissible way for the people to oppose the dictator. Denial is effected by the abolition of popular elections or the perversion of the electoral process, such as allowing elections but denying any real choice to voters, and resorting to massive fraud and coercion in order to exhibit false, allegedly unanimous—or near-unanimous—electoral support for the dictator or the dictator's party.

Dictatorship creates a situation in which if people are unhappy with its policies, they can only complain at the peril of their lives, their livelihoods, and even the safety of their families. A system in which citizens are not protected by the law in their persons, homes, and effects is generally likely to discourage all but the most desperate and intrepid from challenging the regime.

Dictatorship thus raises the costs of spontaneous political action just as democracy lowers them.

Given the values prevalent in American and most Western cultures, it may seem surprising that dictatorship has been, and continues to be, a significant alternative to democracy within the modern world community of nations. To many people, freedom may seem, as it did to Thomas Jefferson, a self-evident good and widespread popular participation in government the best possible way to manage the business of a community. However, the realities of world political systems have been frequently disappointing for proponents of democracy.

In his detailed 1992 study, political scientist Charles Humana reported on the political profiles of 104 countries, most of them members of the United Nations. Using forty analytical categories including multiparty elections by secret ballot, he evaluated these countries on a scale of one to one hundred, with higher scores effectively denoting more democracy, and lower scores reflecting less (Humana 1992, xvii–xix). Only twenty-three countries in Humana's survey equaled or exceeded the political qualities of the United States (score of 90). Twenty-one countries were below the U.S. score but closer to it than they were to the just dissolved Soviet Union. However,

fifty-nine countries—or 57 percent of Humana's total—were actually closer to the Soviet level than they were to the American, and some even had lower scores.

In considering the appeal—or rationale—of dictatorship, it is useful to focus on the performance aspects of political systems and the expectations of different constituencies with respect to such performance. By "performance," we mean the ability of a political system to carry out important functions of the state such as providing citizens with certain expected necessities, services, or opportunities to engage in life-sustaining economic activity or protection from criminal victimization. When we agree to share power with our neighbors and fellow citizens—which is what we do in a democracy—we cannot be indifferent to the uses to which such power may be put. If any significant component of the society has reason to fear the power of other components, democracy is in serious trouble. Dictatorship, in one version or another, may be seen as a desirable alternative by those who are either threatened or frustrated by the broadly inclusive, "sensitive," democratic political system. Unfortunately, such zero-sum alternatives do arise from time to time in various societies—some arise with respect to socioeconomic divisions, some with respect to ethnic divisions, some with respect to religious and cultural divisions.

For example, much of Latin America's historic and periodic difficulty in maintaining democratic governments has revolved around the fear of wholesale expropriation, the loss of land and other private property by the middle and upper classes at the hands of empowered, radicalized, and impoverished masses. This was an important element in the emergence of the dictatorship in Chile in 1973 under the leadership of General Augusto Pinochet. It was also an important concern in Italy before Mussolini's takeover in 1922, and in Germany in Hitler's ascent to power in 1933: the fear that democracy would open the door to a Communist or Communist-led revolutionary transformation of society in which the relatively privileged would lose their possessions and status, and, given the examples furnished by the Russian Revolution of 1917, perhaps even their lives, too.

The single most important reason why, after the "fall of Communism" in 1989, Yugoslavia did not follow the path of all-inclusive democratization—as had happened in Poland, Hungary, Romania, and Bulgaria—but instead erupted into bitterly contested civil wars, was ethnic conflict between the hitherto dominant Serbs, on the one hand, and Croats, Slovenians, Bosnians, Macedonians, and Albanians on the other.

Among religious-cultural causes of democratic failure, and the rise of a dictatorship consequent upon it, one of the most dramatic occurred in Spain in 1936, under its then democratic republic. The democratically elected majority at that time, the so-called Popular Front, was unwilling to

Francisco Franco overthrew the democratic republic of Spain in the Spanish Civil War (1936–1939). He ruled Spain until his death in 1975. (Library of Congress)

sanction a place in Spanish society for the Catholic Church, which it viewed as reactionary, obstructionist, an ally of the rich, and an opponent of social progress. By its rhetoric, legislation, and conduct (seemingly tolerant of the killing of priests and the burning of churches), the democratically elected Spanish government deeply offended and alienated millions of Spaniards, most of them actually quite poor. These people provided an important base of popular support and military volunteers for General Francisco Franco's rising against the republic in 1936–1939 and one of the critical foundations of his nearly forty-year dictatorship.

Beyond the problem of division, democracy confronts the issue of competence. Many democracies have proved that they can govern themselves very effectively over long periods of time. Certainly countries such as the United States, Sweden, and Switzerland have shown this to be feasible. But the matter is hardly axiomatic. If there are many fractures in the body politic causing people difficulty in agreeing on any policies, whatever they might be, and encouraging chaotic protests, strikes, demonstrations, land seizures, and the proverbial "specter of anarchy," some people—many people—are likely to feel a sense of frustra-

tion, a yearning for order, security, and for peace and quiet in the streets. It is situations such as these that create the demand for dictatorial power.

Contemporary German historian Joachim Fest observed with respect to Hitler: "After the Weimar confusion, people yearned for the return of the many German 'punctualities' they had missed for fourteen unbearably long years" (Fest 2004, 38).

FASCISM

Among its several meanings, Fascism is a blueprint for dictatorship—of a certain kind. It is also a compendium of several fundamental principles, with what may be termed "local modifications." (The reader should keep in mind that the more locales, the more modifications—precisely the reason why general definitions are difficult.) One of its principles is the primacy of the national community, which is seen as the critical civilization-creating and -maintaining entity. In Fascism, the individual is transitory and ephemeral; the nation is significant and enduring.

Fascist nationalism is linked to xenophobia, that is, profound hostility to foreigners and all those who, although they might be citizens or residents of the "nation," are not seen as truly or genuinely belonging to the *real* national community. Such people might be immigrants, for example, or naturalized citizens, or those belonging to marginalized minorities (in the United States, African Americans, Hispanic Americans, Jews, and Catholics have often filled this role.) Nazi racism, with Germans at the top of the racial pyramid, was an extreme illustration of the tendency. So was rabid anti-Semitism. (In the Italian case, Jews were persecuted only from 1938 onwards as Mussolini opportunistically attempted to align himself more closely with Hitler's Nazism.) All nationalist movements are concerned about protecting, maintaining, and extending a core identity. For many of them language, religion, customs, or political loyalties may be more important than physical-biological traits or "race." That was the situation in Italy until 1938.

Fascism is hostile to cosmopolitanism, internationalism, globalism, and regionalism because all these are seen as opposed to or subversive of the nation. Fascism is analogously hostile to democracy and socialism because these ideologies are seen as promoting class warfare and domestic conflict. Democracy glorifies individualism, and socialism sees society in terms of classes; each, therefore, undermines national unity and power.

Nationalism and xenophobia are joined in Fascism with authoritarianism. The savior of the nation must be a strong leader who will combat chaos and division within the national community and guide it to greatness, characteristically through internal cohesion as well as external empire and conquest. Leaders are generally extolled and their power glorified. In the Fascist view, politics, and life more generally, is seen in social Darwinist terms, as a pitiless struggle for survival in which the strong must prevail and the weak must perish. Fascism tends to be contemptuous of human rationality and glorifies the use of force and coercion in social relations, whether they are domestic or international.

Fascism is also a somewhat contradictory combination of radical populism and socioeconomic conservatism. The populism is expressed partly in Fascism's organizational outreach to the masses of the people. Fascism promotes political parties aimed at the participation of all social strata. Combined with various auxiliaries, such as mass youth and labor groups, these organizations serve as transmission mechanisms for the Fascist message and are links between "leader" and "people." Fascist organizations, however, are not deliberative or consultative bodies; they are quasi-military in nature. In terms of economic and social ideals, Fascism is also populist in its attacks on capitalist exploitation of workers and farmers, but this is always balanced by denunciations of Communists and Socialists for their allegedly anti-national, destructive activities and objectives. Fascism characteristically promises to rectify free-market capitalist "disorder" and "excesses" by state oversight and regulation of the economy ("in the interest of the nation") and by expanded welfare measures analogously directed to the same ends.

Fascist populism, however, is always balanced (some would say compromised) by its reactionary alliances. Regulatory rhetoric notwithstanding, Fascism has generally defended private property and profit. Fascist movements and leaders have characteristically cultivated as allies important status quo elites in the societies within which they have hoped to establish power or in which they actually succeeded in achieving it. Culturally, Fascism has always tended to look approvingly on the past and very much askance at modernist and avant-garde trends.

Much of our understanding of Fascism derives from the actual experience of the Hitler and Mussolini regimes, from 1933 to 1945 in Germany and from 1922 to 1943 in Italy. Hitler admired Mussolini, whose success predated his own movement and regime, and he adopted various aspects of Italian Fascism, including its characteristic military dress and salute. In each case, the Fascist or Nazi party became the sole political party in the state; all others were prohibited. In each case, the political party created mass youth organizations (most famously the Hitler Jugend in Germany, Balilla in Italy), which became recruiting tools for their adult counterparts and a means for socializing the youth in the values and ideals of Fascists and Nazis. Propaganda and terror networks were enormously expanded. All legitimate media came under Nazi and Fascist scrutiny, management, and coordination—newspapers, magazines, radio, films, book publishing, and virtually all forms of live entertainment. Dissent became a crime against the state. In each case, police forces could, in effect, arrest, detain, and even kill people without any reference to laws or regular courts, although terror was considerably more severe and ruthless in Germany than in Italy. In Germany, part of Hitler's terror apparatus involved so-called concentration camps, where anyone considered hostile, dangerous, or undesirable could be incarcerated, wholly at the mercy of the regime's policemen.

Despite some early slogans about national welfare replacing the class struggle, both Hitler and Mussolini were, at best, indifferent to redistributive social change. Independent trade unions were taken over by the state and deprived of all their powers. Fascism and Nazism identified themselves distinctly with male chauvinism. The position of women in society, in various fields, and especially in public life, was significantly diminished. Women's place was said to be in the home and in the nursery. Men's work was, at its best, behind a rifle. No efforts were made to improve access to higher education for the poor and the relatively disadvantaged. The larger business firms were seemingly secured through the new corporationist economic organizations (allegedly bringing together business, labor, and government in various industrial or economic associations, but more frequently promoting business-party collusion). The burden of taxation fell more heavily on the poorer strata.

What Fascism and Nazism also accomplished, however, was to bring order and quiet to the streets, a certain important sense of outward stability at whatever price it may have been purchased. By and large, trains did run on time. Life was pleasantly predictable—for most people. Especially during massive rearmament in Germany and Italy in the 1930s, high levels of employment with opportunities for overtime pay also became one of the observable aspects of Fascist rule. State-operated welfare programs, however mixed and modest in actual benefits, received a lot of publicity.

Finally, there were many intangible gratifications for the masses. One of these was the chance to "belong"—to the all-powerful, victorious party and to its feeder auxiliaries. One could march with the Leader. And there was also the satisfaction one could have about the country's seemingly enhanced status as a "great power," apparently always moving toward ever greater conquests and world prestige.

Prior to their seizures of power, both Mussolini and Hitler carefully cultivated their connections to industrialists, landowners, the military, aristocrats, and bureaucrats. The cooperation and support of these elements were important to them in the process of achieving ultimate control of the state. In both cases, the willingness of the armed forces to stand aside for the purpose of enabling Mussolini and Hitler to seize and consolidate power was critical. During the Second World War, as defeats mounted, these domestic alliances began to strain and unravel, culminating in the overthrow of Mussolini in 1943 and the anti-Hitler conspiracy of 1944.

Both Hitler and Mussolini succeeded in recruiting followers from virtually all social strata. But in relative terms, that is, in proportion to the size of each class or category of participant, Fascist movements tended to be more upper class, middle class, and lower middle class (as opposed to working class) compared to their political competitors on the Communist and Socialist left.

Alexander J. Groth

See Also African American Freedom Struggle; American Revolution; Chilean Socialist Revolution, Counter-Revolution, and the Restoration of Democracy; Chinese 1989 Democracy Movement; Chinese Revolution; Cinema of Revolution; Cuban Revolution; Documentaries of Revolution; East European Revolutions of 1989; European Revolutions of 1848; French Revolution; Guatemalan Democratic Revolution, Counter-Revolution, and Restoration of Democracy; Haiti's Democratic Revolution; Human Rights, Morality, Social Justice, and Revolution; Italian Fascist Revolution; Japanese New Order Movement; Nazi Revolution: Politics and Racial Hierachy; Paris Commune of 1871; Philippines: The 'People Power' Revolution of 1986; Polish Solidarity Movement; Population, Economic Development, and Revolution; Russian Revolution of 1917; Russian Revolution of 1991 and the Dissolution of the U.S.S.R.; South African Revolution; Spanish Revolution and Counter-Revolution; South Korean Democracy Movement; Student and Youth Movements, Activism and Revolution; Transnational Revolutionary Movements; Trends in Revolution; Women's Movement of the United States

References and Further Readings

Cob, A. 1939. *Dictatorship: Its History and Theory.* New York: Scribner's.

Fest, J. 2004. *Inside Hitler's Bunker: The Last Days of the Reich.* New York: Farrar, Strauss and Giroux.

Friedrich, C., and Z. Brzezinski. 1965. *Totalitarian Dictatorship and Autocracy.* Cambridge, MA: Harvard University Press.

Groth, A. 1964. "The Isms in Totalitarianism," *American Political Science Review* 58: 888–901.

———. 1971. *Comparative Politics: A Distributive Approach.* New York: Macmillan.

Hamilton, R. F. 1982. *Who Voted for Hitler?* Princeton, NJ: Princeton University Press.

Humana, C. 1992. *World Human Rights Guide.* New York: Oxford University Press.

Linz, J. 2000. *Totalitarian and Authoritarian Regimes.* Boulder, CO: Lynne Rienner Publishers.

Lipset, S. M. 1965. *Political Man: The Social Basis of Politics.* Garden City, NY: Anchor Books.

Mayo, H. B. 1960. *An Introduction to Democratic Theory.* New York: Oxford University Press.

Payne, S. 1995. *A History of Fascism, 1914–1945.* Madison: University of Wisconsin Press.

Rabb, T. K., and E. N. Sulemain. 2003. *The Making and Unmaking of Democracy: Lessons from History and World Politics.* New York: Routledge.

Salvemini, G. 1967. *The Fascist Dictatorship in Italy.* New York: H. Fertig.

Schoenbaum, D. 1966. *Hitler's Social Revolution: Class and Status in Nazi Germany.* Garden City, NY: Doubleday.

Schweitzer, A. 1964. *Big Business in the Third Reich.* Bloomington: Indiana University Press.

Documentaries of Revolution

Throughout most of history, revolutions could only be understood or studied through the written or oral accounts of participants or witnesses and the literature, music, and works of art of the revolutionary periods. During the nineteenth century, photographs of leaders and followers provided an additional exciting dimension. In the twentieth century, new technologies permitted motion picture and then also audio recordings of actual events. Film and video documentaries have become a common and useful medium for learning about major social movements and associated social conflicts.

Beyond serving as an additional source of information, documentaries can bring us much closer to the subject matter. Through film, a student of revolution can follow a movement from its birth, viewing the emergence of the leaders and groups involved, hearing crucial speeches and explanations of ideals and goals as well as expressions of the feelings and thoughts of participants, witnessing the social environment that fostered the movement, and experiencing the successes and failures of revolutionaries. Documentaries can provide comprehensive descriptions of the social backgrounds of important revolutionary leaders. They can identify the events that influenced the leaders' lives, investigate why they became revolutionaries and how they rose to positions of leadership, and provide explanations of their key roles and contributions. They can also describe the influence leaders have had on their peoples, whether they were successful in achieving their ideals or original goals, and how they responded to expected or unforeseen challenges.

A recent documentary biography of Lenin, for example, describes how his gifted older brother, a brilliant university science student, became involved in a plot to assassinate Czar Alexander III, refused to ask for mercy, and was executed with several of his comrades when he was only twenty-one and his younger brother Lenin was seventeen. Undoubtedly this experience played a major role in shaping Lenin's unwavering commitment to revolution. Another documentary describes how French colonial persecution resulted in the deaths of the father, sister, and daughter of

Vo Nguyen Giap, who would one day turn the knowledge gained from his study of history and military tactics to the creation of Vietnam's revolutionary Viet Minh army. Giap's forces overcame the French at the Battle of Dien Bien Phu in April–May of 1954, the first time a revolutionary army defeated the armed forces of a colonizing power in a major battle since the American revolutionary army forced the surrender of the British at Yorktown.

Other documentaries describe the revolutionaries' initial attempts to free their people through peaceful means, such as Ho Chi Minh's optimistic effort to present the victorious Allied leaders with a proposal for Vietnamese self-rule at the 1919 Paris Peace Conference after World War I, or Nelson Mandela's leadership in the 1952 civil disobedience Defiance Campaign against South Africa's policies of racially segregated social and commercial facilities. In reaction to the failure of peaceful methods, Ho and his associates turned to an armed struggle against occupying foreign forces, a strategy that resulted in the deaths of over three million Vietnamese between 1941 and 1975. Nelson Mandela and his comrades also reacted to the failure of nonviolent methods and the continued brutal and institutional repression of South Africa's non-European peoples by resorting to revolutionary warfare. In 1961 the African National Congress, together with its ally, the South African Communist Party, created the armed revolutionary force Umkhonto we Sizwe ("the Spear of the Nation"), eventually led by Chris Hani, the future chairperson of the South African Communist Party who was assassinated by white extremists in 1993. As documentaries on Mandela indicate, he and many of his associates were arrested and sentenced to life in prison as terrorists for opposing South Africa's apartheid system. Both Ho Chi Minh and Nelson Mandela were the targets of dehumanizing propaganda efforts by the powerful states that attempted to crush the revolutions they led. But documentaries now available give us a fuller understanding of their lives, motivations, and struggles to supplement what we can learn from books.

Documentaries about revolutionary leaders include those on Latin Americans, such as Cuba's Fidel Castro, the Argentine Che Guevara, Chile's Salvador Allende, and Venezuela's Hugo Chavez. Middle Eastern film biographies have been produced on relative secularists, such as Yasser Arafat and Saddam Hussein, and on revolutionaries asserting more prominently religious inspiration, such as Ayatollah Khomeini and Osama bin Laden. Besides biographies on Asian revolutionaries such as Mao Zedong and Ho Chi Minh, others describe the lives of a spectrum of figures as different as Pol Pot and Gandhi.

Issues of importance to the large masses of people are depicted in documentaries. These include factors such as foreign oppression and exploitation; racial discrimination; war;

poverty; inequality; joblessness; and ideological, religious, and moral concerns. For example, the apparently first-ever documentary of a revolution, *Russian Revolution: Czar to Lenin,* depicted the misery, mass slaughter, and demoralization of millions of peasant and worker Russian soldiers, incompetently sent to war by the czar's regime, and how the survivors became committed to revolutionary change. *China: Century of Revolution* shows the grinding poverty of China's poor peasants before the revolution, the corruption of the Manchu dynasty, and the privileges enjoyed by the many Europeans who controlled much of the country before the revolutionary struggles led first by Sun Yat-Sen and then later by Mao. Other documentaries on China portray the devastating moral consequences of foreign exploitation, such as the many millions of opium addicts created in great part by the victory of the British in the Opium Wars starting in 1839 and the resulting expansion of British opium trade in China, and the recruitment of tens of thousands of young Chinese girls as prostitutes for European residents and tourists.

Common themes of documentaries on revolution include the description of one group's struggle in a movement, such as *Jackets Green,* about the Irish Republicans. Relying on the documentary camera to convey the cause of the Irish Republicans allows the viewer to see the situation from a different perspective than that portrayed in the corporate news media, which has often been biased against revolutionaries and historically shallow or incomplete. Differing perspectives can be presented, as in *People and The Land,* showing the views of both Israelis and Palestinians in one documentary. The close positioning of opposing perspectives often provides an opportunity to make enlightening comparisons.

In some cases, instead of describing the lives of major revolutionary leaders, one otherwise typical person may be the subject of an entire documentary, such as in *Discovering Dominga,* about a Guatemalan woman's return to her country after living for years as a refugee. The film follows her experiences in Guatemala as she learns about the violent history she escaped as a child. This type of work explores specific aspects of the social conditions, the movement, and the ensuing conflict by portraying an individual's story.

The camera can capture certain crucial events in a revolution and convey the attitudes, shock, excitement, anger, or desperation felt at that moment. A video camera, for example, recorded the murder of ABC newsman Bill Stewart by soldiers of Somoza's Nicaraguan National Guard, thus drastically shifting U.S. popular and congressional support away from his regime and facilitating the victory of the Sandinista-led revolutionaries. Video cameras captured the killings and woundings of dozens of civilian demonstrators on the steps of El Salvador's national cathedral by soldiers in the country's armed forces. Cameras also recorded the pleas of Archbishop Oscar Romero, leader of the Catholic Church in El Salvador, to U.S. President Carter not to send more weapons to the El Salvadoran army because these weapons were being used to commit crimes against innocent people, as well as the archbishop's appeals to soldiers in the El Salvadoran army to refuse orders to carry out such acts. The documentary depiction of these events, rapidly followed by the politically motivated assassination of the archbishop, conveys the emotions provoked by these dramatic incidents to a wide public, including students, richly enhancing written historical accounts.

One of the most beneficial aspects of documentaries as a learning medium is the proximity the viewer often feels to the people and places shown in the film. Footage of the land connects the viewer with the terrain and ecology that gave birth to a movement and that helped shape the psychology and life experiences of the people. Images of trucks or armored vehicles filled with men armed with guns and whips rolling down streets to intimidate or eliminate people on behalf of a ruling oligarchy trigger strong reactions. Watching soldiers jump out of the vehicles and chase unarmed demonstrators, beating or shooting the persons they encounter, stirs fiery emotions. Hearing women's and men's mourning cries as they wail over their fallen friends, lovers, and children burns the spirit and enrages the mind. These responses bring emotional reality to the historical facts in *Mandela's Fight For Freedom* (1995), a film which follows Nelson Mandela's journey as a leader through prison to the presidency of post-apartheid South Africa. The footage demonstrates the outrageous tactics used by the white leadership in South Africa to maintain the apartheid system. Listening to pro-apartheid officials make statements about the violence of the revolutionaries—after seeing their soldiers use aggressive brutality against unarmed protestors—serves as an example to the viewer of how regime propaganda can operate to smear opponents in an attempt to protect an unjust and immoral system. In this way, documentaries can serve to educate people not only about history, but also about the realities of oppression.

Documentaries about South Africa provide an important example of how films can affect world opinion in ways that help determine the success or failure of revolutions. *End of the Dialogue* (1970), for example, exposed the inhumane realities of apartheid to the world. In damaging the regime's ability to manipulate global opinion, this film and others like it contributed significantly to the eventual success of the revolution. The peoples of many nations, informed by documentaries on apartheid, pressured their governments into imposing economic restrictions on trade with or investment in South Africa, which helped to bring about a democratic political system there.

As increasing numbers of people have access to recording equipment, making documentaries is becoming more common. Providing this technology to those living under oppressive regimes is a new branch of peace work, enabling people to capture reality and show it to millions in other nations, with the hope of replicating the process that contributed to the end of apartheid. Internationally the camera has become a useful and crucial tool in fighting oppression. In places such as East Timor, where people have had little or no access to public media to express their opinions, the camera has been important in educating the rest of the world. Oppression of the East Timorese has been extremely severe. They have been the victims of environmental resources abuse, violence, and murder. Only international intervention and assistance had the potential to protect and improve the well-being of the East Timorese, who in the past had only limited access to weapons for self-defense. A better-informed international community, in part created through the effects of documentaries, has put increasing pressure on Indonesia's military to reduce violence against East Timor's people. This result provides another demonstration of the power of world opinion educated and shaped in part through effective documentaries, the significance of the disapproval of other governments, and the possibilities for free peoples to affect human rights around the globe.

Many documentaries aim at breaking through the mainstream perception of a conflict or revolution. A camera has no inherent bias regarding whether an armed person should be viewed as a revolutionary fighting for democracy or social justice, or instead be labeled a terrorist. The camera has the potential to honestly portray a person's story if used without the weight of preconceived opinion.

Ironically, the government of the United States, a nation born from a revolution seeking freedom from Great Britain, has often portrayed revolutionary movements among other peoples as unjustified and repeatedly intervened openly or covertly to repress them, sometimes in the defense of imperialist powers, dictatorships, monarchies or fake democracies whose rule was far harsher than that of the British against whom Americans rebelled in 1775. This portrayal has often been accomplished through pressure on the news media or control of information available to news media. For example, years after the event, the CBS *60 Minutes* report on the massacre at El Mozote revealed that it was El Salvadoran government forces supported by the Reagan administration, in disregard of the pleas of the by-then-murdered Archbishop Romero, who had brutally slaughtered more than 700 unarmed men, women, and children as a way of discouraging support for revolutionaries. The Reagan administration, supposedly committed to fighting terrorism, seemed unconcerned with investigating this act of incredible barbarity by those whom it had armed and financially assisted; instead, pro-Reagan elements in the press attacked the credibility of the *New York Times* and *Washington Post* reporters who dared to report objectively on the massacre.

Beyond describing the social conditions, ideologies, precipitating events, leaders, processes, and histories of revolutionary struggles, as well as the efforts to repress them, documentaries can also describe what happens once a revolution achieves victory over the pre-revolutionary regime. Documentaries on revolutions as diverse and separated in time as the French Revolution, the Russian Revolution of 1917, the Cuban Revolution of the 1950s, the Nicaraguan and Iranian Revolutions of the 1970s, and the Polish Solidarity Revolution of the 1980s have recorded post-victory events. Once a widely opposed regime is overthrown—such as the czar's rule, or the Iranian shah's dictatorship, or the Communist Party monopoly of government in Poland—the revolutionary alliance of groups, often with opposing ideologies and divergent plans for the development of the post-revolution society, usually falls apart. A competition for leadership and power takes place. Documentaries on the lives of Stalin and Trotsky typically describe the struggle between these two men, their supporters, and several other prominent Bolsheviks for control of the revolution after the death of Lenin in 1924. The victory of Stalin, a paranoid man whose psychology reflected a violent upbringing and an alcohol-abusing father, shaped the outcome of the Russian Revolution and created the brutal, bureaucratic, elitist Stalinist state feared by Trotsky and many others.

Documentaries on the Iranian Revolution, as well as the biographical documentary on Ayatollah Khomeini, also illustrate the phenomenon of post-revolution conflict. In Iran, Shia Islamic fundamentalists; Shia modernists, such as the Islamic Liberation Movement and the Iranian Mujahidin; secular democratic groups, such as the National Front; and Marxist organizations, such as the Tudeh and the Fedeyeen, forged a desperate coalition to oust the shah and his much-feared army and secret police force, the SAVAK (Sazman-e Amniyat Va Ittilaat-e Keshvar or Organization of National Security and Intelligence). But no sooner had the shah fled than the struggle for control of the revolution's fate intensified. Since the Shia fundamentalists, in comparison to the other revolutionary groups, had the only nationwide (rural and urban) network among the people, by far the largest revolutionary militia, the Islamic Revolutionary Guard, and also enjoyed the advantage that the central revolutionary leader was the Shia fundamentalist Ayatollah Ruhollah Khomeini, the fundamentalist clergy triumphed over other groups in the revolutionary alliance and installed the Vilayat-e Faqih principle, the political rule of a selected top clerical leader (Khomeini, until his death in 1989).

Valuable documentaries also exist that depict the post-revolution policies of other nations toward a revolutionary society. For example, *Forgotten Wars* deals in part with U.S.

military intervention in the Russian civil war following the 1917 revolution. *Americas in Transition* and Public Broadcasting's *Yankee Years* cover a number of examples of foreign intervention, including the U.S. role in the overthrow of Guatemala's elected reform government in 1954. An episode of the Turner CNN Cold War Series describes the Soviet suppression of the 1956 Hungarian Revolution. *Castro's Challenge* includes coverage of the CIA-orchestrated Bay of Pigs invasion in 1961. *Vietnam: A Television History* covers the years of U.S. involvement there. *CIA: Executive Action,* part of the Time Machine Series, interviews CIA agents who attempted to assassinate Fidel Castro, others involved in the capture and execution of Che Guevara in Bolivia, and the role the U.S. played in helping to destabilize Chile's elected government (destroyed in the military repression of September 11, 1973). Public TV's *War on Nicaragua* describes the Reagan administration's "low intensity war" efforts against Sandinista-led Nicaragua. *Secret Government* depicts, in part, the Iran-Contra operation involving U.S. policies toward both the Nicaraguan and Iranian revolutionary governments. Various films about El Salvador, including *Enemies of War* and *El Salvador,* demonstrate the effects of the use of U.S. tax dollars to prevent revolutionary success.

Documentaries, being the product of human efforts, are susceptible to bias. Those who support a revolution have often produced documentaries glorifying a revolution's achievements or its leaders' virtues while ignoring or glossing over its failures, repressive policies, or even betrayals of original revolutionary ideals or goals. This tendency can be seen in some of the early documentaries on the Cuban Revolution, which often minimized problems associated with Castro's regime. Other documentaries have been produced by persons opposing revolution and have often manifested an opposite tendency of vilifying revolutionary leaders and ignoring the positive achievements of revolutionary governments.

In general, surveys of existing documentaries on the topics mentioned above indicate a discernible tendency over time toward more balance, accuracy, and comprehensiveness. Relatively recent documentaries aired by Public Broadcasting, the History Channel, the Arts and Entertainment Network, and the Discovery Channel generally seem to display minimal bias, with a few exceptions.

Liberty, social justice, and equality of opportunity are ideals for which people around the world continue to strive. All people should understand the struggles and conflicts of the past and how they continue today in order to appreciate the achievements thus far and the challenges still to be confronted and overcome. It is important to uphold the positive ideals of revolutionary movements while also comprehending the fears and reactions of those threatened by these movements. Documentaries can be an essential aspect of this process.

The following list is a collection of documentaries on revolutionary movements and related topics in many parts of the world. It is far from complete, due in part to space limitations, but an effort has been made to include many of the most important, useful, and accessible documentaries. In most cases the source from which teachers, students, or other interested persons can obtain the films, videos, or DVDs is indicated (see source list on page 203). Additional sources for documentaries on revolutions include university or college film libraries and organizations dedicated to various social issues, including human rights.

DOCUMENTARY LIST

Afghanistan Revolution (1978–)

Afghanistan: The Lost Truth. 2003. 64 min. (Afghan people after the Taliban government.) – WMM.

Afghanistan Unveiled. 2003. 52 min. (Afghan women after the Taliban government.) – WMM.

Soldiers of God. (Islamic revolutionists in Iran in the late 1970s and in Afghanistan in the 1980s.) – CNN Cold War Series, episode 20.

Algerian Islamic Revolt (1992–)

Algeria: Women at War. 1992. 52 min. (Algerian women's participation in the independence struggle.) – WMM.

Algeria's Bloody Years. 2003. 59 min. (Algeria since independence and through the Islamic Revolt.) – FRIF.

Rachida. 2002. 100 min. (Women threatened by and resisting extremist violence in Algeria.) – FRIF.

Algerian Revolution (1954–1962)

100 Years of Terror: Wars against Colonialism. 200 min. Section on Algerian Revolution, 50 min. – AETV.

American Revolution (1775–1789)

The American Revolution. 482 min. (Five-volume set of ten documentaries: DVD.) – HC or AETV.

The American Revolution. 300 min. (VHS) – HC.

Benedict Arnold. 50 min. (His war career and his switch to the British side.) – BIO.

Benjamin Franklin. 2002. 210 min. 3 parts. (Franklin's life from Boston to Philadelphia to France.) – PBS.

Benjamin Franklin: Citizen of the World. 50 min. (Based on Franklin's writing.) – BIO.

Benjamin Franklin: Founding Brother. 300 min. – HC.

Founding Brothers. 200 min. (Washington, Franklin, Hamilton, Jefferson, Adams, Madison, and Burr.) – HC.

Founding Fathers. 200 min. (Leaders of the American Revolution.) – HC.

Founding Mothers. 50 min. (Women in the American Revolution.) – AETV.

Freedom: A History of the U.S: Fighting for Freedom. 90 min. (The Revolutionary War as the beginning of a long fight for freedom in the United States.) – PBS.

George Washington: American Revolutionary. 50 min. – BIO.

George Washington: Founding Father. 50 min. (Youth to inauguration.) – BIO.

George Washington Remembers. (Based on his autobiography.) – PBS.

John and Abigail Adams. 50 min. – BIO.

Liberty! The American Revolution. 400+ min. (Re-creation of the events leading up to the revolution.) – PBS.

Patrick Henry: Voice of Liberty. 50 min. (Includes parts of speeches and writings.) –BIO.

Paul Revere: The Midnight Rider. 50 min. – BIO.

POWs of the American Revolution. 100 min. – HC.

Thomas Jefferson. 1996. 200 min. Ken Burns film. – PBS.

Thomas Jefferson. 50 min. – BIO

Valley Forge. 50 min. – HC.

Angolan Revolution (1974–)

Chain of Tears. 1989. 50 min. (The effects of war and violence on children in Angola, Mozambique, and South Africa.) – SAMC.

Good Guys, Bad Guys. 46 min. (Cold War conflict in the Third World, including Angola.) – CNN Cold War Series, episode 17.

Arab Nationalist Revolution (1916–1918)

Lawrence of Arabia. 50 min. (Briton who helped in Arab overthrow of Ottoman rule.) – BIO.

Brazil

Americas. Number 2: *Capital Sins: Authoritarianism and Democratization.* 1993. 60 min. (Problems and development in Brazil.) – Americas Series.

The Comrade: The Life of Luiz Carlos Prestes. 1997. 105 min. (About a famous Brazilian revolutionary and related struggles for social change in Brazil.) – FRIF.

Key to codes of sources for purchase or rental of documentaries

AETV (Arts and Entertainment Television (includes History Channel): *www.aetv.com*

AFSC (American Friends Service Committee): *www.afsc.org/resources/video-film.htm*

Amazon: *www.amazon.com*

BIO: *www.biography.com* or through AETV.

BU: Boston University

BUYIN: *buyindies.com*

CNR: California Newsreel: *www.newsreel.org*

CWU: Central Washington University Library Media Services: *www.lib.cwu.edu/media*

DCTV (Discovery Times Channel): *www.dctvny.org*

DEL: Del Canton: *www.delcanton.com*

FF: Faction Films: *www.factionfilms.co.uk*

Filmakers: *www.filmakers.com*

FRIF: First Run Icarus Films: *www.frif.com*

HC: History Channel: *www.historychannel.com*

Indie: *www.indiedocs.com*

ISU: Iowa State University Media Resource Center: *www.lib.iastate.edu*

ITVS: Independent Television Service: *www.itvs.org*

IU: Indiana University: *www.dlib.indiana.edu*

KSU: Kent State University Audio Visual Services: *www.kentlink.kent.edu*

NAATA: National Asian American Telecommunications Association: *www.capaa.wa.gov/naata.html*

PBS: Public Television Service: *www.pbs.org*

POV: Point of View, under PBS: *www.pbs.org/pov*

PSU: Pennsylvania State University Audio Visual Services: *www.medianet.libraries.psu.edu*

PTTV: Paper Tiger Television: *www.papertiger.org*

PU: Purdue University Audio Visual Center: *www.lib.purdue.edu*

PVS: Public Video Store: *www.publicvideostore.org*

SAMC: Southern African Media Center, Resolution Inc./California Newsreel: *www.newsreel.org*

SEG: Sterling Entertainment Group: *www.sterlingentertainmentgroup.com*

SUN: Sunrise Media LLC: *www.sunrisemedia.tv/films*

SUNY-B: State University of New York at Buffalo

SYRU: Syracuse University Film Rental Center *http://libwww.syr.edu/information/media/film/main.htm*

UARIZ: University of Arizona Film Library: *www.library.arizona.edu*

UC-B: University of California/Berkeley, Extension Media Center: *www.lib.berkeley.edu/MRC*

UI: University of Illinois/Urbana: *www.library.uiuc.edu*

UIOWA: University of Iowa Audiovisual Center: *www.uiowa.edu/~avcenter*

UMINN: University of Minnesota Audio Visual Services: *www.classroom.umn.edu/cts/avrental*

UMISSOURI: University of Missouri/Columbia Academic Support Center: *www.missouri.edu/~ascwww*

UMONT: University of Montana Instructional Materials Services: *www.libcat.lib.umt.edu*

UNEVR: University of Nevada/Reno, Film Library: *www.innopac.library.unr.edu/search/X*

USF: University of Southern Florida, Film Library: *www.lib.usf.edu*

UT-A: University of Texas/Austin, Film Library: *www.lib.utexas.edu*

UT-D: University of Texas at Dallas, Media Services: *www.utdallas.edu/library*

UWASH: University of Washington Instructional Media Services: *www.lib.washington.edu*

UWISC-L: University of Wisconsin/Lacrosse Audiovisual Center

UWISC-M: University of Wisconsin/Madison Bureau of Audio-Visual Instruction: *www.library.wisc.edu*

UWY: University of Wyoming Audio Visual Services: *www-lib.uwyo.edu/uwlibs/av.htm*

WMM: Women Make Movies: *www.wmm.com*

WSU: Washington State University: *www.wsulibs.wsu.edu*

Cambodian Khmer Revolution (1967–1979)

Cambodia: Return to Year Zero. 1993. 60 min. (UN Cambodian Peace Plan.) – AFSC.

From the Killing Fields. 1990. 50 min. (With Peter Jennings; civil war in Cambodia and U.S. involvement.) – AFSC.

Pol Pot. 50 min. (The life of the Khmer Rouge leader.) – BIO.

Pol Pot's Shadow. 2002. 60 min. (Searching for an executioner.) – PBS (Frontline).

The Road from Kampuchea. 1998. 44 min. (A disabled Cambodian attempts to aid other Cambodians.) – FRIF.

S21: The Khmer Rouge Killing Machine. 2002. 105 min. (Revisiting Cambodia with survivors and former guards.) – FRIF.

Year Zero: The Silent Death of Cambodia. 1979. 60 min. (Rise to power of the Khmer Rouge and consequences.) – AFSC.

Chechen Revolutionary Movement (1994–)

Terror Strikes Moscow. 2003. 50 min. (Chechen extremists take 800 people hostage at a Moscow theater.) – HC.

Chilean Democratic Socialist Movement and Counter-Revolution (1970–)

Americas. Number 5. *In Women's Hands: The Changing Roles of Women.* 1993. 60 min. (Women's roles and efforts in Chile during the rule of General Pinochet.) – Americas Series.

Battle for Chile. 1976. 184 min. (b/w) (Parts 1 and 2: The efforts at peaceful social revolution and the violent overthrow of the elected government and democracy in 1973.) – FRIF.

Chile: Hasta Cuando? 1987. 57 min. (The overthrow of Allende, mostly documenting Pinochet's violent oppression.) – Filmakers.

Chile, Obstinate Memory. 1997. 58 min. (Chile years after the military takeover.) – FRIF.

CIA—The Secret Files: Part 3 Executive Action. 45 min. (Describes CIA willingness to take action against foreign leaders, including Castro, Guevara, and the Allende government in Chile; includes interviews with CIA officials and agents as well as Cuban counterintelligence.) – Time Machine.

Don't Threaten Me. 1990. 52 min. (Forming democracy in Chile.) – FRIF.

People Power. 1989. 53 min. (Looking at the "people's power" movements in the Philippines, the overthrow of Pinochet in Chile, and the Palestinian *intifada*, this film examines nonviolent revolutionary movements.) – FRIF.

The Pinochet Case. 2001. 109 min. (Begins two years before the actual case.) – FRIF.

Chinese Democracy Movement

China after Tiananmen. 1992. 90 min. (Economic reform while maintaining Communist Party control.) – PBS.

China in the Red. 2003. 50 min. (The human side of China's economy, from Socialism to free trade.) – PBS (Frontline).

China: Unleashing the Dragon. 1995. 200 min. (Four-part series about the opening of China's economy, Deng Xiaoping, Chinese traditions, cultural changes, and an outlook to the future.) – FRIF.

Democracy Crushed: Tiananmen Square. 50 min. – HC.

The Gate of Heavenly Peace. 1995. (A study of the demonstrations at Tiananmen Square and the many killings that followed.) – NAATA.

Chinese Revolutionary Movements (1900–2005)

The Boxer Rebellion. 50 min. – HC.

Chiang Kai Shek. 50 min. – HC or BIO.

China: 1949-1972. 1998. 46 min. (The Chinese Revolution and post-revolution movements.) – CNN Cold War, episode 15.

China: Century of Revolution. Part 1: *Agonies of Nationalism, 1800–1927.* 1972. 24 min. (Foreign involvement, Republican movement, the Communist Party.) – UC-B, UI, ISU, KSU, UMISSOURI, SUNY-B, PSU, PU, WSU.

China: Century of Revolution. Part 2: *Enemies Within and Without, 1927–1944.* 1972. 26 min. (Chinese civil war and Japanese invasion.) – UC-B, UI, ISU, KSU, UMISSOURI, SUNY-B, PSU, PU, UT-A, WSU.

China: Century of Revolution. Part 3, *Communist Triumph and Consolidation, 1945–1971.* 1972. 20 min. – UC-B, ISU, KSU, UMISSOURI, SUNY-B, PSU, PU, WSU.

China Rising. 150 min. (History of modern China.) – HC.

China Yellow, China Blue. 1998. 104 min. (History of the twentieth century in China using original footage.) – FRIF.

Mao: Long March to Power. 1978. 24 min. (Mao's political philosophy and rise to power.)–BU, UI, IU, UIOWA, KSU, SYRU, UWISC-L.

Mao: Organized Chaos. 1978. 24 min. (Post-revolutionary China through the Cultural Revolution.)–BU, UI, IU, UIOWA, KSU, SYRU, UWISC-L.

Mao Tse Tung. 50 min. – BIO.

Morning Sun. 2003. 117 min. (A "psychological history" of those who grew up during the formation of the People's Republic of China.) – NAATA.

Small Happiness: Women of a Chinese Village. 1984. 58 min. (Changes in women's lives since the revolution, and persistence of tradition.)

Sunrise Over Tiananmen Square. 1998. 29 min. (Artistic portrayal of China's modern history.) – FRIF.

Through the Consul's Eyes. 1999. 50 min. (1896–1905 original footage of historical events in urban and rural China, including Yi uprising against China in Tibet.) – FRIF.

Colombia

Colombians Speak Out about Violence and U.S. Policy. 2003. 23 min. – AFSC.

Good Intentions, Bad Results. 2002. 15 min. (*60 Minutes* looks into Plan Colombia.) – AFSC.

Hidden Story: Confronting Colombia's Dirty War. 2001. 30 min. (Investigating corrupt incentives for war.) – AFSC.

The Pipeline War. 2002. 60 min. (Oil and conflict.) – PBS (Frontline).

Plan Colombia: Cashing In on the Drug War Failure. 2003. 58 min. – AFSC.

Welcome to Colombia. 2003. 65 min. (Conflicts among the Revolutionary Armed Forces (FARC) of Colombia, the government army, and paramilitary forces.) – FRIF.

Congo Revolution (1959–)

Lumumba. 2000. 115 min. (Feature film about the first Congolese prime minister, his short term and his tragic fall.) – Indie.

Lumumba: Death of a Prophet. (Lumumba: la morte du prophete.) 1992. 69 min. (French with English narration and subtitles.) – CNR.

Mobutu, King of Zaire. 1999. 162 min. (Three-part series on Mobutu's youth, his reign, and his overthrow.) – FRIF.

Zaire: The Cycle of the Serpent. 1992. 58 min. (Peasants working for survival must also be concerned about the threat of oppression.) – FRIF.

Cuban Revolution (1953–2005)

Americas in Transition. 1981. 29 min. (Covers Cuba, Nicaragua, Chile, the Dominican Republic, El Salvador, Guatemala. Includes U.S. involvement.) – AFSC, FRIF.

Bay of Pigs Declassified. 50 min. (Failed U.S. attempt to intervene in Cuba.) –AETV (History Undercover).

Castro's Challenge. 1985. 60 min. Part 2 of 4 in *Crisis in Central America.* The revolution and post-revolutionary struggle to achieve and maintain ideals.) – AFSC.

Conflict in Cuba: The Bay of Pigs and the Cuban Missile Crisis. 50 min. – AETV.

Cuba. 46 min. (The Cuban missile crisis of October 1962.) – CNN Cold War Series, episode 10.

Cuba and Castro. 50 min. (Portrait of Castro as the leader in Cuba.) – AETV.

Cuba—In the Shadow of Doubt. 1987. 58 min. (Covers Cuba's history, the formation of the revolution, and post-revolutionary Cuba under Castro's rule.) – Filmakers.

Cuba: The Uncompromising Revolution. 1990. 54 min. (Positive and negative effects of Castro's policies in Cuba; comparison with Cuba before the revolution.) – AFSC.

Fidel. 2001. 91 min. (A look at the man, touching on history along the way.) – FRIF.

Fidel Castro. 2004. 120 min. (Portrait of the leader.) – PBS (American Experience).

Fidel Castro: El Comandante. 50 min. (Castro as revolutionary, prime minister, and president.) – BIO.

The Last Communist. 1992. 60 min. (Castro, from guerrilla leader to the leader of a nation.) – PBS.

The Yankee Years. 1985. 60 min. (Part 1 of 4 in *Crisis in Central America.* The First half of the twentieth century in Cuba, Guatemala, Nicaragua, and El Salvador, including U.S. involvement.) – PBS.

East European Revolutions of 1989

Lech Walesa. 50 min. (Solidarity leader and 1990–1995 president of Poland) – BIO.

Pope John Paul II: Statesman of Faith. 50 min. – BIO.

East Timor Revolution

East Timor: Turning a Blind Eye. 1993. (About both the situation and the lack of media coverage in the United States.) – PTTV.

Islands on Fire. 1996. 26 min. (Filmed after 1996 riots; examines the systems that allow for the continuation of the abusive government.) – NAATA.

Punitive Damage. 1999. 77 min. (A mother sues the Indonesian government over her son's murder in the massacre at Santa Cruz Cemetery, revealing the military's tactics.) – FRIF.

Tuti. 1999. 20 min. (A mother's endless search for information about her disappeared son; includes testimony by members of Suharto's military.) – FRIF.

El Salvadoran Revolutionary Conflict (1979–1992)

Americas. Number 9: *Fire in the Mind.* 1993. 57 min. (Revolutionary movements in El Salvador and Peru.) – Americas Series.

Battle for El Salvador. 1985. 60 min. (Part 4 of 4 in *Crisis in Central America.* Development of the conflict and U.S. involvement.) – PBS (Frontline).

Denial. 1993. 57 min. (El Mozote massacre.) – FRIF.

El Salvador: A Country in Crisis. 1981. 30 min. (Focuses on social inequality and government oppression.) – AFSC.

El Salvador: Another Vietnam? 1981. 50 min. (U.S. policy and intervention in Central America since the late 1940s and aftermath of the 1979 military coup.) – AFSC, FRIF.

El Salvador in Crisis. 1989. 33 min. (History of the conflict, focusing on social inequality as the initial cause; analysis of U.S. anti-Communist policy and its effects; Salvadoran government's persecution of rebels.) – AFSC.

El Salvador: Revolution or Death. 1982. 60 min. (Graphic presentation of violence and murder by the government; the uprising against historical oppression.) – AFSC.

El Salvador: The Seeds of Liberty. 1981. 30 min. (The rape and murder of four U.S. churchwomen by El Salvador's National Guard in the context of the history of governmental oppression against the church.) – FRIF.

Enemies of War. 1993. 60 min. (Realities of the civil war through interviews with Salvadoran civilians, political activists, U.S. officials, and Jesuit priests.) – ITVS, PBS.

Justice and Generals. 2002. 86 min. (Seeking justice for the murder of three nuns and an American religious worker.) – FRIF.

Maria's Story. 1991. 58 min. (About the female guerrilla leader Maria Serrano.) – POV, Filmakers.

Media War in El Salvador. 1989. 22 min. (Presidential candidates use media to sway voters with the help of U.S. advertising consultants.) – FRIF.

Remembering Romero. 1992. 28 min. (Interviews with those who had met Archbishop Oscar Romero before he was assassinated in 1980.) – FRIF.

Stories from Cuscatlan. 1989. 52 min. (Three families' stories demonstrate the realities of the civil war.) – FRIF.

Eritrean Revolution (1962–1991)

Eritrea: Hope in the Horn of Africa. 1993. 28 min. (The founding of a nation.) – FRIF.

The Forbidden Land. 1990. 53 min. (War and resulting devastation; highlights projects creating solutions for the people.) – FRIF.

Ethiopian Revolution (1974–1991)

Imperfect Journey. 1994. 88 min. (A survey of Ethiopia demonstrating hardships during and since the Soviet-backed junta.) – FRIF.

Politics Do Not a Banquet Make. 1997. 52 min. (Ethiopians continue their struggle for survival after political change.) – FRIF.

French Revolution (1789–1815)

The French Revolution. 150 min. – AETV or HC.

Marie Antoinette: The Tragic Queen. 50 min. – BIO.

Napoleon Bonaparte. 50 min. – BIO.

German Nazi Revolution (1933–1945)

Adolf Eichmann. 50 min. – BIO.

Hitler and Stalin: Roots of Evil. 2005. 50 min. (Investigates the backgrounds and psychologies of Adolph Hitler and Joseph Stalin.) – HC.

Hitler's Holocaust. 300 min. – HC.

Last Secrets of the Axis. 100 min. (Origins of Nazi ideology and plans; Professor Karl Haushofer's important role as formulator of aspects of Nazi geopolitical goals. – AETV.

The Nazis: Warning from History. 300 min. (History of the Nazi movement.) – AETV.

Plotting to Kill Hitler. 50 min. – HC.

Why Did Hitler Murder Ernst Roehm? 50 min. (Why did Hitler kill one of his most loyal supporters?) – HC.

Greek Civil War

In Search of Greece. 50 min. (Greek History, many topics.) – HC.

Guatemalan Democratic Revolution (1944–)

Approach of Dawn: Portraits of Mayan Women Forging Peace in Guatemala. 1997. 52 min. (Human rights abuses, shortcomings of the 1998 peace accord, and these women's work for lasting peace.) – AFSC.

Dirty Secrets: Jennifer, Everardo, and the CIA in Guatemala. 1998. 56 min. (Jennifer searches for information on her disappeared husband, making discoveries about the CIA.) – AFSC.

Discovering Dominga. 2002. 60 min. (A Guatemalan woman returns home, facing her own history as well as that of her country.) – ITVS.

Guatemala: Deadly Connections. 1995. 13 min. (Former U.S. DEA agent talks of the U.S. role in Guatemala and corruption of the Guatemalan military. Justification of the aid by U.S. officials.) – AFSC.

If the Mango Tree Could Speak. 1993. 60 min. (Community discussion about losses during the war while a mass burial is being uncovered.) – AFSC.

Journey Home: Accompaniment in Guatemala. 1994. 29 min. (Refugees return to their country years after fleeing genocide in the 1980s. Includes speech by Rigoberta Menchu.) – AFSC.

Long Road Home. 1992. 30 min. (Provides background on what the refugees fled, life in the Mexican refugee camps, and the journey back to Guatemala.) – AFSC.

Under the Gun: Democracy in Guatemala. 1987. 40 min. (Military influence in Guatemala after decades of civil war.) – FRIF.

Haitian Democratic Revolution (1986–)

Haiti. 1991. 6 min. (Comments from Aristide.) – FRIF.

Haitian Independence Revolution (1791–1804)

Black Dawn. 1979. 20 min. (Animated story of two slaves, their capture, escape, and freedom in Haiti as it gained independence.) – FRIF.

Hungarian Revolution of 1956

After Stalin. 46 min. (Eastern European resistance to Soviet domination in the 1950s, including the 1956 Hungarian Revolution.) – CNN Cold War Series, episode 7.

Personal Belongings. 1996. 52 min. (Reflections on the Hungarian Revolution from U.S. suburbia.) – POV.

Indian Independence Movement (1885–1947)

Mahatma Gandhi. 50 min. – BIO.

Indonesia

Indonesia: One Struggle, One Change. 1997. 30 min. (Interviews with otherwise voiceless Indonesians about life under the repressive Suharto regime.) – NAATA.

Iranian Revolution (1953–)

Anatomy of a Coup: The CIA in Iran. 50 min. (CIA actions in Iran in 1953 in support of the monarchy.) – AETV (History Undercover).

Holy War, Holy Terror. 1985. 60 min. (Fundamentalist Islam and Shiism in Iran and the war with Iraq.) – PBS.

Iran. 1979. 22 min. (Iran and U.S. policy from the 1950s to the revolution of 1979.) – UI, BU, UMINN, PSU, UWISC-M.

Iran and the Bomb. 1993. 60 min. (Iran replenishes its military while world attention is focused on Iraq.) – PBS.

Iran: Veiled Appearances. 2002. 58 min. (Iran twenty-three years after the Islamic Revolution.) – FRIF.

Mohammed Reza Pahlavi: Politics of Oil. 1986. 24 min. (The shah of Iran's rise and fall.) – BU, UIOWA, IU, UMINN, PSU, SYRU, UNEVR.

Oliver's Army with Eric Mendelson. 1987. (What wasn't in the Iran-Contra hearings.) – PTTV.

The Secret Government: The Constitution in Crisis. 1987. 90 min. (An impressive investigation into secret government activities, including the Iran-Contra operation.) – SUN.

Soldiers of God. 46 min. (Islamic revolutionaries in Iran in the late 1970s and in Afghanistan in the 1980s.) – CNN Cold War Series, episode 20.

Iraqi Revolution (1958–)

The Gulf War. 1996. 4 hours. (History of how it began, interviews with military and governmental officials.) – PBS.

Saddam Hussein. 50 min. – BIO.

Irish Independence and Social Movements (1790–)

Getting Away with Murder: Northern Ireland and the US Media. 1988. – PTTV.

Irish Ways. 1988. 52 min. (Persistence of the conflict in Northern Ireland.) – FRIF.

The Jackets Green. 1988. 14 min. (Irish Republicans and their cause.) – FRIF.

One Island, Two Irelands. 1998. 104 min. Two parts: 1916–1969 and 1969–1995. (All original footage. The history, culture, and movements behind the "troubles.") – FRIF.

The Patriot Game. 1979. 93 min. (History of Ireland from colonization, focusing on the period from 1968 through the late 1970s.) – FRIF.

Spoken by an Actor. 1993. (About biased, incomplete media coverage on Northern Ireland.) – PTTV.

War and Peace in Ireland. 1998. 88 min. and 52 min. versions. (1968 through 1998, focusing on the civil rights movement, the 1969 war, the peace process, and Irish Republican Army cease-fire.) – FRIF.

World History: Endgame in Ireland. 240 min. (The peace process.) – PBS.

Islamic Fundamentalist Revolutionary Movements (1928–)

Osama Bin Laden. 50 min. – BIO.

Party of God. 2003. (Report investigates the Hezbollah.) – PBS (Frontline).

Saudi Time Bomb. 2001. 60 min. (Saudi Arabia and Wahabi international educational activities.) – PBS (Frontline).

Soldiers of God. 46 min. (Islamic revolutionaries in Iran in the late 1970s and in Afghanistan in the 1980s.) – CNN Cold War Series, episode 20.

Son of Al Qaeda. 60 min. (An al-Qaeda associate who turned against the organization.) – PBS (Frontline).

The Women of Hezbollah. 2000. 49 min. (Women activists in Hezbollah.) – FRIF.

Israeli-Zionist Revolution (1896–)

Israel: Birth of a Nation. 100 min. (Israel's early years.) – HC or AETV.

Slaves of the Sword. 2003. 56 min each. Three parts. (Ariel Sharon, Yitzhak Rabin, Moshe Dayan.) – FRIF.

Yitzhak Rabin. 50 min. – BIO.

Italian Fascist Revolution (1919–1945)

Mussolini. 50 min. (The life of the founder of Fascism, Benito Mussolini.) – BIO.

Japanese New Order Movement (1920–1945)

Hirohito. 50 Min. – BIO.

Kenyan Mau Mau Rebellion (1952–1960)

100 Years of Terror: Wars against Colonialism. 50 min.; four sections, 200 min. (Section on Mau Mau Revolt.) – AETV.

Korean Civil War

Battle for Korea. 120 min. (Looking back to understand the war.) – PBS.

Homes Apart: The Two Koreans. 1991. 56 min. (A brother separated from his sister searches for her.) – POV.

Kim Jong Il. 50 min. (North Korean leader.) – BIO.

Korea. 46 min. (The Korean War.) – CNN Cold War Series, episode 5.

Suspicious Minds. 2003. 60 min. (A reporter visits North Korea.) – PBS (Frontline).

Mexican Revolution (1910–)

A Cry for Freedom and Democracy. 1994. (Activists, journalists, and others explore the history of military violence and continuing repression.) – PTTV.

Mexico: Dead or Alive. 1996. 53 min. (Exposing violent political repression in Mexico through the story of Dr. Mario Rojas Alba, now in exile.) – FRIF.

Pancho Villa: Outlaw Hero. 50 min. (Historians, descendents, and rare film footage create an image of the rebel.) – BIO.

Mozambique Revolution (1964–)

Chain of Tears. 1989. 50 min. (The effects of war and violence on children in Angola, Mozambique, and South Africa.) – SAMC.

Samora Machel, Son of Africa. 1989. 28 min. (Interview with Machel, a leader of the revolution in Mozambique, includes footage of political rally and commentary from close friend, Professor John Saul.) – FRIF.

Waiting for the Caribou. 1991. 30 min. (A city-dweller returns to war-torn rural areas in a relief mission.) – FRIF.

Nicaraguan Revolution (1961–1990)

Deadly Embrace: Nicaragua, the World Bank, and the International Monetary Fund. 1996. 28 min. (Thorough analysis of free trade, debt, their effect on people.) – AFSC.

Did They Buy It? Nicaragua's 1990 Elections. 1990. 45 min. – AFSC.

Fire from the Mountain. 1988. (About Omar Cabeza—his journey from student activist to guerrilla to government official.) – POV.

Forgotten Wars. 50 min. (Includes U.S. military intervention in Nicaragua in the 1920s and 1930s.) – AETV or HC.

Guns, Drugs and the CIA. 1988. 60 min. (Investigations concerning possible connections between the CIA and drug operations in Central America and Southeast Asia.) – PBS (Frontline).

Revolution in Nicaragua. 1985. 60 min. (Part 3 of 4, *Crisis in Central America.* U.S. involvement and attempts to influence the revolution.) – PBS (Frontline).

Robin Anderson Exposes the Real Deal. 1990. (The CIA-Contra-cocaine connection as illuminated by Fordham University media scholar Robin Anderson.) – PTTV.

Second Revolution: Women in Nicaragua. 1983. 27 min. (Women's lives in Nicaragua after the revolution.) – AFSC.

The Secret Government: The Constitution in Crisis. 1987. 90 min. (An impressive investigation into secret U.S. government activities, including the Iran-Contra operation.) – SUN.

Ten Days/Ten Years: The Nicaragua Elections of 1990. 1990. 54 min. (Clear analysis of the elections, why Chamorro won, and the U.S. role.) – AFSC.

U.S. Foreign Policy: Projecting U.S. Influence. 30 min. (U.S. in Nicaragua.) – PBS.

War on Nicaragua. 1987. 55 min. (The development of the U.S.-sponsored Contra War.) –AFSC.

Palestinian Independence Movement (1936–)

Al Nakba: The Palestinian Catastrophe. 1997. 56 min. (Hundreds of thousands of Palestinians lose homes and land and become refugees after the 1948 Arab-Israeli war.) – BUYIN.

Battle for the Holy Land. 2002. 60 min. (Interviews with Israelis and Palestinians regarding tactics and strategies.) – PBS.

Edward Said: The Last Interview. 2004. 114 min. (Lengthy interview with Columbia University literature professor and prominent spokesperson for the Palestinian cause shortly before his death.) – FRIF.

The Palestinian People Do Have Rights. 1979. 48 min. (Introduction to the Palestinian-Israeli conflict.) – FRIF.

People and the Land. 1997. 60 min. (Palestinian-Israeli Conflict: border crossing to get opinions from both sides.) – ITVS.

People Power. 1989. 53 min. (Looks at "people's power" movements in the Philippines, the overthrow of Pinochet in Chile, and the Palestinian *intifada;* examines non-violent revolutionary movements.) – FRIF.

The Search for Peace in the Middle East. 50 min. (Traces the careers of Yitzhak Rabin and Yasser Arafat). – AETV (Twentieth Century Series.)

Shattered Dreams. 2001. 120 min. (History of the peace process.) – PBS.

Paris Commune Movement (1871)

La Commune. 2000. 345 min. (b/w) (Reenactment of events; actors portray participants and leaders of the movement.) – FRIF.

Peruvian Shining Path

Americas. Number 9: *Fire in the Mind.* 1993. 57 min. (Revolutionary movements in El Salvador and Peru.) – Americas Series.

Peru: Fire in the Andes. 1985. 35 min. (History of the conflict; human rights abuses.) – FRIF.

Peru—Inca Indians Return Home. 15 min. (Incan descendents rebuild their lives after being forced into the Shining Path movement.) – Filmakers.

Philippine Democratic Movement (1986–)

People Power. 1989. 53 min. (Looks at "people's power" movements in the Philippines, the overthrow of Pinochet in Chile, and the Palestinian *intifada;* examines nonviolent revolutionary movements.) – FRIF.

Philippine Islamic Rebellion

Islands under Siege. 2003. (Reporter's meeting with Muslim rebels.) – PBS (Frontline).

Polish Solidarity Movement (1980–)

Lech Walesa. 50 min. (Leader of Solidarity and president of Poland, 1990–1995.) – BIO.

Pope John Paul II. 50 min. (Life of the Polish pope and his impacts.) – BIO.

Russian Revolution I (1905–1989)

The Bolshevik Victory. 1969. 20 min. (b/w) (The October Revolution.) – KSU, UI, UMONT, UWASH, UWISC-L.

Forgotten Wars. 50 min. (Includes U.S. military intervention in the Russian Civil War.) – AETV or HC.

Lenin. 1980. 39 min. (b/w) – KSU, UI, UWASH, UWISC-L, UWISC-M.

Lenin and Trotsky. 1964. 16 min. – KSU, SYRU, UI, UWISC-L, UWY.

Lenin's Revolution. No. 5, Unit 2 of *History 1917–67.* 1970. 20 min. (b/w) – KSU, UI, WASH, UWISC-L.

Marx for Beginners. 1978. 7 min. (Humorous and informative animated explanation of Marx's most influential concepts.) – FRIF.

Nicholas and Alexandra. 100 min. (Last Romanov rulers of Russia.) – AETV.

Rasputin. 50 min. (Life of the "mad" monk who was blamed for helping to destroy the Romanov dynasty.) – BIO.

The Rise and Fall of the Soviet Union. 124 min. – SEG.

The Romanovs. 50 min. (Final period of the Romanov dynasty.) – AETV.

Russia: Land of the Tsars. 200 min. (Russia's imperial past.) – AETV.

The Russian Revolution: Czar to Lenin. 1966. 33 min. (b/w) – PSU.

Stalin. 50 Min. – BIO.

Stalin and Russian History (1879–1927). 1974. 29 min. (b/w) (Biography of Stalin and his involvement in the Bolshevik Revolution.) – PSU, UARIZ, UI, UWASH, UWISC-L.

Stalin: Red Terror. 50 min. (Original footage and interviews with those who knew him create this portrait of the Soviet tyrant.) – AETV.

Stalin vs. Trotsky: Struggle for Power. 1964. 16 min. (b/w) KSU, UARIZ, UI.

Stalin's Revolution. No. 6, Unit 2 of *History 1917–67* 1971. 22 min. (b/w) – KSU, UI, UWASH, UWISC-L.

Vladimir Lenin. 50 min. – BIO.

Yanks for Stalin. 50 min. (American companies and individuals who helped build the Soviet Union.) – HC.

Russian Revolution II (1990–)

After Gorbachev's USSR. 1992. 60 min. (Social change in Russia.) – PBS.

Boris Yeltsin. 50 min. (First elected president of Russia.) – BIO.

Children of Perestroika Trilogy. Includes *Loveletters from a Children's Prision 2005; A Beautiful Tragedy 2006; Killing Girls 2007* (Russia's younger generation.) – FF (Sales: info@firsthandfilms.com).

Mikhail Gorbachev. 50 min. (Life of the Russian reformer.) – BIO.

The Rise and Fall of the Soviet Union. 124 min. – SEG

Struggle for Russia. 1994. 120 min. (Social, economic, and political problems in Russia in the 1990s.) – AFSC.

Vladimir Putin. 50 min. (Russia's second elected president.) – BIO.

Rwanda Civil Wars (1959–)

Chronicle of a Genocide Foretold. 1996. 141 min. (Documents the Genocide before, during, and after.) – FRIF.

Gacaca: Living Together Again in Rwanda? 2002. 55 min. (Implementing fairness, equality, and justice through Gacaca tribunals.) – FRIF.

Ghosts of Rwanda. 120 min. (Ten years later, Frontline investigates the genocide and the conditions that allowed it to happen.) – PBS (Frontline).

A Republic Gone Mad. 1996. 60 min. (Examining historical relations between Hutu and Tutsi peoples.) – FRIF.

Rwandan Nightmare. 1994. 41 min. (Causes of the massacres.) – FRIF.

Shake Hands with the Devil. 2005. 91 min. (Rwanda 1994.) – CNR.

Saudi Arabia and the Wahhabi Movement (1744–)

The Arming of Saudi Arabia. 1993. 60 min. (The development of the U.S.-funded military.) – PBS.

House of Saud (The royal family from the beginning.) – PBS (Frontline).

Saudi Time Bomb. 2001. 60 min. (Saudi Arabia and Wahabi international educational activities.) – PBS (Frontline).

Slave Rebellions in the United States (1776–1865)

Cinque. 50 min. (Leader of the successful Amistad Rebellion.) – BIO.

Frederick Douglass. 50 min. (Historians and photos portray the man.) – AETV.

Frederick Douglas: When the Lion Wrote History. – PBS.

John Brown's Holy War. 2000. (His life and efforts to end slavery.) – PBS.

Nat Turner: A Troublesome Property. 2002. 60 min. (A recreation of the man using interviews and historical footage.) – CNR.

South African Pro-Democracy and Anti-Apartheid Movements (1948–)

Amandla!: A Revolution in Four Part Harmony. 2002. 103 min. (The power of music for the revolution against apartheid.) – Indie.

Apartheid's Last Stand. 1998. 60 min. – (Ingrid Gavshon) Black Film Center, Indiana University, PBS.

Biko: Breaking the Silence. 1988. 52 min. (History of the Black Consciousness Movement and Steve Biko's role.) – AFSC, SAMC.

Chain of Tears. 1989. 50 min. (The effects of war and violence on children in Angola, Mozambique, and South Africa.) – SAMC.

Changing This Country. 1988. 58 min. (Four union leaders are interviewed on their goals for the future of their people and country.) – SAMC.

Children of Apartheid. 1987. 50 min. (Interviews with black and white youths in a demonstration of apartheid's effects on a child's mind.) – AFSC, SAMC.

Classified People. 1987. 55 min. – AFSC.

Cry of Reason: An Afrikaner Speaks Out. 1987. 58 min. (The white Reverend Beyers Naude teaches about apartheid through his own experiences as he evolved from supporting apartheid to working against it.) – AFSC, SAMC.

The Deadline. 1996. 52 min. (Final hours before finalizing the new constitution.) – FRIF.

End of the Dialogue. 1970. 44 min. (Record of apartheid which opened the eyes of the world to the atrocious reality in South Africa.) – FRIF.

Generations of Resistance. 1980. 52 min. (A history of resistance to white rule in South Africa.) – AFSC, SAMC.

Land Affairs. 1995. 26 min. (Displaced farmers in South Africa want their land back, now owned by whites.) – FRIF.

Last Grave at Dimbaza. 1974. 55 min. (Showing suffering caused by apartheid, especially of the children.) – AFSC.

The Long Walk of Nelson Mandela. 120 min. – PBS.

Maids and Madames. 1986. 52 min. (Black women served white women in apartheid South Africa.) – AFSC, Filmakers.

Mandela: Free at Last. 1990. 79 min. – AFSC.

Mandela: Son of Africa, Father of a Nation. 1997. 118 min. – Indie.

Mandela's Fight For Freedom. 1995. 150 min. – DCTV.

Nelson Mandela: Journey to Freedom. 50 min. – AETV.

Regopstaan's Dream. 2000. 52 min. (Indigenous people's struggle to regain their homelands.) – FRIF.

The Ribbon. 1987. 50 min. (An educational and political tool, the Peace Ribbon was created by black and white South African women in opposition to apartheid.) – FRIF.

Rights and Wrongs: South Africa. 1994. 26 min. (The beginning of a new government and the problems it must correct.) – AFSC.

South Africa Belongs to Us. 1980. 57 min. (Women in South Africa—workers, activists, mothers—struggle for subsistence and respect.) – FRIF.

Spear of the Nation: History of the African National Congress. 1986. 50 min. – SAMC.

Twelve Disciples of Nelson Mandela. 70 min. – ITVS.

White Laager. 1978. 58 min. (Development of white-dominated South Africa.) – AFSC.

Spanish Revolution and Counter-Revolution (1931–1939)

Caudillo: The History of the Spanish Civil War. 111 min. (General Franco's Revolt and the war from Republican and Falangist perspectives.) – UC-B.

The Good Fight: The Abraham Lincoln Brigade in the Spanish Civil War. 1984. 98 min. (U.S. volunteers fight for the republic in the Spanish Civil War.) – UC-B.

The Spanish Civil War. 27 min. (Major events leading up to, during, and at the end of the war.) – UC-B.

The Spanish Civil War. 312 min. (Extensive history with original footage and personal experiences.) – UC-B.

The Spanish Civil War: Blood and Ink. 50 min. (History through poetry of the time.) – UC-B.

Sri Lankan Tamil Revolutionary Movement (1977–)

Living in Terror. 2002. (Conflict in Sri Lanka.) – PBS (Frontline).

Sudanese Civil War

Waiting. 1996. (Dinka people's struggle during the civil war; waiting for aid.) – FRIF.

Uruguay

Tupamaros. 1996. 93 min. (One of South America's major guerrilla movements.) – FRIF.

U.S. Civil Rights Movement (1954–)

At the River I Stand. 1993. 56 min. (The Labor Movement and the Civil Rights Movement come together as sanitation workers strike in Memphis, 1968.) – CNR.

Berkeley in the Sixties. 1990. 118 min. (Using interviews with 15 previous student leaders to document the decade and the various battles fought.) – CNR.

Black Panther and *San Francisco State: On Strike.* 1969. 34 min total. (*Black Panther:* created by the Black Panther Party to communicate their cause and *On Strike:* made by students during the six-month student strike for the creation of the first ethnic studies department in the U.S.) – CNR.

Breaking the Ice: The Story of Mary Ann Shad. 1999. 23 min. (Story of the abolitionist, suffragette, and integrationist.) – FRIF.

Brother Outsider: The Life of Bayard Rustin. 1995. 83 min. (Rustin fought for equality in the Labor Movement and the Civil Rights Movement, while struggling for acceptance as a homosexual.) – CNR.

CBS Tries the New York Three (NY3): Racist Lies on Prime-time TV. 1988. (Analysis of the trial of the three Black Panther Party members) – PTTV.

Citizen King. 2004. 120 min. (The last five years of Dr. King's life, using interviews to draw an intimate portrait.) – PBS.

February One: The Story of the Greensboro Four. 2004. 61 min. (Four black college freshmen catalyze the Civil Rights Movement with at sit-in at Woolworth's.) – CNR.

Finally Got the News. 1970. 55 min. (The League of Revolutionary Black Workers.) – FRIF.

Freedom on My Mind. 1994. 110 min. (Mississippi Freedom Struggle leading to the 1965 Voting Rights Act.) – CNR.

Fundi. 1986. 48 or 63 min. (About Ella Baker's influence in the Civil Rights Movement.) – FRIF.

George Wallace: Setting the Woods on Fire. 2000. (The segregationist's political life and ideological turnaround.) – PBS.

Hate Across America. 50 min. (The KKK and other groups.) - AETV.

The Huey P. Newton Story. 2002. (About the cofounder and leader of the Black Panther Party.) – PBS.

I Am Somebody. 1970. 28 min. (South Carolina female hospital workers strike in 1969.) – FRIF.

Ida B. Wells: A Passion for Justice. 1989. 53 min. (Pioneering African American journalist, suffragist, and civil rights activist.) – CNR.

In Remembrance of Martin. –PBS.

The Intolerable Burden. 2003. 56 min. (Segregation, desegregation, and re-segregation of schools, the story of one family's experiences in the 1960s.) – FRIF.

Jesse Jackson. – BIO.

Ku Klux Klan: A Secret History. 100 min. – AETV.

A Litany for Survival: The Life and Work of Audre Lorde. 1996. (The poet and her work from the 1960s to the 1990s.) – POV.

Malcolm X: A Search for Identity. 50 min. (From childhood to his career as an activist and a leader.) – BIO.

Marcus Garvey: Look for Me in the Whirlwind. 90 min. – PBS.

Martin Luther King, Jr.: The Man and His Dream. 50 min. (How he and his dream evolved through the Civil Rights Movement.) – BIO.

The Murder of Emmett Till. (Story of the fourteen-year-old's murder.) – PBS.

Of Civil Wrongs and Rights: The Fred Korematsu Story. 2004. (Resistor of Japanese internment's long struggle to victory.) – POV, NAATA.

A Panther in Africa. 2004. (Former Black Panther Pete O'Neil reflects on his past and his life in exile in Tanzania.) – POV/PBS.

The Pilgrimage of Jesse Jackson. – PBS (Frontline).

Public Enemy. 1999. 50 min. (Four former Black Panthers reflect.) – FRIF.

The Rise and Fall of Jim Crow. 2002. 4 parts, each 56 min. "Promises Betrayed"; "Fighting Back"; "Don't Shout Too Soon"; "Terror and Triumph." (From the Civil War to the Civil Rights Movement, complete history of Jim Crow.) – CNR.

The Road to Brown (Brown vs. the Board of Ed.). 1990. 56 min. – CNR.

Rosa Parks: Mother of a Movement. – AETV.

Scottsboro: An American Tragedy. (Story of the young African American boys charged with raping two white women in a train car in 1931 Alabama.) – PBS.

Seven Songs for Malcolm X. 1993. 52 min. (A tribute to his life and work.) – FRIF.

Strange Fruit. 2002. 57 min. (History of the song, its influence, and the world that fostered its creation.) – CNR.

Thurgood Marshall: Justice for All. – AETV.

W. E. B. Du Bois: A Biography in Four Voices. 1995. 116 min. (Four parts: "Black Folk and the New Century"; "The Crisis and the New Negro"; "A Second Reconstruction"; "Color, Democracy, Colonies, and Peace.") – CNR.

U.S. Southern Secessionist Rebellion and Civil War (1861–1865)

Abraham Lincoln: Preserving the Union. 50 min. – AETV.

Civil War Journal: The Commanders. 200 min. (Lee, Sherman, and Stonewall Jackson.) – AETV.

Ken Burns Civil War. 690 min. – PBS.

Lincoln: Man or Myth. 50 min. – AETV (Investigating History).

New England and the Civil War. – PBS.

Quantrill's Raiders. 50 min. (Confederate guerrilla warfare.) – AETV or HC.

Robert E. Lee. 50 min. – BIO.

Smithsonian's Great Battles of the Civil War. 520 min. – PBS.

U.S. Women's Movement

America's Victoria: The Victoria Woodhull Story. 1995. 52 min. (The first woman to campaign for U.S. presidency in 1872.) – WMM.

Anthony. 1998. (Fight for women's suffrage.) – PBS.

Clare Booth Luce: Hell on Heels. 50 min. – AETV.

Fly Girls. (U.S. women fly for the U.S. during WWII.) – PBS.

Let the Women Vote! 1997. 60 min. – ITVS.

Louder Than Our Words. 1983. 36 min. (Civil disobedience and Women's Rights.) – WMM.

Mary Cassat: A Brush with Independence. (Nineteenth century.) – PBS.

National Desk: Politics and Warriors: Women in the Military. – PBS.

National Desk: Title IX & Women In Sports: What's Wrong with This Picture. – PBS.

'Not for Ourselves Alone: The Story of Elizabeth Cady Stanton and Susan B. Anthony. 210 min. (Their work and their cause.) – PBS.

One Woman, One Vote. (U.S. suffrage movement.) – PBS.

Ourselves, Our Bodies: The Feminist Movement and the Battle over Abortion. 50 min. – AETV.

The Pill. 1999. 45 min. (The history of the birth control pill.) – WMM.

Some American Feminists. 1980. 56 min. (Includes interviews with Betty Friedan and Rita Mae Brown.) – WMM.

Step by Step: Building a Feminist Movement. 1998. 56 min. (Eight women's personal tales portray the extensive history of the movement.) – WMM.

Susan B. Anthony: Rebel for the Cause. 50 min. – BIO.

With a Vengeance: The Fight for Reproductive Freedom. 1989. 40 min. (History of the fight.) – WMM.

Womanhouse. 1974. 47 min. (Documentary of Judy Chicago and Miriam Shapiro's artistic look beyond the chores and into the minds of female homemakers.) – WMM.

Women of the World. (Outstanding women around the world.) – PBS.

Venezuela's Bolivarian Revolution (1998–2005)

Venezuela: Revolution in Progress. 2005. Approx. 50 min. (The revolution of Venezuela's president Hugo Chavez and related social conflict.) – DCTV.

Vietnamese Revolution (1919–1975)

Guerilla Warfare: Vietnam. 1997. 46 min. (From the Masters of War Series featuring General Vo Nguyen Giap and his adversary, General William Westmoreland.) – Amazon.

Guns, Drugs and the CIA. 1988. 60 min. (Investigations concerning possible connections between the CIA and drug operations in Central America and Southeast Asia.) – PBS (Frontline).

Hearts and Minds. 1974. 112 min. (Effects of the war on people in Vietnam and the U.S.) – UMICH, UT-D.

Ho Chi Minh. 1998. 50 min. – BIO.

Ho Chi Minh. 1968. 26 min. (b/w) (CBS documentary on his life.) – UMINN, UWISC-M.

LBJ and Vietnam. 100 min. – AETV.

Time of the Locust. 1966. 13 min. (b/w) (United States, Japanese, and National Liberation Front coverage of the violence in Vietnam.) – FRIF.

Vietnam: A Television History. 1983. Edited to 11 parts in 1997, 60 min. each. (A thorough portrayal of the war. (1) Roots of a War, (2) America's Mandarin, (3) LBJ Goes to War, (4) America Takes Charge, (5) America's Enemy, (6) Tet, 1968, (7) Vietnamizing the War, (8) Laos and Cambodia, (9) Peace Is at Hand, (10) Homefront USA, (11) End of the Tunnel.) – WGBH, PBS.

Vietnam: An Historical Development. 1975. 56 min. (History of U.S. involvement in Vietnam.) – UARIZ, UC-B, USF, UIOWA, KSU, PSU.

Vietnam: Chronicle of a War. 89 min. (CBS News.) – Amazon.

Vietnam: Faces of Development. 1994. 24 min. (Life in Vietnam in the 1990s and projects supported by the American Friends Service Committee.) – AFSC.

Vietnam Passage: Journeys from War to Peace. 60 min. (How the war affected the Vietnamese.) – PBS.

Vietnam: The Ten Thousand Day War. 1980. (Twenty-six parts. Part 1, 55 min. Parts 2–26, 26 min. each. (1) America in Vietnam, (2) France in Vietnam, (3) Dien Bien Phu, (4) Early Hopes, (5) Assassination, (6) Days of Decision, (7) Westy's War, (8) Uneasy Allies, (9) Guerrilla Society, (10) Ho Chi Minh Trail, (11) Firepower, (12) Village War, (13) Air War, (14) Siege, (15) Tet, (16) Frontline America, (17) Soldiering On, (18) Changing the Guard, (19) Wanting Out, (20) Bombing of Hanoi, (21) Peace, (22) Prisoners, (23) Unsung Soldiers, (24) Final Offensive, (25) Surrender, (26) Vietnam Recalled.) – Part 1 available from UI, ISU; parts 2–26 UI.

Vietnam—The Vietnam Conflict. 46 min. – CNN Cold War Series, episode 11.

The World below the War. 1996. (Villagers in Vietnam relocated underground to escape the fighting.) – NAATA.

Yugoslavian Communist Revolution

Joseph Broz Tito. 50 min. (The life of the Yugoslav Communist leader.) – BIO.

Yugoslavian Dissolution

Death of Yugoslavia. 2005. 50 min. – AETV.

Zapatista Rebellion

Alonso's Dream. 2000. 71 min. (Conflict in Chiapas and the Zapatista National Liberation Army.) – FRIF.

The Sixth Sun: Mayan Uprising in Chiapas. 1996. 56 min. (About the Zapatista Movement; diverse interviews; questioning the real benefits of "progress.") – ITVS.

Super Barrio. 1995. (Chiapas, indigenous poverty, government corruption.) Spanish with English subtitles. – PTTV.

Ya Basta! The Battle Cry of the Faceless. 1997. 50 min. (The Chiapas uprising, the Zapatistas' demands, and the situation three years after the takeovers.) – FRIF.

Zimbabwean Revolution (1966–)

Keeping a Live Voice: 15 Years of Democracy in Zimbabwe. 1995. 54 min. (Zimbabwean people on their independence.) – FRIF.

Notes on Zimbabwe. 1990. – PTTV.

RELATED TOPICS

Capitalism, Revolution, and Counter-Revolution

Controlling Interest. 1978. 40 min. (Multinational corporations: their influence and manipulation in Latin American countries, on U.S. policies, and on workers in both areas.) – AFSC.

Getting Out of the Sand Trap. 1990. (Political and economic analysis of the U.S. role in the Middle East.) – PTTV.

Lines in the Sand. 1990. (In the Middle East, international effects on area, history, war.) – PTTV.

Human Rights

Faces of the Enemy. 1987. 57 min. (Psychology of dehumanizing the enemy and rationalizing war.) – CNR.

Hitler's Holocaust. 300 min. – HC.

Holocaust: The Untold Story. 50 min. (Was coverage of the murder of European Jews suppressed during WWII?) – AETV (History Undercover).

Inside Pol Pot's Secret Prison. 50 min. (Abuses of the Khmer Rouge regime.) – AETV (History Undercover).

Nightmare in Manchuria: Unit 731. 50 min. (Unpunished crimes against humanity. Japanese biochemical warfare.) – AETV (History Undercover).

Quest for Change. 1994. (Five Middle Eastern scholars discuss conflicts and prospects for democracy.) – FRIF.

Rape of Nanking. 50 min. (One of the worst wartime atrocities of WWII, perpetrated by Japanese soldiers.) – AETV (History Undercover).

Trials of Henry Kissinger. 2002. 80 min. (Bombing Cambodia, East Timor violence; the murder of the pro-democracy General Schneider of Chile and other topics: Did Kissinger engage in criminal activity?) – FRIF.

Media and Revolution

The Black Press: Soldiers without Swords. 1998. 86 min. (History of the black press from the Civil War through the Civil Rights Movement.) – CNR.

KFPA on the Air. 2000. (The liberal, independent, outspoken California community radio station.) – POV.

Keyan Tomaselli on Media and Resistance in South Africa. 1990. – PTTV.

Low Power Empowerment: Neighborhood Radio in Ireland and the United States. 1993. – PTTV.

Luis R. Beltran Tunes In to Bolivian Miners' Radio. 1991. – PTTV.

Media Machete: The Chiapas Media Project. 1998. – PTTV.

Mercenaries

Soldiers for Hire. 100 min. (Mercenaries in wars and revolutions: past, present, and future.) – HC.

Music and Revolution

Amandla! A Revolution in Four Part Harmony. 2002. 103 min. (The power of music in the revolution against apartheid.) – Indie.

Freedom: A History of the US: Songs from the Heart of America (CD). – PBS.

I Talk about Me, I Am Africa. 1980. 54 min. (Music, theater, identity of black South Africans, and counter-apartheid movement.) – FRIF.

I'll Sing for You. 2001. 76 min. (Boubacar Traore, revolutionary musician in Mali.) – FRIF.

The Internationale. 2000. 30 min. (Tracing this one song from creation in Paris 1871 through the end of the Cold War.) – FRIF.

Ken Burns Civil War. (CD) 690 min.– PBS.

The Singing Sheikh. 1991. 10 min. (Egyptian Sheikh Imam Mohammad Ahmad Eissa said, "If a beautiful thing is oppressed today, it will rise tomorrow.") – FRIF.

Songs of the Spanish Civil War. Audio. – UC-B.

Strange Fruit. 2002. 57 min. (History of this song, its influence, and the world that fostered its creation.) – CNR.

The Underground Orchestra. 1998. 108 min. (Political exiles in Paris as street musicians.) – FRIF.

Nonviolent Revolution

People Power. 1989. 53 min. (Looks at the "people's power" movements in the Philippines, the overthrow of Pinochet in Chile, and the Palestinian *intifada;* examines nonviolent revolutionary movements.) – FRIF.

Peasants and Workers

Controlling Interest. 1978. 40 min. (Multinational corporations: their influence and manipulation in Latin American countries, on U.S. policies, and on workers in both areas.) – AFSC.

The Fight in the Fields: Cesar Chavez and the Farmworkers' Struggle. 1997. (UFW, Latino civil rights in the 1960s and 1970s.) – ITVS.

Joe Hill's Story: The Man behind the Martyr. 2000. (Executed for murder in Utah, with highly questionable evidence, Joe Hill had been active in the Labor Movement of the early 1900s, fighting for workers' rights and equality.) – University of Utah, KUED-TV.

Land Affairs. 1995. 26 min. (Displaced farmers in South Africa want their land back, now owned by whites.) – FRIF.

Passing the Message. 1981. 47 min. (Black unions in apartheid South Africa.) – FRIF.

Seeds of Revolution. 1979. 28 min. (Examining the successful banana industry in Honduras in the face of extreme poverty among Hondurans.) – FRIF.

The Take. 2004. 88 min. (Workers illegally take over and restart the auto parts factory that was abandoned after the economic crisis in Argentina.) – FRIF.

The Uprising of '34. 1995. (500,000 mill workers went on strike. Continued effects on the Labor Movement.) – POV.

Where Do You Stand? Stories from an American Mill. 2004. 60 min. (A North Carolina town's battle against the man who controlled their town.) – CNR.

Terrorism

100 Years of Terror. 200 min. (Overview of modern use of terror.) – AETV.

CIA: 50 Years of Spying. 50 min. – AETV.

In Search of bin Laden. 60 min. (Osama bin Laden and the al-Qaeda network.) – PBS (Frontline).

Inside the Mind of a Suicide Bomber. 50 min. (Interviews with psychologists and failed bombers.) – AETV (History Undercover).

Inside the Terror Network. 60 min. (Investigation of three Sept. 11 terrorists.) – PBS (Frontline).

Terror Strikes Moscow. 2003. 50 min. (Chechen extremists take 800 people hostage at a Moscow theater.) – HC.

Tracking Terror: The CIA in the Middle East. 50 min. – AETV (History Undercover).

Trail of a Terrorist. 60 min. (The al-Qaeda millennium bombing attempt.) – PBS (Frontline).

War on Terror: A Year in Review. 50 min. (Anti-terror efforts after 9/11.) – AETV.

Women and Revolution

Algeria: Women at War. 1992. 52 min. (Algerian women's participation in the independence struggle.) – WMM.

Nicaraguan Women: Contra War. 1988. 28 min. (Three women and their struggles for survival and justice in the face of the Contras.) – KSU.

The Ribbon. 1987. 50 min. (An educational and political tool, the Peace Ribbon was created by black and white South African women in opposition to apartheid.) – FRIF.

South Africa Belongs to Us. 1980. 57 min. (Women in South Africa—workers, activists, mothers—struggle for subsistence and respect.) – FRIF.

The Women of Hezbollah. 2000. 49 min. (Women activists in Hezbollah.)– FRIF.

Deanna Levanti

References and Further Readings

DeFronzo, James, 2007. 1996. *Revolutions and Revolutionary Movements.* Boulder, CO: Westview Press.

———. 1998. "Films and Video Documentaries." Pp. 174–175 in *Encyclopedia of Political Revolutions,* edited by Jack A. Goldstone. Washington DC: Congressional Quarterly.

E

East European Revolutions of 1989

CHRONOLOGY

1917   On November 7, the Bolsheviks, a radical leftist party led by Vladimir I. Lenin, capture power in Russia. A one-party dictatorship is established in the country; the professed purpose of Russia's new rulers is to implement the ideas of Karl Marx and build a new type of society: Communist.

1917–1924   Bolshevik power is consolidated in Russia. Large-scale changes are made, including the nationalization of industry, banking, and commerce; the Bolshevik interpretation of Marxism is established as the official ideology of the state; class struggle is embraced as a guiding principle of foreign policy; an all-powerful political police is created with the power to detain opponents of the regime in concentration camps; all independent social activities are repressed. In 1922, all territories under Bolshevik domination are integrated into a new state called Union of the Soviet Socialist Republics, or Soviet Union (of which Russia is the biggest unit). After Lenin's death in 1924, Joseph Stalin becomes the leader of the Bolshevik movement.

1939   The Second World War begins in September. The Baltic states and parts of Poland and Romania are annexed by the Soviet government.

1941   On June 22, Hitler's armies attack the Soviet Union.

1945   Having occupied eastern Europe, Soviet troops enter Berlin on May 9; World War II ends in Europe.

1945–1949   Pro-Soviet Communist regimes are established in Poland, Hungary, Czechoslovakia, Romania, Bulgaria, Albania, Yugoslavia, and in Soviet-controlled East Germany (called the German Democratic Republic or GDR). After a schism between the Communist leaders of Yugoslavia and the Soviet Union, relations between the two countries are broken off in the late 1940s.

1953   On June 17, anti-Communist riots erupt in East Germany; the Communist regime suppresses them with the help of Soviet tanks.

1954   In March, Todor Zhivkov becomes general secretary of the Bulgarian Communist Party.

1955   On May 14, a military treaty is signed in Warsaw by Bulgaria, Romania, Hungary,

Poland, Czechoslovakia, the GDR, the Soviet Union, and Albania; it is known as the Warsaw Treaty. It establishes a unified military command in Moscow; Soviet divisions are stationed in most of the member nations prior to the signing. (In the 1960s, Albania will withdraw from the Warsaw Treaty.)

1956   October–November: Popular anti-Communist uprising in Hungary. Soviet troops intervene; tens of thousands of people are killed. János Kádár is appointed leader of a pro-Soviet Hungarian government. The leaders of the uprising, including Prime Minister Imre Nagy, are executed.

1961   On August 13, the Berlin Wall is built by the GDR government in order to stop mass emigration to West Berlin.

1965   In March, Nikolae Ceausescu becomes general secretary of the Romanian Communist Party.

1968   Between March and August, a pro-reform faction within the Czechoslovak Communist Party led by Alexander Dubcek gains power and initiates a set of policies intended to create "socialism with a human face," that is, to liberalize and democratize the political system of the country; these policies become known as "The Prague Spring."

On August 21, Warsaw Treaty troops invade Czechoslovakia to extinguish the Prague Spring reforms.

1969   In April, Gustav Husak, a Marxist hard-liner, replaces Dubcek as general secretary of the Czechoslovak Communist Party. A massive wave of reprisals against supporters of the Prague Spring is unleashed; within two years, virtually all pro-reform members of the party are expelled.

1971   In June, Erich Honecker becomes general secretary of the East German Communist Party.

1980–1989   Nikolae Ceausescu begins to implement a series of radical policies in Romania intended to increase the birthrate, improve agricul-

tural productivity, and repay its foreign debt. Romania's economic situation deteriorates dramatically.

1980–1981   Massive anti-government protests begin in Poland. In September 1980, an independent trade union, Solidarity, is legalized. Striking workers demand far-reaching economic and political reforms. General Wojciech Jaruzelski is elected general secretary of the Polish Communist Party.

1981   On December 13, martial law is declared in Poland; Solidarity is banned, hundreds of activists are arrested, workers demonstrating against the government are fired at, and dozens are killed.

1985   In March, Mikhail Gorbachev becomes general secretary of the Communist Party of the Soviet Union.

1985–1988   Gorbachev launches perestroika, a set of comprehensive reforms intended to revitalize the Soviet economy and democratize Soviet politics. He also makes it clear that the Soviet Union will no longer intervene militarily in Eastern Europe to support local Communist regimes.

1987   In December, Milos Jakes, another hard-liner, replaces Gustav Husak as general secretary of the Czechoslovak Communist Party; Husak assumes the largely ceremonial presidency of Czechoslovakia.

1988   On May 19, János Kádár resigns as general secretary of the Hungarian Communist Party and is replaced by Karoly Grosz.

On August 21, an anti-government demonstration in Prague commemorates the twentieth anniversary of the Soviet invasion.

During the summer, strikes clandestinely organized by the now-banned Solidarity erupt in Poland; by September the industrial sector is largely paralyzed.

1989   In January, "Jan Palach Week" begins in Czechoslovakia—a series of anti-Communist demonstrations commemorating a student who immolated himself in 1969 to protest the Soviet invasion. Vaclav Havel is arrested and given a jail sentence. An opposition manifesto, *Several Sentences,* is signed by more than 40,000 people.

After dramatic deliberations, the central committee of the ruling party in Poland authorizes negotiations with the anti-Communist opposition.

In February, the new leadership of the Hungarian Communist Party announces its endorsement of the principles of party pluralism and electoral competition.

On February 6, Round Table Talks begin in Poland.

In April, Round Table Talks end in Poland, Solidarity is relegalized, and semifree general elections are scheduled for June 1989.

On June 13, Round Table Talks begin in Hungary.

On June 16, Imre Nagy is officially reburied in Budapest; more than 250,000 people participate in the ceremony.

On June 4, the anti-Communist opposition wins the Polish elections.

On August 19, Tadeusz Mazowiecki, a Catholic intellectual, is sworn in as Poland's first non-Communist prime minister since the 1940s.

On September 11, the border between Hungary and Austria is opened; tens of thousands of East Germans travel to Hungary and then flee westwards.

On September 18, the Round Table Talks in Hungary end; free multiparty elections for parliament are scheduled for March 1990.

On October 7–8, an official celebration of the fortieth anniversary of the GDR is held in Berlin; thousands of protestors demonstrate against the government and are brutally dispersed by the police.

On October 9, a large anti-government demonstration is held in Leipzig, GDR. Local Communist authorities refuse to carry out Erich Honecker's order to shoot protestors. A week later in Leipzig, 200,000 citizens participate in a similar demonstration.

On October 18, Erich Honecker resigns as head of state of the GDR and is replaced by Egon Krenz.

On November 3, several thousand people participate in an anti-government demonstration in Sofia, Bulgaria.

On November 4, several hundred thousand people demonstrate against the Communist government in East Berlin.

On November 9, GDR officials permit East Germans free access to West Berlin. Thousands of East Berliners pour through the newly opened Berlin Wall into the western part of the city.

On November 10, Todor Zhivkov resigns; Petar Mladenov replaces him as general secretary of the Bulgarian Communist Party.

On November 17, tens of thousands of people demonstrate against the Communist regime in Prague; the crowd is violently attacked by police.

On November 22, 200,000 people take part in an anti-government demonstration in Prague. Simultaneously, protests are held in Bratislava and all major cities in Czechoslovakia.

On November 24, Nikolae Ceausescu reelected general secretary of the Romanian Communist Party.

On November 24, Milos Jakes resigns as general secretary of the Czechoslovak Communist Party and is replaced by soft-liner Karel Urbanek.

On November 26, the anti-Communist forces favoring postponement win the referendum on the presidential elections in Hungary.

On November 25–26, 750,000 people attend an anti-government rally in Prague.

On November 27, a general strike takes place in Czechoslovakia; 70 percent of the workforce joins the protest.

On December 7, an anti-Communist coalition, the Union of Democratic Forces, is formed in Bulgaria.

On December 10, Gustav Husak resigns as president of Czechoslovakia.

On December 15, anti-government riots take place in Timisoara, Romania. The city is occupied by military detachments.

During December, the post-Zhivkov Bulgarian government restores the civil rights of ethnic Turks and announces that Round Table Talks between the Communist Party and the opposition will be held in Sofia.

On December 19, a general strike is declared in Timisoara.

On December 21–22, anti-Ceausescu demonstrations engulf the Romanian capital, Bucharest. The Communist dictator is forced to flee the city, and fierce fighting between armed groups breaks out in Bucharest.

On December 24, Ceausescu is captured by anti-government forces, and after a brief trial, is executed along with his wife. A Committee of National Salvation is formed, headed by Ion Iliescu.

On December 29, Vaclav Havel is elected president of Czechoslovakia.

1990   During March and April, anti-Communist parties win a decisive victory in the Hungarian elections. A non-Communist government headed by Jozsef Antall is sworn in.

In March, anti-Communist parties win the elections in GDR; the new government announces plans to unify with West Germany.

In June, anti-Communist parties win 80 percent of the votes in Czechoslovak elections; Communists are ousted from the government.

In June, Petar Mladenov resigns the Bulgarian presidency and is succeeded by Zhelyu Zhelev, leader of the anti-Communist Union of Democratic Forces.

On August 21–23, Communist hard-liners organize a coup against Mikhail Gorbachev; the coup fails. The Communist Party of the Soviet Union is temporarily banned.

In September, Wojciech Jaruzelski resigns as president of Poland.

On November 3, the two parts of Germany unite.

In December, Solidarity leader Lech Walesa is elected Polish president.

On December 24, Mikhail Gorbachev resigns; the Soviet Union is dissolved, and Russia becomes an independent state.

INTRODUCTION

The title "East European Revolutions of 1989" refers to the rapid and irrevocable collapse of the Communist Party–dominated nations of Eastern Europe and the historical defeat of the ideological agenda they championed. In the aftermath of these revolutions, the former Soviet-dominated Marxist dictatorships became fully autonomous states in which consensus in favor of democracy, economic reforms, and membership in the European Union prevailed. Thus the events of 1989 altered not only the region and Europe as a whole, but also signaled the downfall of a particular vision of modern development and anti-democratic rule, and thus shaped the direction of political change throughout the world. The East European Revolutions have been generally recognized as the last revolutionary episode of the twentieth century.

BACKGROUND: CULTURE AND HISTORY

The East European Revolutions of 1989 were the final chapter in the history of European Communism, a revolutionary ideology that seemed poised to conquer the entire world. The Communist credo drew sustenance from the philosophical teachings of Karl Marx but was also permeated by the passion for progress and justice that animated modern revolutionary movements. According to Marx, the objectively valid laws of history propel humankind to achieve ever higher stages of socioeconomic development through relentless class struggle. The final and decisive battle in this struggle would pit the proletariat, or the working people, against the bourgeoisie, or those who control capitalist means of production. The proletariat was destined to emerge victorious, and its victory would lay the foundation for a new, far-superior type of society—Communist. The Communist vision provided a radical and comprehensive alternative to the order established in developed Western societies. It promised to replace chaotic and wasteful capitalist competition with a more efficient planned economy, shallow liberal democracy with a new set of political institutions more responsive to the needs of the people, and individualistic bourgeois behavior with a more humane ethics of cooperation. In short, Communism was an attempt to create an alternative modernity—a brand new world that would correspond to humankind's loftiest aspirations.

Nineteenth-century Marxists, including Marx himself, were convinced that the Communist revolution would break out in the countries where proletarian forces were most numerous and experienced, that is, Britain and Germany. Instead, the most successful Marxist movement of the first half of the twentieth century was the Bolsheviks (Russian Communist Party). Led by Vladimir Lenin, a skillful organizer and fanatical revolutionary, they successfully seized power in 1917 and immediately set out to turn the dreams of progressive activists from around the world into reality. Private ownership of means of production was abolished; eventually, the economy began to be managed in accordance with a centrally designed and implemented plan. The supremacy of the victorious revolutionary organization was ensured through the "dictatorship of the proletariat," or the unlimited power exercised by the Communist Party on behalf of the working masses. Marxism became the official ideology of the state, and all non-Marxist views and ideas, including religion, were forcefully suppressed. Loyalty to the revolution and the Communist Party were expected from every citizen; those suspected of disloyalty were branded "enemies of the people" and subject to political repression. Rapid industrialization was launched in order to lift citizens from their abject poverty and turn the Soviet Union into a major power.

A main foreign policy goal of the Bolshevik regime was to stoke a global class war. In the 1920s and 1930s, however, Soviet-led attempts to instigate Communist revolution abroad failed. After the end of World War II, with the Soviet army occupying half of Europe, the effort to expand Communist power beyond the boundaries of the Soviet Union was renewed. In eight East European countries Soviet-style Communist regimes were established: Albania, Bulgaria, Czechoslovakia, the German Democratic Republic, Hungary, Poland, Romania, and Yugoslavia. Important features of the Soviet model—planned economy, nationalization of industrial means of production, dictatorship of the proletariat, violent repression of dissent, transformation of society in accordance with Marxist principles, fervent belief in the progressive historical mission of Communism—were more or less replicated under local conditions. Relations between Moscow and Yugoslavia were broken off in 1949, and between Moscow and Albania in the early 1960s (this is the reason developments in these countries are not considered an integral part of the events of 1989). The remaining six states were entrapped in a tightly knit union—the Soviet Bloc—dominated by and subservient to Moscow.

On several occasions during the post-war years, Communist regimes in Eastern Europe had to face various challenges—sometimes pro-democracy social forces rebelled against the dictatorial practices of regimes perceived as Soviet puppets; sometimes frustrated workers forcefully expressed their economic grievances; sometimes reformist factions within the party questioned Marxist dogmas. The ruthless secret police forces were often unleashed against those who dared to protest, and, if that proved insufficient, Soviet tanks were summoned. Moscow, in fact, explicitly claimed that its East European satellites enjoyed only limited sovereignty. Radical attempts at domestic reform were liable to be interpreted as an assault on Communism, and the Soviet Union arrogated to itself the prerogative to send its army to "rescue the people from counter-revolution" (this position became popularly known as the Brezhnev Doctrine, after Soviet general secretary Leonid Brezhnev, who articulated it in 1968). Up until the late 1980s, therefore, the impact of local attempts to dismantle Communism remained limited.

The opposite is true of the East European Revolutions of 1989. The momentum generated by these revolutions not only shattered the periphery of a declining empire, but also reverberated throughout the world. The events of 1989 became possible as a result of the confluence of long-term processes of decay and political factors that played the role of immediate causes of crises. Among the former, extremely important are

- The economic decline that by the 1980s had negatively affected the living standards of all strata except the highest ranking elites;
- The fact that the party-controlled organizations that played the role of transmission belts (such as the

Communist trade unions and Communist youth organizations) rapidly became dysfunctional and therefore useless as tools of social control;

- The spread of corruption and cynicism at all levels of the Communist administrative hierarchy;
- The reassertion of organized pro-democracy constituencies, such as environmentalists, human rights activists, independent trade unions, and religious congregations;
- The rekindling of nationalist sentiment, which gave rise to demands for more autonomy vis-à-vis Moscow; and
- The continuing erosion of Communist legitimacy (particularly among Communist functionaries themselves, the great majority of whom seemed much more willing to indulge in the simple pleasures of Western life-styles than maintain the purity of the revolutionary spirit).

Among the immediate causes, arguably the most salient one was the rise of Mikhail Gorbachev to power in the Soviet Union in 1985. Almost instantly, this relatively young reformer began his "perestroika," or radical restructuring of Soviet society with a view to establishment of a more open, tolerant, diverse, democratic Socialist society. Gorbachev insisted that the revolutionary catechism should make room for "universal values," such as respect for human dignity and peace among nations. Most importantly, he abandoned the Brezhnev Doctrine and announced that Soviet tanks would no longer intervene in the domestic affairs of its satellites. The changes in the Soviet Union engendered a two-pronged effect in Eastern Europe: they encouraged reformers within the Communist parties, and they emboldened pro-democracy forces within society. The perestroika, therefore, played the role of a catalyst for the tumults of 1989.

While the changes in Eastern Europe are amenable to social-scientific explanations, observers could not but be struck by the magnitude, velocity, and unexpectedness of the process. The year 1989 radiates with the mysterious aura engendered by truly revolutionary episodes. In the course of one year, the key structural features of Communist regimes in Eastern Europe were altered irreversibly; the fortunes of Marxism, the dominant revolutionary ideology since the late nineteenth century, appeared to be reversed; and the glow of hitherto lauded alternatives to liberal democracy began to fade. But the wave-like quality of democratization in the region need not obscure the fact that specific developments in each separate country did not follow a single scenario— there were considerable differences in the levels of societal mobilization, modes of interaction between Communist authorities and their opponents, and the extent to which the cadres of the ancien regime were displaced by new political elites. Nevertheless, all six cases displayed the distinct characteris-

tics of revolutionary dramas: clashes between rulers and mobilized anti-regime constituencies; epic collisions of competing normative visions; and large-scale societal confrontations that triggered mutually reinforcing institutional and structural changes. For a student of revolutionary phenomena, therefore, the simultaneous implosions of Communist regimes in Eastern Europe in 1989 constitute one of the most important thresholds in the history of the modern world.

CONTEXT AND PROCESS OF REVOLUTION

The first stirrings of the tidal wave that engulfed Eastern Europe were felt in Poland and Hungary. Several characteristics set these two Communist regimes apart from other Soviet satellites in the region. First, they had a relatively long history of political and economic reforms, which created propitious conditions for the coalescence of pro-reform factions within the Communist parties as well as the consolidation of non-Communist societal forces. The limited freedom, in turn, rendered possible the institutionalization of anti-regime opposition: both in Poland and in Hungary independent, semi-clandestine organizations existed which the authorities could single out for harsh treatment—but also treat as potential partners in an effort to avert impending crises. Finally, the public sphere in both countries was relatively liberalized, a factor that widened the scope of tactical options available to political competitors: in addition to massive mobilization and threats of violence, they could rely on openly propagated arguments, public consultations, and elite bargaining.

Poland

The revolutionary process of change began in Poland. Ever since the expansion of the Soviet empire into eastern Europe in the late 1940s, Poland had been considered the weakest link in the chain of Moscow-backed Marxist-Leninist regimes. While the power of the Communist Party was firmly entrenched, the national tradition of anti-Russian and anti-authoritarian resistance was never fully extinguished. The Soviet Stalinist model was only partially replicated in the country: agriculture was not collectivized, private entrepreneurship was not completely abolished, and intra-party criticism of governmental policies was not violently suppressed. Most importantly, Communist rulers did not destroy Polish civil society—cultural contacts between Poland and the West were restricted but not banned, Catholic ideas and rituals were tolerated, and nonconformist social behavior was treated more or less leniently. Poland, therefore, was the laboratory where an expanding arsenal of oppositional activities and anti-Communist practices was continually tested and perfected.

Beginning with the early 1950s, the party of the Polish Communists, the Polish United Workers' Party (PUWP), had to cope with periodically erupting political crises and mass protests. Until the late 1970s, however, opposition to the one-party regime was segmented: when students were protesting, as in 1968, workers remained at the sidelines, and when workers took to the streets, as in 1970–1971, Catholic churchgoers did not mobilize in their support. During the 1970s, however, various opposition activists launched a comprehensive effort to overcome divisions and form cross-class alliances. That this novel strategy of resistance might unhinge the regime became apparent in 1980, when, after a series of work stoppages and strikes supported by the Catholic Church and the Polish intelligentsia, an independent trade union called Solidarity was formed on September 22, 1980. By the end of 1981, Solidarity had a membership of approximately 10 million (in a country where the *entire* population was 34 million). The leaders of the trade union, including its president, Lech Walesa, insisted that they had the right to form an independent organization and to go on strike if their demands were not met, but they also consciously confined these demands to issues such as wages, food prices, and more active workers' participation in the administration of state-owned enterprises. Within the concrete political context, however, it was clear to everyone that behind what appeared to be a conflict between labor and management loomed the deeper issues that divided society from the ruling Communists—issues such as democracy, political freedom, steadily worsening economic conditions, and Poland's semicolonial status within the Soviet zone of influence. Throughout 1981, the confrontation between Solidarity and the regime escalated. After months of retreat and indecision, the Polish Communists—who were also concerned that the Soviets might intervene militarily—decided to act. On December 13, 1981, the regime declared martial law, Solidarity was banned, its foremost activists were imprisoned, and ensuing anti-government protests were quelled with gunfire (Ekiert 1996, 262). As the 1980s progressed, however, it became clear that re-equilibration of the regime would not be possible. Martial law could hardly mask the fact that the economy was sinking deeper into crisis, Marxist doctrine could yield no solutions to Poland's problems, and the legitimacy of Communist rule had eroded beyond repair. In fact, the demobilization of anti-regime constituencies proved to be temporary. In May 1988, clandestinely organized strikes broke out again in the Gdansk shipyard and the Nova Huta Lenin steel mill near Krakow. Soon thereafter, the strike wave spread around the country, and by September work routines in many Polish factories were disrupted.

The protests of 1988 were not as massive as the strikes that accompanied the rise of Solidarity. On the other hand, the anti-government forces confronted a Communist leadership that was considerably weaker than it had been in 1981. Once oppositional activities exploded again, it quickly dawned on Poland's leaders that their capacity to maintain order had diminished and their political capital had been depleted. As usually happens in revolutionary times, in the face of society's defiant irrepressibility the options of the rulers were reduced to two: either tighten repression or begin a process of rapprochement with social adversaries. Sensing the regime's dilemma, opposition activists signaled that they might be interested in negotiations. In early 1988, Bronislaw Geremek, a prominent Solidarity activist, proposed the idea of a national "anti-crisis pact," which would allow Communist and anti-Communist forces to reach a consensus regarding the proper way to resolve Poland's predicament. This proposal, articulated in the underground press, prompted the minister of internal affairs, General Czeslaw Kiszczak, to personally ask Lech Walesa whether he was ready to talk. On July 21, 1988, Walesa responded positively. The future course of events was to be determined by the balance of power within the PUWP itself.

The prospect of entering negotiations with political rivals heightened tensions within the highest echelons of Communist power. The controversy pitted those who favored the use of violence against those who acknowledged that the opposition was more than a passing phenomenon and argued that caution and responsibility could only be expected from someone who is given a right to participate in decision-making processes. The intra-party conflict climaxed in January 1989, when, during a meeting of leading Communists, PUWP General Secretary Wojciech Jaruzelski, Prime Minister Mieczyslaw Rakowski, and Kiszczak all threatened to resign unless the party sanctioned contacts with representatives of Solidarity. After tumultuous deliberations, the three officials were given a mandate to reach a deal with the opposition.

The victory of the soft-liners within the party in conjunction with Walesa's decision to give his blessing to contacts with the ruling clique paved the way to the Round Table Talks (RTT), a series of negotiations between the regime and various anti-Communist activists that began on February 6, 1989. With the creation of the new forum, massive anti-government activities were suspended and a modicum of normalcy was restored in the country. At the same time, it was clear to everyone involved that a political change of enormous magnitude was under way. The party de facto surrendered its monopoly on political power. All relevant political actors seemed to recognize that Poland's future would no longer be determined by Marxist dogmas.

The main dispute that the RTT had to resolve stemmed from the fact that while the opposition insisted on free elections and the concentration of political power in democratically elected bodies, the regime demanded that the new political arrangements preserve some elements of Communist power regardless of multiparty election results. Debates concentrated on two specific issues: (1) how to limit electoral pluralism to ensure a considerable presence of Communists in the legislature; (2) how to guarantee that, irrespective of the outcome of the elections, the Communists would retain a measure of control over the executive branch. With regard to electoral rules, the following compromise was reached. The Polish legislature was transformed into a bicameral parliament. Elections for the upper chamber, or the Senate, were to be open to candidates from all parties. The 460 seats in the lower chamber, or the Sejm, were to be distributed in accordance with the following formula: 38 percent of the deputies would be allocated to candidates nominated by the PUWP; 27 percent were to be distributed among smaller satellite parties that traditionally gravitated toward the Communists (such as the United Peasant Association and the Democratic Party); and 35 percent of the seats were reserved for other candidates (e.g., for anti-Communist organizations such as Solidarity). In other words, the trade-off was a democratically elected Senate versus a nondemocratically elected Sejm. Regarding the second issue, Communist control over the executive, it was decided that the country would have a relatively strong president elected by both houses of parliament. A consensus was reached at the RTT that the leader of PUWP, General Wojciech Jaruzelski, would be appointed to the position. In the eyes of all participants these complex arrangements constituted a temporary measure designed to meet the contingencies of the historical moment. There was a mutual agreement that the next parliamentary elections, to be held in 1993, would be fully democratic. Elections were scheduled for June, and on April 18 the Communist authorities finally registered Solidarity as an independent political organization.

The results of the semifree elections revealed the revolutionary proportions of Poland's transformation: anti-Communist candidates won all seats in the Senate and all freely contested seats in the Sejm. Despite the fact that, in accordance with the RTT deal, General Jaruzelski was subsequently elected president on July 19, the Communist monopoly over executive power began to unravel when the smaller parties elected to parliament, after playing for decades the role of marionettes in the hands of the Communists, formed a coalition with Solidarity. The realignment of parliamentary forces made possible the appointment, on August 19, 1989, of the first non-Communist government in the Soviet Bloc: a cabinet headed by Tadeusz Mazowiecki, a prominent Catholic intellectual. Its immediate objectives were to abolish censorship, curb the powers of the secret police, promote the rule of law, institutionalize political

pluralism—and thus demolish the political basis of one-party Communist dictatorship. Its program envisaged far-reaching democratization and radical pro-market reforms. Finally, its main foreign policy objective was to re-establish close relations with the "capitalist" West. The last vestiges of Communist power in Poland vanished in 1990: the Communist Party voted to dissolve itself in January, Mazowiecki fired all Communists from the cabinet in June, and Jaruzelski resigned from the presidency in September—to be succeeded three months later by Solidarity leader Lech Walesa.

Hungary

The Polish events of 1988–1989 had enormous effects on Communist elites and opposition forces across Eastern Europe, but their impacts were most powerful in Hungary. In November 1956, Moscow had to send troops into the country in order to suppress a popular revolution. János Kádár, the Hungarian strongman that the Soviets installed, presided over the bloody reprisals against opponents of Communist power; Imre Nagy, the Hungarian prime minister whom the Soviets deposed, was tried for high treason and executed. By the early 1960s, however, Kádár metamorphosed into a reformer who favored pragmatism over doctrinal rigidity. The policies that he championed came to be known as "Goulash communism," after the national Hungarian meal; their most important characteristics were a measure of toleration for private economic activities, an effort to manage the state-owned economy in such a way as to meet some of the basic needs of Hungarian consumers, and acceptance of a certain degree of political and cultural pluralism.

By the mid 1980s, however, the economic situation in Hungary worsened: between 1984 and 1978, the country's foreign debt more than doubled (from $ 8.8 billion to $ 17.7 billion [Tokes 1996, 273]) and the regime's strategy—buying off the population with material benefits without modifying the command structure of the economy and the party's dominant position—no longer appeared to be working. But at the thirteenth congress of the ruling Hungarian Socialist Workers' Party, held in March 1985, Kádár vowed to keep Hungary on the course to Socialism, rejected demands for comprehensive reforms, and reappointed himself general secretary. By the end of 1986, however, he was forced to admit that Hungary consumed more than it produced, thus implicitly acknowledging the need for changes. The Kádár-led defenders of the status quo were compelled to confront the challenge of the young technocrats who emerged victorious.

On May 19, 1988, Kádár resigned, and was replaced by Budapest party secretary, Karoly Grosz, a centrist. Leading reformers, such as Miklos Nemeth, Rezso Nyers, and Imre Pozsgay, were elevated to positions of power. The new leaders found it useful to distance themselves from the Communist past, which in turn compelled them to place topics such as democratization and pro-market reforms on the party's agenda.

As cleavages within the party were becoming manifest, non-Communist constituencies in the country began to coalesce. None of Hungary's oppositional organizations could replicate Solidarity's success. Yet collectively they became a formidable actor with whom the authorities had to reckon. The first meeting of various semi-official and underground organizations was held on June 15–16, 1985, in Monor. A second meeting, held in September 1987 in Lakitelek, was attended by representatives of the reformist wing of the Communist Party. The Hungarian opposition was very heterogeneous, including nationalists, agrarians, leftist intellectuals, and representatives of political parties banned in the late 1940s; anti-Communism provided the common platform necessary for coordinated political action. In March and June 1988, various opposition activists successfully mobilized tens of thousands of people for anti-government rallies in Budapest.

The simultaneous fragmentation of the party and consolidation of anti-regime forces altered the political landscape—political space opened for new voices. Utilizing a loophole in the electoral law, citizen committees in various parts of Hungary began to nominate independent candidates in local and national elections. In 1985, one such candidate, a television reporter from Szeged, won a seat in the Hungarian parliament. Communists now had to contend with parliamentary opposition.

Under conditions of intensified intra-party clashes and anti-government mobilization, the new leaders of Hungary formulated three distinct sets of reformist policies: (1) transfer of prerogatives from the party to the state; (2) reorient the country's foreign policy toward a closer cooperation with Western countries, particularly West Germany and Austria; (3) design electoral procedures in such a way as to maximize the party's prospects in anticipated multiparty competitions.

The shift of power from party to state began when Miklos Nemeth, a young economist, replaced Karoly Grosz as prime minister in November 1988. By the end of the year, all important decision making, except in regard to national security, defense, and foreign policy, was firmly in the hands of technocrats. This development was resisted by hard-liners led by Grosz. In January 1989, the general secretary announced that a "state of economic emergency" should be declared in order to allow the party to stabilize the weakened Hungarian economy. Grosz, however, was rebuffed by Prime Minister Nemeth, who assured the public that "our government of experts" are still in charge of policy making and would not surrender its prerogatives to "emergency committees" (Tokes 1996, 325–326).

The second reformist item was the abandonment of the principle of international class struggle, according to which relations with "bourgeois-capitalist" countries are characterized by unrelenting antagonism, and instead the cultivation of warmer relations with Hungary's Western neighbors. One element of this new policy had a momentous impact: the dismantling of the barricades and other obstacles erected at the Hungarian-Austrian border (a process that began on May 2, 1989, and was completed on September 11, 1989). It was this Hungarian government decision that precipitated the large exodus of East Germans via Hungary to West Germany, a development that inflicted a fatal blow on the East German Communist regime. Western governments provided incentives to Hungarian reformers: on September 17, U.S. president George Bush announced that Hungary's "most favored nation" status would become permanent, and later that same month West German authorities promised Hungary credits amounting to more than $1 billion. Still, there is no doubt that the primary reason Hungary embarked upon this road was because the new leadership of the Communist Party understood that Hungary's future lay not with the Soviet Bloc but with democratic Europe.

The third focal point of reformist efforts was the introduction of electoral competition. Political pluralism was recognized officially by the Communist leadership in November 1988. In February 1989, the party concluded that "a forum of national reconciliation" was necessary. The opposition was invited to join Polish-style RTT, scheduled to begin on June 13, 1989.

The main opposition-sponsored political event of the summer of 1989 was the reburial of Imre Nagy (the Hungarian prime minister whom the Soviets removed in 1956 and whom Kádár's regime later executed). The symbolic impact of this event could hardly be overestimated: it was intended to relegitimize a national tradition of anti-Communist resistance, to discredit both Kádárism (as a regime stained with innocent blood and imposed by a foreign army) and the rule of the party (as despotism based on violent suppression of freedom), and to endorse political, social, and economic reforms in the country. The reburial ceremony, held on June 16, 1989, attracted more than 250,000 people. As in Poland, the rulers had to conclude that the only alternatives were either massive repression against an energized opposition and population, or concessions.

The Round Table Talks (RTT) focused mainly on the upcoming elections. Opinion polls held at the time indicated that the Communist Party's leading reformist, Imre Pozsgay, was by far the most popular politician in the country and would easily win direct presidential elections. That was why the government's representatives at the RTT, unlike their Polish comrades, were willing to allow fully open elections for parliament; they demanded, in return, the creation of a strong, popularly elected presidency, which they hoped to capture. When the RTT ended on September 18, it was announced that direct presidential elections would be held on November 29, 1989, followed by parliamentary elections in March.

Some of the opposition parties, however, refused to recognize the legitimacy of a bargain that clearly benefited the Communists and argued that the question of whether Hungary should have a stronger, popularly elected president or a weaker president elected by the legislature could not be resolved without consulting the people. A grassroots attempt to force a referendum on the issue succeeded. On November 26, the proposal to postpone the decision of when and how a president should be elected until after the parliamentary elections was approved by a slim margin.

In November and December the institutional foundation of the old regime was dismantled. In a symbolic rejection of Marxist ideology, the name of the country was changed from the Hungarian People's Republic to the Republic of Hungary; the ruling party was renamed the Hungarian Socialist Party, and thousands of hard-line Marxists were expelled from it (they formed a party of their own); and the Workers' Guard, the party-run paramilitary detachments used in the past to unleash terror on political opponents, was disarmed by the Hungarian army. But in the face of the political momentum of 1989, these measures proved to be futile. In the two rounds of elections, held on March 25 and April 8, 1990, the renamed Communist Party won only 11 percent of the popular vote and less than 9 percent of parliamentary seats (a newly formed party of unreconstructed Marxists drew 3.5 percent of the votes, below the 4 percent threshold set for parliamentary representation). Overall, more than 80 percent of the newly elected deputies represented anti-Communist opposition parties. On May 22, 1990, when Jozsef Antall, leader of the largest center-right party, was sworn in as prime minister, Communist rule in Hungary officially ended.

German Democratic Republic (East Germany)

Developments in the GDR, Bulgaria, and Czechoslovakia differed from those in Poland and Hungary in several important respects. In these countries the effort to reproduce the Soviet sociopolitical model under local conditions was much more comprehensive: as in the Soviet Union, heavy industry, collectivized agriculture, and strict social control enforced by an aggressive and sizable security force and police constituted the pillars of Communist domination. In none of the three countries did Communist regimes contemplate any serious reforms in the late 1980s. Power remained firmly in the hands of neo-Stalinists, and violent reprisal was still the preferred response to political challenges. These differences notwithstanding, developments in the GDR, Bulgaria, and Czechoslovakia in 1989 generated an outcome similar to that observable in Poland and Hungary: a decisive break with the Communist past. In the course of three dramatic months, these regimes collapsed—swept aside by international developments over which they had little control and, most significantly, mass pressure from below (a factor that was of crucial importance in the GDR and Czechoslovakia but less significant in Bulgaria). Despite the participation of hundreds of thousands of people, the process was orderly. But it did result in a revolutionary overthrow of existing political structures.

In the case of the GDR, the transformations that began in 1989 rapidly led to the disappearance of the country itself. After World War II, Germany had been divided into two countries. On the territory occupied by the Western allies, the Federal Republic of Germany, or West Germany, was formed; its capital was Bonn. The provinces occupied by the Soviet army became the German Democratic Republic (GDR, or East Germany). The city of Berlin was also split in two: the eastern part became the capital of the GDR, whereas the western part, under the control of U.S., British, and French troops, became, for all practical purposes, a part of West Germany.

The Marxist regime that the Soviets installed in Germany made it clear from its inception that it would adhere to the Stalinist sociopolitical model. In 1953, with the help of Soviet troops in Berlin, the regime suppressed an anti-Communist workers' uprising, and in 1961 it erected the infamous Berlin Wall to prevent massive emigration to the western part of the divided city. During the 1950s, the regime was able to rebuild the industrial base of the country and thus ensured its citizens the highest standard of living in the Soviet Bloc. By the early 1970s, however, the country increasingly relied on financial help from West Germany and was less and less capable of competing in world markets. The Berlin Wall had put an end to the massive exodus of people but not to the desire of East Germans to escape to the West. The number of applications for exit visas grew exponentially in the 1980s; in 1984 alone the regime authorized the emigration of 41,000 malcontents (Snodgrass 2000, 78).

At the beginning of 1989, the ruling Communist party, the Socialist United Party of Germany (SED), seemed fully confident that it would weather any political storm. Ignoring developments in Poland and Hungary, the GDR stuck to the traditional practice of holding elections in which the number of candidates was equal to the number of seats—and reported to an incredulous population that the Socialist Unity Party of Germany had won 97 percent of the vote in the May 7 elections. It was during that same month, however, that GDR authorities were informed by their Hungarian comrades that the border between Hungary and Austria was to be opened in September. What that meant was that East Germans would be able to go to Hungary, cross uninhibited into Austria, and then easily reach the Federal Republic of Germany, where they were entitled to instantly receive full citizenship. On September 11, the day when the barriers separating Austria from Hungary were lifted, tens of thousands of East Germans poured into Hungary and then Austria.

The emigration crisis instantly threw the country into a political tailspin. Both those who wanted to flee and those who wanted to stay were provoked to act. The former began to leave en masse, the latter grew determined to demand political and economic reforms from the Communist authorities. Almost immediately, local churches were transformed into centers of resistance, especially St. Nikolas Church in Leipzig. It was there that, on Monday, September 11, several hundred people gathered to take part in peace prayers. As the worshippers were leaving the church, many of them were arrested by the police. Defiantly, the pastor announced that a week later the congregation would assemble to pray for those detained. Thus began a series of Monday evening vigils that soon escalated into a tension-ridden stand-off between the regime's and pro-democracy forces.

Just as the emigration pressure was gnawing away at the very foundations of the regime, the GDR leaders seemed preoccupied with the upcoming celebrations of the fortieth anniversary of "the German workers and farmers state," scheduled for October 7, 1989. Erich Honecker, the leader of the East German Communists, seemed convinced that a ritualistic display of unity would bolster his regime and dismissed the emigration problem as a distraction. Referring with admiration to the bloody suppression of student revolts in China in June 1989, Honecker vowed to follow the "Tiananmen model" and smash anti-government protests.

It was during the carefully orchestrated festivities, however, that the East German Communists realized that they had been abandoned by an important ally. In his official speech, Soviet leader Mikhail Gorbachev reiterated his view that the further liberalization and democratization of existing Communist systems was the political imperative of the day and issued the dire warning that "those who do not change are swept aside by history." Gorbachev's blunt rhetoric simultaneously undermined the position of the East German government and encouraged those who demanded immediate and radical reforms. The celebrations were not yet over when waves of protests disrupted normally tranquil East Berlin. But perhaps the most important action against the regime took place on October 9 in Leipzig. Anticipating yet another "Monday night vigil," Honecker issued an explicit order for the army and the police "to take all measures and use all means to smash the counterrevolutionaries" (Snodgrass 2000, 106). Instead, local party officials sought informal contacts with civic leaders. As a result of the im-

provised negotiations, a "committee of six" was formed, composed of three party secretaries and three respected, politically unaffiliated intellectuals. Apparently, this course of action enjoyed the blessings of Egon Krenz, Honecker's deputy. The committee issued a joint statement offering mutual assurances of restraint and civilized behavior. Army tanks and police barricades were then removed and the demonstrators were allowed to enter the city center. The order to massacre the regime's opponents was thus ignored.

Predictably, the events of October 9 precipitated a groundswell of demands for political change. By next Monday, October 16, protests had spread to all major cities. Having failed to push his colleagues and the army generals into violent action, Honecker resigned on October 18 and was replaced by Krenz (Snodgrass 2000, 131). But pressure against the Communist regime continued to mount. On October 23, the Monday crowd in Leipzig reached 200,000. A week later it grew to 300, 000. It was in the second half of October that throughout the country the popular chants "We are the people!" turned into "We are one people!," indicating that an increasing number of East Germans wanted to end not only the Communist dictatorship, but also the division of Germany. Unable to offer any meaningful response to this demand, the Communist government resigned on November 7.

The most famous episode of the East European Revolutions of 1989 took place in Berlin two days later, on November 9. During a press conference, a leading official of the regime announced that SED would immediately allow East Germans to leave the country without exit visas. In response to a question, he said that this would apply to the crossings between East and West Berlin. His words were taken seriously. Only half an hour later, large crowds gathered at checkpoints in East Berlin and demanded to be let through. Confused and unable to reach their superiors, the border guards decided to lift the barriers. At this point, East Berliners walked into West Berlin, climbed the infamous wall and began to celebrate their newly gained freedom. In a single night, the Berlin Wall became a remnant of the past.

The momentum generated in 1989 crucially shaped the events of 1990. Only days after the fall of the wall, Communist authorities announced that they would seek "to form a contractual community" between Bonn and East Berlin. During Round Table Talks, held between December 7, 1989, and March 12, 1990, an agreement was reached to establish the rule of law, dissolve the state security apparatus, and create the institutional framework for a democratic political system. The main issue that the RTT did not resolve was whether or not the GDR would continue to exist as an independent state. It was the East German electorate that answered this question. When multiparty elections were held on March 18, 1990, the new eastern branches of the largest West German parties, the Social Democratic Party and the

Christian Democratic Union, won more than 70 percent of the votes; the former Communists won 17 percent. The East German parliament was thus dominated by parties that strove for rapid reunification of Germany. On November 3, 1990, the two German states merged and the GDR ceased to exist.

Bulgaria

On November 10, 1989, the day after the fall of the Berlin Wall, more stunning news from Eastern Europe made the headlines: Todor Zhivkov, the aging dictator of Bulgaria, stepped down as general secretary (a position he had held since 1954). This event marked the culmination of yet another subplot within the broader drama of the East European Revolutions of 1989, a subplot that revealed that the transformative energy afoot in the region could overwhelm even the seemingly most stable Communist regimes.

Traditionally, Bulgaria had been the most pliant Soviet ally. Once the anti-Communist opposition was crushed in the late 1940s, a spasm of violence during which, in a country of 6.5 million people, tens of thousands suffered repression, an orthodox Stalinist dictatorship was quickly institutionalized. Harsh measures against opponents combined with a cultural factor, namely widespread sympathy toward all things Russian—a feeling grounded in the common Slavic past of the two nations and in the fact that it was the Russian (imperial) army that liberated Bulgarians from the Ottomans in 1877–1878—allowed the Communist Party to maintain its domination without encountering organized resistance.

Up until the mid 1980s, Zhivkov's regime seemed immune to the turbulence that periodically swept through the Soviet Bloc. The first sign of trouble was the ten-fold increase of the country's foreign debt: from $1 billion in 1982 to $10 billion in 1987. Within the party, voices favoring far-reaching political and economic reforms began to be heard. Zhivkov's response was to purge all alleged reformers, stiffen censorship over the media and academic institutions, and instruct the security forces to systematically suppress opposition activities. In an attempt to stir nationalist passions and thus bolster its legitimacy, the regime unleashed a large-scale assimilation campaign against the country's 800,000 Muslims, most of whom had a Turkish ethnic background. In the winter of 1984–1985, these Bulgarian citizens were forced to adopt Slavic names and abandon their religion.

The ill-conceived brutal attempt to bring about what was described as "rebirth of the Bulgarian nation" encountered the determined resistance of the Turkish minority, without eliciting the support of ethnic Bulgarians. In repeated clashes between ethnic Turks and heavily armed military detachments, several hundred protestors were killed and thousands of people were incarcerated. In the summer of 1989, Zhivkov changed tactics: he ordered the secret services to pressure ethnic Turks to leave the country. By September 1989, almost one-third of them had resettled in neighboring Turkey.

It was also in the late 1980s that organized civic groups began to emerge. Human rights activists criticized the government for its treatment of Muslims. Writers and artists demanded that censorship be abolished, and discussion groups called for more openness and democracy. But the most significant new actors to emerge on the political scene were the independent ecological movements. In an unprecedented display of political dissent, a group of environmental activists began to openly collect signatures for a petition pleading with the government to abandon several large industrial projects that threatened to ruin the ecosystem of Rila Mountain in southwestern Bulgaria. On October 26, these activists were beaten and then arrested by the police. Undeterred, various opposition groups organized a march to parliament on November 3 and presented the environmentalists' petition to bewildered Communist deputies. More than 5,000 people participated in what was clearly a protest against the Communist regime.

The combined effect of popular disturbances at home and the general trend toward democratization in the Soviet Bloc finally spurred Zhivkov's intra-party rivals into action. On November 10, the dictator was deposed by a clique of reform-minded Communists whose leader, Foreign Minister Petar Mladenov, became the party's new general secretary. A week later Zhivkov and his cronies were removed from the party's decision-making bodies. Whether the new elites intended a full-scale democratization of the Bulgarian political system was unclear; just as elsewhere in Eastern Europe in 1989, however, rapidly evolving events rendered futile any hopes that cosmetic changes at the top might prevent the rise of popular resistance to the Communist regime. On November 18, hundreds of thousands of people attended an anti-government rally in Sofia; on December 7, an anti-Communist coalition, the Union of Democratic Forces, was formed, and demands for far-reaching reforms were constantly articulated in the newly liberated public sphere. By late December, the party's new leaders acknowledged that limiting the scope of reforms might be impossible and announced that all political and civil rights of Bulgaria's ethnic Turks would be restored and that Round Table Talks would be held with the organized opposition.

The results of the first multiparty elections in Bulgaria, held in June 1990, were different than those in Poland, Hungary, and the GDR. The Communist Party won a plurality of the votes and an absolute majority of the seats in the newly elected legislature. Still, the dramatic events of 1989 ultimately altered Bulgaria's sociopolitical system just as dramatically as the much more rapid displacement of Communist elites changed its former Warsaw Treaty allies.

Czechoslovakia

The collapse of the neo-Stalinist regimes in the GDR and Bulgaria generated shock waves in Czechoslovakia. Czechoslovakia was among the better-developed countries in the Socialist camp—prior to 1939, it was an industrially developed, thoroughly Westernized, well-institutionalized liberal democracy. In the aftermath of World War II, Socialist ideas were more popular in the country than anywhere else in the region, and the Communist Party won a plurality of the votes in general elections. In 1948, however, the Communists organized a coup, abolished democratic institutions and practices, and established a party dictatorship. But in January 1968, the Stalinist leadership of the Communist Party was replaced by a team of young reformers, who launched "The Prague Spring," a set of reforms intended to produce "socialism with a human face," or a revitalized Socialist system based on respect for pluralism, law, freedom of artistic expression, and individual rights. This reformist program, however, ultimately proved unacceptable to the Kremlin, and on August 21, 1968, Soviet troops intervened to quash the reform movement. What followed was a series of large-scale, if nonviolent, purges that stifled dissent in the party and reaffirmed the primacy of the Communist Party.

Discontent, however, continued to simmer. In Slovakia, dissent came mainly from among the ranks of Catholic Christians. Throughout the 1980s, the Czechoslovak primate, Frantisek Cardinal Tomasek, repeatedly protested the mistreatment of religious believers. In March and December the tensions between the government and Catholics provoked demonstrations by elderly women Catholics in Bratislava and Olomouc. In the Czech lands, the tradition of dissent was continued by intellectuals, some former Communists associated with the Prague Spring. The most important event was the publication of Charter 77, which demanded that the Communist authorities respect human rights and individual freedoms.

On August 21, 1988, the twentieth anniversary of the Soviet invasion, 10,000 citizens demonstrated in Prague, chanting slogans in favor of freedom and demanding democratic elections, abolition of censorship, and rehabilitation of the victims of political repression. The crowd was dispersed with tear gas, and hundreds of protestors were beaten by the police and arrested. Milos Jakes, the hard-line Marxist leader, announced that further protests would encounter harsher measures. On October 28, 1988, when 5,000 people tried to demonstrate, the beatings were more severe. But in early January,

Vaclev Havel, president of the Czech Republic, 1993–2003. (Embassy of the Czech Republic/Alan Pajer)

various opposition activists announced a "Jan Palach Week"—seven days of anti-Communist protests commemorating the Czech student who immolated himself in 1969 to protest Soviet occupation. In response, the regime began to arrest opposition figures; renowned playwright Vaclav Havel was given a nine-month prison sentence. Persecutions did not quell resistance: a petition in defense of Havel began to circulate, and more than 40,000 Czechoslovak citizens signed an anti-government manifesto, *Several Sentences,* which demanded the release of political prisoners, implementation of basic political reforms, and re-evaluation of the events of 1968.

In March 1989, students organized a petition demanding the end of the monopoly of the Socialist Union of Youth and the formation of a system of academic self-administration. An alternative student organization called STUHA (Studentske hnuti or Student Movement) was formed. Its purpose, according to activist Martin Benda, was "to awaken the sleeping universities to a struggle against communism" (Wheaten and Kavan 1992, 40). It was the students who, after the summer developments in Poland and Hungary, relaunched protests in the fall. On November 17, 1989, the first large-scale demonstration against the regime was held. The crowd grew to 50,000. After a two-hour stand-off, the police attacked, and thousands of peaceful protestors were injured and detained.

In response, the students decided to initiate a two-hour national strike on November 27. The national strike campaign rapidly gained momentum. A newly formed independent organization, Citizen Forum, began to synchronize anti-government activities. The regime was confident that the call for a general strike would be ignored. Government-controlled media repeatedly stated that workers supported the police. But print workers from the Prague paper mills supplied students with everything they needed to produce posters. The students refuted the party's claim that they were "economic saboteurs": they baked bread, cleaned the parks, and swept streets, thus gaining the sympathy of broader constituencies within Czechoslovak society.

The next anti-government rally, held in Prague on November 22, 1989, attracted 200,000 supporters of democracy. As many participants later reminisced, the spectacle of flowers, flags, and flickering candles forged a bond that made everyone reluctant to disperse. A sense of belonging to a community seemed to allay the fear of police violence; a spirit of goodwill and gallantry eclipsed revengeful sentiments and hatred for the Communist authorities (notably, between midNovember and midDecember the police reported a stunning 75 percent drop in crime: Wheaton and Kavan 1992, 74). It is this remarkable mass display of gentleness of manners and firmness of political conviction that brought to life the term "Velvet Revolution", which is how the events of November 1989 in Czechoslovakia came to be known.

Confronted with hundreds of thousands of "Velvet Revolutionaries," the ruling clique began to crack. Various low-ranking Communists demanded official investigation of police brutality. Army generals made it clear that they would not order their troops to shoot at unarmed civilians. It became clear that in order to survive, the regime would have to unleash a violent crackdown. On November 24, 1989, this option was voted down by the collective leadership of the Communist Party, and hard-liner Milos Jakes was removed as general secretary and replaced with the soft-liner Karel Urbanek.

During the weekend of November 25 and 26, as a build-up to the national strike declared for Monday, the biggest rally of the East European Revolutions of 1989 was held in Prague. More than 750,000 people, 5 percent of the country's population, showed up to demand an end to the party's dictatorship. On November 27, the national strike began. Overall, more than 70 percent of the workforce, either by stopping work for short periods or through other actions, joined the coordinated effort to unseat the Communist government. Later that same day, the most prominent hard-liners were dismissed from leadership positions, and the party's para-military People's Militia was ordered to surrender its weapons to the national army.

In early December, seven members of the Citizen Forum were invited to join the government, bringing an end the one-party dictatorship. On December 10, Gustav Husak, the hated Communist functionary who had invited the Soviets to invade his country in 1968, resigned as president of Czechoslovakia. On December 28, parliament elected as its speaker Alexander Dubcek, the venerated and persecuted leader of the Prague Spring. On the next day, former political prisoner Vaclav Havel was elected president. In his New Year address to the people, he declared: "Citizens! Your government has returned to you!"

Romania

Events in Romania followed a different pattern, one that more closely approximated a classical revolutionary scenario featuring armed insurgents, violent clashes, and the execution of disgraced despots. The Communist dictatorship established by Nikolae Ceausescu in Romania was the most brutal in Eastern Europe. He had come to power in 1965, initially perceived as a reformer. When, in defiance of Moscow, he refused to send Romanian troops to Czechoslovakia in 1968, Ceausescu was praised in the West as an independent and liberal ruler (in fact, Romania was the first Communist country to be visited by a U.S. president when Nixon flew there to meet Ceausescu in 1969). But by the late 1970s, Ceausescu's rule had degenerated into an ugly despotism involving a series of brutal attempts to mobilize the population in pursuit of grandiose projects. In 1984, for example, Ceausescu announced that by the end of the century Romania's population should increase by one-third. The regime then proceeded not only to ban the sale of contraceptives and almost all legal abortions, but also to introduce monthly compulsory gynecological examinations of all working women of childbearing age at their workplaces in order to determine when a woman became pregnant and force her to carry the pregnancy to term. At about the same time, Ceausescu declared a policy that envisaged the destruction of thousands of villages and concentrating peasants in labor camp–like compounds. When in the late 1980s the regime decided to repay the $10 billion it owed Western creditors, a series of austerity measures was introduced that caused immense hardships: heat, gas, and medical care were rationed as if the country were at war, and all kinds of foodstuffs, including those that constituted the normal daily diet of the average Romanian citizen, were exported. Famine and malnutrition became endemic.

In March 1989, six party veterans circulated an open letter criticizing Ceausescu's economic policies. In November

1989, however, Ceausescu was re-elected as general secretary. In a militant speech, he lambasted developments in Eastern Europe and declared that his country remained committed to the revolutionary principles of Marxism-Leninism.

A month later, however, the dictator was dead. The terminal crisis of Ceausescu's regime began in Timisoara, a university town, home to 20,000 students and a sizable ethnic Hungarian minority. On December 15, 1989, Laszlo Tokes, an ethnic Hungarian minister in the local Reformed Church—and also a champion of the rights of the Hungarian minority—was supposed to be forcefully transferred to a remote village. He asked his congregation to help him resist the eviction. Several hundred ethnic Hungarians responded to his request. They were later joined by an even larger number of ethnic Romanians. The authorities rescinded the eviction, but this did not placate the growing crowds. When on the next day, more than 5,000 Timisoarans headed toward the local party headquarters, they were attacked by Interior Ministry troops. But by midnight, there were 10,000 men and women in the city's central square.

Early on Sunday, December 17, all of the city's important intersections were controlled by military personnel, and Tokes was arrested. Later that day, Ceausescu's order "to open fire on the counter-revolutionaries and the foreign spies" resulted in several hundred people being killed (Ratesh 1991, 27). On the next day, somewhat reassured, the dictator left for an official visit to Iran.

At least some opponents of the regime, however, interpreted Ceausescu's departure as an escape. On December 19, 1989, a general strike spontaneously erupted in Timisoara. On the next day, huge columns of people began to converge on the center of the city. The army let them pass without interfering. Negotiations did not break the stalemate. There was no one to ensure the main demand, Ceausescu's resignation, would be met.

Ceausescu came back from Iran on the following day. He accused "foreign secret services," the Hungarians in particular, of plotting to overthrow his regime. He called for a mass meeting of support in Bucharest the next day, December 21. During this nationally televised event, however, his speech was interrupted by shouts, chants, and commotion. Eventually, he simply abandoned it and left the rally.

Immediately after the sudden end of the pro-government event, many people gathered at a nearby square and began an anti-Communist demonstration. As the afternoon grew into evening, tensions rose. Eventually troops loyal to the regime attacked the protestors. Many demonstrators were killed or wounded. By early December 22, 1989, it was clear that the final clash was coming. Huge columns of citizens, mainly workers, descended on the center of Bucharest. The crowds gathered in front of the Central Committee building. Ceausescu decided to speak to them. As he was about to begin his address, however, dozens of people rushed into the building and ran toward the balcony from which he was trying to speak. In haste, Ceausescu went to the roof of the building, where a helicopter was waiting for him.

Later on December 22, fierce fighting erupted around the national television and the Central Committee buildings. The same evening, the formation of a National Salvation Front was announced, headed by Ion Iliescu, a former high-ranking Communist official purged by Ceausescu in the 1970s. The National Salvation Front promised free elections, the establishment of a constitutional system of checks and balances, and respect for minority rights. Iliescu and his government were able to win the acquiescence of the army and the secret police. Two days later, Ceausescu was apprehended by military units loyal to the National Salvation Front, and after a four-hour-long trial, he and his wife, who was his first deputy within the Communist hierarchy, were executed. By the end of December the fighting subsided.

The abrupt break did not result in a radical transformation in Romania. For years, politics in the country continued to be dominated by cadres affiliated with the old regime. But the popular rebellion of December 1989, the concluding act of the East European Revolutions of 1989, did lead to the extinction of the Communist regime. Romania became more democratic than it had ever been.

IMPACTS

The Communist experiment that engulfed Eastern Europe in the 1940s was animated by the fervor of a utopian pursuit, the ardency of large-scale social conflict, the energy attendant to rapid modernization, and the drama of a geopolitical clash of rivals espousing irreconcilable values. For over four decades this experiment stood at the core of political, economic, and ideological conflicts raging within and between societies across the globe. It is not surprising, then, that the East European Revolutions of 1989 had far-reaching consequences.

The most dramatic change took place in Eastern Europe itself. During 1989, at varying speeds but with tenacious persistence, these societies embarked upon the road to democratization. A decade of struggles ensued, but ultimately all countries evolved into stable European liberal democracies (Hungary, Poland, and the two independent states into which Czechoslovakia split in 1993, the Czech Republic and Slovakia, all gained full membership in the European Union in 2004, and Bulgaria and Romania were slated to attain the same status in 2007). The transformations that began in 1989 did not spell prosperity for everyone: economic reforms were much more painful than anyone anticipated, and beneath the veneer of political change, analysts detected essential continuities with the old order (that is, in patterns of dependence on entrenched strongmen in the countryside, high levels of distrust of elected authorities, and reliance on informal institutions rather than official procedures). But there is little doubt that these societies became better equipped to face the challenges of the future than they would have been under Communist regimes.

The collapse of the Soviet Bloc also dramatically changed the face of Europe. Germany was reunited, East-West rivalries abated, and channels of communication and cooperation were reopened. The zeal of newly liberated nations for full membership in the European Union energized the process of European integration. The East European Revolutions of 1989, therefore, are among the decisive factors that propelled the most fascinating experiment in transnational and cross-cultural governance in the modern world.

Finally, the events of 1989 brought about the end of the Cold War. Since 1989, the West has not been threatened by a rival military alliance, but by rogue regimes, subnational actors, and organized criminal groups. It is undeniable that after 1989 we think in a new way about the dangers of war and the prospects of peace.

For some, the significance of 1989 is that it led to expansion of the global territory of democracy, and that is a positive development. For others, the same events narrowed the global space available for progressive-Socialist experiments, and that is something to be lamented. More broadly, the ideological impact is difficult to ascertain. On the one hand, the East European Revolutions of 1989 boosted the legitimacy of liberal democracy and economic freedom. On the other hand, there is ample evidence that radical doubts about democracy and markets have not been extinguished in the aftermath of 1989. Several ideas that guided the Soviet experiment—that capitalism is the source of all social evils, that liberal democracy is inherently repressive and should be supplanted by a Socialist democracy, that markets allow the few to grow rich while impoverishing the many and should therefore be abolished, that violence committed in the pursuit of progressive goals or as an act of resistance against capitalism is morally justified—remain deeply ingrained in dominant intellectual and academic discourses. It remains to be seen, therefore, whether the East European Revolutions of 1989 brought about the demise of Marxism as a guiding progressivist paradigm or constituted nothing more than a temporary setback.

Not everyone agrees that the term revolution is applicable to what transpired in Eastern Europe in 1989. For some, these events were too peaceful to qualify. Moreover, politically relevant elites eventually sought to reach a compromise rather than physically eliminate each other. Other observers charge that the events of 1989 produced no new ideas that would justify radical political change. In response, analysts who champion the view that 1989 was a genuinely revolutionary year point out that, armed or not, the people were the major collective actor to emerge on the political scene. A history of 1989 from which the role of mass rallies, demonstrations, and collective acts of dissent is expunged would be an analytical travesty. In the course of several months, tiny opposition groups did mushroom into crushing majorities that actively participated in a seizure of power that transformed the sociopolitical order. Deliberate avoidance of violence may be construed as a result of political learning: one of the lessons drawn from historical precedents was that peaceful protests may be more effective than alternative modes of action, and that physical assaults on regime officials may be less liberating than previously believed. The events of 1989 were driven by popular demands for freedom, democratic accountability, and respect for individual rights. In this sense, the East European Revolutions of 1989 may be considered a manifestation of a broader revolutionary phenomenon: citizens resisting dictatorial power in the name of a set of values believed to be universal.

Overall, the most important consequence of 1989 may be the renewed faith in the efficiency and justice of mass actions in defense of popular freedom, an ideal that East Europeans have continued to defend after 1989. The organized actions of mobilized pro-democracy forces may bring about radical political change, even when opposed by ostensibly immutable structures of power. This conclusion might be the most important legacy of the East European Revolutions of 1989.

PEOPLE AND ORGANIZATIONS

Antall, Jozsef (1932–1993)

Prominent anti-Communist activist in Hungary. After the decisive victory of the pro-democracy forces in the elections of March 1990, he became the country's prime minister.

Ceausescu, Nikolae (1918–1989)

Ceausescu became general secretary of the Romanian Communist Party in 1965. He established an orthodox Marxist dictatorship that increasingly relied on harsh police measures and was characterized by a growing personality cult. After a popular rebellion, he was forced to escape Bucharest on December 22, 1989; two days later he was captured and executed.

Citizen Forum

A civic organization organized in November 1989 in Czechoslovakia. It became the focal point of anti-government and pro-democracy activities during the Czechoslovak Velvet Revolution.

Dubcek, Alexander (1921–1992)

Dubcek became general secretary of the Czechoslovak Communist Party in 1968. He launched a series of policies known as "The Prague Spring" that were intended to liberalize and democratize the political system. In August 1968, the Soviet army intervened in order to put an end to Dubcek's reforms. In 1969 he was removed from power and stripped of his party membership. In the aftermath of the Czechoslovak Velvet Revolution, he was elected speaker of the Czechoslovak parliament (December 1989).

Gorbachev, Mikhail (Born 1931)

Gorbachev became general secretary of the Communist Party of the Soviet Union in 1985 and president of the Soviet Union in 1990. He championed radical reforms— popularly known as perestroika—in virtually all spheres of Soviet life. Although he pressured Communist dictators in Eastern Europe to follow his example, outside of Poland and Hungary, he elicited only lukewarm responses. He also announced that the Soviet Union would no longer intervene militarily in order to protect Communist power in Eastern Europe. Removed from power as a result of a military coup in August 1991, he was subsequently restored to his position with the help of Boris Yeltsin. He could not prevent the disintegration of the Soviet Union, however, and resigned as president in December 1991.

Grosz, Karoly (1930–1996)

Grosz replaced János Kádár as general secretary of the Hungarian Communist Party in 1988. Initially he allied himself with the reformist wing of the party but subsequently spearheaded attempts to block further democratization of the regime. When the former Communist Party was renamed the Socialist Party in November 1989, he left it and set up a radical left-wing party.

Havel, Vaclav (Born 1936)

A Czech playwright and anti-Communist activist, Havel was one of the leaders of the opposition; he was repeatedly arrested and imprisoned. During the Velvet Revolution he emerged as the nationally recognized leader of the Citizen Forum, an umbrella coalition that synchronized pro-democracy activities in Czechoslovakia. Havel was elected president of Czechoslovakia on December 29, 1989.

Honecker, Erich (1912–1994)

Honecker became general secretary of the Socialist Unity Party of Germany (Communist Party of East Germany) in 1971. He favored orthodox Marxist economic policies and massive repressions as the ultimate guarantee of the party's supremacy. When his orders to massacre anti-government protestors were ignored, he resigned on October 18, 1989.

Hungarian Socialist Workers' Party

Official name of the Hungarian Communist Party.

Husak, Gustav (1913–1991)

Husak became general secretary of the Czechoslovak Communist Party in 1969; he supported the Soviet invasion of Czechoslovakia and presided over a series of repressive policies intended to reverse the reforms associated with the Prague Spring and reinstate dictatorial party rule. He stepped down as general secretary in 1987 and became president of Czechoslovakia. On December 10, 1989, he resigned from the presidency.

Iliescu, Ion (Born 1930)

A high-ranking Communist official in Romania until Ceausescu removed him from power in the mid-1970s, Iliescu emerged as the leader of the anti-Ceausescu insurgency of December 1989. He became chairman of the National Salvation Front and subsequently president of Romania.

Jakes, Milos (Born 1927)

Jakes, who favored a hard-line approach in domestic and international politics, replaced Gustav Husak as general secretary of the Czechoslovak Communist Party. He ordered the police to suppress with violence pro-democracy rallies in Czechoslovakia in November 1989. When his suggestion to use the military against the Velvet Revolution was rejected, he resigned on November 24, 1989.

Jaruzelski, Wojciech (Born 1923)

Polish military officer Wojciech Jaruzelski became general secretary of the Polish United Workers Party in 1981. In December of the same year, he declared martial law in Poland

and tried to suppress the Solidarity movement. In 1988, Jaruzelski favored a soft-line approach toward the anti-Communist opposition and was instrumental in organizing the Round Table Talks. Appointed president by the semi-democratically elected parliament in 1989, he resigned a year later.

Kádár, János (1912–1989)

Kádár became general secretary of the Hungarian Socialist Workers Party in 1956. He presided over the bloody repression of the Hungarian Revolution of 1956 and organized the execution of members of the deposed non-Communist government. Later he became a reformer and tried to relax the ideological and economic rigidity of the Communist system through a set of policies known as "Goulash communism." He resigned from his position in 1988, which made possible the ascendancy of a pro-reform faction within the Communist Party.

Kiszczak, Czeslaw (Born 1925)

General Czeslaw Kiszczak was minister of interior during the period of martial law in Poland in the 1980s. He ordered troops to shoot at protesting workers in 1981, for which he was convicted in 2004. After 1981, he adopted a soft-line approach toward the pro-democracy opposition and was instrumental in setting up the Round Table Talks in Poland.

Krenz, Egon (Born 1937)

Krenz replaced Erich Honecker as general secretary of the East German Communist Party on October 18, 1989. He favored a more soft-line approach toward the anti-government protestors and authorized the dismantling of the Berlin Wall. Krenz was expelled from the party in 1990.

Lenin, Vladimir Ilich Ulyanov (1870–1924)

A Russian Marxist revolutionary, Lenin was founder of the Bolshevik Party and the first leader of the Soviet Union.

Mazowiecki, Tadeusz (Born 1927)

A Catholic activist affiliated with Solidarity, he became the first non-Communist prime minister in Poland since the 1940s when his cabinet was sworn in on August 19, 1989.

Mladenov, Petar (1936–2000)

Mladenov replaced Todor Zhivkov as general secretary of the Bulgarian Communist Party on November 10, 1989. Subsequently he was elected president, and he had to face charges that he planned to use the military against the democratic opposition. He resigned from the presidency in 1990.

Nagy, Imre (1896–1958)

Nagy was prime minister of the anti-Communist government established as a result of the Hungarian Revolution of October–November 1956. He was later captured by the Soviet army and executed in 1958. His official reburial on June 16, 1989, marked the climax of anti-government protests in Hungary and reopened public debates regarding the legitimacy of the Communist Party's rule.

Polish United Workers' Party

The official name of the Polish Communist Party.

Round Table Talks (RTT)

A series of official negotiations between Communist governments and democratic opposition that devised policies intended to promote democratic reforms and established mutually acceptable rules of electoral competition. RTT were held first in Poland, then in Hungary, Bulgaria, and the GDR.

Socialist Unity Party of Germany

Official name of the East German Communist Party.

Solidarity

An independent trade union formed in Poland in 1980. In the course of a few months, its membership grew to approximately 10 million people. Solidarity organized strikes throughout the country and pressed the Communist regime for political, economic, and social reforms. Banned after the declaration of martial law on December 13, 1981, it continued to operate underground. In 1988, Solidarity organized a new wave of strikes in Poland. Ultimately it was recognized by the regime, and its leaders were invited to take part in the Round Table Talks held in 1989. It participated in and won the first multiparty elections in Poland.

Stalin, Joseph Vissarionovich Dzhugashvili (1879–1953)

Stalin succeeded Lenin as supreme leader of the Soviet Union and institutionalized a despotic system based on terror and violence against social groups and individuals. He guided the process of Sovietization of the East European countries occupied by the Soviet army in the aftermath of World War II.

Walesa, Lech (Born 1943)

A Polish electrician who became an activist in the anti-Communist labor movement, Walesa ultimately became president of the independent trade union Solidarity. Imprisoned and harassed after the declaration of martial law in Poland (December 1981), he re-emerged as an opposition leader of national stature in 1988. He was elected president of Poland in 1990.

Warsaw Treaty

A military alliance of Communist countries in Eastern Europe, formed in 1955, that included the Soviet Union, Albania, Bulgaria, Czechoslovakia, the German Democratic Republic, Hungary, Poland, and Romania; Albania officially withdrew in 1968.

Zhelev, Zhelyu (Born 1935)

A Bulgarian dissident, Zhelev led the Bulgarian anti-Communist coalition, the Union of Democratic Forces (founded on December 7, 1989). In June 1990, he was elected president of Bulgaria.

Zhivkov, Todor (1911–1998)

Appointed general secretary of the Bulgarian Communist Party in 1954, Zhivkov was removed from power on November 10, 1989, as a result of an intra-party coup—an event that marked the beginning of democratization in Bulgaria.

Venelin Ganev

Acknowledgments This text is dedicated to the memory of my father, Iordan Ganev (1926–2004), who taught me everything important I needed to know about the political history of the twentieth century.

See Also Cinema of Revolution; Democracy, Dictatorship, and Fascism; Documentaries of Revolution; Hungarian Revolution of 1956; Polish Solidarity Movement; Russian Revolution of 1991 and the Dissolution of the U.S.S.R.; Student and Youth Movements, Activism and Revolution; Trends in Revolution; Yugoslavia: Dissolution

References and Further Readings

Ash, Timothy Garton. 1990. *The Magic Lantern: The Revolutions of '89 Witnessed in Warsaw, Budapest, Berlin and Prague.* New York: Random House.

Bradley, J. F. N. 1992. *Czechoslovakia's Velvet Revolution: A Political Analysis.* New York: Columbia University Press.

Calinsecu, Matei, and Vladimir Tismaneanu. 1991. "The 1989 Revolution and the Collapse of Communism in Romania." Pp. 279–297 in *The Romanians: A History,* edited by Vlad Georgescu. Columbus: Ohio State University Press.

Crampton, R. J. 1994. *Eastern Europe in the Twentieth Century.* London: Routledge.

Ekiert, Grzegorz. 1996. *The State against Society: Political Crises and Their Aftermath in East Central Europe.* Princeton, NJ: Princeton University Press.

Elster, Jon, ed. 1996. *The Round Table Talks and the Breakdown of Communism.* Chicago: University of Chicago Press.

Ganev, Venelin I. 1997. "Bulgaria's Symphony of Hope," *Journal of Democracy* 8 (4): 125–139.

Habermas, Jurgen. 1990. "What Does Socialism Mean Today? The Rectifying Revolution and the Need for New Thinking on the Left," *New Left Review* 183: 3–17.

Hall, Andrew Richard. 1999. "The Uses of Absurdity: The Staged War Theory and the Romanian Revolution of December 1989," *East European Politics and Societies* 13 (3): 501–542.

Kaminski, Bartolomej. 1991. *The Collapse of State Socialism: The Case of Poland.* Princeton, NJ: Princeton University Press.

Kenney, Pradaic. 2002. *A Carnival of Revolution: Central Europe, 1989.* Princeton, NJ: Princeton University Press.

Kubik, Jan. 1994. *The Power of Symbols against the Symbols of Power: The Rise of Solidarity and the Fall of State Socialism in Poland.* University Park: Pennsylvania State University Press.

Kumar, Krishan. 2001. *1989: Revolutionary Ideas and Ideals.* Minneapolis: University of Minnesota Press.

Kuran, Timur. 1991. "Now out of Never: The Element of Surprise in the East European Revolutions of 1989," *World Politics* 44 (1): 7–48.

McFalls, Laurence. 1995. *Communism's Collapse, Democracy's Demise? The Cultural Context and Consequences of the East German Revolution.* New York: New York University Press.

Meier, Charles. 1997. *Dissolution: The Crisis of Communism and the End of East Germany.* Princeton, NJ: Princeton University Press.

Osmond, Jonathan, ed. 1992. *German Reunification: A Reference Guide and Commentary.* Harlow, Essex, UK: Longman.

Ratesh, Nestor. 1991. *Romania: The Entangled Revolution.* New York: Praeger.

Roper, Steven D. 2000. *Romania: The Unfinished Revolution.* Amsterdam: Harwood Academic Publishers.

Snodgrass, Warren. 2000. *Swords into Plowshares: The Fall of Communist Germany.* Huntington, NY: Nova Science Publishers.

Stokes, Gale. 1993. *The Walls Came Tumbling Down: The Collapse of Communism in Eastern Europe.* Oxford: Oxford University Press.

Sztompka, Piotr. 1996. "The Year 1989 as a Cultural and Civilizational Break," *Communist and Post-Communist Studies* 29 (2): 115–129.

Tismaneanu, Vladimir. 1992. *Reinventing Politics: Eastern Europe from Stalin to Havel.* New York: Free Press.

Todorova, Maria. 1992. "Improbable Maverick or Typical Conformist: Seven Thoughts on the New Bulgaria." Pp. 148–167 in *Eastern Europe in Revolution,* edited by Ivo Banac. Ithaca, NY: Cornell University Press.

Tokes, Rudolf. 1996. *Hungary's Negotiated Revolution: Economic Reform, Social Change and Political Succession.* Cambridge: Cambridge University Press.

Wheaton, Bernard, and Zdenek Kavan. 1992. *The Velvet Revolution: Czechoslovakia, 1988–1991.* Boulder, CO: Westview Press.

East Timor Independence Movement

CHRONOLOGY

Late 1500s	Portuguese traders and Catholic missionaries establish a presence on Timor.
1702	First Portuguese governor takes up office in the enclave of Oecusse.
1769	Dili is founded as capital.
1911	Last major tribal rebellion against Portuguese.
1942–1945	Japanese occupy neutral Portuguese Timor.
1959	Indonesia-promoted rebellion in remote Viqueque district in May leads to the exile of sixty rebel leaders to Angola.
1974	On April 25, the "Carnation Revolution" in Portugal endorses de-colonization for East Timor.
	On May 5, the governor calls for the establishment of political parties.
	The Timorese Democratic Union (UDT) is formed on May 11.
	The Timorese Social Democratic Association (ASDT) is formed on May 12.
	On September 12, ASDT becomes Fretilin (Revolutionary Front for an Independent East Timor).
	In October, Indonesia commences a covert destabilization operation.
1975	On January 20, the UDT-Fretilin coalition is established.
	UDT withdraws from the coalition May 26.
	On August 11, the UDT stages a coup.
	On August 27, the governor withdraws the administration from Dili to the offshore island of Atuaro.
	In September, Fretilin regains control and consolidates its rule over East Timor.
	In October, Indonesia begins armed attacks across the common border.
	On November 28, Fretilin declares independence, which is recognized by fifteen countries but not Portugal or the United Nations.
	On December 7, Indonesian forces launch a full-scale invasion.
	On December 22, the UN Security Council condemns the illegal invasion and calls for Indonesian withdrawal.
1976	On January 13, Indonesia convenes a puppet assembly in East Timor, which invites Indonesia to proclaim sovereignty over the annexed territory.
	On July 17, the Indonesian parliament ratifies annexation of East Timor as twenty-seventh province of Republic of Indonesia.
1978	August 30, founding Fretilin president Xavier do Amaral is captured.
1976–1982	The UN General Assembly adopts annual resolutions affirming East Timor's right to self-determination.
1982	The UN General Assembly invites the Secretary-General to undertake regular discussions between Indonesia and Portugal.

1986   On February 6, Bishop Carlos Ximenes Belo writes to the UN Secretary-General calling for referendum.

On March 18, Fretilin and UDT create the Convergência Nacionalista Timorense (Timorese National Convergence).

1991   On November 12, the Dili (or Santa Cruz) massacre takes place.

1992   In November, Xanana Gusmão is captured in Dili.

1996   The Nobel Peace Prize is awarded to Bishop Belo and José Ramos-Horta.

1998   In May, Indonesian president Suharto is forced out of office in the midst of the Asian economic crisis.

In June, incoming Indonesian president B. J. Habibie announces the possibility of autonomy for East Timor.

1999   On May 5, the New York Agreement on East Timor referendum is reached.

On June 1, the UN Security Council announces UNAMET (United Nations Mission In East Timor).

On August 26, militia rampage in Dili.

On August 30, the historic referendum takes place.

On September 4, the results are announced (78.5 percent for independence) and a coordinated Indonesian National Army (TNI)–militia campaign of killing, kidnap, and arson throughout East Timor is unleashed.

On September 15, the UN Security Council authorizes a multinational force to restore order and deliver humanitarian assistance.

On September 20, first INTERFET (International Force East Timor) troops arrive.

On October 25, the Security Council mandates UNTAET (United Nations Transitional Administration in East Timor).

On October 30, the last Indonesian personnel depart East Timor.

In November, Brazilian diplomat Sergio Vieira de Mello heads UNTAET with brief to prepare East Timor for independence.

2000   During August and September militia violence flares and UN workers are slain.

2001   In August, the Fretilin party is victorious in first democratic elections.

2002   In February, José Xanana Gusmão triumphs in the first presidential elections, defeating former comrade-in-arms Francisco Xavier do Amaral.

On May 20, the "restoration" of independence celebration takes place in Dili with proclamation of Republica Democratica Timor-Leste (RDTL), attended by the UN Secretary-General, and the presidents of Portugal and Indonesia, among others.

INTRODUCTION

Timorese history is replete with heroic but doomed rebellions against foreign occupiers, but uniquely in the age of decolonization, the Fretilin-led independence movement on the half-island state never fired a shot in anger against the dominant colonial power, Portugal; it developed as a reflex to the bloody invasion and occupation in 1976 by an Asian state, the Indonesia of General Suharto. While the armed wing of the movement was checkmated by superior Western-supplied Indonesian armor, East Timorese youth backed by the Catholic Church skillfully exploited Indonesia's own pro-democracy movement. At the same time, East Timorese in the diaspora along with an increasingly activist global solidarity movement successfully rallied in favor of a new international consensus that would, in September 1999, see eventual UN intervention and supervision pending fully fledged independence in May 2002.

BACKGROUND: CULTURE AND HISTORY

The theme of rebellion against colonial authority ran deep in the near-half-millennium of European contact with Timor

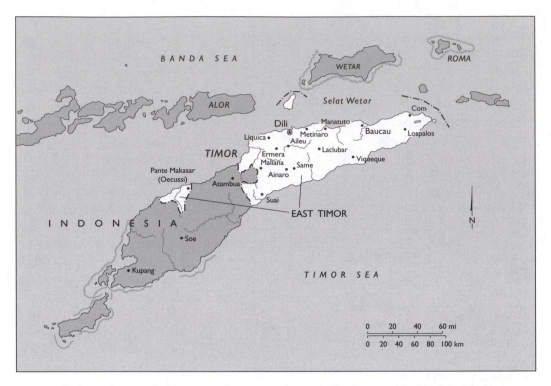

East Timor, formerly controlled by Portugal. Many residents of East Timor perished in the struggle to resist incorporation into Indonesia.

island. Nevertheless, with the establishment of the capital in Dili in 1769 the Portuguese were able to consolidate their control over the eastern half of the island through the adroit manipulation of alliances. Although the Portuguese introduced Portuguese as a language of administration and missionaries introduced Catholicism, the vast majority of the mixed Melanesian-Indonesian population of East Timor remained close to their animist traditions and loyal to their clan leaders across some dozen quasi-feudal principalities outside of Western influences. Even so, it was the Portuguese and Catholic legacy that gradually gave identity to the people of the eastern half of Timor island, separate from that inculcated by the Protestant Dutch who won control over west Timor.

It could be argued that Portugal ran Timor more as a protectorate than as a classic colony. The major economic innovation, and one which endures, was the introduction of coffee plantations in the late nineteenth century. But whereas the Portuguese had been content to collect taxes in the form of jungle produce, by the twentieth century they also began to impose tax in money along with compulsory labor, much resented by the Timorese and the cause of numerous rebellions.

With the crushing of the last great rebellion in 1912 the Portuguese moved to break the traditional lineages of native chiefs. Even so, the invasion and occupation of the island by Japanese military forces in 1942–1945 reawakened ancient

animosities against the colonial power. The occupation and Allied bombing also took its toll upon the population, leaving the colony economically devastated at war's end. But unlike in other occupied Southeast Asian countries, such as the former Dutch East Indies, Japan succored no counter-elite nor prepared the way for independence in East Timor. Neither did the Allies protest Portugal's resumption of political control at war's end.

Portuguese Timor's colonial status was also exploited by the Republic of Indonesia, which inherited Dutch (west) Timor, in 1950. While Indonesia under its first president, Sukarno, emerged as a champion of the Afro-Asian bloc of newly independent countries, the Portuguese dictator António de Oliveira Salazar offered no political space for opposition at home or in the colonies. Neither did he heed United Nations opinion on de-colonization.

CONTEXT AND PROCESS OF REVOLUTION

Strengths and Weaknesses of the Colonial Regime

The major post-war test of Portuguese control came from an Indonesian-fomented tribal rebellion in 1959, which was ruthlessly crushed by the Portuguese, leading to the exile of some sixty of the leaders to a penal colony in Angola. Even so, some urban Timorese, chafing at discrimination and lack of local opportunities, were sympathetic to this rebellion. One was future independence leader Francisco Xavier do Amaral, then a student in Macau. But in 1960, with the installation in Dili of an office of PIDE, the Portuguese secret police, surveillance of activities against the Portuguese state became even more intense. Not only was PIDE concerned to track subversive activities mounted from across the common frontier with Indonesia, but it also closely monitored the writings and other activities of the Timorese elite, including a younger generation of mostly church-educated student radicals. One source of opposition came from members of the small Arab community, including future RDTL prime minister Mari Alkatiri, who claims to have headed a shadowy underground liberation movement from January 1970.

Change came inevitably and swiftly with the end of the dictatorship in Portugal in the April 1974 "Carnation Revolution" mandating the de-colonization process in the empire. In response, a number of political parties were created in this period. First was UDT (Timorese Democratic Union), followed by ASDT (Timorese Social Democratic Association) turned Fretilin (Revolutionary Front for an Independent Timor), and Apodeti (Timorese Popular Democratic Association). UDT attracted such personalities as political leader Francisco Lopez da Cruz and João Carrascalão, descendant of a plantation-owning family. Pro-independence Fretilin attracted a spectrum of young political activists including the Lobato brothers; Mari Alkatiri, the former exiled journalist; centrist José Ramos-Horta; and the Maoist Abilio Araujo. Fretilin's leader was Xavier do Amaral.

The Apodeti party stood for integration with the Republic of Indonesia. While Fretilin (leftist and demanding rapid independence) and UDT (favoring a more lengthy transition to independence) enjoyed a short-lived pact of unity around independence, UDT leaders were seduced by Indonesian propaganda falsely discrediting Fretilin as Communist, just as Indonesian security services commenced to unleash a destabilization campaign in the colony. Although there were many flaws in the hastily conceived de-colonization program, it was also the case that populist Fretilin won handsomely in district elections. But the de-colonization process took a fateful turn with the Indonesian-backed UDT coup of August 11, 1975. In the ensuing bloody civil war, Fretilin regained control of the territory; UDT members, along with significant numbers of refugees, fled to west Timor. The flare-up of fighting in Dili caused the Portuguese administration to withdraw to the offshore island of Atauro. By the end of the month, Fretilin became the de facto rulers of the territory.

Causes of the Revolution

Paradoxically in the history of de-colonization, the enemy of the revolution now became not the colonial oppressor, but a foreign aggressor, Indonesia, apparently motivated in part by the fear of a leftist-led independent East Timor on its border and responding to requests for assistance from the defeated UDT. While the Portuguese governor on Atauro resisted calls by Fretilin to return to the mainland, the Portuguese flag remained flying in Dili as Indonesian commandos stepped up their raids across the border. Among the first casualties were an Australian-based television crew who filmed the Indonesian invasion. Not surprisingly, the UDT coup, the civil war, and the invasion gave the upper hand to the radicals within Fretilin. Hardly Communist as their detractors made out, they were nevertheless in solidarity with—and inspired by—the independence struggles of the peoples of Guinea-Bissau, Angola, and Mozambique. On November 18, 1975, as Fretilin/Falintil (Armed Forces for the Liberation of East Timor) forces were pushed back from the frontier, and with evidence of full-scale Indonesian invasion mounting, Fretilin's first president, Xavier do Amaral, issued a unilateral declaration of independence, recognized by fifteen countries but, crucially, not by Portugal or the United Nations. U.S. and Australian fears of a Fretilin-dominated Southeast Asian "Cuba" also played into the hands of Indonesian propaganda, just as the West backed the invasion.

Mobilization for the Revolution

While Fretilin/Falintil forces in the mountainous hinterland of East Timor could never hope to defeat the Western-supplied armor of the invader, the survival of the ragged band of guerrillas was mythic in the imagination of East Timorese people. Guerrilla strategy undertaken by Fretilin/Falintil obviously adapted to circumstances. The opening years of the invasion saw major attrition of both Falintil and the population it desperately tried to protect. In December 1978, with the death of Commander Nicolau Lobato following an Indonesian annihilation campaign in the eastern mountains, and the loss of radio contact with the outside world, José Xanana Gusmão successfully adopted the strategy of leading small mobile guerrilla units while establishing a network of bases among a supportive population. In 1982 the first tentative contacts were made by the armed resistance with the outside world. In 1983 Gusmão also initiated a series of cease-fires with weary Indonesian commanders, although that tactic was also abandoned. In 1987–1988 Gusmão formed the non-party National Council of Maubere Resistance (CNRM) declaring Falintil a "national" army, a successful ploy to expand the popular appeal of the resistance. When Gusmão was captured in November 1992, he was replaced as leader by Ma Hunu (later captured) and, in turn, by the legendary Nino Konis Santana, killed in 1998.

It is not to say that the occupier did not win over collaborators. As in many situations of foreign occupation, there were also those who benefited from the new circumstances. Most East Timorese were obliged to play double roles, and many would undoubtedly have accepted some kind of autonomy if it were not for the heavy TNI (Indonesian Armed Forces) presence and the counterproductive activity of the TNI in inflicting massive human rights abuses. A particular divisive strategy mounted by the TNI was to create armed militias drawn from criminal gangs and including many west Timorese with a view to coercing the East Timorese to reject independence.

Eventually, in the run-up to the historic August 1999 ballot, the Falintil guerrillas accepted voluntary territorial restrictions so as not to provoke Indonesian claims of civil war. Falintil did not intervene in the TNI-militia violence of this period although it did heroically offer protection to the civilians who fled the post-ballot violence. Falintil survivors reluctantly accepted disarmament at the hands of UN peacekeepers pending recruitment into the ranks of the future independent nation's armed forces.

Role of the "Clandestine" and the Church

While Falintil fought a classic guerrilla war against all odds, the pro-independence struggle mounted by East Timor civil society was essentially nonviolent, largely because of the central role of the Catholic Church as the protector of the people—a reference not only to the high-profile role of Bishop Belo, but also to the pastoral role of the clergy in the rural districts. The Indonesian occupation also corresponded with a surge in converts from animism to Catholicism, helping to forge a common Timorese-Catholic identity, along with the use of Tetum, the major indigenous language, as the language of liturgy. But it is also significant that it was the first generation of Timorese schooled by Indonesia that became the first to rebel. Known as the "clandestine," their underground activities included networking on college campuses in Bali and Java and finding, toward the end, important allies in Indonesia's own pro-democracy movement. Inside East Timor, beginning in 1985, the clandestine initiated the first contacts with Falintil. They also staged daring protests during the period when East Timor was closed to foreign journalists and tourists. They also paid the price when, on November 12, 1991, over 200 young people were gunned down in the Dili or Santa Cruz Cemetery massacre. The advent of the Habibie administration in Indonesia in May 1998 also offered space for East Timorese students to show their hand and present their claims for independence to the first visiting UN envoys. By staging spectacular embassy break-ins in Jakarta, the clandestine groups also helped to raise the international media profile for their cause.

External Delegation and Global Solidarity

The third arm of mobilization was the external delegation of Fretilin, later joined by an expanding global solidarity movement of support groups, lobbyists, the global human rights community, and, eventually, nations. In a broader sense it was also the solidarity of nations in support of East Timor independence working through the UN which, after a twenty-year hiatus, eventually reintervened in the East Timor issue. From the outset, Mozambique was a steadfast supporter of East Timor independence, offering sanctuary and passports to such external leaders as Mari Alkatiri. Undoubtedly, however, the external delegation of Fretilin was personified by José Ramos-Horta, acknowledged even by his detractors as the consummate diplomat.

Portugal's re-engagement in the East Timor issue, after years of drift that allowed Indonesian diplomats to win over a large bloc of countries, especially Islamic countries, only gathered momentum under President Mario Soares. Especially after entry into the European Union in January 1986, Portugal successfully pushed for a common position on East Timor in that forum. By taking Australia to the World Court in 1991 over its presumption to divide hydrocarbon spoils in the Timor Sea with Indonesia, Portugal won confirmation of the right of East Timor for self-determination. The global coalition of support groups gathered further momentum with media exposure of the 1991 Dili massacre and the awarding of the 1996 Nobel Peace Prize to two sons of Timor. The personal activism of UN Secretary-General Kofi Annan cannot be discounted, notably in appointing a special envoy, Pakistani diplomat Jamsheed Marker, to canvass opinion on a settlement of the situation. But as Marker (2003) acknowledges, it was the resignation of the authoritarian President Suharto in May 1998 amidst the Asian economic crisis that facilitated a window of opportunity for the UN to organize a referendum to ascertain the people's aspirations as to independence or "autonomy" within the Republic of Indonesia.

IMPACTS

Impacts on Local Society

The impacts upon local society of the Indonesian military occupation of East Timor and the Falintil resistance were deadly and destructive. Deadly, because as rigorously inves-

East Timorese raise their fists while singing their national anthem during a freedom celebration in Dili November 28, 2001. East Timor president-in-waiting Xanana Gusmão, in a visit to Indonesia's west Timor, called on tens of thousands of East Timorese refugees who fled from the bloodbath in East Timor after the independence ballot in 1999 to return to the territory and rebuild their shattered land. (Reuters/Corbis)

tigated by researchers at CAVR (Commission for Reception, Truth, and Reconciliation), the UN-backed "truth commission" in East Timor, some 25–30 percent of the population perished at the hands of the TNI. Destructive, because Indonesia plundered East Timor's forest resources, exploited and neglected its coffee plantations, and also demographically changed East Timor by introducing mostly Muslim immigrants. Culturally, local society was also "Indonesianized" through schooling, mass media, and other assimilationist programs. The Portuguese language was declared illegal and Indonesian language generalized.

The CAVR's "truth-seeking" division sought to reconstruct a retrospective mortality analysis of the events of 1975–1999 around the following themes: the "civil war," hunger and forced displacement, crimes against women, crimes against children, crimes against humanity committed by the TNI, complicity of international actors in supplying weapons, and imprisonment. Several peaks were discerned in the demographic loss. The major attrition bordering upon genocide occurred in the first two years of the invasion. Certain categories of people were targeted, namely Chinese and members of Fretilin and their families. But thousands of civilians were also victims of TNI bombardments and countless others died from malnutrition and sickness. Other peaks of demographic loss coincided with famines of 1982–1983. Owing to a freeze on the activities of nongovernmental organizations and a ban on foreign visits, little of this was reported. However, the TNI-militia killings peaking in September 1999 following the UN-conducted ballot on East Timor's future sovereignty were witnessed by international observers. Adding to the international outrage, the TNI who were entrusted by the UN to provide a secure environment for the historic referendum actively abetted pro-independence militias to sway the result of the ballot through intimidation. In this outpouring of violence, some 1,500 supporters of independence were killed, 80 percent of national housing and infrastructure was destroyed, one-third of the population displaced to the highlands, and another third of the population forcibly removed to west Timor where they long languished in refugee camps. Under the Indonesian occupation, between one-quarter and one-third of East Timor's population perished, a record that borders on genocide. In 2004, UN investigators handed down indictments for crimes against humanity to a number of senior Indonesian military figures.

Impacts on International Society

The impacts of the East Timor Revolution on international society were complex and contradictory. Certainly Indonesia was condemned for its annexation of the territory in a number of Security Council resolutions, commencing in 1975, and it was a revived UN process guided by Secretary-General Kofi Annan that eventually sanctioned a UN-conducted ballot on East Timor's future. But flaws in that process also led to the destruction of September 1999. UN initiatives also led to a successful humanitarian rescue of East Timor, paving the way for two-and-a-half years' stewardship as a virtual UN protectorate pending political preparation for independence on May 20, 2002. Successful UN stewardship over East Timor was also upheld as a model for future UN missions in post-conflict situations. But, looking back, the international community, including the former colonial power, failed the East Timorese people on a number of critical junctions. Portugal long failed to prepare East Timor for eventual de-colonization. While pro-reform activists inside Indonesia linked East Timor's liberation with Indonesian democracy, until today, East Timor's "separation" offers ammunition to Indonesian nationalists to allow no quarter for secession of other provinces. The Western powers, eager to court the Jakarta government over military sales, business deals, and even, in the case of Australia, control over East Timor's rich petroleum sources, failed to act on human rights abuses. The UN was naive to entrust security of the ballot to the Indonesian security forces without preparation for a worst-case scenario.

PEOPLE AND ORGANIZATIONS

Alkatiri, Mari Bin Amude (Born 1949)

Founding member of ASDT and Fretilin. Fretilin minister for political affairs. Long based in Maputo, and traveling on a Mozambique passport, Alkatiri played a prominent role in the Fretilin external delegation. Economics minister and chief minister of East Timor under the UN administration, became prime minister of RDTL upon independence.

Amaral, Francisco Xavier do (Born 1937)

First president of Fretilin and proclaimer of Timor-Leste independence. Expelled from Fretilin after disagreements over strategy, he was placed in custody in September 1977. In August 1978 he was captured by the TNI and removed to Jakarta where for twenty years he was used as a propaganda tool by the TNI and the Indonesian government. Returning to Dili in 2000, he re-entered the political arena with the support of his ethnic Mambae but also linked his name with the CPD-RDTL or "false Fretilin" faction. Unsuccessful contender in presidential elections of 2001.

Apodeti (Associação Popular Democratica Timorense; Timorese Popular Democratic Association)

Apodeti was the East Timorese party that favored integrating the former Portuguese colony into Indonesia. Launched on May 27, 1974, early support for the party came from individuals associated with an Indonesian-promoted rebellion of 1975, certain of the Arab community of Dili, along with a number of *luirai,* or little kings, the most important of which was Guiherme Gonclaves. The first president of the party was Arnaldo dos Reis Araujo, a former collaborator with the Japanese. Minuscule in membership, Apodeti nevertheless became a major instrument through which Indonesian intelligence services mounted their subversion and later annexation of the territory.

ASDT(Associação Social Democratica Timorense; Timorese Social Democratic Association)

Founded on May 20, 1974, by José Ramos-Horta, Justino Mota, and Nicolau Lobato. The ASDT was a leftist East Timorese political party which advocated independence from Portugal in line with a lengthy process of decolonization. Later the ASDT became Fretilin, the Revolutionary Front for an Independent East Timor, the leftist revolutionary organization that worked to achieve rapid independence for East Timor. In 2001, ASDT was reborn as a political party, separate from Fretilin, under the leadership of Francisco Xavier do Amaral to contest elections for a new East Timor constituent assembly held under UN auspices on August 30, 2001.

Belo, Carlos Filipe Ximenes (Bishop) (Born 1948)

Ordained as priest in Lisbon (1980); named Apostolic Administrator of Dili (1983); named bishop (1988); February 6, 1989, appealed to UN for referendum on East Timor; co-winner of 1996 Nobel Peace Prize; member of CNRT; September 1999 evacuated to Australia after deadly TNI-militia attack on residence; returned as interlocutor with UNTAET, resigned position in 2003. The most highly respected church leader in East Timor.

Carrascalão, João Viegas (Born 1945)

President of UDT party.

CAVR (Comissão de Acolhimento, Verdade e Reconciliação; Commission for Reception, Truth, and Reconciliation)

Set up in March 2002, CAVR was a UN-backed commission to seek the truth regarding human rights abuses committed in East Timor between April 1974 and October 1999 and, where possible, attempt to work out compensation and reconciliation between victims and perpetrators. As such, CAVR was the first "truth commission" established in an Asian nation, although strongly modeled along the lines of its South African counterpart. Certain novel features of CAVR included community-based hearings with apologies offered by perpetrators. Another first was a graveyard count as part of a retrospective mortality investigation. Having completed its mission in October 2005, CAVR presented its findings and recommendations in the form of a final report to the president of the Democratic Republic of Timor-Leste, in turn transferred to the East Timor parliament with the expectation that the report be further presented to the UN Secretary-General prior to its being made public to the people of East Timor. But by 2005 even the need to know the unpalatable truth was seen by the political leadership as secondary to the expediency of good relations with Muslim-majority Indonesia.

CNRM (Conselho Nacional da Resistência Maubere; National Council of the Maubere Resistance)

Founded under adverse conditions in 1986 by Xanana Gusmão as a new broad-based nationalist organization, CNRM was intended to stand above party politics such as represented by a strictly Fretilin-based struggle. Nevertheless,

Xanana Gusmão retained his leadership of Falintil, as the armed wing of CNRM. As a truly nationalist organization, including Fretilin, student organizations, exiles, and a newly pro-independence UDT party, CNRM represented mainstream East Timorese opinion both inside and outside East Timor. José Ramos-Horta long acted as CNRM's external spokesperson.

CNRT (Conselho Nacional da Resistencia Timorenses; National Council of the Timorese Resistance)

Nonpartisan umbrella organization bringing together different political organizations, notably including UDT. Founded in April 1998 at a convention held in Portugal to replace CNRM, Xanana Gusmão was elected president. The CNRT spearheaded the pro-independence campaign in the UN-sponsored "popular consultation" of August 1999 and many youthful members became victims of the Indonesian-orchestrated violence. The CNRT was dissolved at a congress held in Dili in August 2000.

CPD-RDTL (Conselho Popular pela Defesa da República Democrática de Timor-Leste; Popular Council for the Defense of the Democratic Republic of Timor-Leste, or "false Fretilin")

Faction which denied UN stewardship over East Timor and continues to mount civil disturbances against the elected authorities.

Falintil (Forcas Armadas de Liberação Nacional de Timor-Leste; Armed Forces for the National Liberation of East Timor)

The Fretilin resistance army which, over 24 years, and in great adversity, spearheaded the defense of the nation against the Western-backed Indonesian occupier. Originally headed by Nicolau Lobato, Falintil had declined from a force of some 4,000 to several hundred by 1981. Reorganized under the leadership of Xanana Gusmão, Falintil survived through a shift to more mobile tactics. As the armed wing of Fretilin, Falintil became the armed wing of the CNRM with the advent of that organization in 1986. Largely fighting a defensive war, Falintil offered protection to urban dwellers fleeing militia violence in September 1999. By 2000–2002 Falintil were either encadred into the RDTL armed forces or entered various veterans' associations.

Fretilin (Frente Revolucionária de Timor-Leste Independente; Revolutionary Front for an Independent East Timor)

With its origins in ASDT, Fretilin emerged in September 1974 as a more avowedly revolutionary Socialist organization along the lines of and inspired by the Frelimo movement in Mozambique. Two founder members of ASDT/Fretilin, José Ramos-Horta and Mari Alkatiri, had spent time in Mozambique. Not a Communist party as made out by detractors, it is also true that certain of the Fretilin leadership looked to radical solutions. Above all, Fretilin stood for immediate de jure independence but was also prepared to follow Portugal's de-colonization timetable. Victorious in crushing an Indonesian-backed armed coup by UDT party in August 1975, Fretilin was the de facto government of East Timor with the departure of the Portuguese government to Atauro Island. Although never recognized by Portugal, Fretilin's unilateral declaration of independence on November 28, 1975, by its founding president Francisco Xavier do Amaral, days ahead of the full-scale Indonesian invasion, is today proclaimed a national holiday in the RDTL. Victorious in the UN-sponsored Constituent Assembly elections of August 30, 2001, Fretilin headed the new RDTL government which came into being with independence on May 20, 2002.

Gusmão, José Alexandre (Xanana) (Born 1946)

Former poet-journalist fled with Fretilin/Falintil to the mountains ahead of the Indonesian invasion. As one of the last surviving members of the Fretilin central committee, took charge of a dwindling group of veterans. From 1981 he became commander in chief of Falintil. First contacted by an outside journalist in the 1980s, Gusmão's name became synonymous with the struggle. A hero to ordinary Timorese, he achieved Nelson Mandela–like status following his capture and imprisonment in Jakarta from 1992 until October 1999. Still in prison, he was elected president of CNRT. In 2001, the charismatic Gusmão was elected president of RDTL, winning 82.7 percent of the vote.

Habibie, B. J. (Born 1936)

President of Republic of Indonesia, following resignation of President Suharto in May 1998.

INTERFET (International Force East Timor)

September 15, 1999–February 28, 2000. INTERFET was mandated on September 15, 1999, by UN Security Council Resolution 1296/1999 under the chapter 7 "peace enforcement" provisions of the UN Charter. This followed intense international pressure on Indonesian president B. J. Habibie to offer consent to the insertion of an international peacekeeping force into East Timor, still under Indonesian military occupation. While the lead role played by Australia in INTERFET was vital, the multinational character of the force was exemplified by smaller contributions from such countries as Thailand, the Philippines, and South Korea, along with a number of Western countries. The U.S. role, though important, was confined to logistics and intelligence. Although not a direct participant, Japan provided vital financial assistance. Headed by an Australian general and seconded by a Thai counterpart, at peak deployment some 9,000 troops participated in INTERFET, of which 5,500 were Australian. As security was successfully established, INTERFET was eclipsed by the UNTAET mission.

Lobato, Nicolau (1952–1978)

Founder of ASDT and Fretilin central committee member. Becomes second president of Fretilin; killed in December 1978. Remembered as national hero as in "Presidente Nicolau Lobato International Airport" (Dili).

Mello, Sergio Vieira de (1948–2003)

Brazilian diplomat; special representative of the Secretary-General and transitional administrator of UNTAET. Killed in attack on UN headquarters in Iraq in August 2003.

PIDE (Policia Internacional e Defesa Estado; International Police in Defense of the State)

Portuguese secret police.

Ramos-Horta, José (Born 1949)

Fretilin external affairs and information minister, foreign minister of RDTL, co-winner of 1996 Nobel Peace Prize. Indefatigable efforts at lobbying on East Timor on the part of the former-journalist-turned-diplomat undoubtedly were crucial in keeping East Timor on the international agenda.

RDTL (Republica Democratica Timor-Leste; Democratic Republic of East Timor)

Official name of the country as proclaimed on May 20, 2002.

Suharto (Born 1921)

General-president of Republic of Indonesia, seized power in 1965–1966. Forced to relinquish power in May 1998.

TNI (Tentera National Indonesia; Indonesian National Army)

Backed by U.S.-supplied armor, TNI led the invasion of East Timor. In their 24-year occupation the TNI not only were complicit in crimes against humanity as determined by UN prosecutors but also suffered many casualties themselves. Many serving Indonesian generals won their spurs in East Timor before being deployed to such restive provinces of Indonesia as Aceh and Papua.

UDT (União Democratica Timorense; Timorese Democratic Union)

Founded on May 11, 1974, the UDT was an East Timor political party with an anti-Communist orientation that originally favored a gradual transition of East Timor to independence. Founding president was Mario Carrascalão, joined by his brother João Viegas Carrascalão, along with Francisco Lopez da Cruz and Cesar Agusto da Costa Moushino. As a party of conservative landowners, the UDT quickly lost support to the populist Fretilin. Tragically, with Indonesian backing, UDT launched a coup in August 1975, sparking off a short but bloody civil war in which Fretilin forces triumphed, largely pushing the UDT rump into exile. Only in the late 1980s would UDT enter into a political convergence with its former rival, Fretilin, in order to pursue a coordinated diplomatic approach to independence.

UNAMET (United Nations Mission in East Timor—June 11, 1999–October 25, 1999)

Headed by Ian Martin, UNAMET was charged to organize and conduct the "popular consultation" on whether East Timorese would accept or reject integration with the Republic of Indonesia.

UNTAET (United Nations Transitional Administration in East Timor)

Under the leadership of Sergio Vieira de Mello, UNTAET was charged in October 1999 with preparing East Timor for independence. A virtual protectorate under UNTAET, East Timorese frequently chafed at the lack of demonstrable development. But the UN was also obliged to rebuild human capacity while mentoring the formation of new government bureaus. To satisfy East Timorese impatience for independence, the UN progressively Timorized the administration, organized elections for a constituent assembly and presidential elections while waiting out the approval of a new constitution. After independence on May 20, 2002, a successor mission, United Nations Mission in Support of East Timor, or UNMISET, remained in East Timor to build on successes but acknowledging deficiencies in the legal system and in the training of police and defense forces. UNMISET was in turn replaced on May 20, 2005, by a smaller United Nations Office in Timor-Leste (UNOTL).

Wiranto (General) (Born 1947)

In February 1998, Wiranto was appointed armed forces commander, minister of defense, under President Suharto, positions maintained under President Habibie. Indicted by UN prosecutors in Dili in February 2004 for command-control of crimes against humanity.

Geoffrey C. Gunn

See Also Documentaries of Revolution; Human Rights, Morality, Social Justice, and Revolution; Indonesian Counter-Revolution; Indonesian Independence Revolution

References and Further Readings
Chomsky, Noam. 2000. *A New Generation Draws the Line: Kosovo, East Timor and the Standards of the West.* London: Verso.
Cotton, James. 2004. *East Timor, Australia and Regional Order: Intervention and Its Aftermath in Southeast Asia.* London and New York: RoutledgeCurzon.
Dunn, James. 1983. *Timor: A People Betrayed.* Milton, Australia: Jacaranda Press (1996. Sydney: ABC Books).
Gunn, Geoffrey C. 1997. *East Timor and the United Nations: The Case for Intervention.* Trenton, NJ: Red Sea Press.
———. 1999. *Timor Loro Sae: 500 years.* Macau: Livros do Oriente.
———. 2000. *New World Hegemony in the Malay World.* Trenton, NJ: Red Sea Press.
Jolliffe, Jill. 1978. *East Timor: Nationalism and Colonialism.* St. Lucia, Australia: University of Queensland Press.
Marker, Jamsheed. 2003. *East Timor: A Memoir of the Negotiations for Independence.* Jefferson, NC, and London: McFarland.
Martin, Ian. 2001. *Self-Determination in East Timor: The United Nations, the Ballot, and International Intervention.* International Peace Academy Occasional Paper Series. Boulder, CO: Lynne Rienner.
Ramos-Horta, José. 1987. *Funu: The Unfinished Saga of East Timor.* Trenton, NJ: Red Sea Press.
Tanter, Richard, Mark Selden, and Stephen R. Shalom, eds. 2001. *Bitter Flowers, Sweet Flowers: East Timor, Indonesia, and the World Community,* Lanham, MD: Rowman and Littlefield.
Taylor, John G. 2001. *Indonesia's Forgotten War: The Hidden History of East Timor.* London: Zed.

Egyptian Revolution of 1952

CHRONOLOGY

639 A.D.   An Arab army under Amr ibn al-As conquers Egypt and begins the Islamization of the country.

1250–1517   The Mamluk period.

1517   Ottoman conquest of Egypt by the Sultan Selim II.

1798   The French expedition led by Napoléon Bonaparte defeats the Mamluks and occupies Egypt for the next three years.

1805   An Ottoman officer, Muhammad Ali, is appointed governor of Egypt and extends his personal authority across the country. He will rule until 1848 and establish a dynasty.

1869   The Suez Canal, a waterway connecting the Mediterranean and Red seas, is completed, but the cost of construction adds to Egypt's financial difficulties.

1877   The establishment of the system of dual control gives British and French representatives the authority to supervise Egyptian government expenditure and revenue.

1882   The 'Urabi Revolution; British forces defeat 'Urabi and occupy Egypt. Despite their declared intention to soon depart the country, the British consolidate their control over the following decades. Formally, Egypt remains part of the Ottoman empire.

1914   With the outbreak of the First World War, Britain declares Egypt a British protectorate.

1919–1921   The 1919 or National Revolution, a series of widespread protests throughout Egypt that calls for the evacuation of British forces and full independence for Egypt. Led by Sa'd Zaghlul, it fails to achieve its aims but forces the British government to grant Egypt limited self-government, including its own constitution and monarchy.

1936   In April, King Fu'ad dies and is succeeded by his son Faruq.

In August, the Anglo-Egyptian Treaty establishing a mutual defensive alliance is signed between a Wafdist government and the British.

1942   Prompted by concerns of pro-Axis sentiments in the palace, British tanks surround Abdin Palace in February and force Faruq to install a pro-Allied Wafdist government. The event vividly demonstrates the impotence of Egypt.

1948   The declaration of the Israeli state in May marks the beginning of the Palestine War, in which Egypt is defeated.

1952   On January 25, a gun battle breaks out between Egyptian police and British troops in Ismailia.

On January 26, an anti-British riot sees a fire break out in Cairo, which burns down a large part of the city center. Faruq dismisses the Wafdist government of Mustafa al-Nahhas and appoints a series of weak cabinets.

In the early hours of July 23, the Free Officers, a group of junior officers led by Gamal Abdel Nasser but with Muhammad Nagib as its public spokesman, seizes power in a virtually bloodless coup. A military junta takes power and forces Faruq to abdicate three days later. A regency is established.

1953   On January 17, all political parties are banned.

On June 18, Egypt is declared a republic.

1954   In March a political struggle between Nasser and Nagib sees Nasser triumph.

On October 19, Britain and Egypt sign an accord that provides for the withdrawal of British troops from Egyptian soil.

On October, 26, an attempt on Nasser's life by a member of Muslim Brotherhood provides the pretext for a campaign of repression against the organization. Nagib is dismissed from the presidency and placed under house arrest.

1955	In April, Egypt plays a prominent role at the Bandung conference.
	In September, the Czech arms deal is concluded.
1956	In June, the British withdraw all forces from Egypt, ending an occupation of seventy-four years. The same month a new constitution takes force and Nasser is confirmed as president of the republic.
	On July 26, following the withdrawal of financial support for the Aswan High Dam project by the U.S. government, Nasser nationalizes the Suez Canal.
	In response, the British government, in collusion with the French and Israelis, invades Egypt in October.
1958–1961	The period of the United Arab Republic, an organic union of Egypt and Syria.
1961	In July, a series of decrees nationalizes a wide range of banks, insurance firms, shipping companies, and industries.
1962	In June, the National Congress of Popular Forces approves the national charter and sets up the Arab Socialist Union as the official political party.
1967	In June, Egypt is defeated by the Israelis and loses the Sinai.
1970	On September 28, Nasser dies; he is succeeded by his vice president, Anwar Sadat.
1979	Egypt signs a peace treaty with Israel and is expelled from the Arab League.
1981	Sadat is assassinated in October; he is succeeded by Husni Mubarak.
1989	Egypt is accepted back into the Arab League.

INTRODUCTION

The Egyptian Revolution of 1952, also known as the July or 1952 Revolution, brought an end to the dynasty of Muhammad Ali and set up a republic in its place. Launched by a group of junior military officers led by Gamal Abdel Nasser, it embarked on a program of constitutional change, social reform, and Socialist transformation using the rhetoric of national independence and Arab nationalism.

BACKGROUND: CULTURE AND HISTORY

In 1952 Egypt had a population of 21 million people made up of different ethnic groups—the original inhabitants of the pharaonic period, Arabs, Nubians— and a more recent foreign resident presence. It was predominantly Muslim, but with a significant Coptic (Christian) minority and a small Jewish community of long standing. The political and social elite were large landowners with a modest urban middle class, but the great majority of the population were peasants (*fellahin*).

The center of the ancient pharaonic civilization based in the Nile Valley of Egypt has always been influenced by outside forces because of its geographical position. From the Roman period onward, the country was ruled by a succession of foreign dynasties. The Arab conquest in 639 A.D. brought an end to Byzantine rule and began a process of steady Islamization and an accompanying decline of Coptic culture. A series of Muslim dynasties followed, notably the Fatimids and Ayyubids, before a succession of Mamluk rulers, a Turkic slave caste, ruled the country. The invasion by the Ottoman Sultan Selim the Grim in early 1517 saw Egypt's incorporation into an expanding empire that would stretch from North Africa to the Balkans and the edge of Persia at its height. Ottoman rule, regularly characterized by struggle for political advantage between the Ottoman-appointed governor and the local Mamluks, continued until the end of the eighteenth century.

In 1798 Napoléon Bonaparte launched the French expedition in an attempt to set up a colony in Egypt. The French occupation of Egypt lasted only three years, but the direct exposure to Western influence had a lasting impact on the country. In the political vacuum that followed the French withdrawal, an Ottoman officer, Muhammad Ali, first secured appointment as Ottoman governor in 1805 and then proceeded to establish personal superiority over his rivals. In the course of a long reign, he lay the foundations of a family dynasty and the modern state of Egypt, which formally was still part of the Ottoman empire.

Muhammad Ali embarked on an ambitious program of modernization, reforming the military forces and establishing a series of institutions for the administration of the state. He sought to put the Egyptian economy on a sounder basis by reforming the system of land tenure, improving the transport system and infrastructure, and developing Egyptian industry. In order that Egypt had people with the necessary skills, he encouraged foreigners, particularly Greeks, Italians, and Levantines, to settle in the country, where many could benefit under the Capitulations, a regime of legal and economic privileges for foreign nationals. These policies were continued by his successors; one of the most spectacular infrastructure projects was the construction of the Suez Canal, completed in the reign of the Khedive Isma'il Pashain, 1869. However, such grand projects put the Egyptian treasury increasingly into debt, and in the 1870s, British and French representatives were given control over Egyptian state revenues to secure the interests of European bondholders. Increasing resentment at the foreign interference in the country and tensions between elements of the Egyptian and the local Turko-Circassian elite saw Ahmad 'Urabi emerge as leader of a nationalist group. His appointment as war minister and his subsequent military defeat by invading British forces resulted in the occupation of Egypt in 1882.

Despite its declared intention to stay only until the national finances were put in order, the British showed no signs of leaving Egypt. In response, by the first decade of the twentieth century an Egyptian national movement began to call for the withdrawal of British forces, though with little success. Instead, following the Ottoman entry into the First World War on the side of Germany in 1914, Britain formalized its presence by declaring Egypt a British protectorate. With the end of hostilities in November 1918, there were renewed demands for independence. An Egyptian delegation (*wafd*) sent to the Versailles Conference was not received but came to play the chief role in representing nationalist aspirations. Britain was unwilling to accede to Egyptian demands. But following a series of nationwide protests in 1919 and again in 1921 known as the 1919 Revolution, the British government became convinced to grant Egypt self-government unilaterally. Egypt was permitted a monarchy and its own constitution, even if Britain reserved for itself important powers relating to defense matters, the Suez Canal, the Sudan, and the protection of foreign interests and minorities.

The period between the two revolutions, 1922–1952, the so-called liberal period, witnessed a prolonged political stalemate. The Wafd, the nationalist party with genuine mass support and led by Sa'd Zaghlul, and his successor Mustafa al-Nahhas held office on a number of occasions. But the Wafd was regularly kept out of office by the machinations of an interfering monarchy, the British high commissioner, and rival political parties. The Wafdist leadership, many of them

landowners, also failed to use its popular support to great advantage and showed that even though it sought political independence, the Wafd was far from being a radical party on economic and social issues. Limited progress was made on the question of Egyptian-British relations with the signing of the 1936 Anglo-Egyptian treaty that provided for mutual defense arrangements and, while not granting Egypt complete independence, did allow the Egyptian government greater authority in certain matters. British forces were now largely confined to the Canal Zone, and a timetable was laid down for the abolition of the Capitulations in the following year and of the Mixed Courts (set up originally in 1876 to deal with cases involving both Egyptians and resident foreign nationals) in 1949. With the outbreak of war in Europe in 1939, Britain invoked the treaty. Egypt served as its base in the eastern Mediterranean for the next six years.

CONTEXT AND PROCESS OF REVOLUTION

Pressing political and economic issues were put on hold until 1945, when increasing political and social instability framed the lead-up to revolution. The continuing British presence was the most politically urgent matter. In February 1946 a demonstration of students and workers calling for the abrogation of the 1936 treaty had resulted in the death of a number of protesters, but negotiations with the British government later the same year failed to make any headway. In May 1948 the general situation further deteriorated with Egypt's entry and subsequent defeat in the Palestine War. Political violence escalated, culminating in the assassination of Egyptian prime minister al-Nuqrashi by a member of the Muslim Brotherhood later that year. Too late, the Wafd finally abrogated the 1936 treaty in October 1951.

This political volatility was fed by serious economic and social problems. Foremost was the need for land reform. The large landowning class had continued to amass wealth and property in the late 1940s and the early 1950s as they had in the past through higher rents on land, while peasants became more indebted or forfeited their small landholdings. The legacy of the British policy of promoting Egypt as an agricultural economy, and particularly as a producer of cotton, meant that Egyptian industrialization had failed to keep pace with a growing population. The practice of monopoly capitalism and the existence of a prominent comprador bourgeoisie had resulted in inadequate industrial development, with poverty and unemployment on the increase. Many Egyptians had little access to education and most were illiterate. Inter-communal tensions re-emerged between Muslims and Copts.

The failure of the traditional political class to effectively address these issues had triggered the emergence of new political forces even before 1945. Foremost among these were the Communists and the Muslim Brotherhood. The Communist movement, first established in the early 1920s, had revived in the 1940s and, though splintered, introduced Socialist ideas into the public debate, addressing issues of land reform and social inequality. The Society of Muslim Brothers, established by Hasan al-Banna in 1928, called for Egypt to be an Islamic state as the solution to its problems. Both of these currents expanded in size and influence after the Second World War, using demonstrations and an active press to promote their policies.

However, it was from the military that the revolution would be launched. The 1936 treaty had allowed for the enrollment of some lower-middle-class Egyptians into the Military Academy. Over the next decade, some of these new entrants became politicized by two events in particular: (1) the February 1942 incident when the British forced the appointment of a pro-Allied Wafdist government; and (2) the defeat of Egyptian forces in Palestine in 1948, with its ensuing arms scandal in which the Egyptian government was accused of providing its soldiers with defective weapons. By late 1949, a group of officers barely in their mid-thirties led by Gamal Abdel Nasser and calling itself the Free Officers began to organize itself.

In January 1952, events testified to an increasingly corrupt and impotent political order. A shootout between Egyptian police and British troops in Ismailia on January 25 was followed the next day by "Black Saturday," when a fire apparently set by anti-British activists destroyed much of the modern center of Cairo. The Wafdist government was dismissed, but a series of coalition governments over the following months seemed only to reinforce the failure of the liberal system. In the early hours of July 23, the Free Officers decided to move. They launched a virtually bloodless coup, arresting senior officers and securing control of the country. The conspirators felt that they needed a figure of greater seniority than Nasser to lend their action authority, and prior to the coup had approached a much older officer, General Muhammad Nagib, who agreed to act as its public spokesman.

Muhammad Nagib (second from right), Gamal Abdel Nasser (third from right, seated) and Anwar Sadat (fourth from left) meet with other Egyptian Free Officers in Cairo in 1952. The Free Officers forced King Faruq to abdicate his throne on July 23, 1952. (AFP/Getty Images)

Though influenced by the contemporary political currents of the day, the coup leaders had no fixed ideology beyond a broad nationalist program. They quickly forced the abdication of Faruq and initially invoked the 1923 constitution, making claims not to a revolution but a "blessed movement." The monarchy was maintained in form and a civilian, Ali Mahir, appointed as prime minister. The hanging of two workers who had participated in a workers' demonstration in August at Kafr al-Dawwar and were accused of murder, arson, and incitement to riot showed that the new regime's inclinations were not so radical. In the following months the junta sought to define its aims and policies, drawing on a wide range of civilian experts for advice on legal, constitutional, and economic issues, and effectively playing civilian politicians off against one another.

In time, the revolution would develop six principles: the end of imperialism, the abolition of feudalism, the breakup of monopolies, social justice, the strengthening of the military, and a return to democratic rule. However, as the old political parties proved unwilling to reform by purging themselves of corrupt elements, the junta moved away from its proposed program to restore democracy. In December 1952, it abrogated the 1923 constitution and set up a Treason Court to try cases of corruption and the abuse of power under the old regime. In January all political parties (except the Muslim Brotherhood) were banned, and the Liberation Rally, the first of a series of government political parties, was created. Only at this time did the term *revolution* gain official currency and the Revolutionary Command Council (RCC) become formally established.

During 1953 the RCC consolidated its power, abolishing the monarchy and appointing Nagib as Egypt's first president in June. The crisis of March 1954 was a showdown between the forces that favored authoritarian rule, led by Nasser and backed by most of the army and certain elements of the labor movement, and those that sought a return to parliamentary democracy, led by Nagib and Khalid Muhyi al-Din. For a time the result was in doubt, but through skillful maneuvering Nasser ultimately prevailed. Following an assassination attempt on Nasser in October by a member of the Muslim Brotherhood, the regime cracked down on political opposition. Nagib was dismissed and placed under house arrest, and Nasser came increasingly to dominate political affairs.

Despite its inexperience, the RCC showed itself adept in international negotiation. In 1954, an agreement was reached with the British for the evacuation of the last troops in the Canal Zone. The attempt to secure arms from the West was less successful, and the subsequent Egyptian purchase of Czech arms caused a souring of relations with the Americans. Indeed, Nasser's refusal to join the pro-West Baghdad Pact and his participation in the nonaligned Bandung conference aroused American unease. When the U.S. government reneged on an agreement to provide financing for the building of the Aswan High Dam, Nasser responded by nationalizing the Suez Canal on July 26, 1956. The decision was greeted with indignation and hostility by the British and French governments, who hatched a plan with Israel to launch a military attack on Egypt in October. Although Egyptian forces were defeated in the field, the U.S. government forced an end to the fighting, allowing Nasser a diplomatic victory. The affair propelled Nasser onto the international stage as the dominant Arab leader and lay the foundation for a closer relationship between Egypt and the Soviet Union that would remain in place throughout the 1960s. This turn to the left was evident domestically at the beginning of the 1960s, when Nasser embraced the ideology of Arab Socialism, formalized at the National Congress of Popular Forces that convened in 1962 and agreed on a new program of action set out in the National Charter. Among other things, it set up the Arab Socialist Union as the new government party.

In his *Philosophy of the Revolution,* Nasser had described Egypt's three circles of orientations: the Arab, the African, and the Muslim. Of these, the first was given the greatest emphasis, particularly after 1956. In February 1958, the United Arab Republic, a union between Egypt and Syria, was established, though it lasted little more than three years. Nevertheless, Nasser continued to promote and serve as a political inspiration for radical nationalism, anti-imperialism, and anti-Zionism throughout the Arab world. He supported the cause of Algerian independence, sent troops to Yemen to assist the republicans in 1962, sponsored the establishment of the Palestinian Liberation Organization, and criticized conservative Arab regimes. He cultivated close relations with Africa's newly independent leaders and with leaders of other nations as well. The Voice of Free Africa was broadcast out of Cairo, and Egypt hosted the Afro-Asian Peoples' Solidarity Conference in Cairo in 1957.

IMPACTS

At the political level, the revolution of 1952 replaced a constitutional monarchy and a liberal parliamentary system dominated by the large landowning class with an authoritarian military regime. Despite its appeal to the 1923 constitution, the regime came to favor the notion of a guided democracy that sought to mobilize and control the masses through one-party rule, popular organizations, the elitist Vanguard, and the state bureaucracy. The nationalization of the press in 1959 gave the regime greater control over public expression. Where necessary, it used co-optation, as with the labor movement, or repression, using the security services to arrest and imprison political opponents, particularly Communists, Muslim Brothers, and liberals. Although the regime could point to some successes—women first received the vote and sat in parliament in 1956—the political legacy of the revolution has had a most deleterious impact on Egyptian political life.

The economic record of the revolution was more impressive. The land reform of September 1952 limited individual landholdings, and the fixing of rents allowed for significant land redistribution among the Egyptian peasantry. Other laws further limiting land ownership were issued during the 1960s. Such measures were significant steps in alleviating the problem of social inequality and poverty, but they served the dual purpose of reducing the power of the landowning class. Industrial policy was also a priority. Initially the new regime sought cooperation with foreign and native capitalists, but a move to more central planning and public ownership flowed from the nationalization of foreign businesses during the Suez affair. The first five-year plan, launched in 1960, was based heavily on state ownership and an import substitution strategy. Further nationalizations in July 1961 reinforced this trend. The building of the Aswan High Dam not only served the needs of Egyptian agriculture but with other public projects, such as the Hilwan Iron and Steel Works, was an important symbol of economic transformation. These policies proved successful in expanding opportunities for employment and consolidating state planning, but inefficient industries, the demands of the welfare system, the burden of military expenditures, and an increasing population created significant difficulties for the Egyptian economy. By the late 1960s, the economy was beginning to stagnate. Education was also an important plank of government policy, promoted as a means of social advancement. This link was reinforced by a decree passed in 1964 obliging the public sector to offer employment to all university and higher education graduates. Yet, over time employment was unable to keep pace with the numbers of graduates produced, and public service efficiency was consequently undermined.

Egypt's shift from virtual colonial status to an independent state in the 1950s had a significant impact on society. The revolutionary regime's approach to the religious character of Egyptian society was resolutely secular and the inter-communal tensions evident prior to 1952 were quickly dissipated. However, the revolutionary leadership, based as it was in the military, meant that Copts were unrepresented at the highest level. Conscious of this imbalance, Nasser appointed Copts to the cabinet on a regular basis—a practice that has now become standard. The departure of the resident foreign communities beginning in the 1950s, triggered by the nationalizations, the increasingly strident Arab nationalism, and the instability caused by the ongoing Arab-Israeli conflict, meant Egyptian society became more narrow in its social composition.

The revolution came to exercise a considerable influence in public culture. Literature, film, and song reflected much of the new spirit. The press, especially *al-Ahram* under the editorship of Muhammad Haykal, became an important forum for intellectual discussion within certain limits. Specialized institutions such as the Institute of Arabic Studies and the Higher Institute of Socialist Studies were set up to promote official visions of Egyptian history and culture. Although the state was ultimately unwilling to dictate to the universities, new trends in Egyptian scholarship reflected the impact of the political changes and provided the basis for an exploration of social history by locally trained scholars.

The image of a strong, confident Egypt was dealt a stunning blow with its defeat by Israel in the June War of 1967, a setback from which arguably Arab nationalism has not recovered and one of the factors in the revival of political Islam. Although Nasser ultimately stayed in power, the debacle effectively marked the end of the spirit of the July revolution. In his March 30 declaration the following year, Nasser acknowledged that the Arab Socialist Union had failed as a popular institution and promised greater democracy, though this did not materialize. Internationally Egypt became more dependent on the Soviet Union and more conciliatory toward the conservative Arab regimes.

With the death of Nasser in September 1970, Muhammad Anwar Sadat, an original member of the RCC, became president. He charted his own course, launching a "Corrective Revolution" in May 1971 to purge his leftist rivals and granting greater toleration for the Muslim Brotherhood as a political counterweight. Ejecting Russian military advisers in 1972, and leading a surprise attack on Israel in 1973, Sadat gambled further with a peace treaty with Israel in 1979 that saw Egypt expelled from the Arab League. Domestically, he presided over an economic liberalization (*infitah*) and a limited political pluralization, but his policies met with increasing opposition from a broad section of Egyptian society. His assassination in October 1981 was mourned more internationally than in Egypt. Since then, President Husni Mubarak has presided over a country that again faces pressing economic and social problems with little freedom of political action, as it attempts to play the dual role of leading the Arab world and being a reliable American ally.

PEOPLE AND ORGANIZATIONS

Arab Socialism

The official state ideology in Egypt during the 1960s.

Arab Socialist Union (ASU)

Set up at the National Congress of Popular Forces in 1962, the ASU was the official political party during the 1960s. Under Sadat it was dismantled and replaced by the National Democratic Party.

Communist Movement

First active in Egypt in the early 1920s, the Communist movement resurfaced during the Second World War and, though plagued by factionalism, played a very significant role in propagating Socialist ideology. Following sustained repression under Nasser, a now-united Communist Party agreed to dissolve itself in early 1965 in return for individual cadres being given a special place in the regime.

Faruq (1920–1965)

The last king of Egypt, Faruq ascended the throne in 1936 after the death of his father, King Fu'ad. Initially he proved a popular monarch, but his inept political skills and dissolute personal life saw him squander this advantage. He was forced to abdicate by the Free Officers on July 26, 1952, and went into exile in Europe were he died.

Free Officers

The secret organization of military officers formed by Gamal Abdel Nasser in late 1949, with the broad platform of Egyptian independence. Its seizure of power in July 1952 became known as the July Revolution.

Haykal, Muhammad Hasanayn (Born 1923)

Political journalist, writer, and intimate of Nasser, in 1957 Haykal became editor of *al-Ahram*, the most influential newspaper in the Arab world. From this position he served as an unofficial voice of the regime. He fell out of favor with Sadat in 1974 but has continued to maintain his position as a trenchant commentator on Arab and international affairs and an upholder of the Nasserist legacy.

Liberation Rally

The first state political party established by the RCC in January 1953. It was replaced by the National Union in 1957.

Muslim Brotherhood

An Islamic modernist organization set up by Hasan al-Banna in 1928, the Muslim Brotherhood emerged as a significant political force in the late 1940s. With the coming to power of the Free Officers, the Muslim Brothers enjoyed some favor with the regime. But the organization was banned following the assassination attempt on Nasser in October 1954, its members imprisoned and its activities repressed. Under Sadat, the Muslim Brotherhood was tolerated but not granted legal status—an ambiguous status that continues today.

Nagib, Muhammad (1901–1984)

An officer in the Egyptian army since 1918, Nagib was approached before the coup by the Free Officers, who needed a more senior officer than Nasser as a figurehead for the new regime. He served as prime minister from 1952–1953 and as president 1953–1954. In March 1954 he was outmaneuvered by Nasser and dismissed as president in November, following his alleged implication in an assassination attempt on Nasser. He was put under house arrest until 1971 and played no further public role.

Nahhas, Mustafa al- (1879–1965)

The successor of Sa'd Zaghlul as leader of the Wafd, al-Nahhas served as Egyptian prime minister on five occasions from the late 1920s until January 1952. A committed nationalist, he nevertheless presided over a party that became increasingly conservative. His last term (1950–1952), in some ways the last throw for the ancien regime, proved a failure. He was dismissed by Faruq following the Cairo fire in January 1952 and banned from political life by the revolutionary regime.

Nasser, Gamal Abdel (1918–1970)

The chief architect of the 1952 revolution and its leader until his death, Nasser was the son of a postal clerk and entered the Military Academy in 1938. He served during the Palestine War campaign, an experience that did much to politicize him. A colonel at the time of the 1952 coup, he stayed in the background during the first two years of the revolution. With the fall of Nagib, he assumed executive power and in the following years cut a charismatic figure on the world stage. The 1960s were less successful for him, and his leadership reached a nadir with Egypt's defeat by Israel in June 1967. He resigned in the wake of the defeat but was persuaded to resume office following mass public demonstrations. He died suddenly in September 1970 and was succeeded by Anwar Sadat. A towering figure in modern Egyptian history, he presided over significant economic progress and steps toward social equality, though his pattern of dictatorial rule established an unwelcome precedent.

National Charter

The document that set out the ideology and goals of the regime's "turn to the left." Approved by the National Congress of Popular Forces in 1962.

Revolutionary Command Council (RCC)

The body made up of twelve men by which the Free Officers ruled Egypt in the period following their successful seizure of power in July 1952. Not formally known as the RCC until early 1953, it was dissolved in June 1956, when Nasser was elected president.

Sadat, Muhammad Anwar (1918–1981)

Nasser's successor as president of Egypt, Sadat had been politically active since the 1940s and a member of the RCC. He served in a series of posts during the 1950s and 1960s, and in 1969 was appointed vice president. His term as president, (1970-1981), was marked by a move toward the United States and domestic economic liberalization. His controversial decision to make peace with Israel in 1979 and his clampdown on political opposition were the prelude to his assassination by an Islamic militant in 1981.

United Arab Republic (UAR)

The name given to the union between Egypt and Syria but in which Egypt had the dominant role. It lasted from February 1958 until September 1961. Ostensibly inspired by the ideology of Arab nationalism, it also served a range of domestic political interests in both Egypt and Syria. It collapsed following a coup d'état in Syria.

Vanguard Organization

An elite, secret group set up within the Arab Socialist Union to promote the revolutionary ideology of the regime.

Wafd

Originally formed to represent Egypt at the Versailles Conference in 1919 (the name means "delegation"), the Wafd developed into the mass-supported nationalist movement of the 1919–1952 inter-revolutionary period. Led by Sa'd Zaghlul, then Mustafa al-Nahhas, it held power on six occasions but was more often kept out of office by the hostility from the palace and other parties. A broad coalition of progressive landowners, bourgeoisie, and representatives of the masses, it was always more interested in national independence than in social and economic revolution.

Zaghlul, Sa'd (1857–1927)

Though of a peasant background, Zaghlul married well and served as a government minister before the First World War. During the 1919 Revolution he emerged as the leader of the Wafd and was exiled on two occasions by the British. Following the establishment of the 1923 constitution, the Wafd won the first parliamentary elections and Zaghlul formed his only government in January 1924. He resigned in response to Allenby's ultimatum in November of that year after the assassination of Sir Lee Stack and died in 1927.

Anthony Gorman

See Also Colonialism, Anti-Colonialism, and Neo-Colonialism; Islamic Fundamentalist Revolutionary Movement; Transnational Revolutionary Movements

References and Further Readings

Abdel-Malek, Anouar. 1968. *Egypt: Military Society.* New York: Random House.

Beattie, Kirk J. 1994. *Egypt during the Nasser Years: Ideology, Politics and Civil Society.* Boulder, CO: Westview Press.

Daly, M. W., ed. 1998. *The Cambridge History of Egypt.* Vol 2. Cambridge: Cambridge University Press.

Gordon, Joel. 1992. *Nasser's Blessed Movement: Egypt's Free Officers and the July Revolution.* New York: Oxford University Press.

Gorman, Anthony. 2003. *Historians, State and Politics in Twentieth Century Egypt.* London: RoutledgeCurzon.

Kerr, Malcolm. 1971. *The Arab Cold War: Gamal 'Abd al-Nasir and his rivals, 1958–1970.* London: Oxford University Press for the Royal Institute of International Affairs.

Louis, W. R., and Roger Owen, eds. 1989. *Suez 1956: The Crisis and Its Consequences.* Oxford: Clarendon Press.

Meijer, Roel. 2002. *The Quest for Modernity, Secular Liberal and Left-Wing Political Thought in Egypt 1945–1958.* London: RoutledgeCurzon.

Mohi El Din, Khaled. 1995. *Memories of a Revolution: Egypt 1952.* Cairo: American University at Cairo Press.

Naguib, Mohammed. 1984. *Egypt's Destiny,* Westport, CT: Greenwood.

Nasser, Gamal Abdel. 1959. *Philosophy of the Revolution.* Buffalo, NY: Smith, Keynes, and Marshall.

Rejwan, Nissim. 1974. *Nasserist Ideology, Its Exponents and Critics.* Jerusalem: Israel Universities Press.

Sadat, Anwar. 1978. *In Search of Identity.* London: Collins.

Sayyid, Mustapha Kamil al-. 1999. "The Rise and Fall of the United Arab Republic." Pp. 109–127 in *Middle East Dilemma,* edited by M. Hudson. New York: Columbia University Press.

Waterbury, John. 1983. *The Egypt of Nasser and Sadat: The Political Economy of Two Regimes.* Princeton, NJ: Princeton University Press.

Elites, Intellectuals, and Revolutionary Leadership

Whatever the actually existing social, political, economic structures, the ideologies extant, international conditions, even the grand sweep of history—it seems clear that revolutions are fundamentally about people: created by people, led by people, fought and died for by people, and consciously and intentionally constructed by people (which is not to deny the profusion of unconscious and unintentional aspects of the process). As a result, within the dynamic matrix evoked by the term *revolution,* there are any number of relationships of varying degrees, intensities, and durations. Assuming the reference is to "traditional" (i.e., since 1789) conceptions of revolution in which the ultimate goal is state power for the purpose of transforming society, there are myriad connections across and within the (at least) three distinct phases of most revolutions: the struggle for power, the toppling of the old regime, and the effort to create the new society.

Few relationships are more complex and convoluted than that between revolutionary leaders and followers: leaders can go neither farther nor faster in pursuing their goals than the willingness of their followers. Yet visionary and organizational leadership is necessary across all phases of the revolutionary process. Leaders find that they must bargain, compromise, and negotiate in efforts to make the revolution, not just with the population as they attempt to win them over, but among themselves.

And the leaders are hardly a uniform lot. Commonly a collection of dissident elites, radical (or at least renegade) intellectuals, and a cadre of people committed to the revolutionary process because of the material conditions of their everyday lives, they comprise an ever-evolving cast of characters, though those we most associate with revolutionary processes remain vital and relevant across all phases of revolution. Often fraught with crosscutting allegiances, shared frustrations, similar (though rarely identical) visions, and sometimes disparate desires and competing convictions, dissident elites, intellectuals, and revolutionary leaders have been inextricably bound together in most revolutionary situations and processes to date.

The construction of such categories suggests far more clear-cut and readily discernable groupings than one often finds in reality. Here *elites* refers to those members of society privileged by socioeconomic (class) background, characterized by culturally designated leadership traits and often possessing political power. *Intellectuals* includes those involved in "intellectual" careers and often charged with the justification of the state and society (and entrusted with the education of young people). Thus they are often closely allied with the elite. *Revolutionary leaders* are those men and women who take it upon themselves to direct, or are charged with directing, the efforts to seize state power and fundamentally transform society.

ELITES

Revolutionary leaders have often, but not always, been disaffected members of the pre-revolutionary society's elite. But why should this be true? After all, aren't the elites the "haves" who revolutionaries, in the name of the "have-nots," are seeking to displace? While the great majority of elites remain loyal to the old regime, working to assure they will maintain their place and power in society, it is also the case that there are often divisions among the elite for various reasons. If such divisions become serious enough, the pre-revolutionary state can be critically weakened by being deprived of the loyalty and service of many of its most able citizens. This situation can provide an opportunity for revolutionary leaders. A member of the elite may betray his or her class interests for any number of reasons. Practically, we can group them into several broad categories.

One set might be described as disgruntled elites whose fortunes have faded, who feel themselves marginalized, or simply have been ill incorporated into the system. Disaffected nouveau riche played a leadership role in the French Revolution. A variation on this occurs when the traditional elites believe that the regime has betrayed them. In Nicaragua during 1978–1979 and in Cuba in the late 1950s, elites perceived that their governments had been disloyal, thereby justifying their alliance with the rebels. Another type of alienated elite is children of elite families who become morally outraged at inequalities, injustices, and corruption in the pre-revolutionary regime and feel compelled to "right the wrongs" perpetuated by their class and to renounce their class privilege(s). Here again, Nicaragua is an instructive case, with elite youth flocking to the revolutionary cause. This type of disaffection can also include children of lesser elites who attain the trappings of elite status. Such revolutionary leaders include Cuba's Fidel Castro, a lawyer, and Argentina's Che Guevara, a doctor, as well as Colombia's Father Camilo Torre, a priest and sociologist.

Dissident members of the pre-revolutionary elites can perform any number of functions in the revolutionary process. Perhaps one of the most critical roles of elites who "go over" to the revolution is to lend a certain legitimacy, both domestically and internationally, to the revolution. The appearance, for example, of the elite's children in revolutionary leadership positions can call into question some of the fundamental assumptions about the old regime, its legitimacy and its stability. The defection of elites not only deprives the pre-revolutionary regime of people with exceptional intellectual abilities and talents, thereby further weakening it, but it also brings these critically needed skills and capabilities to the revolutionary movement. Nonetheless, the presence of elite persons in revolutionary leadership should not obscure the fact that the majority of the elite usually remain loyal to the old regime, not only during the revolutionary conflict but typically well beyond the transfer of power, often fleeing to external allies and potentially constituting a significant threat to the new regime.

INTELLECTUALS

In a society in the midst of revolution, there may be no more contested, convoluted position than that occupied by the intellectuals. Typically, intellectuals—those in society who specialize in mentally intensive pursuits such as producing works of literature or art, interpreting history, conducting scientific research, or educating the young—function socially to protect and enhance the power of the existing government and the interests of the elite. Intellectuals are usually the preeminent rationalizers and defenders of the status quo. It is, after all, the elite who provide their salaries, workplaces, and prestige. Intellectuals, however, are also those best positioned by both training and inclination to criticize the old regime and proffer plans for the day to come. As a result, intellectuals occupy a strange role in the revolutionary process, coming from positions of privilege but rarely power, and possessing critical faculties and facility. Intellectuals find themselves a contested, compromised, and at times coveted crowd.

Intellectuals are hardly a monolithic group. The most relevant for revolution are academics (including professors and students, sometimes at the secondary as well as at the university level) and "public" intellectuals, who can vary greatly depending on the society but may well include prominent writers and thinkers (Lenin, Trotsky), those with legal (Castro) or academic (Cabral) training, medical people (Che Guevara), or respected or revered religious figures such as priests (Camilo Torres or Gasper Garcia Laviana), shamans, pastors, rabbis, imams (Ayatollah Khomeini), lamas, elders, etc. But preceding the outbreak of a revolutionary conflict, some intellectuals typically produce works that seriously criticize and undermine the legitimacy of the pre-revolutionary regime. Thus they play an essential role in creating the revolutionary situation that sets the stage for the revolutionary process. The abandonment of the old regime by popular intellectuals in some cases has constituted a critical juncture of sorts in undermining the legitimacy of the pre-revolutionary state and in arousing and mobilizing the young people, in particular, for a revolutionary struggle. Certain French political philosophers, such as Montesquieu and Rousseau, attacked the absolute monarchy before the French Revolution. The young Chinese intellectuals of the New Youth Movement, whose slogan was "Democracy and Science" (DeFronzo 1996, 86), played a key role in assaulting the old Confucianist political culture and system, and many later joined China's Communist Party, some becoming important leaders. Ali Shariati, the brilliant Iranian sociologist, writer, and lecturer, helped set the stage for Iran's revolution by reinterpreting Shia Islamic concepts and popularizing the idea that Shiism could play a role in the revolutionary effort. But generally intellectuals have been even more important in the development, articulation, and ongoing refinement of revolutionary ideologies and revolutionary strategies.

Lenin elevated the role of intellectuals in revolutionary leadership in his modification of Marxist concepts. On their own, he argued, workers were unlikely to develop a truly revolutionary view or consciousness. They tended, instead, to focus on issues such as demands for higher wages and better working conditions rather than on comprehending the need to transform society's economic and political systems. The vision, organization, mobilization of the masses, and plan for revolution, in Lenin's view, would be the task of revolutionary intellectuals who would communicate their scientific understanding of society and the necessity of sweeping structural change to workers and peasants. Ironically, although Bolshevik intellectual leaders succeeded in bringing the Communist Party to power in Russia, after Lenin's death in 1924, the original top intellectual leadership of the party, including Trotsky, was virtually wiped out at the hands of Stalin and his associates, who ultimately determined the outcome of the revolution.

It merits mention that focusing on publicly recognized pre-revolutionary intellectuals ignores Gramsci's compelling argument for the importance of "organic" intellectuals, distinguished not by their profession or position, but by their ability to articulate the dreams and desires of the class to which they belong. Regardless, the role of revolutionary intellectuals, whether as revolutionary leaders or simply as articulate foot soldiers, seems to be a critical one. The loss of the people who are, in a very real sense, charged with the rationalization and justification of the existing system is an enormous blow to any regime.

Russian revolutionary Leon Trotsky, commissar of war and leader of the Red Army during the Russian Civil War. (The Illustrated London News Picture Library)

REVOLUTIONARY LEADERSHIP

In most conceptions of revolution, the process is an organized one. The most "successful" cases—France, Russia, China, Cuba, and Iran seem to enjoy the broadest consensus—suggest that strong leadership is necessary if not sufficient. It is the revolutionary leaders, rarely a static group, who make the choices. They consider the wants and needs of the population in whose name the revolution is being made, the most effective way to propagate their revolutionary vision(s), and the domestic and international factors that inevitably and inexorably encroach on the realization of the revolution. Historically, a powerful vision without organization and strategy can not succeed and, conversely, organization and strategy without a guiding vision seems to degenerate into stultifying bureaucracy. What this means in practice is that successful revolutions require both visionary (usually charismatic) and organizational leadership. Visionary leaders articulate the critique of the old regime, the revolutionary ideology, and the vision of the future; they are often verbal

and dynamic people with broad popular appeal. Organizational leaders, charged essentially with translating the revolutionary visions to a revolution on the ground, are methodical, perhaps taciturn people, busy at work behind the scenes. Both types of leaders display various combinations of quixotic idealism, aversions to compromise, pragmatic realism, and deft touches. All come into play as they maneuver to maximize popular support.

Visionary leadership derives in part from the rare capacity to conjure up scenarios in which actually existing circumstances are transformed into an image of a better future. What this means in practice is that prior to political victory, the visionary leadership must articulate popular grievances and discontent with the status quo and propose a vision of the future in which these are redressed and rectified. The goal is both to undermine the old regime and to call the population to the revolutionary project, eliciting from them the necessary commitment for the arduous struggle. Their role remains critical after victory: society's institutions have been undermined and people's consciousness challenged. The transformation of society necessitates daring, commitment, creativity, and adaptability. Visionary leaders are expected to provide inspiration (and direction) to those mobilized by the revolutionary project and to others they hope to attract to the struggle. They must exhort, energize, and emotionally empower members of the population to take control of their own lives and determine their destiny. The reconstruction of the social consensus, torn during the struggle, requires visionary leaders to promote and sell the revolutionaries' agenda. Hence they seek to kindle dramatic visions of the future to justify the sacrifices of the present, and to evoke the fervor of community in place of the oppression of an alienated and atomistic past.

Visionary leadership is virtually always charismatic in nature, though the nature of the charisma may vary from culture to culture. Charismatic leadership helps to promote and facilitate the revolutionary process by portraying in a compelling manner people's needs and giving voice to popular aspirations, albeit wedded to the vision of the future that the revolutionary leaders propose. A charismatic figure who has heroic qualities and resonates with the people can be invaluable.

Charismatic figures raise the promise and the potential of rejecting convention and creating future possibilities. Such leadership may vary dramatically over time and from one location or stage in the revolutionary struggle to another. The factors that denote it are often elusive: a tone of voice, certain gestures, a pattern of anticipating how to address an audience and adapt to its response, a special relationship to the population rooted in a knowledge of its history and experiences, shared pain and suffering, shared joy, or people's association of their lives with that of the leader. It is difficult in any given situation to identify and categorize whatever combination of these factors is present, partly because different people may discern different appealing elements. But the impact is undeniably real.

Charisma in and of itself is not sufficient to guarantee a successful leader or account for the vagaries of any revolutionary process. For that matter, exaggerating the power and gifts of visionary leaders readily degenerates into the "great person of history" fallacy, in which the success of a revolution is unrealistically credited to the role of one person. It seems unlikely that visionaries, no matter how charismatic, can themselves propel any society into or through a revolutionary process; it is more likely that they may find themselves scurrying not to be left behind as events unfold, as in Russia in 1917, when the Bolshevik leadership was caught unprepared by the spontaneous uprising. A compelling vision of great power and beauty, even articulated by a charismatic figure, is not enough.

If it is visionary leaders who engage and mobilize the population, it is the organizational leaders who draw on that commitment in an attempt to make real the promise of the revolution. Prior to political victory, the organizational leadership must arrange for basic necessities (including food, arms, medicine), coordinate military activities, establish and maintain communication, and provide internal discipline and justice, all under duress; the task is essential and typically monumental. After victory, it is their charge to create and maintain the structures necessary to realize the social transformations promised by the revolution.

Thus, once the old regime is defeated, organizational leadership is often focused on the development of the structures of the new state. Legitimization of the revolution is sought through maintenance of or even an increase in popular allegiance. In particular, state institutions must be made accessible to the population and services provided. As a result, the revolutionary vision must be matched, perhaps at times even superseded, by a revolutionary strategy for constructing the new society. Such a strategy is almost certainly related to, but inevitably also somewhat distinct from, the often idealistic conceptions of the transformation process that the revolutionaries had before achieving victory. In the struggle for power, the revolutionary leadership typically advocates broadly popular programs with little or no notion of how they might be actualized. In addition, conditions on the ground have an enormous impact on what is possible. Pragmatism often begins to vie with possibilism as organizational leaders confront the "new" world.

It is important not to exaggerate the difference or distance between the two types of leadership outlined here; these categories are obviously not exclusive. Visionary and organizational leadership may be found in the same person. V. I. Lenin and Leon Trotsky in Russia, Mao Zedong in China, Ho Chi Minh in Vietnam, and Fidel Castro in Cuba resist easy categorization, and it is no coincidence they would likely top any list of "great" revolutionary leaders. Such leaders seem to embody both vision and organization, thereby guaranteeing the presence of these necessary elements and consequently reducing the difficulty of the revolutionary leadership in attempting to balance one with the other. In Russia, though, Stalin is more usefully understood as an organizational genius than as a visionary. Cuba was, arguably, blessed with an abundance of visionary and organizational leadership. Fidel Castro combined both qualities. Raul Castro is an organizational leader of great ability. Camilo Cienfuegos was a prodigious organizer with an appealing visionary streak. Che Guevara was a powerful organizer globally renowned as a visionary leader.

Myriad elements bind the stages of the revolutionary process to each other; chief among these are the leaders who may, but do not necessarily, carry over from one phase to another. Some leaders flourish during the insurrection, able to rally people to the process or organize the groundwork for the process; others thrive during the battle for political victory, and still others come to the fore in the effort to fundamentally transform society. Not all leaders can lead across all stages, but no stage can be bereft of leaders; when leaders fail to emerge, the revolutionary process stalls. Although each revolutionary period is defined in part by its specific reality and populated with people suited to the particular demands of that phase, those leaders we most associate with revolutionary processes are those who are prominent in all phases.

Revolutionary leaders confront an impressive array of obstacles before and after they attain power, and it is nearly impossible to predict which conditions will be present or have an impact in any one case. What is never in doubt is that their situation will demand of them great skill—a deft touch, an ear for nuance, sophisticated eyes—as they rely on their creativity, verve, and élan to fashion the tools necessary to realize their aims. Who these people are and how and why they emerge as they do remain fascinating questions.

Eric Selbin

See Also Anarchism, Communism, and Socialism; Cinema of Revolution; Democracy, Dictatorship, and Fascism; Documentaries of Revolution; Ideology, Propaganda, and Revolution; Student and Youth Movements, Activism and Revolution; Transnational Revolutionary Movements

References and Further Readings

Brinton, Crane. *The Anatomy of Revolution.* New York: Random House.

Cabral, Amilcar. 1980. "The Weapon of Theory." Pp. 115–123 in *Revolutionary Thought in the 20th Century,* edited by Ben Turok. London: Zed.

DeFronzo, James. 1996. *Revolutions and Revolutionary Movements.* Boulder, CO: Westview Press.

Gramsci, Antonio. 1971. "Intellectuals." Pp. 5–23 in *Selections from the Prison Notebooks,* edited and translated by Quintin Hoare and Geoffrey Nowell Smith. New York: International Publishers.

Guevara, Ernesto "Che." 1997. "Notes for the Study of the Ideology of the Cuban Revolution." Pp. 106–115 in *Che Guevara Reader: Writings on Guerrilla Strategy, Politics, and Revolution,* edited by David Deutschmann. New York: Ocean Press.

Lenin, V. I. 1969. *What Is to Be Done?* New York: International Publishers.

Rejai, Mostofa, and Kay Philips. 1988. *Loyalists and Revolutionaries: Political Leaders Compared.* New York: Praeger.

Selbin, Eric. 1999. "Social Revolutionary Leadership: Ideology and Strategy." Pp. 66–91 in *Modern Latin American Revolutions,* 2nd edition. Boulder, CO: Westview Press.

Weber, Max. 1968. *On Charisma.* Edited by S. N. Eisenstadt. Chicago: University of Chicago Press.

Wilson, Edmund. 2003. Part III. Pp. 343–466 in *To the Finland Station: A Study in the Writing and Acting of History.* New York: New York Review of Books.

Ethiopian Revolution

CHRONOLOGY

1st century	Rise of Aksum, Ethiopia's forerunner.
1270	Invention of the Solomonic dynasty.
1855	Tewodros II lays the foundation of the modern Ethiopian state.
1890	Italy creates Eritrea out of northern Ethiopia.
1896	Ethiopia defeats Italy at Adwa.
1930	Haile Selassie I becomes emperor and grants the first written constitution in 1931.
1936–1941	Italy occupies Ethiopia; emperor flees to England.
1941	Ethiopia is liberated, Solomonic dynasty restored, and Britain occupies Eritrea.
1952	Independent Eritrea is federated with Ethiopia in accord with a United Nations vote.
1960	The emperor survives a military coup.
1961	Eritrean armed struggle for secession begins.
1962	Emperor dissolves Eritrean-Ethiopian federation.
1965	Rise of the student movement.
1968	Formation of the All Ethiopia Socialist Movement (Meison).
1972	Ethiopian People's Revolutionary Party (EPRP) is created.
1974	On January 12, first army mutiny triggers the revolution.
	On February 18, the popular uprising begins.
	In June, the Coordinating Committee of the Armed Forces, Police and Territorial Army (Derg) is constituted.
	During 1974 EPRP and Meison appear in Addis Ababa.
	On September 23, emperor is deposed, and the Provisional Military Administrative Council (PMAC) is established.
	On November 23, General Aman Mikael Andom, chairman of the PMAC, is executed.
	On December 20, the PMAC embraces "Ethiopian Socialism."
1975	January–August. All rural land and all major industrial and financial enterprises are nationalized.
	On August 27, Haile Selassie dies.
	During 1975 Ethiopian Democratic Union (EDU) is founded in London.
1976–1977	Violence erupts, leading to the Red Terror.
1977	On February 3, Teferri Banti, chairman of the PMAC, is eliminated.
	On February 11, Mengistu Haile Mariam seizes power.

1977–1978	Ethiopian-Somali war.
1981	Ethiopian People's Democratic Movement (EPDM) is organized.
1984	In September, the Workers Party of Ethiopia (WPE) is formed.
1987	In September, the People's Democratic Republic of Ethiopia (PDRE) is established, with Mengistu as its president.
	The alliance between the Eritrean People's Liberation Front (EPLF) and the Tigray People's Liberation Front (TPLF) is formed.
1988–1989	The Ethiopian Revolutionary Army is defeated in Eritrea and Tigray.
1990	In March, the WPE renounces Marxism-Leninism.
1991	In May, Mengistu flees into exile and the army collapses. The EPLF liberates Eritrea, and the Ethiopian People's Revolutionary Democratic Forces (EPRDF) capture Addis Ababa.
1993	In May, Eritrea becomes independent.
1995	On August 5, the Federal Democratic Republic of Ethiopia (FDRE) is established.
1998–2000	War between Eritrea and Ethiopia.

INTRODUCTION

The Ethiopian Revolution was a profound social upheaval. It deposed a long-reigning autocrat, abolished an iniquitous social order, separated politics from religion, and radically altered the country's international relations. Yet what started as the dawn of a new era of progress and prosperity ended as an unmitigated disaster. Today, most Ethiopians remember the revolution more for its grand failures than for its grandiose ambitions.

BACKGROUND: CULTURE AND HISTORY

With an area of 435,186 square miles and a population of 70 million, Ethiopia is one of Africa's largest countries. Much of it is a plateau dissected by canyons and mountain ranges rising to 15,000 feet. Most of the people live in the temperate highlands. There are more than 70 linguistic groups, but the Amhara and Oromo make up nearly two-thirds of the total. The population is split almost evenly between Orthodox Christians and Sunni Muslims, with tiny fractions of Catholics, Protestants, and those retaining their traditional African beliefs.

Ethiopia's historical identity stretches back for at least two millennia. The historical core was Aksum, a kingdom that rose to grandeur by the first century A.D. in what is today Tigray and southern Eritrea, then declined by the eighth century. In the mid thirteenth century, Amhara rebels of Shewa ousted the Zagwes (1135–1270), successors of the Aksumites, erecting what came to be known as the Solomonic dynasty, which claimed direct ties with ancient Israel. According to legend, King Solomon's intimate encounter with the Queen of Sheba gave birth to Menelik I, the mythological founder of the dynasty that was abolished in 1975. The Amhara and Tigray, descendants of the Aksumites, have ruled the country for more than 700 years, the former for most of the time.

The relationship of the pre-capitalist polity to the community that supported it was hierarchical and inequalitarian. Farmers and herders lived in widely scattered villages where everyday life has changed little in centuries. Peasant households worked on the communal land, which the community controlled through kinship relations. They produced crops and livestock for themselves and for a hierarchy of nobility as tribute. Since estates granted by the monarch were revocable, there was no aristocracy of birth. The tenure system nonetheless generated competition for control or enlargement of fiefs and of the surpluses extracted from the peasantry. This system led, in the mid eighteenth century, to the political and religious fragmentation of the kingdom. But only eighty years later, Kassa of Gondar re-established monarchical authority.

The history of modern Ethiopia began in 1855, when Kassa crowned himself Tewodros II, King of Kings of Ethiopia. He was a reformer, but the gentry and clergy, unwilling to give up their inherited privileges, obstructed his policies. Even though they lost part of the northern historical heartland in 1890 to the Italians, who named the colony Eritrea, his successors reunified and vastly expanded the kingdom southward. The result was a multiethnic and multilingual empire in which the Amhara occupied a privileged position in their relationship with both the central authority and the subordinate peoples. National domination had a material base, of course. The imperial state allotted most of the expropriated lands to itself, the northern conquerors, and their local collaborators. These new landlords collected rent from their tenants, the majority of the southern peoples,

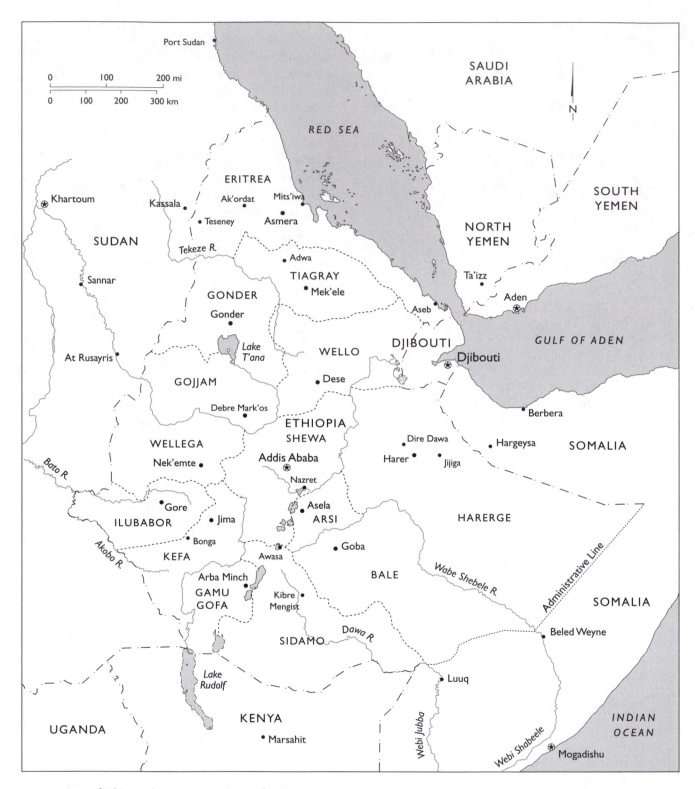

Pre-1991 map of Ethiopia showing major cities and regions.

whose obligations were more onerous than those of their northern counterparts. The conquered had been reduced to near-serfdom.

The modern empire-state was forged in the face of European imperialism. The Ethiopians preserved their independence by defeating Italy at Adwa (1896) but failed to reclaim Eritrea. Nevertheless, Ethiopia's legal and physical boundaries were delimited and national sovereignty recognized. Menelik II ruled until 1913, establishing the basis of rudimentary modernization. But it was Haile Selassie I who brought the country into the modern age.

Haile Selassie (1892–1975) was a modernizing autocrat who awkwardly superimposed imported ideas and state paraphernalia over existing ones. The early phase of his reign, interrupted by the Italian invasion, was marked by a zeal to imitate Europe and Japan. But later he became a retrograde autocrat. The emperor erected an autocratic dynastic state by destroying regional autonomies. The diminution of the fragmented world of feudal loyalties produced possibilities for a new and broader consciousness. For the first time, the peasantry was incorporated into national life, even if central authority remained distant and uncaring. But the detachment of the monarchical state from its rural social base of landed gentry would haunt him later.

The pillars of monarchical absolutism were the military and civilian bureaucracy. The armed forces and their auxiliaries numbered about 120,000 strong. The professional soldiers were organized, trained, and equipped with foreign assistance, mainly from the United States. The civilian bureaucracy, which numbered about 100,000 by 1973, was headed by a prime minister appointed by and responsible to the emperor (Ottaway and Ottaway 1978, 174). Though functionally differentiated, the bureaucracy was not fully developed. Nepotism was widespread and corruption pervasive, implementation of laws lacked consistency and predictability, and administrative decisions and actions were often arbitrary.

Despite bureaucratization, the expansion of secular education, and the country's incorporation into the world economy, Haile Selassie's Ethiopia remained predominantly agrarian, technically backward, and proverbially poor. Peasants made up more than 90 percent of the population, and even though the average family holding was one hectare, farmers surrendered as much as 75 percent of their produce to landlords (Gebru 1991, 78). They were taxed heavily, and cries for land reform were ignored. By the early 1970s, food production was falling behind population growth. This agrarian crisis was the cumulative result of technical archaism, an iniquitous land tenure system, and insufficient capital investment. Rural Ethiopia was abysmally poor and perennially vulnerable to devastating famines, as in 1958, 1973, and 1984.

The capitalist sector was negligible, and the new social classes were minuscule and fractious. Economic development was sluggish and uneven, both within and between regions. State-sponsored industrialization had been expanding steadily since the 1950s, but it still accounted for less than 4 percent of gross domestic product (GDP) and scarcely 5 percent of exports (Gebru 1991, 57; Keller 1988, 109). Foreign capital dominated the industrial and commercial sectors, and an Ethiopian middle class that could have served as a midwife of liberal democracy did not exist. Industry employed about 100,000 workers, scarcely 1 percent of the active population (Lefort 1983, 26–27). Wages were meager and working conditions degrading. Though these incipient classes were tiny, the social cleavages that state-directed modernization spawned were deep enough to cause a crisis in feudalism. Haile Selassie could not meet the increasing demands of the social forces he had set in motion. To contain them, he resorted to despotism.

Autocracy allowed little room for dissent. Even though the Revised Constitution of 1955 provided for a popularly elected lower house, the Ethiopian Parliament was an innocuous institution. The emperor had the right to initiate or veto its legislation, and he could even suspend the constitution. There were no legal political parties and no free press. The growing rift between state and society, along with the absence of public space for permissible political activity, pushed more and more individuals and groups into radicalism and violence. Agrarian agitation became a recurring phenomenon, and the aborted coup of 1960 heralded a decade of social activism.

Two dissident movements served as catalysts of the revolution. Following independence in 1952, Eritrea was federated with Ethiopia. The arrangement proved unworkable, and Ethiopia annexed the autonomous territory, triggering a thirty-year civil war. The Eritrean Liberation Front (ELF) started it in 1961, and the Eritrean People's Liberation Front (EPLF) won the war in 1991. The other enduring opposition came from the schools. Both at home and abroad, radical Ethiopian students resolutely challenged despotism by creating new forms of activism that shaped the lives of a generation and influenced society to the present. They gave rise to the Left, which provided the revolution with both its main guiding ideas and the ethnoregional insurgents who are now in power.

CONTEXT AND PROCESS OF REVOLUTION

The scale and the subsequent course of the revolution came as a surprise. It began bloodlessly but soon turned violent, costing tens of thousands of lives in 1977–1978 and hundreds of thousands more in the subsequent years. The scale and subsequent course of the uprisings were certainly not intended by the agitators, but once they reached a certain point, those who started them could not contain them. What began as scattered and uncoordinated events slowly meshed to produce the most convulsive African social upheaval.

It all began on January 12, 1974, in a provincial military outpost. The mutiny over squalid living conditions might have passed unnoticed, had not a similar rebellion occurred at the main air force base close to the capital just one month later. The soldiers revolted because of poor pay, harsh conditions in the barracks, and the unending Eritrean insurgency. Memories of the 1960 coup inspired them, as did the progressive ideas borrowed from the radical intelligentsia. These soldiers legitimated sedition as patriotic. Their action set off a successive wave of spontaneous and sectional public demonstrations and strikes in Addis Ababa.

First to take to the streets on February 18 were the ever-defiant students, who seized upon the famine of 1973 to both highlight the plight of the peasantry and discredit the regime by inflaming popular passion. On their heels came the teachers and taxi drivers, who were reacting to the spiraling cost of food partly caused by the drought, and to the sudden hike in the price of gas, the result of the Arab oil boycott subsequent to the Arab-Israeli War of October 1973. A week later, the Second Division in Eritrea revolted. Emboldened Muslims overwhelmed Addis Ababa's streets, demanding legal equality with Christians. Then state civil employees and organized labor entered the fray, asking for constitutional reform. The urban protesters had moved from sectarian to collective political demands. The peasantry, however, remained passive.

The authorities could not immediately fathom the discordant voices. All frenetic attempts to halt the tide failed for lack of imagination and resolve. If the emperor's reaction was bewilderment, that of his prime minister, Aklilu Habte Wold, was fright and vacillation. His unexpected resignation only helped to encourage public clamor for change. Mass mobilization in public life rose to an unprecedented scale.

Amid the escalating political turmoil the autocrat quickly lost his grip on power. Several factors allowed the popular upsurge to gain greater social depth, to expand its geographical reach, and to succeed eventually. First, at eighty Haile Selassie had lost his vitality and charisma, and none of his offspring had his strength of character or Machiavellian talents. Second, the dominant political class was fractious and byzantine, individuals or groups frantically vying for power even as they strove to stave off a revolution. Third, by maintaining an initial outward stance of neutrality, the United States, which had propped up the regime since the 1950s, may have emboldened the agitators while disheartening the defenders of the old order. Finally, the desertion by the military deprived the regime of its repressive organs.

The movement, still without a leader or ideology to guide it, had nonetheless attained a momentum of its own. No governmental reshuffling would mollify the protestors. Endalkachew Makonnen, an Oxford-educated aristocrat who became prime minister on February 28, tried to outmaneuver the dissidents tactically by introducing piecemeal reforms. He could not restore political order, however. As the disparate protesters pressed on, the dissident soldiers seized the moment by demanding the detention of all ministers, an action that presaged the regime's end.

In June, the soldiers formed a coordinating committee or Derg (council) with 120 members, all men, and all below the rank of lieutenant colonel. Majors Atnafu Abate and Mengistu Haile Mariam became its vice-chairmen. General Aman Mikael Andom, a popular officer, was drafted to become its chairman. The Derg adopted *Itiopia Tikdem* ("Ethiopia First") as its motto, exemplifying its nationalist character. In July it replaced Endalkachew with Mikael Imru, another aristocrat albeit with liberal credentials. Soon the Derg became a parallel government, dismissing or appointing officials at will. The state of dual power ended only when the emperor was deposed on September 12. Parliament was dissolved, the constitution discarded, and the monarchy abolished. Although it renamed itself the Provisional Military Administrative Council (PMAC), the Derg would not relinquish power for sixteen years. The PMAC was able to seize power and to hold on to it for two reasons: (1) no social class was willing to defend the old regime, and (2) the civilian opposition was hopelessly factionalized.

Before year end, two landmark events occurred: the first internal crisis within the Derg led to the killing of its chairman, two members who supported him, and fifty-seven high-ranking officials of the fallen regime. The crisis was the result of policy differences toward Eritrea as well as a power struggle between the chairman and the Derg, especially its first vice-chairman Mengistu. It augured the times of terror. Second, the Derg embraced Ethiopian Socialism, a foggy ideology that nevertheless indicated its political orientation.

The years 1975–1978 saw the passage of radical reforms and an alarming escalation of gruesome violence that coincided with external hostility in the form of the July 1977 Somali invasion of Ethiopian territory. Between January and August 1975, the PMAC expropriated all major industrial plants, corporations, and banks, as well as all urban land and surplus housing. However, no other project was more significant and permanent than the decree of March 4, 1975, which nationalized all rural land. By abolishing landed property, the decree erased the material base of the old social order, foreclosing its restoration. This action was the result of the students' struggle for "land to the tiller." It also affirmed the PMAC's irreversible radicalization.

Protestors carry posters which read "Land to the tiller, the laborer" and "Land is communal, not private." (Courtesy Gebru Tareke)

Yet as the leadership of the PMAC tilted toward the left, it clashed with the organized Left, inaugurating one of the bloodiest episodes in Ethiopian history. The popular upsurge had given rise to numerous organizations of varied political persuasions. In the urban areas the main actors were the Ethiopian People's Revolutionary Party (EPRP) and the All-Ethiopia Socialist Movement (AESM), better known as Meison, its Amharic acronym. Both were products of the student movement. In their struggle for power, the EPRP agitated for a people's government, in the hope that the EPRP would lead it. Meison struck a "tactical" alliance with the PMAC, but only until it could gain the upper hand and topple the PMAC. The internecine fighting they initiated, as well as the EPRP's futile attempt to kill Mengistu on September 23, 1976, backfired dreadfully. Having appropriated EPRP's ideas and organizational skills, Mengistu created the Revolutionary Flame (RF) to counter them. Meanwhile, on February 3, 1977, in the second round of power struggles, Mengistu eliminated his rivals in the PMAC, including the chairman, General Teferri Banti, and seized supreme power. Against the vi-

olence the rival parties had authored, Mengistu fought back with greater ferocity. Mengistu's Red Terror decimated the leftist organizations, first the EPRP and then Meison, and Mengistu established a sturdy dictatorship.

Peace eluded him, however. The periphery could not be subdued, and the protracted civil war in Eritrea spread to the rest of the country. But of all the ethnonationalist organizations, only the Tigray People's Liberation Front (TPLF) grew to become as dauntless as the EPLF, and northern Ethiopia became the crucial arena of combat. For Mengistu, defeating the dissident nationalists fighting for either independence or autonomy took priority over other objectives, and that decision was his undoing.

Unpopular government policies estranged civil society and precipitated military defeat. Claiming to act on behalf of the oppressed masses, the government instituted new organs of state that the population regarded as even more oppressive and exploitative than those of the previous regime.

In 1984, the Workers Party of Ethiopia (WPE) was established. Party and affiliated mass associations mobilized the

Protestors carry posters which read "We Ethiopian women in a struggle to end class and gender oppression" and "The Revolution will not be secured unless the masses are organized." (Courtesy Gebru Tareke)

peasantry for war and to procure taxes and resources. The demands of state, party, and government accelerated as the war escalated. The state levied multiple taxes, the associations exacted dues, and the officials demanded bribes. Universal conscription, instituted in 1983, was regarded by the peasants as the most burdensome form of taxation.

But the peasants had reasons other than taxation to become disenchanted with the government. An official marketing board bought agricultural produce cheaply, sold it profitably, and used part of it to placate urban society. Besides the hated collectivization, the government implemented two controversial policies in the mid 1980s as part of its counter-insurgency strategy. It forcibly resettled about a half million people from the famine-ravaged areas. And between 1985 and 1987 it moved no less than 8 million people, roughly 22 percent of the rural population, to consolidated villages in order to deprive the rebels of support (Clapham 1988, 176). Consequent peasant dissatisfaction tipped the balance of forces on the battlefields. As the number of government volunteers and conscripts shrank, guerrilla ranks swelled. A dispirited army began to lose ground precipitously.

In 1987, as the short-lived People's Democratic Republic of Ethiopia (PDRE) was declared, the EPLF and TPLF forged a tactical alliance. At that point, the end of the regime became imminent. The Second Revolutionary Army (SRA) suffered a major defeat in Eritrea in 1988. A year later, the Third Revolutionary Army (TRA) was defeated in Tigray. In May 1991, the EPLF seized Asmara, Eritrea's capital, and declared independence in 1993. The Ethiopian People's Revolutionary Democratic Forces (EPRDF), a coalition of the TPLF, the Ethiopian People's Democratic Movement (EPDM), and several other organizations, seized the government in Ethiopia in May 1991. It subsequently established the Federal Democratic Republic of Ethiopia (FDRE), an ethnically based federal state in which power is dispersed, theoretically, among nine equally autonomous regions.

IMPACTS

Although the revolution was essentially an Ethiopian affair, there were external meddlers. Prominent among them were the governments of Saudi Arabia, Sudan, and the United States, which supported the Ethiopian Democratic Union (EDU), the only significant counter-revolutionary organization. But the EDU proved too feeble to counter the Ethiopian Revolution. More dangerous was the irredentist state of Somalia with territorial ambitions in northeast Africa. Ignoring the counsel of the Cubans and Soviets who had helped build its armed forces, Somalia declared war on Ethiopia. Simultaneously, the United States imposed an arms embargo on the victim of aggression. In desperation, Ethiopia turned to the Socialist block for help. Cuba dispatched 18,000 troops, and Russia shipped $1.5 billion worth of armaments. Assistance from such Muslim countries as Egypt, Iran, and Pakistan could not save the day for Somalia, which was decisively defeated in March 1978. The Ethiopian government then switched its allegiance from the United States to the U.S.S.R.

The war led to the militarization of the Ethiopian state, which still had to contend with local insurgencies. Ethiopia emerged as the regionally dominant power, with a half million men in arms, and Mengistu projected that power by funneling arms to the liberation movements of southern Africa. But militarization was a heavy drain on the country's economy. Ethiopia's debt by the end of the civil wars exceeded ten billion dollars. Worse, the military failed to safeguard the country's territorial integrity. Bereft of Soviet aid, which was terminated by 1989, and estranged from society, the demoralized army collapsed, Mengistu fled into exile, and the state broke into two.

Though the revolution erased an exploitative and repressive social system, it failed to deliver either prosperity or equality. Nothing more poignantly revealed the regime's utter failure to deal with the agrarian crisis than the famine of 1984, the worst in a hundred years. The people of Ethiopia have sunk deeper into poverty—today, Ethiopia has forty million more people than in 1974, and more than half of the population lives on a dollar a day, with at least 20 percent permanently undernourished. The revolution's failure was largely due to the civil wars, incompetent and corrupt leadership, and the adoption of untimely or inapplicable Socialist policies in one of the poorest and most backward countries.

Admittedly, some political progress has been made since the end of tyranny. Ethiopia is now more democratic than at any time in its history. It has an enlightened leadership, a vocal legal opposition, a vigorous press, and a thriving civil society. Yet power still tends to be personal, arbitrary, and abusive. Violations of human rights are frequent, official corruption rife. The government, like its predecessors, has so far failed to resolve the country's persistent problem of food insufficiency. The reckless war with Eritrea in 1998–2000 damaged a frail economy and threatened social stability. Peace and democracy are essential to the region's develop-ment, but that calls for some kind of federal or confederal unity between the two countries. The peoples of the Horn are waiting for a new kind of revolution.

PEOPLE AND ORGANIZATIONS

Ethiopians have no last names or surnames. A person's name is simply followed by his or her father's name. So normal procedure among Ethiopians is to alphabetize by the person's name, not by the father's name.

Aklilu Habte Wold (1912–1974)

He was educated in France, where he stayed until 1941, agitating against the Italian occupation. He held several ministerial positions before becoming prime minister (1961–1974). Aklilu was executed in 1974.

All Ethiopia Socialist Movement (Meison)

Meison was founded in July 1968 by Ethiopian students in Europe. It became influential in the revolution by striking a convenient alliance with the Derg, for whom it became an ideological mentor. It fell victim to the Red Terror.

Aman Mikael Andom (1924–1974)

Known as a competent and popular officer in the army, Aman became defense minister, chairman of the Derg and head of state all at the same time in 1974. Following disagreements with the Derg, he was killed in a gun battle at his residence on November 23, 1974.

Atnafu Abate (1937–1977)

A graduate of the Holeta Military Training School (HMTS), Ethiopia, Atnafu was a founding member of the Derg and vice-chairman of the PMAC until his execution on November 13, 1977.

Derg

The coordinating committee of the armed forces, police, and Territorial army. It surfaced in June 1974 and was later replaced by the PMAC, although the expression Derg was still widely used for the PMAC.

Endalkachew Makonnen (1926–1974)

The son of a former prime minister, Endalkachew was educated at Oxford. He held various ministerial and ambassadorial posts until his appointment as prime minister in 1974. He was executed in the same year.

Eritrean Liberation Front (ELF)

Muslim dissidents founded this secessionist movement in 1961. It began the thirty-year armed struggle but was splintered into several competing groups in the early 1970s. In 1981 it lost a violent struggle on the battlefield to the EPLF.

Eritrean People's Liberation Front (EPLF)

Three splintered groups from the ELF joined in 1973 to form the EPLF. It fought until total victory in 1991.

Ethiopian Democratic Union (EDU)

This counter-revolutionary organization was founded in 1975 in London by officials of the old regime. Expelled from Tigray by the TPLF and thrashed in Gondar in 1978 by the Derg (PMAC), it maintained some roving bands in that area until 1990.

Ethiopian People's Democratic Movement (EPDM)—now Amhara National Democratic Movement (ANDM)

Organized in 1981 in Gondar by dissident members of the EPRP.

Ethiopian People's Revolutionary Democratic Forces (EPRDF)

The TPLF and EPDM formed this united front in 1989. It helped create many satellite ethnoregional organizations and became the ruling party.

Ethiopian People's Revolutionary Party (EPRP)

Organized by Ethiopian students in Europe in April 1972. Although it was decimated by the Red Terror and defeated in Tigray by the TPLF in 1978, it waged an armed struggle in Gondar and Gojjam against the Mengistu regime until 1990.

Haile Selassie I (1892–1975)

Teferri Makonnen was the son of Ras (Duke) Makonnen, the cousin of Emperor Menelik II. In 1916 he became regent and heir apparent to the Solomonic throne, which he ascended as king on October 7, 1928. Two years later he was crowned King of Kings (Emperor) with the throne name of Haile Selassie I. He started as a progressive, initiating constitutional, educational, and economic reforms, but later became autocratic and a social conservative. He was deposed in 1974 and died in 1975.

Mengistu Haile Mariam (Born 1938)

Son of a sergeant in the army, Mengistu entered the Holeta Military Training School (HMTS) in 1957 and graduated as second lieutenant in 1959. He was twice (1963 and 1969) sent to the United States for further training in ordinance. Little was known about his politics before the revolution. When he became a member of the Derg, Mengistu was elected its first vice-chairman. On February 11, 1977, he became the undisputed leader, and in 1987 president of a new republic. Mengistu ruled the country with an iron fist until 1991, when he went into exile.

Mikael Imru (Born 1926)

The son of Ras (Duke) Imru Haile Selassie, the emperor's cousin, Mikael was educated at Oxford and gained a reputation, like his father, for liberalism. Mikael served in various positions until his elevation to the short-lived premiership in 1974. But he remained a close adviser of the PMAC.

Provisional Military Administrative Council (PMAC)

It replaced the coordinating committee or Derg in 1975, although many people continued to refer to this council as the Derg.

Revolutionary Flame

Mengistu created the organization in 1977, mainly to counter Meison.

Teferri Banti (1921–1977)

Trained at the Holeta Military Training School (HMTS) and in the United States, Teferri was a competent professional with no known political ambition. He was commander of the Second Division when he succeeded Aman as chairman of the PMAC. Teferri was killed on February 3, 1977.

Tigray People's Liberation Front (TPLF)

Organized by university students, it began armed struggle in February 1975 with assistance from the EPLF. In 1977–1978 the TPLF defeated its rivals to become the sole movement in Tigray. It won total military victory in 1991, emerging as the dominant organization in the EPRDF, currently the ruling party.

Gebru Tareke

See Also Colonialism, Anti-Colonialism, and Neo-Colonialism; Documentaries of Revolution

References and Further Readings
Clapham, Christopher. 1988. *Transformation and Continuity in Revolutionary Ethiopia.* Cambridge: Cambridge University Press.
Gebru Tareke. 1991. *Ethiopia: Power and Protest: Peasant Revolts in the Twentieth Century.* Cambridge: Cambridge University Press.
———. 2004. "From Af Abet to Shire: The Defeat and Demise of Ethiopia's 'Red' Army, 1988–89," *Journal of Modern African Studies* 42 (2): 239–281.
Halliday, Fred, and Maxine Molyneux. 1981. *The Ethiopian Revolution.* London: Verso.
Keller, Edmond. 1988. *Revolutionary Ethiopia: From Empire to People's Republic.* Bloomington: Indiana University Press.
Lefort, Rene. 1983. *Ethiopia: An Heretical Revolution?* London: Zed Press.
Markakis, John. 1987. *National and Class Conflict in the Horn of Africa.* Cambridge: Cambridge University Press.
Ottaway, Marina, and David Ottaway. 1978. *Ethiopia: Empire in Revolution.* New York: Africana Publishing.
Pool, David. 2001. *From Guerrillas to Government: The Eritrean People's Liberation Front.* Oxford and Athens: James Currey Ltd. and Ohio University Press.
Tiruneh, Andargachew. 1995. *The Ethiopian Revolution, 1974–1987: A Transformation from an Aristocratic to a Totalitarian Autocracy.* Cambridge: Cambridge University Press.
Young, John. 1997. *Peasant Revolution in Ethiopia: The Tigray People's Liberation Front, 1975–1991.* Cambridge: Cambridge University Press.

Ethnic and Racial Conflict: From Bargaining to Violence

In pluralistic societies, ethnic and racial conflict is ubiquitous, but not necessarily destructive. Different group interests lead to competition and conflict with respect to the determination of state policies. This competition and conflict remains at manageable levels so long as conflict is bounded, demands are reasonable, and political spokespersons are prepared to abide by societal norms on channeling these claims through established institutions to those in positions of power. However, as bargaining relations increase in difficulty, the intensity of ethnic conflict increases, leading to rising communal demands or to either a lack of state responsiveness or state overreaction. To gain an insight into this shifting pattern of state-society interaction, we will first examine the best case scenarios of stable strategic interactions and then turn to a focus on bargaining failure and, sometimes, the triggering and escalation of violence. In the conclusion we will consider the role of third parties in preventing this pattern of deteriorating relations.

NEGOTIABLE ISSUES

So long as ethnic and racial groups compete over resources that can be divided, norms are shared, and leaders and groups have pragmatic perceptions of each other's intentions, the negotiating process can prove to be a productive one in terms of containing conflict at manageable levels. In these positive encounters, the interethnic or state-ethnic struggle takes place between essentially rational actors prepared to advance their interests in accordance with the prevailing rules. The state establishes and acts as the enforcer of these basic rules, while the demand-bearing spokespersons enter into a complex bargaining relationship with both state leaders and other ethnic patrons. Group leaders and members can then consider potentially divisive questions of allocating resources and positions, enabling them to negotiate the distribution of revenues and positions in government over time. This leads them to feel relatively secure that their group members will not suffer exploitation and victimization. And with disputes regarded as essentially negotiable, the relevant elites are likely to perceive minimal threats to their traditions, cultural practices, or physical survival in the pluralistic context.

In engaging in what is essentially a constructive relationship with other groups, the prevailing political structure encourages leaders and group members to act in a positive way toward others, developing networks of reciprocity among leaders and groups and entering into bargaining relationships with their counterparts. Under favorable conditions, positive relationships can also be promoted by a process of political liberalization within authoritarian regimes. This can lead in some cases to such liberal regimes as majoritarian democracy, power sharing, or a combination of these. Although these transitions may be triggered by a top-down decision within the established ruling elite, these regimes must nonetheless gain general acceptance over time if they are to be accorded political legitimacy (Bratton and van de Walle 1997). Thus, Jerry Rawlings' cautious experiment with managed elections in Ghana in 1992 gradually gained broad popular acceptance, and by the time the 2000 election took place, the process of selection was deemed free and fair.

Although regimes grounded on majority democracy and power sharing have both proved fragile, especially in developing countries, majoritarian and power-sharing democracies do offer decided advantages over their authoritarian counterparts in terms of elite competition and public participation. This advantage also applies to structuring the kind of regularized relationships that promote repeated bargaining encounters. In principle, either of these popularly based regimes can be protective of minority interests, so long as basic rules of free expression, proportionality, inclusion, accountability, and transparency are accepted. At times soft authoritarian regimes can also demonstrate a preparedness to deal with ethnic and racial pluralism in a peaceful manner. In the way that these authoritarian regimes combine elite participation with state control, they can, for a limited time at least, foster a sense of security and well-being among minority ethnic interests that furthers political stability.

In brief, what tends to be common to stable majoritarian and consensus regimes is modest and negotiable demands, effective institutions, shared norms and values, and leadership committed to core liberal values. Ethnic and racial interests remain negotiable because groups remain reasonably secure within the borders of a common state. The combination of the above conditions (e.g., in contemporary South Africa) can result in a mutually beneficial encounter between state and society—even in situations where a high degree of ethnic pluralism, class cleavage, and relatively low per capita incomes prevails.

NON-NEGOTIABLE ISSUES

What causes this conflict to become intense and result, in worst cases, in violence and mass killing? Why have negotiations become problematic and the relations between groups adversarial, leading at times to the triggering and escalation of violence among subethnic, ethnic, racial, religious, and subregional interests? The answer can neither be explained by the coexistence of plural groups in the same society, nor by the existence of ancient hatreds. Lack of economic opportunity or scarcity of land no doubt proved a conflict-creating factor in some instances, as in Rwanda; yet nonmaterial explanations—such as the ideology of ethnic distinctiveness, perceived threats to the group's physical or cultural survival, or challenges to group status, worth, or identity—should not be underestimated. Moreover, the explanations can often be found in the strategic interactions of

elites and in the perceptions that key actors hold about the intentions of adversaries.

It is important to stress at the outset that in most places most of the time, the demands that ethnic and racial entrepreneurs make to those in power are limited and reasonable. Consequently, conflicts remain negotiable. At times, however, as political entrepreneurs place their parochial interests above those of the larger community and manipulate the uncertainties and concerns their constituents hold about the future, they can create a situation where collective fears lead to group polarization. Suspicion and hostility replace a common effort to solve joint problems (Lake and Rothchild 1998). Politicians and their allies bear a heavy responsibility for shaping the dialogue among groups in such a way that their membership feels justified in taking extreme measures to advantage their group at the expense of others.

In a context of state weakness, those who control the political center often become a large part of the problem, championing exclusion and displaying an unwillingness or inability to act as protectors of the minority. A weak state is marked by a number of aspects, most notably a low level of legitimacy, a lack of social cohesion, ineffective public institutions, and limited capacity for economic management and resource extraction (Rothchild 2002, 192–198). Connections among groups are fragile, and the state is unable to safeguard its citizenry from the predatory ambitions of rogue leaders. Group members, searching for increased security, may therefore retreat to their ethnic containers to defend themselves against the perceived aggressive interventions of their adversaries. Ethnic group control of the state and its institutions exacerbates this sense of vulnerability. It causes marginal members to rally around the ethnic leadership in an effort to increase their sense of security.

When the strategic interactions among elites lead to extreme polarization, the result is unreliable information about the adversary and its intentions. This heightens a sense of insecurity and complicates the management of conflict through bargaining. With suspicion high, group leaders tend to be secretive, even to send out misleading information in order to confuse their rivals about their strength or purposes. This breakdown in communications further exacerbates a sense of vulnerability and contributes to uncompromising postures and bargaining failure (Lake and Rothchild 1998, 9–11).

The failure to share information contributes directly to another source of bargaining failure, namely the inability of the adversary parties to make a credible commitment to uphold what may be described as the ethnic contract. A commitment to uphold a formal or informal agreement may not be credible in the eyes of weaker parties. Future leaders may not be prepared to honor the commitments made by other intermediaries in earlier times. Majority leaders simply can not be effectively hemmed in by legal safeguards made earlier under different circumstances. To be sure, majority ethnic elites may be a prepared to offer concessions to weaker parties to get them to sign on to cease-fires and peace accords, but the reassurances given them may not be enforceable at a later phase as new conditions come to the fore. As the balance of power between ethnic groups shifts, assurances given by the more powerful bargaining actor may no longer be viewed as in its interests, leading the stronger party to renege on its commitments (Lake and Rothchild 1998, 13–17).

THE TRIGGERING AND ESCALATION OF VIOLENCE

Bargaining failure becomes manifest with the triggering of violence. The actions of elites are usually critical in explaining the deterioration of bargaining relations and the triggering of violence, although at times, in Sierra Leone or Liberia, thugs and child soldiers have been known to organize violent initiatives on their own. Violence can be said to be ethnic in nature when a group, mobilized in most cases by elites on behalf of their ethnic membership, acts in a violent manner toward another group on the basis of its ethnic identity. States may at times be parties to ethnic violence when they engage a subgroup on the basis of ethnic criteria. Although riots and disturbances can be spontaneous phenomena, ethnic elites usually play a significant role in mass ethnic violence, pushing their membership to take action and making critical decisions on the launching of attacks. In both Bosnia and Rwanda, these attacks were well planned and orchestrated by ambitious elites who urged their constituents to carry out assaults on helpless victims.

Nevertheless, efforts to organize violence are most likely to be effective when predisposing conditions are present that lend credence to the call to action. Such predisposing conditions include the following factors: conflicting claims and objectives, hatred or fear of adversaries, conviction that there is no alternative to violent measures, a sense that the group can prevail in a military contest, an assessment that fighting will provide better prospects for the future, the availability of weaponry, and access to hate radio (Carnegie Commission 1997, 30). As violence ensues, broadly accepted norms and values from the past give way to suspicion and distrust. This phenomenon of aggressive action and intensifying insecurity is heightened by the emotionally laden denunciations of elites who use the mass media to evoke communal sensitivities regarding old hurts and humiliations. In the former Yugoslavia and Rwanda, ambitious politicians made effective use of the mass media to rouse their supporters to take violent measures against neighboring communities. As a consequence, the bargaining practices prevailing earlier were undercut and the linkages that bound communities together in a common enterprise were gravely weakened.

Certainly chance and unanticipated provocations can have disastrous results, but by and large it seems clear that the predispositions and conscious decisions of political elites are usually critical in triggering major instances of violent ethnic conflict. Not only do bargains become difficult to strike, but they are hard to maintain. Agreements among ethnic leaders may prove unenforceable, especially in a situation where the state is weak and lacking in legitimacy and where it has limited capacity to maintain the rules of relationship. In the wake of intra-state wars, with information about the intentions of adversaries largely unavailable and commitments by adversary elites unreliable, it becomes extremely difficult to implement peace agreements.

Since negotiations are viewed as potentially risky and one side perceives its influence to be declining, group demands may harden and become non-negotiable. The costs of compromise may appear higher than that of direct forms of action. This adversarial encounter can lead to a full breaking of connections, which finds expression in various forms of non-cooperation, calls for partition and secession, and the triggering of inter-group violence. The trigger phase is short-term in duration, leaving open the possibility that external actors can intercede and prevent the crisis from worsening. If, however, the spiral of organized violence is not contained and ethnoregional warfare endures, the escalation phase sets in and frequently the war widens. In these prolonged encounters, civilians have been especially vulnerable to assaults by irregular forces, such as the 2004 Jingaweit militia attacks on civilians in Darfur. The dynamics of escalation tend to draw neighboring countries into the spreading military encounters, as seen in the long-running and highly destructive wars of Liberia, Sierra Leone, and the Democratic Republic of the Congo (Sriram and Wermester 2003).

GENOCIDE

As the strategic interactions of ethnic groups continue on a trajectory of intensifying conflict and, in worst cases, result in ethnic-inspired mass killing, bargaining failure reaches its ultimate point. Although it shares characteristics with ethnic wars (Harff 2003, 57), genocide represents an extreme in ethnic and racial relations because it is a point of no return: the genocidists seek to eliminate a rival group physically in an effort to end the encounter with it once and for all. Genocide is distinct from sporadic killings or atrocities in that those controlling the state or another ethnic group seek to murder the members of another ethnic group intentionally and systematically. As defined by the UN Genocide Convention, genocide consists of acts intended to destroy a national, ethnical, racial, or religious group in whole or in part. Genocide includes the following actions: killing members of the group, causing serious bodily or mental harm to members of the group, deliberately inflicting the conditions of life calculated to bring about a group's physical destruction in whole or in part, imposing measures intended to prevent births within the group, and forcibly transferring children of the group to another group. Such acts occur more regularly than many observers might assume. By Barbara Harff's (2003, 57) account, nearly fifty such events have taken place since World War II, causing over 12 million deaths.

Certainly many of the factors leading to the triggering and escalation phases of ethnic conflicts apply readily to experiences with genocide. High on the list of characteristics is the lack of state legitimacy and an unwillingness on the part of the state or opposition groups to abide by the rules. The weak state's inability and unwillingness to protect its citizens leaves the ethnic groups with the responsibility to provide for their own security. Such self-reliance can in turn contribute to aggressive action when elites perceive their greatest security to lie in a preemptive attack. Other similar characteristics include a regime insecure about its hold on state power, the accession to power of a regime committed to radical change, political memories of past victimization, and a lack of international constraints. But genocide is also distinctive as a political and social process, for it is a calculated series of actions, organized and directed by bureaucratic agencies that seek to dehumanize the members of rival communal groups with the intention of appropriating their property, altering their country's political composition, and eliminating their cultural and physical presence in the society (Kuper 1977).

With the international community hanging back and staunchly resisting appeals to intervene, those planning genocide invoke the domestic jurisdiction principle to ward off international pressure or intercession. Although external actors have been loath to intercede—on behalf of the Armenians in Turkey or the Kurds in Iraq, or in Nazi Germany, Rwanda, or Bosnia—there is increasing international agreement that sovereignty must be exercised responsibly, that it is not a protection for those committing mass murder. Over time, the legitimacy of the military intervention norm has gained increasing (but grudging) approval. Acceptance of the principle that human rights are to be respected globally has been used to justify external armed intercession as a last resort to protect the vulnerable from mass displacement and murder (Evans and Sahnoun 2002), but, as seen with the cautious UN and European Union response to the widespread killings in 2004 in Sudan's Darfur region, the world community is only slowly learning how to react to severe ethnic violence.

CONCLUSION

The bargaining relations of ethnic groups are marked by complexity and variety. In the most stable of situations, bargaining encounters are predictable and regularized over time. So long as group leaders compete over resources that can be divided, have pragmatic perceptions of one another, and are buttressed by supporting institutional norms and arrangements, a process of ongoing interactions holds out the prospect of stable and beneficial relations into the future. But this prospect begins to change and unleashes a process of bargaining failure when ethnic champions mobilize their members for political action and when elite ambitions and group grievances are sufficiently strong to cause intense conflict and possibly to trigger violence. If state or international actors are not able to restrain these attacks, bargaining failure may become more pronounced, leading to a protracted phase of escalation. Many of the characteristics of intense and highly polarized conflict remain in place as the strategic interactions shift toward mass killing and genocide. To be sure, mass killings may also take place during the escalation phase, but genocide is a distinctive phase that features planned and systematic efforts by one ethnic actor to destroy another.

Clearly, it is difficult for political actors caught up in the phases of escalation and genocide to extricate themselves from these violent encounters. Such grim episodes limit the possibilities for effective bargaining politics, since the intensity of conflict and lack of information about the intentions of rivals make accommodations extremely difficult. Agreements reached in such an environment are often viewed as motivated by strategic concerns and their commitments lacking in credibility. To overcome this looming prospect of bargaining failure, it is necessary for third parties to take the initiative and intercede to contain the spiraling conflict by facilitating negotiations and overseeing the implementation process. Even under these circumstances, there can be no guarantee that durable bargaining relations can be restored, for the local parties themselves must have a minimal level of confidence that the institutions and norms of encounter will be respected over time.

Donald Rothchild

See Also Chechen Revolt against Russia; Cinema of Revolution; Documentaries of Revolution; Indian Independence Movement; Irish Revolution; Kenyan Mau Mau Rebellion; Kurdish Movements; Nazi Revolution; Pakistan Independence and the Partition of India; Palestinian Movement; Rwanda Civil Wars; Slave Rebellions in the United States; South African Revolution; Terrorism; Yugoslavia: Dissolution; Zapatista Movement; Zimbabwean Revolution; Zionist Revolution and the State of Israel

References and Further Readings
Bratton, Michael, and Nicolas van de Walle. 1997. *Democratic Experiments in Africa: Regime Transitions in Comparative Perspective.* Cambridge: Cambridge University Press.

Carnegie Commission on Preventing Deadly Conflict. *Preventing Deadly Conflict: Final Report.* 1997. Washington, DC: Carnegie Commission on Preventing Deadly Conflict.

Evans, Gareth, and Mohamed Sahnoun. 2002. "The Responsibility to Protect," *Foreign Affairs* 81 (6) (November–December): 99–110.

Harff, Barbara. 2003. "No Lessons Learned from the Holocaust? Assessing the Risks of Genocide and Political Mass Murder Since 1955." *American Political Science Review*, Vol. 97, No. 1:57–71.

Kuper, Leo. 1977. *The Pity of It All: Polarization of Racial and Ethnic Relations.* Minneapolis: University of Minnesota Press.

Lake, David A., and Donald Rothchild. 1998. *The International Spread of Ethnic Conflict: Fear, Diffusion, and Escalation.* Princeton, NJ: Princeton University Press.

Power, Samantha. 2002. *A Problem from Hell: America and the Age of Genocide.* New York: Basic Books.

Rothchild, Donald. 1997. *Managing Ethnic Conflict in Africa: Pressures and Incentives for Cooperation.* Washington, DC: Brookings Institution Press.

———. 2002. "The Effects of State Crisis on African Interstate Relations (and Comparisons with Post-Soviet Eurasia)." Pp. 189–214 in *Beyond State Crisis? Postcolonial Africa and Post-Soviet Eurasia in Comparative Perspective,* edited by Mark R. Beissinger and Crawford Young. Washington, DC: Woodrow Wilson Center Press.

Sriram, Chandra, and Karin Wermester, eds. 2003. *From Promise to Practice: Strengthening UN Capacities for the Prevention of Violent Conflict.* Boulder, CO: Lynne Rienner.

European Revolutions of 1848

CHRONOLOGY

1848   January Revolt in Sicily: King of Two Sicilies allows creation of a constitution.

In February, the *Communist Manifesto* of Karl Marx and Friedrich Engels is published.

On February 22–24, the February revolution in Paris forces King Louis-Philippe's abdication. The Second Republic is proclaimed, and the provisional government is invested at Paris city hall, headed by Alphonse de Lamartine.

On February 26, the French government establishes national workshops to provide jobs for unemployed persons.

On February 27, the Mannheim popular assembly of Baden demands freedom of press, trial by jury, right of assembly, an army of the people, and a German parliament. Similar assemblies take place in Wurtemberg , Hesse-Darmstadt, Nassau, and other German states.

On March 2, Bohemian noblemen in Prague demand calling of Bohemian Diet (assembly).

On March 4, Charles Albert proclaims constitution (*Statuto*) for Piedmont at Turin.

On March 6, Czech radicals in Prague call for a meeting on March 11 to draft reform petition.

On March 7, Berlin popular assembly "under the tents" begins.

On March 8, German Confederation in Frankfurt declares the Black-Red-Gold the German flag.

On March 13–15, the Vienna Revolution takes place; Metternich flees to exile in England.

On March 15, the Pressburg (Bratislava) Hungarian Diet demands reforms transforming Hungary into a modern constitutional monarchy.

Also on March 15, Pest Revolt leaders proclaim 12 Demands for political and social change.

On March 18, street fighting breaks out in Berlin.

On March 18–22, Milan Revolt "Five Glorious Days;" General Radetzky withdraws Austrian forces from Milan.

On March 19, Prussian troops withdraw from Berlin. Prince William of Prussia flees to England.

On March 20, following street protests in Munich, King Ludwig I of Bavaria abdicates in favor of his son Maximilian II. In Poznan, the Polish rising against Prussia begins.

On March 22, the Venice Arsenal Revolt takes place. Daniele Manin becomes leader of Venetian Republic.

On March 23, Charles Albert declares war on Austria to liberate Italy.

On March 24, Frederick William agrees in Berlin to national reorganization of Poznan.

On March 31, members of various German assemblies gather in pre-parliament and call for elections of representatives to a German national assembly to write a constitution for a united Germany.

In April, a republican rising in Baden is put down by troops of the German Confederation.

On April 11, the Austrian emperor agrees to the demands of Hungarian Diet, the April Laws, that creates constitutional government for Hungary.

On April 16, *Champs de mars* demonstration in Paris marks a decisive turning point. Democrats are defeated. Resurgence of reaction.

On April 23, French election results in a majority of conservative, pro-monarchist deputies, which will lead to the defeat of the more radical urban workers and their demands.

On April 27, the end of slavery in French colonies is proclaimed in Paris.

On May 9, the last of the Polish insurgents in the Poznan Revolt capitulate at Bardo, and the Polish Revolt is defeated.

On May 15, the Second Revolt in Vienna forces the calling of an Austrian parliament. Emperor Ferdinand escapes to Innsbrück.

On May 18, the German National Assembly opens in Frankfurt.

On May 22, the Prussian National Assembly opens in Berlin.

On June 1 in Cologne, the first issue of the liberal newspaper *Neue Rheinische Zeitung* is published, edited by Marx and Engels.

On June 2–12, the Pan-Slav Congress in Prague calls for the transformation of Austrian empire into a confederation of peoples with equal rights; repression ends efforts of Czech liberals to get reforms.

On June 2–6, the first Representative Assembly of the North German Artisans and Trades takes place in Hamburg.

On June 7, Prince William of Prussia returns from London to a tide of reaction in Prussia.

On June 13, the Prague Revolt of Czech radicals is put down by Alfred Prince zu Windischgrätz.

On June 14, the Berlin armory is stormed by revolutionary workers and craftsmen, who are ultimately defeated.

On June 22–26, during the so-called June Days, many French workers stage insurrections against the government's closing of the national workshops, which benefited the unemployed. The rebellion is defeated by government forces, with several thousand killed.

On June 27, Archduke Johann of Austria is voted imperial vicar by Frankfurt Assembly. He names a Reich cabinet.

On July 15–August 18, the Frankfurt German artisan and trade congress is held (excludes journeymen).

On July 23–25, the Battle of Custozza takes place. Radetzky's Austrian forces defeat the Sardinian-Piedmont army, which must accept an armistice providing for vacating Austrian-held territory of Lombardy.

On July 22–September 20, the Journeymen Congress is held in Frankfurt.

On August 23–September 3, the first General German Worker Congress is held in Berlin, at the initiative and under the leadership of Stephan Born.

On August 27, Venice falls to Radetzky.

On September 18, two deputies are murdered by a Frankfurt mob; the assembly is forced to call in German armies to protect it from the revolutionary crowd.

From October 6 to October 30, the Third Revolt takes place in Vienna, but is put down after heavy fighting. The Austrian assembly is transferred to Kremsier. Felix zu Schwarzenberg takes over Austrian government ministry.

On November 8, Robert Blum, revolutionary delegate from the Frankfurt assembly, is executed in Vienna by Habsburg imperial government troops.

On November 9, King Frederick William IV closes the Berlin assembly.

On November 10, General Wrangel moves into Berlin to crush all popular opposition.

On December 2, Ferdinand of Austria abdicates in favor of his nephew Franz Joseph.

On December 5, King Frederick William IV dissolves the Prussian assembly and calls for new constitutional assembly.

1849   On March 4, the Kremsier assembly dissolved.

On March 7, Schwarzenberg disregards the April Laws of 1848 to proclaim a constitution for the entire Austrian empire, precluding a voice for German, Hungarian, or any other peoples.

During March Charles Albert resumes war. His forces are decisively defeated by the Austrians at Novarra on March 23.

On March 28, the Frankfurt assembly votes on a constitution for a German state that excludes Austria and names Frederick William IV emperor of the Germans.

On April 3, Frederick William IV declares that he can accept only with the approval of the other German sovereigns. The final refusal by Frederick William IV occurs on April 28.

On April 5, Schwarzenberg orders all Austrian deputies to return from Frankfurt.

On May 3–9, a revolt with bitter street fighting takes place in Dresden.

On May 12, an outbreak of republican revolts with armies joining the revolution takes place in Baden and the Palatinate. A provisional government is formed.

On May 13, a popular assembly takes place in Offenburg. Archduke Leopold of Baden flees to Frankfurt and asks Prussia to send troops.

On May 14, Prussian deputies are ordered to return from Frankfurt.

On May 19, the last issue of the *Neue Rheinische Zeitung* appears. The paper is forced to close by Prussian government.

On May 30, the remaining delegates at the Frankfurt assembly (the "Rump" assembly) close the assembly and move meetings to Stuttgart.

On June 10, Mannheim is occupied by Prussian troops.

On June 14, Prussian troops invade the Palatinate.

On June 18, Wurtemberg closes the Rump parliament in Stuttgart.

On July 23, Rastatt capitulates; Prussian martial law is declared. Twenty-seven leaders of the revolt are executed. Carl Schurz escapes to the United States. The German Revolution ends.

In August, the Roman republic is defeated by French forces and papal rule is re-established; Austrians force the surrender of Venice.

On August 9, Temesvar Bem defeat seals fate of Hungarian Revolution.

INTRODUCTION

Following the defeat of Napoléon, the victorious allied monarchs at the 1814–1815 Congress of Vienna re-established monarchies in France and several nations that had been under French control. In 1820–1821 and then on a somewhat wider scale in 1830, rebellions occurred in several European countries for more democratic political systems and, in several cases, for independence from foreign control. With few exceptions, the insurrections failed or fell far short of the participants' aspirations. By the late 1840s, rapid population growth, poor harvests, and the difficulties faced by many workers and peasants in the transition from traditional modes of production to increasingly capitalistic forms of industry and agriculture set the stage for new collective upheavals.

In 1848, the longings for democracy and independence, coupled with the spread of more radical economic and political ideologies and the effects of the generally difficult economic conditions, brought about the greatest number of nearly simultaneous revolutionary movements in Europe's history. Initially, the upper- and middle-class liberals and urban workers and some of the peasants were united in a fragile revolutionary alliance against a common enemy, the absolutist governments that seemed unwilling to make way for even slight reforms. But the participants had differing goals. Upper- and middle-class liberals basically sought greater civil liberties, separation of church and state, increased political participation; in nations dominated by foreign powers, such as Poland, parts of Italy, and Hungary, they sought political independence. Except for a small number of radical intellectuals, they had no interest in significant economic reforms, particularly those that might threaten private property rights. In contrast, many workers who were unemployed or whose livelihoods were threatened by technological or economic trends sought major state intervention to provide them with jobs. A large number of workers became attracted to Socialist ideologies, which advocated collective ownership of resources and industries and government-supported economic security. Once the revolutionary forces were temporarily victorious, they began fighting each other, opening the door for the political and military forces of reaction to suppress the revolutions. Ultimately the middle classes and many peasants, when faced with the prospect of the urban workers' economic radicalism, preferred restoration of conservative, authoritarian governments. Although most of the rebellions were suppressed within a year, the issues that inspired them continued to motivate later revolutionaries into the twentieth century. Furthermore, revolutionary ideologies, organizations, and political strategies of twentieth-century revolutionaries often developed directly from the ideas, experiences, failures, and repression of the 1848 revolutionaries.

BACKGROUND: CULTURE AND HISTORY

The Congress of Vienna in 1815 attempted to restore the old absolutist system of the eighteenth century. The Austrian prince Klemens von Metternich used diplomacy and repres-

Giuseppe Mazzini, founder of Young Italy, a nineteenth-century secret society that worked for the unification of Italy. (Library of Congress)

sion to suppress revolutionary movements. Key was the solidarity of the Three Northern Courts of Austria, Russia, and Prussia, founded on the eighteenth-century division of Poland by the three monarchs. Austria was at the juncture of all centers of unrest. Not merely divided Poland, Italy, and Germany, but the Austrian empire would have problems with ethnic minorities of Magyars, Czechs, Serbs, Croats, Slovenes, Romanians, Ukrainians, and Slovaks. The Wartburg Festival of the German students' fraternities called for German unification. When Karl Sand, a former student, assassinated an anti-liberal Russian spy, August von Kotzebue, in 1819, political violence entered a new phase. In Italy and France the conspiratorial Carbonnari, secret societies opposed to absolutist rule, romanticized rebellion. The governments particularly feared the French army as a potential threat. The entire diplomatic system of Metternich sought to isolate France as the seat of revolutions. Mazzini's Young Italy society was another source of revolutionary martyrs. The multinational and multireligious Ottoman empire was the sick man of Europe. Autonomous Serbia and the successful Greek Revolt led to Bosnia and Herzegovina and Albania becoming potent centers of future conflict. Great

Britain had a permanent center of discord in Ireland, scene of the horrible Great Famine of 1846. Even Russian autocracy was attacked by revolution in the Decembrist rising of 1825.

The democratic and equalitarian ideals of the French Revolution, along with the desires of occupied peoples for independence from foreign control, continued to motivate sectors of the populations of several nations to repeatedly rise up against autocracy. During 1820–1821 rebellion broke out first in Spain, whose 1820 revolt coined for freedom the term *liberalism,* and then in Portugal and Naples and, in 1821, in Piedmont. The rebels included discontented army officers who generally hoped to establish constitutional monarchies in which the people would have some democratic participation in government. But in all four countries most of the peasants, urban workers, aristocracy, and clergy remained loyal to the ruling dynasty. Foreign military intervention, by Austria in Piedmont and Naples, and France in the case of Spain, played a central role in defeating three of the revolutions. After the 1820 rebellions, the monarchal regimes in Russia, Prussia, and Austria, whose foreign minister, Prince Klemens von Metternich, played an important role in formulating policy, agreed to intervene militarily to protect other monarchies in Europe and help them suppress domestic revolutions.

The next major rebellion against autocratic rule occurred in France in 1830. Charles X of the Bourbon dynasty had maintained a parliament (Chamber of Deputies), although only a limited number of men who paid sufficient taxes could vote for its members. After an economic crisis during 1826–1827, the parliament became too disagreeable for the king, and he disbanded it twice in 1830 and finally deprived most of the small electorate of the right to vote. In response, a rebellion broke out and Charles X was forced to abdicate, ending the Bourbon dynasty. Liberal deputies then offered the throne to the duke of Orleans, Louis-Philippe. The new monarch proved somewhat less conservative and expanded the right to vote to more members of the middle class. But in response to demands for more liberal reforms and broader suffrage, he turned to repression. As a result, many people lost faith altogether in the concept of preserving the monarchy, and radical ideologies such as republicanism and Socialism, which would play prominent roles in the revolutions of 1848, began to grow in popularity.

The fall of the conservative Bourbon dynasty in France encouraged several rebellions and reforms by nationalists and liberals in several other countries. Belgium successfully broke away from Holland, and in Switzerland universal male suffrage was enacted. In Poland military cadets began a rebellion against Russian domination that quickly drew much popular support, though generally not from the Polish aristocracy. Although the Polish Sejm (assembly) declared independence, Russian troops suppressed the Poles in the summer of 1831. Rebellions also occurred in some Italian cities against papal rule and in some German states for constitutions, but these were also suppressed.

The 1830 revolutions, which overthrew and forced into exile the French king Charles X, shook Europe to its foundations. The simultaneous nationalist revolts in Poland, the German Confederation, and the various Italian states had forced Metternich to allow the Belgians to set up a breakaway state independent of the Netherlands' monarch. The Three Northern Courts had to concentrate their attention on Poland, the great epicenter of all the revolts. The Polish exiles were welcomed across Europe by liberals as heroes of freedom, and they maintained a system of conspiratorial envoys in east central and southern Europe from the home of Prince Adam Czartoryski in Paris, the Hotel Lambert. For the better part of a century, a Pole and a revolutionary were synonymous terms.

The new king of the French installed by the 1830 July Revolution, Louis-Philippe, was a disappointment to revolutionaries. Many French called for a new Napoléon to once more liberate Europe. From Paris exile, the poet of freedom, Heinrich Heine, wrote that they lived in an Age of Emancipation. Not just the Caribbean slaves, but all of humanity needed to be freed from the iron leading-strings of the aristocracy. French democrats sought more than merely doubling the male electorate from 100,000 to 200,00 in a country of 24 million. They took up the British Chartist call of "One man, one vote!" France was rocked by assassination attempts on King Louis-Philippe and street barricades during the 1830 Revolution. Victor Hugo popularized a new term for the oppressed poor who took out their frustration on the Parisian barricades: *les miserables.*

Conservative prime minister Francois Guizot brought stability to France, attempting to make it a worthy ally of Metternich in the 1840s. But his management of elections by alleged bribery brought a call for reform, particularly from a former supporter of the deposed Charles X but now an orator of the opposition in the French assembly, another great Romantic poet, Alphonse de Lamartine. In France at least, Romanticism was poetry in politics.

The great topic of conversation of the 1840s was the Social Question. All Europe read of the great experiment of Robert Owen in Lanark, where workers were treated with dignity. When Nicholas I, czar of Russia, visited Britain, one of his first wishes was to see with his own eyes Owen in Scotland. Louis Napoléon, claiming to be a Socialist, wrote *The Extinction of Poverty.* The age of Socialism made household names of the utopian Socialists Saint Simon, Fourier, and others. In 1847, the Communist League authorized Marx and Engels to draft a party program, which was published in London at the end of February 1848 as the *Manifesto of the Communist Party.*

CONTEXT AND PROCESS OF REVOLUTION

The 1848 revolutions were an intensely interconnected and complex Europe-wide phenomena. Four separate types of revolutions overlapped. First, social revolutions touched off by severe economic dislocations. Second, an awakening of national self-consciousness among a wide range of European peoples. Third, political revolutions among peoples demanding civil rights in an open society. Fourth, in a few constitutional states with developed parliamentary regimes, reform forces called for wide-ranging extension of suffrage to groups hitherto excluded from the political process.

A major source of discontent arose from the widely held perception that the elites of the existing social order opposed all efforts at peaceful change. Across Europe reform was blocked. The obstinate police state presided over by Austrian chancellor Klemens von Metternich in Vienna, the inability of London's parliament to deal with mass famine in Ireland or the call for "One man, one vote!" by British Chartists, the frustrations of Prussians at the refusal of their king, Frederick William IV, to inaugurate a constitutional regime all provoked anger. But most of all, the French were outraged by the perceived immobility of the Guizot cabinet in Paris. Discontent with the refusal to consider reform exploded in violence when the French monarch decided to prohibit a public protest for electoral change set for February 22. Much of the military refused or was unable to suppress the demonstrators, leading to larger numbers of people joining the protests. All Europe was shocked when a crowd invaded the Tuilleries Palace in Paris to send the king of the French into exile and to chase his prime minister, Guizot, from office.

On March 2, the French provisional government of the Second Republic, headed by the Romantic poet Alphonse de Lamartine, electrified the European public with a *Manifesto of Peace,* which promised liberation to the oppressed peoples of all Europe. The manifesto was seconded by the Christian Socialist Jules Bastide, who replaced Lamartine as foreign minister. The French sent out secret agents, including the notorious Russian anarchist Mikhail Bakunin, to observe the expected collapse of the existing social and political order. Certainly the French never fooled themselves into believing that they were more than bystanders, but they saw within the month that indigenous and independent revolts did break out throughout Germany and in certain urban centers, notably Milan, Venice, and Budapest. For a moment it seemed that the oppressed peoples whom Lamartine had promised their liberty were indeed successfully imitating the example set in Paris. According to a German observer, everyone walked around as though his or her head was an explosive with a wick ready for anyone to light and explode. Crowds of central Europeans rejoiced at the newly won right of free speech after decades of censorious repression.

The official leaders of the thirty-nine disunited German states stood by while liberal members of their various state legislatures (Landtag) took the initiative. A gathering of prominent opposition spokespersons from across the German Confederation bypassed their sovereigns to gather in Heidelberg, where they called on all German governments to hold elections by universal manhood suffrage for the first all-German parliament to meet in the crowning city of Frankfurt am Main.

Under pressure from crowds in Milan and Venice, General Radetzky withdrew Austria's armed forces from the riotous capitals of Lombardy and Venetia to the safety of the garrison cities of the quadrilateral centered on Verona. Meanwhile, from across the several Italian states came a call to King Charles Albert of Sardinia-Piedmont to lead an armed struggle to push out the hated Austrians. Charles Albert in Turin responded to the challenge by rejecting any French support and promised all Italians that "*Italia fara da se*" ("Italy will do it by itself"). He took command of the volunteers who joined the cause of Italian liberation. His small army of 60,000 took on Austria, which fielded the greatest army in all Europe, close to a half-million troops. The French gathered an "Army of the Alps" on the border, which never participated in the hopelessly unequal struggle between Charles Albert (a latter-day David) and the mighty Austrian Goliath of the north.

Nationalism

In March, ministries in the various German states allowed opposition deputies to replace the old regimes. Most notably, in Berlin the former Prussian ambassador in Paris, the "lame" Arnim (because of a leg wound in the Napoleonic wars) promised autonomy to the Polish provinces. King Frederick William IV alone held out against a Berlin March Ministry ready to cede Poles their freedom. The Prussian king told his most trusted military attaché that the new Prussian cabinet unanimously sought a war of German unification against Russia. Across Germany the entire nation was caught up in a "revolutionary psychosis" (Stadelmann 1975). Men rushed to join in the battle for German unity that would place the Prussian monarch at the head of a united German empire and lead them to victory in a war against eastern despotism. The reluctant Frederick William IV stood alone as the cold wind of German war enthusiasm swept over the land.

Troops charge workers in Berlin (then the capital of Prussia) during the revolution of 1848. Already experiencing riots born of years of poor harvests, famine, and disease, Prussia was ignited by news of unrest in France. Violence broke out in Berlin on March 18, and 200 people were killed before the king's troops were withdrawn from the city. (Library of Congress)

In Vienna, the Austrian emperor was forced to promise Magyars (Hungarians) constitutional autonomy in the April Laws. Attacked in the south by Italians and in the east by Magyar nationalists, and menaced in Vienna itself by a mob that included workers calling for bread and work, the Austrian empire tottered on the brink of disaster. Likewise, the entire old order of the alliance of the Three Northern Courts of Russia, Prussia, and Austria wavered. In Paris, Prince Adam Czartoryski placed his entire underground conspiratorial quasi-diplomatic corps at the service of the French provisional government, as all awaited the sound of guns in the east at the expected march of Russia to counter the Polish-German provocation. But Nicholas I, without his Prussian and Austrian allies, refused to respond in arms.

Instead of the united war against czarism, civil war broke out. It began first in the Prussian eastern provinces, where ethnic Germans relied on the Prussian army to subdue Polish insurgents. Likewise, the non-Hungarian Slavic and Romanian populations mistrusted the revolutionary Hungarian government, and fighting broke out in the southern provinces of the Austro-Hungarian empire. By the summer, Josip Jellacic commanded border units of Croats and Serbs who resisted what they feared was Hungarian domination.

The Social Revolution

The economic cause of the revolution was the disastrous harvest of 1846, setting off the last great western European famine and an economic downturn that continued into 1847, leading to a severe economic dislocation. The French response to widespread unemployment was the creation of national workshops in late February 1848 to meet the immediate problem of preventing starvation. But with no planning, there was work for only a small proportion of the unfortunates. The republican provisional government raised taxes to pay for what was, in effect, a dole. The experiment in universal manhood suffrage, however, doomed any hope of a social revolution. April elections in France and in the various

German states divided the revolutionary forces. Superb studies by historians Kale and Stadelmann (1975) detected the seeds of the revolutions' demise in their early stages. Steven Kale identified local elites who began to organize a counter-revolution soon after the French February Revolution as the source of conservative reaction. Rudolf Stadelmann likewise determined that the relatively few acts of violence in Germany ultimately drove the bourgeois movement for freedom and a constitution into the arms of reaction, and that this shift was already visible by the end of March 1848.

The rapid elections in Germany and France by universal manhood suffrage resulted in the election of an overwhelming majority of moderates and conservatives seeking social and economic stability and protection of property rights. The delegates to the first German parliament and to the French assembly were largely provincial and politically moderate notables, rather than men from the urban working class that had precipitated the revolutions. At the center of the new German political parties was the Pius Association, founded by a Hessian priest in 1846, which was instrumental in calling for an organized Roman Catholic movement in March 1848. Likewise, in Protestant Prussia the Kreuzzeitung Party organized the masses to support King Frederick William IV and resist the revolution, which was portrayed as a threat to both Christianity and economic well-being.

The moderate-conservative majority in the French assembly, which opened in early May, sought a quick showdown with the social revolutionaries and moved rapidly to close the national workshops. The workers of Paris rose again spontaneously in a new revolt against the prospect of the starvation of their families. The French assembly turned to General Eugene Cavaignac to suppress the workers in the bloody June Days. In the aftermath of the violent repression, a number of Socialist leaders were arrested and thousands of the rebels were deported to Algeria.

In Frankfurt, the German parliament spent its life in debating whether to offer the German crown to the monarch of Prussia or that of Austria. The deeply conservative nature of the assembly was manifested in its choice of an Austrian Habsburg prince as its executive. By July 1848 the social revolution was a spent force.

The Triumph of Anti-Revolutionary Reaction

The fates of the national revolutions were decided by the victory of the deeply conservative Prussian and Austrian armies. The various attempts of revolutionaries to confront a professional army with popular militias were uniformly unsuccessful, even when heroic resistance seeded historic myth making. The Prussian army's suppression of the Poznan Revolt once more thwarted Polish hopes of a reconstitution of Poland. Austrian generals rallied the imperial army to suppress the revolts in Prague and Vienna. Likewise, the hopelessly outmanned Sardinian-Piedmontese military was no match for Radetzky's Austrian forces in northern Italy. Lajos Kossuth and the Magyars were caught in the contradiction inherent in constructing a national homeland in multinational Hungary. Ban Josip Jellacic and his Croats rallied loyally to their Austrian king and emperor.

In the summer, Czar Nicholas I moved his army into Walachia and Moldavia to crush the popular Romanian uprising against the Ottoman sultan. The September revolutionary insurrection in Frankfurt forced the largely moderate Frankfurt parliament to call on the armies of the German states for protection. The counter-revolution in Vienna in October and in Berlin in November overwhelmed democratic forces and set the stage in December for a full retreat. Prince Felix zu Schwarzenberg's order for Austrian delegates to withdraw from the Frankfurt assembly and the popular election of Louis Napoléon as prince-president in France in December demonstrated the demise of all revolutionary hopes. Conservative reaction was in firm control by the close of the year.

In the winter of 1848–1849, the German Left pulled together in the organization of the Central March Associations. The armed crisis came after Frederick William IV refused the crown "from the gutter" of united Germany, offered by a delegation from the Frankfurt parliament. The outrage unleashed the civil war of May 1849. The defeat of the various uprisings incited a mass escape of German "48ers" abroad, in particular to the United States.

Lajos Kossuth called for a popular uprising of the Magyar nation, which led to his exile in the U.S., England, and Italy, where he, like many other revolutionists, reconsidered the lessons of the 1848 revolutions.

IMPACTS

The workers' movements were crushed. Later two types of workers' movements resulted from 1848: a democratic-parliamentary wing and a radical-revolutionary movement calling for the dictatorship by the proletariat.

In France, the parliamentary leftist movement was successful in electing Democratic Socialists in the 1849 elections after the fiasco of the 1848 events. But after Louis Napoléon's coup of December 2, 1851, they were driven underground or into exile. The repression and the absence of democracy attracted more people to Socialist movements, which grew in strength and finally took power, though temporarily, in the first workers' state, the Paris Commune of 1870–1871.

The repressions in central Europe caused the exile of Marx to London, because he unwisely renounced his Prussian citizenship in protest. With Engels and Bakunin, Marx helped organize the Workers International (First International). Its song, "The Internationale," is a call for freedom for the downtrodden of the earth.

The great workers' movement was centered in Germany. The trade union movement that emerged during the revolution was instrumental in supporting democratic Socialism. Savage repression of Socialists in German states during the latter half of the nineteenth century increased the strength of Socialist political activist and leader Ferdinand Lassalle's moderate German Workers Party. Despite Bismarck's anti-Socialist laws, by the end of the nineteenth century, Lassalle's party, renamed the German Socialist Party (SPD), attracted more voters than any other party of the German Reichstag. The SPD that governed Germany in 2005 traces its roots to the 1848 revolution's moderate Socialism. The PDS (Party of Democratic Socialism—the former Communist Party of East Germany), which is very strong in the eastern areas of Germany, traces its roots to Marx and Engels' more radical wing of Socialism.

The March 1848 Berlin martyrs and the Parisian June Days became potent symbols of the continuing myths of 1848 and the fight for worker justice.

The French Fourth Republic wrote into its constitution of 1945 the right to work, the principal demand of French workers in 1848. The right to work means the responsibility, symbolized in the national workshops, of the state to guarantee employment to every person. In 2005, this right was part of extensive "Solidarity" legislation in France to provide a wide range of support to those seeking employment.

National Revolutions

Austrian chancellor Schwarzenberg, with Russian help, temporarily ended Prussian efforts to dominate the German Confederation at the November 29, 1850, conference known later as Humiliation of Olmuetz. Otto von Bismarck, in response, changed from a defender of Austria within Prussia to her enemy. He brought about Prussian military victories during 1862–1871 that created a German state. In his famous and widely quoted declaration Bismarck stated that Germany would not be created by speeches and parliamentary resolutions "but by iron and blood" (Gall 1986, 204) Likewise, Camillo Cavour, prime minister of Sardinia-Piedmont, with a sterner plan and more skillful diplomacy than Charles Albert, unified Italy in 1859–1870. Bismarck's defeat of Austria forced the Compromise of 1866, giving the Magyars the autonomy that escaped Kossuth in 1848. The Czechs, Slovaks, Croats, Slovenes, Serbs, Ukrainians, Bulgarians, and Romanians today all enjoy the national liberties sought in movements that began in the violence of 1848. But the greatest

champions of freedom and justice in all ages are the Poles. Poland's 1848 rebellion is sandwiched between great risings of 1830, 1846, and 1863, which are in the heroic Polish tradition of resistance.

Popular Democracy and Popular Dictatorship

The various constitutions written in 1848 set up a number of parliaments elected by popular votes, with various results. Democratic parties like the SPD in Germany date themselves to the first democratic elections to the Frankfurt parliament.

Austria's Schwarzenberg-devised Kremsier Constitution of 1849, which preserved absolutism in the face of demands for freedom, met with Magyar resistance. Many years later, after Vienna allowed separate Magyar rule in 1866, the Austrian Reichstag was the scene of popular opposition from other peoples, especially the Czechs. Tensions in Budapest after World War I, when the Austro-Hungarian empire came to an end, eventually led to the Trianon Treaty of 1920 that dissolved the old Hungarian state, greatly reducing the country's size by taking away territories that were not almost purely Magyar in population composition.

After World War I, friction in all the successor states to Austria-Hungary with large German minorities was instrumental in leading to World War II, since Nazi Germany claimed it was concerned about protecting Germans living in countries such as Czechoslovakia and Poland. But expulsion of the German minorities after World War II did not materially contribute to the Cold War because of the brilliant diplomacy by Konrad Adenauer, Willi Brandt, and other builders of the European Union. The Polish-Magyar-French plan for a "Danubian Confederation" of free and equal states is the basis of today's European Union. The father of united Europe could have been Napoléon III, Jules Bastide, Lajos Kossuth, and, above all, Prince Adam Czartoryski. Their vision of a peaceful union of the European peoples did triumph in the May 2004 celebrations of the European Union along the lines born in the Hotel Lambert in Paris in 1848.

In 1848 France led the world in universal manhood suffrage. Louis Napoléon was elected president, not by divine right, but an overwhelming majority. As Napoléon III, he inaugurated a new type of political system of popular dictatorships behind a deceptive veneer of mass elections to a parliament. A majority of the countries of the world were ruled by such facade democratic political systems in 2005. Napoléon III's manipulation of elections and skillful choice of "official candidates" became the rule and actual parliamentary democracy the rare exception.

The ideas pioneered by the British Chartists triumphed peacefully through various reform bills after 1867 that changed the British system from a representative to a democratic parliament. The 1848 Young Ireland martyrs inspired Home Rule for Ireland.

Government rule before 1848 was founded on censorship and repression of all open opposition. In 1848, conservatives were forced to organize to stand for elections and to propagandize. The Berlin *Kreutzzeitung* of 1848 was the model for present tabloid journalism and an electronic media controlled by wealthy elites, as Napoléon III was the model for the new manipulation of voters by elites. The back-up weapons of conservatives were always the iron fists of police and army, and the administration of laws, especially in the courts, and the churches. The Roman Catholic political movement dates to 1848 in reaction to leftist political movements. The major political parties in much of continental Europe were organized by the church, in particular the German Center Party and the present German Christian Democratic Union (CDU) and the Christian Social Union (CSU). The more recent Muslim resurgence in Europe is a continuation of this tendency of organizing politics along religious lines. The European conservative political parties date from the 1848 Revolution, when governments learned to rule by persuasion rather than by force alone.

PEOPLE, ORGANIZATIONS, CONSTITUTIONS, AND CONCEPTS

Albert, Charles (1798–1849)

Duke of Savoy, Piedmont, and Aosta and king of Sardinia from 1831 to 1849. His military defeat by the Austrian army led to the sterner plan for Italian unity of 1859–1870 of Camillo Cavour. Charles Albert's *Statuto* gave Piedmont a constitution and the admiration of liberals. After military defeat, his cause was ultimately victorious.

Arnim, Heinrich von (1803–1868)

Known as the "lame" Arnim because of wound in the Napoleonic Wars, he was the Prussian ambassador in Paris in February 1848 and returned to Berlin in March with a plan to free the Poles and to unite Germany in a war against Russia. Headed the Prussian cabinet united in seeking the "liberal alliance" of Prussia with Great Britain and France to carry out the grand design. His dream probably ended with October 1848 events. Frederick William IV alone opposed war with Russia. Arnim was the great Prussian visionary of a united Europe.

Bakunin, Mikhail (1814–1876)

Anarchist opponent of Marx and Engels who was instrumental in breaking up the the Workers International by defending terrorism as a tactic. Marx and Engels strongly opposed Bakunin's followers and dissolved the International to prevent him from taking control.

Bastide, Jules (1800–1879)

Jules Bastide was French foreign minister and assistant to Lamartine in 1848. He sought the liberation of all oppressed peoples, whom he thought by the summer of 1848 were "sovereign" rather than the old princes (Chastain 1988).

Bismarck, Prince Otto von (1815–1898)

Conservative opponent of liberalism and democracy, Bismarck was a demagogue of *Kreuzzeitung* Party who saw the value of public support for the Prussian monarch. In 1848, he championed Austrian supremacy in Germany, but after the Olmuetz Humiliation of Prussia he became an opponent of Austria. Instead, he followed Cavour's example of iron and blood to counter the Austrian domination of central Europe.

Blum, Robert (1807–1848)

Robert Blum, from the German state of Saxony, was a leftist leader in the Frankfurt Assembly of 1848. He was sent by the assembly to Vienna and participated in the insurrection there against Austrian imperial forces in October. When the insurrection was defeated, he was captured and executed by imperial troops. He is considered a hero of the revolution.

Born, Stephan (1824–1898)

Labor leader of *Verbruderung* (Fraternity), a forerunner of the great trade union movement. He led the organized fight for labor justice.

Cavaignac, General Eugene (1802–1857)

Brother of the deceased republican leader Godfrey Cavaignac, he came from the French army in Algeria to suppress the rising of the June Days. He was made head of the government by the national assembly.

Cavour, Count Camillo (1810–1861)

Cavour took command of the Piedmontese government after the fiasco of the 1848–1849 wars to unify Italy. Conspired with Napoléon III and Bismarck to expel Austria from the Italian peninsula.

Czartoryski, Prince Adam (1770–1861)

Exiled "king of Poland" after 1848. His Parisian home, the Hotel Lambert, included headquarters for envoys, especially from the Balkans, seeking to free the Slavs from Austrian, Ottoman, and Russian tyranny. He proposed the "Danubian Confederation" to free the peoples of east central Europe. Great Polish visionary of a freely united Europe.

Danubian Confederation

Adam Czartoryski's proposal of a federation of autonomous and free states in east central Europe would have united the entire area with eventual alliance ties to France, united Italy, and united Germany. This union would form the basis of a united continental Europe that could help to bring the eventual overthrow of absolutist autocracy in czarist Russia. The main outline of the Danubian Confederation was achieved on May 1, 2004, with the proclamation of the extension of the European Union to new member states.

Duties of Man

Joseph Mazzini's work that included a call for sacrifice of the individual and martyrdom if necessary to the highest ideal, the nation. The organization he created, Young Italy, sought to sacrifice young people whose deaths would inspire Italians to throw off the Austrian yoke and to free and unite Italy.

Fourier, Charles (1772–1837)

Fourier was an advocate of Socialism. His Socialist commune would divide work by the interests of the individuals. He emphasized the innovative idea of making work an extension of the individual's need for creativity. The utopian Socialists, such as Fourier, inspired scientific management of industry by investigating the psychological forces behind work.

Frankfurt Parliament

Liberal members of the various state legislatures of the thirty-nine disunited German states called on all German governments to hold elections by universal manhood suffrage for the first all-German parliament to meet in the city of Frankfurt am Main, May 18, 1848. Parliament members attempted, but failed, to unite Germany in a constitutional monarchy. The parliament called out troops to suppress rebellious workers September 18, 1848, reflecting a damaging split in the middle class–urban worker alliance that had begun the 1848 revolutions.

Frederick William IV, King of Prussia (1795–1861)

He was ruler of Prussia at the time of the 1848 revolutions. Though initially forced to appoint some liberal government ministers, he opposed both the unification of the German states under a constitutional monarchy system and war with the absolute monarchy of Russia. He refused the Frankfurt Parliament's offer to become emperor of a united Germany. Thus he delayed the unification effort for more than twenty years, when it would take place through the military efforts of Bismarck and lead to Frederick's brother Wilhelm being crowned kaiser of united Germany in 1871.

Garibaldi, Giuseppe (1807–1882)

Giuseppe Garibaldi was a member of Mazzini's Young Italy society and a daring and skillful revolutionary military leader. Though defeated in 1848, he played a crucial role in the unification of Italy in the 1860s.

Hotel Lambert

Hub of a Polish conspiratorial network to free Poland by reorganizing east central Europe into a Danubian Confederation.

Jellacic, Ban Josip (1801–1859)

Croat Ban (governor) whose army was instrumental in preserving the Austrian monarchy and defeating the Hungarian and October Viennese revolutions. Ultimately he was also responsible for blocking the negotiations of Orthodox Primate of Croatia Rajacic to seek national autonomy for southern Slavs.

Kossuth, Lajos (Louis) (1802–1894)

He was a Hungarian leader who negotiated with secret Polish envoys and the French government to gain autonomy for all the national minorities of Austria and Hungary in a "Danubian Confederation." In exile he publicly proposed the Danubian Confederation very closely along the lines peacefully proclaimed on May 1, 2004, with accession of Hungary and other new members to the European Union. Kossuth is one of the heroic founders of a united Europe. (Sam Wilson, "Danubian Confederation" www.ohio.edu/~chastain/dh/danconf.htm)

Kremsier Constitution

Schwarzenberg's answer to the Austrian Reichstag draft constitution. It preserved absolutism in the face of demands for freedom by most of the people of the Austrian empire.

Kreuzzeitung

Berlin newspaper edited by Friedrich Julius Stahl, who skillfully mobilized the masses against democracy and liberalism.

Lamartine, Alphonse de (1790–1869)

Defender of Charles X before the 1830 Revolution and major voice of opposition in assembly to Louis-Philippe. He gave rousing addresses to crowds at political rallies disguised as "banquets" (to avoid the ban on political assemblies), which were organized in pursuit of extending the right to vote, leading up to 1848 revolution. Leader of the provisional government that promised to liberate the oppressed peoples of Europe in a public declaration of March 2, 1848.

Manin, Daniele (1804–1857)

Daniele Manin, a lawyer and author, was a Venetian patriot who led the Venetian Republic during its 1848–1849 rebellion against Austrian control. Manin was also an advocate of the unification of Italy under a republic form of government. After reinforced Austrian empire forces defeated the Venetian Republic, Manin was exiled to France. There he continued to participate in the effort to free Italy from foreign domination and bring about its unification, but he accepted the concept that these goals could be achieved under the leadership of the Piedmont royal family and result

in a monarchy rather than a republic form of government in Italy. Manin is considered a hero of the struggle for Italian independence.

March Revolutions

The March Revolutions in central Europe ushered in liberal March Ministries that passed sweeping reforms. Monarchs stayed in power by temporizing until the revolutionary storm passed. The reactionary governments, especially in Prussia and Vienna, replaced the March liberal government ministers with open reactionaries and then suppressed the revolutions with armed force.

Marx, Karl (1818–1883)

Father of scientific Socialism, author with Friedrich Engels of the *Communist Manifesto* and editor of *Neue Rheinische Zeitung* in 1848. Marx blamed Austrian imperial forces for failure of the 1848 Revolutions. (For a lengthier biography, see the entry for the Russian Revolution of 1917.)

Mazzini, Giuseppe (1805–1872)

Giuseppe Mazzini was a revolutionary who advocated the expulsion of foreign armies from Italy and its unification under a republican form of government. He created the secret Young Italy society to work for this goal. But during the 1848 revolutions, the rebellions in parts of Italy that Mazzini encouraged were defeated.

Metternich, Prince Klemens von (1773–1858)

Austrian chancellor before 1848, champion of absolutism, and enemy of liberalism and nationalism. Driven from power by the 1848 revolution in Vienna.

National Workshops

Controversial French response to mass unemployment in Paris. The workshops largely enrolled skilled artisans, for whom there was no gainful employment because of the economic depression. Attacked by the conservative press as waste of money, the national workshops had few supporters in the elected April National Constituent Assembly. The conservative majority immediately sought to dissolve the workshops in June. In response, desperate French workers launched the June Days (June 22–26) insurrection, which was crushed with several thousand killed. Disappointment and frustration on all sides led to dissolution of the workshops.

Nicholas I, Czar of Russia (1796–1855)

An absolute autocrat. The czar's Russian army was the ultimate enemy of national freedom and liberalism in all of Europe.

Owen, Robert (1771–1858)

Industrialist and Socialist whose humane and paternalist respect for workers' dignity in Lanark, Scotland, inspired widespread interest.

Palacký, František (1798–1876)

Austroslav Bohemian proponent of autonomy for Czechs in a reorganized Austrian monarchy. Organizer of the Pan-Slav Congress in Prague in 1848 to propose Slavic autonomy within the Austrian empire. Palacký's efforts in 1848 were crushed by General Windischgrätz. Palacký was the great Bohemian visionary of a united Europe.

Punktation of Olmuetz (Olmounc)

This Russian diplomatic intervention in November 1850 aided the Austrian effort to prevent any constitutional changes in the German Confederation and frustrated Prussian hopes to unite Germany through the peaceful cooperation of the various German princes.

Radetzky, Joseph (1766–1858)

Radetzky was an Austrian general of Czech ancestry. His military defense of Austrian absolutism and victory in the field over the Italians' army prevented the unification of Italy in 1848, the reform of the Austrian state, and peaceful evolution to a multimonarchy of free and autonomous nations.

Risorgimento Newspaper

Calling for regeneration and unity of the Italian peninsula, this newspaper gave its name to the movement that was crowned with success by the wars of 1859–1860 and 1866.

Saint Simon, Claude Henri de Rouvroy, Comte de (1760–1825)

A founder of French Socialism, he emphasized the creative process of "industrialists," the builders of capital. He would have dynamized society by eliminating inherited wealth in favor of the marketplace of invention. His followers were responsible for great industrial enterprises, notably digging the Suez Canal.

Schwarzenberg, Prince Felix von und zu (1800–1852)

Principal architect of reaction. Savior of the Austrian monarchy, Chancellor Schwarzenberg took office with the bloody suppression of the Viennese 1848 October Revolution. Schwarzenberg and Franz Joseph's refusal to contemplate national autonomy for the Slavic majority of the empire doomed the Danubian monarchy to destruction. Schwarzenberg's short-range rescue was in shambles with Austrian losses in Italy in 1859–1860 and the military defeat of 1866. As a result, Austria was closed out of united Germany and forced to grant equal status to the Magyars in the doomed compromise of 1866. With Nicholas I of Russia, Franz Joseph I and Schwarzenberg were among the most short-sighted "victors" of 1848–1849.

Socialism

A social system which, according to its proponents, would be characterized by collective ownership of resources and the means of production and be relatively free from the injustices and great inequalities of capitalist society.

Statuto

Piedmont constitution of 1848 that later provided a basis for the united Italian constitutional monarchy.

Utopian Socialism

Term used by Marx in the *Communist Manifesto* to describe what he perceived as an impossible type of Socialism advocated by Fourier, Owen, Saint Simon, and others which was supposed to result from the subjective will of people, independent of objective economic conditions. Marx's "scientific" Socialism, in contrast, would result from the development of certain historical circumstances and inevitable class conflict between workers and capitalists. (For a description of the Marxist conception of scientific Socialism, see the entry on the Russian Revolution of 1917.)

Workers' International

The Workers' International, a federation of international working class organizations, grew out of the desire to organize for the next great revolution after 1848. It broke up over Marx's opposition to anarchists' defense of the use of political terror. It inspired the Second International, which today is the coordinating caucus of Democratic Socialist political parties ruling in states like Sweden, Germany, and Britain (Labour Party).

Young Italy (see *Duties of Man*).

James Chastain

See Also Anarchism, Communism, and Socialism; Democracy, Dictatorship, and Fascism; Documentaries of Revolution; French Revolution; Italian Risorgimento; Literature and Modern Revolution; Nationalism and Revolution; Paris Commune of 1871

References and Further Readings

Chastain, James G. 1988. *Liberation of Sovereign Peoples: French Foreign Policy of 1848*. Athens: Ohio University Press.

———. 1999, 2004. *Encyclopedia of the 1848 Revolutions*. http://www.cats.ohiou.edu/~chastain.

Coppa, Frank J. 1973. *Camillo di Cavour*. New York: Twayne Publishers.

de Luna, F. A. 1969. *The French Republic under Cavaignac, 1848*. Princeton, NJ: Princeton University Press.

Deak, Istvan. 1979. *The Lawful Revolution: Louis Kossuth and the Hungarians, 1848–1849*. New York: Columbia University Press.

Deme, Laszlo. 1976. *The Radical Left in the Hungarian Revolution of 1848*. New York and Boulder, CO: Eastern European Quarterly, distributed by Columbia University Press.

Eyck, Frank. 1968. *The Frankfurt Parliament, 1848–1849*. New York: St. Martin's Press.

Flaubert, Gustave. 1964. *Sentimental Education*. Trans. Robert Baldick. New York: Penguin Books.

Gall, Lothar. 1986. *Bismarck: The White Revolutionary*. Vol. 1. London: Allen and Unwin.

Ginsborg, Paul. 1979. *Daniele Manin and the Venetian Revolution of 1848–49*. New York: Cambridge University Press.

Gooch, Brison. 1963. *Belgium and the February Revolution*. The Hague: Nijhoff.

Jelavich, Barbara. "The Russian Intervention in Wallachia and Transylvania, September 1848 to March 1849," *Rumanian Studies* 4 (1976–1979): 16–74.

Kale, Steven. 2005. "Conservative Resistance to Revolution in France." http://www.ohiou.edu/~chastain/dh/danconf.htm (accessed February 24, 2006).

Pflanze, Otto. 1990. *Bismarck and the Development of Germany*. Princeton, NJ: Princeton University Press.

Rath, R. John. 1957. *The Viennese Revolution of 1848*. Austin: University of Texas Press.

Sheehan, James J. 1989. *German History 1770–1866*. Oxford: Oxford University Press.

Sperber, Jonathan. 1984. *Popular Catholicism in Nineteenth-Century Germany*. Princeton, NJ: Princeton University Press.

———. 1994. *The European Revolutions, 1848–1851*. Cambridge: Cambridge University Press.

Stadelmann, Rudolf. 1975. *Social and Political History of the German 1848 Revolution*. Trans. James G. Chastain. Athens: Ohio University Press.

Wilson, Sam. 2005. "Danubian Confederation." http://www.ohiou.edu/~chastain/dh/danconf.htm (accessed February 24, 2006).

F

French Revolution

CHRONOLOGY

1748   The jurist and philosopher Charles Louis de Secondat, Baron de Montesquieu, publishes *De l'Esprit des Lois* (*The Spirit of the Laws*).

1756–1763   The Seven Years War opens after colonial clashes in North America and India brought France and Britain into conflict. France allies with her traditional enemy, Austria.

1762   Jean-Jacques Rousseau publishes *Du Contrat Social* (*Social Contract*).

1764–1766   Opposition to tax reforms from the *parlement* (aristocratic sovereign court) of Brittany leads to the arrests of its leading magistrates, sparking protests from the *parlement* of Paris. Louis XV's response is to declare his authority absolute (the Flagellation Session).

1770   In an effort to strengthen the Franco-Austrian alliance, the dauphin (heir to the throne), the future Louis XVI, is married to the Habsburg archduchess Marie-Antoinette.

1771   In an effort to break aristocratic resistance to reform, Chancellor René de Maupeou breaks up the *parlements*.

1774   Louis XV dies, and his grandson and heir is crowned Louis XVI. He recalls the *parlements*. Anne Robert Jacques Turgot is appointed controller-general of finances.

1775   The *guerre des farines* (Flour War) erupts over high food prices and against Turgot's liberalization of the grain trade.

1776   A beleaguered Turgot is dismissed by the king. He is eventually replaced by the Genevan Jacques Necker.

1778   France enters the American War of Independence, which first explodes in 1775, on the side of Britain's rebellious colonies.

1781   Necker publishes his version of the royal accounts, the *Compte rendu au Roi* (*Account Submitted to the King*), in which he paints a rosy picture of royal finances. The Franco-American victory at Yorktown galvanizes public opinion.

1783   Charles Alexandre de Calonne is appointed controller-general of finances. The Treaty of Versailles ends the American War of Independence.

1786   In August, Calonne reveals the extent of the royal deficit to Louis XVI.

1787   The Assembly of Notables stymies Calonne's reforms. Louis XVI replaces him with Cardinal Étienne Loménie de Brienne. In November, Louis XVI resorts to pushing the reforms through the *parlements* but provokes a storm of opposition.

1788   In May, Louis XVI exiles leading magistrates of the Paris *parlement,* sparking national protests.

In August, Brienne attempts to calm public opinion by calling the Estates-General to meet in May 1789. He is replaced by Necker.

In September, public opinion turns against the *parlements* when they seek to ensure the domination of the clergy and the nobility over the representatives of the commoners, the Third Estate, in the Estates-General.

1789   In February, Emmanuel Sieyès publishes *What Is the Third Estate?*

In the spring, an economic crisis gathers pace and there are food riots across the country.

In May, the Estates-General meets at Versailles.

On June 17, the Third Estate declares itself the "National Assembly." Three days later, with the "Tennis Court Oath," the National Assembly swears never to separate until it finds a constitutional settlement for the kingdom.

On July 14, at the peak of the economic crisis, the Bastille is taken by the Paris crowd. The king capitulates and authority falls to the National Assembly, which, now calling itself the Constituent Assembly, sets to work to reform France under a constitutional monarchy. As royal authority collapses, the countryside explodes into violence.

On August 4, to calm the peasantry, the Constituent Assembly abolishes seigneurialism and sweeps away all provincial, corporate, and personal privileges.

On August 26, the principles of the new order are proclaimed with the Declaration of the Rights of Man and the Citizen.

On October 5–6, protesting against continued food shortages and aiming to force the king to accept the new laws, Parisian women march on Versailles and force the royal family to move to the Tuileries Palace in the capital city. The Constituent Assembly restricts the vote to "active citizens," meaning those adult males who pay sufficient taxes. The assembly divides France into eighty-three roughly uniform departments.

In November, the assembly nationalizes church property to tackle the debt, with a view to auctioning it as *biens nationaux* (national property). Meanwhile, the state's creditors are paid in paper (*assignats*), redeemable at the sales of *biens nationaux.*

1790   In June, titles of nobility are abolished.

In July, in order to find a way of supporting the church now that its lands are confiscated, the Civil Constitution of the Clergy makes the clergy elective and salaried by the state.

In August, as part of the reform of the judiciary, the *parlements* are abolished. The cumulative effect of these measures is to polarize opinion between those who support the revolution and those for whom it has already gone too far.

In November, the assembly introduces an oath of loyalty to the Civil Constitution, to be taken by the clergy in France. The clerical oath splits the clergy down the middle, reflecting the deeper division within the country between supporters and opponents of the revolution.

1791   In March, trade guilds are abolished. That same month, the royal family makes an attempt to flee the country, following a number of royalists who had already slipped into Germany (the *émigrés*). The king and his family are caught at Varennes and brought back to Paris. The Constituent Assembly temporarily suspends Louis from his duties as executive. There is an upsurge of republicanism, particularly in Paris.

In July, Paris radicals organized by the Cordeliers club sign a petition demanding a referendum on the king's constitutional role. The authorities panic, and the citizens' militia, the National Guard, fires on the crowd, killing some fifty protesters. The republican movement is suppressed for now.

In August, this campaign for war is given momentum by the Declaration of Pillnitz, issued jointly by the Prussian king Frederick William II and the Austrian emperor Leopold II. It calls on European monarchs to act in concert with them to restore monarchical authority in France. That same month, a slave uprising breaks out in France's most lucrative Caribbean colony, Saint-Domingue, where Toussaint-Louverture emerges as the leader of the rebellion.

In September, the Constituent Assembly finishes drafting the constitution, which the reinstated king approves. Elections are held for the new Legislative Assembly, which meets in October and includes a vocal minority of radicals from the Jacobin club who are convinced that the king's acceptance of the constitution is a sham. Their leader, Jacques-Pierre Brissot, leads the charge by demanding urgent action against the *émigrés,* who are forming their own army, and the German princes harboring them. In a war, the king would be forced to choose between backing the new regime in France or being exposed as a traitor.

1792   In March, Louis XVI is forced to appoint a government of Jacobin ministers, who declare war on Austria on April 20.

In June, Prussia enters the fray. In the military crisis, republicanism stirs once more and when Louis dismisses his Jacobin ministers the same month, the Tuileries Palace is invaded by a crowd of militant Parisians *sans-culottes.*

In July, the Legislative Assembly declares the country in danger ("*la patrie en danger*") and unleashes emergency measures, including the mobilization of provincial National Guard units. The allied commander, the Duke of Brunswick, threatens "forever memorable vengeance" should the king be harmed. This deepens the crisis.

On August 10, the National Guard units, backed by *sans-culottes* mobilized by the Paris municipality (the Commune), storm the Tuileries and topple the monarchy. Prisons are filled with monarchists, Swiss Guards who have survived the attack on the Tuileries, and refractory priests (those who have refused to take the clerical oath).

In early September, in the climate of fear brought by the news of the Prussian advance into France, a mob breaks into these prisons and slaughters the inmates.

On September 21, the day after the French army turns the Prussians back at Valmy, the National Convention meets, made up of representatives chosen in elections based on near-universal male suffrage.

On September 22, the convention declares a republic in France.

During September, the French invade Savoy and Nice, belonging to the Kingdom of Sardinia.

In November, the Austrians are defeated at Jemappes and the French are now advancing into Belgium and Germany.

In December, the convention puts Louis XVI on trial for treason against the nation.

1793   Louis XVI is found guilty, but the death penalty splits the republicans between moderates (known as Girondins) and radicals (the Mountain, who now control the Jacobin club). The death penalty passes by one vote.

On January 21, Louis is guillotined. Meanwhile, the surge of French military power in western Europe alarms other European powers.

On February 1, France declares war on Britain and the Netherlands.

On March 7, France declares war on Spain.

During March, the war brings renewed crisis to the revolution. The imposition of conscription sparks a royalist insurrection in western France (the *chouannerie* in the Vendée, Brittany, and Normandy), and the French are defeated by the Austrians at Neerwinden. At the same time, food shortages and inflation spark *sans-culottes* violence in Paris, as the militants demand price controls (the "Maximum").

Between March and May, the convention passes measures that create the institutions of The Terror, including the Revolutionary Tribunal, local surveillance committees, and the executive committees of Public Safety and of General Security.

On May 31–June 2, an alliance of *sans-culottes,* Parisian National Guard units, and Jacobin deputies in the convention topple the Girondin government in a coup and have the leading Girondin deputies arrested. Most escape to their home departments, sparking "Federalist" revolts against the convention. These are crushed over the summer and the autumn.

In August, the new constitution, providing universal male suffrage, is ratified but immediately suspended. The Parisian *sans-culottes,* led first by the Enragés, then by the Hébertists (the journalist Jacques-René Hébert and his cronies), keep up the pressure, threatening an insurrection in early September and forcing the assembly to declare government by terror. A Law of Suspects broadly defines those liable to arrest and a General Maximum, which fixes prices on a broad variety of commodities, is passed.

In the autumn, the convention begins to get a grip on the domestic and military situation, with the rebels of the Vendée defeated in battle, inflation under control, and victories against the British and Austrians.

In October, Marie-Antoinette and then the Girondins are executed, but an outburst of attacks on religious belief (the dechristianization campaign) and reports of atrocities committed in the provinces convince the government that the time has come to rein in the worst excesses of The Terror.

On October 5, a new revolutionary calendar is introduced.

In December, the Law on Revolutionary Government centralizes control of The Terror under the Committee of Public Safety, whose members include Maximilien Robespierre.

1794   The government faces demands for "indulgence" from leading Jacobins, including Georges-Jacques Danton, but also calls from the Hébertists for more radical measures to prosecute the war and deal with the economic crisis.

In March, the government strikes, first to the left, having Hébert and his supporters arrested, tried, and executed.

In April, it is the turn of Danton and his friends. The Terror becomes increasingly a means of imposing political conformity rather than a response to the crisis.

In May, the government launches the cult of the Supreme Being to forge a civic religion.

That same month, the Law of 22 Prairial (June 10 in the revolutionary calendar introduced in October 1793) reforms the Revolutionary Tribunal to speed up trials, and the rate of executions accelerates.

On June 26, the French defeat the Austrians and then reconquer Belgium. Yet as the external crisis abates, the government itself begins to fall apart under the strain of The Terror.

In July, the government loses what popular support it has left by introducing controls on wages.

On July 27 (9 Thermidor) a combination of extremists, surviving friends of Danton, and the middle ground (the "Plain") in the convention vote for the arrest of Robespierre and his closest colleagues on the Committee of Public Safety. They and other Robespierrists are guillotined the following day. The Thermidorians, the surviving members of the convention, start to dismantle the apparatus of The Terror.

In September, church and state are formally separated.

In December, the surviving Girondins are allowed to return to the convention, and the Maximum is repealed. The French strike into the Rhineland and overrun the Netherlands.

1795   Truces are brokered with the counter-revolutionaries in western France.

In April and May, the Paris crowds twice rise up (the Germinal and Prairial insurrections), demanding "Bread and the Constitution of 1793." Forces loyal to the Thermidorian Convention crush the revolt. Jacobins in some southern regions are killed in an outbreak of "White Terror."

In April, Prussia signs a peace treaty with France.

In May, France transforms the Netherlands into a "sister republic."

In June–July, a British-backed royalist force lands in Brittany but is defeated by the republicans.

In July, France signs a peace treaty with Spain.

In October, France annexes Belgium, and the royalist Vendémiaire insurrection is crushed in Paris. A new constitution provides for a two-chamber legislature based on an indirect suffrage of male taxpayers. The executive is in the hands of a five-man Directory, which first meets in November.

1796   General Napoléon Bonaparte invades Italy in April.

In May, a proto-Socialist 'Conspiracy of the Equals', led by Gracchus Babeuf, is foiled.

1797   In the elections of 1797, the monarchists win a large number of seats.

In September, the republicans respond with the coup of Fructidor, in which loyal army units purge the legislature of monarchists.

In October, Napoléon forces Austria to make peace in the Treaty of Campo Formio, which allows France to annex the Rhineland.

1798   In the spring, Jacobins threaten an electoral resurgence.

In May, the elections of Jacobin candidates are annulled in the coup of Floréal. A French attempt to support an insurrection against British rule in Ireland fails. Bonaparte's invasion of Egypt brings both Turkey and Russia into the war.

1799   A new coalition is formed when Austria, Russia, Britain, and Turkey counterattack.

In June, the Jacobins get their revenge in the parliamentary coup of Prairial, forcing the resignation of three directors.

By the summer, France is threatened with renewed invasion. Domestically, the Directory reforms the tax system, abolishes the inflation-prone *assignats,* and lays some foundations for Napoléon's later reforms in education, but it enjoys only a narrow base of support among a population weary of war and social unrest. Facing renewed military crisis, worried by the resurgence of the Jacobins and threatened with a royalist insurrection in the south, moderate republicans, including Sieyès, turn to Bonaparte to help them force a major revision of the constitution.

November 9–10, Napoléon overthrows the Directory in the Brumaire coup and establishes the Consulate. He comes to power as first consul.

1800–1804   As first consul, Napoléon forges the machinery of his dictatorship. The Constitution of 1800 gives him executive powers, with two other consuls having a consultative voice. The legislature includes the Tribunate, the Legislative Body and the Senate. Real power resides in the Senate, which is appointed by Bonaparte and empowered to issue *Senatus Consulta,* by which Napoléon can amend the constitution at will and so control the legislature. Prefects are introduced into the departments to act as the eyes and ears of the central government and to carry out its will. Censorship is imposed, many newspapers are closed down, and agents report on public opinion and political dissent to Napoléon's police minister, Joseph Fouché.

1800   In December, a royalist bomb plot against Bonaparte gives him an excuse to crush the Jacobins. Bonaparte increases his support, first by bringing peace. He is victorious at Marengo.

1801   Austrians sign the peace treaty of Lunéville.

1802   A peace treaty with Britain is sealed at Amiens in 1802. Bonaparte heals the religious schism by signing a Concordat with the Pope. It recognizes Catholicism as the religion of the great majority of French citizens and provides state salaries for the Catholic clergy, but offers toleration of other faiths and secures papal recognition for the sale of the *biens nationaux.* He also obtains support from the elites by offering status and wealth to those, whether of the old nobility or of the new revolutionary elites, who serve him well. Secondary schools, the *lycées,* intended to prepare the sons of these elites for training as army officers, state officials, and engineers, are established.

1804   Another royalist conspiracy leads Bonaparte to eliminate some counter-revolutionary enemies. The Civil Code is published, which enshrines some of the key principles of the French Revolution in law. It is in this constructive, relatively peaceful, phase that plebiscites are held making Bonaparte consul for life in 1802 and hereditary emperor in 1804.

Yet by that year, the War of the Third Coalition, the first of the Napoleonic Wars, has been kindled and warfare will scar the Napoleonic empire until its final collapse in 1815.

INTRODUCTION

The French Revolution destroyed the absolute monarchy of the Bourbon dynasty in 1789 and in 1792 led to the founding of the First French Republic, which witnessed the rise to power of Napoléon Bonaparte in 1799. During France's revolutionary decade of 1789–1799, the institutional and legal foundations for modern France were laid. The ideals and the events of the revolution have been equally the source of inspiration and abhorrence across the world, for both contemporaries and generations up to the present day. Its institutions were spread, by force and by imitation, to far-flung parts of the world, and its political language and practices have helped to forge modern political culture.

BACKGROUND: CULTURE AND HISTORY

Eighteenth-century France was predominantly rural, Catholic, and hierarchical. In 1789, peasants accounted for more than 80 percent of the population and owned about half the land, but they differed widely, from well-to-do peasant landowners to sharecroppers and the landless laborers who migrated in search of work. There were only a few thousand serfs. A little more than 11 percent of the population was urban, consisting of domestic servants, journeymen (waged workers), artisans and master craftsmen, and a diverse "bourgeoisie" of people engaged in the liberal professions (particularly law), civil service, finance, commerce, and manufacturing. Nobles, about 1.5 percent of the population, owned approximately 20 percent of the land. They varied from the courtiers at the royal court at Versailles to impoverished provincial squires, sometimes indistinguishable from their peasant neighbors.

The vast majority of French people were Catholic, while 2 percent were Protestants and about half a percent were Jews. The Catholic clergy consisted of less than 2 percent of the population but owned up to 10 percent of the land. The clergy taxed their parishioners through the *dîme* (tithe), which in theory amounted to 10 percent of incomes. The village priest was often the leader of the community, the only educated man who could be expected to articulate his parishioners' concerns before the authorities. The church provided education and most of the welfare services, such as hospitals and charity for the poor. Within the clergy there was a world of difference between the bishops and wealthiest abbots and abbesses from noble families and the parish curates, who were frequently educated peasants.

The French population was theoretically organized into a "society of orders," where one's place was defined by one's function. At its crudest, it consisted of three orders, or estates: the clergy, the nobility, and the "third estate," which comprised all commoners—non-noble town dwellers and all the peasantry, together amounting to well over 90 percent of the population. The first two estates, called the "privileged orders," enjoyed the most tax exemptions and, in theory, exclusive access to high office. Yet in practice, most French people enjoyed some privilege, by virtue, for example, of living in a province or a town with certain tax exemptions, or by being a member of a guild that regulated entry into a craft or a trade.

The least privileged group was the peasantry: the poorest town dweller did not have to perform the *corvée* (labor service on the royal highways), but peasants did. In addition to royal taxation, the *corvée,* and the tithe, peasants were subjected to the seigneurial rights and dues of their landlords, who were both nobles and well-to-do non-nobles ("bourgeois"). While often pecuniary, such as payments for the upkeep of the lord's château, they also may have included the right to hunt across peasant land and the lord's monopoly on the winepress or mill (which a peasant had to pay to use). The lord could impose these rights and dispense justice on the peasants through manorial courts. In the decades before the French Revolution, landlords resurrected old rights that had fallen into disuse, seeking to wring as much profit out of their estates as possible. Tensions increased in the countryside.

But other factors also contributed to peasant restiveness in 1789. The population was rapidly growing, from around 21 million people in 1715 to 28 million by 1789. For the poor, this caused great hardship, particularly in periods following bad harvests. In general, food production did not keep pace with population growth, which meant that prices outstripped wages. This was especially hard on those peasants who owned no land to grow their own food (perhaps half of the entire population) and the urban poor (Andress 1999, 19). In times of scarcity, such as 1789, the misery was all the sharper.

There was some economic dynamism, however. Bordeaux and Nantes were expanding commercial cities whose trade was bound up with the produce of the French overseas colonies. There were signs of industrial development (but no "industrial revolution") in manufacturing towns like Lyon (silk), Saint-Etienne and Le Creusot (large-scale iron foundries), and Rouen (cotton). It was once argued (Lefeb-

vre 1939) that economic development created a confident, capitalist bourgeoisie whose ambitions, frustrated by the restraints of the old aristocratic regime, caused the revolution. More recently, however, it has been suggested that the bourgeoisie, who made up some 8.5 percent of the population, shared much in common with the nobility. Sections of the nobility invested in large-scale commerce. Both groups also shared a common culture in the eighteenth-century Enlightenment, and the wealthy bourgeoisie was not seeking to destroy the nobility, but to join it. The monarchy had admitted increasing numbers of commoners to the nobility as a reward for state service. Middle-class people without noble titles tried to emulate the aristocracy by investing money in land, of which the bourgeoisie owned about 20 percent. This gave them a further interest in common with the nobles. Rather than two hostile classes, the upper reaches of the nobility and bourgeoisie were forming a common, landowning elite. It was they, some suggest, who took political control of France in the revolution (Lucas 1973).

If the French Revolution was not a dramatic social transformation, then its "revolutionary" nature came in the way French politics was transformed. This political transformation sprang from the cultural milieu of eighteenth-century France. In 1715 average literacy rates stood at 29 percent for men and at 14 percent for women. By 1789 they were 47 percent for men and 27 percent for women (in Paris they may have been as high as 90 and 80 percent respectively). This expansion in literacy presented writers and publicists with the opportunity to spread political, religious, and social concepts among a wider audience than ever before. Above all, the very notion of a "public opinion," independent of church and state to which one could appeal for legitimacy, evolved in the eighteenth century.

In the eighteenth century, the Enlightenment, a broad, inchoate movement of social and moral criticism, stressed the importance of reason and tolerance. In the widely read *De l'Esprit des Lois* (1748), Montesquieu praised limits on royal authority. During the mid eighteenth century, public opinion viewed the *parlements* (aristocratic sovereign courts) as the main brake on royal power. Yet more radical ideas were also circulating. Rousseau's *Du Contrat Social* (1762) depicted the ideal form of government as that which reflects the consensus of all in society—the general will—rather than individual or sectional interests. The implications were far-reaching. As a democratic thinker, Rousseau suggested that civil society consisted of equals who submitted to the same laws upon which they had all agreed. Each citizen, therefore, shared an equal stake in the body politic, which left no room for privileges. But he who broke the laws agreed upon by the general will could be treated "less as a citizen than as an enemy," because once he broke the rules of society, he was no longer a member of the state (Rousseau 1968, 79). This idea had ominous implications in light of The Terror and later totalitarian regimes. Meanwhile Voltaire supported royal power as the best way of destroying institutions based on bigotry, but at the same time he relentlessly assaulted The Catholic Church. Publicists, such as the future revolutionary Brissot de Warville, produced newspapers, pamphlets, cartoons, and song sheets (Darnton 1982, 70) and helped spread these ideas as well as political pornography, which did much to drag the monarchy through many a Parisian gutter (Darnton 1996).

In the late eighteenth century, these ideological and cultural developments accompanied a growing crisis of confidence in the monarchy. Its roots were financial. When Louis XIV died in 1715, his wars left debts estimated at 2,000 million *livres*. French foreign policy, particularly involvement in wars, and the failure of reforms to raise revenue to meet the costs ensured that the debt would balloon dangerously. The War of Austrian Succession, the Seven Years War (the latter disastrous for France), and other foreign policy commitments were financed by deeper indebtedness, which could only be reduced by tax reform and economic growth. These measures implied an assault on those with tax exemptions, particularly on the clergy and nobility, and on trade guilds, municipal corporations, and provincial estates, some of which had some role in allocating the tax burden in the lands under their authority. The strongest obstacle to reform, however, were the aristocrat-dominated *parlements,* the thirteen sovereign courts with the right to register all royal edicts before they became law in their particular jurisdictions. The most powerful was the Paris *parlement,* covering a third of the kingdom. In 1764, when the *parlement* of Brittany objected to reforms, Louis XV had their leaders arrested, spurring the Paris *parlement* to protest. Louis reacted angrily in the "Flagellation Session" of 1766, stating that the courts derive all their authority from him. In 1771, Chancellor René de Maupeou exiled the Paris *parlement* and dismissed the others when they objected. In the government's view, this measure destroyed the most important obstacle to reform. Yet to the public, the fact that the *parlements* could be so easily brushed aside showed that there were no real barriers to the "despotic" tendencies of the monarchy.

Royal claims to absolutism made the monarchy appear increasingly out of touch with the public. The Bourbon dynasty had lost much support because of failures in its foreign policy. The Seven Years War marked a change in France's diplomatic alignments that would have severe reverberations in domestic politics. France allied with her old rival, Austria, but the war ended in humiliation. At the Treaty of Paris in 1763, French territories in Canada, along with other colonial possessions in India and the Caribbean, were lost to Britain. In the wake of the debacle, the Austrian alliance was deeply unpopular in France. The monarchy would be damaged still more when it sought to strengthen the alliance with the marriage of the future Louis XVI to the Habsburg archduchess, Marie-Antoinette, in 1770. She became queen when Louis XV died in 1774, and her husband was crowned king. The young woman quickly became a target for the venom of those hostile to the Austrian alliance, and unfounded rumors about the queen's sexual shenanigans did further damage to the prestige of the monarchy among the French public.

On his accession, Louis XVI sought to curry public opinion by recalling the *parlements,* but he also appointed the reformist Anne Robert Jacques Turgot as controller-general of finances. Influenced by the progressive ideas of the Enlightenment, Turgot embarked on a program of fiscal and economic reform, seeking to free the peasants of such burdens as the *corvée* and to liberate manufacturing from the grip of the guilds. Overall, he tried to pursue policies that would ease poverty and encourage economic growth. His measures provoked strong opposition in the *parlements* and from the guilds, but also a violent outbreak of food riots (the "Flour War") in 1775, when his liberalization of the grain trade coincided with a poor harvest and high food prices. Louis dismissed him in 1776. Turgot's ultimate successor was Jacques Necker, a Genevan Protestant who was controlling the royal purse strings when France entered the American War of Independence against Britain in 1778. The war was a military triumph, ending in 1783 with American independence. Yet at the same time, public enthusiasm for the American Revolution, which appeared to be bringing eighteenth-century political ideas to fruition, gave wider currency to such notions and terms as *liberty, nation, patriotism,* and *citizen* and subverted the concept of the king as lord over his *subjects.* Moreover, through what today would be called "creative accounting," Necker had hidden the loans that financed the war.

Charles Alexandre de Calonne, controller-general of finances from 1783, finally discovered in August 1786 the true size of the deficit. He proposed a reform program to stimulate the economy for long-term growth and to increase tax revenue. To bypass opposition from the *parlements,* public support would be expressed by an Assembly of Notables, a hand-picked gathering of the kingdom's great nobles and clergy, which met in 1787. Yet its members suspected the king was attempting to increase royal power. His device failing, Calonne was replaced by Cardinal Brienne, but the Assembly of Notables insisted that it was not competent to decide matters of reform and taxation. It demanded the convocation of the Estates-General, the full representative assembly of the realm, to discuss these matters.

Brienne convoked the Estates-General for May 1, 1789, but the state's creditors refused to lend the government any more money. Brienne was dismissed and replaced by the still-popular Necker. The aristocratic opposition, however, lost public support by insisting that the Estates-General should meet according to 1614 procedures, whereby the two privileged orders, the clergy and the nobility, would always be able to outvote the representatives of the commoners, the Third Estate. All male taxpayers over the age of twenty-five could vote in the elections (which opened in January), making them "the most democratic spectacle ever seen in the history of Europe . . . nothing comparable occurred again until far into the next century" (Doyle 1989, 97). Supporters of the Third Estate organized into political clubs and sought to mobilize public opinion by declaring their opposition to privilege and their support for the people ("the nation") and its interests. The most important contribution to the debate was published in February 1789. Heavily influenced by Rousseau, Emmanuel Sieyès' pamphlet *What Is the Third Estate?* stridently condemned privilege and suggested that the entire nation was alone the source of all sovereignty. The tract would prove to be one of the ideological cornerstones of the French Revolution.

CONTEXT AND PROCESS OF REVOLUTION

The Estates-General met on May 4, 1789. Debate was dominated by the issue of whether the three orders should meet together and vote by head (giving the advantage to the Third Estate) or meet separately, with each order expressing a single, collective opinion (whereby the clergy and nobility would usually agree and so outvote the Third Estate). The Third Estate defiantly proclaimed itself the "National Assembly" on June 17 and, three days later, its members, meeting at the royal tennis court, swore never to disperse until they had framed a constitution for France. The regime was also beset by an economic crisis, which stemmed from a desperately bad harvest in 1788. Food supplies began to dwindle in the spring of 1789. Riots spread across the kingdom. A slump in demand for manufactured goods sent unemployment shooting upwards. When the frustrated king dismissed Necker on July 12, Parisians saw the removal of the popular minister as the opening move in a royal coup. Seeking to defend themselves against troops they expected to attack, the Paris crowd stormed the Bastille on July 14 to secure its stocks of gunpowder. When military commanders warned him that they could not rely on their troops against French civilians, Louis had no way to restore his evaporating authority. Royal power also collapsed in the provinces. Resentment against landlords was aggravated by the "Great Fear" of foreign invasion or of armed brigands in the pay of aristocrats. Peasants took up arms and burned châteaux, destroyed symbols of privilege, and made bonfires of legal titles to seigneurial rights and dues. The peasant revolution shattered the authority of the absolute monarchy in the countryside. With France in chaos, Louis XVI capitulated to the National Assembly, now also calling itself the Constituent Assembly, which had approximately 1,200 members. It began the reform of France.

The French Revolution witnessed the constitutional monarchy (1789–1792) and the turbulent life of the First Republic (1792–1804). The latter was governed first by the National Convention (1792–1795), which oversaw The Terror of 1793–1794. From 1795, a moderate republican regime, the Directory, failed to bring political and social stability to the weary country. It was toppled in 1799 by General Napoléon Bonaparte, who under the authoritarian Consulate laid the foundations for his imperial dictatorship. He ended the republic when he crowned himself emperor of the French in 1804. These successive revolutionary regimes were all faced at various times with factors that made the task of finding a viable political settlement nearly insurmountable: counter-revolution, a religious schism, the challenges mounted by the political Left, a series of economic crises, and above all, France's entanglement in an intense European war, which exacerbated all the other problems. In these circumstances, the revolution's achievements in laying the foundations of the modern French state and in making strides toward the creation of modern political ideas and practices seem all the more remarkable.

The Constituent Assembly tried to restore order to the countryside by abolishing what it called "feudalism" in a tumultuous session on the night of August 4, 1789. The extent of the reform was then carefully defined on August 11 by a decree that completely destroyed dues related to personal servitude but recast others as property rights, for the loss of which peasants had to make redemption payments. The August decrees also abolished personal, provincial, and corporate privilege (titles of nobility were abolished in June 1790). On this blank slate, the Constituent Assembly was able to construct a fresh, rational, and uniform administrative, fiscal, and political structure, quickly achieving what the monarchy had been struggling to build for decades. The new system was based on roughly uniform departments, which replaced the old provinces, and which still exist today. The Declaration of the Rights of Man and the Citizen (August 26, 1789) laid out the principles upon which the new order was to be based, proclaiming civil (not social) equality and basic civil rights, including freedom of religious worship and freedom of expression. While it also proclaimed that the nation was the source of all sovereignty, most revolutionaries believed that only those with a certain amount of property or commerce should dominate political life. This idea was entrenched in France's first constitution, which was ratified in September 1791. The vote was given to male "active citizens" (those paying sufficient taxes)—about 15 percent of the population. Royal power was severely reduced. The king enjoyed only a suspensive rather than an absolute veto over the National Assembly, but no decree would become law without royal sanction. These achievements, however, were overshadowed by problems. First, Louis XVI was never reconciled to his loss of absolute power. His prevarication over sanctioning the August decrees and the Declaration of Rights, combined with continued food shortages, led the women of Paris to march on Versailles on October 5–6, 1789, and force the royal family to live in the Tuileries Palace in the city, where they would effectively be hostages of the Paris crowd. Louis was alarmed by the radical left-wing press and political clubs (including the Jacobins and the Cordeliers) and, a devout Catholic, he was dismayed by the revolution's reform of the church and by the clerical oath. Prevented in April 1791 from leaving the city to celebrate Easter with his own confessor, he and his family fled the city on the night of June 20–21. The royal family were arrested at Varennes and hauled back to the capital. Louis was temporarily suspended from his official functions. The king's constitutional powers were soon restored, and while he gave royal sanction to the Constitution of 1791 in September, the political Left doubted his sincerity.

From July 1789, courtiers, including the king's two brothers, and aristocrats fled France into Germany. Among these *émigrés* were army officers who brought soldiers with them, forming the nucleus of a royalist army at Koblentz. Counter-revolution was given wider support by the most divisive issue of all: the reform of the church. In November 1789 the revolutionaries nationalized all church property as *biens nationaux,* to be auctioned as a means of paying off the state debt. (Meanwhile, state creditors would be paid in *assignats,* paper bills redeemable at the auctions, but they became legal tender in April 1790). Its wealth gone, the church needed another form of support and, with the Civil Constitution of the Clergy in July 1790, priests became salaried civil servants, elected by the "active citizens" among their parishioners. The conservative press attacked this system as an assault on Catholicism, mobilizing the devout in the process. The National Assembly decreed that all priests swear an oath of loyalty to the Civil Constitution. The clerical oath split the French church down the middle, and priests who refused it ("refractories") were generally responding to pressure from their own parishioners (Tackett 1986). In rural France, refractory priests would emerge as leaders of counter-revolution, which henceforth had a popular basis.

Meanwhile, the Left, seeking a more democratic political settlement, protested through its newspaper press and its political clubs against the limited suffrage and the royal veto. It attacked both *émigrés* and the refractory clergy. The flight to Varennes was a boon to the Left: the Jacobin club, which had 200 affiliated societies across France, mushroomed into a network of 900 clubs. The more radical Left swerved openly toward republicanism, including the Cordeliers club, which, though restricted to Paris, could mobilize the artisans and workers who formed the backbone of the popular movement. The Cordeliers drafted a petition calling for a referendum on the king's fate, though the Jacobins split between a radical minority, led by Maximilien Robespierre, who wanted to support the petition, and the majority who remained loyal to the constitutional monarchy and went off to form the Feuillant society. When protesters gathered to sign the petition on the *Champ de Mars* in Paris on July 17, 1791, fifty of them were killed by the National Guard, after which the incipient republican movement was forced underground.

With the constitution ratified in September, the work of the Constituent Assembly was over. Following elections, the new, 745-strong Legislative Assembly first met on October 1. The simmering political divisions of the summer bubbled to the surface in a developing international crisis. After the flight to Varennes, Marie-Antoinette's brother, Emperor Leopold II of Austria, had joined with King Frederick William II of Prussia to issue the Declaration of Pillnitz in August, in which they resolved to restore the rights of the French monarchy if they received support from other monarchs. To the French Left, this looked like a prelude to a foreign-backed invasion by *émigré* forces gathering across the frontier. In the Legislative Assembly, the Jacobins, led by Jacques-Pierre Brissot, campaigned for war against the German princes harboring the *émigrés* as a means of removing the threat and of forcing the king to choose between the revolution and his suspected desire to restore the absolute monarchy in the wake of an enemy victory. Most of the Feuillants wanted peace in order to give the new constitution a chance to work. Louis XVI wanted war, because he believed that the forces of Austria would easily defeat the now ill-disciplined and disorganized French army and restore the absolute monarchy.

On April 20, 1792, war was declared against Austria, which was joined by Prussia in May. This conflict now drove the revolution on its radical course. As the crisis mounted, republicanism began to emerge into the open once again. The king and queen were accused of betrayal, and the Left began to mobilize the Parisian militants, the *sans-culottes.* Popular enthusiasm for the defense of the revolution was unleashed in July, when the Legislative Assembly declared *la patrie en danger* (the fatherland in danger), a state of emergency in which National Guard units from across France were mobilized and sent to the front. The allied commander, the Duke of Brunswick, issued an inflammatory manifesto warning that if the royal family were harmed, Paris would suffer "exemplary and forever memorable vengeance." On August 10, radical National Guard units provided the firepower for an insurrection organized by the radical Parisian districts. The insurgents stormed the Tuileries Palace and toppled the monarchy. New elections, based on near-universal male suffrage, were held for a Convention of 749 deputies to draft a new constitution. As the military crisis grew worse, a Parisian mob, at once fearful and vengeful, massacred some 1,500 prisoners held in the capital's jails in the first week of September. The Prussians, however, were at last turned back by the French army at Valmy, and on September 22, the Convention proclaimed the French Republic. In December, it tried Louis XVI for treason and found him guilty. The king was guillotined on January 21, 1793.

Although the French were winning military victories, their very triumph exacerbated the conflict. With the Prussians in retreat and the Austrians defeated at Jemappes in November, the French invaded both Belgium and Germany while, in the south, they conquered Savoy and Nice. This surge of French power alarmed the British, Dutch, and Spanish. By March, France was at war with these three powers and was soon invaded on every territorial frontier, while British ships blockaded its ports. The republic was also confronted with an acute domestic crisis. There was a desperate need for recruits. When the Convention imposed conscription, however, the smoldering hostility of devout peasants in Normandy, Brittany, and the Vendée finally exploded into a full-scale Catholic-royalist revolt led by nobles and refractory priests. Although the open rebellion was defeated by December, it continued as a guerrilla war for almost a decade. Meanwhile, the disastrous inflation of the *assignat* and the scarcity of food in Paris sparked riots that were turned against the government by radicals who articulated the fears and desires of the *sans-culottes* for price controls and for more direct democracy. Among them were the Enragés (literally, the madmen) and the journalist Jacques-René Hébert.

The government was in the hands of the moderate Girondins, who had been swept into power by the revolution of August 10, 1792. Since they had opposed the king's execution, they were expelled from the Jacobin club, which was now dominated by radicals like Robespierre and whose members in the Convention formed a group called the "Mountain." The political struggle over the military and domestic crisis would become a fight to the death between the Girondins and the Jacobins. The latter proposed most of the drastic, authoritarian measures to deal with the crisis that would, collectively, form the machinery of The Terror:

- two committees—Public Safety and General Security—to take emergency measures for, respectively, the war effort and internal policing;
- a Revolutionary Tribunal to try those accused of treason;
- the dispatch of members of the Convention to the provinces as "representatives on mission" to mobilize the population and to crush counter-revolution;
- and the organization of local surveillance committees, to watch and report on suspects.

Eventually, to garner support in their struggle with the Girondins, the Jacobins supported some *sans-culotte* demands, including the Maximum, which fixed prices on bread and grain.

In the coup of May 31–June 2, 1793, the *sans-culottes* and the Parisian National Guard brought the Jacobins to power when they purged the leading Girondins from the Convention and the government. A new constitution was drafted, providing for universal male suffrage, but it was never implemented. The purge of the Girondins, who represented constituencies in the provinces, plunged France into civil war as an anti-Jacobin "Federalist" revolt exploded in the country's leading provincial cities.

The Jacobins responded to the confluence of military defeat, economic misery, counter-revolution, and civil war with The Terror, which was extraordinary, emergency government. At the same time, however, the Jacobin Convention was not allowed to forget that it was the popular movement that had removed the Girondins. The *levée en masse,* the universal conscription decreed in August, was originally a *sans-culotte* idea. Many of the measures taken in autumn were taken under the threat of a further insurrection by the *sans-culottes,* such as the proclamation of Terror, the General Maximum (fixing prices on a range of goods), the death penalty for hoarders, a forced loan on the rich, and the mobilization of the "revolutionary armies" (units of militants that scoured the countryside requisitioning food supplies). The Law of Suspects of September 17, 1793, defined those liable to arrest in the broadest of terms, ensuring that prisons across the country, and especially in Paris, would be overcrowded. In October, Marie-Antoinette and then the Girondins were tried and guillotined. Outside Paris, the Convention's representatives committed mass executions as they suppressed the Federalist revolts and tried to crush the counter-revolution in western France.

By the end of 1793, the crisis was slowly abating: the French won some victories along the northern frontier, the Federalist revolts had been stamped out, the counter-revolution contained, and the economic crisis was under control. Meanwhile, the regime was also forcing the pace of a cultural transformation, expressing a break with the past and the advance to a new, purportedly more rational republican order. Among the most dramatic of these expressions was the introduction of a new revolutionary calendar to replace the Gregorian version. The new age was held to have dawned with Year I on September 22, 1792, with the proclamation of the republic. Year II, therefore, was that of The Terror in 1793–94. The year was divided into regular thirty-day months, each with names representing the climate or agricultural activities of the season. Hence the first month of the revolutionary year, straddling late September and most of October, was "Vendémiaire" (the month of the harvest); "Thermidor" (astride July and August) captured the stifling heat of high summer. Each month was divided into three ten-day weeks (*décades*), with one rest-day a week (the *décadi*) to replace the religious festivals on Sundays. Napoléon Bonaparte eventually did away with this calendar in 1806.

With the immediate crisis receding, some Jacobin voices (the Indulgents) around Georges-Jacques Danton and Camille Desmoulins began to call for clemency. They were opposed by extremists around Jacques-René Hébert, who sought *sans-culotte* support by demanding an intensification of The Terror and of the war effort. The latter went too far for the government, however, when they sponsored an atheistic "dechristianization" movement. For Robespierre and his colleagues on the Committee of Public Safety, this and the more extreme measures taken in its name threatened to create more enemies for the republic. On December 4, a law on revolutionary government centralized control of The Terror, placing all initiative in the hands of the Committee of Public Safety and its agents. Finally, in March 1794, the government struck, arresting Hébert and his associates, who were tried and guillotined. With that, the government decapitated the *sans-culotte* movement and was able to abolish the notorious "revolutionary armies." Yet Robespierre and his colleagues saw no reason to end The Terror altogether. They also destroyed the Indulgents, who were arrested, tried, and executed in April. The destruction of the Hébertists was accompanied by a brief, but barely implemented, program of social reform that included the Ventôse Laws, which ordered, first, that all the property of "enemies of the revolution" be seized by the state, that this apply to all those arrested since the beginning of the revolution, and that the property be distributed among "indigent patriots." These decrees primarily aimed to steal extremist thunder and to secure popular support, for a law was also passed that punished with death anyone who proposed an "Agrarian Law" (for a more radical redistribution of property).

By now, The Terror was becoming a means of killing off all dissent rather than an extraordinary response to the crisis. The Law of 22 Prairial (June 10) decreed that those unfortunates arraigned before the Revolutionary Tribunal would not be permitted defense counsel. Consequently, while in the entire period of The Terror between March 1793 and late July 1794, 2,639 people were guillotined in Paris, 1,515 of them perished in the seven-week period following the Law of 22 Prairial (Doyle 1989, 275). The resentment among the government's broadening ranks of enemies could not be contained for long, especially when there was a growing sense that The Terror had achieved its purpose. The French defeated the Austrians at the Battle of Fleurus on June 26 and reinvaded Belgium. In Paris, the government's fearful opponents in the Convention finally combined their parliamentary forces. On 9–10 Thermidor (July 27–28), Robespierre and his associates were overthrown and executed. The surviving members of the Convention, who became known as the Thermidorians, dismantled The Terror. Moderate republicanism was given a boost in December 1794, when the seventy-one surviving Girondins were reinstated in the Convention.

The moderate revolutionary regimes after the Thermidorian reaction had to deal with the perennial problems of economic and social dislocation, counter-revolution, opposition from the Left, and above all, they had to bring the war to a successful conclusion. Without peace, the other problems would persist. Napoléon Bonaparte came to power on the ruins of the efforts to solve these problems.

The Jacobin club was shut down in November 1794 and, in the South, the Thermidorians did little to stop royalist mobs wreaking bloody vengeance on the Jacobins in the "White Terror." The Paris crowd was finally spent as a political force after a final insurrection in the spring of 1795, driven largely by a surge in the price of dwindling food supplies caused by a combination of the repeal of the Maximum in December 1794 and the coldest winter in a century. That summer, a royalist force was defeated in Brittany, and a royalist insurrection in Paris in October (the Vendémiaire uprising) was crushed by gunners under Napoléon Bonaparte.

A new constitution, to replace the more democratic, but never implemented, document of 1793, came into force in November 1795. The Constitution of 1795 established the Directory and sought to avoid both the "anarchy" of direct democracy and royalist counter-revolution. All male taxpayers were given the right to vote for delegates to local departmental electoral colleges, which would choose the deputies to a two-chamber legislature consisting of a Council of Five Hundred and a Council of Elders. The legislature elected a five-man Directory, which acted as the executive: one member was replaced by election annually. Real power lay with the 30,000 wealthiest government officials, army officers, manufacturers, and landowners who had done well out of the revolution and who benefited most from the system of indirect suffrage (meaning that the voters chose delegates to electoral colleges, who then selected the members of the legislature) (Doyle 1989, 319). The Directory therefore rested on narrow social foundations and seemed to offer little to the peasant or urban masses, who were thus receptive to royalist or Jacobin propaganda. With its slender popular base, the government needed the support of either monarchists or Jacobins, so the regime swung between left and

Influenced by their American counterparts, French citizens proclaim a new constitution on September 14, 1791, during the French Revolution. Less than a month earlier, the National Assembly adopted the Declaration of the Rights of Man and the Citizen, a watershed document in the history of human rights legislation. (Library of Congress)

right. In 1796, it survived a radical left-wing "Conspiracy of the Equals" led by Gracchus Babeuf, who sought to create a proto-Socialist republic. In the coup of Fructidor (September 1797), the army was used to purge the legislature and the Directory of suspected monarchists. In May (Floréal) 1798, it was the turn of the Jacobins to be denied their seats. The military crisis and the resurgence of both Jacobinism and royalism convinced many people that the constitution needed revision. Among them was the director, Emmanuel Sieyès, who engineered the downfall of the Directory in the coup of Brumaire (November 9–10, 1799), bringing Napoléon Bonaparte to power.

The authoritarian regime of the Consulate (1799–1804) sought to keep some of the revolution's achievements while providing strong executive government. From 1800, a complex system of indirect male suffrage ensured that Bonaparte,

as first consul, named all officials and representatives from village mayors to senators. Prefects were appointed in each department in 1800 to carry out the will of the first consul in the provinces. The legislature consisted of a Tribunate, a Legislative Body, and a Senate. This last was hand-picked by Bonaparte, and it was through the Senate that Napoléon could effectively rule by decree. Press restrictions were strict: sixty Parisian newspapers were shut down in 1800, leaving only thirteen in print. In the provinces, royalists, deserters, and brigands were pursued ruthlessly: those caught were summarily tried by military commissions and shot. A secret police system watched and arrested dissidents, while workers were controlled from 1803 by the obligation to carry an internal passport, the *livret,* which included an individual's employment record and personal details and without which no one could get a job.

Portrait of Napoléon Bonaparte. (Library of Congress)

Yet Bonaparte also secured some acquiescence from both the revolutionary elites and the people at large. First, he made brief but victorious peace with all of France's enemies, bringing respite to a war-weary population. While these proved to be no more than truces, the Napoleonic Wars did not begin in earnest until 1805. It was in the years of relative peace that Bonaparte held plebiscites to secure his appointment as consul for life (1802) and then hereditary emperor (1804). He also healed the religious schism, signing a Concordat with the Pope in 1801 that recognized Catholicism as "the religion of the great majority of citizens." The French state promised to salary French bishops and parish priests; there was to be no clerical oath, but only a promise to obey the laws. In return, the Pope recognized the sale of church lands. Now secure in the possession of their *biens nationaux,* the elites were also wooed by creation of the *lycées* in 1802. These were secondary schools that would train the sons of the elites as officials, engineers, and military officers. Napoléon also codified the 15,000-odd decrees passed since 1789 in the Civil Code, promulgated in 1804. This "Napoleonic Code" recognized equality before the law, the abolition of privilege, the principle of careers open to talent, and property rights, and it maintained, though in much stricter terms, provisions for divorce, which the revolution had legalized in 1792. Together, these reforms bound the old revolutionary elites to the Napoleonic regime. The revolution was over.

IMPACTS

In 1789, most intellectuals hailed the revolution as the embodiment of Enlightenment ideas, the triumph of freedom and reason over despotism and ignorance. Reformers across Europe urged their governments to amend social and political institutions. In Britain and Ireland, numerous societies campaigning for peaceful parliamentary reform were either galvanized by events in France or founded in response to them (Dickinson 1985). The hopes of Dutch and Swiss "patriots" in exile in France were raised as their French friends now appeared to be in control of French foreign policy. They were soon joined by Belgians who fled a failed revolution against Austrian rule, though their insurrection was little inspired by the French Revolution (Rapport 2000). The Anglo-Irish politician and writer Edmund Burke was one of the few to spoil the festivities, denouncing the revolution from the outset in his *Reflections on the Revolution in France* (1790) for leveling the Old Regime and for trying to create an entirely new order based, not on France's political traditions, but on abstract principles (Burke 1790). Radical writers reacted strongly: in Britain, Thomas Paine's reply to Burke in *Rights of Man,* published in two parts in 1791 and 1792, made the most impact. Paine defended the French constitution and the notion of natural rights while attacking monarchy and aristocracy (Paine 1791–1792). For reactionaries, the revolution was providential punishment for the freethinking permitted by the Old Regime. Apart from the hostility of Catherine II ("the Great") of Russia, governments at first reacted cautiously. Initially, the revolution seemed to weaken one of Europe's most powerful and dangerous states. In February 1792, the Turkish Sultan Selim III's private secretary wrote in his diary: "May God cause the upheaval in France to spread like syphilis to the enemies of the [Ottoman] Empire, hurl them into prolonged conflict with one another, and thus accomplish results beneficial to the Empire Amen" (Blanning 1986, 184).

Yet radicals and reformers who applauded the French Revolution began to look downright dangerous from 1792, when the republic was proclaimed and the revolution became more violent. Worse, they seemed like pro-French subversives once the French Revolutionary Wars developed, from November 1792 with the "Propagandist Decrees," into a war ostensibly of liberation but in reality of French expansionism. Repression came swiftly. In Spain, laws were passed expelling French citizens (Herr 1958). Russia did the same in February 1793, also forbidding trade with France and recalling all Russian subjects from French soil. In Britain, the government started to prosecute "subversive" writers and subsidized loyalist publications and associations, particularly that founded by John Reeves, the Association for the Preservation of Liberty and Property against Republicans and Levellers in late 1792. A convention of primarily Scottish radicals was closed down in Edinburgh at the end of 1792 and its leaders were put on trial. A volunteer militia was authorized for home defense against both French invasion and domestic revolution. In 1795, the "Two Acts" placed restrictions on public meetings and defined verbal or written attacks on the king as treason (Mori 2000, 99). In 1799, a persistent radical organization, the London Corresponding Society, was outlawed, as were trade unions. In Italy, governments arrested and executed leading radicals, reversed reform programs, and imposed censorship. Poland, which promulgated Europe's first written constitution on May 3, 1791, did not have time to enjoy it, since the following year Catherine II of Russia, on the pretext of destroying Jacobinism in eastern Europe, sent in her army to occupy the country. A national uprising led by Tadeusz Kosciuszko and inspired by the French war effort in 1794 was crushed, and Poland was completely partitioned between Russia, Prussia, and Austria. Even the republic of the United States succumbed to fear of subversion, passing the Alien and Sedition Acts in 1798. Yet in some countries, government repression and the failure of peaceful reform forced some radicals to form a revolutionary underground. The United Irishmen, which sought independence for Ireland, tried to lead an unsuccessful insurrection against British rule in 1798.

The vast majority of radicals, however, were overwhelmed not only by government repression, but also by the strength of popular conservatism. While governments feared the threat of domestic revolution and Jacobinism, for many ordinary Europeans, first-hand experience of the French Revolution came in the terrifying shape of war and military occupation by the French. While Belgium (1795), the German Rhineland (1798), and Piedmont (in northern Italy, 1800) were annexed directly onto France, other countries conquered by the French were converted into "sister republics." These satellite states were subjected to French interference and were expected to raise taxes and armies for the French war effort. Conscription and economic exploitation, as well as efforts to secularize society and thus attack religious beliefs, combined to persuade most Europeans to reject the brave new world offered by the revolutionaries. Major popular uprisings against French dominance and against their local Jacobin allies took place in Belgium in 1798 and in Italy in 1799. It was only under the Napoleonic empire, when much of western Europe settled under long-term French rule, that the more constructive legacies of the French Revolution, such as rational administration, effective policing, and an even-handed, accessible legal system, began to be appreciated by more than a tiny minority of Europeans.

This was especially true of the principles of the French Revolution as presented in the Napoleonic Code, which implied the abolition of seigneurialism and the freedom of worship implicit in the Concordat. When they were exported to Napoléon's European conquests and satellite states, the impact was potentially revolutionary, though in practice their radical effects were softened by Napoléon's need to conciliate local elites. Nonetheless, the code, in particular, was especially appreciated in the German Rhineland and Poland, where it was retained after 1815. The code influenced legal systems in places as far flung as South America, Romania, Turkey, Egypt, and the former French colonies of Louisiana, Haiti, and Quebec. In the French overseas empire of the later nineteenth century, however, indigenous people were subjected to a separate *code de l'indigénat* and could only benefit from French law if they obtained French citizenship.

If the institutional legacy of the French Revolution is ambiguous, its political and cultural inheritance is even more so. On the one hand, The Terror can be seen as a prototype for modern totalitarian dictatorships, and the attempts by the revolutionaries to spread their gospel by force as a precursor to France's self-proclaimed "civilizing mission," which justified French overseas imperialism in the later nineteenth century. Indeed, Napoléon's invasion of Egypt in 1798 has been identified as a key moment in efforts of the West to dominate non-Europeans, both politically and culturally (Said 1985). The concept of *revolution* was also irreversibly altered to mean an event resulting in dramatic change. Before 1789, even after the American Revolution, the term had been used to describe a variety of political changes, from palace coups to upheavals like the "Glorious" Revolution in Britain of 1688–1689, which purported to restore an older, better system rather than create a new one. Since 1789, too, revolution has usually been associated with violence until the revolutions in Eastern Europe in 1989, which were relatively non-violent (an exception being Romania). The French Revolution also produced the first professional revolutionaries, the Babouvists, who were dedicated to sparking a revolution, overthrowing the existing order through conspiracy and violence, and who spawned generations of imitators, from Auguste Blanqui in mid-nineteenth-century France to Lenin in the early twentieth century.

One particular legacy of the revolutionary wars was double-edged. The French adopted the idea (first proposed by the Old Regime military theorist Jacques de Guibert) that "all citizens would be soldiers, and all soldiers citizens." On the one hand, this principle encouraged the reform of the army, including better conditions for the troops (flogging was abolished), but on the other hand, it brought forth the notion of the "nation in arms," with the mass recruitment of the *levée en masse* in 1793 and the Jourdan Law of 1798, which established a regular system of universal conscription. It was this law that provided Napoléon with much of his cannon fodder, and it presaged the rise of the mass armies of the modern era.

Nonetheless, the French Revolution had emancipating power. It was not the first political movement to proclaim national sovereignty as the legitimizing principle for states and governments and as the basis of citizenship. But its expression as a universal principle, at a time when Europe was mostly divided between dynastic states, was truly radical. It has therefore provided an ideological foundation for movements of national liberation ever since and also offered an overarching ideal of citizenship that could transcend religious and ethnic divisions within any polity. The Declaration of the Rights of Man and the Citizen of 1789 and that of 1793 (which gave citizens rights to social welfare) have been imitated or adapted ever since, most notably by the United Nations Declaration of Human Rights of 1948 (Best 1988, 111–122). The French Revolution gave full civil rights to religious minorities (French Jews were emancipated in 1791), both in France and its conquests. Slavery was abolished in the French colonies in 1794, though that was admittedly a response to the great slave insurrection led by Toussaint-Louverture in Saint-Domingue (Haiti). Although women were not granted the suffrage during the revolution (and not until 1945), the logic of French revolutionary principles suggested that they should have been—a point not lost on feminists of the French Revolution, such as Olympe de Gouges, who penned her own Declaration of the Rights of Women in response to women's exclusion from political rights.

In France, after the downfall of Napoléon in 1815, many people sought to keep the revolutionary legacy at arms length: a French schoolbook during the Bourbon Restoration (1815–1830) pithily disposed of the entire era: "1789–1815— During this period France was a prey to disorder" (Cobban 1946, 8). Even when France appeared to return to its revolutionary tradition in the 1830 Revolution, which sent the restored Bourbon monarchy scurrying into exile, few people wanted a republic, which was associated with The Terror. Another dynasty, the cadet Orléans line, was brought to the throne instead. By 1848, however, republicanism had regained respectability after more than thirty years of constitutional monarchy. The short-lived Second Republic (1848–1851) saw the reintroduction of universal male suffrage, which France has had ever since, except for the hiatus of the Nazi occupation (1940–1944). After revisiting another legacy of the revolutionary era, the Bonapartist regime of Napoléon III (1852–1870), France was once again ruled by a republic that explicitly drew its principles from those of 1789. For nineteenth-century conservatives, reactionaries, liberals, and radicals alike, the French Revolution was an unavoidable point of reference, because society had passed through the fiery trial of political upheaval and revolutionary war and could not emerge unaltered. While liberals accepted 1789 as a foundation for constitutional principles and institutions, radicals were more likely to rhapsodize about the Jacobin constitution of 1793 as the inspiration for a democratic republic. Early Socialists, like Pierre-Joseph Proudhon, saw an antecedent in the redistributive, self-governing communes envisaged by Babeuf in 1796–1797. Jacobinism and Babouvism remained a source of inspiration for French Socialists through the Paris Commune in 1871, though from 1917 the Russian Revolution offered a more recent and, for Communists, a more promising example in the twentieth century.

Nonetheless, the French Revolution still held a critical place in what historian François Furet scathingly described as the Marxist "revolutionary catechism" (Furet 1978). For Karl Marx and Friedrich Engels and for the Russian revolutionaries, the French Revolution was the flawed, bourgeois forerunner of the greater upheaval of the masses (Marx and Engels 1848; Shlapentokh 1997). On the eve of the First World War, the French Revolution was the most popular historical topic for the Russian reading public (Keep 1968–1969, 25). For Marxist historians (like Lefebvre 1939 and Soboul 1974), the French Revolution represented the triumph of the capitalist bourgeoisie over a feudal aristocracy, which in a Marxist framework implied that the next revolution would see a proletariat destroying the bourgeoisie and forging a new, egalitarian society. This view was challenged by the revisionist British historian Alfred Cobban and subsequently by others who either denied the existence of a coherent, capitalist, revolutionary middle class altogether, or claimed that the bourgeoisie had so much in common with the nobility that it was, in fact, a common elite of landholding "notables" who seized power. The revolution did not, therefore, represent a transition from feudalism to capitalism (Cobban 1964, and Doyle 1980).

The rupture of the orthodox Marxist interpretation has brought on a glorious anarchy among historians, who have embarked on a wide range of approaches in explaining the legacy of the French Revolution. One, but by no means the only, new answer is the idea that the legacy of the French Revolution is to be found less in its social consequences than in the transformation of politics: the revolution, it is argued, bequeathed political vocabulary (among them, the terms *Left* and *Right*, which first arose in the Constituent Assembly, from the seats chosen by the radicals, who sat to the president's left, and by the more conservative monarchists, who sat to his right), symbols (the *tricolore*), ideology (such as notions of human rights, national sovereignty, revolution and, arguably, totalitarian democracy), and practices (popular participation in elections, the explosion of the press) that have helped to shape modern political culture. As historian Douglas Johnson writes: "Whether the French Revolution was the model for all revolutions or not, whether it is a myth or not, whether it is a jumble of unpredictable events or not, it is an inescapable subject. Every historian, whatever his particular speciality, has at some time to take account of the French Revolution. It is always there. It is always with us" (Sutherland 1985, 10).

PEOPLE AND ORGANIZATIONS

Babeuf, François-Noël "Gracchus" (1760–1797)

François-Noël Babeuf was a lawyer who, ironically, worked on cases asserting the seigneurial rights for landlords. His radical conscience was pricked by the revolution, and he worked for the government during The Terror on the commission responsible for procuring food supplies. After Thermidor, he remained a Jacobin, and he led the Conspiracy of Equals against the Directory, which envisaged a coup d'état to establish a republic of small, self-sufficient communes in which each member had only enough property to live comfortably. He was arrested in May 1796, tried, and guillotined in May 1797.

Bonaparte, Napoléon (1769–1821)

Napoléon Bonaparte was born in Corsica, son of a nobleman, Carlo Buonaparte, who was secretary to Pasquale Paoli, the leader of the Corsican independence movement. He was sent to military school in France, first at Brienne and then in Paris, where he graduated as an artillery officer in 1785. Sympathetic to the revolution (he had Jacobin leanings), during the French Revolutionary Wars, he distinguished himself in 1793 for his part in driving the British from Toulon. He commanded the artillery against the royalist Vendémiaire uprising in Paris in 1795, and he was appointed to lead the Army of Italy, which crossed the Alps in April 1796. He drove the Austrians out of Italy, forcing them to make peace at Campo Formio in October 1797. He led an expedition to Egypt in 1798, which proved to be a military disaster. Bonaparte escaped from Egypt in 1799, arriving in time to fulfill the role of military champion in the Brumaire coup against the Directory. He became first consul, then emperor of the French in 1804. The Napoleonic Wars proved to be his undoing. He was exiled to Elba in 1814. Then, after his escape and final defeat in 1815, he was exiled to the Atlantic island of Saint Helena, where he died in 1821.

Brissot de Warville, Jacques-Pierre (1754–1793)

A journalist and pamphleteer before 1789, Jacques-Pierre Brissot was also involved in the anti-slavery movement. His newspaper, *Le Patriote Français (The French Patriot)* gave him prominence in Paris during the Constituent Assembly. He was elected to the Legislative Assembly, where he launched a campaign for war against the German princes who harbored the *émigrés.* His political followers in the Convention would join with provincial deputies and become known as the Girondins. Expelled from the Jacobin club in October 1792, Brissot was arrested during the purge of the Girondins of May 31–June 2, 1793, and guillotined with other leading Girondins on October 31.

Chouans

Counter-revolutionary guerrillas in western France, mostly devout Catholic peasants led by priests and local nobles.

Committee of General Security

During The Terror, the Committee of General Security was first elected by the Convention in the spring of 1793 from among its own members. It gathered reports from the surveillance committees and intelligence on political subversion and public order, supervised arrests and censorship, and proposed measures to the Convention on these matters. From September 1793, its members were nominated by the Committee of Public Safety. After Thermidor, it supervised the release of prisoners and the disarming of Jacobins before it was abolished with the installation of the Directory.

Committee of Public Safety

During The Terror, a nine-man Committee of Public Safety was elected by the Convention from April 1793 to supervise the government ministries and the war effort. Its membership was renewable every month. At first the dominant voice was that of Danton, though he retired from the committee in June. From July, the main personality was that of Robespierre, under whom the Committee of Public Safety effectively became the executive government. Its powers were enhanced by the Law of 14 Frimaire (December 4, 1793), which gave it central control over the machinery of The Terror through its "national agents" and by the obligation of all subordinate bodies to report to the committee every ten days. In April 1794, government ministries were superseded by administrative commissions reporting to the Committee of Public Safety. After Thermidor, the committee was shorn of most of its powers and restricted to supervising the war effort and foreign policy. It was abolished when the Directory was installed.

Committees of Surveillance

Committees of surveillance were originally established spontaneously by the Paris sections immediately after August 10, 1792, in order to keep watch over suspected counter-revolutionaries. They were given a formal role and established all over France on March 21, 1793, to keep an eye on foreigners and suspects (defined in dangerously broad terms by the Law of Suspects of September 17, 1793). They reported to the Committee of General Security. After Thermidor, they were reduced in number before being abolished outright.

Commune

The smallest administrative division in rural districts (of which 44,000 were created in 1789), but in Paris, the Commune was the municipal government of the entire city.

Cordeliers Club

The Society of Friends of the Rights of Man was founded in May 1790 in the heartland of Parisian radicalism, the Cordeliers district. It denounced the distinction between "active" citizens (those adult males who paid sufficient taxes) and the rest of the population and admitted both men and women to its debates. In 1791, it was at the forefront of the republican movement, sponsoring the petition that led to the Champ de Mars massacre on July 17. It coordinated the invasion of the Tuileries on June 20, 1792, and after the fall of the monarchy, it became increasingly the voice of revolutionary extremism, first of the Enragés, then of the Hébertistes. It was cowed after the execution of the latter in March 1794.

Danton, Georges-Jacques (1759–1794)

Danton trained as a lawyer and discovered his vocation for radical politics in Paris, where he was a leading member of the early Cordeliers club and then a Jacobin. After the fall of the monarchy, he was minister of justice in the provisional government before being elected to the Convention, where he sat with the Mountain. He sponsored the creation of the Revolutionary Tribunal and was a member of the Committee of Public Safety before stepping down in June 1793. He withdrew from politics briefly due to exhaustion, then returned to Paris where he campaigned for less bloodshed during The Terror. Tarnished with corruption and accused of treason, he was arrested with other Indulgents and guillotined in April 1794.

Directory

The regime that ruled the French Republic from November 1795 until November 1799, when it was overthrown by Bonaparte's Brumaire coup. It was an executive of five directors, elected by the two legislative councils (the Council of Five Hundred and the Council of Elders). Every year, the directors would draw lots to decide who among them would stand down. He would then be replaced by a candidate chosen by the legislative councils. These councils were elected on the basis of annual elections, in which the membership of each chamber was renewed by a third. The lower chamber, the Five Hundred, initiated legislation; the 250-member-strong upper house, the Elders, whose members had to be aged over forty (sometimes rather harshly translated as the "Ancients"), could discuss, reject, or accept the laws proposed by the Five Hundred. All male taxpayers had the right to vote, but suffrage was indirect, meaning that voters chose delegates (who had to meet a stiff property qualification), who met in departmental colleges. These colleges then selected the deputies to the two councils.

Émigrés

Those, notably (though not exclusively) aristocrats and clergy, who fled France for political reasons during the revolution.

Enragés

Literally "mad men," the Enragés articulated the program of the *sans-culottes* in the spring and summer of 1793. Led by the ex-priest Jacques Roux and Jean Varlet, extreme democrats, they demanded the death penalty for hoarders and speculators, price controls, the utmost prosecution of the war, and a more egalitarian society with direct democracy. They also had close ties with the radical women's club, the Society of Revolutionary Republican Women. Although they took over the Cordeliers club in the summer of 1793, they were weakened by the arrest of Roux and Varlet as dangerous extremists in September. Leadership of the popular movement was then assumed by the Hébertistes.

Girondins

A left-wing group, originally from the Jacobin club, consisting of politicians around Brissot in the Legislative Assembly (the Brissotins) and around a nucleus of deputies from the Gironde region. The Girondins took the lead in the campaign for war in 1791–1792 and formed a short-lived ministry from March to June 1792. They were swept into power after August 10, 1792, but fell out with their Jacobin colleagues over the fate of the king and then over how best to deal with the crisis of 1793. The leading Girondins were purged from the government in the coup of May 31–June 2, 1793. Seventy-five members of the Convention who signed a protest against the coup in a secret declaration in June would also be defined as Girondins. When the "Federalist" revolts (supported by those Girondins who had escaped from Paris) faltered in the autumn, twenty-one leading Girondins were guillotined on October 31. The survivors remained in jail or in hiding until after The Terror, returning to the Convention only in December 1794, after which they lent considerable weight to the moderate republicanism of the Thermidorian Convention.

Hébert, Jacques-René (1757–1794)

In 1789, Jacques-René Hébert was living in poverty in Paris. But with the revolution, his journal, *Le Père Duchesne,* gained him popularity. A member of the Cordeliers club, he took up the Enragé program in the summer of 1793 and was heavily involved in the mass demonstration of September 5, which forced the Convention to decree government by Terror and subsequently to enact measures to placate the *sans-culottes.*

His supporters were strong in the Cordeliers club, the war ministry, and the Paris Commune. Active in the dechristianization campaign in Paris, urging an intensification of The Terror, and implicitly suggesting a coup against the government, he and other Hébertistes were arrested in March 1794 and guillotined.

Jacobins

As the Estates-General met, patriotic deputies from Brittany met to discuss policies and tactics at Versailles. This "Breton Club" became the nucleus for the more left-wing deputies in the early months of the revolution. When the National Assembly moved to Paris in October 1789, the Breton Club took over premises of the monastery of the Jacobins in Paris for its meetings—hence its popular name. Its formal title was the Society of the Friends of the Constitution. It became the center of a network of affiliated societies across the country: from twenty such clubs early in 1790, the number of corresponding societies rose to 300 a year later, and in the surge of radicalism after the flight to Varennes, to 900 by July 1791. It suffered a schism when the more moderate members broke away to form the Feuillant society in protest against the radicals' flirtations with the republican movement in the summer of 1791. Nonetheless, the Jacobins' lower membership

dues and opening of meetings to the public gave it wider popularity than the Feuillants, though its membership was predominantly middle class and exclusively male.

During The Terror, the Jacobins became the sounding-board for the policies of the Mountain, and expulsion from the club was a serious fall from grace. In November 1794 (after The Terror), the Thermidorian Convention closed the organization down, but Jacobin fortunes revived after the shock of the royalist Vendémiaire uprising in October 1795 and, though tarnished by Babeuf's Conspiracy of the Equals in 1796, the Jacobins enjoyed a brief revival in 1799, when a new Manège Club was founded in July, before being suppressed by the Directory in August. Jacobin leadership was almost totally silenced by Bonaparte who, as first consul, reacted to an attempt on his life at the end of 1800 by arresting some 130 of them, exiling most to Guiana. Outside France, the term *Jacobin* was applied, often misleadingly, to reformers and revolutionaries suspected of sympathy with or ties to the revolution in France.

Lafayette, Marie-Joseph Paul Yves Roche Gilbert De Motier, Marquis De (1757–1834)

Lafayette won accolades for his role in the American War of Independence while a young army officer. He was appointed to the Assembly of Notables in 1787, where he was among those who called for the Estates-General. Elected for the nobility in 1789, he was among the patriotic wing of the second estate, and he was appointed to command the Paris National Guard on July 14. The Champ de Mars massacre occurred under his command, and he was distrusted equally by the court and by the radical movement. In 1791–1792, he was at the center of a group of "Fayettists," who cast him in the role of a military strongman who could crush Jacobinism and restore some authority to the crown. With the outbreak of war, he was back in the army. After August 10, 1792, he considered an attempt to lead his troops against Paris, but the new republican government dismissed him. Before word reached him, however, he had deserted to the Prussians, who imprisoned him. Released in 1797, he returned to France under Napoléon. After 1815, he was involved in the left-wing liberal opposition to the restored Bourbon monarchy and was adopted as a symbolic leader of the 1830 Revolution.

Louis XVI (1754–1793)

Louis XVI was the grandson of Louis XV. He was married to Marie-Antoinette of Austria in 1770, crowned king in 1774, and despite some efforts at reform prior to 1789, was unable to save the absolute monarchy. After 1789, he never fully accepted his role as a constitutional monarch and tried to flee with his family in June 1791. Overthrown and imprisoned on August 10, 1792, he was tried by the Convention in December and guillotined on January 21, 1793. His son and heir, Louis XVII, died in captivity in 1795, and he was eventually succeeded by his younger brothers Louis XVIII (1814/15–1824) and Charles X (1824–1830).

Marat, Jean-Paul (1743–1793)

Swiss by origin, Jean-Paul Marat was both a doctor and a radical writer before the revolution. In 1789, he started publishing his journal, *Ami du Peuple (Friend of the People),* which became more incendiary as the revolution progressed. Popular with the *sans-culottes,* he was forced into hiding after the Champ de Mars massacre, was involved in the insurrection of August 10, 1792, and was the prime mover behind the September massacres. A member of the Convention, he was arraigned by the Girondins before the Revolutionary Tribunal in April 1793, but he was acquitted in triumph. Assassinated by the Girondin sympathizer, Charlotte Corday, on July 13, 1793, he briefly became an idol of the Jacobins.

Marie-Antoinette

Marie-Antoinette (1755–1793) was the youngest daughter of Maria-Theresa of Austria. Married to the future Louis XVI in 1770, she was the butt of rumor and scandalous gossip because she was Austrian and because, until 1777, the marriage had failed to produce an heir. In 1789, she advocated the use of force against the insurrection in Paris and in the popular mind became associated with the counter-revolutionary cabal at court. When war broke out in 1792, she maintained correspondence with Austria and was suspected of being at the center of a treasonous "Austrian Committee" in the Tuileries. Imprisoned with Louis XVI and her children on August 10, 1792, she was guillotined on October 16, 1793.

National Guard

A citizens' militia created in Paris in July 1789 to keep law and order in the capital while also defending the city against royal troops during the revolutionary upheavals. Poorer sections of the population were excluded, but the ranks were thrown open to them during the military crisis of the summer of 1792. Provincial detachments of the National Guard, known as *fédérés,* were instrumental in the overthrow of the monarchy on August 10, 1792.

Necker, Jacques (1732–1804)

A Genevan banker, Jacques Necker was French finance minister from 1777 to 1781, and he published the first-ever public accounts. For this, and because he hid the costs of French intervention in the American War of Independence, he earned a reputation for financial genius. He was recalled to office in 1788, and his subsequent dismissal by the king in July 1789 was one of the catalysts for the popular uprising that led to the fall of the Bastille in Paris. Remaining as finance minister, he was discredited when he opposed the nationalization of Church lands and when state finances were hit by a shortfall in tax revenue. He resigned in September 1790 and returned to Geneva.

Refractory Priests

Priests who refused to take the clerical oath: also known as "non-jurors."

Robespierre, Maximilien

A lawyer from Arras in northern France, Maximilien Robespierre (1758–1794) espoused enlightened causes in his early legal career before being elected to the Estates-General. Elected as the public prosecutor of Paris in 1791–1792, he retained heavy political influence through the Jacobin club. He opposed Brissot in his campaign for war and was involved in the insurrection of August 10, 1792. Elected to the Convention, he sat with the Mountain and joined the Committee of Public Safety in July 1793. He became one of the leading spokesmen for The Terror in the government, in the Convention, and among the Jacobins. He was arrested and guillotined along with his closest associates when the Convention asserted itself against The Terror in the parliamentary coup of Thermidor, July 27–28, 1794.

Saint-Just, Louis-Antoine (1767–1794)

A young revolutionary idealist and acolyte of Robespierre, Saint-Just was elected to the Convention and then to the Committee of Public Safety in May 1793. He became one of its spokesmen in the Convention, defending the policies of The Terror. He was guillotined along with Robespierre and his other associates during the coup of Thermidor.

Sans-culottes

Called *sans-culottes* ("without knee-breeches") because they disdained "aristocratic" breeches in favor of long trousers, the Parisian popular militants were mobilized by the Paris sections and the popular political clubs. Driven by anger at economic scarcity and high prices, they demanded drastic measures, such as the death penalty for hoarders and speculators and the creation of "revolutionary armies" to requisition food supplies from the countryside. But the *sans-culottes* also had a democratic, egalitarian program of direct democracy and supported the utmost prosecution of the war. They were a coalition of master craftsmen and the journeymen who worked and lived with them. They also had leadership in the form of the radical Enragés and then the Hébertistes. Cowed after the execution of the latter, the *sans-culottes* met their final defeat when the insurrection of Prairial in 1795 was crushed.

Sections

Electoral wards in larger cities. There were forty-eight sections in Paris. Each had an assembly, a police commissioner, a justice of the peace and, from August 1792, "revolutionary" committees of surveillance alongside a "civil committee" that ran day-to-day affairs. Also endowed with popular political societies, the sections proved to be the bedrock of the *sans-culotte* movement. After Thermidor, they were replaced by larger *arrondissements*, of which there were twelve in Paris.

Sieyès, Emmanuel (1748–1836)

A clergyman by training, Emmanuel Sieyès wrote pamphlets condemning privilege during the great debate surrounding the Estates-General in 1788–1789; the most influential, *What Is the Third Estate?* He was a deputy to the Estates-General and one of the prime movers behind the Tennis Court Oath and the Declaration of the Rights of Man and the Citizen. He was elected to the Convention, but he kept his head down ("J'ai vécu"—"I survived," he later replied when asked what he did during the revolution). Elected to the legislative councils under the Directory, he also served as a diplomat before being chosen as a director in 1799. He used this position to engineer the Brumaire coup and, though he helped to draft the Napoleonic constitution of 1800, he refused to play second fiddle to Bonaparte and rejected a position as a consul.

Michael Rapport

See Also Democracy, Dictatorship, and Fascism; Documentaries of Revolution; European Revolutions of 1848; Human Rights, Morality, Social Justice, and Revolution; Inequality, Class, and Revolution; Music and Revolution; Nationalism and Revolution; Paris Commune of 1871; Population, Economic Development, and Revolution; Reform, Rebellion, Civil War, Coup D'etat, and Revolution; Russian Revolution of 1917; Terrorism; Trends in Revolution; War and Revolution

References and Further Readings

Andress, David. 1999. *French Society in Revolution 1789–1799*. Manchester: Manchester University Press.

Aston, Nigel. 2004. *The French Revolution 1789–1804: Authority, Liberty and the Search for Stability*. Basingstoke, England: Palgrave Macmillan.

Best, Geoffrey, ed. 1988. *The Permanent Revolution: The French Revolution and Its Legacy, 1789–1989*. London: Fontana Press.

Blanning, Tim. 1986. *The Origins of the French Revolutionary Wars*. London: Longman.

———. 1996. *The French Revolutionary Wars 1787–1802*. London: Arnold.

Broers, Michael. 1996. *Europe under Napoléon 1799–1815*. London: Arnold.

Burke, Edmund. 1790 (1968 ed.). *Reflections on the Revolution in France and on the Proceedings in Certain Societies in London Relative to that Event*. Harmondsworth, England: Penguin.

Cobban, Alfred. 1946. *Historians and the Causes of the French Revolution*. London: Historical Association.

———. 1964. *The Social Interpretation of the French Revolution*. Cambridge: Cambridge University Press.

Darnton, R. 1982. *The Literary Underground of the Old Regime*. Cambridge, MA: Harvard University Press.

———. 1996. *The Forbidden Bestsellers of Pre-Revolutionary France*. London: Harper Collins.

Dickinson, H. T. 1985. *British Radicalism and the French Revolution, 1789–1815*. Oxford: Blackwell Press.

Doyle, William. 1980. *Origins of the French Revolution*. Oxford: Oxford University Press.

———. 1989. *The Oxford History of the French Revolution*. Oxford: Oxford University Press.

———. 2001. *The French Revolution: A Very Short Introduction*. Oxford: Oxford University Press.

Furet, François. 1978 (trans. 1981). *Interpreting the French Revolution*. Cambridge: Cambridge University Press.

Gough, Hugh. 1998. *The Terror in the French Revolution*. Basingstoke, England: Macmillan.

Herr, R. 1958. *The Eighteenth-Century Revolution in Spain*. Princeton, NJ: Princeton University Press.

Jones, Colin. 2002. *The Great Nation: France from Louis XV to Napoléon*. London: Penguin.

Keep, John. 1968–1969. "1917: The Tyranny of Paris over Petrograd," *Soviet Studies* 20 (1968–1969): 22–35.

Lefebvre, Georges. 1939 (trans. 1947). *The Coming of the French Revolution*. Princeton, NJ: Princeton University Press.

Lucas, Colin. 1973. "Nobles, Bourgeois and the Origins of the French Revolution," *Past and Present* 60 (August 1973): 84–126.

Marx, Karl, and Friedrich Engels. 1848 (1948). *The Communist Manifesto*. New York: International Publishers.

Mori, Jennifer. 2000. *Britain in the Age of the French Revolution, 1785–1820*. Harlow, England: Pearson.

Paine, Thomas. 1791–1792. *Rights of Man*. London: J. S. Jordan.

Rapport, Michael. 2000. *Nationality and Citizenship in Revolutionary France: The Treatment of Foreigners, 1789–1799*. Oxford: Oxford University Press.

Rousseau, Jean-Jacques. 1762 (trans. 1968). *The Social Contract*. Harmondsworth, England: Penguin.

Rudé, George. 1964. *Revolutionary Europe 1783–1815*. Glasgow: Fontana.

Said, Edward W. 1985. *Orientalism*. Harmondsworth, England: Penguin.

Shlapentokh, Dmitry. 1997. *The French Revolution and the Russian Anti-Democratic Tradition: A Case of False Consciousness*. New Brunswick, NJ: Transaction Publishers.

Simms, Brendan. 1998. *The Struggle for Mastery in Germany, 1779–1850*. Basingstoke, England: Macmillan.

Soboul, Albert. 1974. *The French Revolution 1787–1799*. 2 vols. London: NLB.

Sutherland, Donald. 1985. *France 1789–1815: Revolution and Counterrevolution*. London: Fontana.

Tackett, Timothy. 1986. *Religion, Revolution and Regional Culture in Eighteenth Century France: The Ecclesiastical Oath of 1791*. Princeton, NJ: Princeton University Press.

G

Ghana's Independence Revolution: De-colonizing the Model Colony (1946–1972)

CHRONOLOGY

1471 The Portuguese arrive on the West Coast of Africa and soon after begin construction of Castle of São Jorge da Mina, now known as Elmina Castle.

1637 The Dutch capture the Castle of São Jorge da Mina from the Portuguese.

1665 The English capture Cape Coast Castle from the Swedes. The castle becomes the headquarters of the Royal African Company.

1808 The British government abolishes the transatlantic slave trade.

1844 The British government takes over the administration of those coastal settlements under the control of her merchants and signs the Bond of 1844 with local chiefs.

1870 The British purchase all the Dutch castles and forts on the coast.

1874 The British settlements become the Colony of the Gold Coast.

1901–1902 Ashanti Protectorate and Northern Territories become part of the Gold Coast Colony.

1925 Governor Guggisberg introduces a new constitution for the colony that creates provincial councils of chiefs and expands chiefly representation in the legislative council.

1946 Governor Burns introduces a new constitution that gives Africans a majority in the legislative council.

1947 The United Gold Coast Convention (UGCC) is founded. Kwame Nkrumah is recruited by the UGCC to be the full-time organizing secretary.

1948 Demonstration by ex-servicemen ends in shooting and riots that leave twenty-nine dead and vast amounts of property destroyed. Executive of UGCC arrested.

1949 Nkrumah breaks from the UGCC and forms the Convention People's Party (CPP). The CPP initiates "Positive Action," and the government imprisons Nkrumah and the CPP leadership.

1951	The CPP wins a majority of the seats in the newly expanded legislative council. Nkrumah is released from prison and becomes the leader of government business.
	Five-Year Development Plan drawn up to cost $330 million.
1954	The CPP wins 72 out of 104 seats in the expanded legislative council.
1955	The National Liberation Movement (NLM), primarily an Asante political party, unites with other anti-CPP groups to form the United Party. They advocate a federal form of government.
1957	The CPP wins the final election before independence with 71 of the 104 seats contested. On March 6, the Gold Coast becomes the independent country of Ghana.
1958	The CPP government passes the Preventive Detention Act, which allows for the detention of opponents without trial.
1959	Nkrumah announces a new Five-Year Development Plan that is to cost $700 million.
1960	Ghana becomes a republic with Nkrumah its first president.
1961	The Ghana-Guinea-Mali Union announced.
1962	Attempted assassination of Nkrumah at the border town of Kulungugu.
1964	A national referendum makes Ghana a one-party state.
	The construction of the Akosombo Dam is completed.
1965	Ghana hosts the Organization of African Unity (OAU) meeting in Accra.
1966	Nkrumah overthrown by the army and the police. They establish the National Liberation Council (NLC).
1972	Exiled former president Nkrumah dies while seeking medical treatment in Romania.

INTRODUCTION

Kwame Nkrumah organized the movement that forced the British to grant independence to what they had thought of as their model colony, the Gold Coast. In 1957 it became the independent country of Ghana, the first European colony in West Africa to achieve this status. Nkrumah attempted to employ a Socialist development approach to industrialize Ghana and modernize its agriculture. He also pushed for unity among the African states that subsequently followed Ghana's path to independence. These pan-African efforts achieved limited success, and his economic policies were bitterly criticized. His increasingly authoritarian government was accused of corruption and ineffectiveness, and in 1966 it was overthrown by members of Ghana's armed forces and police. Nevertheless, Nkrumah is still viewed as the main hero of Ghana's independence struggle, a champion of the aspirations of Africa's poor, an opponent of colonialism and neo-colonialism, and a pioneer in the movement for African unity.

BACKGROUND: CULTURE AND HISTORY

Ghana is situated on the middle of the West African coastline a few degrees north of the equator. The only major seasonal change is the difference between the rainy season and the dry season. Much of the southern part of the country consists of various types of rain forest, while the north is predominantly savanna woodland. The highest point in the country is less than 3,000 feet above sea level, with the result that the climate all over the country is tropical, and in spite of the area's long contact with Europeans, it was never attractive to white settlers as was the case for highland areas in East Africa.

In 1471, when the Portuguese were the first Europeans to arrive on the West African coast, the area was only sparsely populated. Akan people had been moving into the rain forest from the savanna from as early as the fourteenth century. They came in contact with people who had preceded them, like the Ga-Dangme, and centralized societies gradually began to emerge in the rain forest and on the coast. In general this coincided with the coming of Europeans, who were to have a profound impact on how these societies developed. Initially, contact northward with the savanna was of predominant importance for the Akan people. For example, the gold that the rain forest yielded was traded in this direction. But as the European presence on the coast expanded in the seventeenth century to include the Dutch, the French, the English, the Danes, the Swedes, and the Brandenburgers, this focus began to change.

Kwame Nkrumah, first president of Ghana, being interviewed by reporters at New York International Airport, after he arrived from Accra, 1960. (Library of Congress)

For the next two centuries European contact with this part of West Africa remained very much peripheral. Around the castles and forts Europeans constructed on the coast to protect their trading interests, small towns developed that originally were fishing or salt production settlements for inland states. In the eighteenth century, as the transatlantic slave trade became the major European trading activity with the coast, these towns began to rival and later superceded their inland counterparts in importance. They were the entry point for European merchandise like firearms, liquor, metal goods, and cloth. Europeans also introduced new food crops—cassava and maize from the Americas, and bananas, coconuts, and sweet potatoes from Asia—that spread into the interior and became a major supplement to the various kinds of yams that had been the staple food crops of this region.

An important cultural interaction followed from this contact. Europeans brought their languages, education, and Christian proselytizing. During the era of the slave trade, this influence was confined to the settlements immediately around the European forts and castles. However, in the nineteenth century, when the slave trade came to an end, European missionary organizations expanded their activities into the interior. Christianity was coupled with Western education and proved extremely successful, so that today the vast majority of the people in southern Ghana are members of some Christian denomination.

In the nineteenth century the British began to emerge as the dominant European power on the coast. As the nation pioneering the way into the industrial era, it was not surprising that this was so. New products like palm oil, tropical hardwoods, and later wild rubber became important items of trade for Britain's expanding industrial economy and drew her merchants to this area. After a period of hesitation in the earlier part of the century, in 1844 the British government took formal control of the forts and castles its merchants had established on the coast. In 1850 it bought the Danish counterparts, and in 1870 it did the same thing with the Dutch possessions. At that point, the coastal area from

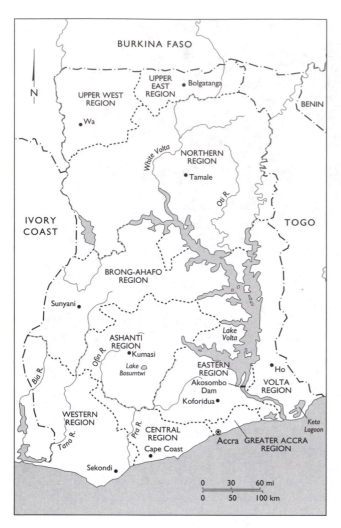

Major cities and regions of Ghana.

the Volta River in the east to the Tano River in the west was under British control.

Britain's emergence as the dominant power on the coast upset relationships with the Asante confederation, the major centralized African state in the interior. In the early part of the nineteenth century the Asante tried to extend their power all the way to the coast, but they were checked by the British, who worked with coastal peoples to prevent this. The British also made a number of attempts to invade the Asante state but did not succeed until 1874. Even then, the victory was inconclusive, but enough for the British to feel that they had eliminated the Asante threat to their settlements on the coast. In that year they proclaimed this area a British colony.

In 1896 and 1900 hostilities once again broke out with the Asante, resulting in the Asantehene, the ruler of the Asante people, eventually being deported and exiled to the Seychelles Islands in the Indian Ocean for over twenty years. At that time, the scramble for Africa was on, and other European

nations, such as the French and the Germans, had designs on the hinterland. To prevent the colony from being separated from its interior, in 1901–1902 the British established a protectorate over what had been the main area of the Asante state, which became known as the Ashanti Colony, and over a large area farther north that came to be known as the Northern Territories Protectorate. These areas were administered separately but were under the control of the colony's governor. In essence, the entire area became the British colony of the Gold Coast.

Initially, there was an attempt to administer the colony directly using British officials. But as the size of the area under British control increased, this became impractical, and a system of indirect rule developed in which African chiefs were incorporated into the colony's administration. At the same time the British believed that the "civilized coast," which had been affected by long contact with Europeans, required Western-style municipal government. The educated coastal elite—doctors, newspaper editors, and most of all lawyers who had received their training in Britain—filled the positions for Africans on the town councils that were established. But they were always outnumbered by the traditional African elite officials who were also appointed to sit on these bodies. This divided system of African participation in the colony's government created tension between what came to be known as the "traditional" elite and the Western-educated elite or "intelligentsia." Constitutional changes in the 1920s favored the traditional elite over the intelligentsia and did much to continue the rivalry between these competing groups. On the other hand, indirect rule created a highly localized political environment in which members of a wide and diverse section of the colony's population competed to control its institutions, such as courts and treasuries. Nationalist politicians were later able to take advantage of this politicized population to create the mass movement for independence.

In the 1930s, stimulated by the harsh conditions that the Great Depression created, pan-Africanist and anti-imperialist ideas gave a much more radical slant to African political expression in the colony. There were newspapers, organizations, and individuals who made what became increasingly strident attacks on colonial rule. Attempts by the large metropolitan firms that dominated the colony's economy to regulate the buying of cocoa, which had become the Gold Coast's number one export, also precipitated resistance. In 1931, and again in 1937, there were major efforts to challenge these initiatives. "Hold ups" were organized (refusals to sell cocoa crops to the metropolitan firms); they had little success in increasing prices but did much to increase local hostility toward these firms and toward colonial rule in general.

The Second World War also played an important role in heightening opposition to colonial rule. Allied war aims, which emphasized the principle of self-determination for all people, served to raise expectations in the colony that when the fighting was over, the Gold Coast could expect major advances in its political status. Over 65,000 Africans from the Gold Coast saw service during the Second World War. Many of them fought in North Africa and in the Far East, an experience that had a radicalizing effect on these men, as they came into contact with colonial subjects from India, Burma, and Ceylon, British colonies that were on the verge of independence. However, conditions immediately after the war did not live up to their expectations. Return to a peacetime economy with consumer items in short supply, inflation rampant, and a colonial government that seemed once again to favor the interests of the large metropolitan firms furthered discontent with colonial rule. The rapid development of the Cold War added an ideological component to the postwar political world that gave colonial peoples an ideal battleground for attacking colonial powers.

CONTEXT AND PROCESS OF REVOLUTION

From before the Second World War Africans had begun to anticipate that some sort of change in the colony's status was inevitable. This was the motivation behind the establishment in the 1930s of the youth movement. Dr. J. B. Danquah, a nephew of the colony's most important chief and the first Gold Coast African to obtain an academic doctorate, was the driving force behind this movement. In 1938 and 1939 he organized two conferences. Danquah made a conscious effort to bring the chiefs and the intelligentsia together, but there was no attempt to bring in newly formed organizations like labor unions. He was more interested in bringing the "thinking people" together than he was in "doing something" (Holmes 1972, 463).

In 1944, 100 years after the signing of the Bond of 1844, Governor Alan Burns introduced a new constitution that gave Africans a majority in the legislative council. The promise of further constitutional advance inspired six members of the educated elite, including Dr. Danquah, to form in 1947 the United Gold Coast Convention (UGCC), the colony's first nationwide political movement. Shortly afterward, the convention made the momentous decision to appoint a full-time organizing secretary. The man they chose was Kwame Nkrumah, who at the time was making a reputation for himself in Great Britain as one of the leading critics of British colonial rule in Africa. Nkrumah had followed a somewhat unique path for members of the educated elite in the Gold Coast. In 1935 he had gone to America rather than Great Britain for higher education. He had spent ten

years obtaining a bachelor of arts from Lincoln University in Pennsylvania, a bachelor of theology from Lincoln Seminary, and a master of arts from the University of Pennsylvania. In 1945 he had gone to Great Britain to study law as well as for a doctorate in philosophy from the London School of Economics. Anti-colonial politics rather than academic study had become his main focus, and in 1945 he enhanced his political reputation by becoming the joint secretary, with George Padmore, the veteran revolutionary from Trinidad, West Indies, of the Fifth Pan-African Congress, held in Manchester, England.

When Nkrumah arrived in the Gold Coast, the colony was on the brink of an explosion. In the colony's cocoa-growing areas, the colonial government's approach to dealing with a devastating outbreak of cocoa swollen-shoot virus was extremely unpopular. The only method of preventing the spread of this virus, spread by mealy bugs, was to cut down all the cocoa trees in affected areas, regardless of whether they were infected or healthy. The compensation that the government offered fell far short of what even infected trees could produce at a time when cocoa prices had finally begun to rise. There were violent clashes between cocoa farmers and the Agriculture Department's cutting-out gangs.

The situation in the urban areas was no better. In the immediate postwar economy, consumer goods were in short supply and inflation was rampant. In 1947 Nii Kwabena Bonne II, a traditional chief in the colony's capital, Accra, began a boycott campaign directed against the big metropolitan firms and Lebanese merchants. It did manage to get these parties to agree to reduce their profit margins, but this meant only a small reduction in prices. Early in 1948, after the end of the boycott, disgruntled ex-servicemen staged a demonstration to protest their lack of jobs and inadequate pensions. It quickly got out of control, and major rioting broke out and spread to other towns in the colony. Before the colonial government was able to restore order, twenty-nine people had been killed and millions of dollars worth of damage had been done to property.

The colonial government quickly sought out scapegoats and arrested the leaders of the UGCC, including Nkrumah. It also established a commission of inquiry to investigate "the recent disturbances." In hearings before this body (the Watson Commission, named after its chairman, Aiken Watson), the friction that had already developed between Nkrumah and the executive of the UGCC rapidly came to the surface (Watson, et al., 1948, 5). They blamed Nkrumah for what had happened, and they made every effort to disassociate themselves from what they felt was his dangerous radicalism. From the start they had disagreed over his "pan-Africanism." His use of the term *comrade* also upset them, but most of all they felt threatened by his organizing of youth groups (Nkrumah 1957, 89). In the 1940s there had been a proliferation of youth groups as a flood of elementary-school graduates had moved into southern towns and villages. Few could find jobs, and they were easily radicalized. They were people, not always that young, who were hostile to the chiefs and suspicious of the professionals. Nkrumah had brought many of these youth organizations together to form the Committee on Youth Organization (CYO), which adopted the slogan "Full self-government now," in contrast to the UGCC's "Self-government within the shortest time" (Nkrumah 1957, 97). Not surprisingly in the atmosphere of recrimination that the Watson Commission created, these differences could no longer be ignored. Just before the executive of the UGCC moved to expel him in 1949, Nkrumah broke away from the UGCC and, using the nucleus provided by the CYO, formed his own party, the Convention People's Party (CPP).

The first major challenge the CPP faced was how to react to the new constitution proposed by an all-African committee under the chairmanship of the colony's most senior African judge, Justice Henley Coussey. Initially Nkrumah rejected it as a "Trojan gift horse," and called for "Positive Action," which was to consist of civil disobedience (Austin 1964, 87). With the memory of the 1948 riots still vividly in mind, the government quickly moved to preempt this action and arrested Nkrumah and most of the CPP executive. In spite of his being incarcerated and having dismissed the new constitution as "bogus and fraudulent," Nkrumah led his party to participate in the elections that took place in 1951 (Austin 1964, 87). The CPP won twenty-nine seats to the UGCC's two. With a very comfortable majority, Nkrumah, who had to be released from prison, became the leader of government business in the new legislature. A year later, after a modification to the constitution, he was allowed to acquire the more substantive title of prime minister.

The party quickly shifted from Positive Action to what Nkrumah described as Tactical Action. The early 1950s was a period of unparalleled prosperity for the colony, and this helped to reduce friction between the CPP and colonial officials. Indeed, Nkrumah and Governor Arden-Clarke developed a close working relationship. A five-year development plan that was to cost $336 million was drawn up, and there was considerable expansion of the colony's infrastructure.

Nevertheless, criticism began to surface. There were those who felt that the CPP, now that it was in power, had forsaken its policy of self-government. The rate of Africanization of the civil service also seemed to have slowed down. The financing plan for the Volta River Dam project was criticized as "economic enslavement," and there were ugly rumors about corruption, with Nkrumah himself implicated (Gold Coast Legislative Assembly Debates, February 23, 1953, cited in Austin 1964, 166).

Nevertheless, the CPP was able to score an even more commanding victory in the election of 1954, winning 74 of the 104 constituencies in a now even larger legislature. The road to independence seemed clear. But before it could happen, there developed a major challenge to CPP government in the Ashanti region. Ironically, it was a dramatic increase in the world price of cocoa that precipitated this challenge. The CPP tried to stabilize the price paid to cocoa farmers, ostensibly to prevent inflation and to use the surplus to fund development projects. Cocoa farming areas all over the country were up in arms, particularly the Ashanti region, where most of the colony's cocoa was grown, and where there was already opposition to the CPP. Cocoa farmers, chiefs, members of the UGCC opposition, and young men who had become disgruntled with the CPP came together to form the National Liberation Movement (NLM). They appropriated the symbols of Asante nationalism, and most importantly got the support of the *asantehene*. The NLM called for a federal form of government and forced the colonial government into holding one more election in 1956 before granting independence.

However, the CPP was able to play on the historic fear of Asante domination and once again scored a major electoral victory, winning 71 of the 104 contested seats. The British government sought to reassure the NLM that in an independent Ghana, constitutional safeguards would protect regional autonomy. With the promise of this compromise, Ghana became independent on March 6, 1957.

IMPACTS

Rather than compromising, as had been promised, Nkrumah took advantage of the divisions that existed in Ashanti and divided it into two regions (Ashanti and Brong Ahafo) to weaken the potential threat of Asante nationalism. He very effectively played off chiefly and ethnic rivalries in this area, and in general moved to bring the country's chieftaincy to heel by stripping them of their political and judicial functions. To curb opposition from other opponents, in 1958 his government passed the Preventive Detention Act, which allowed for detention for up to five years without appeal to the courts for conduct considered prejudicial to the defense and security of the state. The government also moved to control civic organizations, like labor unions, and in 1959, Nkrumah proclaimed that the party was the state and the state was the party (10th Anniversary Address, Evening News, June 14, 1959, cited in Austin 1964, 383). In 1960 the CPP conducted a plebiscite to determine whether Ghana should become a republic. It was a foregone conclusion that this would pass, and the new constitution gave the state even more power to appoint and dismiss civil servants. Five years later, in protest at Great Britain's inability to suppress the unilateral declaration of independence by the white minority in Rhodesia, Ghana severed its remaining ties with its former mother country by withdrawing from the British Commonwealth.

Nkrumah had promised Ghanaians that the CPP would transform the country "into a paradise in ten years," and right after independence a massive Second Five-Year Development Plan was unveiled (*Ashanti Pioneer,* March 5, 1949). Luckily, the country enjoyed significant reserves that had built up after the Second World War. High cocoa prices had contributed to this, and the assumption was that this situation would continue. A major effort was made to expand the cocoa industry, which was still suffering from the swollen-shoot virus. Unfortunately, however, the price for cocoa declined dramatically, and Ghana also failed to attract significant foreign investment from the capitalist West. As a result, in 1961 the country adopted a much more Socialist orientation, which in 1963 resulted in a Seven-Year Development Plan that called for a massive increase in taxation.

Nkrumah had also maintained that Ghana's "independence [was] meaningless unless it [was] closely linked up with the total liberation of Africa," and he committed himself to forging pan-African unity (Nkrumah 1997, 67). Ghana hosted conferences that inspired leading nationalists from all over Africa. In 1958 Nkrumah formed a union with Guinea that had voted no to joining a French-inspired community of African nations. Two years later Mali also joined this union. However, in the 1960s, as the floodgates of independence opened up, Ghana was challenged as the leader of the pan-Africanist movement. The most important challenge came from Nigeria, and bitter disputes soon erupted over the fate of institutions that they shared in common, such as the West African Currency Board, the West African Court of Appeal, and the West African Military Command. Eventually Ghana withdrew from membership in these organizations to prevent the country from being exposed to what Nkrumah described as dangerous neo-colonial influences. In general, independent African nations divided into two camps: the Monrovia group and the Casablanca group, which was politically more radical in its economic and political policies and in its vision of what pan-African union meant. The political crisis that developed in the Congo, after it became independent in 1960, did much to exacerbate the tensions between these different groups. Ghana wanted this crisis resolved by African nations and to keep out others, particularly Belgium, the former colonizing power. However, Ghana's deep involvement in the crisis served to isolate Nkrumah from most of his West African neighbors to the extent that when the Organization of African Unity was formed, Nkrumah was little more then a critic of what he felt was a woefully diluted African union.

By the 1960s Ghana's collapsing economy coupled with rampant corruption and increasing isolation abroad had dramatically undermined Nkrumah's popularity. His in-creasingly authoritarian government had eliminated all forms of legitimate protest, and his enemies turned to assassination. In 1962, at the border town of Kulungugu, he was nearly killed in a grenade attack. In 1964 he narrowly missed being shot by a police constable on guard duty in his office. These assassination attempts were followed by arrests and purges of those perceived as opponents. The most notable victim after the 1964 attempt was Dr. J. B. Danquah, who was to die in prison one year later.

In the midst of the Cold War, the CIA was inevitably linked to these assassination plots, and revelations about the CIA's role in Africa in the 1970s lent substantial credence to these suspicions. However, there was obviously considerable local opposition to a government that many felt was destroying Ghana. In 1966, while Nkrumah was out of the country engaged in perhaps one of his most quixotic endeavors, to negotiate a peace between North Vietnam and the United States, members of the Ghanaian military and the police overthrew his government.

In spite of this ignominious ending, there was clearly more to Nkrumah than the sum of his many failures. He was the towering figure of the independence movement, and it is not surprising that he was wooed both by the West and by the East. Undoubtedly the most important indication of his enduring status is how much better he looks in retrospect than those who overthrew and succeeded him. Unfortunately, his violent removal brought Ghana into line with what was to emerge as the dominant trend in the continent in the 1960s and 1970s—the military intervention in politics.

PEOPLE AND ORGANIZATIONS

Afrifa, Akwasi Amankwaa (1936–1979)

Afrifa was one of the major leaders of the coup that overthrew Nkrumah in 1966. He received his military training in Great Britain, and he served in the Ghana contingent in the Congo in 1961.

Botsio, Kojo (1916–2001)

Botsio became one of Nkrumah's close confidants in England and returned to the Gold Coast with him in 1947. He was one of the founders of the Convention People's Party (CPP) and its first general secretary. He was arrested by the colonial authorities as a result of the CPP's Positive Action campaign. He was elected to the legislature in 1951 and became the first minister of education and social welfare. He subsequently held other ministerial positions in the CPP government. He spent some time in custody after the 1966 coup.

Busia, Dr. Kofi Abrefa (1913–1978)

Busia obtained a doctorate in social anthropology from Oxford University. In 1949 he joined the faculty of the newly created University College of the Gold Coast. In 1951 he was elected to the legislative assembly. He became an important voice in the National Liberation Movement and went to London in 1955 to represent their interests. In 1957 he became the leader of the United Party that opposed the CPP. In 1959 he went into exile and only returned after the coup of 1966. In 1969, as the leader of the Progress Party, he became president of what then was Ghana's Second Republic.

Convention People's Party (CPP)

The CPP was created in June 1949 in a break away from the United Gold Coast Convention. It won elections in February 1951 and stayed in power until 1966, when it was disbanded. When political parties re-emerged in Ghana in the 1990s, there was considerable struggle among those who considered themselves Nkrumahists to claim the party's name. Eventually a CPP party did emerge in the 2000 elections, but it won only 1.8 percent of the vote.

Danquah, Dr. Joseph Boakye (1895–1965)

Danquah studied in London, where he obtained a doctorate in ethics from London University and qualified as a lawyer. In the 1930s he was active in newspaper publication in the Gold Coast. In 1937 he founded the Gold Coast Youth Congress, and in 1947 he was one of the founders of the United Gold Coast Convention (UGCC). In 1948 he was arrested with Nkrumah and four other members of the UGCC as a result of the riots in the colony. Nevertheless, he was appointed a member of the Coussey Committee to design a new constitution for the colony. By this time he had parted ways with Nkrumah. He ran unsuccessfully for election in 1954 and 1956. In 1960 he was the leader of the United Party but lost badly against Nkrumah. He was imprisoned in 1961 and released in 1962, and imprisoned again in 1964. One year later, while still in prison, he died. Danquah was most responsible for Ghana adopting this name when the country became independent. He argued that there was a historical connection between the ancient empire of Ghana (located several hundred miles to the northwest) and modern-day Ghana. When the former state collapsed in the thirteenth century, supposedly some of its members had migrated to present-day Ghana.

Gbedemah, Komla Agbelli (1912–1998)

Gbedemah in 1948 became the chairman of the Committee on Youth Organizations. He joined the UGCC and was a founding member of the CPP. While Nkrumah was in prison, he ran the CPP and edited the party's newspaper. He won a seat in the 1951 election. From 1951 to 1952, he was the minister of health and labor, from 1952–1954 he headed the ministry of commerce and industry, and from 1954–1961 he was finance minister. When Nkrumah moved to the left the two became estranged, and eventually Nkrumah fired him and he went into exile. He returned to Ghana after the 1966 coup and organized the National Alliance of Liberals but was barred from taking the seat he won in the 1969 elections.

Grant, "Pa" George Alfred (1878–1956)

Grant was a wealthy timber merchant and often referred to as the "the father of Gold Coast politics." He was one of the founding fathers of the UGCC and its first president.

Lewis, Sir William Arthur (1915–1991)

Lewis was born in Saint Lucia, West Indies, and received a Ph.D. in economics from the London School of Economics in 1940. He was an expert in developmental economics, and in 1953 he advised the Gold Coast government on industrialization. In 1957 he was appointed economic advisor to the Ghana government. His ideas about stimulating economic development through increasing agricultural productivity and encouraging foreign investment were, in theory, the basis for Ghana's first development plan.

National Liberation Movement (NLM)

NLM was the political movement formed in Asante in September 1954 under the leadership of K. A. Busia. It was made up of those in favor of a federal system of government versus the centralized system that Nkrumah wanted. In October 1957 it joined with other parties in opposition to the CPP to form the United Party with Busia as its leader.

Nkrumah, Kwame (1909–1972)

Nkrumah was born at Nkroful, a small village in the Western Region of Ghana. He was educated in Roman Catholic schools and at Achimota College, the premier secondary school in the

Gold Coast in the 1930s. He attended university in the United States and then in Great Britain. In 1945 he was the joint secretary of the Fifth Pan-African Congress, held in Manchester, England. In 1947 he returned to the Gold Coast as the general secretary of the UGCC. In 1949 he organized his own party, the CPP, which demanded "Self-Government Now." He was imprisoned in 1950 but was elected to the legislative assembly. In 1951 he became the leader of government business and in 1952 the prime minister. In 1953 he introduced his "Motion of Destiny" for Ghana's independence, but it was three years before this was achieved. Quickly his rule became more authoritarian. In 1959 the opposition was expelled from parliament. He became president for life in 1962, and in 1964 Ghana became a one-party state. While he was away on a trip to China in 1966 he was overthrown by a military coup. His main supporter, Sékou Touré of Guinea, proclaimed him co-president, and Nkrumah spent the rest of his life in Guinea. Stricken with cancer, he was flown to a clinic in Bucharest, Romania, where he died on April 27, 1972.

Padmore, George (Née Malcolm Nurse) (1903–1959)

Padmore was born in Trinidad, West Indies, and studied in the United States. He became a member of the Communist Party and received training in the Soviet Union. Eventually he settled in Great Britain, where he became a leader of pan-African resistance to British imperialism. Along with Nkrumah he organized the Fifth Pan-African Congress in Manchester, England. Shortly after Ghana's independence, Nkrumah appointed him to be the head of Ghana's new African Bureau to advance the cause of African unity. When he died in England, his body was brought back for burial in Ghana.

Trades Union Congress (TUC)

In September 1945 a number of labor unions in the Gold Coast came together to form the TUC. It collapsed after the Positive Action of 1950, but in 1953 reunited and soon became an important adjunct to the CPP. After the fall of the CPP, the union had a checkered career, but it is presently the most important organization of labor unions in Ghana.

United Gold Coast Convention (UGCC)

UGCC was founded in 1947 and was the first political party in the Gold Coast to talk about self-government. Its immedi-
ate aim was to replace chiefs on the legislative council with members of the educated elite. In 1947 it hired Kwame Nkrumah to be its organizing secretary and was soon overtaken by the CPP. It was defeated in the election of 1951 and was dissolved the following year.

Volta River Dam Project

Construction of the Volta River Dam, located near the town of Akosombo on the Volta River, Ghana's largest river, began in 1961 and was completed in 1965. Lake Volta, which was formed by the earth-and-rock fill structure of the dam, extends 250 miles to the north and is one of the world's largest man-made lakes. Nkrumah hoped that the hydroelectricity generated from the dam would provide the nucleus for Ghana's industrialization. To ensure that the loans for building the dam would be repaid, most of the power generated was sold to the Volta Aluminum Company (VALCO), a consortium of aluminum interests created by Kaiser Aluminum of the United States. Though Ghana has large aluminum-ore deposits, the bauxite for smelting is brought from Jamaica in the West Indies. Resettlement of people displaced by the creation of Lake Volta, the terms of the power-supply agreement with VALCO, and failure to develop Ghana's own bauxite reserves made the project controversial.

Roger Gocking

See Also Colonialism, Anti-Colonialism, and Neo-Colonialism; Nationalism and Revolution

References and Further Readings
Adamafio, Tawia. 1982. *By Nkrumah's Side: The Labour and the Wounds.* London: Rex Collings.
Alexander, Henry T. 1965. *African Tightrope: My Two Years as Nkrumah's Chief of Staff.* London: Pall Mall Press.
Allman, Jean. 1993. *The Quills of the Porcupine: Asante Nationalism in an Emergent Ghana.* Madison: University of Wisconsin Press.
Austin, Dennis. 1964. *Politics in Ghana: 1946–1960.* London: Oxford University Press.
Bing, Geoffrey. 1968. *Reap the Whirlwind: An Account of Kwame Nkrumah's Ghana from 1950-1966.* London: MacGibbon and Kee.
Birmingham, David. 1998. *Kwame Nkrumah: The Father of African Nationalism.* Rev. ed. Athens: Ohio University Press.
Bretton, Henry. 1966. *The Rise and Fall of Kwame Nkrumah: A Study of Personal Rule in Africa.* New York: Frederick Praeger.
Davidson, Basil. 1973. *Black Star: A View of the Life and Times of Kwame Nkrumah.* London: Allen Lane.
Fitch, B., and M. Oppenheimer. 1966. *End of an Illusion.* New York: Monthly Review Press.
Gocking, Roger. 2005. *The History of Ghana.* Westport, CT: Greenwood Press.
Hadjor, Kofi B. 1988. *Nkrumah and Ghana: The Dilemna of Post-Colonial Power.* London: Kegan Paul International.

Holmes, Baron A. 1972. *Economic and Political Organizations in the Gold Coast, 1920–1945.* (PhD diss. University of Chicago).

James, C. L. R. 1977. *Nkrumah and the Ghana Revolution.* Westport, CT: Lawrence Hill.

Jones, Trevor. 1976. *Ghana's First Republic 1960–1966: The Pursuit of the Political Kingdom.* London: Methuen.

Le Vine, Victor T. 1975. *Political Corruption: The Ghana Case.* Stanford, CA: Hoover Institution.

Nkrumah, Kwame. 1957. *Ghana: The Autobiography of Kwame Nkrumah.* New York: International Publishers.

———. 1968. *Dark Days in Ghana.* London: Lawrence and Wishart.

———. 1997. "Africa Must Be Free." Pp. 67–68 in *Selected Speeches of Kwame Nkrumah,* vol. 2. Edited by S. Obeng. Accra, Ghana: Afram Publications.

Padmore, George. 1953. *The Gold Coast Revolution: The Struggle of an African People from Slavery to Freedom.* London: D. Robson.

Rathbone, Richard. 2000. *Nkrumah and the Chiefs: The Politics of Chieftaincy in Ghana 1951–1960.* Athens: Ohio University Press.

Rooney, David. 1989. *Kwame Nkrumah: The Political Kingdom in the Third World.* New York: St. Martin's Press.

Sherwood, Marika. 1996. *Kwame Nkrumah: The Years Abroad 1935–1947.* Legon, Ghana: Freedom Publications.

Thompson, Scott W. 1969. *Ghana's Foreign Policy 1957–1966.* Princeton, NJ: Princeton University Press.

Watson, Aiken, A. Dalgleish, and Keith A. Murray. 1948 *Report of the Commission of Enquiry into Disturbances in the Gold Coast: 1948.* London: HMSO.

Greek Civil War

CHRONOLOGY

1821	Greek uprising against Ottoman rule.
1832	Greek independence recognized internationally.
1912–1913	Balkan Wars. Greece doubles its territory.
1916	Liberal prime minister Eleftherios Venizelos clashes with King Constantine I over Greece's participation in WWI. This dispute becomes known as the National Schism.
1918	Socialist Workers Party of Greece founded. In 1920 the Party affiliates with Comintern and in 1924 it renames itself the Communist Party of Greece (KKE).
1920	Treaty of Sevres signed between Greece, Turkey, and other Allied powers. Greece expands territorially in Eastern Thrace and Asia Minor.
1922	The Greek army is defeated by the forces of Mustafa Kemal, leader of the Turkish Nationalists, and forced out of Asia Minor.
1923	Treaty of Lausanne signed between Greece, Turkey, and other Allied powers, precipitating a massive population exchange between Greece and Turkey, with roughly 380,000 Muslims expelled from Greece and some 1.1–1.2 million Greek Orthodox refugees expelled from Turkey. King George II leaves the country.
1924	Greece becomes a republic.
1935	On March 1, Venizelist officers launch a military rebellion against the Peoples' Party government. The coup fails and Venizelos flees Greece. Massive purges of Venizelist public officials ensue. A rigged plebiscite restores the monarchy under George II.
1936	In January, general elections lead to parliamentary deadlock, as fifteen Communist deputies hold the balance in the 300-seat parliament. (The People's Party and its allies win 143 seats versus the 141 seats of the Liberal Party and its allies).
	In April, an overwhelming parliamentary majority (but none of the Communist deputies) gives Prime Minister Ioannis Metaxas the power to govern by decree while parliament adjourns until September 30. Metaxas convinces King George II to suspend civil liberties and the parliament.
	On August 4, Metaxas establishes a dictatorship. The regime's police under Konstantinos Madiakis prove effective in neutralizing the KKE.
1940	On October 28, Italy invades Greece from Albania. The Greek army repels the invasion and pushes the Italian forces back into Albania.
1941	Metaxas dies in January.

On April 6, Germany invades Greece, assisted by Bulgaria, which had agreed in January to join the Axis in return for receiving territory in Thrace and Macedonia.

On April 27, German forces enter Athens. Germany and its allies occupy Greece until late 1944. King George II and the Greek government flee to Crete and then to Egypt.

KKE establishes the National Liberation Front (EAM) as an umbrella organization for several smaller leftist parties. Along with its military force (the yet-to-be-established National Popular Liberation Army, ELAS), EAM will dominate the resistance movement.

1942   In February, the KKE establishes ELAS. Small-scale guerrilla fighting begins.

On November 25, the first major act of sabotage at the Gorgopotamos Bridge, involving both ELAS and another resistance group (EDES), takes place under British command.

1943   ELAS successfully attacks and eliminates several small non-Communist resistance groups across the country; major clashes between ELAS and EDES in September.

Ioannis Rallis appointed prime minister of the collaborationist government in April. He initiates a major effort to assist the German occupation through the formation of a collaborationist militia, the Security Battalions.

Italy capitulates in September and Germany takes over throughout Greece.

1944   On February 29, a cease-fire is signed between ELAS and EDES. EDES survives but is confined to the Epirus region.

On March 10, EAM establishes a provisional government known as the Political Committee of National Liberation (PEEA) to antagonize the Greek government in exile.

Between May 17 and 20, a conference between politicians and resistance leaders takes place in Lebanon, ending in a major setback for the Communists. The KKE signs the Lebanon Charter, which calls for the unification of resistance forces under the exiled government and offers a minority of ministries in the post-occupation government to the KKE.

During the spring and the summer a major expansion of the Security Battalions results in clashes between ELAS and Security Battalions, especially in the Peloponnese and Macedonia.

In September, German forces begin to withdraw from Greece.

On September 26, KKE representatives, the exiled government, and British representatives sign the Caserta Agreement in Italy. This provides for the arrival of British forces to support the exiled government (now led by Georgios Papandreou), combines ELAS forces with Greek armed forces under the command of British general Ronald Scobie, and prohibits ELAS forces from entering Athens and EDES territory.

On November 4, the last German forces exit Greece. Several clashes between ELAS and the Security Battalions and other collaborationist militias result in the collaborationists' defeat. Several massacres ensue.

In early December violent clashes break out in Athens after a disagreement on the terms of the ELAS demobilization. ELAS launches a full-fledged assault, defeats EDES, neutralizes the police in Athens, and arrests tens of thousands of civilian hostages, many of whom it executes. The ELAS is ultimately defeated by the British in street battles in Athens.

1945   On January 8, the KKE flees Athens and calls for a truce.

On February 15, the Varkiza Agreement is signed, which provides for the demobilization of the ELAS. A persecution of Communist members and sympathizers ensues.

In May, Nikos Zahariadis returns to Greece from the Dachau concentration camp where he was held and resumes leadership of the KKE.

1946   At the KKE Second Plenum in February, Zahariadis announces the stepping-up of sporadic guerrilla activities.

In March, general elections are boycotted by the KKE. Highly symbolic guerrilla attacks take place, and the Peoples' Party wins and takes over the government.

In September, a plebiscite restores the monarchy.

In December, the KKE establishes the Democratic Army of Greece (DSE) and steps up the attacks.

1947   On March 12, the United States announces the Truman Doctrine, allocating $300 million to Greece for reconstruction and fighting the Communist insurgency.

In September, the KKE opts for a full-scale insurgency.

1948   The civil war is in full swing. The DSE fails in all its attempts to conquer an urban center and make its Provisional Democratic Government a credible contender, but the government army fails in its campaign to dislodge the DSE from the mountains of central and northern Greece.

1949   In August, a successful army offensive against the DSE produces a decisive victory. The DSE retreats into Albania. At the close of the war, roughly 140,000 people, including many leftist fighters, supporters, and peasants in villages controlled by the DSE, leave the country for the countries of the Soviet Bloc.

1958   The United Democratic Left (EDA), a front party for the outlawed KKE, becomes the official opposition in elections held that year.

1967   Military coup establishes right-wing dictatorship.

1968   KKE splits following the Soviet invasion of Czechoslovakia. The splinter party is called KKE Interior after its leadership, which is composed of the clandestine "interior" bureau, operating from within Greece.

1974   Greek-Cypriot armed forces in Cyprus, supported by the military government in Greece, overthrow the government of the Cypriot Republic. In response, Turkish military forces invade Cyprus and partition the island. This disaster for Greece discredited the military government in Greece, resulting in a transition to democracy. KKE is legalized and wins 9.5 percent of the vote as part of a coalition with other leftist parties. The KKE hovers around 10 percent of the votes in the subsequent elections.

1989   In June, inconclusive elections lead to the formation of a short-lived but historic coalition government between the Right and the Communist Left.

INTRODUCTION

The Greek Civil War is one of the four major contemporary European civil wars, along with the Finnish, Russian, and Spanish ones. Like them it was primarily an ideological civil war pitting Right against Left. Unlike the other three wars, however, its origins lie in the Second World War and the Cold War.

BACKGROUND: CULTURE AND HISTORY

The independence of Greece was internationally recognized in 1832. Parliamentary rule was established early, in 1844, and universal male suffrage followed soon. Between 1844 and the Greek Civil War there were only a few periods of departure from parliamentary rule. A series of land reforms provided for a largely egalitarian distribution of Ottoman lands. This helped create a large class of peasant yeomen cultivating their small family-operated farms. This social outlook combined with the country's political institutions to produce personalistic parties based on patronage networks. Unlike other Balkan countries, no strong regionally based or peasant parties developed. The role of the state was critical: by 1870 the number of state officials in relation to the population was seven times that of Britain and growing (Close 1995, 14).

At the same time, Greece remained economically backward throughout the first half of the twentieth century. Low per capita income, low literacy, high rural underemployment, and a low average life expectancy were entrenched features of Greek society. Mass immigration to the United States at the turn of the century helped relieve the social pressure caused by population growth.

The political establishment promoted an irredentist project of territorial enlargement known as the *Megali Idea* (Great Idea), which was implemented to an important degree by the end of the Second Balkan War, in 1913. As a result of the two Balkan wars, Greece doubled its territory and expanded in the north. At the same time, large Christian Greek Orthodox populations remained outside Greece, mainly in Asia Minor.

The onset of World War I precipitated what became known as the National Schism. This division would influence Greek politics for years to come and affect the course of the Greek Civil War. The schism began as a dispute between Liberal prime minister Elefthérios Venizelos and King Constantine over whether Greece should align with Germany or the Western powers in World War I. Venizelos advocated joining the Western powers in the hopes of annexing Eastern Thrace and Asia Minor territories, whereas Constantine, who was closer to Germany, saw alignment with the West as risky. Relying on entente troops, Venizelos forced Greece's entry into the war on the side of Western powers and was rewarded with territorial gains following the signing of the Treaty of Sèvres in 1920. However, Greece was now divided into two intensely antagonistic political camps that eventually were associated with a highly destabilizing institutional cleavage: the followers of Venizelos and his Liberal Party, also known as Venizelists, would increasingly be associated with a preference for republicanism, while the supporters of the king became royalists.

These territorial gains were lost in 1922, after Greece's failed campaign against the Turkish Nationalists of Mustafa Kemal. Over a million people were forced out of what became Turkey, and the Christian presence in Anatolia came to a definitive end. Absorbing the refugees was not easy for a poor country like Greece, but their resettlement primarily in Macedonia turned this region into Greek territory. The great majority of refugees became staunch Venizelists, adding an additional dimension to the main cleavage of Greek politics, that between natives and refugees, "Old Greece" and "New Lands" (Mavrogordatos 1983, 182–225).

Socialist ideas had circulated among the tiny urban working class as well as among urban artisans since the late nineteenth century. Union membership remained fragmented and small, since the country's industrial base was limited. In 1918 the Socialist Workers Party of Greece was founded in Thessaloniki. In 1920 the Party affiliated with Comintern, and in 1924 accepted the full Communist program and renamed itself the Communist Party of Greece (KKE). By 1936 KKE membership had increased to roughly 15,000, and the party was making inroads among the urban Asia Minor refugees living in the slums of Athens. But the KKE's support

of independence for newly acquired territories with large non-Greek minorities, such as Macedonia and Thrace, was a source of tension for the party and precipitated accusations of treason.

Still, the KKE remained a marginal force before World War II. Always a target of suspicion and fear, it was increasingly persecuted from the late 1920s onwards. The *Idionym* Law of 1929, passed by a Liberal government, penalized attempts to develop, implement, or propagate ideas that aimed at violently overthrowing the established social order or detaching part of the state's territory. In 1932–1933 the government began making release for imprisoned leftists contingent on signing declarations of repentance, which stigmatized signers. Instability during the 1930s gave way to the Metaxas dictatorship of 1936–1941; it was extremely successful in cracking down on the KKE, which was virtually eliminated.

CONTEXT AND PROCESS OF REVOLUTION

It is possible to distinguish four distinct phases of the civil war. The first phase took place during the German occupation of Greece, pitting leftist forces led by the KKE against non-Communist resistance groups, the German occupiers, and Greek collaborationists. This phase ended with the German withdrawal in September–November 1944. The second phase took place in December 1944 and January 1945, when the KKE launched an uprising against the British-backed government that resulted in a Communist defeat. During the third phase, in 1945–1946, various attempts to institutionalize the new political system failed, and leftist supporters were persecuted by right-wing militias with the tacit support of the gendarmerie. The fourth and final phase began in February 1946, with the KKE decision to step up guerrilla activities, and was sealed in March, when Communist guerrillas launched highly symbolic attacks against the gendarmerie. The war ended with a total Communist defeat in 1949.

The proximate cause of the Greek Civil War is clear and uncontroversial: it lies in Greece's defeat in World War II, which led to the collapse of the state and its replacement by a triple occupation—German-Italian-Bulgarian—in April 1941. Hence, any account of the Greek Civil War must include a description of the occupation and the resistance.

In October 1940 Italy invaded Greece. Surprisingly, Greek forces held off the invasion and forced Italy to retreat beyond Greek borders. In March 1941 British expeditionary forces arrived in Greece, and on April 6 Germany invaded Greece. The Greek defenses collapsed quickly, and the Germans entered Athens. King George II and the Greek government fled to Crete, which they had to abandon after the Germans conquered Crete. They eventually ended up in Egypt, where they remained throughout the occupation.

The occupiers' presence was thin, particularly in Greece's mountain hinterland; this caused widespread banditry and a general collapse of security. Descriptions of life in the mountains during 1941 and 1942 are rife with complaints about cattle-thieving and banditry (Kalyvas 2006). In addition, a terrible famine hit Greece during the winter of 1941–1942. Indifferent to the well-being of the population, German forces had seized all public and private stocks of food, apparel, medical supplies, military materiel, means of transport, and fuel. The German-controlled Greek government was responsible for paying the costs of occupation, leading to high rates of inflation. Population loss from increased deaths and reduced births in 1941–1942 is estimated at 300,000 (Mazower 1993, 41). The famine was deadliest in food-deficit locales, particularly in Athens and the islands. Many mountain villages suffered as well.

In spite of the grievances caused by the defeat, the famine, and the humiliation that many Greeks felt at being occupied by the Italians —an enemy it had defeated on the battlefield—no armed resistance emerged. In fact, compared to neighboring Yugoslavia, the resistance movement in Greece was slow to develop. A few isolated actions by rogue Communist bands in Eastern Macedonia triggered collective German reprisals and massive Bulgarian repression. As a result, all resistance momentarily ceased. In 1942, however, this began to change, and once the course of the war shifted, in 1943, this trend was completely reversed.

Early resistance took two distinct forms. On the one hand, several clandestine urban networks emerged. Most sought to engage in intelligence collection in close coordination with the Allies, while a few chose the path of spectacular actions, the most notable of which was the bombing of the Athens headquarters of ESPO, a Greek Nazi organization, in February 1942. Generally, urban networks were small in size, bourgeois in membership, and pro-British in their politics. They were also vulnerable to penetration and dismantlement and suffered repeated blows from the Germans. On the other hand, several bands of guerrilla fighters emerged in the mountainous hinterland, especially in central and northern Greece. Some were local and decentralized bands that drew on homegrown traditions and skills; a few were formed by local army officers. The two bands that developed into the biggest resistance armies—the Popular Liberation Army known by its Greek acronym of ELAS and the National Democratic Greek League or EDES—had clear political roots.

The advent of the occupation caused the revival of the KKE. In 1941, the KKE established the National Liberation Front (EAM) as an umbrella organization for smaller leftist parties, and in early 1942 it set up its military wing, ELAS.

Initially, the KKE kept its leadership of the EAM and ELAS secret to avoid alienating less radical segments of society. Critical to the early success of ELAS was a Communist operative named Thanasis Klaras, best known by his military alias of Aris Velouchiotis. Using a combination of nationalist discourse and coercive practices, he succeeded in establishing a political and military authority in the mountains of central Greece. His success was reinforced by his ability to suppress the criminal wave caused by the collapse of the Greek state and to absorb several independent local bands. By 1943, ELAS emerged as the largest and most powerful guerrilla army in Greece—more so following the Italian capitulation in the fall of 1943.

EDES proved no match for ELAS. Formed by an ex-officer of the Greek army, Napoleon Zervas, it was built on traditional local networks in his home region of Epirus. In this respect, EDES was not unlike many similar efforts by royalist and republican officers. In contrast, EAM was the work of a handful of highly committed Communist cadres who relied on a highly effective organizational technology that combined political organization in every village, guerrilla action, and a nationalist (as opposed to Communist) message.

By 1943, the echo of the German defeats in the Eastern Front was clearly audible in Greece; coupled with persistent rumors of an Allied landing in Greece, it created a perception that the occupation was coming to an imminent end. From that point on, power in post-war Greece overshadowed the occupation as the main preoccupation of most organizations. In this context, the elimination of rivals became a priority. In the spring and fall of 1943, ELAS attacked the other guerrilla resistance bands and destroyed almost all of them. Unlike most non-Communist groups, EDES managed to parlay its close British collaboration into survival but was reduced to a marginal role. The exact causes behind these attacks remain unclear; what is unambiguous, however, is EAM's intolerance of any group that refused to submit to its authority. This intolerance can be explained, in turn, as resulting from a combination of competition for scarce local resources and KKE's Stalinist mentality.

Once it defeated them, ELAS usually offered the officers of these other organizations the possibility of joining its ranks. Indeed, the military leader of ELAS, Colonel Stefanos Sarafis, was previously the leader of a band defeated by ELAS. In some instances, the leading officers were shot, but most of them either fled Greece and joined the Greek army in Egypt or sought refuge in Athens and other towns. Particularly notorious was the destruction of the small organization EKKA, whose military leader Colonel Dimitrios Psarros was shot alongside 150–200 of his fighters. Many among the surviving officers would later join the collaborationist Security Battalions. Thus, accusations of collaboration with the Germans proved to be a self-fulfilling prophecy: used liberally by

EAM's propaganda machine, such false accusations justified attacks that often ended up producing mass collaboration. The resulting polarization and lack of political alternative led thousands of officers, many of whom had been staunch republicans, to side with the collaborationist government as the only bulwark against the Communist onslaught. This explains the puzzle of collaboration literally exploding in the spring and summer of 1944, when the Germans were clearly losing the war and in a country with no pro-Nazi ideology or mass movement.

By 1944, EAM was fully dominant: it now effectively ruled close to 70 percent of Greece, while the occupation authorities were confined in the main cities, coastal areas and plains, and a few points of strategic interest. At the same time, it set upon the task of enlisting thousands of Greek peasants into various mass organizations with the intent of turning them into KKE supporters.

The only force challenging EAM was now the Security Battalions. The spring and summer of 1944 was a time of violent strife across Greece, as the Security Battalions clashed with ELAS. The highest price was paid by civilians, who were killed and abused by both sides; hundreds of villages were destroyed, and the country became deeply polarized. As soon as the Germans began withdrawing from Greece in September 1944, ELAS attacked the collaborationist militias and executed thousands of militiamen.

In May 1944, the KKE suffered what, in retrospect, was clearly a strategic defeat: it signed the Lebanon Charter. This agreement called for the creation of a national unity government led by the prime minister of the government in exile, Georgios Papandreou, in which the Communists would hold a minority stake. The charter was reinforced by the Caserta Agreement signed in September 1946, which prohibited ELAS from entering Athens. According to these agreements, ELAS was to demobilize and a new army would be formed, blending elements of ELAS, EDES, and the Greek army in exile. Exactly why the KKE compromised at this point remains a matter of contention (Iatrides 1972), particularly after recently opened KKE archives show that already in the autumn of 1943, the party had drawn up a military plan for the capture of Athens. On the one hand, the Soviets recommended caution and, on the other, the Communists thought that they could win power without recourse to force: their control of the country would have easily translated into an electoral victory. The key element, of course, was preserving this control, which hinged on their ability to keep their army intact.

Under these conditions it is not surprising that the demobilization process turned into a highly contentious issue, ultimately triggering a collision between KKE and the Papandreou government backed by the British. On December 3, in an atmosphere of heightened polarization, the Communists organized a massive demonstration in Athens that was fired upon by the police; at the same time, ELAS troops infiltrated Athens and attacked police stations and army garrisons. Many thousands of Athenian civilians were taken as hostages and a few thousand were executed by OPLA, EAM's notorious death squads. While a few of the hostages were accused of collaboration with the Germans, most had simply been denounced as hostile to the KKE (Gerolymatos 2004).

Eventually, the British flew in thousands of troops and defeated the Communist uprising. With its position weakened, EAM signed the Varkiza Agreement on February 15, 1945, which provided for the demobilization of the ELAS. Though this agreement outlined a peaceful end to fighting and normalized politics, it was ultimately violated by all sides. The government allowed the persecution of leftist supporters, while the Communists did not surrender their best weapons.

In 1945–1946, hundreds of right-wing paramilitary bands emerged throughout the country, harassing the supporters of the Left. In response, the Communists organized new guerrilla bands known as "self-defense." At the same time, several thousands of Communist cadres were evacuated to Yugoslavia and assembled in the town of Bulkes.

In 1946, the charismatic Communist leader Nikos Zahariadis, who had returned from the Dachau concentration camp, opted for a course of collision with the government; exactly why he did so remains unclear. The Yalta "percentages agreement" placed Greece in the British sphere of influence; nevertheless, Stalin sent ambivalent signals to the Greek Communists, encouraging them to take bold action without guaranteeing that he would help them. As a result, the Communists boycotted the parliamentary elections of March, which resulted in a landslide for the conservative Peoples' Party, while Communist guerrilla bands launched highly symbolic attacks against government forces. A rigged plebiscite restoring the monarchy signaled the country's rightward turn. In December the KKE established the Democratic Army of Greece (DSE) and opted for waging a full-scale insurgency against the government and its supporters, officially abandoning its earlier commitment to gain power through legal channels. The Communists failed to conquer any urban center they could use as their capital so that they could gain international recognition for their Provisional Democratic Government.

Compared to ELAS, DSE had access to a much smaller proportion of the country's territory. The Greek government was able to control most of the country; where that proved impossible it adopted a policy of mass population displacement, moving thousands of peasants from their mountain villages to the outskirts of towns. As a result, the Communists lost access to manpower. They tried to solve this problem by resorting to forcible recruitment, by massively recruiting women, and by aggressively courting Greek Macedonia's

Throngs of supporters of the Greek Communist party dominated National Liberation Front, Ethnikón Apeleftherotikón Métopon (EAM), gather for a protest rally in Athens on the eve of the general elections in March 1946. (Library of Congress)

ethnic Slav minority. None of these solutions, however, helped them solve their problem.

The fighting continued throughout 1949 with both sides experiencing victories and defeats. The Tito-Stalin fallout turned out to be an important determinant of the final outcome: the KKE sided with Stalin and, by doing so, lost its access to the Yugoslav territory that was used as a supply route and a place from where to stage attacks. By August 1949 almost all of the remaining 17,000 DSE troops were arrayed on the northern frontier; they were attacked by a government force of roughly 100,000 troops. Many of the DSE troops were killed and the rest, including Zahariadis, retreated into Albania. In September the last large DSE formations fled into Bulgaria, and in October Zahariadis announced an end to the war. At the close of the war roughly 140,000 leftists escaped into the Soviet Bloc (Close 1995, 219).

The most crucial element contributing to government victory in the civil war was international assistance. British funding, training, and forces supplemented the weak Greek military into 1947. With the British planning to withdraw from Greece in late March 1947, on March 12 the United States announced the Truman Doctrine, which allocated 300 million dollars to Greece for reconstruction and the fight against the insurgency. A little known but critical aspect of U.S. military assistance were thousands of mules imported from the United States, which proved crucial in moving supplies across the rough terrain of central and northern Greece. U.S. military assistance spilled over into the society at large by generating high levels of economic development.

The civil war caused enormous damage to the country. It is still impossible to estimate the full extent of the human cost. The available evidence suggests fatality rates approaching 100,000. During the occupation period, close to 30,000 civilians were killed in reprisal actions or mass executions by the occupying forces, sometimes assisted by local collaborators; several thousands were incarcerated or were sent to Germany as slave labor; during the occupation and up to February 1945, EAM killed 15,000–20,000 civilians and imprisoned several thousands in makeshift concentration camps it set up in the mountains. Up to 1,000 collaborating militiamen and 5,000 guerrillas were also killed in combat. The December 1944 uprising cost 3,000–4,000 lives on ELAS's side and 3,500 on the government's side, plus 3,000–5,000 civilians killed by ELAS. In 1945–1946, up to 3,000 civilians were killed, mainly by right-wing militias. The last phase of the war claimed the lives of up to 15,000 members of the government army and 20,000 leftist rebels; up to 4,000 civilians were killed by the rebels, while the state executed up to 5,000 leftists, mainly captured guerrillas (Kalyvas 2006, Chapter 9; Close 1995, 220). Thousands more served prison sentences or spent time in the notorious Makronisos island concentration camp where enlisted soldiers of the regular Greek army suspected of having leftist sympathies were deported to be "re-educated."

IMPACTS

The Greek Civil War had a powerful effect on Greek politics, society, and economics.

On the political front, the civil war signaled the destruction of the Left and the mass movement it had spawned during the occupation. Post–civil war Greece was a parliamentary democracy, but a restricted one. The civil war caused a number of distortions. First, it bequeathed a large set of paramilitary organizations that became known as the "parastate"; second, it turned the army into a de facto protector of the institutions of the Greek state and its official ideology; third, it transformed rabid anti-Communism into a discourse of legitimation that could be used for any purpose.

The KKE was outlawed and its members could only operate clandestinely. Leftists were discriminated against and had little access to state jobs, the main source of employment. A series of decrees enacted from 1946–1948 were used to this end as well. For example, Law 516 of 1948 required a certificate of sound social opinions to obtain licenses and state jobs. Widespread surveillance was carried out by Greek security forces, which compiled files on the majority of the population. As in the pre–World War II era, large numbers of suspected Communists were arrested and imprisoned or deported without trial.

Yet these discriminations were far from watertight. The dynamism of EAM found an outlet in a new political party of the Left established in 1950: the United Democratic Left (EDA). EDA was really a front party for the outlawed KKE, whose headquarters were located in Eastern Europe. Yet the Greek government allowed the EDA to operate partly because the party took votes from the centrist parties, thus favoring the Right (Close 1993, 218). EDA was quite successful, so much so that in the 1958 elections it won 25 percent of the vote and became the official opposition.

On the economic front, the post–civil war years were a time of economic development that changed the face of Greece. Per capita income rose at an average rate of nearly 6 percent per year for thirty years after the civil war (Close 1993, 221). In combination with the mass population movements from mountain villages to the cities, especially to Athens, the civil war helped transform Greece from a backward rural country into the urban service economy it became in the second half of the twentieth century.

The disjunction between political immobility and economic and social development created a political crisis in the early 1960s. The army stepped in to prevent political change: the military coup of 1967 led to a dictatorship that lasted until 1974. Its collapse, in the wake of the Cyprus debacle in 1974, led to mass radicalization, which was expressed in the rejection of the monarchy in the 1974 referendum (69 percent of voters chose to abolish it) and culminated in the 1981 electoral landslide of the Socialist Party PASOK (Panhellenic Socialist Movement). This party dominated Greek political life in the last quarter of the twentieth century. It remedied the absence of a Socialist tradition in Greece by appropriating EAM's history from the KKE and transforming the first phase of the civil war into a story of "national resistance" that glossed over EAM's darker spots. With PASOK's victory, this leftist version of the civil war became enshrined as official history—despite the fact that PASOK's leader, Andreas Papandreou, was the son and political heir of Georgios Papandreou, the prime minister who had squashed EAM's armed bid for power in December 1944.

PEOPLE AND ORGANIZATIONS

Communist Party of Greece (KKE)

Established in 1924 out of the Socialist Workers Party of Greece. Persecuted heavily and essentially destroyed by the government in the inter-war years, the KKE resurfaced during German occupation and led the largest force in the resistance, the EAM. After the civil war with the Greek government, the KKE was made illegal and the majority of its remaining members went into exile. From exile KKE leaders secretly controlled the successor party to the EAM in Greece, the United Democratic Left (EDA), which enjoyed moderate electoral success in the 1950s. In 1974, the KKE was re-legalized.

Democratic Army of Greece (DSE)

Established in December 1946 to replace the dissolved ELAS. At its height in the spring of 1948 the DSE had roughly 26,000 troops in Greece. Most DSE combatants were young, and over a quarter were female. A substantial proportion were ethnic Slavs from Greek Macedonia. They were defeated by government forces in 1949, and the majority of troops fled into Albania and Bulgaria.

ESPO

Greek Socialist Patriotic Organization. Short-lived Greek Nazi organization.

King George II (1890–1947)

When the monarchy was restored in 1935, he returned from exile in England and became king. He was instrumental in bringing about Metaxas's dictatorship. He was the official head of the Greek government in exile during the occupation and returned to power after the plebiscite of September 1946.

Liberal Party

The primary political party representing Venizelists.

Metaxas, Ioannis (1871–1941)

Right-wing dictator from 1936–1941. He persecuted the Communists and attempted to mold his regime after the Italian Fascist regime. He died in 1941 during the German occupation, after having redeemed himself by opposing the Italian invasion and presiding over the victorious resistance of the Greek army.

Mountain Brigade

The main unit of the exiled Greek army, it fought against EAM in December 1944.

National and Social Liberation (EKKA)

Established 1942 as a resistance organization, it was destroyed by ELAS in 1944.

National Democratic Greek League (EDES)

A non-Communist resistance organization during German occupation, led by Napoleon Zervas; a major rival of the ELAS.

National Liberation Front (EAM)

Established in 1941 and controlled by the KKE, EAM came to dominate the resistance movement in Greece.

National Popular Liberation Army (ELAS)

The armed wing of EAM, established under German occupation. ELAS was dissolved by the Varkiza Agreement of February 1945.

OPLA

Organization for the Protection of the People's Struggle. EAM's organization entrusted with the assassination of its opponents.

Papandreou, Georgios (1888–1968)

Appointed prime minister of the exiled government April 26, 1944, he successfully faced EAM's challenge in December 1944.

Peoples' Party

The main conservative party during the inter-war and immediate post-war years.

Political Committee of National Liberation (PEEA)

Provisional government established in March 1944 by EAM; formally lasted until November 1944.

Rallis, Ioannis (1878–1946)

Appointed prime minister of the collaborationist government by Germany in April 1943. Rallis was an anti-Venizelist, belonged to an old political family, and had long ministerial experience. He was instrumental in organizing the Security Battalions.

Sarafis, Stefanos (1890–1957)

Former officer of the Greek army who became the military leader of ELAS after his own resistance organization was destroyed by ELAS.

Security Battalions

Military units that collaborated with the German occupiers against EAM.

Siantos, Giorgos (1890–1947)

Assumed leadership of the KKE in November 1941 and consequently held great power within EAM.

Sofoulis, Themistoklis (1859–1949)

Prime minister of a Liberal government November 1945 to April 1946. His appointment was secured by British influence.

United Democratic Left (EDA)

A leftist party established in 1950. KKE leaders exerted a good deal of control over the EDA.

Vafiadis, Markos (1906–1992)

Also known as General Markos, he was the military leader of DSE.

Velouchiotis, Aris (1905–1945)

Key military leader of ELAS. Committed suicide in 1945 when he was about to be captured by government forces following his decision to ignore the KKE's demand to lay down his arms.

Venizelos, Elefthérios (1864–1936)

Prime minister in 1914, his dispute with King Constantine over Greek alignment in World War I caused the National Schism. Died in exile in 1936.

Zahariadis, Nikos (1903–1973)

Leader of the KKE after 1931, except during periods of exile and imprisonment. A charismatic and autocratic leader, he admired Stalin. He returned to Greece in May 1945 after a period of imprisonment in the Dachau concentration camp and made the decision to launch an insurgency in 1946.

Zervas, Napoleon (1891–1957)

A former republican officer, he founded and led the EDES resistance organization.

Stathis N. Kalyvas

See Also Documentaries of Revolution; Italian Fascist Revolution; Nazi Revolution: Politics and Racial Hierarchy; War and Revolution

References and Further Readings
Close, David H., ed. 1993. *The Greek Civil War, 1943–1950: Studies in Polarization.* New York: Routledge.
_____. 1995. *The Origins of the Greek Civil War.* New York: Longman.
Gerolymatos, André. 2004. *Red Acropolis, Black Terror: The Greek Civil War and the Origins of Soviet-American Rivalry, 1943–1949.* New York: Basic Books.
Iatrides, John O. 1972. *Revolt in Athens: the Greek Communist "Second Round," 1944- 1945.* Princeton, NJ: Princeton University Press.
_____, ed. 1981. *Greece in the 1940s: A Nation in Crisis.* Hanover, N.H.: University Press of New England.
Jones, Howard. 1989. *"A New Kind of War:" America's Global Strategy and the Truman Doctrine in Greece.* New York: Oxford University Press.
Kalyvas, Stathis N. 2000. "Red Terror: Leftist Violence during the Occupation." Pp. 142–183 in *After the War Was Over: Reconstructing Family, State, and Nation in Greece, 1944–1960.* Edited by Mark Mazower. Princeton, NJ: Princeton University Press.
_____. 2006. *The Logic of Violence in Civil War.* New York: Cambridge University Press.
Koliopoulos, Ioannis S. 1999. *Plundered Loyalties: Axis Occupation and Civil Strife in Greek West Macedonia, 1941–1949.* London: Hurst & Company.
Mavrogordatos George Th. 1983. *Stillborn Republic: Social Coalitions and Party Strategies in Greece, 1922–1936.* Berkeley: University of California Press.
Mazower, Marc. 1993. *Inside Hitler's Greece: The Experience of the Occupation, 1941–1944.* New Haven and London: Yale University Press.
McNeill William H. 1947. *The Greek Dilemma: War and Aftermath.* Philadelphia: J. B. Lippincott.
Woodhouse, C. 1948. *Apple of Discord: A Survey of Recent Greek Politics in their International Setting.* London: Hutchinson & Co.

Guatemalan Democratic Revolution, Counter-Revolution, and Restoration of Democracy

CHRONOLOGY

1524	Pedro de Alvarado of Spain conquers Guatemala.
1821	Guatemala declares independence from Spain.
1837	Peasant rebellions empower conservative Rafael Carrera, who reverses liberal reforms to defend the interests of the Maya.
1873–1885	President Justo Rufino Barrios reintroduces liberal reforms that privatize communally held indigenous land.
1904	Guatemalan dictator Manuel Estrada Cabrera grants United Fruit Company (UFCO) a contract to build and operate a railway connecting the banana plantations to the eastern port of Puerto Barrios.
1931	Jorge Ubico establishes a dictatorship.
1944	October Revolution led by students, nationalist army officers, and the middle class topples the Ubico dictatorship.
1945	Juan José Arévalo assumes the presidency after winning Guatemala's first democratic election.
1949	Major Francisco Arana is killed in a mysterious gun battle near Guatemala City, trigger-

ing an unsuccessful officer revolt against the Arévalo government.

1950   In November, Jacobo Arbenz elected president.

1951   March 15, Jacobo Arbenz inaugurated president.

1952   Arbenz enacts Decree 900, the largest land reform in Guatemalan history.

1954   Colonel Carlos Castillo Armas ousts President Arbenz in a coup orchestrated by the U.S. Central Intelligence Agency (CIA).

1957   Palace guard assassinates President Castillo Armas.

1958   President Miguel Ydígoras Fuentes elected president.

1960   In November, a major military rebellion (MR-13 rebellion) is thwarted by the U.S. Central Intelligence Agency. In December, the General Treaty of Economic Integration is signed, leading to the formation of the Central American Common Market (CACM).

1962   Remnants of the MR-13 rebellion form the first guerrilla organizations, which eventually merge into FAR (Rebel Armed Forces).

In March and April students and labor leaders wage national strike to protest electoral fraud; police kill several student leaders.

1963   Colonel Enrique Peralta Azurdia seizes power in a military coup designed to prevent Arévalo from being re-elected president. FAR opens guerrilla fronts in Zacapa and Izabal.

1966   Revolutionary Party candidate Julio César Méndez Montenegro elected president after signing a secret pact giving the military jurisdiction over the counterinsurgency campaign.

In May, internal security forces execute twenty-eight leftists. In October, guerrilla leader Luis Turcios Lima is killed in auto accident.

1968   FAR kills two U.S. military attachés. Guatemalan government expels several Maryknoll priests for conspiring with the guerrillas.

In August, U.S. ambassador Gordon Mein is killed attempting to flee FAR kidnappers.

1970   West German ambassador Karl Von Spreti assassinated by guerrillas. FAR leader Yon Sosa is assassinated in Mexico.

1971   Death squads assassinate opposition congressman Adolfo Mijangos López.

1972   Guerrilla Army of the Poor (EGP) launches guerrilla fronts in the highlands.

1976   Earthquake strikes Guatemala City, killing more than 22,000.

1977   U.S. Congress restricts military aid to Guatemala.

1978   CUC (Committee for Campesino Unity) formed. Military massacres dozens of indigenous protestors in the town of Panzós, Alta Verapaz.

1980   Guatemalan internal security forces firebomb the Spanish embassy, killing several dozen peasant protestors; CUC responds by organizing massive strikes on sugar plantations.

1980–1983   Guatemalan military conducts a scorched-earth campaign against Mayan communities.

1981   To prevent the guerrillas from contacting highland communities, the army forces villagers to join Civilian Self-Defense Patrols (PACs).

1982   Guerrilla factions unite to form URNG (National Revolutionary Union of Guatemala). General Efraín Ríos Montt seizes power in a military coup and institutes the "rifles and beans" program.

1983   Defense Minister General Oscar Humberto Mejía Víctores ousts Montt in a military coup.

1985	U.S. Congress resumes economic and military aid to Guatemala, which adopts a new constitution.
1990	Anthropologist Myrna Mack is murdered.
1992	Mayan activist Rigoberta Menchú wins the Nobel Peace Prize.
1996	URNG rebels and government sign peace agreement ending the civil war.
1998	Bishop Juan Gerardi is murdered after issuing a human rights report for the Archdiocese of Guatemala.
1999	CEH (Commission for Historical Clarification) publishes report accusing the Guatemalan government of committing genocide against the Mayans and blaming the military and its paramilitary allies for more than 90 percent of the deaths in the civil war. President Clinton declares that the United States should not have supported the Guatemalan security forces during the civil war.
2001–2004	Homicides and vigilante killings climb to record levels with more than 2 million illegal weapons circulating within the country.

INTRODUCTION

The Guatemalan Revolution of 1944 that toppled dictator Jorge Ubico ushered in a decade of political, economic, and social reforms that was terminated by a CIA-sponsored military coup in 1954. After installing a new dictator, the Eisenhower administration then initiated a counter-revolution, which spawned a civil war that killed more than 200,000. The peace agreement of 1996 created a political opening for the Left and facilitated a Mayan cultural resurgence; however, human rights violations, crime, and extreme poverty still continue to plague the country.

BACKGROUND: CULTURE AND HISTORY

The roots of the Guatemalan conflict can be traced to the ethnic division of the population, unequal distribution of land, and the extreme external dependency of the Guatemalan economy—all legacies of the colonial period.

Guatemala, the most populous country in Central America (14 million in 2004), is divided between two main ethnic groups: indigenous (Maya) and ladino (mestizo, or persons of mixed European-Indian descent). Ladinos wear Western clothing, speak Spanish, and generally embrace Western values and theology; indigenous people wear traditional clothing, speak a Mayan language most of the time, and follow Mayan cultural customs. Although the civil war induced some Mayan Indians to convert to ladinos (ladinoization) or to adopt evangelical Protestantism, the majority of the Indians have fused their older religious beliefs with some form of Christianity (syncretism).

The Mayans descended from a civilization that was initially located in the present-day department called the Petén, a northern region of flat jungle. The mysterious collapse of the Maya empire prior to the Spanish conquest of the sixteenth century led to a scattering of indigenous people, who eventually resettled into more than twenty different language groups. The majority of the Indians came to reside in the mountainous regions of the country (Altiplano), where they survived by cultivating small plots of corn and beans. During the colonial period, the Spanish crown granted large tracts of land to criollos (persons of Spanish descent born in the New World) who conscripted Indian labor. Although Indians had to convert to Christianity, Mayans maintained a physical and cultural form of autonomy that one anthropologist has labeled a "closed corporate community" (Smith 1990, 18–21).

Ten years after Guatemala obtained its independence from Spain (1821), liberal governments introduced a new education system, revised the civil code, reduced the power of the Catholic Church, and imposed taxes. An attempt to sell off indigenous communal land triggered a peasant rebellion in 1837 headed by Rafael Carrera, a Conservative who reversed the Liberal reforms. After Carrera's death in 1865 Liberals resumed their modernization efforts. To promote the development of a coffee oligarchy, the Liberals required Indians to work several days per year either on public works projects or on coffee plantations. Those who failed to fulfill their labor obligations faced imprisonment or stiff fines. Landowners also sought to entrap Indians by luring them with alcohol into signing labor contracts that perpetuated debt peonage. In 1877, the government began a massive assault upon Indian land by forcing peasants to either buy the land they were using or forfeit it to the government. Most Indians were poor and lacked formal land titles, so the bulk of their land was confiscated and sold on the private market. By the late nineteenth century, land shortages and the debt peonage system forced Indians to migrate seasonally from the Altiplano to the lowlands to work on coffee plantations.

Liberal governments of the nineteenth century also attempted to attract European immigrants and foreign investment. Although the immigration schemes largely failed, Guatemala fell into the U.S. economic orbit during the regimes of Justo Rufino Barrios (1873–1885) and Manuel Estrada Cabrera (1898–1920). By the early twentieth century the United Fruit Company (UFCO), established by U.S. entrepreneur Minor Keith, had gained control of Guatemala's fledgling banana industry. Dictator Jorge Ubico (1931–1944) granted UFCO tax exemptions and land to encourage its expansion. To consolidate his monopoly, Keith bought an unfinished railway and charged competitors higher rates for shipping freight of the same weight. By constructing the railroad to serve the coastal ports, not the interior, UFCO delayed the development of an internal transportation network needed for the establishment of a national market. In short, Guatemala emerged in the first half of the twentieth century under a cruel dictatorship that perpetuated U.S. economic dependency and empowered a local agrarian elite over disenfranchised Indians and poor ladinos.

CONTEXT AND PROCESS OF REVOLUTION AND COUNTER-REVOLUTION

Ubico's subservience to United Fruit and his brutal suppression of all dissidence eventually sparked a middle-class revolution in 1944 that led to a decade of democratic reforms known as the ten years of spring. The rebels wrote a new constitution that guaranteed free speech, the right to organize labor unions, and established a public education system. Guatemala's first open and fair election was won by Juan José Arévalo, a populist, who built health clinics, established a social security institute that covered urban workers, drafted a permissive labor code favorable to allowing workers to unionize, and increased educational funding. Arévalo's talk of "spiritual socialism" and his encouragement of a labor movement that challenged U.S. economic interests such as UFCO greatly alarmed U.S. diplomats. Suspicions about Guatemala deepened after the death of Major Francisco Arana, chief of the armed forces. In 1949 President Arévalo instructed Defense Minister Jacobo Arbenz to capture Arana, who was plotting against the government. Rather than submit to arrest, Arana perished in a gun battle at a blocked bridge on the outskirts of Guatemala City. Arana's supporters then tried unsuccessfully to stage a military coup. After Arbenz won the 1950 presidential election, U.S. officials became convinced that he had killed Arana to gain power.

President Arbenz continued Arévalo's reforms, but he also moved the Guatemalan Revolution further to the left. Between the beginning of Arévalo's presidency and his own election in 1950, Arbenz, through his reading of Marxist literature and the influence of his wife and their friends in the Guatemalan Communist Party (PGT), had become attracted to Communist ideology. PGT members convinced Arbenz that Guatemala was still mired in feudalism and had to pass through capitalism before making the transition to Socialism. Consequently, Arbenz eagerly carried out capitalist reforms, including World Bank recommendations to build more highways, ports, and houses. In 1952 he enacted the largest land reform (Decree 900) in Guatemalan history. Decree 900 broke the hold of the agrarian elite by redistributing 1.4 million acres of land to more than 500,000 individual campesinos (peasants) (Streeter 2000b, 19). The Arbenz administration also expropriated UFCO property and offered financial compensation based on the value of the property that the company had declared on its tax returns. As UFCO had long undervalued the value of its holdings to evade taxes, the government viewed this expropriation arrangement as just retaliation for decades of fraudulent reporting by a foreign monopoly. Outraged at this scheme, UFCO publicly condemned the Arbenz government and lobbied the State Department to intervene on its behalf.

The UFCO case notwithstanding, Arbenz's land reform and his close association with the PGT convinced the Dwight D. Eisenhower administration that Guatemala had become a Soviet beachhead. U.S. officials ignored that Moscow did not control the PGT, which held only 4 out of 54 congressional seats, and that Arbenz himself did not belong to the PGT. In the anti-Communist atmosphere of the early Cold War, such exaggerations and misrepresentations of the Communist threat prevailed in U.S. diplomatic circles. The U.S. ambassador to Guatemala, for example, used the "duck test" to determine that Arbenz was a Communist: if a strange animal looked, walked, swam, and quacked like a duck, then it must be a duck; likewise, because Arbenz talked, thought, and acted like a Communist, he had to be one.

In 1954, President Eisenhower authorized a covert operation (PBSUCCESS) to overthrow Arbenz. The CIA trained, equipped, and financed a mercenary force headed by Colonel Carlos Castillo Armas, an ex–Guatemalan military officer who had been imprisoned for plotting against the government but had escaped into exile in 1951. With the CIA's logistical assistance, Castillo Armas invaded Guatemala from a base in Honduras with a ragtag band of 150 peasant soldiers and toppled the Arbenz regime within ten days. The Eisenhower administration claimed that the "liberation" represented a spontaneous popular uprising against Communism, but in truth PBSUCCESS would have flopped had the CIA not bribed Guatemalan army officials into cooperating with the coup. Because high-level Eisenhower administration officials had financial ties to United Fruit (Secretary of

Jacobo Arbenz Guzmán, president of Guatemala, 1951–1954, addresses a crowd of supporters. (Library of Congress)

State John Foster Dulles, for example, owned UFCO stock), some observers concluded that the fruit company had masterminded the downfall of Arbenz. Declassified State Department and CIA records, however, have since revealed that U.S. officials were not acting solely on behalf of one company's financial interests. The greater fear was that Arbenz's land reform might serve as a model for other Latin American revolutionaries, thus spreading domestic unrest and challenging U.S. hegemony in the hemisphere.

After seizing power, Castillo Armas held a rigged referendum and began a counter-revolution against the ten years of spring. His government executed hundreds of political prisoners and temporarily incarcerated thousands of campesinos who had participated in Arbenz's land reform. The Castillo Armas regime also reversed Decree 900, revoked free speech, dismantled the labor movement, and drew up a blacklist naming 10 percent of the adult population (Streeter 2000b, 39). The Eisenhower administration, which played a crucial role in shaping and financing this counter-revolution, sought a stable anti-Communist government in Guatemala that would open its economy to foreign investment, provide the United States with strategic raw materials, align itself with Washington in the United Nations, and welcome U.S. military training and assistance. To weaken the appeal of Communism in Guatemala, the Eisenhower administration also sponsored an economic development assistance program to improve the standard of living.

The U.S. attempt to transform Guatemala into a democratic "showcase" for capitalism in Latin America did foster macroeconomic growth, but the country became less rather than more stable. The politically mobilized constituencies of the ten years of spring (campesinos, students, labor leaders) refused to accept Washington's mandate, which actually hurt the poor. The U.S. emphasis on the agro-export sector, for example, meant devoting more land to growing coffee instead of subsistence crops like corn and beans. Guatemalans resented U.S. interference in local affairs, especially after the State Department infiltrated Guatemalan government ministries in order to control legislation and government spending. When social activists took to the streets to protest the results of the counter-revolution, they met fierce police and military repression. In 1957 Castillo Armas was assassinated by a palace guard. A year later, after several disputed elections, Miguel Ydígoras Fuentes, a former candidate to lead PBSUCCESS, was elected president.

By 1960 conditions were ripe for a civil war between the oligarchy (agrarian elite and the industrial bourgeoisie) and the survivors of the ten years of spring. The Guatemalan military was initially divided, as the younger officers grew disenchanted with low salaries and the government's increasing subservience to the United States. In November 1960, a group of dissident officers launched a barracks rebellion (MR-13) against President Ydígoras for having agreed to help the United States invade Cuba. Earlier that May the CIA had established a secret base in Guatemala where it began training several hundred Cuban exiles for the ill-fated Bay of Pigs operation.

With the CIA's assistance, Guatemalan army loyalists suppressed the MR-13 rebellion within a few days, but its leaders managed to flee the country. Over the next few years, these junior military officers evolved from narrow-minded nationalists into Marxist-Leninist revolutionaries who believed that only armed struggle could defeat the counter-revolution. Two of the main leaders, Turcios Lima and Yon Sosa, had actually received U.S. military training, so they were familiar with U.S. counterinsurgency doctrines. In 1962 they organized Guatemala's first guerrilla units, known as FAR (Rebel Armed Forces). Following the Cuban model, FAR attempted to establish *focos* (bases) in several remote regions where they could escape detection by the authorities. These *focos* gained little popular support, however, as few Indians were attracted to a ladino-led movement that spoke of class oppression but did not address discrimination against the Maya. The rebels also suffered from internal divisions and committed tactical errors that enabled the Guatemalan military to eradicate some of the *focos*.

As the guerrilla war began to heat up, avenues for peaceful change dwindled. In April and March 1962 students and labor organizers protesting electoral corruption were shot down by the police. A year later, Colonel Enrique Peralta Azurdia seized power in a military coup designed to prevent Juan José Arévalo from running for president again. The John F. Kennedy administration, which had just embarked on a $20 billion development assistance program for Latin America known as the Alliance for Progress, embraced Peralta by funding rural civic action programs and promoting the formation of a Central American Common Market. At the same time, the State Department dispatched dozens of U.S. police, military, and intelligence advisers to help reorganize the Guatemalan internal security forces.

In early 1966, FAR decided to support Revolutionary Party candidate Julio César Méndez Montenegro in the upcoming presidential election. Méndez Montenegro won but then signed a secret pact granting the military full impunity to pursue the guerrillas. After this betrayal, FAR moved some of its units to Guatemala City and began kidnapping wealthy Guatemalans and foreign diplomats to exchange them for ransom and political prisoners. In retaliation, the military organized anti-Communist death squads, such as the White Hand, to capture and eliminate suspected subversives. These paramilitary organizations targeted not only guerrillas but also student activists, labor leaders, and campesinos, often torturing their victims in a gruesome but distinguishable manner in order to intimidate other leftists.

The State Department justified the repression as necessary to check a Cuban-backed insurgency. While FAR leaders identified with Third World revolutions and many did visit Cuba to receive guidance and military training, the Guatemalan guerrillas did not take orders from Moscow or Havana, and most of the popular resistance to the counterrevolution did not draw its inspiration from Communism. U.S. officials, however, did not make such distinctions, especially after the assassination of U.S. ambassador Gordon Mein, who was shot by FAR during a botched kidnapping attempt in 1968. Mein's death strengthened Washington's resolve to bolster Guatemala's armed forces with ammunition, machine guns, helicopters, uniforms, radios, computers, and other military equipment. Under its Public Safety Program, the U.S. Agency for International Development (AID) dispatched dozens of special counterinsurgency experts to teach the internal security forces how to track suspected subversives, control crowds, and interrogate suspects. The Guatemalan armed forces received $14 million in U.S. Military Assistance Program aid between 1964 and 1972 (Jonas 1991, 205).

To lure peasants away from the guerrillas, AID also built roads, wells, and schools, and established community leadership training programs. The Peace Corps, which entered Guatemala in the mid 1960s, helped coordinate many of AID's soft development projects, including the formation of hundreds of agricultural cooperatives. Although AID failed

to achieve the specific goals stipulated in the Punta del Este charter of the Alliance for Progress, its development assistance programs contributed to the formation of a popular movement that began to flourish under the influence of a religious reform movement known as Catholic Action.

The Guatemalan Catholic Church had created Catholic Action after World War II to convert potentially rebellious Indians into passive and respectful Christians. The program changed radically after 1954, however, when Castillo Armas invited dozens of foreign priests to Guatemala because of a shortage of local priests. In the 1960s, religious orders such as the Maryknoll Brothers and Sisters, which had long operated missions in the northwest department of Huehuetenango, began organizing Christian base communities that encouraged the poor to read the Bible in ways that developed a collective social conscience, a process known as *concientización*. In these communities, thousands of catequists (local Catholic leaders) established literacy programs, Indian cooperatives, and campesino leagues, often relying indirectly on AID funding.

The development programs sponsored by the Alliance for Progress and Catholic Action proved explosive in a country like Guatemala, where the oligarchy did not take kindly to challenges to its rule. Helping Indians to organize agricultural cooperatives, for example, challenged the control of the fertilizer market by wealthy ladinos and indirectly interfered with the recruitment of migrant laborers. Increased agricultural yields enabled peasants to remain in the highlands, rather than descend to the coast to endure back-breaking work under miserable living conditions. Soon thousands of Catholic priests, community leaders, and labor organizers began to disappear as the civil war expanded into the countryside. In 1968 the Guatemalan government deported several radical Maryknoll priests and one Maryknoll sister for conspiring with the guerrillas. As the expelled Maryknollers later explained to the press, peaceful avenues of change no longer existed in Guatemala; they had felt compelled by their Christian consciences to begin a dialogue with FAR. The Maryknoll incident proved somewhat misleading—few priests and catequists advocated armed struggle—but it helped cast suspicions on anyone in the religious community working for social justice.

A major reorganization of the guerrilla movement in the early 1970s contributed to the oligarchy's perception that the countryside had become a hotbed of Communism. Some members of FAR decided that the guerrillas needed to build greater support among the Indians. They formed a new organization called Guerrilla Army of the Poor (EGP), which began recruiting in the Ixcán region of El Quiché for several years before initiating military operations. The EGP gained notoriety for executing plantation owners with reputations for brutal treatment of the peasantry. Several more revolutionary organizations soon sprouted with similar goals and tactics, but by 1982 they had all coalesced into the URNG (National Revolutionary Unit of Guatemala). The URNG's broad political platform clearly challenged the oligarchy: guarantees of basic civil and human rights, an end to discrimination against Indians, and a major land reform.

Also frightening to Guatemala's rulers was the formation in 1978 of CUC (Committee for Campesino Unity). This national peasant organization, which included poor ladinos but was led mostly by Indians, concerned itself mainly with rectifying Guatemala's grossly unequal distribution of land. According to the 1979 agricultural census, just 2.5 percent of the population held 65 percent of the land, while 88 percent of the population had to grind out a living on 16 percent of the land. (World Bank 1995, v). In May, CUC organized a peaceful demonstration of several hundred Q'eqchi' Indians in the town of Panzós to present land claims against local planters. The Guatemala military fired on the unarmed crowd, killing dozens. The Panzós massacre, as it became known, represented an ominous turning point in the civil war, as political violence began to engulf Mayan communities. In 1980, the Guatemalan riot police firebombed the Spanish embassy, burning to death several dozen peasant protestors. In response, CUC organized massive strikes on South Coast plantations that brought the sugar harvest to a halt.

The threat of a broad-based revolution that included workers, campesinos, and Indians convinced the Guatemalan oligarchy by the early 1980s to support a scorched-earth counterinsurgency campaign against the Maya. The armed forces dispatched units to the Altiplano, where they massacred the inhabitants of more than 400 villages. More than 90 percent of the victims of Guatemala's civil war died between 1978 and 1984 (CEH 1999, 5:42). The army claimed it was targeting only those communities suspected of having collaborated with the guerrillas, but the massacres were so widespread and so transparently aimed at indigenous groups that most human rights investigators concluded that the Guatemalan state was waging a genocidal campaign of terror against the Maya.

Violence in the countryside peaked under the regime of Efraín Ríos Montt, a right-wing evangelical who seized power in a military coup in 1982. President Ronald Reagan praised Montt for his commitment to democracy and complained that the general had received a "bum rap" from human rights organizations. Reagan shifted the blame for the violence in Guatemala to the guerrillas and out-of-control death squads, and he lobbied the U.S. Congress to lift the restrictions it had placed on military aid to Guatemala in 1977. While Congress balked, Reagan administration officials found legislative loopholes that permitted the sale of military spare parts to Guatemala. At the same time, the Guatemalan military relied more heavily on Israel, Argentina, and Taiwan for security assistance so that it could continue the counter-revolution.

The extreme violence began to subside in 1984, when General Oscar Mejía Víctores deposed Ríos Montt in a military coup. To prevent a resurgence of guerrilla activity, the military organized PACs (Civilian Self-Defense Patrols) among the Indian communities. These patrols forced villagers to monitor the surrounding area and report suspicious activity. The army also created "development poles," which were concentrations of "model villages," or resettlement camps subjected to military discipline (Jonas 1991, 150). In these villages AID provided food and electricity, and sponsored civic-action development projects to build roads, schools, and wells. The system succeeded insofar as it prevented the URNG from expanding its base, but the guerrillas, skilled at moving camp quickly, evaded capture and continued to fight into the 1990s.

Soon after the Guatemalan government returned to formal civilian rule in 1985, the U.S. Congress resumed military aid on the grounds that Guatemala had reformed itself. In fact repression against the popular movement continued, but instead of conducting open massacres, the internal security forces (especially an army intelligence unit known as G-2) continued to torture and murder selected students, labor leaders, and other highly visible social activists, such as Guatemalan anthropologist Myrna Mack.

The civil war remained deadlocked until the 1990s when several developments prodded the two sides to come to terms. The collapse of the Soviet Union in 1991 helped undermine the pretext that outside Communist agitators were propping up the Guatemalan guerrillas. At the same time, the Latin American Left realized that an era had ended. No longer could any revolutionary group expect to seize control of the state through armed struggle. The electoral defeat of the Nicaraguan Sandinista Revolution in 1990 and the peace settlement in El Salvador two years later left the URNG isolated in Central America. Despite optimistic pronouncements over the years by the URNG and the Guatemalan armed forces, a decisive battlefield victory by either side did not appear imminent. Bill Clinton's victory in the 1992 presidential election and the Jennifer Harbury case, a scandal which revealed that the CIA still had ties to the death squads, also weakened the military option. For all these reasons, the Guatemalan government and the URNG signed a peace agreement formally ending the war on December 30, 1996.

No sooner had Guatemalans agreed to peace than an academic war erupted in the United States. In 1999, anthropologist David Stoll published an exposé of Rigoberta Menchú, an indigenous activist from Quiché who had won the Nobel Peace Prize in 1992. Stoll disputed many of the factual details of Menchú's *testimonio* (autobiography), including her claim that her personal story represented the general experience of the Mayan community. According to Stoll, solidarity groups, human rights organizations, and North American scholars romanticized indigenous revolutionaries such as Menchú while ignoring that most Indians felt trapped "between two armies." Conservative pundits applauded Stoll's account as an important blow against "political correctness." Most academics, however, disputed Stoll's research methods, questioned his logic, decried his inattention to history, and impugned his intentions.

As the Menchú controversy raged in the United States, Guatemalans joined with the United Nations to begin a process of national reconciliation and healing through the establishment of a truth commission. The Oslo Accords of 1994 created the Commission for Historical Clarification (CEH) to assess the effects of the civil war on the population and make recommendations for reparations. Five years later, the CEH published a report that traced the origins of the war to Guatemala's racist colonial legacy and the state's failure to mediate between divergent social and economic interests. The commission charged the Guatemalan government with genocide: 83 percent of the victims in the civil war were Mayan; state forces and related paramilitary groups had committed 93 percent of the arbitrary executions and forced disappearances (CEH 1999, 5: 21, 25). The report also rejected the "between two armies" thesis, because it failed to address the causes of the violence, its persistence, and the disproportionately large number of deaths among the popular organizations, the Christian base communities, and Mayan villages.

IMPACTS

The Guatemalan October Revolution of 1944 demonstrated that it was possible to break from the colonial past, as the ten years of spring established political and cultural institutions that laid the foundation for modern democracy. During this reform period, Guatemalans learned that political power could be transferred peacefully through honest elections instead of military coups, land reform could be achieved on a national scale, and U.S. hegemony was not absolute. The political opening provided by the revolution enabled the development of peasant, student, and labor organizations that eventually became the bedrock of resistance to the counter-revolution.

The 1954 coup reversed many, but not all, of the gains of the ten years of spring at a gruesome cost to the population. More than 200,000 Guatemalans perished during the thirty-six-year civil war, the vast majority of the victims from Mayan communities in the highlands. Survivors continue to suffer emotional and physical scars from having been beaten, raped, and tortured. The war created 200,000 orphans and up to 1.5 million internal refugees. Another 150,000 fled to

refugee camps along the Mexican border. An untold number of Guatemalans migrated to U.S. cities such as Los Angeles, Houston, New York, and Washington, D.C. (CEH 1999, 2: 285, 5: 38).

The Eisenhower administration's suppression of the Guatemalan Revolution had important international consequences. It signaled other Third World countries that Washington would not tolerate challenges to U.S. hegemony, even if they were democratic. Ernesto "Che" Guevara, who personally witnessed Arbenz's downfall in 1954, learned that the United States would likely attempt to suppress any future revolution in the hemisphere. The Bay of Pigs operation, which the CIA modeled on PBSUCCESS, failed in part because supporters of the Cuban Revolution such as Che were better prepared for the U.S.-backed invasion.

The civil war greatly damaged Guatemala's environment. The military's use of defoliants, state-sponsored relocation projects requiring the clearing of land, and the flight of peasants (Committees of Peoples in Resistance) into the jungle to escape the violence, all contributed to deforestation. In a region just to the south of the Petén known as the "Zone of the Generals," the military encouraged logging to clear the land for cattle ranches. This ecological disruption has led to severe soil erosion and climate modification that threatens many endemic animal and plant species.

An important but perhaps unexpected consequence of the civil war has been the massive conversion of Guatemalans from Catholicism to evangelical Protestantism. While this phenomenon certainly has many complex causes, the counter-revolution appears to have accelerated the trend. The fierce repression against the Catholic Christian base communities and the ascension of Ríos Montt to the presidency appear to have induced some Catholics to convert to Protestantism as a form of refuge.

Economic costs of the civil war, difficult to estimate precisely, include physical damage to the infrastructure, loss of production, capital flight, and diversion of government resources from social services to military spending, thus straining a tax system that was already highly regressive. Lost opportunity costs in the 1980s amounted to 14 percent of the GDP (CEH 1999, 5: 40). The counter-revolution also helped consummate Guatemala's neo-liberal economic transformation. Neo-liberalism is an economic philosophy that advocates the privatization of social services and deregulation of the economy to encourage private investment. Whereas the Latin American Left had formerly championed the statist strategies of development recommended by the Economic Commission on Latin America, most revolutionaries gave up that goal by the 1980s in exchange for political concessions such as honest elections and respect for human rights. This was certainly the case in Guatemala, as business candidates have dominated the electoral process since the peace settlement.

The restoration of democracy in Guatemala since 1996 has been a very troubled process. Although the peace accords greatly reduced state violence and committed the nation in principle to building a democracy, continuing human rights violations against social activists suggest that the Guatemalan oligarchy has still not agreed to share power. The very socioeconomic conditions that fostered the civil war in the first place—namely unequal land distribution, high unemployment, and racial discrimination—remained largely unaddressed by the post-1996 governments, which have catered primarily to the business sector. The homicide rate and vigilantism have skyrocketed, in part because of the proliferation of guns, but also because poverty, insecurity, and the failure of the justice system have generated a climate of despair. One ray of hope has been the revitalization of the popular movement, including Pan-Mayanism, which is diversifying political representation and challenging neo-liberal globalization.

PEOPLE AND ORGANIZATIONS

Arbenz Guzmán, Jacobo (1913–1971)

Arbenz, from a middle-class background, was a graduate of the Guatemalan national military academy who helped lead the 1944 revolution against Ubico. Later, his staunch nationalism, reading of books on revolution and history, and the influences of his wife and their Communist friends attracted him to Marxist-Leninist ideas. Elected president in 1950, Arbenz enacted the largest land reform in Guatemalan history. His term was abruptly terminated in 1954 by a CIA-backed coup. Arbenz did not enjoy exile. He eventually moved to Cuba, but was forever tainted for having failed to arm the workers against Castillo Armas. The next generation of Guatemalan revolutionaries viewed Arbenz as old-fashioned because he did not embrace Che Guevara's guerrilla *foco* theory. He died in Mexico in 1971.

Arévalo, Juan José (1904–1990)

Arévalo, a philosophy professor, returned from exile in 1944 to become the first democratically elected president following the overthrow of Ubico. Arévalo advocated "spiritual socialism," but he acted more like a New Deal Democrat. His government built schools and health clinics, encouraged the formation of unions, and established a social security institute. Arévalo was forced into exile by the 1954 coup. He returned in 1963 to run for president again, but a military coup forced him back into exile, whereupon he retired from politics. Arévalo died in Guatemala City in 1990.

Army Intelligence (G-2)

G-2 is a branch of the Guatemalan military ostensibly responsible for collecting intelligence, but also known informally as the "army's death squad." The unit, which has been operating at least since the 1960s, received considerable technical and military assistance from various U.S. agencies, including the CIA. Several of G-2's leading officers were trained in the School of the Americas, a combat training institute located in Fort Benning, Georgia. (In 2001, the School of the Americas was replaced by the Western Hemisphere Institute for Security Cooperation.)

Castillo Armas, Carlos (1914–1957)

Castillo Armas was an anti-Communist Guatemalan army colonel chosen by the CIA to lead the 1954 coup against Arbenz. His regime initiated the counter-revolution with the economic and military assistance of the Eisenhower administration. While publicly heaping praise on the "liberator," U.S. officials privately regarded Castillo Armas as a pathetically weak leader who literally had to be held by the hand. He was assassinated by a palace guard in 1957.

Catholic Action

Catholic Action was an important religious movement that helped organize Christian base communities in the 1960s and 1970s. The leaders of these communities organized peasant leagues, cooperatives, and literacy programs in the highlands in order to help the poor achieve a higher standard of living. Under the influence of Liberation Theology, many Catholic Action workers attempted to raise peasant consciousness through critical readings of the Bible and self-help discussion groups. The movement was decimated by the government's internal security forces, which murdered radical priests and their followers under the pretext that they had become Communist sympathizers.

César Montes, Julio (Born 1942)

Julio César Macías (alias César Montes), is one of the oldest surviving Guatemalan guerrilla commanders. His memoirs provide valuable insight into the guerrilla movement. As one of the founders of FAR, Montes witnessed the convoluted transformation of the various guerrilla organizations that culminated in the formation of the URNG in 1982.

Chambers of Commerce, Industry, and Finance (CACIF)

CACIF is a business association that unites the agrarian and industrial elite. As the most powerful representative of the Guatemalan oligarchy, CACIF encouraged the military to conduct the counter-revolution to preserve the social order. Composed of wealthy planters, industrialists, and bankers, this coalition became the driving force behind the neoliberal transition following the peace accords.

Civilian Self-Defense Patrols (PAC)

PACs were mandatory paramilitary organizations formed by the Guatemalan military in the early 1980s as part of the highlands scorched-earth campaign. The program, which included more than a million participants at its peak, was designed to force the population to support the counterinsurgency effort. All males above the age of sixteen were required to spend several days each week patrolling the areas surrounding their towns and reporting on suspected subversives. The PAC system was highly abusive and widely hated by most Indians, who tried to resist its implementation. PACs were officially disbanded by the Peace Accords of 1996, but they soon re-emerged in the form of Community Security Committees, which are currently suspected of violating human rights.

Commission for Historical Clarification (CEH)

CEH was created by the 1994 Oslo Accords to investigate human rights violations during the civil war, determine their causes, and make recommendations for reparations. CEH's final report, published in 1999, stunned the world with the revelation that more than 200,000 Guatemalans had perished in a genocidal war conducted by the Guatemalan state on behalf of the oligarchy.

Committee for Campesino Unity (CUC)

CUC was a national peasant organization that formed in 1978. The organization was created largely by church groups concerned with indigenous issues, but it also incorporated poor ladinos. CUC organized the demonstration that resulted in the Panzós massacre. In January 1980 several CUC protes-

tors were burned alive in the Spanish embassy, including the father of Mayan activist Rigoberta Menchú. The following month CUC staged its most successful action, a major strike on the South Coast sugar plantations that gained agricultural workers an increase in the minimum wage.

Guatemalan Labor (Communist) Party (Partido Guatemalteco Del Trabajo—PGT)

The Guatemalan Communist Party, created in the 1920s, became the most persecuted political party in Guatemalan history. The party's heyday was the Arbenz administration (1950–1954), when it enjoyed a close association with the president and helped him to enact a land reform. The PGT was made illegal by the regimes that followed the 1954 coup. The PGT attempted to maintain a loose association with a variety of guerrilla organizations, but factionalism, dogmatism, and severe repression kept the party from regaining its former glory.

Menchú, Rigoberta (Born 1959)

Menchú is an Indian activist from Quiché whose famous autobiography (*testimonio*) explains Mayan culture and details the horrors committed by the military against Indians during the civil war. Menchú's *testimonio*, which was an international bestseller in the 1980s, generated controversy after a U.S. anthropologist claimed that she had partially fabricated her story to appeal to a Western audience. Menchú stood by her account, as have most academics, who still view it as offering a valuable perspective on the indigenous struggle in Guatemala. After winning the Nobel Peace Prize in 1992, Menchú established a human rights foundation.

National Revolutionary Union of Guatemala (URNG)

The URNG was formed in 1982 through the merger of four different rebel organizations. Unlike the earlier guerrilla organizations, which clung to class analysis and ignored indigenous peoples, URNG sought to unite Indians and ladinos in the revolutionary struggle. After agreeing to disarm following the 1996 peace agreement, the organization became a political party by the same name.

Ríos Montt, Efraín (Born 1926)

Montt is a Guatemalan general who seized power in a military coup in 1982. He oversaw the worst massacres in the highlands and implemented the "rifles and beans" program to reward peasants who collaborated with the military and to punish those deemed guerrilla sympathizers. Montt is a born-again evangelical with strong ties to Christian fundamentalists in the United States. He was deposed in a military coup in 1983. He was later elected to congress and made several unsuccessful and illegal bids to run for the presidency.

United Fruit Company (UFCO)

The United Fruit Company was a multinational corporation, headquartered in Boston, that controlled the Guatemalan banana industry during the first half of the twentieth century. Guatemalan critics dubbed UFCO "the octopus" because of its tentacle-like grip over the national economy. Some observers believe the fruit company plotted to overthrow Arbenz because of his land reform, but the Eisenhower administration engineered the 1954 coup to restore U.S. hegemony, not to defend the UFCO estate. Castillo Armas returned expropriated land to UFCO shortly after coming to power, but in 1957 the U.S. Justice Department prosecuted the company under anti-trust laws, forcing it to sell its subsidiaries. UFCO fell into financial difficulties in the 1970s and was eventually purchased by Del Monte.

U.S. Agency for International Development (AID)

AID was created in 1961 to administer the distribution of economic aid in developing countries. To win the "hearts and minds" of the Guatemalan peasantry, AID supported grassroots development programs by building roads, schools, wells, and by sponsoring literacy and local leadership programs. As a branch of the State Department, AID was also in charge of the Public Safety Program, which equipped and trained the internal security forces.

U.S. Central Intelligence Agency (CIA)

The CIA, which was created in 1947, engineered the overthrow of the Arbenz government in 1954. The agency's covert operation in Guatemala, known as PBSUCCESS, became a blueprint for the ill-fated Bay of Pigs operation in Cuba. The CIA was instrumental in organizing and strengthening the intelligence capabilities of the Guatemalan internal security forces during the counter-revolution. The agency maintained close ties to G-2 and other death squads, even keeping on the payroll assets who had killed American citizens, such as Michael Devine, an American businessman who was murdered in 1990.

Stephen M. Streeter

See Also Cuban Revolution; Democracy, Dictatorship, and Fascism; Documentaries of Revolution; Human Rights; Terrorism

References and Further Readings

Arias, Arturo, ed. 2000. *The Rigoberta Menchú Controversy.* Minnesota: University of Minnesota Press.

Carmack, Robert, ed. 1988. *Harvest of Violence: The Maya Indians and the Guatemalan Crisis.* Norman, OK: University of Oklahoma Press.

César Macías, Julio. 1999. *La guerrilla fue mi camino: epitafio para César Montes [The Guerrilla Movement Was My Path: The Epitaph of César Montes].* Guatamala City, Guatemala: Editorial Piedra Santa Arandi.

Comisión para el Esclarecimiento Histórico (CEH). 1999. *Guatemala: memoria del silencio. [Guatemala: Memory of Silence].* Guatemala. *http://shr.aaas.org/guatemala/ceh/gmds_pdf/index.html* accessed June 17, 2005.

Cullather, Nick. 1999. *Secret History: The C.I.A.'s Classified Account of Its Operations in Guatemala.* Stanford, CA: Stanford University Press.

Davis, Shelton, and Julie Hodson. 1983. *Witnesses to Political Violence in Guatemala: The Suppression of a Rural Development Program,* 2nd edition. Boston: Oxfam.

Dosal, Paul J. 1995. *Power in Transition: The Rise of Guatemala's Industrial Oligarchy, 1871–1994.* New York: Praeger.

Falla, Ricardo. 1993. *Massacres in the Jungle: Ixcán, Guatemala, 1975–1982.* Boulder, CO: Westview Press.

Garrard-Burnett, Virginia. 1998. *Protestantism in Guatemala: Living in the New Jerusalem.* Austin: University of Texas Press.

Gleijeses, Piero. 1991. *Shattered Hope: The Guatemalan Revolution and the United States, 1944–1954.* Princeton, NJ: Princeton University Press.

Handy, Jim. 1994. *Revolution in the Countryside: Agrarian Reform and Rural Conflict in Guatemala, 1944–1954.* Chapel Hill: University of North Carolina Press.

———. 2004. "Chicken Thieves, Witches, and Judges: Vigilante Justice and Customary Law in Guatemala," *Journal of Latin American Studies* 36, 3: 533–561.

Jonas, Susanne. 1991. *The Battle for Guatemala: Rebels, Death Squads, and U.S. Power.* Boulder, CO: Westview Press.

Manz, Beatriz. 1988. *Refugees of a Hidden War: The Aftermath of Counterinsurgency in Guatemala.* New York: State University of New York Press.

May, Rachel A. 2001. *Terror in the Countryside: Campesino Responses to Political Violence in Guatemala, 1954–1985.* Athens: Ohio University Press.

McClintock, Michael. 1985. *The American Connection.* vol. 2, *State Terror and Popular Resistance in Guatemala.* London: Zed.

Menchú, Rigoberta. 1984. *I, Rigoberta Menchú: An Indian Woman in Guatemala.* London: Verso.

Nash, June C. 2001. *Mayan Visions: The Quest for Autonomy in an Age of Globalization.* New York: Routledge.

Schirmer, Jennifer. 1998. *The Guatemalan Military Project: A Violence Called Democracy.* Philadelphia: University of Pennsylvania Press.

Schlesinger, Stephen, and Stephen Kinzer. 1999. *Bitter Fruit: The Story of the American Coup in Guatemala.* 2nd edition. Cambridge, MA: David Rockefeller Center Series on Latin American Studies, Harvard University.

Smith, Carol A., ed. 1990. *Guatemalan Indians and the State, 1540 to 1988.* Austin: University of Texas Press.

Stoll, David. 1999. *Rigoberta Menchú and the Story of All Poor Guatemalans.* Boulder, CO: Westview Press.

Streeter, Stephen M. 2000a. "Interpreting the 1954 U.S. Intervention in Guatemala: Realist, Revisionist, and Postrevisionist Perspectives," *History Teacher* 34, 1: 61–74.

———. 2000b. *Managing the Counterrevolution: The United States and Guatemala, 1954–1961.* Athens: Ohio University Press.

World Bank. 1995. *Guatemala: An Assessment of Poverty.* June 17, 2005.

Guerrilla Warfare and Revolution

HISTORIC AND THEORETICAL CONSIDERATIONS

Major sociopolitical upheavals during the twentieth century often led scholars and ordinary observers alike into a casual linkage of revolutionary movements with guerrilla warfare (from the Spanish, meaning "little war"). This combination of movements' goals with a particular military strategy was encouraged, in particular, by those Marxist revolutionaries who wrote systematically on the subject, including Vladimir Lenin, Mao Zedong, Vo Nguyen Giap, Ernesto "Che" Guevara (1997), and Carlos Marighella in his manual for the urban guerrilla. The linkage remains strong, even if we recognize that precisely the same tactics have also been used by fighters of the right to attack left-wing regimes, notably against the Sandinista government of Nicaragua in the 1980s.

Yet the practice of guerrilla warfare antedated by millennia those twentieth-century revolutionary struggles, and even very old military theories like those of Sun Tzu seem to be describing, even advocating, something like guerrilla warfare. Guerrilla warfare is almost surely the most ancient form of war, and humankind has consistently been able to reinvent it whenever a people is faced with a violent struggle against a foe superior in numbers, technology, or both. Thus handicapped, the almost natural inclination is to reinvent the strategy: "to avoid direct, massed engagements with the enemy and instead to concentrate on slowly sapping the enemy's strength and morale through ambushes, minor skirmishes, lightning raids and withdrawals, cutting of communications and supply lines, and similar techniques" (Wickham-Crowley 1992, 3). These combatants quickly discover that the technique is also an excellent means by which to arm your own forces, often with far more potent weaponry. Thus we should not be surprised that Walter Laqueur (1976), in his sweeping historical review of guerrillas, draws our attention all the way back to the ancient Hittites, whose king commented bitterly on enemies who only struck at his sleeping people at night and then vanished into the darkness. Various "barbarian" forces also typically resorted to guerrilla warfare in the ancient world to fight the Roman legions—usually without success, it should be noted. Yet in the battle of the Teutoberg Forest (dramatized in the miniseries *I, Claudius*), Vercingetorix and the Gauls inflicted a huge defeat on the Roman legions trapped in an inferior tactical position, even though those same Gauls later succumbed when they resorted to non-guerrilla strategies, in allowing themselves to be besieged and later defeated at Alesia. Such historical exemplars are simply too numerous to recount here (but see Asprey 1994).

In those past centuries, a populace usually employed guerrilla warfare in response to foreign invaders and conquerors, and thus ethnic cohesion could provide strong guarantees of cooperation and support for those who took up arms to oppose invaders. The crucial development during the last century or two has been the use of guerrilla warfare in the context of internal struggles for power, civil wars, and revolutionary upheavals. With the increasingly common use of revolutionary insurgency by portions of the local populace seeking to unseat incumbent indigenous rulers, those elements of ethnic solidarity no longer assure the silent consent (minimally) or the vigorous active participation (maximally) of one's own people with the insurgents.

Unsurprisingly then, modern-day theorists of insurgency and of counterinsurgency devote much of their prose in trying to understand when, where, from whom, and how such support will be provided, either to the revolutionaries or to the incumbent regime and its armed defenders. Thus we have Mao's famous dictum that the revolutionaries should move through the supportive population like "a fish through water" and to pursue policies that ensure such environs; or Giap's assertion that a revolutionary struggle seeks to become a "people's war," so that the armed forces of governments (whether colonial or native-run) face, not just the relatively few armed insurgents, but a massive, popularly supported "infrastructure" as well; and we have Che Guevara's oft-criticized *foco* theory of revolution, which also insists that popular support is crucial to eventual success, where a very small initial nucleus of fighters can rapidly expand its numbers, weaponry, support, and power by commencing an armed revolutionary effort even before a popularly supported revolutionary infrastructure exists. In general, however, each of these theories and all of these guerrilla organizations foresaw a generally similar scenario of expansion: they would begin by controlling the more peripheral national areas where the power and reach of the state apparatus is weakest; later they would add more and more national terrain to their "holdings," perhaps best measured by which armed forces control the area at nighttime; and finally they would control very large segments of the national

Argentinian rebel Ernesto "Che" Guevara, who helped Fidel Castro's forces win the Cuban Revolution, with his left arm in a sling, January 7, 1959, Havana, Cuba. Shortly before this picture was taken, Guevara had led a force of Cuban revolutionary guerrillas to victory at the Battle of Santa Clara.

terrain with many more fighters and arms added to their side of the conflict, eventually forcing the incumbent regime and its defenders into either surrendering or, more strikingly, militarily switching sides in the course of the conflict, thus hastening the regime's downfall.

In a more recent climate of political conflict and discourse, however, guerrilla-revolutionaries are viewed through a different lens, often automatically labeled as "terrorists." Such a labeling surely suggests the politicization of our language, not a carefully considered concept. If we reserve the terms "terror" and "terrorist" for acts of violence that systematically injure or kill unarmed civilian populations—whether those actions consciously target civilians or simply engulf them indiscriminately—then we can see that terror is a narrow tactic more than a general strategy for seizing power. Some guerrilla groups may use terror, others may

not: very little terror was used by Fidel Castro's guerrillas during the Cuban struggle of the 1950s; a great deal was employed by the Shining Path in the 1980s in Peru; and the Cambodian Khmer Rouge used terror both in opposition and (more overwhelmingly) as a government in the 1970s.

Based upon worldwide comparative analyses, we can also generally assert that government armed forces (including thinly disguised offshoots of government like certain paramilitary forces and some death squads) are more likely to visit terror upon civilians during an insurgency than are the insurgents themselves. To be more precise: government terror against civilians is more likely to be indiscriminate and to take more lives, while insurgents' use of terror is more likely to be precisely targeted against those seen as opposing the cause of revolution. While we have little careful theorizing about terror, sociologist Wickham-Crowley has argued that either side in a revolutionary struggle is most likely to use terror when its claim to be a legitimate government (the incumbents) or a legitimate counter-state-in-formation (the revolutionary insurgents) is "opposed" by the civilian population in acts of noncompliance, resistance to commands, active disobedience, or even support for one's foes. Thus "governments-in-decline," whether the incumbent regimes or "guerrilla governments," tend to use terror more frequently and to take more lives than those polities whose standing among the populace is stable and secure (Wickham-Crowley 1991, chapters 2, 3).

In the later decades of the twentieth century, "urban guerrilla warfare" appeared as a new approach (yet now is rarely advocated seriously as a strategy for revolution). Rather than a return to the urban-barricades tactics of European revolutionaries of the past, the urban guerrillas saw their strategy (at least in Latin America) as a step beyond Guevara's peasant-and-countryside *foco* theory. Especially they saw in it a method far more suited to the overwhelmingly urban societies of more developed areas of Latin America (and Europe), where 70 percent or more of the populace lived in large cities and where land-tenure issues were thoroughly marginal ones in the national consciousness. Thus the most prominent urban guerrilla groups arose in Germany, Italy, the "Southern Cone" countries of South America (that is, Argentina, Chile, and Uruguay), and also in Brazil. These groups often resorted to bank robberies and kidnappings, and in many instances indiscriminate forms of bombings and suchlike that typically earned them the label of "terrorist" from the authorities, often appropriately (Russell and Miller 1977).

Yet such alternative revolutionary strategies soon faded, for at least two good reasons. First, urban guerrillas never had any clear means or theory by which to convert nuisance activities or even wide-scale bombings into direct confrontations with the incumbent state. Second, they remained exceptionally vulnerable to repressive state actions, since they operated where the state presence was strongest and were often quickly dismantled once the military or the security forces were given a freer hand in pursuing them. Thus most of these groups were shattered and their leaders captured or killed after less than a decade of operations, a fate which also often befell the urban wings of otherwise rural guerrilla-revolutionary groups, notably in 1950s Cuba and 1980s Guatemala.

THE SOCIAL COMPOSITION OF REVOLUTIONARY GUERRILLA FORCES

The leaders and the rank and file of revolutionary organizations are generally not drawn from similar social backgrounds, as observers have noted since the time of Karl Marx and Frederick Engels (themselves drawn, respectively, from upper-middle-class and propertied upper-class backgrounds). Thus, while earlier urban-based revolutionaries may have drawn their greatest number of supporters and participants from the working classes in places as diverse as Russia and Germany in the 1910s and Bolivia in 1952, the leadership there and elsewhere was still drawn from the well-educated sons (occasionally daughters) of the relatively privileged, with scarcely a worker found among the higher echelons of revolutionaries. Sociologist Alvin Gouldner (1979, 53–73) not only confirmed those leadership patterns for a number of twentieth-century revolutionary groups, mostly guerrilla organizations, but also developed a theory linking their paradoxical revolutionism to their educations in universities where highly critical views of the status quo, critiques both theoretical and moral, are nurtured, sustained, and further elaborated.

For numerous Latin American revolutionary guerrilla organizations operating over the past fifty years, Wickham-Crowley (1992, chapters 2, 9, appendixes A, B) provides further evidence of the elite or upper-middle-class background of most revolutionary leaders. The peasants who came to be the mainstays of support (almost everywhere) and of membership (usually) for more than a dozen different revolutionary guerrilla groups in the region almost never were leaders when the movements were founded and rarely rose to the highest ranks thereafter; various guerrilla groups in Colombia provide the only clear, major exceptions to that rule. Even later groups like the Zapatistas, who went into action in 1994 in Chiapas, Mexico, clearly echo this long-established pattern. The urban, privileged, and well-educated character of revolutionary leaders was even more pronounced for the urban guerrilla organizations (Russell and Miller 1977).

With regard to the gender and racial/ethnic composition of guerrilla groups, most of them began as overwhelmingly male-staffed organizations, whether in Latin America or elsewhere, with women often left in thoroughly marginal roles when permitted to join. Beginning with the urban guerrilla groups that appeared circa 1970 in both Europe and Latin America, there was a distinct shift: women entered in far higher percentages, and many became more central to the overall command structure. By the 1970s and 1980s the Latin American (and perhaps African) guerrilla organizations became ever more gender-egalitarian in membership and command opportunities, in both urban and rural wings (Wickham-Crowley 1992, chapters 2, 9), even if many issues and conflicts about gender remained. The increased numbers of women in revolutionary guerrilla armies reflected a shift away from what many regarded as the flawed quick-road-to-revolution-guerrilla-*foco* approach (after the death of its main advocate Guevara in Bolivia in 1967) to the prolonged war effort of the Nicaraguan Sandinistas and the Farabundo National Liberation Front in El Salvador, "which implies a greater emphasis on the sheer, long-term accumulation of human support" (Wickham-Crowley 1992, 215). The trend toward greater women's participation also likely resulted from the effects of the globalization of feminism and the efforts of leftist revolutionaries to cope with the apparent contradiction of fighting for equality while not significantly addressing the issue of the subordination of women in society. The ethnic and racial composition of guerrilla groups often came to be slowly more aligned with the populations of the territories where the guerrillas operated most securely (as with the Guatemalan or Peruvian indigenous peoples who moved into these groups in the 1970s). But in many world conflicts, the revolutionary movements' foundations were rooted in ethnic differences and conflicts as such, as in most of Africa and much of Asia (e.g., Sri Lanka's Tamil Tigers). Hence an element of ethnic irredentism or separatist nationalism characterized these revolutionary civil wars, with corresponding echoes of those age-old, inter-ethnic settings for guerrilla warfare.

WHEN WILL REVOLUTIONARY GUERRILLA MOVEMENTS WIN POPULAR SUPPORT OR STATE POWER?

Professional revolutionaries also considered that there might well be specific economic circumstances (especially of the peasantry) and political scenarios (the varied forms of national governance) that would either enhance or damage the insurgents' chances for success. Scholars and other analysts see such theories naturally dovetailing with questions already long raised in formal studies of social movements (and their supporters) and of revolutions (and the conditions for their failures and successes).

Many writers have argued for economic correlates of support for, and the success rate of, revolutionary insurgencies. Those economic conditions for revolution could be of a macroeconomic sort wherein, for example, the overall living standards of rural populations are systematically damaged not only by economic depressions, but also by deepening exactions made by landlords and by central government tax collectors that leave fewer and fewer resources in the hands of cultivating classes. That latter source of economic "assault" on peasant living standards became the centerpiece of "moral economy" theories seeking to explain peasant uprisings (Scott 1976, on Southeast Asia, is the foundational work). Similarly, for Central American and Peruvian guerrilla insurgencies, political scientists Booth (1991) and McClintock (1998) confirm the radical consequences of the economic damages caused both by landlord actions and by government actions or inactions, even if the peasants' outright loss of land itself figures more prominently in these Latin American cases than in the Southeast Asian ones. But such "living-standard" theories also tend to place these localized, national economic trends in the context of a world capitalist economy whose routine operations can pressure landlords and states to seek more resources from rural populations but which also provides new market opportunities and incentives for landlords and others to reorient the use of land away from subsistence use to export agriculture.

The expansion of export agriculture is seen by both moral-economy theory and in sociologist Jeffery Paige's (1975) class-conflict theory of agrarian revolution as a prime mover behind massive and increasing forms of peasant discontent and rural uprisings. While neither theory's focus concerns peasants joining revolutionary guerrilla organizations, both theories can deeply illuminate the actual patterns of peasant support and non-support for Latin American guerrilla movements over the last half-century (Wickham-Crowley 1992, chapters 6, 10), and the work of sociologist John Foran (1997) suggests a broader, more global applicability of these ideas. Wickham-Crowley (1992, chapters 6, 10) also confirms many of Paige's correlations between sharecropping and migratory-labor forms of cultivation and a predisposition to support revolutionary groups, but also suggests a similar pattern for squatters as well. Beyond those extensions, Paige's own statistical analysis of sharecropper-based revolutionary Socialist movements and their tactics points toward their regular resort to (guerrilla) warfare in the period he studied, 1948–1970, involving 135 world export-agricultural regions (Paige 1975, 104–120).

Yet all strictly economic theories of guerrilla warfare and revolution necessarily leave out the political elements whereby incumbent rulers are unseated and replaced by their revolutionary opponents. Those theorists who have most called into question such economic theories of revolution and argued for largely political causes (or geopolitical ones) have been sociologists Theda Skocpol and also Jeff Goodwin (2001); his work engages us more directly, focusing on guerrilla movements as such, including "persistent insurgencies," a situation of regime-insurgent stalemate. From Goodwin's perspective, the very structure of regimes and also the political actions taken by state managers (notably indiscriminate violence) are likely to predict whether or not insurgencies as such develop and come to challenge incumbent governments. Exceptionally violent state actions in remote rural areas, he argues, are likely to lead to persistent insurgencies, regardless of other conditions, including nominal elections or economic upturns. He also argues carefully, in a complex comparative analysis of four cases each from Central America and from Southeast Asia, that only "exclusionary dictatorial regimes" with narrow support bases are likely to be overthrown by such revolutionary insurgencies (for related views, see Loveman and Davies in Guevara 1997; Foran 1997; and Wickham-Crowley 1992, chapters 8, 11). This overarching view allows him to treat four post-war anti-colonial rebellions in Southeast Asia; the insurgents seized power only where the colonial state apparatus excluded the participation of native elites (the French in Vietnam). He also considers four cases from Central America, where a Marxian-led insurgency succeeded only in Nicaragua—and not because economic conditions there were worse or the insurgency militarily strongest—but because a "sultanistic" or personalistic form of civilian-cum-military rule by Anastasio Somoza Debayle systematically excluded all other participants and proved uniquely vulnerable to an assault from below, unlike more bureaucratic-military or vaguely democratic forms of government elsewhere (for similar conclusions, see Wickham-Crowley 1992, chapters 8, 11, 12). Analyses by Goodwin and many other scholars have also resoundingly confirmed that democratic systems, with governments elected in fair and free elections, seem to be invulnerable to overthrow by revolutionary insurgencies.

Timothy P. Wickham-Crowley

See Also Angolan Revolution; Chinese Revolution; Cinema of Revolution; Cuban Revolution; Documentaries of Revolution; Elites, Intellectuals, and Revolutionary Leadership; Malayan Rebellion; Mozambique Revolution; Nicaraguan Revolution; Palestinian Movement; Philippine Huks and the New People's Army; Philippine Muslim Separatist Rebellions; Salvadoran Revolution; Student and Youth Movements, Activism and Revolution; Terrorism; Vietnamese Revolution; Women and Revolution; Zapatista Movement; Zimbabwean Revolution

References and Further Readings
Asprey, Robert B. 1994. *War in the Shadows: The Guerrilla in History.* New York: W. Morrow. (Originally: 2 vols. 1975. New York: Doubleday.)

Booth, John. 1991. "Socioeconomic and Political Roots of National Revolts in Central America," *Latin American Research Review* 26 (1): 33–73.

Foran, John. 1997. "The Comparative-Historical Sociology of Third World Social Revolutions: Why a Few Succeed, Why Most Fail." Pp. 227–267 in *Theorizing Revolutions,* edited by John Foran. London and New York: Routledge.

Goodwin, Jeff. 2001. *No Other Way Out: States and Revolutionary Movements, 1945–1991.* Cambridge and New York: Cambridge University Press.

Gouldner, Alvin W. 1979. *The Future of Intellectuals and the Rise of the New Class.* New York: Continuum.

Guevara, Ernesto "Che." 1997. *Guerrilla Warfare.* 3rd edition. Revised and updated introduction and case studies by Brian Loveman and Thomas M. Davies, Jr. Wilmington, DE: Scholarly Resources.

Laqueur, Walter. 1976. *Guerrilla: A Historical and Critical Study.* Boston: Little, Brown.

McClintock, Cynthia. 1998. *Revolutionary Movements in Latin America: El Salvador's FMLN and Peru's Shining Path.* Washington, DC: United States Institute of Peace Press.

Paige, Jeffrey, 1975. *Agrarian Revolution: Social Movements and Export Agriculture in the Underdeveloped World.* New York: Free Press.

Russell, Charles A., and Captain Bowman H. Miller. 1977. "Profile of a Terrorist," *Military Review* 57 (August): 21–34.

Scott, James C. (1976) *The Moral Economy of the Peasant: Rebellion and Subsistence in Southeast Asia.* New Haven: Yale University Press.

Wickham-Crowley, Timothy P. 1991. *Exploring Revolution: Essays on Latin American Insurgency and Revolutionary Theory.* Armonk, NY: M. E. Sharpe.

———. 1992. *Guerrillas and Revolution in Latin America: A Comparative Study of Insurgents and Regimes since 1956.* Princeton, NJ: Princeton University Press.

Guinea-Bissau: Revolution and Independence

CHRONOLOGY

1250s	Formation of the kingdom of Kaabu in Guinea-Bissau.
1400s	Portuguese establish fortified trading centers in Bissau and Cacheu.
1884–1885	Partition of Africa by European powers meeting at the Berlin Congress.
1880s–1930s	Portugal wages violent "pacification" wars in Guinea-Bissau to assert control.
1926	Portuguese republican government overthrown and a Fascist state is established.
1928–1930	António de Oliveira Salazar consolidates Fascist power in Portugal.
1945	PIDE (International and State Defense Police) created to fight the opponents of colonialism and Fascism.
1951	Status of Guinea changes from "colony" to "overseas province."
1954	MING (National Independence Movement of Portuguese Guinea) is created.
1956	Amilcar Cabral and associates create a liberation movement, PAIGC (African Party of Independence for Guinea and Cape Verde) to free Guinea-Bissau and Cape Verde.
1963–1974	Period of national liberation and armed struggle in Guinea-Bissau.
1973	Assassination of Amilcar Cabral. Guinea-Bissau admitted as the forty-second member of the Organization of African Unity (OAU).
1974	The Portuguese MFA (Armed Forces Movement) overthrows the Fascist military government there and recognizes the independence of Guinea-Bissau.
1975	Cape Verde achieves independence.

INTRODUCTION

For centuries, the people of the Republic of Guinea-Bissau have resisted domination from a series of overlords, slave traders, and Portuguese colonialists. This strong tradition of resistance has been a unifying theme in Guinea-Bissau's history, and nothing exemplifies this tradition better than its eleven-year war for national liberation. In September 1974, more than 400 years of Portuguese colonial rule was brought to an end by the Partido Africano de Independência de Guiné e Cabo Verde or PAIGC (African Party of Independence of Guinea and Cape Verde), long led by revolutionary theoretician and practitioner Amilcar Lopes Cabral.

BACKGROUND: CULTURE AND HISTORY

The area known today as the Republic of Guinea-Bissau has a long and complex history. Guinea-Bissau was once home to the powerful kingdom of Kaabu, a vassal state of the great medieval Malian empire, and often served as a major entry point for European explorers, missionaries, and traders. The first Europeans to reach the shores of Guinea-Bissau were the Portuguese in the 1400s. But for many years Portuguese influence in Guinea-Bissau was limited to a small number of fortified trading centers in Bissau and Cacheu.

During the Berlin Congress of 1884–1885, European powers such as Portugal, Germany, France, and England formally and arbitrarily partitioned Africa. As a result, no new European colony would be recognized unless its territory was effectively occupied, which meant that European officials had to establish visible and effective power in the areas claimed. This requirement precipitated a military "scramble for Africa" with colonial wars of "pacification." From the 1880s to the 1930s, Portugal waged a series of brutal "pacification" campaigns against the people of Guinea-Bissau. Nevertheless, at the turn of the century, Portuguese authority in Guinea-Bissau was purely nominal, for the spirit of resistance among the people of Guinea remained strong. It was further enhanced by the clandestine acquisition of modern firearms from coastal traders.

In the next decade, the new republican government in Portugal placed a greater emphasis on crushing Guinean resistance. The colonial administration succeeded in conquering most of the land through manipulation and force, and with the arrival of Captain João Teixeira Pinto in 1912, Portugal began to effectively occupy Guinea-Bissau. The infamous Captain Pinto led colonial troops in a pillaging rampage across Guinea, for which he was awarded the highest Portuguese military honor, Cavaleiro da Ordem da Torre e Espada (Noble of the Order of the Bull and Sword). Now under the command and guidance of colonial agent José Ferreira Diniz, Guinea moved toward a system not unlike apartheid as it was constituted in South Africa. Nonetheless, the people of Guinea continued to resist.

The Nature of Portuguese Colonialism

After the military conquest of Guinea, the Portuguese sought to quickly extend colonial administration to all parts of the territory. For instance, in 1918, an office of Negócios Indigenas (Native Affairs) was established in the coastal city of Boloma, then the capital of the colony. Although the Portuguese controlled the colonial administration, Cape Verdeans and mestiços (people of mixed race) held the vast majority of the administrative posts and were responsible for collecting all colonial taxes, maintaining all public works, recruiting labor, and establishing law and order throughout the colony. Meanwhile, the Portuguese inflicted the harshest forms of forced labor (for the production of cash crops such as rice and palm oil), racial degradation (by its policy of "assimilation"), cultural destruction (via its missão civilizadora or "civilizing mission"), and economic exploitation (which left the overwhelming majority of Guineans without adequate food, shelter, or means to subsist). The Portuguese showed little interest in developing the area for the welfare of its inhabitants, who were regarded as no more than a source of unlimited labor.

By all accounts, Portuguese Guinea was a highly stratified society. The inhabitants of Guinea were classified into the following categories: civilizados (civilized) or não civilizados (uncivilized), as well as assimilados (assimilated) or indigenas (natives). The majority of the indigenous population of Guinea was classified as "uncivilized" and "native." Under the missão civilizadora, Guineans received a colonial education aimed at creating, not an African intelligentsia, but obedient colonial collaborators. Through education, employment, land ownership, and/or military service, Guineans could attain the privilege of civilizado or assimilado status. But only a small portion of the Guineaen population (less than 5 percent) assimilated.

Portugal's political environment and colonial aspirations changed dramatically on May 28, 1926. The Portuguese republicans were overthrown and Fascism was established under General Gomes da Costa. In 1928–1933, António de Oliveira Salazar consolidated Fascist power in Portugal under the banner of the Estado Novo (New State). This blueprint for Portuguese Fascism and colonialism prevailed in Guinea-Bissau until the revolutionary period (1963–1974). As a result of the newly created Estado Novo regime, political repression occurred in Portugal and increased in its African colonies, and colonial exploitation intensified.

Following World War II, the Cold War atmosphere gave rise to the repressive Portuguese state security apparatus known as Polícia International e de Defesa do Estado (PIDE, International and State Defense Police) in 1945. PIDE's mission was to crush anti-colonial and anti-Fascist resistance in Portugal and Africa under the banner of "fighting Communism." Yet, a Pan-African conference in Manchester, England, in 1947 called for the complete independence of Africa, and Henrique Galvão, a Portuguese republican, reported on the abhorrent labor conditions in Portuguese Africa. To drown out these voices, in 1949 the Portuguese opened a high security prison in Tarafal, Cape Verde Islands, for their many political opponents and anti-colonial sympathizers.

In 1950 Amilcar Cabral completed his studies in agronomy at the University of Lisbon and returned to Praia, Cape Verde. Meanwhile, at the Third Pan-African Congress in London, representatives protested Portuguese colonialism. In response, the Portuguese changed the status of Guinea from "colony" to "overseas province" in 1951.

CONTEXT AND PROCESS OF REVOLUTION

Early Anti-Colonial Resistance

Despite Portuguese efforts to stunt any movement expressing anti-colonial and nationalist sentiments, Guineans and their Cape Verdean counterparts carried on with aspirations for freedom and liberty. They began to study the revolutionary writings of Karl Marx, Friedrich Engels, V. I. Lenin, C. L. R. James, and others in order to formulate their own political strategies for national liberation. Early leaders from Lusophone Africa (Portuguese-controlled Africa) included Agostinho Neto, a medical doctor and first president of the Movimento Popular de Libertação de Angola (MPLA, Popular Movement for the Liberation of Angola); Eduardo Mondlane, founder of Frente de Libertação de Mocambique (FRELIMO, Liberation Front for Mozambique); and Amilcar Cabral. Often meeting in Lisbon, these three revolutionaries, along with many others, discussed the plight of colonial subjects and ways to end Portuguese Fascism and colonialism.

Although the PAIGC was the dominant and best-known nationalist party in Guinea-Bissau, it was not the sole party to articulate anti-colonial sentiments. In 1954 Amilcar Cabral and Henri Labéry clandestinely organized the Movimeto para Independência Nacional da Guiné Portuguesa (MING, National Independence Movement of Portuguese Guinea) in the capital of Bissau. Although its program was ineffective and its tenure short-lived, MING was the organizational predecessor of the PAIGC. Then on September 19, 1956, Cabral, his brother Luís Cabral, Fernando Fortes, Aristides Pereira, Rafael Barbosa, and others met secretly in Bissau to form the PAIGC (or PAI) and to begin clandestine organizing. The main difference between the MING and the PAIGC was the latter's inclusion of independence for the Cape Verde Islands in its platform. Labéry went on to found Frente de Luta Pela Independência Nacional da Guine-Bissau (FLING, Front of the Struggle for National Independence of Guinea-Bissau) in 1962, a persistent rival to the PAIGC.

Due to increasing nationalist sentiments, in 1957 PIDE arrived in Guinea-Bissau to assist in intelligence, counterinsurgency operations, and to arrest suspected nationalists. In 1961, the Política de Segurança Pública (PSP, Public Security Police) were added. PIDE became so notorious that its name was changed to the Direção Geral de Segurança (DGS, General Directory of Security). The Cold War rivalry between the Western capitalist nations and Eastern Socialist nations was also part of the context for Guinea's independence struggle. The U.S. led North Atlantic Treaty Organization (NATO) provided military and political support to Fascist Portugal,

Amilcar Cabral won independence for his homeland of Guinea-Bissau as the leader of the political party that overthrew decades of colonial rule by Portugal. (Hulton Archive/Getty Images)

which was still holding on to its global colonial empire. Areas to the south of the equator were officially out of NATO's jurisdiction, but NATO contributed significant aid to Portugal as long as the African nationalist wars were viewed as part of Portugal's anti-Communist campaign.

Before 1958, Portugal spent about 4 percent of its GNP on its military, an amount comparable to that spent by other Western nations. By 1964 Portugal's "defense" requirements reached 8 percent of GNP. In 1965 more than half of the state revenues went to the military. Portugal also received military loans and grants from (West) Germany and the United States. The American military aid to Portugal through NATO between 1949 and 1968 officially reached $349 million, not including other aid to ease Portugal's hard-pressed economy. In 1972 alone, the United States arranged financial assistance to Portugal of well over $400 million. Most of Portugal's NATO military forces and equipment were in Africa, especially artillery, armored vehicles, aircraft, and American-trained counterinsurgency specialists during the wars from 1961 to 1974.

Meanwhile the Organization of African Unity (OAU) and United Nations tried to support de-colonization but had limited military capacity. The OAU, the first modern Pan-African organization, was formed on May 25, 1963, by the recently independent African nations. Its African Liberation Committee coordinated practical support for the liberation movements such as the PAIGC, which, after 1967, the OAU recognized as the only effective party in Guinea.

Africans burdened by racism and colonial occupation in southern and Portuguese Africa advertised the inherent legitimacy of their struggle, which was obscured by Cold War banners. Cabral stressed that he had no quarrel with the Portuguese people, or Portuguese language, but was an opponent of the Portuguese colonialism and Fascism that burdened millions of Portuguese workers, youths, peasants, draft resisters, and democrats. Just as the "anti-Communist" scarecrow diverted the contemporaneous civil rights and anti-war struggles in the United States, the same tactic was used in Africa and the Middle East to block national independence and struggles against colonialism and apartheid; meanwhile, NATO military vehicles, planes, arms, napalm, and cannons streamed into Guinea-Bissau, Mozambique, and Angola. But as the old West African adage states, the "eyes of this crocodile" could not stop Cabral from "crossing the river."

Amilcar Cabral, the PAIGC, and the War of Liberation

The central figure of the PAIGC was its cofounder and leader Amilcar Lopes "Abel Djassi" Cabral (September 12, 1924–January 20, 1973). He was born in Bafatá, Guinea-Bissau, to Cape Verdean parents. His father was an educated man. Cabral went to the Liceu Gil Eanes in São Vicente, Cape Verde, for his secondary education, and at twenty-one he entered the University of Lisbon, Institute of Agronomy, and graduated with honors in 1950. In the early 1950s in Lisbon, Cabral was associated with the Casa dos Estudantes do Império (CEI, House of Students from the Empire), where he met with other African revolutionary intellectuals. Cabral entered the colonial agricultural service in 1950, and from 1952 to 1954 he traveled extensively in Guinea to conduct its first agricultural census and to gain detailed knowledge of the land and people. This was a great asset to future PAIGC mobilization. Cabral's first effort to build a nationalist movement in Guinea was the Recreation Association in 1954, which led to the short-lived MING.

Around this time the Portuguese Communist Party endorsed anti-colonial movements. In 1957 the former Gold Coast became independent Ghana and provided a West African site for an anti-colonial congress held in Accra in 1958. Neighboring Guinée-Conakry gained its independence and was to become critically involved in the following years of struggle. By 1959 Amilcar Cabral and the nascent movement were also supported by the British Communist Party. Meanwhile Fascist Portugal raised the anti-Communism banner to rally NATO support against African nationalism. Propaganda battles were waged by both sides. The hope of the PAIGC was to put more pressure on Portugal through international bodies, especially the United Nations, to get it to withdraw, since in West Africa only Guinea-Bissau was not free.

On August 3, 1959, at the Pidjiguiti dockyards of Bissau, striking workers were shot down, with many killed, wounded, and arrested. The PAIGC responded from December 1960 to September 1961 by calling for a peaceful end to colonial rule. They distributed some 14,000 nationalist flyers and wrote two open letters to the Portuguese people, as well as sending the same proposal to the United Nations. But by the end of 1961, the PAIGC determined that only armed struggle would bring national independence. To block this move, the PIDE arrested Rafael Barbosa in March 1962, the same month the PAIGC had planned an attack on Praia. In June and July the PAIGC carried out a few small attacks in Guinea-Bissau. This escalation put Bissau under martial law with some 2,000 suspected activists arrested. Portuguese military strength reached about 10,000 soldiers. In order to respond, Amilcar Cabral's PAIGC joined with fellow nationalists from Mozambique, Angola, and São Tomé and Principe in 1961 to form the Conferência das Organizações Nacionalistas das Colônias Portuguesas (CONCP, Conference of Nationalist Organizations of the Portuguese Colonies), an umbrella organization linking all African liberation groups fighting against Portuguese colonialism in Africa.

The PAIGC's new political links were coupled with military training in North Africa, Eastern Europe, China, and Cuba in preparation for the military campaign set to open in 1963. PAIGC leaders hoped it would be a brief military campaign, but it turned into eleven years of bloody guerrilla warfare. After only one year of fighting, the First National Congress of the PAIGC was held inside liberated Guinea territory at Cassacá. Problematic divisions in the PAIGC were eliminated. FLING also conducted attacks in Guinea-Bissau.

In April 1964 the PAIGC attacked the Portuguese on the large southern coastal island of Como. This sixty-five-day offensive forced the Portuguese to withdraw 3,000 troops after losing hundreds. By 1965 approximately half of the countryside was under PAIGC control, even though Portuguese soldiers now numbered about 25,000. In 1965 nearby Gambia became independent. From 1965 to 1966 there was a military standoff until the PAIGC regained the initiative in the newly opened eastern front that included parts of the former northern and southern regions. By 1966 the war in Guinea had grown from automatic rifles to mortars, bazookas, small canons, and 75mm recoilless rifles. PAIGC military headway accounted for political gains at the OAU, which in 1967 gave its full support to the PAIGC and abandoned its efforts to reconcile PAIGC with FLING. Other accomplishments in that year included the PAIGC's new Radio Libertação. In 1968, the main thrust was political consolidation and strengthening the infrastructure in the liberated zones.

The PAIGC boldly attacked the strategic Bissalanca Airport serving Bissau on February 19, 1968. This was a symbolic turning point that helped the PAIGC to gain the military initiative. By February 1969, the Portuguese were forced out of Medina Boé in the south, which gave the PAIGC a much broader area of entry. Throughout 1969 and 1970, the PAIGC achieved more notable military and political victories, although the Portuguese claimed 614 PAIGC were killed in 1969 and 895 in 1970. On July 1, 1970, Amilcar Cabral and his associates met with the pope in Rome. Portuguese officials were enraged at this diplomatic victory for the liberation forces. On November 22, 1970, a Portuguese raiding party from Bissau invaded the capital city of Conakry to overthrow the supportive government of President Sekou Touré and to kill leading members of the PAIGC who were based there. The invasion failed after bloody fighting but served to underscore the fact that Portugal was growing desperate to stop the PAIGC. The Portuguese made another attempt to defeat the PAIGC in the early 1970s with the introduction of General Spinola's "Better Guinea" program, which proclaimed certain minimal reforms. The PAIGC response in 1971 was rocket and artillery attacks against the main towns of Farim, Bafatá, and Bissau. The Portuguese claim for PAIGC killed in 1971 reached 1,257, the highest such statistic for the war. Revisions of the Portuguese constitution in 1971 and the Overseas Organic Law of 1972 gave more formal autonomy to the "overseas provinces," but the advance of the PAIGC was now beyond Lisbon's control.

Although military action did not take place in Cape Verde, in 1971 the PAIGC started a campaign of nationalist wall slogans there. By April 1972 a special mission of the United Nations visited the liberated areas, assessed the extent of PAIGC territorial control, and took testimony about colonial atrocities. Also in the early 1970s the PAIGC military expanded attacks at Farim in the east and strengthened its positions in the north and south. Then, only the capital and some major towns were under Portuguese control. Even Portugal's control of the air was challenged when the PAIGC introduced Estrella surface-to-air missiles and anti-aircraft guns from the Soviet Union. These weapons reduced the effectiveness of Portuguese helicopters and attacks with napalm and white phosphorus dropped by fighter-bombers. Now the PAIGC could bring down two or three enemy aircraft each month. Portugal quickly lost some twenty aircraft, while PAIGC

ground units attacked Bula, Catio, Cadique, Gadamael, and Guidage.

In April 1972 a unique mission of the United Nations visited the liberated zones, and the UN De-colonization Committee again recognized PAIGC achievements. The observations and recognition of the special mission were endorsed by the twenty-seventh session of the United Nations General Assembly later that year. This was a major diplomatic triumph for the PAIGC's long effort to isolate and discredit Portuguese colonial rule. In August 1972 in the liberated zones the first elections occurred for 273 regional commissioners and 99 representatives to the PAIGC's Assembléia Nacional Popular (ANP, Popular National Assembly).

In Praia, Cape Verde, on September 21, 1972, a big anti-colonial demonstration shocked the Portuguese, who launched a campaign of PIDE repression there. Amilcar Cabral's 1972 speaking tour in the United States enraged Portugal further. The desperate Portuguese plotted to kill Cabral, invade Guinea-Conakry, and kidnap PAIGC leaders. The murder of Amilcar Cabral on January 20, 1973, brought a response on May 25, when in Operation Amilcar Cabral the PAIGC captured the strategic border fort at Guiledge with heavy Portuguese losses in life and war materiel. Cabral soon came to rank with Lumumba, Mandela, Mondlane, Nasser, Nkrumah, Neto, Nyerere, Touré, and others known for their fearless revolutionary resolve. Amilcar Cabral's birthday is now an official holiday in Guinea and Cape Verde.

American journalist Richard Lobban crossed Guinea-Bissau on foot from Senegal to Guinea-Conakry in June 1973 by staying in liberated zones. PAIGC military progress permitted the Second PAIGC Congress to be held from July 18 to 22 in Medina Boé and the election of Aristides Pereira as the new secretary general. The congress prepared for the historic September 23–24, 1973, first meeting of the ANP, which declared an independent constitutional state. By October diplomatic recognition had been granted by sixty-one nations. While Portuguese troops still occupied some towns, General António Spinola was relieved of his command of the war. On November 2, 1973, the United Nations General Assembly called on Portugal to cease all military activity in Guinea-Bissau. Portugal refused, and on November 6 PAIGC units attacked Bula and Bafatá. On November 19, Guinea-Bissau was admitted as the forty-second member of the OAU.

By 1974 Portugal was also devastated by the advance of other African liberation movements. In response, on April 25, 1974, the Portuguese Movimento das Forças Armadas (MFA) led by General Vasco Gonçalves overthrew Prime Minister Caetano and made General Spinola, recently dismissed from Guinea-Bissau, the new president of Portugal. The MFA restored democracy to Portugal and promised decolonization. The new leader of the Portuguese Socialist Party, Mario Soares, met with Aristides Pereira on May 15 to negotiate Portugal's recognition of Guinea-Bissau and withdrawal protocols. By August, Portugal officially agreed to grant independence and the final details were determined. On September 10 Portugal gave de jure recognition to the new Republic of Guinea-Bissau, and Luís Cabral and Aristides Pereira entered Bissau on October 19, 1974. On May 1, 1974, political prisoners were released from Tarrafal, Cape Verde. Cape Verde also became independent on July 5, 1975.

IMPACTS

As leader of the PAIGC, Cabral saw the world as a place connected by potential forces of opposition and forces of potential friendship. Cabral typically viewed social, political, and economic relationships from a dialectical perspective. As a result, he carefully appraised his opponents as well as his allies. He saw that circumstances and relationships always had the revolutionary possibility of turning into their opposite. This view was at the bedrock of his revolutionary optimism and his personal capacity to formulate tactics and strategies that would bring the intended result while anticipating and fomenting failures and errors by his opponents.

Cabral's masterstroke was the creation of the PAIGC. He overcame a number of more narrowly defined parties that focused exclusively on either Cape Verdean or on Guinean independence. Not only did he link these two nations, Cabral linked himself with the African continent and its peoples. This highest sense of internationalism was a real hallmark of Cabral and his political action. From this base he cemented ties with the OAU as well as progressive and Socialist nations. In addition, Cabral aligned himself with trade unions and a wide variety of anti-racist, pro-labor, anti-colonial, and anti-imperialist movements. Cabral identified personally and politically with the raging contemporaneous struggles in Vietnam and Southeast Asia, Cuba, and South America. In forum after forum he expressed his international solidarity with the movements that were fighting for independence, nationhood, and human rights.

Cabral was also an architect and cofounder of the important CONCP. This was a brilliant move of internationalism that sought to unify all of the movements fighting against Portugal's colonial enterprises in Cape Verde, Guinea-Bissau, São Tome, Principe, Cabinda, Angola, and Mozambique. Internationalism was not only his personal spirit, but also a tactic in his strategy to unite friends and disperse and weaken the enemy. This sense of practical internationalism was sensitively manifest when Cabral discussed the now famous topic "National Liberation as an Act of Culture" at Syracuse University in 1970.

The policies of Cabral and the PAIGC included non-alignment with military blocs and measures to protect the citizens of Guinea-Bissau and Cape Verde at home and in their various host nations. He and his followers clearly favored a progressive, Socialist, and Third World outlook that would improve economic, cultural, social, and infrastructural development in practice. These practices continued in modern Cape Verde and, in different ways, in Guinea-Bissau.

Cabral and the PAIGC promised a resolute anti-colonial struggle that would lead to the political independence of Guinea-Bissau and Cape Verde. They achieved even more, for they not only contributed directly to the last major de-colonization of Africa, but also advanced the struggle for anti-Fascist democracy in Portugal itself. Under the PAIGC's leadership, both the Republic of Guinea-Bissau and the Republic of Cape Verde not only gained freedom from Portuguese colonial rule, but became members of the international community, joining such organizations as the OAU and the UN.

Despite the success of the eleven-year war for liberation and resulting international visibility, Guinea-Bissau struggled throughout its post-colonial existence, while Cape Verde thrived. Today, Guinea-Bissau is one of the poorest nations in the world, while Cape Verde is a beacon of light in the post-colonial milieu of West Africa. Nevertheless, it cannot be forgotten that Cabral and the PAIGC led a successful campaign against Portuguese Fascist and colonial rule, brilliantly exemplifying the strong tradition of resistance to oppression illustrated throughout Guinea-Bissau's history.

PEOPLE AND ORGANIZATIONS

Assembléia Nacional Popular—ANP (People's National Assembly)

The ANP was first constituted in the liberated areas of Guinea-Bissau in 1972. Officially the highest political body in Guinea-Bissau, the ANP passes laws, ratifies decrees, and can revise the constitution.

Cabral, Amilcar (1924–1973)

Amilcar Lopes "Abel Djassi" Cabral was born September 12, 1924, in Bafatá, Guinea-Bissau. Born of Cape Verdean parents, Amilcar attended the Liceu Gil Eanes in São Vincente, Cape Verde, for his secondary education. Cabral would later enter the Institute of Agronomy at the University of Lisbon, graduating with honors in 1950. Following his university training, Cabral worked for the Portuguese colonial administration as an agronomist traveling throughout Guinea between 1952–1954 conducting the country's first agricultural census. Using this position he obtained detailed knowledge of the Guinean land and people, which in turn helped him develop a strategy for national liberation to be carried out by the PAIGC.

Before the formation of the PAIGC, Cabral founded in 1954 the "Recreation Association" and the ephemeral MING, followed in the mid 1950s by the Movimento Anti-Colonialista (MAC). On September 19, 1956, Amilcar and others formed the most enduring nationalist revolutionary party in Guinean history, the PAIGC. In the same year, as Cabral lived and worked in Angola, he and Angolan nationalists organized the MPLA.

As the architect and undisputed leader of the PAIGC, he called for the total independence of both Cape Verde and Guinea-Bissau from Portuguese colonial control. During the armed struggle (1963–1973) Cabral served as secretary general of the PAIGC and wrote extensively on Guinean history and African liberation and culture, all while traveling to the United States, U.S.S.R., Cuba, and Italy to express his desire for all oppressed people to be liberated from Fascist, colonial, racist, and imperial forces. He can easily be labeled an international humanist; his ideas and actions were not only instrumental in the liberation movement that brought independence to the peoples of Cape Verde and Guinea-Bissau, but also important to people and activists worldwide. However, just months before the victory of national independence, Cabral was assassinated on January 20, 1973, with the assistance of Portuguese agents within the PAIGC.

As one of the most important revolutionary leaders, theoreticians, and practitioners of the twentieth century, Cabral received the Nasser Award at the fifth annual Pan-African Congress, the Joliot-Curie Medal, and honorary doctorates from the Soviet Academy of Sciences and Lincoln University (U.S.A.). Today, educational centers continue to be named in his honor and his birthday (September 12) is celebrated as a national holiday in Guinea-Bissau.

Cabral, Luís De Almeida (Born 1931)

Luís De Almeida Cabral was born in Guinea-Bissau of Cape Verdean parents. Cabral was originally trained as an accountant but would later join his brother Amilcar Cabral as one of the founding members of the PAIGC. Following the formation of the PAIGC, PIDE sought to apprehend Cabral. In response, Cabral left his homeland for neighboring Guinea-Conakry. In 1961 he was founder and secretary general of Uniao Nacional dos Trabalhadores da Guiné (UNTG), a pro-PAIGC trade union.

In 1963, Cabral would become commander of the strategic liberated zone and member of the PAIGC war council. He would also become a member of the Comité Executíve da Luta (CEL), therefore in part responsible for national recov-

ery and reconstruction programs (e.g., medical and educational services and *armazens do povo,* "People's Stores.") Following the independence of Guinea-Bissau, Luís Cabral became the deputy secretary of the PAIGC and first president of the newly formed nation-state. Cabral would be overthrown by General Joao "Nino" Vieira in 1980 and later exiled to Cuba and then to the Cape Verde Islands.

Organization of African Unity (OAU)

Founded in 1963, the OAU, now called the African Union, is a continent-wide watchdog organization similar to the United Nations.

Partido Africano De Independência De Guiné E Cabo Verde—PAIGC (African Party of Independence for Guinea and Cape Verde)

Founded in 1956 by Amilcar Cabral and others in Bissau, the PAIGC was the victorious nationalist organization in Guinea-Bissau and Cape Verde. The PAIGC espoused a radical ideology very much influenced by Marxism; thus the fundamental principles of the PAIGC were Socialist in character. Furthermore, the party emphasized "revolutionary democracy," Pan-African unity, and education for all.

Pereira, Carmen (Born 1937)

Carmen Pereira was born in Guinea-Bissau to a well-off and respected family; her father was a well-known African lawyer. In 1961, she heard of the PAIGC and joined in 1962. Carmen and her husband, Umaru Djallo, were both party activists. As repression escalated in 1962, Carmen and her three children were able to leave Bissau for neighboring Senegal. In Zinguinchor (Senegal) she worked as a seamstress, enabling her to feed her children as well as thirty party comrades.

By the end of 1963, Carmen was sent to the Soviet Union for political and medical training. One year later she served as a health cadre in the liberated areas and opened the first PAIGC hospital in Guinea-Bissau. She also headed a nurses' training delegation to the Soviet Union in 1965. In 1967 Carmen became the political commissar for the entire southern front, thus responsible for all political mobilization in the area. Pereira then became the only woman to be appointed to the Comité Executívo da Luta (CEL). She was also elected deputy for Bissau, second vice president of the ANP in Guinea, and one of the fifteen members of the state council in 1973.

Polícia International E De Defesa Do Estado (PIDE)

PIDE was the secret police organization of Portugal during its Fascist/colonial period. In 1957, PIDE arrived in Bissau to assist in intelligence, counterinsurgency operations, and arrests of suspected nationalists.

Richard Lobban, Jr., and Paul Khalil Saucier

See Also Angolan Revolution; Cinema of Revolution; Colonialism, Anti-Colonialism, and Neo-Colonialism; Elites, Intellectuals, and Revolutionary Leadership; Mozambique Revolution; Nationalism and Revolution; Student and Youth Movements, Activism and Revolution

References and Further Readings

Cabral, Amilcar. 1969. *Revolution in Guinea: Selected Texts by Amilcar Cabral.* NewYork: Monthly Review Press.

———. 1979. *Unity and Struggle: Speeches and Writings of Amilcar Cabral.* New York: Monthly Review Press.

Castanheira, Jose Pedro. 1995. *Quem Mandou Matar Amilcar Cabral?* Lisbon: Relogio d'Agua.

Chabal, Patrick. 1983, *Amilcar Cabral: Revolutionary Leadership and People's War.* New York: Cambridge University Press.

Chaliand, Gerard. 1969. *Armed Struggle in Africa: With Portuguese Guerrillas in "Portuguese" Guinea."* New York: Monthly Review Press.

Davidson, Basil. 1984, *No Fist Is Big Enough to Hide the Sky: The Liberation of Guinea-Bissau and Cape Verde.* London: Zed Press.

Lobban, Richard, and Peter Karibe Mendy. 1997. *Historical Dictionary of the Republic of Guinea-Bissau.* 3rd edition. Lanham, MD: Scarecrow Press.

Index

Editor Biography

James V. DeFronzo of the Sociology Department at the University of Connecticut has taught over 7,000 students in his revolutions course and over 9,000 students in his criminology course and is preparing the third edition of his textbook on revolutions, *Revolutions and Revolutionary Movements*. He has written dozens of research articles published in various academic journals dealing with topics such as criminology, social policy related to crime, demography, gender issues, teaching, and social stratification. Born in New Britain, Connecticut, he received a B.A. in Sociology from Fairfield University, Connecticut, and attended graduate school at Indiana University on a federal quantitative methodology fellowship and later on a research assistantship. He taught for three years in the Sociology Department at Indiana University-Purdue University at Fort Wayne, Indiana, and also taught as an adjunct instructor at Indiana University in Bloomington. He completed his Ph. D. the year after he began teaching at the University of Connecticut at Storrs. His teaching experience at Indiana University or the University of Connecticut includes Introductory Sociology, Social Problems, Social Psychology, Social Conflict, Criminology, Methods of Social Research, Social Stratification, and Revolutionary Movements Around the World. He is a member of the American Sociological Association and the American Society of Criminology. His writing and research interests include social movements, criminology, general sociology, social problems and political and historical sociology and developing textbooks for several of these areas.